ZAGAT®

Boston
Restaurants
2011/12

Including Cape Cod,
Martha's Vineyard, Nantucket
and The Berkshires

LOCAL EDITORS
Eric Grossman, Liza Weisstuch, Naomi Kooker
and Lynn Hazlewood

STAFF EDITOR
Bill Corsello

Published and distributed by
Zagat Survey, LLC
4 Columbus Circle
New York, NY 10019
T: 212.977.6000
E: boston@zagat.com
www.zagat.com

ACKNOWLEDGMENTS

We thank William P. DeSousa-Mauk, Demaris Kooker, Gerrish Lopez, Daniel Newcomb, Sara O'Reilly, Charlie Perkins, Ellen Roberts, Jenn Smith and Ian Turner, as well as the following members of our staff: Danielle Borovoy (editorial assistant), Brian Albert, Sean Beachell, Maryanne Bertollo, Sandy Cheng, Reni Chin, Larry Cohn, Nicole Diaz, Alison Flick, Jeff Freier, Michelle Golden, Matthew Hamm, Justin Hartung, Marc Henson, Natalie Lebert, Mike Liao, James Mulcahy, Polina Paley, Chris Walsh, Jacqueline Wasilczyk, Art Yaghci, Sharon Yates, Anna Zappia and Kyle Zolner.

The reviews in this guide are based on public opinion surveys. The ratings reflect the average scores given by the survey participants who voted on each establishment. The text is based on quotes from, or paraphrasings of, the surveyors' comments. Phone numbers, addresses and other factual data were correct to the best of our knowledge when published in this guide.

Our guides are printed using environmentally preferable inks containing 20%, by weight, renewable resources on papers sourced from well-managed forests. Deluxe editions are covered with Skivertex Recover® Double containing a minimum of 30% post-consumer waste fiber.

SUSTAINABLE FORESTRY INITIATIVE
Certified Sourcing
www.sfiprogram.org
SFI-00993

ENVIROINK™

The inks used to print the body of this publication contain a minimum of 20%, by weight, renewable resources.

Maps © Antenna International™

© 2011 Zagat Survey, LLC
ISBN-13: 978-1-60478-350-6
ISBN-10: 1-60478-350-8
Printed in the
United States of America

Contents

Ratings & Symbols

Zagat Top Spot	Name	Symbols	Cuisine	Zagat Ratings			
				FOOD	DECOR	SERVICE	COST

Area, Address & Contact

Z Tim & Nina's ☻ *Eclectic* ▽ 25 | 4 | 13 | $15

Fenway | 1000 Thatcher St. (Margin St.) | 617-555-1234 | www.zagat.com

Review, surveyor comments in quotes

T&N "sent their fleet of funky food trucks to the junkyard" and built this Fenway "shack" where the "cut-rate" Eclectic eats are still "capricious" and "succulent", particularly the signature alligator-and-sheep kebab; the "tangy trace of exhaust" is absent from the new iteration's fare ("somehow, I miss it!"), but the staff is as "tired" as ever.

Ratings **Food, Decor** & **Service** are rated on a 30-pt scale.

0 – 9 poor to fair

10 – 15 fair to good

16 – 19 good to very good

20 – 25 very good to excellent

26 – 30 extraordinary to perfection

▽ low response | less reliable

Cost The estimated price of a dinner with one drink and tip. Lunch is usually 25% less. For unrated **newcomers** or **write-ins,** the price range is shown as follows:

I $25 and below   E $41 to $65

M $26 to $40   VE $66 or above

Symbols Z highest ratings, popularity and importance
☻ serves after 11 PM
Ⓢ Ⓜ closed on Sunday or Monday
⊄ no credit cards accepted

Maps Index maps show restaurants with the highest Food ratings in those areas.

Menus, photos, voting and more – free at ZAGAT.com

About This Survey

 Here are the results of our **2011/12 Boston Restaurants Survey,** covering 1,369 eateries in Boston and its surroundings, as well as on Cape Cod, Martha's Vineyard, Nantucket and in The Berkshires. Like all our guides, this one is based on input from avid local consumers – 7,465 all told. Our editors have synopsized this feedback, highlighting representative comments (in quotation marks within each review). To read full surveyor comments – and share your own opinions – visit **ZAGAT.com,** where you'll also find the latest restaurant news plus menus, photos and lots more, all for free.

THREE SIMPLE PREMISES underlie our ratings and reviews. First, we believe that the collective opinions of large numbers of consumers are more accurate than those of any single person. (Consider that our surveyors bring some 970,000 annual meals' worth of experience to this year's survey. They also visit restaurants year-round, anonymously – and on their own dime.) Second, food quality is only part of the equation when choosing a restaurant, thus we ask surveyors to separately rate food, decor and service and report on cost. Third, since people need reliable information in a fast, easy-to-digest format, we strive to be concise and we offer our content on every platform – print, online and mobile. Our Top Ratings lists (pages 7–18) and indexes (starting on page 226; Berkshires page 310) are also designed to help you quickly choose the best place for any occasion, be it business or pleasure.

ABOUT ZAGAT: In 1979, we started asking friends to rate and review restaurants purely for fun. The term "user-generated content" had not yet been coined. That hobby grew into Zagat Survey; 32 years later, we have over 375,000 surveyors and cover airlines, bars, dining, fast food, entertaining, golf, hotels, movies, music, resorts, shopping, spas, theater and tourist attractions in over 100 countries. Along the way, we evolved from being a print publisher to a digital content provider, e.g. **ZAGAT.com, ZAGAT.mobi** (for web-enabled mobile devices), **ZAGAT TO GO** (for smartphones) and **nru** (for Android phones). We also produce customized gifts and marketing tools for a wide range of corporate clients. And you can find us on Twitter (twitter.com/zagat), Facebook and just about any other social media network.

THANKS: We're grateful to our local editors, Eric Grossman, a Boston-based food and travel writer; Liza Weisstuch, Boston-based food, drinks and travel writer; Naomi Kooker, Boston-based food, wine and travel writer; and Lynn Hazlewood, former editor-in-chief of *Hudson Valley* magazine. We also sincerely thank the thousands of surveyors who participated – this guide is really "theirs."

JOIN IN: To improve our guides, we solicit your comments; it's vital that we hear your opinions. Just contact us at **nina-tim@zagat.com.** We also invite you to join our surveys at **ZAGAT.com.** Do so and you'll receive a choice of rewards in exchange.

New York, NY
April 20, 2011

Nina and Tim

Nina and Tim Zagat

What's New

After a relatively sharp 4.6% increase in 2008 to $33.64, the average price of a meal in Boston is now slightly lower at $33.56, comfortably below the $35.62 national average. Bostonians report eating out 2.5 times a week, which is down from 2.6 two years ago, but just a bit. Luckily for them, restaurateurs continue to offer exciting new choices, the majority of which are reasonably priced.

TRENDING TOPICS: The gastropub-style eatery – in which craft cocktails and serious beer lists share focus with typically more upscale grub – is this year's most conspicuous trend, with affordable additions **American Craft, Canary Square, Citizen Public House & Oyster Bar, Foundry on Elm, The Gallows, The Haven** and **Russell House Tavern** all riffing on the theme. Also geared to these value-conscious times are newcomers **Back Bay Social Club, Cognac Bistro, Darryl's Corner Bar & Kitchen, Jacky's Table** and **The Regal Beagle.** But that doesn't mean luxe dining is a thing of the past, as evidenced by high-profile, high-priced premieres **Bergamot, Bondir, Deuxave, Island Creek Oyster Bar** and **Noche.** Also commanding top-tier tabs is a small crop of celebrity-chef-backed premieres: Lydia Shire and Jasper White's **Towne** and Barbara Lynch's **Menton.** Making its Survey debut, Menton nabs the No. 1 ratings for both Decor and Service, while **O Ya,** surveyed for just the second time, pulls off a similar coup by earning the coveted No. 1 Food score.

MEALS ON WHEELS: Though fetishized in cities like New York, Los Angeles and Austin, the food truck phenomenon hasn't quite caught on in Boston, with 79% of respondents having never tried one. However, there are signs that a scene may be on the horizon, with the city relaxing some of the ordinances that can make mobile meals an ordeal. One success story: the vegetarian Clover Food Trucks proved so popular that a brick-and-mortar offshoot, **Clover Food Lab,** has opened in Harvard Square.

DINING OUT IN THE DIGITAL AGE: Eighty-one percent of respondents visit a restaurant's website before dining there, while 45% make reservations via the Internet, up from 38% two years ago. When it comes to taking pictures in restaurants, 13% feel it's rude, while 68% say it's ok in moderation and 15% feel it's perfectly acceptable. But as for chatting on phones or texting at the table, 63% think it's inappropriate.

SURVEY ALSO SAYS: Though 65% of surveyors peg service as their No. 1 dining-out irritant, Bostonians are still fairly generous tippers, leaving an average 19.4% gratuity (vs. the 19.2% national mean) . . . 59% would pay more for food that's locally sourced, organic or sustainable, while 27% seek out restaurants specializing in such 'green' cuisine . . . 74% think Boston should follow New York and Los Angeles' example and require eateries to prominently display their health-inspection results.

Boston, MA
April 20, 2011

Eric Grossman

Most Popular

Plotted on the map at the back of this book.

BOSTON

1. Legal Sea Foods | *Seafood*
2. Abe & Louie's | *Steak*
3. Craigie on Main | *French*
4. Blue Ginger | *Asian*
5. Oleana | *Mediterranean*
6. L'Espalier | *French*
7. No. 9 Park | *French/Italian*
8. Capital Grille | *Steak*
9. Hamersley's Bistro | *French*
10. B&G Oysters | *Seafood*
11. Mistral | *French/Mediterranean*
12. Aquitaine | *French*
13. Grill 23 & Bar | *Steak*
14. Neptune Oyster | *Seafood*
15. Oishii | *Japanese*
16. EVOO | *Eclectic*
17. Lumière | *French*
18. Ten Tables | *American/European*
19. Union Oyster | *New Eng./Seafood*
20. Cheesecake Factory | *American*
21. Sel de la Terre | *French*
22. Anna's Taqueria | *Tex-Mex*
23. Giacomo's | *Italian/Seafood*
24. Elephant Walk | *Cambodian/Fr.*
25. Sorellina | *Italian*
26. Toro | *Spanish*
27. Hungry Mother | *Southern*
28. Clio | *French*
29. La Campania | *Italian*
30. Eastern Standard | *Amer./Euro.*
31. Petit Robert Bistro | *French*
32. Blue Ribbon BBQ | *BBQ*
33. Il Capriccio | *Italian*
34. Atlantic Fish Co. | *Seafood*
35. O Ya | *Japanese*
36. Flour Bakery | *Bakery*
37. Locke-Ober | *Amer./Continental*
38. Anthony's | *Seafood*
39. Bergamot | *American*
40. East Coast Grill* | *BBQ/Seafood*
41. Radius | *French*
42. Fugakyu | *Japanese*
43. Ruth's Chris | *Steak*
44. Durgin-Park | *New England*
45. Davio's | *Italian/Steak*
46. Rialto | *Italian*
47. Harvest | *American*
48. Not Your Average Joe's | *Amer.*
49. Morton's | *Steak*
50. Rendezvous | *Mediterranean*

CAPE COD, MARTHA'S VINEYARD & NANTUCKET

C=Cape Cod; M=Martha's Vineyard; N=Nantucket

1. Abba/C | *Mediterranean/Thai*
2. American Seasons/N | *Amer.*
3. Chatham Bars Inn/C | *American*
4. Brewster Fish/C | *Seafood*
5. Impudent Oyster/C* | *Seafood*
6. Straight Wharf/N | *Seafood*
7. Black-Eyed Susan's/N | *Amer.*
8. Arnold's Lobster/C | *Seafood*
9. Ocean House/C | *American*
10. Cape Sea Grille/C | *American*
11. Topper's/N | *American*
12. Galley Beach/N | *Eclectic*
13. Mews/C | *American*
14. Brant Point/N | *Seafood/Steak*
15. 28 Atlantic/C* | *Amer.*
16. Art Cliff Diner/M | *Diner*
17. Chillingsworth/C* | *French*
18. Co./Cauldron/N* | *Amer.*
19. Alchemy/M | *American*
20. Lobster Pot/C* | *Eclectic/Seafood*
21. Red Inn/C | *New England*
22. Chart Room/C | *New Eng./Seafood*

* Indicates a tie with restaurant above

KEY NEWCOMERS

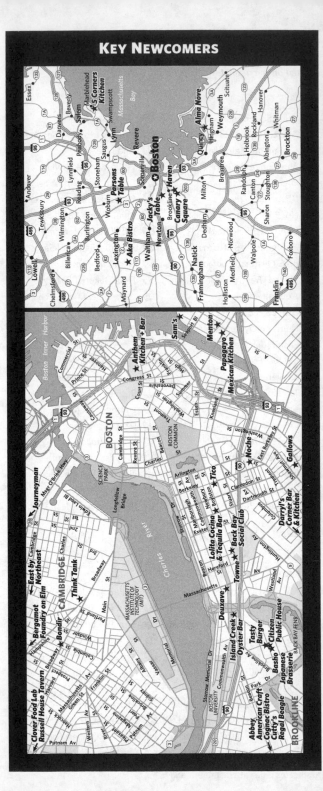

Menus, photos, voting and more - free at ZAGAT.com

Key Newcomers

Our editors' favorites among this year's arrival. See full list at page 279.

Abbey | *American* | comfort food with a twist in Brookline

Aka Bistro | *French/Japanese* | upscale addition to Lincoln

Alma Nove | *Italian/Mediterranean* | waterside dining in Hingham

American Craft | *Pub Food* | Brookline's latest brew mecca

Anthem Kitchen + Bar | *American* | affordable option for Faneuil Hall

Back Bay Social Club | *American* | retro drinks and speakeasy vibes

Basho Japanese Brasserie | *Japanese* | pre-Fenway stop for sushi

Bergamot | *American* | sophistication in Somerville

Bondir | *American* | Central Square spot serving sustainable fare

Canary Square | *American* | Jamaica Plain's newest 'green' joint

Citizen Public House | *American* | cozy pub near Fenway Park

Clover Food Lab | *Vegetarian* | food truck sets down roots in Harvard Square

Cognac Bistro | *French* | sexy space in a residential part of Brookline

Cutty's | *American/Sandwiches* | already popular Brookline shop

Darryl's Corner Bar & Kitchen | *American* | jazzy South End hangout

Deuxave | *American* | fashionable Back Bay boîte with a French accent

East by Northeast | *Chinese* | modern Sino fusion comes to Inman Square

5 Corners Kitchen | *French* | new fine-dining option for Marblehead

Foundry on Elm | *American* | watering hole near Tufts in Somerville

Gallows | *American* | gastropub-style dining in the South End

Haven | *Scottish* | fare that's rare for Boston in Jamaica Plain

Island Creek Oyster Bar | *Seafood* | bivalves in Kenmore Square

Jacky's Table | *French* | Brighton sibling of Petit Robert Bistro

Journeyman | *American* | Luxe tasting menus in cool Somerville environs

Lolita Cocina & Tequila Bar | *Mexican* | alluring Back Bay basement

Menton | *French/Italian* | Barbara Lynch's Seaport District instant winner

Noche | *American* | gorgeous digs and a sizzling South End scene

Papagayo Mexican Kitchen | *Mexican* | funky Seaport District destination

Parsons Table | *American* | Chris Parsons reimagines Catch in Winchester

Regal Beagle | *American* | providing creative food and drink to Brookline

Russell House Tavern | *American* | pub for grown-ups in Harvard Square

Sam's | *American/French* | harborside haunt in the Seaport District

Tasty Burger | *Burgers* | hip hamburger joint near Fenway Park

Think Tank | *American/Asian* | stylishly retro Kendall Square nightspot

Tico | *American/Latin* | Michael Schlow's new Back Bay venture

Towne | *Eclectic* | chic Back Bay scene from Lydia Shire and Jasper White

Top Food

29 O Ya | *Japanese*

28 Oleana | *Mediterranean*
La Campania | *Italian*
Neptune Oyster | *Seafood*
Lumière | *French*
Hamersley's Bistro | *French*
Uni Sashimi Bar | *Japanese*
T.W. Food | *American/French*
Menton | *French/Italian*
Mistral | *French/Mediterranean*

27 L'Espalier | *French*
Sofra Bakery | *Mideastern*
Duckworth's | *American*
Oishii | *Japanese*
Craigie on Main | *French*
Clio | *French*
No. 9 Park | *French/Italian*
Bergamot | *American*
Ithaki Med. | *Greek/Med.*
All Seasons Table | *Asian*
Carmen | *Italian*
Sorellina | *Italian*
Grill 23 & Bar | *Steak*
Bistro 5 | *Italian*
Toro | *Spanish*

Grapevine | *American/Italian*
Salts | *American/French*
Ten Tables | *Amer./European*
Flour Bakery | *Bakery*
Ecco | *American*
L'Andana* | *Italian*
Parsons Table* | *American*
Il Capriccio | *Italian*
Blue Ginger | *Asian*
Prezza | *Italian*
Barker Tavern | *American*

26 Carlo's Cucina | *Italian*
Trattoria Toscana | *Italian*
Taranta | *Italian/Peruvian*
Abe & Louie's | *Steak*
Rendezvous | *Mediterranean*
Neighborhood Rest. | *Portugese*
Delfino | *Italian*
B&G Oysters | *Seafood*
Hungry Mother | *Southern*
Coppa | *Italian*
Garden at The Cellar | *Amer.*
EVOO | *Eclectic*
Troquet | *American/French*
Rialto | *Italian*

BY CUISINE

AMERICAN (NEW)

28 T.W. Food
27 Duckworth's
Bergamot
Grapevine
Salts

AMERICAN (TRAD.)

27 Barker Tavern
25 Cutty's
24 Mr. Bartley's
Sorella's
23 Ashmont

ASIAN

27 All Seasons Table
Blue Ginger
24 Myers + Chang
Maxwells 148
22 Grasshopper

BARBECUE

26 East Coast Grill
Blue Ribbon BBQ
24 Redbones BBQ
22 Soul Fire
21 Village Smokehse.

BURGERS

24 Mr. Bartley's
23 Boston Burger Company
22 UBurger
21 Christopher's
20 Five Guys

CAMBODIAN/
VIETNAMESE

25 Xinh Xinh
24 Pho Pasteur
Pho Hoa
23 Elephant Walk
21 Le's

Excludes places with low votes

Menus, photos, voting and more – free at ZAGAT.com

CHINESE

25 Peach Farm
Bernard's
Gourmet Dumpling House
Sichuan Gourmet
East Ocean City

ECLECTIC

26 EVOO
25 Centre St. Café
Scutra
24 Blue Room
Metropolis Cafe

FRENCH

28 Menton
Mistral
27 No. 9 Park
Salts
26 Pigalle

FRENCH (BISTRO)

28 Hamersley's Bistro
27 Craigie on Main
26 Troquet
5 Corners Kitchen
24 Chez Henri

FRENCH (NEW)

28 Lumière
T.W. Food
27 L'Espalier
Clio
26 Radius

INDIAN

24 Punjabi Dhaba
Punjab Palace
Kashmir
Kebab Factory
India Quality

ITALIAN

28 La Campania
Menton
27 No. 9 Park
Carmen
Sorellina

ITALIAN (NORTHERN)

27 Bistro 5
L'Andana
Il Capriccio
26 Trattoria Toscana
Grotto

JAPANESE

29 O Ya
28 Uni Sashimi Bar
27 Oishii
26 Super Fusion
25 Douzo

MEDITERRANEAN

28 Oleana
Mistral
27 Ithaki Med.
26 Rendezvous
Caffe Bella

MEXICAN

26 El Sarape
25 El Pelón Taqueria
Tacos Lupita
Angela's Café
24 Taqueria Mexico

NEW ENGLAND

25 Gibbet Hill Grill
24 Café Fleuri
Parker's
23 Henrietta's Table
22 Green Street

PIZZA

26 Galleria Umberto
25 Emma's
Santarpio's Pizza
Posto
24 Figs

PUB FOOD

24 Druid
23 Plough & Stars
22 Matt Murphy's
20 Johnny D's
Black Cow

SEAFOOD (AMERICAN)

28 Neptune Oyster
26 B&G Oysters
East Coast Grill
24 Clam Box
Atlantic Fish Co.

SEAFOOD (ETHNIC)

25 Peach Farm
Giacomo's
East Ocean City
24 Daily Catch
23 Tamarind Bay

SPANISH

27 Toro
25 Taberna de Haro
   Dalí
23 Tasca
   Tapéo

STEAKHOUSES

27 Grill 23 & Bar
26 Abe & Louie's

Capital Grille
Mooo . . .
Ruth's Chris

THAI

24 Brown Sugar
   Khao Sarn Cuisine
   Rod Dee
23 Dok Bua
   Bangkok City

BY SPECIAL FEATURE

BRUNCH

26 Abe & Louie's
   East Coast Grill
25 Centre St. Café
   Harvest
24 Café Fleuri

CHILD-FRIENDLY

27 Flour Bakery
26 Neighborhood Rest.
   Galleria Umberto
   Blue Ribbon BBQ
25 Peach Farm

CHOWDER

28 Neptune Oyster
24 Clam Box
   Atlantic Fish Co.
   Captain's Table
21 Summer Shack

DESSERT

27 Flour Bakery
26 Bristol Lounge
24 Picco
   Hi-Rise
21 Finale

HOTEL DINING

28 Uni Sashimi Bar
      (Eliot Hotel)
27 Clio
      (Eliot Hotel)
26 Rialto
      (Charles Hotel)
   Meritage
      (Boston Harbor Hotel)
   Mooo . . .
      (XV Beacon Hotel)

LANDMARKS

25 Locke-Ober
24 Pizzeria Regina
22 Charlie's Sandwich
21 Union Oyster
20 Durgin-Park

LATE DINING

27 Oishii
26 Coppa
25 Peach Farm
   Douzo
   Santarpio's Pizza

NEWCOMERS (RATED)

28 Menton
27 Bergamot
   Parsons Table
26 5 Corners Kitchen
25 Cutty's

PEOPLE-WATCHING

28 Mistral
27 Clio
   No. 9 Park
   Sorellina
   Grill 23 & Bar

POWER LUNCH

26 Abe & Louie's
   Radius
   Bristol Lounge
25 Harvest
21 Towne

WINNING WINE LISTS

28 La Campania
   Lumière
   Hamersley's Bistro
   Uni Sashimi Bar
   Menton

BACK BAY

28 Uni Sashimi Bar
27 L'Espalier
Clio
Sorellina
Grill 23 & Bar

BEACON HILL

27 No. 9 Park
26 Grotto
Mooo . . .
25 Scampo
Toscano

BROOKLINE/ CHESTNUT HILL

27 Oishii
26 Capital Grille
Super Fusion
25 La Morra
Lineage

CENTRAL/INMAN SQS./ EAST CAMBRIDGE

28 Oleana
27 Craigie on Main
Salts
Flour Bakery
26 Rendezvous

CHARLESTOWN

24 Figs
Navy Yard Bistro
23 Sorelle
22 Tangierino
19 Warren Tavern

CHINATOWN

25 Peach Farm
Xinh Xinh
Gourmet Dumpling House
East Ocean City
24 Taiwan Cafe

DOWNTOWN CROSS./ FINANCIAL DISTRICT

26 Radius
Ruth's Chris
25 Chacarero
Locke-Ober
KO Prime

FENWAY/KENMORE SQ.

26 Trattoria Toscana
24 India Quality

Olecito
23 Petit Robert Bistro
Woody's Grill

HARVARD SQ.

27 Ten Tables
26 Garden at The Cellar
Rialto
25 Harvest
24 Sandrine's

JAMAICA PLAIN

27 Ten Tables
25 Centre St. Café
24 El Oriental/Cuba
Sorella's
22 Bukhara

NEEDHAM/NEWTON/ WELLESLEY

28 Lumière
27 Blue Ginger
26 Café Mangal
Sweet Basil
Blue Ribbon BBQ

NORTH END

28 Neptune Oyster
27 Carmen
Prezza
26 Taranta
Mare

PARK SQ.

26 Erbaluce
25 Davio's
Via Matta
Fleming's Prime
24 Da Vinci

SEAPORT/ WATERFRONT

28 Menton
27 Flour Bakery
26 Meritage
25 Morton's
Sportello

SOMERVILLE

27 Bergamot
26 Neighborhood Rest.
25 Highland Kitchen
Tacos Lupita
Dalí

SOUTH END

28 Hamersley's Bistro
    Mistral
27 Oishii
    Toro
    Flour Bakery

THEATER DISTRICT

26 Troquet
    Pigalle
    Market
24 Tantric
23 Avila

WALTHAM/
WATERTOWN

28 La Campania
27 Il Capriccio
26 Super Fusion
24 Pizzeria Regina
    Taqueria Mexico

OUTLYING SUBURBS

27 Duckworth's
    Oishii
    Ithaki Med.
    All Seasons Table
    Grapevine

CAPE COD

28 Bramble Inn
    PB Boulangerie Bistro
    Abba
27 Glass Onion
    Cape Sea Grille

MARTHA'S VINEYARD

28 Larsen's Fish Mkt.
    L'Étoile
    Détente
26 Bite
    Art Cliff Diner

NANTUCKET

28 Pearl
    Òran Mór
27 Co./Cauldron
    Topper's
    Straight Wharf

THE BERKSHIRES

27 Old Inn/Green
    Blantyre
25 Wheatleigh
    Nudel
    Tratt. Rustica*

Top Decor

27| Menton
Bristol Lounge
Sorellina
L'Espalier
Oak Room

26| Top of the Hub
Cuchi Cuchi
Gibbet Hill Grill
Noche
Meritage
Square Café
Alibi
Clio
Tosca
Bond
Barker Tavern
Alma Nove

25| Mistral
Asana
Longfellow's Inn

Locke-Ober
Parker's
Radius
Rowes Wharf Sea Grille
All Seasons Table
Dalí
No. 9 Park
Mooo . . .
Eastern Standard
W Lounge
Davio's
L'Andana
Rialto
Post 390
Tangierino
Hamersley's Bistro

24| Upstairs on the Square
Grill 23 & Bar
Scampo
Bistro du Midi

OUTDOORS

Abe & Louie's
B&G Oysters
Barking Crab
Dante
Eastern Standard
Harvest

Henrietta's Table
KingFish Hall
La Voile
Oleana
Stella
Stephanie's

ROMANCE

Bristol Lounge
Carmen
Casa Romero
Chez Henri
Cuchi Cuchi
Dalí

Hungry I
Lala Rokh
Mamma Maria
Oleana
O Ya
Pigalle

ROOMS

Avila
Clio
Dali
Dante
Eastern Standard
Gaslight Brasserie

KO Prime
La Campania
L'Espalier
Mooo . . .
Sorellina
Upstairs on the Square

VIEWS

Anthony's
Back Eddy
Barking Crab
Blu
Dante
Mamma Maria

Meritage
Red Rock
Ristorante Fiore
Sam's
Tavern/Water
Top of Hub

Top Service

<u>29</u> Menton	Meritage
<u>27</u> L'Espalier	Grill 23 & Bar
No. 9 Park	Maxwells 148
T.W. Food	Abe & Louie's
Bristol Lounge	Trattoria Toscana
Lumière	Rialto
O Ya	Capital Grille
<u>26</u> Salts	<u>25</u> Davide Rist.
Hamersley's Bistro	Oleana
Mistral	Il Capriccio
Clio	Grapevine
Bergamot	Tosca*
Bistro 5	La Campania
Ithaki Med.	Radius
Craigie on Main	Rendezvous
Parsons Table	Troquet
Mooo . . .	Hungry Mother
Sorellina	Blue Ginger
Locke-Ober	Oak Room
Barker Tavern	Duckworth's

Best Buys

In order of Bang for the Buck rating.

1. 1369 Coffeehouse
2. Chacarero
3. Anna's Taqueria
4. Pinocchio's Pizza & Subs
5. Boloco
6. El Pelón Taqueria
7. Boca Grande
8. Dorado Tacos & Cemitas
9. Galleria Umberto
10. B. Good
11. Mr. Crepe
12. Neighborhood Rest.
13. Sorelle
14. Cutty's
15. Flour Bakery
16. UBurger
17. Tacos Lupita
18. Athan's Café
19. Paris Creperie
20. Darwin's Ltd.
21. Charlie's Sandwich
22. Pho Hoa
23. Sorella's
24. UFood Grill
25. Boston Burger Company
26. Mike's
27. All Star Sandwich
28. El Oriental/Cuba
29. Dosa Factory
30. Sofra Bakery
31. Blue Ribbon BBQ
32. Vicki Lee's
33. Hi-Rise
34. Rod Dee
35. Victoria's Diner
36. Xinh Xinh
37. Punjabi Dhaba
38. Sound Bites
39. Sweet Tomatoes Pizza
40. Noodle Street

OTHER GOOD VALUES

Addis Red Sea
Anchovies
Baja Betty's
Basta Pasta
Border Cafe
Brother's Crawfish
Brown Sugar
Cafe Jaffa
Caffe Belo
Caffe Paradiso
Cantina La Mexicana
Captain's Table
Charlie's Kitchen
Courthouse Seafood
Delux Cafe
Deluxe Town Diner
Dok Bua
Druid
Grendel's Den
Haley House Bakery + Cafe
India Quality
Istanbul'lu
Kebab Factory
Le's
Lower Depths

Mr. Bartley's
Muqueca
9 Tastes
Other Side Cafe
Pho Lemongrass
Pho Pasteur
Pizzeria Regina
Purple Cactus
Rami's
Redbones BBQ
Rosebud Diner
Santarpio's Pizza
Shabu-Zen
Shawarma King
Silvertone B&G
South Street Diner
Sultan's Kitchen
Tacos El Charro
Taiwan Cafe
Taqueria Mexico
Trident Booksellers + Cafe
Upper Crust
Veggie Planet
Volle Nolle
Wagamama

PRIX FIXE MENUS

Call for availability. All-you-can-eat options are for lunch and/or brunch.

PRIX FIXE LUNCH

26 Radius ($29)
 Market ($22)
25 Harvest ($22)
24 Sandrine's ($20)
 Upstairs on the Square ($20)
23 Sel de la Terre ($23)
 Elephant Walk ($17)
 Basho Japanese ($14)
22 Les Zyomates ($17)

PRIX FIXE DINNER

28 Lumière ($35)
 T.W. Food ($45)
27 Clio ($49)
 Ten Tables ($33)
 L'Andana ($38)

26 Rendezvous ($38)
 EVOO ($38)
 Pigalle ($40)
 Grotto ($35)
25 La Morra ($25)

ALL YOU CAN EAT

26 Neighborhood Rest. ($12)
24 Kashmir ($10)
 Parker's ($22)
 Blue Room ($23)
 Kebab Factory ($8)
 Mela ($10)
 Masala Art ($12)
 Tantric ($11)
23 Henrietta's Table ($45)
 Kathmandu Spice ($10)

BEST BUYS: CAPE COD

In order of Bang for the Buck rating.

1. Karoo Kafe
2. Dunbar Tea Room
3. Capt. Frosty's
4. Betsy's Diner
5. Marshland Restaurant
6. Squealing Pig
7. Sir Cricket's
8. Wicked Fire Kissed Pizza
9. Liam's at Nauset
10. D'Parma Italian Table

BEST BUYS: MARTHA'S VINEYARD

1. Art Cliff Diner
2. Larsen's Fish Mkt.
3. Bite
4. Net Result
5. Newes from America
6. Zapotec
7. Offshore Ale
8. Giordano's
9. Sharky's Cantina
10. Lattanzi's

BEST BUYS: NANTUCKET

1. Fog Island Cafe
2. Even Keel Cafe
3. Pi Pizzeria
4. Sconset Café
5. Brotherhood/Thieves
6. Black-Eyed Susan's
7. Arno's
8. Sea Grille
9. Figs
10. Ropewalk

BEST BUYS: BERKSHIRES

1. Haven
2. Baba Louie's
3. Pho Saigon
4. Siam Sq. Thai
5. Mission Bar/Tapas
6. John Harvard's
7. Aroma B&G
8. Truc Orient
9. Barrington Brew
10. Flavours of Malaysia

BOSTON/
CAPE COD & THE ISLANDS
RESTAURANT
DIRECTORY

Boston

NEW Abbey, The ● *American*
`- | - | - | M`

Brookline | 1657 Beacon St. (Washington St.) | 617-730-8040 |
www.abbeyrestaurant.com

With owners who honed their craft around the corner at Washington
Square Tavern, this Brookline newcomer is a similarly casual "little
gem" serving moderately priced New American "comfort food with
a twist" until 1:30 AM nightly; the bar includes several local craft
beers as well as a wide selection of scotches and Irish whiskeys.

Abbondanza Ristorante Italiano ☒ *Italian*
`23 | 15 | 21 | $31`

Everett | 195 Main St. (Forest Ave.) | 617-387-8422 |
www.abbondanzaristorante.com

"Someone was paying attention to nana when she was cooking" coo
acolytes of this "jewel" in Everett, because the "rustic, delicious"
Italian fare is "the real thing" – plus, it's doled out in "large helpings"
and sold for "moderate prices"; while there's "nothing fancy about
the decor", the "awesome staff" "makes you feel right at home."

Abby Park ● *American*
`19 | 21 | 18 | $36`

Milton | 550 Adams St. (Franklin St.) | 617-696-8700 |
www.abbypark.com

In the "desert of dining options" that is East Milton Square, this
fairly priced New American bistro is a "welcome oasis", with "gorgeous decor" and a "happening" vibe, especially in the "wonderful
bar"; the dishes may be "nothing spectacular", but most palates
deem them "delish", and while service can be "spotty", at its best
it's "friendly" and "informed."

☑ Abe & Louie's *Steak*
`26 | 24 | 26 | $64`

Back Bay | 793 Boylston St. (Fairfield St.) | 617-536-6300 |
www.abeandlouies.com

If you have an "über expense account", "you really can't go wrong"
at this Back Bay "landmark" serving "sensational steaks" and
"equally impressive everything else" in "huge portions", plus an "extensive wine list" that offers many "reasonable prices"; "impeccable" "professional service" and "dark" "gentleman's-club" decor
impart a "classic feeling", but be prepared for "excessive decibel
levels", particularly from the "hot scene at the bar."

Addis Red Sea *Ethiopian*
`22 | 20 | 20 | $26`

South End | 544 Tremont St. (bet. Hansom & Waltham Sts.) |
617-426-8727 | www.addisredsea.com
Porter Square | 1755 Massachusetts Ave. (Linnaean St.) | Cambridge |
617-441-8727 | www.addisredseacambridge.com

"Be ready to eat with your hands" at these "frugal-eaters' dreams" in
Porter Square and the South End, where "spongy injera" bread "sops
up the aromatic and spicy Ethiopian" fare, honey wines wash it down
and everything's brought by "helpful" servers; "adventurous" types
like that the settings are "suitably exotic", though some surveyors

have issues with tables reminiscent of "enormous baskets" and "small stools" that make their "butts fall asleep."

Aegean *Greek*   20 | 18 | 20 | $28

Watertown | 640 Arsenal St. (bet. Coolidge Ave. & Greenough Blvd.) | 617-923-7771
Framingham | 257 Cochituate Rd. (bet. Caldor Rd. & Greenview St.) | 508-879-8424
www.aegeanrestaurants.com

"Everyone in the family, from kids to grandparents", feels "comfortable" at this "roomy" Watertown Greek "standby" and its even more "spacious", "contemporary" Framingham offshoot that also boasts a "hip-ish", "lively" bar; "accommodating", "friendly service" also pleases, but it's the "consistent" fare that "really shines", as it comes in "huge portions" that make for a "great value."

Aji *Japanese*   ∇ 23 | 19 | 22 | $40

Newtonville | 340 Walnut St. (Washington Park) | 617-965-2801 | www.ajisushibar.com

"Who would have thought Newtonville would have a first-class sushi joint?" ask locals who've discovered this "relaxing, quiet" spot specializing in "creative rolls"; "simple", "dim" and "spacious" describes the dining room, which is filled with "plenty of tables" and "attentive, patient servers."

NEW Aka Bistro *French/Japanese*   25 | 21 | 23 | $55

Lincoln | 145 Lincoln Rd. (Ridge Rd.) | 781-259-9920 | www.akabistrolincoln.com

In the "leafy suburb of Lincoln" resides this "unique surprise" and "great addition to the Metrowest dining scene", where worldly palates can "mix and match" from separate menus of "classic French bistro fare" and "imaginative sashimi" (the former "quite reasonably priced", the latter leaning toward "stratospheric" cost levels); the "bustling", somewhat "sterile" interior often gets "noisy", which is why most ask for the "lovely" patio in warm weather.

Al Dente *Italian*   22 | 18 | 22 | $36

North End | 109 Salem St. (Cooper St.) | 617-523-0990 | www.aldenteboston.com

"Go in and feast" encourage supporters of this "homey" Italian "throwback" where "huge portions" of "basic", "dependable" "red sauce" are delivered for "good prices" by staffers who "make you feel like family"; "cramped quarters" mean "you have to squeeze in", but to most surveyors, that represents "everything you learn to love about North End eateries."

Z Alibi *American/Mediterranean*   19 | 26 | 20 | $37

Beacon Hill | Liberty Hotel | 215 Charles St. (bet. Cambridge & Fruit Sts.) | 857-241-1144 | www.alibiboston.com

"The old drunk tank never looked so swank" testify Beacon Hill imbibers about this "über-cool" nightlife venue ensconced in a former jail, whose "preserved cell bars and exposed brick" make for an "architecturally dramatic" environment; "expensive" American-

Med nibbles and "interesting" cocktails plus "good-looking" "people-watching" lure "hordes" of "fashionable" folks, with which "it can get too crowded", leading to sometimes "slow service."

☒ All Seasons Table *Asian*

27 | 25 | 23 | $32

Malden | 64 Pleasant St. (bet. Dartmouth & Washington Sts.) | 781-397-8788 | www.astrestaurant.com

Malden locals are "excited" that they "don't need to go into Boston" for an "excellent variety" of "beautifully prepared", "inventive" Asian cuisine, including "melt-in-your-mouth sushi", thanks to this spot whose moderate prices seem like a "bargain" due to the "large" portion sizes; an "attentive" staff helps maintain a "relaxed atmosphere" in the "artfully decorated" space, which springs to life with live jazz Thursday–Saturday evenings.

All Star Sandwich Bar *Sandwiches*

23 | 15 | 19 | $17

Inman Square | 1245 Cambridge St. (Prospect St.) | Cambridge | 617-868-3065 | www.allstarsandwichbar.com

"Masterpieces between two pieces of bread" is how "true connoisseurs" of sandwiches describe the "creative concoctions" whipped up at this "small", "frenetic" Inman Square shop, where the "wide variety" includes "rotating specials" and "irresistible" sides ("awesome poutine", hell fries, etc.); there's "no ambiance" in the "small space", and though some calculate it's "overpriced" for what it is, "gargantuan portions" compensate, as does the "friendly service."

☒ NEW Alma Nove *Italian/Mediterranean*

22 | 26 | 20 | $43

Hingham | 22 Shipyard Dr. (Rte. 3A) | 781-749-3353 | www.almanovehingham.com

The "wonderful vistas" afforded by its "location on the water in the old Hingham shipyard" "mesmerizes" as much as the "fabulous decor" and "outdoor seating with fire pit" at this "already popular", "upscale" Italo-Med newcomer; though a few respondents claim there are "kinks" to "work out" in the food and service, for the most part, they're "impressive" (if a wee bit "expensive for suburbs").

Alta Strada *Italian*

22 | 19 | 22 | $41

Wellesley | 92 Central St. (Weston Rd.) | 781-237-6100 | www.altastradarestaurant.com

"Sophisticated Italian" fare – like "deeply flavored pastas", "innovative antipasti" and other "enjoyable small plates" – from chef Michael Schlow is "promptly served" (and "a tad pricey") at this "modern" venue in Wellesley Center; with "lots of wood, hard surfaces and cramped tables", the dining room is often "noisy", which is why some folks stick to takeout from the "fantastic downstairs market."

Amarin of Thailand *Thai*

21 | 17 | 20 | $26

Newton | 287 Centre St. (Jefferson St.) | 617-527-5255
Wellesley | 27 Grove St. (bet. Central & Spring Sts.) | 781-239-1350
www.amarinofthailand.com

These "old reliables" in Newton and Wellesley are "convenient" stops for a "broad selection" of "boldly flavored", "easy-on-the-wallet" Thai "standards"; "take-out service is quick and friendly", but the "soothing decor" and "pleasant atmosphere" make them equally "appealing" for dining in.

Amelia's Kitchen *Italian*   18 | 14 | 17 | $26

Somerville | Teele Sq. | 1137 Broadway (Curtis St.) | 617-776-2800 | www.ameliaskitchen.com

Regulars revere the "wonderful" Italian "home cooking" doled out for "reasonable prices" at this Somerville neighborhood haunt; on the other hand, detractors deem it "nothing to write home about", citing "standard" eats, "spotty service" and "decor in need of an update."

Amelia's Trattoria 🗷 *Italian*   21 | 17 | 19 | $38

Kendall Square | 111 Harvard St. (Portland St.) | Cambridge | 617-868-7600 | www.ameliastrattoria.com

"Affordably priced", "inventive Italian cooking" "satisfies" hearty appetites at this Kendall Square spot whose "decor has a modern flair"; service is for the most part "good", leaving only the space to complain about: respondents "wish the restaurant was a little larger" (so "don't let the secret out!").

NEW American Craft *Pub Food*   17 | 17 | 18 | $27

Brookline | 1700 Beacon St. (Tappan St.) | 617-487-4290 | www.eatgoodfooddrinkbetterbeer.com

Although its hops list is "not quite as extensive" as that at The Publick House, this younger sibling "down the street" in Brookline harbors its own "fantastic selection" of brews, plus "bartenders who know their stuff", making it a "beer snob's dream"; to accompany is "hearty", "reasonably priced" pub grub that's "undistinguished", though "generally good", with "customizable burgers" that can be "great"; P.S. fans raise a glass to the "seasonal patio seating."

Amrheins *American*   19 | 17 | 19 | $29

South Boston | 80 W. Broadway (A St.) | 617-268-6189 | www.amrheinsboston.com

For a taste of "old-time Southie", head for this "casual, cozy" "institution" where the Traditional American fare is offered in "big portions" that are "easy-on-the-wallet"; it "can be noisy" due in part to the "enormous" screens playing sports at the "popular bar" (a "magnificent" specimen "from the 1800s"), while in summer, there's a "relaxing patio" "decorated to help you forget it's in a parking lot."

Anchovies ● *Italian*   19 | 15 | 20 | $23

South End | 433 Columbus Ave. (bet. Braddock Park & Holyoke St.) | 617-266-5088

This "tiny South End mainstay" with a "dive-bar setting" is often "packed" with "young" "locals", many of whom label the "no-frills", "flavorful" Italian food some of the "best cheap, late-night eats in town"; "strong drinks" and an "entertaining staff" add to the "quirky, fun" atmosphere, for which it's "worth the wait" on busy nights.

	FOOD	DECOR	SERVICE	COST

Angela's Café *Mexican* `25` `14` `22` `$25`

East Boston | 131 Lexington St. (Brooks St.) | 617-567-4972 |
www.angelascaferestaurant.com

"Mama can cook" assure devotees of this "family-run" spot in East
Boston that's "a bit off the beaten track, but worth the effort" for
"amazing, authentic Mexican" breakfasts, lunches and dinners with
"a few twists"; a "welcoming" staff and prices that "won't put too big
a dent in your wallet" are further advantages, making it easy to overlook the "small", "no-frills environment."

Angelo's ⊠ *Italian* ▽ `27` `18` `21` `$37`

Stoneham | 237 Main St. (bet. Elm & William Sts.) | 781-279-9035 |
www.angeloristorante.com

With its "amazing pastas", "well-organized wine list" and "high
standards of service", this Italian "gem" in Stoneham is regarded by
some to be "possibly even better than North End" competitors;
while the setting has been "spiffed-up to be more modern", a few
patrons find it "a bit hard to ignore the comings and goings" from the
"take-out pizza" side "depending on the table", so rather than
chance it, they too "take it home."

☒ Anna's Taqueria *Tex-Mex* `23` `11` `18` `$10`

Beacon Hill | 242 Cambridge St. (Garden St.) | 617-227-8822
Cambridgeport | MIT Stratton Student Ctr. | 84 Massachusetts Ave.
(Vassar St.) | Cambridge | 617-324-2662 ◑
Porter Square | Porter Exchange Mall | 822 Somerville Ave. (Mass. Ave.) |
Cambridge | 617-661-8500
Brookline | 1412 Beacon St. (Summit Ave.) | 617-739-7300
Brookline | 446 Harvard St. (bet. Coolidge & Thorndike Sts.) |
617-277-7111
Somerville | 236 Elm St. (bet. Bower Ave. & Chester St.) | 617-666-3900
www.annastaqueria.com

For "huge", "addictive" burritos, "tasty tacos" and "amazing quesadillas" "made to order" "fast" and "as you like" them, supporters get
on line at this "counter-service" Tex-Mex chain "institution"; true,
the settings are "functional" at best, but for a "super deal", you
"can't beat Anna's"; P.S. Cambridgeport is cash only.

NEW Anthem Kitchen + Bar ◑ *American* `19` `19` `19` `$33`

Faneuil Hall | Faneuil Hall Mktpl. | 101 S. Market St. (Merchants Row) |
617-720-5570 | www.anthem-boston.com

"Tourists" and "local patriots" alike heed the siren song of this
"great addition to Faneuil Hall", where "pleasant", "decently portioned" New American comfort food is brought by a mostly "friendly
staff" in "spacious", "trendy-elegant" digs; people-watching is a
particular treat from the "nice outdoor" area, but the best feature
may be the prices: "reasonable", especially considering the area.

☒ Anthony's Pier 4 *Seafood* `18` `19` `19` `$50`

Seaport District | 140 Northern Ave. (Pier 4) | 617-482-6262 |
www.pier4.com

"After all these years", this "Boston landmark" in the Seaport District
still claims acolytes who value "spectacular harbor views", "quality"

seafood, "to-die-for popovers", "formally attired waiters" and other bits of "comforting" "nostalgia"; however, critics label it a "tired" "tourist trap" with an "overpriced" menu that's "stuck in the '80s" and service that's "lacking" in every way but "attitude."

Antico Forno *Italian/Pizza*   23 | 18 | 20 | $33

North End | 93 Salem St. (bet. Cross & Parmenter Sts.) | 617-723-6733 | www.anticofornoboston.com

The "smell of the wood-burning oven will lure you inside" this "homey" North End "gem", and the "reliably tasty", "reasonably priced", "traditional" Southern Italian cuisine "will keep you coming back", particularly the "to-die-for brick-oven pizza"; most staffers remain "good sports" when the dining room gets "crowded and noisy", and if some become "brash", well, that's "part of the charm."

Antonio's Cucina Italiana ⊠ *Italian*   23 | 16 | 22 | $28

Beacon Hill | 286 Cambridge St. (bet. Anderson & Grove Sts.) | 617-367-3310 | www.antoniosofbeaconhill.com

This "no-frills" Beacon Hill Italian provides "generous" helpings of "delicious" "red sauce" to "hungry families" and scrubs (it's "across from Mass General") at a "low cost" and "without the North End hustle"; the "staff makes you feel like family", but "with one small room", it gets "crowded" and "noisy" easily, so some folks peg it as "best for takeout."

Apollo Grill & Sushi ❶ *Japanese/Korean*   ∇ 19 | 13 | 13 | $30

Chinatown | 84-86 Harrison Ave. (Kneeland St.) | 617-423-3888

The atmosphere at this all-night Chinatown joint is "nothing to write home about", the sushi and Korean barbecue served is "ok, not great" and "you can get better service elsewhere"; but "the prices are so good that you won't care", especially at 3 AM, when hunger strikes after clubbing.

Appetito *Italian*   17 | 15 | 17 | $34

Newton | 761 Beacon St. (Langley Rd.) | 617-244-9881

"Consistently wonderful year after year" cheer devotees of this "convenient" "neighborhood Italian place" in Newton Center whose "friendly" ambiance is "great for a romantic night out"; however, detractors deem it "overpriced for what you get", namely "uneven food", "tired", "tight" digs and "slow", sometimes "cranky" service.

⊠ Aquitaine *French*   23 | 22 | 22 | $43

South End | 569 Tremont St. (bet. Clarendon & Dartmouth Sts.) | 617-424-8577 | www.aquitaineboston.com

Chestnut Hill | Chestnut Hill Shopping Ctr. | 11 Boylston St. (bet. Hammond Pond Pkwy. & Hammond St.) | 617-734-8400 | www.aquitainebis.com

Dedham | Legacy Pl. | 500 Legacy Pl. (Providence Hwy.) | 781-471-5212 | www.aquitainededham.com

At this bistro bunch – the "hip", "noisy" South End original, the more "cozy" Chestnut Hill branch that enlivens a "colorless strip mall" and the "charming" Dedham sophomore – "artfully constructed", "fabu" French cuisine, "cool cocktails" and "great wines" come via "friendly", "attentive service"; brunch is particularly "delightful", so overall, the main debate is about cost: "a bit expensive for what it is" vs. "reasonable."

Artú *Italian*
22 | 17 | 20 | $33

Beacon Hill | 89 Charles St. (Pinckney St.) | 617-227-9023
North End | 6 Prince St. (Hanover St.) | 617-742-4336
www.artuboston.com

With a "cute little basement" location on "equally quaint Charles Street" and another "in the heart of the North End" with a "relaxed bar", this Italian duo provides a "dazzling array of creative antipasti", "rave"-worthy rotisserie meats and "solid pastas" at "great prices"; "service is friendly and timely", but "it's a bit cramped" (especially the Beacon Hill haunt), so some utilize it primarily for takeout.

Z Asana *New England*
22 | 25 | 24 | $61

Back Bay | Mandarin Oriental | 776 Boylston St. (Fairfield St.) | 617-535-8888 | www.mandarinoriental.com

"Upscale elegance without the attitude" is the name of the game at this Back Bay New Englander where fans say that the staff is as "doting" and "charming" as the design is "sleek", "chic" and "gorgeous" (after they peel their eyes from "people-watching" through the floor-to-ceiling windows); additionally, the fare is "interesting and tasty", albeit "pricey" – but this is the Mandarin Oriental after all.

Ashmont Grill *American*
23 | 21 | 22 | $34

Dorchester | 555 Talbot Ave. (Ashmont St.) | 617-825-4300 | www.ashmontgrill.com

Choose from "delicious comfort food" or more "sophisticated" American entrees – either way you will "not spend a fortune" at this "delightful" "Dorchester oasis" that habitués say just "gets better with the years"; the "cool", artistically designed dining room, "vibrant bar" (the milieu of "wonderful wines" and "excellent signature cocktails") and "cozy backyard patio with a fire pit" get "pretty crowded", but luckily, the "friendly staff" is adept at staying "on top of things."

Asmara *Eritrean/Ethiopian*
22 | 15 | 23 | $26

Central Square | 739 Massachusetts Ave. (bet. Pleasant & Temple Sts.) | Cambridge | 617-864-7447 | www.asmararestaurantboston.com

"Adventurous" "students, faculty and yuppies" rave about the Eritrean-Ethiopian "taste and tactile sensations" supplied at this "warm, inviting" Central Square spot where the fare is served without utensils but with "spongy bread"; the interior is "not fancy", but that fits the "family-owned business vibe", as do the "attentive" servers and moderate prices.

Assaggio ◑ *Italian*
23 | 20 | 22 | $40

North End | 29 Prince St. (Hanover St.) | 617-227-7380 | www.assaggioboston.com

Everyone says "try to sit upstairs and near the window" for "the full North End experience" at this "classic Italian place", while opinions about the "dim" "wine cellar" with "plastic grapes hanging from the "ceiling" are divided between "proves to be romantic" and "kinda tacky"; the bar is also "great", but wherever you end up, the fare is "consistent", the staff is "friendly" and the "prices are reasonable."

Atasca *Portuguese*   20 | 20 | 21 | $32

Kendall Square | 50 Hampshire St. (Webster Ave.) | Cambridge | 617-621-6991 | www.atasca.com

"Why it isn't always packed to the gills is a mystery" to those "charmed" by this Portuguese spot in Kendall Square, where the seafood and steaks are "nothing less than delicious" and "reasonably priced" to boot; everything's served with "pride" and "attention to detail" by "friendly" servers, who bounce between the "pleasant", "intimate" interior and "lovely", "lushly planted patio."

Athan's European   22 | 18 | 17 | $14
Bakery & Café *Bakery/Mediterranean*

Brighton | 407 Washington St. (bet. Leicester & Parsons Sts.) | 617-783-0313
Brookline | 1621 Beacon St. (Washington St.) | 617-734-7028
www.athansbakery.com

"Desserts that are as delicious as they are beautiful" "lure" like "sirens" at these Brookline and Brighton Mediterranean bakeries that whip up "yummy coffee drinks" too (407 also offers a "slim" selection of panini and salads); despite the "minimal decor" and "not-too-friendly" service, fans "sit for hours" "pretending they're in Europe."

Atlantica ⓜ *Seafood*   ▽ 20 | 25 | 21 | $39

Cohasset | 44 Border St. (Summer St.) | 781-383-0900 | www.cohassetharborresort.com

While "you won't find anything particularly cutting-edge" on the "extensive" seafood menu at this Cohasset eatery, it's "reliable", with Sunday brunch providing particularly "excellent" options; the "fun, friendly" bar area is a draw, but it's the "stunning views" that keep acolytes "coming back", as the "lovely" venue with a "wonderful" deck "literally hangs out over the harbor."

ⓩ Atlantic Fish Co. *Seafood*   24 | 21 | 23 | $46

Back Bay | 761 Boylston St. (bet. Exeter & Fairfield Sts.) | 617-267-4000 | www.atlanticfishco.com

"After a day of shopping" in the Back Bay, "rest your feet" (if "not your credit card") at this "reliable" destination for a "real Boston seafood" experience (e.g. "amazing clam chowder in a bread bowl"), complete with "welcoming", "attentive service"; everyone from "business" types to "college kids with visiting parents in tow" keeps the "classy" "wood-and-brass" interior and "great" sidewalk-dining area "buzzing", and while that causes some to label it "a tourist trap", connoisseurs find it simply "sensational."

Audubon Circle *American*   21 | 19 | 19 | $24

Kenmore Square | 838 Beacon St. (Arundel St.) | 617-421-1910 | www.auduboncircle.us

"With a variety of food and drink options for every taste and budget" ("creative touches" abound, but the "super burgers and potstickers" are the stars) and a "trendy-gastropub" environment, this American spot is a "welcome" "alternative" to Kenmore Square's "proliferation of sports bars" ("the minimal TV presence" is "appreciated"); both the "cute patio" and "long, narrow, dark" interior are "great first-date" or "perfect pre-Fenway" places, and the mostly "responsive" service is another plus.

Aura *American* 22 | 20 | 22 | $53

Seaport District | Seaport Hotel | 1 Seaport Ln. (bet. Congress St. & Northern Ave.) | 617-385-4300 | www.aurarestaurant.com

"Terrific" New American fare by a "creative chef" makes this "expensive" Seaport District spot a "step up from your ordinary hotel" restaurant, even if its setting is "decidedly hotellike"; nevertheless, it "exudes a warm and comfortable aura" thanks mainly to servers who "could not be more obliging."

Avenue One *American* ∇ 19 | 17 | 19 | $46

Downtown Crossing | Hyatt Regency Boston | 1 Ave. de Lafayette (bet. Chauncy & Washington Sts.) | 617-422-5579

The Hyatt Regency's all-day restaurant "does not get enough love" according to admirers who deem it "a gem" for its "well-done" New American fare, "professional" staff and "accessible location in Downtown Crossing"; indeed, it's "nice" for a "leisurely" meal, as "one never feels rushed here."

Avila *Mediterranean* 23 | 24 | 24 | $50

Theater District | 1 Charles St. S. (Stuart St.) | 617-267-4810 | www.avilarestaurant.com

"Strikingly tasty, creative" Mediterranean cuisine is the métier of this "go-to restaurant in the Theater District" (an "offshoot of Davio's"), where full meals are "slightly expensive" but the "delicious small dishes" at the "happening bar" are a "great value"; the "elegant", "bright", "airy" setting features "high ceilings, huge windows" and a "friendly" staff that's "accommodating" "if you want to have a leisurely meal" and "prompt" if you have "tickets to a show."

Bacco *Italian* 21 | 19 | 19 | $40

North End | 107 Salem St. (Parmenter St.) | 617-624-0454 | www.bacconorthend.com

Its "great location in the North End" explains why this Italian eatery with two "pleasant" though somewhat "tight" floors and a bar is "extremely crowded" on most nights, which means you should "be prepared to wait", "even with a reservation"; as for the fare, though by most accounts it's "genuinely good", many deem it nonetheless "a tad overpriced."

NEW Back Bay Social Club ❷ *American* 18 | 20 | 22 | $36

Back Bay | 867 Boylston St. (bet. Fairfield & Gloucester Sts.) | 617-247-3200 | www.backbaysocialclub.com

"Fantastic" "creative" and "trendy-throwback" cocktails are the "highlights" of this "classy addition" to the Back Bay offering an "upbeat" "speakeasy atmosphere" on two levels, plus what some call "tasty" American fare; naysayers claim it "focuses far more on the social scene than it does its food", but most everyone applauds the "well-oiled team" of servers.

Back Eddy, The *Seafood* | 23 | 21 | 21 | $38

Westport | 1 Bridge Rd. (Rte. 88) | 508-636-6500 | www.thebackeddy.com

"Après-beach", "get seated outside or next to a window" and "watch the sun set over the marshes" at this "ultimate summer restaurant" in Westport, whipping up "wonderfully fresh", "imaginative" seafood dishes; you might have to "wait for a table", but there are "places to hang out" on the dock while "having a drink or two", "quite a special" experience in and of itself.

Baja Betty's Burritos ⊄ *Mexican* | ▽ 23 | 12 | 22 | $13

Brookline | 3 Harvard Sq. (Davis Ave.) | 617-277-8900 | www.bajabettys.com

"Starving students" and families with kids descend upon this "cheap" Brookline shop for "ginormous" burritos with a "tantalizing" selection of "creative fillings" plus other "Californian-style" Mexican fare; "friendly folks" man the counter, but "the place is tiny with not many places to sit", so count on taking it out.

Bakers' Best Cafe *American* | 22 | 14 | 16 | $20

Newton | 27 Lincoln St. (bet. Hartford & Walnut Sts.) | 617-332-4588 | www.bakersbestcatering.com

"A known quantity" among the "ladies who lunch in Newton", this New American bakery/cafe serves up "an excellent variety" of "somewhat pricey" breakfasts, lunches, brunches and desserts; it's "comfort food at its finest", though the storefront environs are "less than comfortable", so let the "efficient" counter staff wrap it up to go.

Bambara *American* | 21 | 22 | 22 | $41

East Cambridge | Hotel Marlowe | 25 Edwin H. Land Blvd. (Rte. 28) | Cambridge | 617-868-4444 | www.bambara-cambridge.com

Finicky folks who "normally eschew hotel restaurants" say "don't miss this one" when in East Cambridge, as its New American fare is "innovative, delicious" and "good value for the quality", particularly considering the "generous portions"; what's more, there's a "beautiful" setting that's as notable for its "designer decor", "comfortable banquets" and "nice bar" as it is for "friendly", "attentive service."

Bamboo *Thai* | 23 | 18 | 22 | $24

Brighton | 1616 Commonwealth Ave. (Washington St.) | 617-734-8192 | www.bamboothairestaurant.com

"Consistently fresh, delicious" Thai with some "healthy touches" earns this affordable Brighton eatery "cut-above" status; attention is paid to the "friendly staff", but some diners say "dining in can be uncomfortable", partly because the setting feels "a little old."

☑ B&G Oysters *Seafood* | 26 | 20 | 22 | $47

South End | 550 Tremont St. (Waltham St.) | 617-423-0550 | www.bandgoysters.com

"So shucking good" say surveyors of this Barbara Lynch "pearl" in the South End, where "a wonderful array" of "hard-to-find" "oysters and other sea creatures of that ilk" from "around the world" star on the "limited" seafood menu (the "lobster roll rocks" too, as does the "creative wine list"); yes, there are usually "long waits" to get a table in the "miniature, cramped", "informal" digs or on the "delightful" patio, and "you'll pay dearly" too, but most agree "the hassles" are "well worth it."

Bangkok Bistro *Thai*
∇ 18 | 13 | 17 | $26

Brighton | 1952 Beacon St. (Chestnut Hill Ave.) | 617-739-7270
Given its "unassuming location" in Brighton's Cleveland Circle and "outdated decor", this cheap eatery "surprises" with "consistent, well-prepared" Thai fare; it's particularly "great for a quick lunch", but most locals keep it on the list strictly as a "take-out joint", not least of all because service can swing from "friendly" to "snooty."

Bangkok Blue *Thai*
20 | 13 | 20 | $24

Back Bay | 651 Boylston St. (bet. Dartmouth & Exeter Sts.) | 617-266-1010 | www.bkkblueboston.com
"Weekday lunch crowds" swarm this Back Bay Thai for "large portions" of "super-affordable", "dependably good food"; "pleasant servers" buzz between the "typically decorated" dining room and the "nice" patio, a "great spot for people-watching" due to its "location overlooking the Boston Public Library."

Bangkok City *Thai*
23 | 20 | 23 | $28

Back Bay | 167 Massachusetts Ave. (Belvidere St.) | 617-266-8884 | www.bkkcityboston.com
"Before the symphony" or a "Berklee show" are "convenient" times to hit this Back Bay venue offering "low-priced", "great-tasting" Thai cuisine, including "spicier, more complex meals at the back" of the "huge menu"; the space is marked by "decorative artwork", an atrium and servers who are "accommodating" whether you desire an "unhurried" meal or are "rushing" to make a curtain.

Baraka Cafe Ⓜ 🏱 *African*
25 | 18 | 18 | $24

Central Square | 80½ Pearl St. (bet. Auburn & William Sts.) | Cambridge | 617-868-3951 | www.barakacafe.com
An "inexpensive" "trip to another world" comes via this "tiny" Central Square spot where "amazing, unusual" North African fare is served in "quirkily decorated" digs; "everyone raves" about the "crave-worthy" rose-petal lemonade, but still, some find "no alcohol" "a bummer", just like the "sometimes long waits" to get in (due to no reservations, not many tables and occasionally "slow" service).

🄩 Barker Tavern Ⓜ *American*
27 | 26 | 26 | $44

Scituate | 21 Barker Rd. (Brookline Rd.) | 781-545-6533 | www.thebarker.com
"For a special evening", this "old-school" Scituate tavern "has it all": "wonderful" Traditional American fare, "a nice wine list", "caring staff" and an "outstanding", "historical" Colonial setting; the main dining room is somewhat "formal", but things are more "relaxed" in the adjoining pub, plus you'll "save a couple of bucks" there.

Barking Crab *Seafood*
17 | 16 | 16 | $31

Seaport District | 88 Sleeper St. (bet. Northern Ave. & Seaport Blvd.) | 617-426-2722 | www.barkingcrab.com

"Always loud and raucous" with "younger" folks and "tourists" (expect "long waits"), this Seaport District spot serves "really cold beers" and "basic fried and boiled fish" (with "a wide spectrum of prices") "served at picnic tables" by sometimes "spotty" staffers; befitting the "seafood-in-the-rough experience", "the place is nothing much to look at", but "if you can sit outside, the atmosphere is great."

BarLola ● *Spanish*
17 | 19 | 18 | $33

Back Bay | 160 Commonwealth Ave. (Dartmouth St.) | 617-266-1122 | www.barlola.com

"Groups of friends" "love" this Back Bay Spaniard for its "beautiful patio" and "sexy, subterranean dining room", especially "after-work" and "Sunday nights, with live flamenco performances"; though tipplers recommend the "delish sangria", foodies disagree about the tapas: "solidly yummy" vs. "uninspired", therefore "pricey."

NEW Barlow's ● *American*
16 | 18 | 18 | $31

Seaport District | 241 A St. (Binford St.) | 617-338-2142 | www.barlowsrestaurant.com

American "standards" are "dressed-up" and "done pretty well" at this Seaport District addition serving "gorgeous cocktails" in an "open, airy", "industrial" interior and on a patio; though it occasionally can be "quiet" due to its "off-the-beaten-path" location, it's oftentimes "crowded" and "noisy", especially "after work."

NEW Barracuda Tavern ● *Seafood*
- | - | - | M

Downtown Crossing | 15 Bosworth St. (bet. Province & Tremont Sts.) | 617-482-0301 | www.barracudatavern.com

The affordable menu at this Cajun-kissed Downtown Crossing seafooder runs the gamut from fish tacos with chipotle aioli to clam po' boys to Caribbean chicken; it's all accompanied by wine and a dozen or so microbrews and served in an ocean-themed setting with a hanging rowboat and pictures of the beach until 1:30 AM nightly.

Bar 10 ● *Mediterranean*
21 | 22 | 20 | $33

Back Bay | Westin Copley Pl. | 10 Huntington Ave. (Dartmouth St.) | 617-424-7446 | www.westin.com

Thanks to its "cozy booths" and "beautiful decor" with "lots of cocoa/mocha colors", this "relaxing" Back Bay hotel lounge makes a "nice first-date place"; but it's also "great" for "-after-work" or "catching up" with friends thanks to its "massive bar" where "decent drinks" are sopped up with "tasty" Mediterranean small plates.

NEW Basho Japanese Brasserie ● *Japanese*
23 | 22 | 20 | $41

Fenway | 1338 Boylston St. (bet. Jersey & Kilmarnock Sts.) | 617-262-1338 | www.bashosushi.com

"Wonderful sashimi", "fantastic" "sushi concoctions" and cooked fare from a glass-enclosed robata grill comprise the "huge menu" proffered at this "big" Fenway Japanese; some dropping by "before a Red Sox game" find the prices "a little high for the Fenway" (and the "minimal decor" "too hip"), but most think it's "worth it", particularly when factoring in the "attentive service" and "large portions."

Basta Pasta Italian
22 | 10 | 17 | $17

Central Square | 319 Western Ave. (Montague St.) | Cambridge | 617-576-6672 | www.bastapastacambridge.com
NEW Quincy | 150 Hancock St. (Kendall St.) | 617-479-7979 | www.bastapastaenoteca.com **M**

"Ignore" the decor and join the "loyal following" of this Central Square spot for "generous portions" of "Italian comfort food" "prepared skillfully with fresh ingredients"; it's "among the best values in the area", and it's "amazing for takeout", thanks in large part to the "quick service"; P.S. the new, "fancier" Quincy enoteca displays a "slightly more extensive menu and somewhat higher prices."

Beacon Hill Bistro French
23 | 21 | 22 | $43

Beacon Hill | Beacon Hill Hotel | 25 Charles St. (Branch St.) | 617-723-1133 | www.beaconhillhotel.com

"All things local and sustainable" go into the "reliable, unpretentious" French bistro fare crafted at this "neighborhood gem" in the Beacon Hill Hotel, where "knowledgeable servers" proffer the "affordable menu" (even those who deem it "a little pricey" say it's "worth it") and "impressive wine list"; the "casually elegant" environs are as "easygoing" as they are "intimate", and particularly "cozy" "on a snowy winter night."

Beacon Street Tavern American
19 | 18 | 18 | $30

Brookline | 1032 Beacon St. (bet. Carlton & St. Mary's Sts.) | 617-713-2700 | www.beacon1032.com

The "trendy" takes on "classic" American pub food are wholly "decent" at this "cozy", "lively" Brookline tavern with a "large sidewalk patio for balmy summer evenings"; service runs the gamut from "cheerful" to "indifferent", but since the tabs are typically "not expensive", it usually doesn't matter much either way.

Beehive American
20 | 24 | 20 | $35

South End | Boston Center for the Arts | 541 Tremont St. (Clarendon St.) | 617-423-0069 | www.beehiveboston.com

"Super arty" "twenty-" and "thirtysomething" "hipsters" depend on this "funky", "sexy", "bohemian" New American restaurant/ "high-end night club" as a "place to bring a date or find one in the South End"; the New American fare has "flair", but most of the "buzz" is reserved for the "cutting-edge" cocktails and "killer" nightly live music performances; P.S. it's "wonderful for brunch" too.

Bella Luna Restaurant & Milky Way Lounge Italian
19 | 21 | 19 | $25

Jamaica Plain | The Brewery | 284 Amory St. (Minton St.) | 617-524-6060 | www.milkywayjp.com

"Located in the same brick complex as the Sam Adams brewery", this "lively", "eye-catching" "Jamaica Plain staple" pairs "reliable"

FOOD   DECOR   SERVICE   COST

Italian fare like "tasty pizza" with "specialty beers on tap"; live music, a dance floor, video games and "friendly" servers who "have no issues with kids" make it a "gathering place" "for family and friends" alike, as does the fact that the "bill doesn't break the bank."

Bella's *Italian* | – | – | – | M |

Rockland | 933 Hingham St. (Commerce Rd.) | 781-871-5789 |
www.bellasrestaurant.com

Behold "the hidden jewel of the South Shore" say Rockland diners of this "old-fashioned Italian" haunt harboring "solid", affordable "red-sauce" fare, a "helpful staff" and a setting that's as appropriate for "a big group" as it is for "a romantic dinner"; furthermore, with a bar that's "a great place for drinks, Keno" and to watch "a game", there's no need to go "all the way to the North End."

NEW Benevento's *Pizza*   ▽ | 21 | 18 | 21 | $22 |

North End | 111 Salem St. (Cooper St.) | 617-523-4111 |
www.beneventosboston.com

"Excellent pizza" with a side of "friendly service" makes this Italian a "great addition" to the North End, though some feel other items "don't live up to expectations"; "copper ceilings and a granite bar" help craft a "warm" ambiance, but the space is small and "crowded", so beware if you "don't love sitting on top of the next table."

Z NEW Bergamot *American* | 27 | 23 | 26 | $51 |

Somerville | 118 Beacon St. (Kirkland St.) | 617-576-7700 |
www.bergamotrestaurant.com

"Nuanced, creative" seasonal New American fare featuring "interesting juxtapositions of tastes and textures" is "backed by a sound wine list" and "well-trained, friendly" service at this "sophisticated but unpretentious", "wonderful addition" to Somerville; all in all, "prices are not outrageous", although the "portions are on the smallish side" so big appetites recommend you "get three courses or you may leave hungry."

Bernard's *Chinese* | 25 | 14 | 22 | $35 |

Chestnut Hill | The Mall at Chestnut Hill | 199 Boylston St. (Hammond Pond Pkwy.) | 617-969-3388

"Exquisite" "gourmet Chinese" fare that's "light, fresh and non-greasy" plus "pleasant, helpful" servers equals an experience that's "so much better than the setting suggests" at this "delight" in the Chestnut Hill Mall; indeed, the "sparse decor" is "badly in need of an update", but with "great value" practically guaranteed, it's "always crowded" – and "noisy" too.

Bertucci's *Italian* | 18 | 15 | 17 | $23 |

Faneuil Hall | Faneuil Hall Mktpl. | 22 Merchants Row (bet. Chatham & State Sts.) | 617-227-7889
Kenmore Square | 533 Commonwealth Ave. (Brookline Ave.) | 617-236-1030
Central Square | 799 Main St. (bet. Cherry & Windsor Sts.) | Cambridge | 617-661-8356

(continued)

(continued)

Bertucci's

Harvard Square | 21 Brattle St. (Mt. Auburn St.) | Cambridge |
617-864-4748
Huron Village | 5 Cambridgepark Dr. (Alewife Brook Pkwy.) |
Cambridge | 617-876-2200
Braintree | 412 Franklin St. (West St.) | 781-849-3066
Chestnut Hill | Atrium Mall | 300 Boylston St. (Florence St.) |
617-965-0022
Medford | 4054 Mystic Valley Pkwy. (Fellsway) | 781-396-9933
Newton | 275 Centre St. (Pearl St.) | 617-244-4900
Framingham | 150 Worcester Rd. (Caldor Rd.) | 508-879-9161
www.bertuccis.com
Additional locations throughout the Boston area

It's "rug-rat heaven" at this "decent" Italian chain that's a "surefire
thing" with the kids (who get to "play with dough" at the table); just
"stick with" the brick-oven pies, "hot rolls" and "nice salads" (the
other selections can seem "processed"), and you'll get a "predictable" meal for a "fair price."

Betty's Wok &
| 17 | 14 | 17 | $26 |
Noodle Diner *Asian/Nuevo Latino*

MFA | 250 Huntington Ave. (bet. Gainsborough St. & Mass. Ave.) |
617-424-1950 | www.bettyswokandnoodle.com

Set near the MFA, this "funky" Asian–Nuevo Latino "retro diner" ca-
ters to "picky eaters" with "inexpensive" "build-your-own noodle
bowls"; however, some cite "disappointing" dishes in which "everything's glopped together", not to mention "worn" digs, as proof the
"convenient" "location is the best thing going for it", especially for a
"quick bite" "before the symphony or the theater."

B. Good *Burgers*
| 18 | 13 | 18 | $11 |

Back Bay | 131 Dartmouth St. (bet. Columbus Ave. & Stuart St.) |
617-424-5252
NEW Back Bay | 137 Massachusetts Ave. (Boylston St.) |
617-236-5480
Back Bay | 272 Newbury St. (bet. Fairfield & Gloucester Sts.) |
617-236-0440
NEW Downtown Crossing | 255 Washington St. (Water St.) |
617-227-1006
Harvard Square | 24 Dunster St. (bet. Mass. Ave. & Mt. Auburn St.) |
Cambridge | 617-354-6500
Dedham | Legacy Pl. | 950 Providence Hwy. (Elm St.) |
781-251-0222
NEW Hingham | Derby Street Shoppes | 94 Derby St. (off Pilgrims Hwy.) |
781-741-5393
www.bgood.com

Salubrious surveyors are "obsessed" with this local "healthy fast-
food" chain's "all-natural burgers", "non-fried fries", "inventive
sandwiches" and "great shakes"; however, there is a vocal contingent that thinks the "concept is better in theory than in practice",
because it's "overpriced" not only "for what you get", but also
"relative to yummier competitors."

Bhindi Bazaar Indian Cafe *Indian*   20 | 16 | 20 | $22

Back Bay | 95 Massachusetts Ave. (bet. Commonwealth Ave. & Newbury St.) | 617-450-0660 | www.bhindibazaar.com

"Bring your appetite", because the "great curries, lovely breads" and "excellent dosas" are ladled out in "large portions" at this "good deal" in the Back Bay; you probably "wouldn't make a special trip" for its "unremarkable digs", but for those heading to "a Sox game" or a Berklee show, it's quite "handy."

Bia Bistro ☑ *Mediterranean*   ▽ 25 | 19 | 21 | $45

Cohasset | 35 S. Main St. (Elm St.) | 781-383-0464 | www.biabistro.com

Advocates of this rustic, "casual" restaurant in Cohasset admit to having "always a pleasant evening", because although the Mediterranean fare is a bit pricey, it's "fantastic"; the location also helps it earn "best option" status, as it's "convenient if you're going to the nearby" South Shore Music Circus.

Big Papi's Grille *American*   13 | 19 | 16 | $33

Framingham | Worcester Rd./30 Rte. 9 E. (Shoppers World Dr.) | 508-620-9990 | www.bigpapisgrille.com

Sox fans say when slugger/owner David 'Big Papi' Ortiz "stops by with some of his baseball buddies", this "bright" Framingham New American sporting "awesome memorabilia" is a "treat"; however, foodies feel that, though "moderately priced", the Latin-tinged fare is "mediocre", and "slow service" is another strike against the place.

Billy Tse *Asian*   21 | 15 | 21 | $32

Revere | 441 Revere St. (Pierce St.) | 781-286-2882 | www.billytse-revere.com ☻
North End | 240 Commercial St. (Fleet St.) | 617-227-9990 | www.billytserestaurant.com

"In an area known for Italian and seafood places", this North Ender (with a Revere sibling) offers a "full range" of "something-for-everyone" Pan-Asian fare, including "quality sushi" and "tasty" "Americanized Chinese food"; it's "reliable" for "efficient service" and "reasonable prices" too, which helps "make up" for "no atmosphere."

Biltmore Bar & Grille, The *American*   21 | 19 | 20 | $28

Newton | 1205 Chestnut St. (Oak St.) | 617-527-2550 | www.thebiltmoregrill.com

"Solid" American "comfort food", "inventive cocktails" and a "great beer selection" make for a "winning combination" at this "warm", "dark, woodsy" "neighborhood pub" in Newton; "reasonable prices", "friendly" service and a "pleasant atmosphere" mean the dining room is "ok" for "families", but things can get "noisy on the bar side", which hosts "many young professionals' after-work bonding rituals."

Bina Osteria & Alimentari *Italian*   18 | 19 | 17 | $49

Downtown Crossing | 581 Washington St. (Avery St.) | 617-956-0888 | www.binaboston.com

A "great" location in Downtown Crossing makes this a "pre-theater choice", but surveyors split on whether the Italian fare is "delicious" or "bland" (therefore, "overpriced"); likewise, some applaud staffers who get you "in and out pretty quickly" and the "modern" digs, while others boo "inattentive service" and decor that's "surprisingly cold for an Italian restaurant"; P.S. the alimentari, the attached gourmet food-and-wine shop, offers take-out breakfasts, light lunches and gelato.

Bin 26 Enoteca *Italian*
21 | 22 | 21 | $45

Beacon Hill | 26 Charles St. (Chestnut St.) | 617-723-5939 | www.bin26.com

"Knowledgeable oenophiles" on staff suggest selections from the "expertly constructed, thoughtfully chosen" *vini* list at this Beacon Hill wine bar that also prepares "sophisticated", "slightly pricey" Italian plates (the "fresh pastas" are a particularly "perfect complement"); labels, corks and bottles are the design highlights of the otherwise "minimalist" space, which offers a few "stylish" surprises, e.g. "check out the ceilings in the bathrooms."

Birch Street Bistro *American*
∇ 20 | 20 | 18 | $33

Roslindale | 14 Birch St. (bet. Belgrade Ave. & Corinth St.) | 617-323-2184 | www.birchstbistro.com

"Love this place!" cheer Roslindale locals who cite "well-prepared", affordable American fare and a "wine list that's very good for such a small spot"; but its best feature may be the "friendly", "homey, neighborhood" setting (dark hues, exposed brick), which can get "crowded on music nights" (Thursdays); P.S. check out the patio in summer.

Bison County Bar and Grill *BBQ*
18 | 13 | 16 | $24

Waltham | 275 Moody St. (Crescent St.) | 781-642-9720 | www.bisoncounty.com

It "doesn't reach any heights", but BBQ junkies "have yet to be disappointed" at this Waltham joint where the portions are "generous" and the "prices are reasonable"; "strong" drinks and a "laid-back atmosphere" are constants, though not service, which runs the gamut from "prompt" to "slow."

Bistro Chi ◑ *Chinese*
- | - | - | M

Quincy | 37 Cottage Ave. (bet. Dennis Ryan Pkwy. & Hancock St.) | 617-773-3000 | www.bistrochi.com

While "there are a lot of Chinese restaurants in Quincy", supporters argue "this one is a step above the rest", as the affordable, authentic fare is augmented with "interesting", "tasty" "fusion-esque alternatives"; the "restful, spare", cream-colored setting features a small bar, soft lighting, bamboo and "comfortable banquettes", plus "efficient service" that adds to the "all in all satisfying experience."

Bistro du Midi *French*
23 | 24 | 23 | $57

Back Bay | 272 Boylston St. (bet. Arlington St. & Hadassah Way) | 617-426-7878 | www.bistrodumidi.com

Though it's "rather formal for a bistro", habitués are wholly "happy" with this Back Bay venture's "relaxing", "sophisticated" second-floor dining room with "beautiful views" of the Public Gardens and "well-prepared" Provençal fare, "a perfect combination" of "rustic" and "modern"; there's a "different menu" in the "casual street-level bar", but the staffers are universally "charming" and the prices generally "too expensive for bistro food."

☑ Bistro 5 ☒Ⓜ *Italian*　　| 27 | 23 | 26 | $48 |
West Medford | 5 Playstead Rd. (High St.) | 781-395-7464 | www.bistro5.com
In a "surprising" (ok, "weird") location "near the commuter rail" in West Medford lies this "warm, elegant" Northern Italian "gem" where "passionate" chef-owner Vittorio Ettore's "high-concept", "fabulous" "seasonal menus highlight the freshest ingredients"; "knowledgeable, friendly" staffers can recommend "incredible pairings" of wine that, like the fare, is priced "extremely reasonably" "for the quality and presentation."

Black Cow Tap & Grill *American/Pub Food* | 20 | 21 | 20 | $35 |
South Hamilton | 16 Bay Rd. (bet. Linden St. & Railroad Ave.) | 978-468-1166
Newburyport | 54R Merrimac St. (Green St.) | 978-499-8811
www.blackcowrestaurants.com
"Beef it up" at this pair of "bustling" "neighborhood" taverns where "fabulous burgers" are the highlights of the "fine" American pub grub selection; "you can't beat the deck" with its "priceless water views" at the Newburyport location, the South Hamilton outpost offers an "inviting beamed dining room", and you'll find "friendly service" and moderate fees at both.

Black Sheep Restaurant *American* | ▽ 21 | 22 | 19 | $31 |
Kendall Square | Kendall Hotel | 350 Main St. (Dock St.) | Cambridge | 617-577-1300 | www.kendallhotel.com
"One of the cutest restaurants in Cambridge", this "pleasant" "little" red-colored spot in the Kendall Hotel serves an "expansive menu" of American classics from breakfast through dinner; it's a particularly "good option for business lunches" "if you work in the neighborhood" because it's affordable, but just know that's when service can "get easily overwhelmed."

Blarney Stone, The *Pub Food* | ▽ 20 | 19 | 19 | $25 |
Dorchester | 1505 Dorchester Ave. (bet. Faulkner & Park Sts.) | 617-436-8223 | www.blarneystoneboston.com
"If you have reasonable expectations", you'll be "happy" with the "typical pub fare" dished out at this "neighborhood emerald" in Dorchester; "friendly, efficient service" and an "attractive, comfortable setting" mean it's a "great place to meet friends or watch a game", but it can get "noisy" once in a while.

Blu *American* | 21 | 21 | 20 | $48 |
Theater District | Millennium Complex | 4 Avery St. (bet. Mason & Washington Sts.) | 617-375-8550 | www.blurestaurant.com
Though it's "a little expensive for what you get" (some say the portions are "small"), this Theater District haunt has fans who call its New American fare "creative and delicious" and its location "conve-

nient" "before a show" or "after working out" next door (truth be told, it's "kind of weird to walk through the gym" to get here); the "ultramodern" environment gets a shout-out too, what with its "wonderful views" from "floor-to-ceiling windows."

Blue Fin *Japanese*   22 | 15 | 19 | $28

Porter Square | Porter Exchange Mall | 1815 Massachusetts Ave. (Roseland St.) | Cambridge | 617-497-8022
Middleton | 260 S. Main St. (bet. Log Bridge & Lonergan Rds.) | 978-750-1411
www.bluefin-restaurant.com

"Wonderful cooked entrees" are listed alongside "terrific sushi" on the "huge menu" proffered at these "consistent", "affordable" Japanese ventures in Middleton and Porter Square; indeed, "the quality and price", not to mention the "unflappable staff", easily "make up for" the "meh" strip-mall settings.

☑ Blue Ginger *Asian*   27 | 23 | 25 | $58

Wellesley | 583 Washington St. (Church St.) | 781-283-5790 | www.ming.com

"Taste-bud-tickling", "highly creative" Asian fusion fare comes from this Wellesley destination's open kitchen, where "justifiably famous" "wizard" chef Ming Tsai "actually cooks" when he's not "mingling with his guests"; "professional, polished service" reigns, even though the "unpretentious" setting is often "packed" – indeed, you need to "make a reservation well in advance" or try for the bar and its "more casual", "less expensive" but no less "intriguing menu"; P.S. "the foie gras shumai and the Alaskan butterfish may be the best appetizer–main course combination" ever.

Blue on Highland *American*   20 | 21 | 21 | $34

Needham | 882 Highland Ave. (Mark Lee Rd.) | 781-444-7001 | www.blueonhighland.com

From its perch "on a busy suburban street", this "fairly priced" Needham "staple" serves "solid", "well-presented" New American fare in a "spacious", "attractive" and "somewhat loud" setting with a "window wall" that opens in summer; "friendly, efficient service" is the norm, whether for a "group luncheon", "after-work" drinks at the "nice bar" or a "quick dinner."

☑ Blue Ribbon BBQ *BBQ*   26 | 12 | 19 | $17

Arlington | 908 Massachusetts Ave. (Highland Ave.) | 781-648-7427
Newton | 1375 Washington St. (Elm St.) | 617-332-2583
www.blueribbonbbq.com

These "funky", "low-priced" BBQ joints are "the real deal" according to those "blown away" by the "generous portions" of "smoky, tender" "slow-cooked meats" backed by "a variety of tasty sauces" and "creative side dishes"; both the Arlington and Newton branches have "limited seating" and "basic" decor – which "doesn't matter", since most folks get their "gluttony to go" via the "fast" counter service.

Blue Room, The *Eclectic*
24 | 21 | 22 | $43

Kendall Square | 1 Kendall Sq. (Hampshire St.) | Cambridge | 617-494-9034 | www.theblueroom.net

"Still going strong after all these years", this "sophisticated" yet "casual" Kendall Square "mainstay" "deftly prepares" "bold, creative" Eclectic fare that emphasizes "locally sourced" "artisanal ingredients"; the "cozy", "rustic" setting, "swift service" and "reasonable prices" cancel out the fact that its often "crowded and noisy", especially during the "fascinating" "all-you-can-eat Sunday brunch" buffet.

Bluestone Bistro ◗ *Pizza*
▽ 18 | 12 | 16 | $20

Brighton | 1799 Commonwealth Ave. (Chiswick Rd.) | 617-254-8309 | www.bluestonebistro.com

Located in a "residential area" of Brighton, this "small shop" sells pizza and pitchers of beer for "cheap"; many locals peg it as "mediocre in every way", but it's "great" for "BC students" who "crave comfort food" and don't mind "abrupt service" from their classmates.

Blue22 Bar & Grille *American/Asian*
▽ 14 | 13 | 14 | $24

Quincy | 1237 Hancock St. (Saville Ave.) | 617-774-1200 | www.blue22-barandgrille.com

"Folks from the neighborhood" come to this "low-key" Quincy hangout for "cheap" drinks, "trivia nights", "karaoke" and a generally "friendly" atmosphere; too bad then that many are "never really satisfied" by the "limited menu" of "bland" American and Asian eats, "affordable" though it may be.

Boca Grande *Tex-Mex*
21 | 11 | 16 | $10

Kenmore Square | 642 Beacon St. (Commonwealth Ave.) | 617-437-9700
East Cambridge | 149 First St. (Bent St.) | Cambridge | 617-354-5550 | www.bocagranderestaurant.com Ⓢ
Porter Square | 1728 Massachusetts Ave. (Linnaean St.) | Cambridge | 617-354-7400 | www.bocagranderestaurant.com
Brookline | 1294 Beacon St. (bet. Harvard & Pleasant Sts.) | 617-739-3900 | www.bocagranderestaurant.com

"Bust out your grade-school Spanish and order up some authentic *comida*" at this "casual", "spartan" local Tex-Mex chain that delivers "outstanding value" in "huge burritos", quesadillas, enchiladas and tacos that are "cheap" yet made with "high-quality" ingredients; the folks running the counter are "kind of disinterested", but they're "fast", and that's all that really matters.

Bokx 109 American Prime *Steak*
21 | 23 | 20 | $60

Newton Lower Falls | Hotel Indigo | 399 Grove St. (Rte. 128) | 617-454-3399 | www.bokx109.com

"Hidden" away in a Newton Lower Falls hotel, this "slick", "modern" suburban spot is "a real surprise" for "great steaks" and a "hip" bar that's "quite a scene for older singles"; however, "for what you get", the "prices are questionably high", notwithstanding the "professional" service, "impressive wine list" and "complimentary cotton candy at the end"; P.S. in summer, check out the "spectacular outdoor area" by the pool.

Boloco *Eclectic/Tex-Mex*   19 | 13 | 18 | $10

Back Bay | 1080 Boylston St. (Mass. Ave.) | 617-369-9087
Back Bay | 247 Newbury St. (bet. Fairfield & Gloucester Sts.) |
617-262-2200
Downtown Crossing | 27 School St. (Province St.) | 617-778-6750
Fenway | 283 Longwood Ave. (Blackfan St.) | 617-232-2166
Fenway | Marino Ctr. | 359-369 Huntington Ave. (bet. Forsyth St. &
Opera Pl.) | 617-536-6814
Financial District | 133 Federal St. (Matthews St.) | 617-357-9727 ⑤
Financial District | 50 Congress St. (Water St.) | 617-357-9013 ⑤
Theater District | 2 Park Plaza (Boylston St.) | 617-778-6772
Harvard Square | 71 Mt. Auburn St. (Holyoke St.) | Cambridge |
617-354-5838
Medford | Tufts University | 340 Boston Ave. (Winthrop St.) |
339-674-9740
www.boloco.com
Additional locations throughout the Boston area
"Create your own burrito" at this locally based "fresh fast-food option" that "deviates from the Tex-Mex tradition" with a "diverse"
"variety" of "wholesome" Eclectic fillings and "delicious smoothies"
too; it gets "crazy during lunchtime", but the "industrious staff"
works "speedily", and though some snicker that it's "not anything to
go loco over" (a few even deem it "rather bland"), the endeavor gets
respect for being "reliable, reasonably priced" and "green."

Bon Caldo *Italian*   20 | 20 | 21 | $40

Norwood | 1381 Providence Tpke. (Sumner St.) | 781-255-5800 |
www.boncaldo.com
Sometimes unfairly "overlooked", this Norwood "find" executes
"solid", "old-world" Italian dishes for "affordable" tabs, maintains
an "extensive wine list" and employs a "friendly", "professional"
staff; as for the setting, there's a modern-rustic dining room, a "fun"
bar and a "relaxed atmosphere" throughout.

Ƶ Bond *Eclectic*   22 | 26 | 18 | $43

Financial District | Langham Hotel Boston | 250 Franklin St.
(Pearl St.) | 617-451-1900 | www.boston.langhamhotels.com
With a "striking", "sexy ambiance", this "upscale" Financial District
hotel lounge attracts "celebrities", "hedge-fund managers" and
scenesters "from all over the world", who wash down the "unique"
Eclectic small plates and mains with "delicious", "pricey" cocktails;
indeed, it's a "happening" "place to feel trendy without the cover
charge and pulsing music", albeit with service that can seem "a bit
lacking"; P.S. afternoon tea is "amazing."

NEW Bondir *American*   - | - | - | E

Central Square | 279A Broadway (bet. Columbia & Elm Sts.) |
Cambridge | 617-661-0009 | www.bondircambridge.com
Chef-owner Jason Bond brings his sustainable New American cuisine to Central Square, offering a daily changing pricey menu that includes both small plates for sharing and full entrees, accompanied
by a petite but ambitious drink list with a focus on seasonal beers;
the quaint cream-and-green dining room includes a portrait of a

beloved pig painted by Bond's grandfather, and there's an alcove with tree stumps for tables and a fireplace.

Bon Savor *French/S. American* | 22 | 16 | 21 | $30 |

Jamaica Plain | 605 Centre St. (Pond St.) | 617-971-0000 | www.bonsavor.com

"If you want something a little different" in Jamaica Plain, check out this "cozy" "neighborhood spot", which "lovingly prepares" a "satisfying" yet "curious blend of French and South American food"; "friendly, efficient service" contributes to the "charming atmosphere", and best of all, the tabs are a "great value", especially for the "big hit" weekend brunch.

Border Cafe *Cajun/Tex-Mex* | 20 | 18 | 19 | $20 |

Harvard Square | 32 Church St. (Palmer St.) | Cambridge | 617-864-6100 ✪

Saugus | 356 Broadway (Lynn Fells Pkwy.) | 781-233-5308

Burlington | 128 Middlesex Tpke. (Burlington Mall Rd.) | 781-505-2500

www.bordercafe.com

"Happy hordes" of "families" and "students" head for this trio for "huge portions" of Tex-Mex-Cajun "staples" served with "never-ending bowls of fresh chips and salsa" and "mind-numbing" "margaritas the size of your head"; despite the "uneven service" and "corny decor", they remain "too popular" because "you can't beat the price", so count on "crazy waits" and "high noise levels."

NEW Bosphorus *Mediterranean* | – | – | – | M |

Inman Square | 1164 Cambridge St. (bet. Norfolk & Tremont Sts.) | Cambridge | 617-945-2730 | www.bosphoruscambridge.com

This midpriced Med arrival in Inman Square offers mounds of mezes (hummus, whipped eggplant) plus a wide variety of appetizers, entrees, vegetarian options and desserts; the sleek, sexy setting has an exotic air with red walls, soft-orange hanging lamps and birchwood booths, and there's a long bar serving beer and wine.

Boston Beer Works ✪ *Pub Food* | 18 | 17 | 18 | $23 |

Fenway | 61 Brookline Ave. (Lansdowne St.) | 617-536-2337

West End | 112 Canal St. (Causeway St.) | 617-896-2337

Hingham Beer Works *Pub Food*

NEW Hingham | Hingham Shipyard | 18 Shipyard Dr. (off Rte. 3A) | 781-749-2337

Salem Beer Works ✪ *Pub Food*

Salem | 278 Derby St. (bet. Congress & Lafayette Sts.) | 978-745-2337

www.beerworks.net

The "typical", "moderately priced" pub food does its job, but "the reason to come" to these "casual" microbreweries is the "interesting", "freshly brewed" "seasonal beers"; while the original location "across from Fenway Park" and its West End brother "around the corner from the Garden" are usually "packed" and "loud" "before the game or show" (hence, service can seem "harried"), the Salem outpost features more of a "family environment"; P.S. the Hingham branch opened post-Survey.

	FOOD	DECOR	SERVICE	COST

Boston Burger Company *Burgers*   23 | 15 | 20 | $16

Somerville | 37 Davis Sq. (College Ave.) | 617-440-7361 |
www.bostonburgerco.com

If you've "ever desired a mac 'n' cheese burger", come to this "small,
cramped", "crazy-busy" Davis Square "joint" that offers a
"seemingly endless menu" of "reasonably priced", "super-creative",
"high-quality" patties; it's "nothing special on the decor front", but
the atmosphere's "fun", thanks in large part to the "friendly staff."

Boston Sail Loft *Seafood*   18 | 18 | 18 | $29

Waterfront | 80 Atlantic Ave. (N. Commerical Wharf) |
617-227-7280

"Hanging in there" after "many years", this Waterfront seafooder
with a "rustic pub environment" offers "standard", "fairly priced",
"mostly fried" fish alongside "beautiful views" and "pleasant" service; however, the "loud, lively crowd" of tipplers that frequents it,
particularly "after work", shores up its reputation as "more of a bar
scene than an eating destination."

Bottega Fiorentina *Italian/Deli*   23 | 12 | 17 | $17

Back Bay | 264 Newbury St. (bet. Fairfield & Gloucester Sts.) |
617-266-0707 | www.botteganewbury.com
Brookline | 313B Harvard St. (Babcock St.) | 617-232-2661 |
www.bottegabrookline.com

"Astoundingly delicious" Tuscan sandwiches, pasta dishes and
antipasti are sold for "deliciously cheap" prices at these Italian
delis; the counter-serve Brookliner has "limited seating" (it's
"primarily takeout"), while the Back Bay offshoot boasts a larger,
"nicer atmosphere" inside and a "great patio" for Newbury
Street "people-watching."

Brasserie Jo *French*   21 | 21 | 22 | $43

Back Bay | Colonnade Hotel | 120 Huntington Ave. (bet. Garrison &
W. Newton Sts.) | 617-425-3240 | www.brasseriejoboston.com

"Smooth" service "without attitude" is the only thing "un-French"
about this "elegant" Back Bay hotel restaurant that "remains a classic" "choice for dining before or after a concert at Symphony Hall";
indeed, the bistro fare is "authentic" (and "delicious" too), the
"price is right" and the "spacious", "attractive" space's "art deco
decor gives it the feel of Paris in the 1930s."

Bravo *Eclectic*   20 | 22 | 20 | $47

MFA | Museum of Fine Arts | 465 Huntington Ave., 2nd fl.
(bet. Forsyth Way & Museum Rd.) | 617-369-3474 |
www.mfa.org

With its "lovely setting", "wonderfully diverse menu" of "delicious,
beautifully presented" Eclectic fare and "fine service", this "classy"
MFA dining spot is a simultaneously "restful" and "invigorating in-
terlude from experiencing great art"; though it may be true that "you
pay for the convenience" of not having to leave the building, menus
that "reflect current exhibits" make it an "excellent complement" to
a day at the museum.

	FOOD	DECOR	SERVICE	COST

Brenden Crocker's
Wild Horse Cafe *American*

▽ 26 | 23 | 23 | $41

Beverly | 392 Cabot St. (Bennett St.) | 978-922-6868 |
www.wildhorsecafe.com

"An amazing find" in Beverly, this "gem" "pleases everyone" with a
"varied" variety of "innovative, delicious" New American cuisine
(perhaps "priced a bit high" for the area, but warranted by its "quality"); the "relaxed" dining room is done up like a "quirky" "cafe",
which is separate from the "lively bar" offering its own menu, "awesome martinis" and "wide selection of beer."

Bricco *Italian*

25 | 21 | 21 | $51

North End | 241 Hanover St. (bet. Cross & Richmond Sts.) |
617-248-6800 | www.bricco.com

"Skip the traditional red-sauce" places in the North End for "something more creative", i.e. this "costly" bastion of "modern Italian"
cuisine, where "incredible handmade pastas" with "diverse ingredients" are served alongside "inventive drinks" that "pack a punch";
the "always busy" atmosphere and "sexy" bar scene make it "noisy"
downstairs, but that's where the "luxe crowd" prefers to sit, as upstairs can seem "isolated from the fun."

Bridgeman's *Italian*

24 | 21 | 23 | $43

Hull | 145 Nantasket Ave. (Bay St.) | 781-925-6336 |
www.bridgemansrestaurant.com

"Inspired" Northern Italian fare is complemented by a "terrific wine
list" and administered by a "professional yet friendly staff" at this
"splurge" "across from the beach in Hull"; downstairs, site of the
"great bar", is airy and "elegant", but "upstairs at the window is the
place to be" for "fantastic" "ocean views."

Brighton Beer Garden *Pub Food*

16 | 19 | 18 | $20

Brighton | 386 Market St. (Henshaw St.) | 617-562-6000 |
www.brightonbeergarden.com

Although the pub food is "nothing special", fans of this Brighton den
say "as far as sports bars go, it runs with the leaders" thanks to
"many TVs", "cheap" tabs and a "fun" atmosphere; though most
cheer a "good selection of beer", some say it's "shockingly small" –
still, it's a "great place to watch a game" thanks to the "cool" folks
behind the bar and a "lotta hotties" in front of it.

Z Bristol Lounge, The *American*

26 | 27 | 27 | $55

Back Bay | Four Seasons Hotel | 200 Boylston St. (Charles St.) |
617-351-2053 | www.fourseasons.com

"Feel like royalty" at this New American "special-occasion place" in
the Back Bay that "lives up to the Four Seasons name" with "wonderful service" and an "elegant, relaxing" setting with "cushy couches",
"terrific views" of the Public Garden and "outstanding people-
watching"; the "high-quality" all-day edibles (including a
"lip-smacking" burger) are "pricey", but it's "worth it" for a "treat",
especially afternoon tea and the "fabulous" Viennese dessert buffet
on Saturday nights.

Brookline Family Restaurant *Turkish* | 22 | 9 | 16 | $21 |

Brookline | 305 Washington St. (bet. Harvard & Holden Sts.) | 617-277-4466 | www.brooklinefamilyrestaurant.com

"Don't judge it by its looks" – this Brookline diner doppelgänger is really an "exotic" "gem" serving "luscious", "crowd-pleasing" Turkish dishes in "huge portions" and for "affordable prices" (the "authentic" menu is augmented with American standards, mostly at breakfast); "service can be slow", but that's usually forgiven because it's "run by real nice people."

NEW Brother's Crawfish Ⓜ *Asian/Southern* | – | – | – | I |

Dorchester | 272 Adams St. (bet. Dickens & Park Sts.) | 617-265-1100 | www.brotherscrawfish.com

Tucked into Dorchester's Field's Corner, this Asian-Southern–fusion newcomer doles out "New Orleans–like" crawfish by the pound accompanied by sides of baby corn and smoked sausage, plus fried seafood and teriyaki dishes; the "small" storefront with glass-topped bistro tables befits the budget-friendly tabs, and though alcohol wasn't available at Survey time, a license was forthcoming.

Brownstone ❶ *Pub Food* | 15 | 15 | 15 | $24 |

Back Bay | 111 Dartmouth St. (I-90) | 617-867-4142 | www.irishconnection.com

"Really just ok" is the consensus of the bar food served at this "relaxed" pub, but its location makes it "convenient for lunch" in both the Back Bay and South End; though "it's nice when they open the front windows and you can people-watch", the "atmosphere is definitely lacking", which isn't helped by "hit-or-miss service."

Brown Sugar Cafe *Thai* | 24 | 17 | 20 | $24 |

Boston University | 1033 Commonwealth Ave. (bet. Alcorn & Babcock Sts.) | 617-787-4242

Similans, The *Thai*

East Cambridge | 145 First St. (bet. Bent & Rogers Sts.) | Cambridge | 617-491-6999

www.brownsugarcafe.com

"Popular with the BU kids and their visiting parents", this "campus hangout" with a "low-key" East Cambridge sibling presents a "wide-ranging menu" of "authentic Thai delicacies" whose "large portions" provide "great bang for the buck"; "fast-paced service" works best "if you're in a rush, but not for a leisurely dinner" – except if it's your birthday, when the staff takes the time to "cut the lights, start up the strobes" and "sing to you" (it's "terribly funny").

NEW Budda C *Asian* | ▽ 20 | 22 | 20 | $31 |

Brookline | 1223 Beacon St. (St. Paul St.) | 617-739-0000 | www.buddac.com

"Diverse groups" chasing a "change of pace" catch it at this Brookline newcomer presenting an "excellent range" of "reasonably priced", "thoughtfully prepared" Asian fusion fare with influences "from Japan to India"; highlights of the "lovely", "welcoming" setting include "a massive Buddha" and an "accommodating staff."

Bukhara *Indian* 22 | 18 | 19 | $23

Jamaica Plain | 701 Centre St. (Burroughs St.) | 617-522-2195 |
www.bukharabistro.com

With such an "extensive", "amazing" lunch buffet comprised of a
"nice mix of standards and less familiar dishes" at this "reasonably
priced" Indian "standby", Jamaica Plain workers can't help but "return to the office in a serious food coma"; dinners are equally "well
prepared", while "service remains, as always, spotty"; P.S. "opt for a
window seat for excellent people-watching."

Bukowski Tavern ◐⇥ *Pub Food* 18 | 16 | 17 | $20

Back Bay | 50 Dalton St. (Boylston St.) | 617-437-9999
Inman Square | 1281 Cambridge St. (Prospect St.) | Cambridge |
617-497-7077

"Poor college students" join "writers looking for liquid inspiration"
at these Back Bay and Inman Square "dives" doling out "quality" pub
grub at "decent prices" – but "really, it's all about the 100-plus
beers" on offer, an "amazing" variety; "bone-crushing" "crowds",
"blasting music" and a "knowledgeable" though "frequently un-
pleasant staff" complete the picture.

Bullfinchs *Eclectic* 21 | 22 | 22 | $36

Sudbury | 730 Boston Post Rd. (bet. Lafayette Dr. & Stone Rd.) |
978-443-4094 | www.bullfinchs.com

"There's a good reason why" this Sudbury Eclectic "where everybody knows your name" has been in business for more than
30 years: the owners (along with the "great" staff) "take personal
care of the customers" while keeping things "fresh" with an ever-
"evolving menu"; the "trendy decor", "lovely" patio, "excellent
value", Sunday jazz brunch and cooking classes make it "a place to
enjoy on a regular basis."

Burren, The *Irish/Pub Food* 17 | 19 | 19 | $20

Somerville | 247 Elm St. (Chester St.) | 617-776-6896 | www.burren.com

"Friendly" "expat servers", "solid" "traditional grub" from the
Emerald Isle, "well-pulled pints" and "Bono" sightings ("seriously")
earn this Somerville "hangout" a reputation as "one of the most authentic Irish pubs" around; "great live entertainment" and "decent"
prices draw a "young college crowd."

Burtons Grill *American* 21 | 20 | 21 | $36

Fenway | 1363 Boylston St. (Kilmarnock St.) | 617-236-2236
North Andover | Eaglewood Shops | 145 Turnpike St. (Peters St.) |
978-688-5600
NEW **Peabody** | Northshore Mall | 210 Andover St. (bet. Prospect
St. & Yankee Division Hwy.) | 978-977-0600
Hingham | Derby Street Shoppes | 94 Derby St. (Cushing St.) |
781-749-1007
www.burtonsgrill.com

A "classy" option for a "pre- or post-game meal", this "reliable"
Fenway grill offers "something for everyone" on its "fairly priced",
"au courant" American menu, from "terrific burgers" to "more inter-

esting fare"; the other branches bring its "city-trendy feel" to the suburbs, while all offer "positive service" and "lively bar scenes" that can sometimes feel a little "too crowded and noisy."

Butcher Shop, The *French/Italian*　　25 | 20 | 23 | $47

South End | 552 Tremont St. (Waltham St.) | 617-423-4800 | www.thebutchershopboston.com

"What a show!" shout "meat lovers" of "food magician" Barbara Lynch's "casual, sophisticated" French-Italian restaurant/vino bar/retailer in the South End, which specializes in "superb" pâtés, antipasti, "upscale hot dogs" and "a few entrees"; "solid service" comes from a staff "knowledgeable" about the "short" but "brilliant wine list", and while "it may be a tad pricey" and "no reservations" plus "few tables" equals sometimes "long waits", the hassles are "well worth it."

Byblos Ⓜ *Lebanese*　　24 | 18 | 22 | $32

Norwood | 678 Washington St. (Vernon St.) | 781-278-0000 | www.byblosrestaurant.com

"Be adventurous" and take a meal at this "authentic Lebanese" in Norwood, which is a real "crowd-pleaser" thanks to "fantastic" fare, "huge portions" and "fair prices"; indeed, "the whole family" "always leaves happy" thanks in part to the "gracious" service and "great fun" belly dancing on weekend evenings.

Cactus Club *Tex-Mex*　　17 | 17 | 17 | $26

Back Bay | 939 Boylston St. (Hereford St.) | 617-236-0200 | www.cactusclubboston.com

"For a fun night of high-octane" "margaritas that hit the spot at a reasonable cost", head to this Back Bay "frat house"; the "typical Tex-Mex" is "nothing memorable" and the "typical colorful decor" could use "updating", but that doesn't stop it from becoming "crowded with lots of people standing" and getting "rowdy"; P.S. when "the weather cooperates", there's "nice outdoor seating" on the sidewalk.

Café Algiers ◗ *Mideastern*　　16 | 21 | 14 | $22

Harvard Square | 40 Brattle St. (Church St.) | Cambridge | 617-492-1557

"Discuss the meaning of life" "for hours without being disturbed" while sipping "fine" Middle Eastern coffee at this "meeting place" that's "one of the last" bastions of "funky" "bohemian" Harvard Square; the hummus and such may be "overpriced" for being merely "mediocre", but they provide fuel for "lingering" in the "eccentric space", "full of off-kilter tables and tiny nooks"; P.S. there's also an "appealing" roof deck.

Café at Taj Boston *Eclectic*　　21 | 23 | 25 | $52

Back Bay | Taj Boston | 15 Arlington St. (Newbury St.) | 617-536-5700 | www.tajhotels.com

"Grown-ups" who bemoan "there's not much elegance left on the Common" "love" this "sunny, posh", "formal" Eclectic Back Bay hotel cafe where you should "treat yourself to a window seat" for "great people-watching"; the "well-prepared", expensive fare includes "a few Indian dishes" to "spice up the menu", and the "gracious" staff aids in making it "always a treat" for "special occasions."

Cafe Barada 🏠🍴 *Lebanese* | 24 | 13 | 21 | $21 |

Porter Square | 2269 Massachusetts Ave. (Dover St.) | Cambridge | 617-354-2112 | www.cafebarada.net

"High-quality Lebanese food" is "created and served by one of the nicest families" around at this "quaint" yet "sparse" Porter Square storefront; the prices represent an "excellent value", but make sure you come prepared for the "courageous no-credit-card policy."

Café Belô *Brazilian* | ▽ 24 | 10 | 17 | $14 |

Allston | 177 Brighton Ave. (bet. Parkvale & Quint Aves.) | 617-202-6816
Somerville | 120 Washington St. (Franklin St.) | 617-623-3696 🌓
Everett | 158 School St. (Broadway) | 617-544-3772 🌓
Framingham | 417 Waverly St. (Concord St.) | 508-283-1451 🌓
www.cafebelo.com

"When you're feeling carnivorous", these Brazilians offer "one of the best deals in the city": a "huge selection" of "flavorful", "hearty" fare that's "cheap" whether you pay "per kilo" or choose the "flat-rate" buffet ("good if you're a big eater"); the environs are "holes-in-the-wall" all the way, which is why many folks stick to takeout.

Café Brazil *Brazilian* | 22 | 15 | 23 | $28 |

Allston | 421 Cambridge St. (Harvard Ave.) | 617-789-5980 | www.cafebrazilrestaurant.com

For a "yummy taste of Brazil", Alston carnivores rely on this "old standby" doling out "huge portions" of "wonderfully prepared, affordable", meat-centric dishes (not the "all-you-can-eat" rodizio style); though there isn't much to recommend in the tropical-themed decor, endorsements are bestowed on the "friendly" staffers as well as the occasional live entertainment.

Cafe Escadrille 🅰 *Continental* | 21 | 21 | 22 | $42 |

Burlington | 26 Cambridge St. (Wayside Rd.) | 781-273-1916 | www.cafeescadrille.com

"Steady as she goes", this nearly 40-year-old Burlingtonian provides suburbanites with a "classy setting" for "special occasions", plus Continental fare to go with – which traditionalists think is "wonderful" and modernists find "boring"; it's "a bit expensive", but "you can eat on the bar side for a lot less money" while partaking in a "hopping" "meat market", if that's your thing.

Café Fleuri *New England* | 24 | 22 | 23 | $46 |

Financial District | Langham Hotel Boston | 250 Franklin St. (Pearl St.) | 617-451-1900 | www.boston.langhamhotels.com

"So elegant" sigh surveyors about this all-day "reliable standard" in the Financial District's Langham Hotel, a "place to linger" over "delicious" New England fare that's ferried by "fine" servers and "not inexpensive but worth every penny"; the "totally decadent" weekend brunch is a "superb" treat for live-jazz lovers, but it's the "beautifully presented" chocolate buffet (Saturdays, September-June) that's really "to die for."

Cafe 47 *American*

19 | 19 | 21 | $23

Back Bay | 47 Massachusetts Ave. (bet. Commonwealth Ave. & Marlborough St.) | 617-536-1577 | www.cafe47.net

"Hidden gem alert!" – though you could easily "walk past" this "tiny" Back Bay cafe without "noticing it", it's a "real find" for its "diverse", "reasonably priced" American menu starring "great pizza"; the setting is "inviting" and "cozy enough that you can go for a date" and "casual" enough to go "alone in your sweats", while "service is usually quick and attentive."

Cafe Jaffa *Mideastern*

21 | 12 | 18 | $18

Back Bay | 48 Gloucester St. (bet. Boylston & Newbury Sts.) | 617-536-0230 | www.cafejaffa.net

"Take a break from Newbury Street shopping" and refuel via "generous portions" of "tasty" Middle Eastern eats served "fast" at this "economical" Back Bay respite; despite the "small", "drab" setting, it's usually "busy at lunchtime", meaning it "can get really loud" (you can always opt for takeout); P.S. "dinner is more relaxed."

Café Mangal ⊠ *Mediterranean/Turkish*

26 | 20 | 23 | $36

Wellesley | 555 Washington St. (Grove St.) | 781-235-5322 | www.cafemangal.com

"Ladies who lunch in Wellesley" "jockey for the limited tables" at this "informal" Med-Turk cafe specializing in "scrumptious" salads and sandwiches alongside some American dishes; come nighttime, the "delightful" staff "converts the place" into a "serene oasis" for "intimate", "beautifully presented" dinners, when BYO helps mitigate the "more expensive" checks.

Cafe of India *Indian*

20 | 17 | 18 | $26

Harvard Square | 52A Brattle St. (Hilliard St.) | Cambridge | 617-661-0683 | www.cafeofindia.com

"Not wonderful in any category", but certainly "reliable", "tasty" and "convenient" sums up this "pleasant", "long-standing" Indian whose best feature is its fees: "midpriced", especially "for Harvard Square", with further value found in the lunch buffet.

Café Polonia *Polish*

24 | 19 | 24 | $26

South Boston | 611 Dorchester Ave. (Southampton St.) | 617-269-0110
NEW Salem | 118 Washington St. (bet. Essex & Front Sts.) | 978-745-0045
www.cafepolonia.com

South Bostonians liken this "sweet little restaurant" to "a Polish grandmother's cozy countryside cottage", with "delectable", "filling" "home cooking" to match; "über-polite" waitresses in "authentic" dress "add to the experience", which commands fittingly inexpensive tabs; P.S. the Salem newcomer opened post-Survey.

Café St. Petersburg Ⓜ *Russian*

21 | 19 | 17 | $40

Newton | 57 Union St. (Langley Rd.) | 617-467-3555 | www.cafestpetersburg.com

For "authentic" "Russian delights" and the "best" "infused vodkas" "this side of the Volga", there's this "hangout" in Newton, where the pianist "thundering out classical tunes" abets "fun, romantic evenings"; however, quite a few surveyors say the staff is as "cold as a Siberian winter" if you don't "speak the language."

Cafe Sushi *Japanese*
▽ 22 | 18 | 19 | $30

Harvard Square | 1105 Massachusetts Ave. (bet. Remington & Trowbridge Sts.) | Cambridge | 617-492-0434

Harvard Square students with "sushi cravings" easily "get over the cheap name" of this humble Japanese joint and fill up on its "fresh, well-cut" fish; true, "there are better places in town", but not many that are this inexpensive.

Cafeteria *American*
18 | 17 | 17 | $29

Back Bay | 279A Newbury St. (bet. Fairfield & Gloucester Sts.) | 617-536-2233 | www.cafeteriaboston.com

"Trendy" people come to this Back Bay New American eatery to "see and be seen", especially on the "lively" patio; however, they can't agree on the quality of what they're getting, be it the "casual", "moderately priced" fare ("tasty" vs. "weak"), the mostly white, modern decor ("chic" vs. "sterile") or the service ("friendly" vs. "lousy").

Caffe Bella ☒ *Mediterranean*
26 | 17 | 23 | $46

Randolph | 19 Warren St. (Main St.) | 781-961-7729

Admirers "can't praise this place enough", citing "big portions of high-quality", "robust" Mediterranean fare, "helpful service" and a "casual atmosphere", all of which makes it "worth the schlep" to Randolph; no reservations mean you'll probably have a "long wait on weekends", but in all other respects, it "never fails to impress."

Caffe Paradiso ◑ *Coffeehouse*
▽ 19 | 17 | 20 | $16

North End | 255 Hanover St. (bet. Cross & Richmond Sts.) | 617-742-1768 | www.caffeparadiso.com

"For a truly international experience", "join the crowd" (particularly "during soccer matches") while partaking in "fantastic pastries" and "to-die-for cappuccinos" at this Italian coffeehouse in the North End; "great service" and "excellent value" are two more reasons that first-timers often "become regulars" before long.

Caffe Tosca ☒ *Italian*
24 | 21 | 22 | $38

Hingham | 15 North St. (Cottage St.) | 781-740-9400 | www.caffetoscahingham.com

"Everything works" at this "casual" offspring of Tosca across the street ("near the harbor" in Hingham), which "excels" at "wonderful handmade pastas, delectable thin-crust pizzas" with "imaginative combinations of ingredients", "fabulous antipasti" and other "Italian bistro" fare; "friendly prices" match the "great service" and "warm", "cozy" setting featuring a "lively bar" and "comfortable" patio.

Caliterra *Californian/Italian*
▽ 15 | 14 | 17 | $37

Financial District | Hilton Boston Financial District | 89 Broad St. (Franklin St.) | 617-556-0006 | www.caliterrarestaurant.com

Though this moderately priced venue in the Hilton Boston Financial District proffers a menu that "sounds unremarkable" to some foodies, many wind up rating the "Californian-inspired" Italian creations as "decent"; others, such as guests of the hotel, say "only go here when you don't have a choice", like for breakfast, which is often "quite packed" with local businesspeople too.

Cambridge Brewing Co. *Pub Food*   16 | 15 | 17 | $25

Kendall Square | One Kendall Square Complex | 1 Kendall Sq. (Hampshire St.) | Cambridge | 617-494-1994 | www.cambridgebrew.com
"Ambrosia" sigh suds-groupies about the "mind-blowing" seasonal microbrews that are offered in "beer towers", "tasting portions" and "take-home growlers" at this "upbeat" Kendall Square brewpub with a "cavernous" interior and a "nice patio"; as for the grub, well, it's "pretty standard", and it comes via "surly service."

Cambridge Common ● *Pub Food*   18 | 14 | 20 | $20

Harvard Square | 1667 Massachusetts Ave. (bet. Sacramento & Shepherd Sts.) | Cambridge | 617-547-1228 |
www.cambridgecommonrestaurant.com
With an "extensive menu" of "cheap as chips" comfort grub and "large selection of ever-rotating taps", this "wicked awesome pub" near Harvard Square is a "perfect burger-and-beer after-work spot"; sports on TV and "concerts in the basement Lizard Lounge" make it "good for groups", which can sometimes get "rowdy" – good thing there's a "no-nonsense" staff on deck to keep everyone in check.

Cambridge 1 ● *Pizza*   22 | 19 | 19 | $23

Fenway | 1381 Boylston St. (bet. Kilmarnock St. & Park Dr.) | 617-437-1111
Harvard Square | 27 Church St. (Palmer St.) | Cambridge | 617-576-1111
www.cambridge1.us
"Innovative" charcoal-grilled "masterpiece" pizzas plus "clever salads" lure "crowds" searching for a "quick", "inexpensive" bite "before a flick" to these pie palaces that also stock a "great beer selection"; set in a "former firehouse", the Harvard Square version is "slick" and "modern", the newer Fenway outpost is equally "cool" and "casual", and both boast "efficient" servers.

NEW Canary Square ● *American*   - | - | - | M

Jamaica Plain | 435 S. Huntington Ave. (Centre St.) | 617-524-2500 |
www.canarysquare.com
Expect classic American with a twist at this rustic yet sleek Jamaica Plain arrival where you can belly up to the reclaimed-wood bar for one of 30 draft beers or settle in the green-minded dining room with recycled chairs; further attractions for locals include a big bike rack out front and mostly-below-$20 entrees on the menu.

Canestaro *Italian*   ▽ 16 | 11 | 17 | $22

Fenway | 16 Peterborough St. (bet. Jersey St. & Park Dr.) |
617-266-8997 | www.canestaro.com
"After a game", many a Sox fan heads to this "old reliable" "close to Fenway Park" for "competent" "red-sauce Italian" entrees and "thin-crust pizza" at a "reasonable price"; the "patio is a major asset when the weather is fine", while "efficient" service makes it "great for takeout" too.

Cantina Italiana *Italian*
22 | 16 | 23 | $41

North End | 346 Hanover St. (Fleet St.) | 617-723-4577 |
www.cantinaitaliana.com

"If it's traditional Italian you want, you can't go wrong" at this "representation of the North End" of yore, a "safe spot" in a "prime location" serving "delicious" "homemade pasta" and "wonderful specials"; indeed, "nothing changes" here, and regulars admit that has its "good" aspects ("great service", "reasonable prices") and its "bad" (the menu and decor can seem "tired").

Cantina la Mexicana *Mexican*
∇ 24 | 19 | 20 | $19

Somerville | 247 Washington St. (Bonner Ave.) | 617-776-5232 |
www.lataqueria.com

"You will not believe the prices" at this "top tamale stop" in Somerville that's "loved" for its "high-quality" Mexican eats brought in "large portions" by "friendly" staffers; "the pitchers of margaritas are great for groups", which keep the "casual setting" "festive."

☑ Capital Grille *Steak*
26 | 24 | 26 | $66

Back Bay | 359 Newbury St. (bet. Hereford St. & Mass. Ave.) |
617-262-8900
Chestnut Hill | 250 Boylston St. (bet. Hammond Pond Pkwy. &
Langley Rd.) | 617-928-1400
Burlington | 10 Wayside Rd. (Cambridge St.) | 781-505-4130
www.thecapitalgrille.com

"Superb" steaks are "served with style" to "lots of suits" at this "topnotch" chain; boasting a "fantastic" wine list, "superior" service and a "manly club atmosphere", it's "wonderful" "for a date" or "impressing a client", so "if you're on an expense account, go for it."

Captain's Table & Take Away *Seafood*
24 | 13 | 20 | $23

Wellesley | 279 Linden St. (Kingsbury St.) | 781-235-3737 |
www.captainmardens.com

"Elegant it ain't", but "fresh, delicious" and "inexpensive" it is! - that's why this "seafood-lovers' legend in Wellesley" gets "crowded with families" and "lots of senior citizens" (it's "hard to find a seat at lunch or early dinner"); BYO adds to the "bang for the buck", and it serves a "terrific" breakfast too.

☑ Carlo's Cucina Italiana *Italian*
26 | 13 | 23 | $31

Allston | 131 Brighton Ave. (bet. Harvard Ave. & Linden St.) |
617-254-9759 | www.carloscucinaitaliana.com

"Townies and visitors" admit to being "addicts" for the "superb oldschool Italian" cuisine dished out in "plentiful" portions for "bargain" rates at this "steady Eddie" in Allston; it's can be a "cute date place" with service that "makes you feel part of the family", but it's so "small" and "crowded", there's "usually a wait."

☑ Carmen Ⓜ *Italian*
27 | 21 | 23 | $48

North End | 33 North Sq. (Prince St.) | 617-742-6421 |
www.carmenboston.com

"Haven't had better, not even in Italy" marvel fans "wowed" by the "amazing" cuisine offered at this "popular" North End "gem" that's also notable for its "dreamily romantic" setting with only a "handful of tables"; "come early, as reservations are treated the same as a doctor's appointment" ("you'll wait forever"), and plan to "not linger" or else "you'll get a glare" from the otherwise "affable" servers; P.S. the "only drawback: no dessert."

Casablanca *Mediterranean*   21 | 20 | 21 | $37

Harvard Square | 40 Brattle St. (Church St.) | Cambridge | 617-876-0999 | www.casablanca-restaurant.com

"Murals of Bogart and Bergman" make heading down to this "longtime Harvard Square" "basement hideaway" like "stepping into the set of the movie" where "fast and courteous" staffers serve students, "professors and young professionals" "high-quality" Mediterranean fare for "modest prices"; "more lively than the dining area" is the "charming" back bar, a "fun place to meet for drinks" and "heaping meze plates."

Casa Portugal *Portuguese*   23 | 16 | 21 | $28

Inman Square | 1200 Cambridge St. (bet. Prospect & Tremont Sts.) | Cambridge | 617-491-8880 | www.restaurantcasaportugal.com

For "big portions" of "authentic, tasty" Portuguese fare, and especially "excellent fish", head to this "always satisfying" "standby" near Inman Square; the setting may be "nothing fancy", but its "homey, unpretentious" feel matches the affordable pricing.

Casa Romero *Mexican*   22 | 22 | 21 | $36

Back Bay | 30 Gloucester St. (bet. Commonwealth Ave. & Newbury St.) | 617-536-4341 | www.casaromero.com

You may "get lost trying to find" this "hidden treasure" in a Back Bay "back alley", but once you do, you're in "true Mexican territory", i.e. "no border food", just "authentic" dishes that are "upscale", "tremendous", ferried by a "friendly staff" and paired with "fresh margaritas strong enough to take the paint of a car"; the interior is a bit of a "cave", but it's a "beautiful" one, while the patio is similarly "quaint and romantic."

CBS Scene Restaurant & Bar ❷ *American*   - | - | - | M

Foxboro | Patriot Pl. | 200 Patriot Pl. | 508-203-2200 | www.cbsscene.com

Whether they come for a quick bite before kickoff at Gillette Stadium next door or to watch the game on TV within, Foxboro sports-lovers call this Patriot Place American nirvana; the ginormous space is dotted with over 135 HDs on three floors, featuring private dining areas on the first, a vast network of booths on the second, a bar setting on the third and a spiral staircase connecting them all; moderately priced pub grub fills the substantial menu, and after the last whistle's blown, the entertainment switches over to other CBS programming.

NEW Ceia Kitchen & Bar *European*   - | - | - | M

Newburyport | 25 State St. (bet. Essex & Middle Sts.) | 978-358-8112 | www.ceia-newburyport.com

This Modern Mediterranean in Downtown Newburyport features Portuguese specialties, housemade Italian pastas and other Euro coastline fare (with a complementary wine list); the cozy, chic, historic setting features exposed-brick walls, recessed mirrors and copper tables covered with butcher paper, plus a banquette overlooking bustling State Street and a bar offering a view of the open kitchen along with signature cocktails.

NEW Center Café, The M *American* ▽ 20 | 15 | 19 | $30

Needham | 1027 Great Plain Ave. (Eaton Sq.) | 781-455-8800 | www.thecentercafe.com

With an "unusual location" "almost right on the train tracks", this casual, "welcome addition to the Needham restaurant scene" offers "grown-up American" fare at "really fair prices"; "friendly management" "really know how to treat their guests", as do the "nice" staffers they employ.

Central Kitchen *American* 23 | 20 | 21 | $37

Central Square | 567 Massachusetts Ave. (Pearl St.) | Cambridge | 617-491-5599 | www.enormous.tv

"Cozy", "dimly lit", "tastefully decorated", environs encourage "conversation and lingering" at this "terrific date-night" option in Central Square, where the New American victuals are as "sophisticated" as they are "satisfying"; it's also a "pleasant" place to just "sit at the bar with a friend" and peruse the "affordable" wine list, with which the "informed, attentive and friendly" staffers can assist.

Centre Street Café *Eclectic* 25 | 15 | 23 | $26

Jamaica Plain | 669A Centre St. (bet. Burroughs & Myrtle Sts.) | 617-524-9217 | www.centrestcafe.com

"A mixed crowd" "on a tight budget" appreciates the "huge portions" of "fab" Eclectic fare doled out at this "tiny", "funky" Jamaica Plain eatery where there are always "queues down the street" for the "famous" brunch ("well worth" the "excruciating wait") and "lunch and dinner are more sane"; "attentive" staffers "make you feel at home", and they can tell you all about how the ingredients are procured "from local farmers and responsible meat purveyors."

Chacarero ∌ *Chilean/Sandwiches* 25 | 10 | 18 | $10

Downtown Crossing | 101 Arch St. (bet. Franklin & Summer Sts.) | 617-542-0392 | www.chacarero.com

Supporters "salivate when thinking about" the "unique", "unbelievable" Chilean sandwiches – featuring "addictive" avocado spread, hot sauce, green beans and "special bread" – constructed at this "awesome value" venue in Downtown Crossing; it's takeout only, and you should "prepare to wait in line" whether you come for breakfast or lunch (open weekdays only).

Changsho *Chinese* 21 | 19 | 20 | $29

Porter Square | 1712 Massachusetts Ave. (bet. Linnaean & Martin Sts.) | Cambridge | 617-547-6565 | www.lotuscuisine.com

Though the "prices are higher than average", they "match the quality" delivered at this Chinese place located between Porter and Harvard Squares, which can be "an excellent-deal" if you do the "popular" daily lunch buffet; the "large", "nice-looking room" is "great for groups" and provides a welcome "bit of space" between tables, and service is usually "quick" to boot.

Charley's American — 18 | 17 | 19 | $30

Back Bay | 284 Newbury St. (Gloucester St.) | 617-266-3000 ◑
Chestnut Hill | The Mall at Chestnut Hill | 199 Boylston St.
(Hammond Pond Pkwy.) | 617-964-1200
www.charleys-restaurant.com

"Bring the kids" to this American eatery from an "era gone past" in the Mall at Chestnut Hill, or "people-watch" from the "pleasant" patio of the Back Bay progenitor, which also happens to be "one of best bargains on Newbury Street"; the "diverse menu" runneth over with "tasty", "reliable" choices highlighted by "big, juicy burgers" and "great" brunch fare, all of which comes with "smiling service" and "homey", "warm" atmospherics.

Charlie's Kitchen ◑ Diner — 17 | 15 | 17 | $17

Harvard Square | 10 Eliot St. (Winthrop St.) | Cambridge |
617-492-9646 | www.charlieskitchen.com

As "one of the last vestiges" of old-time Harvard Square, this "lovable dive" enjoys "institutional status" thanks to its "delicious", "greasy diner-style food" like "awesome burgers" that "won't burn a hole in your pocket", "cheap, generous drinks" and "quick service"; the "laid-back setting" features a "loud", "fabulous jukebox" and a "fun outdoor beer garden", but its best attribute may be that it's "open late."

Charlie's Sandwich Shoppe ☒⊘ Diner — 22 | 15 | 19 | $15

South End | 429 Columbus Ave. (bet. Dartmouth & W. Newton Sts.) |
617-536-7669

"Truck drivers, Boston pols and college kids" "wait on line" to "step back in time" via "big portions" of "reliable", "reasonably priced" diner breakfasts and lunches at this "rough-around-the-edges" "genuine" "greasy spoon" in the South End; a "surly staff" adds a "gruff charm" to the "casual atmosphere", which features "communal seating" and "no bathrooms"; P.S. closed Sundays.

Chart House Seafood — 20 | 22 | 20 | $50

Waterfront | 60 Long Wharf (Atlantic Ave.) | 617-227-1576 |
www.chart-house.com

"Beautiful" views of the Waterfront enhance the "well-prepared" surf 'n' turf selections at this upscale chain seafooder that's "known more for its scenery" than its "consistent" cuisine; "attentive" service helps keep it a "safe" bet, though critics who contend a "pretty space can't mask the lackluster chow" call it "average for the price."

Chau Chow City ◑ Chinese — 22 | 11 | 15 | $22

Chinatown | 83 Essex St. (bet. Kingston & Oxford Sts.) |
617-338-8158 | www.chauchowcity.net

Chau Chow Dim Sum & Seafood Restaurant Chinese

Dorchester | 699 Morrisey Blvd. (Victory Rd.) | 617-288-8188

"Tantalizing dim sum" and an "old-school Chinatown" setting are some of the reasons this spot is "a staple", especially "for those on a slender budget", while the "hilarious" "2 AM" scene makes it "a legend" among "drunkies"; the ravenous like that the "carts move at record speed" – but that's because some staffers "have little patience" for folks "who can't make up their minds" (it "helps to have a native speaker at your table"); P.S. the Dorchester outpost is "just as good."

Cheers *Pub Food*
14 | 17 | 16 | $27

Beacon Hill | 84 Beacon St. (bet. Arlington & Charles Sts.) | 617-227-9605 ☻
Faneuil Hall | Faneuil Hall Mktpl. | Quincy Mkt. (bet. Commercial & Congress Sts.) | 617-227-0150
www.cheersboston.com

"When the souvenirs outnumber the choices on the menu, you know you're in a tourist trap" advise "locals" who "stay away" from this "overrun" Beacon Hill "name-brand attraction", its Faneuil Hall "rerun" and their "adequate beer selection", "mediocre", "overpriced" pub grub and settings that are "not what you saw on TV"; however, "if you're a fan" of the sitcom, it's "worth going" "at least once" – "you might enjoy it."

☑ Cheesecake Factory *American*
18 | 17 | 18 | $28

Back Bay | Prudential Ctr. | 115 Huntington Ave. (Belvidere St.) | 617-399-7777 ☻
East Cambridge | Cambridgeside Galleria | 100 Cambridgeside Pl. (bet. Edwin H. Land Blvd. & 1st St.) | Cambridge | 617-252-3810
Braintree | South Shore Plaza | 250 Granite St. (Forbes Rd.) | 781-849-1001
Chestnut Hill | Atrium Mall | 300 Boylston St. (Florence St.) | 617-964-3001
Peabody | Northshore Mall | 210 Andover St. (Cross St.) | 978-538-7599
Natick | Natick Collection | 1245 Worcester St. (Speen St.) | 508-653-0011
Burlington | Burlington Mall | 75 Middlesex Tpke. (Rte. 128) | 781-273-0060
www.thecheesecakefactory.com

"Humongous portions and humongous lines" characterize this American chain where the "textbook"-size menu offers "lots of choices" and a "broad price spectrum" to keep families "stuffed and happy"; the "herd 'em in, herd 'em out" feel isn't for everyone and critics knock "mass-produced" fare and "overdone" decor, but overall it's a "crowd-pleaser", especially when it comes to the "amazing" namesake dessert – even if you need to "take it home for much later."

Chef Chow's House *Chinese*
20 | 16 | 19 | $22

Brookline | 230 Harvard St. (Webster St.) | 617-739-2469 | www.chefchowshouse.com

"For years and years", this Brookliner "convenient to all things Coolidge Corner" has "maintained its quality" while providing "great value" in "substantial portions" of "delicious", "classic Chinese food"; "fine service" is the norm whether you get it to go or eat in the "comfortable, low-key" dining room.

Chez Henri *Cuban/French*
24 | 20 | 21 | $43

Harvard Square | 1 Shepard St. (Mass. Ave.) | Cambridge | 617-354-8980 | www.chezhenri.com

"Cubano-Franco fusion" fare is the "innovative" métier of this "upscale-casual" Harvard Square "diamond" – but it's "overshadowed by the rightfully praised Cuban sandwich", "available only at the bar", which also offers "wonderful cocktails" and a more "happenin' scene"; prices are by and large "reasonable", whereas servers vary between "obliging, sweet" and "too much attitude."

Chiara Ⓜ *Mediterranean*
24 | 22 | 23 | $44

Westwood | 569 High St. (Barlow Ln.) | 781-461-8118 | www.chiarabistro.com

For Bostonians, "traveling to Westwood to eat at a strip mall may sound strange", but this "charming" "oasis" is "worth the trip" for "excellent Mediterranean cuisine" that's "well presented by a knowledgeable and amiable staff"; though "the prices are on the high side" for the suburbs, "you won't regret" going since it "rivals anything Downtown."

Chilli Duck *Thai*
21 | 13 | 18 | $22

Back Bay | 829 Boylston St. (bet. Fairfield & Gloucester Sts.) | 617-236-5208 | www.chilliduckthai.com

You "can't beat the value" at this Back Bay Thai where everything on the "extensive menu" is "cheap" and "tasty"; it's "easy to overlook" with a "cramped", "dismal basement location" and "wacky decor" "in massive need of a refresh", but "don't let that throw you off", especially "when you want a quick bite" (the "pleasant service" is fast).

China Blossom
Restaurant & Lounge *Chinese*
- | - | - | M

North Andover | 946 Osgood St. (Sutton St.) | 978-682-2242 | www.chinablossom.com

"Don't 'pu-pu' the platter till you've tried it" say punny partisans of this "big, typical-looking suburban" Sino spot that's been servicing North Andover with "high-quality" eats for more than 50 years; "amenable" staffers deliver "course after course" to the tables while "constantly refreshing" what "may be one of the best Chinese buffets in New England", presented at lunch and dinner daily.

China Pearl *Chinese*
21 | 11 | 15 | $22

Chinatown | 9 Tyler St. (bet. Beach & Kneeland Sts.) | 617-426-4338
Quincy | 237 Quincy Ave. (bet. Circuit & Faxon Park Rds.) | 617-773-9838
www.chinapearlrestaurant.com

The "bad banquet decor" isn't why you go to this "cavernous" Chinatown space according to "hard-core dim-summers" who know to "come ridiculously early for the best selection" of "cheap, tasty" bits of Chinese "heaven" (and to "avoid a line that goes down the stairs"); if a "noisy, crowded" atmosphere and service that "leaves something to be desired" (due in part to "language barriers") irk you, "you'll be welcomed" with even "more space" at the Quincy location.

	FOOD	DECOR	SERVICE	COST

China Sky *Chinese/Japanese*   22 | 22 | 21 | $32

Wellesley | 11 Forest St. (Rte. 16) | 781-431-2388 |
www.chinaskyrestaurant.com

"Tucked off the main drag in Wellesley", this "reliable" venue serves "beautifully prepared" Chinese cuisine and sushi in "classy", somewhat "formal" environs; prices seem "higher" than the norm to those who find the portions "on the stingy side", but that's just a quibble in light of the "gracious" service for both eat-in and takeout.

Christopher's ● *Eclectic*   21 | 19 | 20 | $23

Porter Square | 1920 Massachusetts Ave. (Porter Rd.) | Cambridge | 617-876-9180 | www.christopherscambridge.com

"Some of the most original burgers anywhere" are found on the "solid" Eclectic pub menu at this "Porter Square institution", a "friendly neighborhood" "hangout" that also offers a "revolving" selection of beers; "decent prices", "friendly servers and a "warm, homey" setting all add to the "genuine Cambridge collegiate experience."

Chung Ki Wa *Japanese/Korean*   ∇ 23 | 10 | 15 | $28

Medford | 27-29 Riverside Ave. (bet. Main & Oakland Sts.) | 781-391-5606 | www.chungkiwaboston.com

"Tasty spreads" of grill-it-yourself Korean BBQ are laid out for diners at this "reliable staple in Medford", which also tempts with "fresh, well-prepared sushi" and "amazing side dishes"; though the "warehouse-like" space is "uninspiring", the rates are reasonable and the staffers are "always friendly and helpful, even if their English is lacking."

Church *American*   20 | 20 | 17 | $31

Fenway | 69 Kilmarnock St. (bet. Peterborough & Queensberry Sts.) | 617-236-7600 | www.churchofboston.com

Parishioners of this "relaxed" Fenway New American praise its "inspired" decor (e.g. "gargoyles"), "inventive-as-all-get-out" cocktail list "with a 'seven sins' theme" and "quite delicious" dishes, especially those at the "solid weekend brunch"; even those who reprove the "forgetful" members of the staff confess loyalty to the "smart" pricing and "punk rock"–centric live music room.

Cilantro Ⓜ *Mexican*   ∇ 21 | 16 | 23 | $36

Salem | 282 Derby St. (bet. Central & Congress Sts.) | 978-745-9436 | www.cilantrocilantro.com

You'll leave "with a smile on your face" assure fans of this "welcoming" Salem site offering "nicely prepared Mexican dishes" and a setting "convenient to the Peabody Essex Museum"; indeed, "great meals" are the rule here, regardless of what some consider "slightly expensive" tabs for "small portions" (still, they're "worth it").

NEW Citizen Public House &   - | - | - | M
Oyster Bar ● *American*

Fenway | 1310 Boylston St. (bet. Jersey & Kilmarnock Sts.) | 617-450-9000 | www.citizenpub.com

From the owners of Franklin Café and Tasty Burger comes this dinner-only American pub near Fenway Park that specializes in whiskeys and bourbons, plus a half dozen beers on tap, all paired with hearty, moderately priced fare; diners can belly up to the bar or get cozy in a booth close to the gas fireplace to enjoy the likes of prime rib, burgers and raw-bar selections.

City Bar ● _American_ ▽ 19 | 21 | 20 | $33

Back Bay | The Lenox | 61 Exeter St. (Boylston St.) | 617-933-4800
Seaport District | Westin Boston Waterfront Hotel | 425 Summer St. (D St.) | 617-443-0888
www.citybarboston.com

If you're "looking for a scene", you'll most likely find a "sexy" one at these "cozy, dark" Back Bay and Seaport District hotel bar/lounges; upscale yet moderately priced American fare is available for sustenance, but "out-of-this-world drinks" are really what they're all about – well, that and "pickup" opportunities, especially on weekends.

City Table _American_ 22 | 23 | 23 | $38

Back Bay | The Lenox | 61 Exeter St. (Boylston St.) | 617-933-4800 | www.citytableboston.com

"A mixed crowd" of Back Bay locals and visitors "passes through the lobby" of "the beautiful Lenox Hotel" to get to this "cozy, laid-back spot" serving "tempting", "innovative" New American "comfort food" at "affordable prices"; a "solicitous staff" services the "sophisticated" room, which offers everything from "beautiful breakfasts" to a "fantastic late-night scene."

CK Shanghai _Chinese_ 24 | 16 | 20 | $29

Wellesley | 15 Washington St. (River St.) | 781-237-7500 | www.ckshanghai.com

"People come from far" and away for this "popular" Wellesleyite's "delicate", "wonderfully prepared" Shanghainese fare that's definitely "not your run-of-the-mill Chinese"; though it gets "noisy and crowded at peak times", the "friendly servers" help keep things "comfortable" in the "casual", somewhat "plain" environs.

Clam Box of Ipswich ⊄ _Seafood_ 24 | 10 | 14 | $22

Ipswich | 246 High St. (Mile Ln.) | 978-356-9707

You'll have to brave "unbearably long lines", but it's "well worth the wait" for the "clams par excellence" and other "perfectly fried" seafood sold at this "self-serve" "box-shaped" BYO "institution" in Ipswich; there are "some tables" inside where the decor is "rudimentary", but the "best seats are at the picnic tables next to the parking lot."

Clink _American_ 19 | 23 | 20 | $46

Beacon Hill | Liberty Hotel | 215 Charles St. (Cambridge St.) | 617-224-4004 | www.clinkboston.com

"Lock me up and throw away the key!" plead devotees of this "lively, entertaining" all-day Beacon Hill hotel haunt "set in the old Charles Street Jail", who find the "beautifully plated" New American fare as "distinctive" as the decor ("dining among the cells – how cool is

	FOOD	DECOR	SERVICE	COST

that?"); however, there is a contingent that advises "trade in your get-out-of-jail-free card" to avoid occasionally "uppity service" and fare that's "too pricey" for being "mediocre."

❷ Clio ⓧ *French* | 27 | 26 | 26 | $83 |

Back Bay | Eliot Hotel | 370A Commonwealth Ave. (Mass. Ave.) | 617-536-7200 | www.cliorestaurant.com

"As interesting as ever", this "subdued", "luxe" "special-occasion destination" in the Back Bay's Eliot Hotel "sets the standard for contemporary French" fare with chef Ken Oringer's "cutting-edge" "edible art" composed of "unexpected textures with surprising flavors" and paired with an "exceptional wine list"; service strikes most as "attentive" and "knowledgeable" (though a minority finds it "pretentious"), and although it's "hyper-expensive" for "relatively small" portions, it's "well worth it" if you want to "eat like royalty."

🆕 Clover Food Lab *Vegetarian* | - | - | - | I |

Harvard Square | 7 Holyoke St. (bet. Hwy. 2A & Mt. Auburn St.) | Cambridge | www.cloverfastfood.com

What began as a food truck has blossomed into this three-meals-a-day brick-and-mortar vegetarian in Harvard Square, offering quick, flavorful, locally sourced fare at bargain prices, plus housemade lemonade, Melitta-brewed coffee, beer and wine; the open kitchen looks out into an industrial space with booths and a long communal table, while staffers are equipped with iPhones for sending orders to the cooks.

Club Cafe *American* | 19 | 19 | 19 | $35 |

South End | 209 Columbus Ave. (Berkeley St.) | 617-536-0972 | www.clubcafe.com

"Quite a show" is presented at this "straight-friendly gay establishment" in the South End boasting "solid" New American fare, "strong drinks", entertainment and "plenty of eye candy", both in the "fabulous crowd" and the usually "welcoming, funny" staff; "Sunday brunch is fantastic", and "there's even an alfresco option on summer evenings."

Coach Grill, The *Steak* | 24 | 22 | 25 | $50 |

Wayland | 55 Boston Post Rd. (Old Connecticut Path) | 508-358-5900 | www.coachgrillrestaurant.com

For "Downtown quality" "close to home", Waylanders have this "reliable" "sister restaurant of Abe & Louie's" serving "similar" steakhouse eats that "never miss a beat", plus "fine drinks" from the "lively bar"; of course, you'll pay city prices, but with "outstanding service" and "charming, warm" decor with "polished wood and brass", it's "worth it" for a "big treat."

Coda *American* | 21 | 18 | 21 | $30 |

South End | 329 Columbus Ave. (Dartmouth St.) | 617-536-2632 | www.codaboston.com

"Perfectly acceptable" American alimentation listed on a "limited menu" is turned out at this "cozy", "cute" eatery in the South End; it's "reasonably priced" "for a quick bite", but it's also a place to linger on a "date" or with friends at the "comfy bar" where "innovative cocktails" and "wonderful wines and beers" are poured.

NEW Cognac Bistro *French*   - | - | - | M

Brookline | 455 Harvard St. (Thorndike St.) | 617-232-5800 | www.cognacbistro.com

From Nelson Cognac, chef-owner of prized Kouzina in Newton, comes this intimate French arrival in a residential part of Brookline serving moderately priced bistro fare that includes raw-bar items, soups and pastas; guests can sup in a sexy red-walled dining room decorated with antiques or cozy up to the bar for a cocktail.

Columbus Café *Eclectic*   20 | 16 | 21 | $28

South End | 535 Columbus Ave. (Claremont Park) | 617-247-9001 | www.columbuscafeandbar.com

"Friendly locals" fill this "popular, pleasant" South End "neighborhood hang" where the Eclectic "comfort standbys" "won't break the bank"; the "charming", "cozy place" boasts "attentive service" and outdoor seating that's "nice", particularly at the "delicious brunch."

Comella's *Italian*   - | - | - | M

West Roxbury | 1844 Centre St. (W.R. Pkwy.) | 617-327-8600
NEW Arlington | 202 Massachusetts Ave. (Lake St.) | 781-646-3000
NEW Belmont | 43 Leonard St. (Channing Rd.)
Brookline | 417 Harvard St. (Beacon St.) | 617-277-4400
NEW Chestnut Hill | 1 Boylston St. (Hammond Pond Pkwy.) | Newton | 617-278-2400
NEW Needham | 1095 Great Plain Ave. (Chapel St.) | 781-444-2600
West Newton | 1302 Washington St. (Mass. Tpke.) | 617-928-1001
Concord | 12 Walden St. (Main St.) | 978-369-9555
Wellesley | 288 Washington St. (Route 9.) | 781-235-7300
www.comellasrestaurants.com

This local chain provides harried parents with "quick", affordable "Italian comfort food" like pizza and pastas whose servings run from single-portion to family-sized 'buckets'; with only a handful of tables per location, most take their grub to go; P.S. it's "ideal for feeding the masses" at "informal gatherings."

Coolidge Corner Clubhouse ◑ *Pub Food* 17 | 14 | 17 | $19

Brookline | 307A-309 Harvard St. (bet. Babcock & Beacon Sts.) | 617-566-4948 | www.thecoolidgecornerclubhouse.com

"Too many choices" abound at this Brookline sports abode, from the "encyclopedia-sized menu" of "decent" pub food (which comes in "massive portions") to the "huge number of beers on tap"; moderate prices and "pleasant" service make it "good for a lazy Sunday", but if you're hungover, you might want to "avoid it" at "game time", because it "gets busy and loud."

Z Coppa ◑ *Italian*   26 | 20 | 21 | $41

South End | 253 Shawmut Ave. (Milford St.) | 617-391-0902 | www.coppaboston.com

"Prepare" for a "long wait" at Ken Oringer and Jamie Bissonnette's no-reservations South End enoteca where, once you've won the "fight for a table", you'll be "truly wowed" by the "inventive, snout-to-tail" Italian small plates including "amazing" charcuterie delivered by a "hip, attentive staff" – just know that the "costs can run up quickly"; the "wedge"-shaped interior is "tiny", "cramped" and "loud", but it's augmented by "seats at the bar" and a summertime sidewalk patio.

Coriander Bistro *Indian/Nepalese* ▽ 25 | 19 | 23 | $34
Sharon | 5 Post Office Sq. (Billings St.) | 781-784-2300 | www.corianderbistro.net
"After a switch from upscale [French] bistro", this Sharon spot now offers a "nice selection of Indian and Nepalese" fare, "from mild to hot"; while some calculate it's "a little pricey" for the genre, it's "worth every penny" given the "quality" and "friendly service"; P.S. for "great value", "try the lunch buffet."

Corner Tavern, The ● *American* - | - | - | M
Back Bay | 421 Marlborough St. (Mass. Ave.) | 617-262-5555
Nostalgists beg "bring back the dartboards" of this Back Bay haunt's prior incarnation, the more casual Last Drop, but others say "give it a shot" – the New American fare is "better than you would expect at a neighborhood bar"; it's still a "good place to watch football" and the like alongside "friendly bartenders."

Cornwall's ● *British/Pub Food* 16 | 14 | 18 | $20
Kenmore Square | 654 Beacon St. (Commonwealth Ave.) | 617-262-3749 | www.cornwalls.com
"Like everything in Kenmore Square", this "fun" "English-style pub" gets "packed and loud" "on game nights" with "BU students", "professors" and other assorted "regulars" filling up on "hefty portions" of "standard pub fare" and beers (no wonder service gets "overwhelmed"); one can "enjoy the activity of the street" from the "wonderful deck", but there's "plenty to do inside" thanks to "a pool room, darts and closet full of board games."

Cottage, The *Californian* 19 | 20 | 19 | $32
Wellesley Hills | 190 Linden St. (bet. Everett St. & Pine Tree Rd.) | 781-239-1100 | www.cottagewellesley.com
"Ridiculously crowded" with "families, couples, older folks" and everyone else, this "big", "boisterous", "hip place to meet" in Wellesley offers a "diverse" menu of "tasty, consistent" Californian cuisine "priced right"; the "crisp, white, beachy atmosphere" seems like it belongs in "Nantucket", and the daytime "swarms" make you "feel like one of those ladies who lunch" even if you're not.

Courthouse Seafood ✆ *Seafood* ▽ 24 | 7 | 17 | $15
East Cambridge | 498 Cambridge St. (6th St.) | Cambridge | 617-491-1213 | www.courthouseseafood.com
"Awesomely cheap" "fresh seafood" doled out in "huge portions" keeps this "family-run, paper-plates-and-soft-drinks" East Cambridge "joint that shares real estate with a fish purveyor of the same name" "very popular"; it "fills up fast" at lunchtime, "so be prepared for takeout" – it's probably your best option; P.S. no dinner, no alcohol.

Courtyard at the Boston Public Library, The ⓩ *American*

18 | 21 | 18 | $21

Back Bay | Boston Public Library | 700 Boylston St. (bet. Dartmouth & Exeter Sts.) | 617-859-2251 | www.thecateredaffair.com

"You can't beat the atmosphere" at this "pretty, peaceful", "surprising" place for an "enjoyable", "light" New American lunch or high tea in the Back Bay's central library; the "courtyard is special in nice weather" and the adjoining Map Room Café sells takeout "sandwiches, pastries", et al. – meanwhile, service is "nice" and "prices are moderate" throughout.

⚡ Craigie on Main Ⓜ *French*

27 | 23 | 26 | $65

Central Square | 853 Main St. (Bishop Richard Allen Dr.) | Cambridge | 617-497-5511 | www.craigieonmain.com

"Formidable culinary presence" Tony Maws presents "unforgettable dining" at this "compelling" Central Square "destination" where "obsessive attention" to "local, sustainable" ingredients (not to mention a "worship of pig") is obvious in his "luscious" French fare with "mind-boggling flavors"; "with all of this perfection, one might expect snobbery", but the staff's "seasoned professionals" are "hospitable" as they navigate the "lively", "unpretentious" setting, which includes a "fantastic bar" boasting "outstanding drinks" and an "excellent menu with pared-down prices" – but even the normally "costly" tabs are "worth every penny."

C. Tsar's ⓩ *Mediterranean*

- | - | - | M

Newton | 344 Walnut St. (Cabot St.) | 617-332-4653 | www.ariadnerestaurant.com

This casual, cozy, dimly lit addition to Newton offers an affordable menu of gourmet thin-crust pizzas, handmade pastas and other Med meals; there's a small, inviting bar that's a boon for locals who have a limited number of nearby options for drinks and small plates.

⚡ Cuchi Cuchi ⓩ *Eclectic*

23 | 26 | 22 | $40

Central Square | 795 Main St. (Windsor St.) | Cambridge | 617-864-2929 | www.cuchicuchi.cc

"Wear the most outlandish thing in your closet" to match the "kitschy", "flapper-bordello" environment and "slinky waitresses in vintage clothes" at this Central Square "hoot" "for a celebration or a girls' night out"; "all kinds" of Eclectic cuisines represent on the "interesting small-plates menu", which "can add up to a big bill if you don't pay attention" or if you get too juiced on the "vast selection" of "retro and inventive cocktails."

🆕 Cutty's ⓩ *American/Sandwiches*

25 | 15 | 21 | $14

Brookline | 284 Washington St. (Harvard St.) | 617-505-1844 | www.cuttyfoods.com

Devotees say their "dreams are made of" the "fabulous" "gourmet sandwiches" created with "imagination and attention to flavor" at this "welcome" American addition offering breakfast and lunch to Brookline Village; its "take-out setting" features a "little counter", behind which a "friendly staff" provides "quick" "service with a smile."

	FOOD	DECOR	SERVICE	COST

Cygnet *American*   ▽ 23 | 23 | 23 | $49

Beverly | 24 West St. (Hale St.) | 978-922-9221 |
www.cygnetrestaurant.com
"Fairly traditional" American dining is what's offered at this upscale-casual Beverly eatery whose "great" food and "super drinks and wine" are ferried by a "cheery, efficient staff"; it's a tad "expensive for the suburbs", but the majority deems the tabs "worth it" for a "nice" lunch or evening out.

Daedalus *American*   18 | 19 | 18 | $27

Harvard Square | 45½ Mt. Auburn St. (bet. DeWolfe & Plympton Sts.) |
Cambridge | 617-349-0071 | www.daedalusharvardsquare.com
Harvard Square "crowds" agree: the "killer roof deck" of this New American "can't be beat" for "fun" and "creative drinks"; as for everything else, opinions swing from "dependable" to "disappointing" vis-à-vis the "wide array" of food, and "efficient" to "spotty" servicewise, but it remains "busy, busy, busy", not least of all because it's "reasonably priced for the location."

Daily Catch *Italian/Seafood*   24 | 13 | 18 | $35

North End | 323 Hanover St. (bet. Prince & Richmond Sts.) |
617-523-8567 ⊘
Seaport District | Moakley Federal Courthouse | 2 Northern Ave.
(Sleeper St.) | 617-772-4400
Brookline | 441 Harvard St. (bet. Coolidge & Thorndike Sts.) |
617-734-2700 **M**
www.dailycatch.com
"Absurdly long waits" are the norm at this "legendary", "tiny", "no-frills" storefront in the North End, where "kick-ass" Sicilian seafood-and-pasta dishes are "served in the same pans they were prepared in" and at "rational prices" (cash-only); similarly "high-quality, fresh" fare is offered at the roomier Seaport and Brookline locations, the former with an "impressive waterfront view and outdoor seating", the latter with a "quiet neighborhood setting" and both with bathrooms (unlike the original).

Dalí Restaurant & Tapas Bar *Spanish*   25 | 25 | 23 | $37

Somerville | 415 Washington St. (Beacon St.) | 617-661-3254 |
www.dalirestaurant.com
"Your taste buds will have a field day" with the "mouthwatering tapas" on offer at this Somerville Spaniard whose "long waits to get a table" (no reservations) are a little easier at the bar where the "bliss"-inducing sangria "flows"; "outlandish, oddly gorgeous decor to match the name" sets the "funky", "festive" tone, which is suitable to both "romantic" and "special occasions" thanks in part to the "charming staff."

Dalya's ⊠ *American*   21 | 21 | 24 | $42

Bedford | 20 North Rd. (Rte. 62) | 781-275-0700 | www.dalyas.com
Bedford folks "save gas and time getting Downtown" by dining at this "comfortable", "pleasant" and "reasonably quiet" farmhouse look-alike whose New American dishes are "delish"; service is

"solid", and most surveyors label the tabs "affordable", though there are a few who think they're "overpriced."

Dante *Italian*
24 | 22 | 21 | $47

East Cambridge | Royal Sonesta Hotel Boston | 40 Edwin H. Land Blvd. (Charles St.) | Cambridge | 617-497-4200 | www.restaurantdante.com

A "delightful selection" of chef Dante de Magistris' "inventive", "high-end Italian fare" – starring "exquisite housemade pastas" – impresses guests of this East Cambridge hotel restaurant with "prime real estate at water's edge" on the Charles and "amazing views" from both the "coolly modern" interior and "pretty patio"; though service is "iffy", you can rely on the bartenders to churn out "unique libations" from a cocktail list that alone is "worth the visit."

⊠NEW Darryl's Corner Bar & Kitchen Ⓜ *American*
- | - | - | M

South End | 604 Columbus Ave. (Northampton St.) | 617-536-1100 | www.darrylscornerbarboston.com

Back in original owner Darryl Settles' hands, the iconic South End space that was long ago Bob the Chef's has been transformed into this Regional American with midpriced eats, late-night dining on weekends and occasional live music; it has an upscale neighborhood vibe with silver walls, brown-and-cream banquettes and a classy metallic-tiled bar.

Darwin's Ltd. *Coffeehouse/Deli*
21 | 14 | 15 | $13

Harvard Square | 148 Mt. Auburn St. (Brewer St.) | Cambridge | 617-354-5233

Harvard Square | 1629 Cambridge St. (bet. Roberts Rd. & Trowbridge St.) | Cambridge | 617-491-2999
www.darwinsltd.com

"Cleverly named", "masterfully put together" sandwiches comprising "fresh ingredients", plus "excellent coffee and pastries" make these "reasonably priced" delis on opposite sides of Harvard Square "indispensable"; though everyone suggests the help "drop the attitude", the "biggest drawback" actually is that it's "hard to get a seat", so "go early" or "be prepared to wait."

Davide Ristorante *Italian*
25 | 21 | 25 | $51

North End | 326 Commercial St. (bet. Battery & Clark Sts.) | 617-227-5745 | www.daviderestaurant.com

"Located in a basement" on "the outskirts of the North End", this "old-world" venue provides a "cozy" locale for "Italian favorites" that "live up to" the "intimidating prices"; with "white tablecloths", "professional service" and a "lengthy" wine list, the "elegant room" is suitable "for special occasions" as well as "romantic" trysts.

Da Vinci ⊠ *Italian*
24 | 22 | 22 | $53

Park Square | 162 Columbus Ave. (bet. Arlington & Berkeley Sts.) | 617-350-0007 | www.davinciboston.com

The "omnipresent" chef-owner of this Park Square site "really cares, and it shows" in his "high-end", "stellar" "Italian with a twist", plus he "makes a point to say hello" to his guests in the "warm", "classy" dining room; the rest of the staff is just as "terrific" as it presents "welcoming" touches such as "menus that light up when opened."

☑ Davio's *Italian/Steak* | 25 | 25 | 25 | $57 |

Park Square | Paine Furniture Bldg. | 75 Arlington St. (Stuart St.) | 617-357-4810

Foxboro | Patriot Pl. | 236 Patriot Pl. (Rte. 1) | 508-339-4810

www.davios.com

When they "want a big night out", Foxboro and Park Square suppers know they can "depend" on these "big, sexy" "mainstays" for "exquisite", "gourmet" Northern Italian steakhouse fare and "inspired wines" "served up with style and professionalism"; while some prefer the "clubby" dining rooms, others "eat at the bar" for "great people-watching" – just be aware that it's "noisy" and "pricey" throughout.

Dbar *American* | 23 | 19 | 19 | $37 |

Dorchester | 1236 Dorchester Ave. (Hancock St.) | 617-265-4490 | www.dbarboston.com

You "wouldn't know you're on Dot Ave." when ensconced in this "sexy", "dimly lit" "oasis" whose New American fare, fans say, is "dbomb"; however, if you're just looking to sample the "innovative" eats, "go early" because "later in the evening", it "morphs into a gay bar" fueled by "fabulous cocktails" and serviced by "lukewarm" staffers; P.S. "nice outdoor dining in the summer."

Deep Ellum ● *Eclectic* | 23 | 18 | 21 | $25 |

Allston | 477 Cambridge St. (Brighton Ave.) | 617-787-2337 | www.deepellum-boston.com

With its "well-thought-out selection" of "rotating taps", this "dark, simple" Allston haunt with an "awesome patio" is "a go-to for craft-beer lovers" who soak up the suds with Eclectic "gastropub delights" listed on a "limited, interesting menu"; "knowledgeable hipsters" wait on the "upscale hipster crowd" – in fact, "if you're not a hipster", you may "have a hard time getting a table" here!

☑ Delfino Ⓜ *Italian* | 26 | 16 | 22 | $39 |

Roslindale | 754 South St. (bet. Belgrade Ave. & Washington St.) | 617-327-8359 | www.delfinorestaurant.com

"Cramped quarters", "tables too close together" and lots of "noise" mean habitués "hesitate to praise" this Roslindale spot for "fear of never getting in again" to enjoy its "large portions" of "incredible Italian food"; as it stands now, there are already "long waits" (no reservations), so it's wise to "get there early" to experience the "courteous service" and "great value."

Delux Cafe Ⓩ⊄ *Eclectic* | 20 | 20 | 18 | $23 |

South End | 100 Chandler St. (Clarendon St.) | 617-338-5258

"Good times abound" at this "rare cheap option in the South End" serving a "limited menu" of Eclectic fare that's "much better than you would expect" considering it's served in a "tiny" "divelike bar"; locals come in "extremely casual attire", which suits the "funky" setting, "studded with album covers, Elvis busts", "year-round Christmas" decorations and a staff of "characters."

Deluxe Town Diner *Diner*
22 | 15 | 20 | $18

Watertown | 627 Mt. Auburn St. (Aberdeen Ave.) | 617-926-8400 | www.deluxetowndiner.com

"Be prepared to wait during peak times" (e.g. weekend brunch) for this all-day "old-fashioned" Watertown "delight" whose "excellent combination of traditional diner choices and updated classics" are "something special"; it's "a tight fit", but "what should be sheer chaos is instead orderly mayhem" thanks to the efforts of the "pro" staff, whose "friendliness" makes up for the fact that "some of the booths are unbearably difficult" comfortwise.

Demos *Greek*
17 | 6 | 14 | $15

Waltham | 146 Lexington St. (bet. Emerson Rd. & Pond St.) | 781-893-8359
Watertown | 60-64 Mt. Auburn St. (Summer St.) | 617-924-9660

"One step up from a cafeteria", these Waltham and Watertown "old faithfuls" "compensate" for "zero atmosphere" with "generous portions" of "classic Greek" eats at "prices that cannot be beat"; the "no-frills" folk who work the counter get guests in and out "fast", another reason fans keep coming back "year after year."

NEW Deuxave *American*
- | - | - | E

Back Bay | 371 Commonwealth Ave. (Mass. Ave.) | 617-517-5915 | www.deuxave.com

This sophisticated addition to the Back Bay offers a pricey menu of New American cuisine with nouvelle French influences; the fashionable setting features vaulted ceilings, dark wood and metallic accents, plus there's a gas fireplace, a semi-private dining room and a spacious, buzzing marble bar.

Devlin's *American*
20 | 21 | 20 | $25

Brighton | 332 Washington St. (Chestnut Hill Ave.) | 617-779-8822 | www.edevlins.com

For a "pleasant dinner at a pleasant price", Brightonians have this "cute spot" where there's "something for everyone" on the New American menu and the "service is great"; the "cozy" interior features autumnal hues, plus a "bar scene" and "wonderful outdoor dining."

Dillon's *American*
16 | 16 | 15 | $30

Back Bay | 955 Boylston St. (Mass. Ave.) | 617-421-1818 | www.irishconnection.com

A "good place to unwind after work" or "before a Sox game", this "noisy neighborhood joint" with a Prohibition-era motif in the Back Bay serves up "reliable" (though "unremarkable") Traditional American fare at "slightly higher-end prices"; "go on a nice day and sit on the patio" or join the "bar scene" "late at night" when things "can get crazy" – and "servers can vanish for prolonged periods of time."

District ⓈⓂ *American*
- | - | - | M

Leather District | 180 Lincoln St. (bet. Beach & Kneeland Sts.) | 617-426-0180 | www.districtboston.com

Mostly known as a bottle-service-pushing club that's popular with athletes, celebs and other jet-setters, this trendy, colorful Leather

District nightspot also offers a small New American menu of share-able small plates that some foodies find "surprisingly amazing" – which is shocking to those who ask "do they even serve food" here?

Diva Indian Bistro *Indian* | 22 | 20 | 17 | $25 |

Somerville | 246 Elm St. (Chester St.) | 617-629-4963 | www.divabistro.com

For "delicious Indian" dishes "beautifully presented" in "hip" sur-roundings, Davis Square denizens head to this spot whose dinners may be "a little pricey" for the genre, but whose "copious" lunch/brunch buffet is a "bargain"; there's a "decent wine and beer list" to go with – it's just too bad the "uneven service" is "not on par with the food"; P.S. the attached Diva Lounge mixes up exotic cocktails in "funky", "outer-space" environs.

Dog Bar at 65 Main St. ❷ *American* | - | - | - | M |

Gloucester | 65 Main St. (bet. Porter & Short Sts.) | 978-281-6565 | www.dogbarcapeann.com

While surveyors find the Traditional American fare served at this relaxed Gloucester hangout altogether "good", some opine the nightly live music is even "better"; the interior filled with exposed brick and antique photos is quaint and casual, while the "great out-side seating area" is a lively summer oasis.

Dogwood Café *American* | 20 | 16 | 19 | $23 |

Jamaica Plain | 3712 Washington St. (Arbor Way) | 617-522-7997 | www.dogwoodcafe.com

"Fabulous pizza" is the highlight of the "tasty" New American "pub fare" doled out at this "relaxed" Jamaica Plain place that maintains a "great selection of ever-changing draft beers" and an exposed-brick-heavy, "neighborhood-bar atmosphere"; further attractions include live music on Fridays and Saturdays, an "awesome" week-end brunch and "friendly servers" whatever the day.

Dok Bua *Thai* | 23 | 10 | 20 | $19 |

Brookline | 411 Harvard St. (bet. Fuller St. & Naples Rd.) | 617-232-2955 | www.dokbua-thai.com

"If you don't mind" dining amid a "crazy hodgepodge" of "perplex-ing" "kitsch" and sifting through a "huge menu" printed with "color photos" of "every dish", you'll be rewarded with Thai fare that "packs a punch" for "cheap" at this Brookliner; the "friendly" staff-ers are also "fast", even when they're hauling "more food than one should eat", aka the "great value" "combo plates."

Dolphin Seafood *Seafood* | 19 | 14 | 18 | $30 |

Harvard Square | 1105 Massachusetts Ave. (bet. Remington & Trowbridge Sts.) | Cambridge | 617-661-2937
Natick | 12 Washington St. (Rte. 135) | 508-655-0669
www.dolphinseafood.com

"Unfussy, fresh and delicious seafood" for "much lower prices" than its "flashier competition" makes these fish houses a "best buy", es-pecially if you partake in the "amazing early-bird specials"; "don't be put off by" Natick's "unimpressive suburban setting" or Harvard

Square's "spartan" "strip-mall surroundings" – both are salvaged by "pleasant", "quick service."

Donatello *Italian*　　　　　　　　　22 | 19 | 21 | $44

Saugus | 44 Broadway (bet. Salem & Walnut Sts.) | 781-233-9975 | www.donatellosaugus.com

"So old school", "you'll feel like you stepped into a movie" – "*The Godfather*", for instance – this Italian delivers an "upscale" experience for folks on the North Shore; though "it's pricey for Saugus", "consistently wonderful food" and "great service" mean you get your money's worth.

Don Ricardo's ⓈＺ *Brazilian/Peruvian*　　∇ 20 | 14 | 20 | $26

South End | 57 W. Dedham St. (bet. Shawmut Ave. & Tremont St.) | 617-247-9249 | www.donricardoboston.com

A "charming proprietor" oversees a staff that "makes you feel right at home" at this South End "jewel" where the Brazilian, Peruvian and "other Latin dishes" are "made with care" and "value" priced; apropos of the "homestyle" preparations are the "cozy", plant-filled digs.

Dorado Tacos & Cemitas *Mexican*　　24 | 14 | 20 | $12

Brookline | 401 Harvard St. (Naples Rd.) | 617-566-2100 | www.doradotacos.com

"There are a zillion Mexican places in Brookline now", but this fast-food counter "stands out" with "serious", "authentic" eats that are as "crave-worthy" as they are "inexpensive"; and when factoring in the "friendly staff" and "clean, no-frills atmosphere", it's no wonder devotees beg "please expand to other parts of the city!"

Dosa Factory *Indian*　　　　　　　22 | 9 | 14 | $13

Central Square | 571 Massachusetts Ave. (Pearl St.) | Cambridge | 617-868-3672 | www.dosa-factory.com

"Gigantic, crispy, light dosas" draw "authentic" Indian "street food" lovers, who recommend you "don't neglect" the rest of the "range of rarely found dishes" at this unassuming Central Square counter "hidden behind" a subcontinental "grocery-and-spice market"; "quick" service and "cheap" tabs mean it's "good for a fast fix", "especially for take out."

Douzo ◑ *Japanese*　　　　　　　25 | 22 | 21 | $43

Back Bay | 131 Dartmouth St. (Columbus Ave.) | 617-859-8886 | www.douzosushi.com

"Fresh, creative" "designer sushi" made with "impeccable ingredients" is matched with "interesting cocktails" at this "hip, happening" Japanese "heaven" in the Back Bay, where "loud music" sets the "lively" tone; it's "a little pricey", but "not so expensive" considering the "high quality", "attentive service" and "stylish" "modern decor" – and compared to many "upscale" competitors.

Doyle's Cafe *Irish/Pub Food*　　　17 | 21 | 20 | $21

Jamaica Plain | 3484 Washington St. (Williams St.) | 617-524-2345

"Steeped in Boston political history", this 1882 Jamaica Plain "institution" is a "happy" "trip to the past", with decor that's "in line" with its pedigree, plus "undistinguished but comforting" Irish pub fare that's appropriate for the "reasonable prices" (there's a "great drink selection" to boot); likewise, the "friendly service" "matches well" with the "homey", "boisterous atmosphere."

Drink *American* | 21 | 23 | 25 | $31 |

Seaport District | 348 Congress St. (A St.) | 617-695-1806 | www.drinkfortpoint.com

"Cocktail fiends" fill this "speakeasylike" Seaport District lounge where there's "no drinks menu", just "talented", "passionate", "wicked knowledgeable" mixologists who concoct "amazing", "unique" (and "expensive") libations "based on your tastes"; Barbara Lynch's "tasty" New American finger foods are available for those feeling peckish, but as the name indicates, "the drink is the focus."

Druid *Irish/Pub Food* | 24 | 19 | 21 | $21 |

Inman Square | 1357 Cambridge St. (Springfield St.) | Cambridge | 617-497-0965 | www.druidpub.com

"Skip the fake Irish pubs and riverdance over" to this "warm and cozy" "real deal" in Inman Square where there's a "surprising level of accomplishment" in the inexpensive pub food; the "authenticity" continues with "live Irish music", "Irish trivia, Irish beer" and a staff filled with "charming" "Guinness-blooded Irishmen", who help sustain a "chill atmosphere."

Ducali ◑ *Pizza* ▽ | 19 | 18 | 15 | $25 |

North End | 289 Causeway St. (Washington St.) | 617-742-4144 | www.ducalipizza.com

"Good luck getting in at game time", as this North End pizzeria/bar that's "close to the Garden" fills with "noisy, young" fans with their eyes glued to the TVs and their mouths chomping on "crisp, flavorful thin-crust pizza" and "high-quality" Italian "bar food"; however, there are some surveyors who "really want to like this place", but can't because they're too "disappointed" in the service.

☑ Duckworth's Bistrot Ⓜ *American* | 27 | 20 | 25 | $46 |

Gloucester | 197 E. Main St. (Plum St.) | 978-282-4426 | www.duckworthsbistrot.com

Disciples of this "crown jewel" of Gloucester "love that you can order" half portions of chef Ken Duckworth's "sublime" New American fare, "so you can try more stuff" and "save money", just as with half pours from the "terrific wine list"; the "cute", "casual" setting – which is patrolled by a "knowledgeable staff" – is "small" and "popular" to boot, so "make sure you make a reservation, or you'll be eating elsewhere."

☑ Durgin-Park *New England* | 20 | 15 | 16 | $37 |

Faneuil Hall | Faneuil Hall Mktpl. | 340 N. Market St. (Congress St.) | 617-227-2038 | www.durgin-park.com

"Quintessential" "Yankee cuisine" such as the "legendary", "gigantic prime rib" gets "gobs of tourists" into this "must-visit" Faneuil Hall New England "landmark" dating from 1826; the "unique experience" continues with "historic" decor that's "cheesy" down to the "cheap checkered table cloths" and service that includes "notoriously cranky" "waitresses who also served Paul Revere" (plus some "younger" types who are "not as surly").

NEW East by Northeast M *Chinese*   22 | 17 | 21 | $35

Inman Square | 1128 Cambridge St. (Norfolk St.) | Cambridge | 617-876-0286 | www.exnecambridge.com

"Unusual", sometimes "revelatory" "modern Chinese fusion cuisine" – based on "local ingredients" and served in "sort of tapas-sized" portions (prices are "affordable", but they can "add up quickly") – makes this a "welcome addition to Inman Square"; though the "cramped" dining room is "not for lingering", it does boast a "friendly, helpful staff."

Z East Coast Grill & Raw Bar *BBQ/Seafood*   26 | 18 | 22 | $41

Inman Square | 1271 Cambridge St. (Prospect St.) | Cambridge | 617-491-6568 | www.eastcoastgrill.net

"Hot times in Inman Square" happen at Chris Schlesinger's "tried-and-true" home of "reasonably priced", "knocks-your-socks-off" "spicy BBQ and seafood", especially during "not-to-be-missed" Hell Nights, an "extreme food adventure" for "iron stomachs"; "the service is friendly but harried", as the "casual" digs with "kitschy" "'50s Polynesian decor" (matching the "fun party drinks") are "always loud and crowded"; P.S. reservations are only taken for large groups, so "get there early" or risk "waiting until hell freezes."

Z Eastern Standard *American/European*   23 | 25 | 23 | $40

Kenmore Square | Hotel Commonwealth | 528 Commonwealth Ave. (Brookline Ave.) | 617-532-9100 | www.easternstandardboston.com

"Somehow it all works" at this Kenmore Square hotel eatery with an American-European menu "diverse enough to please all tastes and budgets" and a "lively" crowd sporting everything from "black evening dresses to Red Sox jerseys"; the "striking setting" is as "big" and "classy" (and "freakin' loud!") as "Grand Central Station", and it features a "fantastic" bar where "wonderful mixologists" concoct "stellar drinks", an "awesome patio" and "knowledgeable" staffers who "how to treat a customer right."

East Ocean City *Chinese/Seafood*   25 | 12 | 18 | $30

Chinatown | 25 Beach St. (bet. Harrison Ave. & Washington St.) | 617-542-2504 | www.eastoceancity.com

For "a fabulous feast" of "fresh fish right out of the tanks", this "reliable", "comfortable" Cantonese "standby" in Chinatown does an "excellent" job – and it "doesn't put a dent in your wallet"; it "can be busy any time of the day or night", which makes for "fun people-watching" – and occasional "waits" (not long ones, as the "pleasant" servers work "fast").

Z Ecco *American*   27 | 23 | 24 | $39

East Boston | 107 Porter St. (bet. Chelsea & Paris Sts.) | 617-561-1112 | www.eccoboston.com

A "trendy place in a not-so-trendy neighborhood", this "hidden gem" "near the airport" in East Boston is one part "fantastic cocktail bar" offering a "huge martini/mixed drinks selection" and one part "calming" New American restaurant with a "creative" menu of "many delicious treats"; a "friendly", "attentive staff" and "reasonable prices" are two more reasons it's "totally worth the ride through the tunnel."

88 Wharf *American*   19 | 22 | 21 | $42

Milton | 88 Wharf St. (Adams St.) | 857-598-4826 | www.88wharf.com
"Wonderful views" of the Neponset River from both the "warm, stylish interior" and "lovely patio" make this Milton New American a "charming", even "romantic" choice; "accommodating service" and "not too pricey" tabs are boons, and as for the "trendy comfort food", foodies say it can be "great" if you "keep it simple."

⊠ Elephant Walk *Cambodian/French*   23 | 20 | 20 | $35

Fenway | 900 Beacon St. (Park Dr.) | 617-247-1500
Porter Square | 2067 Massachusetts Ave. (bet. Russell & Walden Sts.) | Cambridge | 617-492-6900
Waltham | 663 Main St. (Moody St.) | 781-899-2244
www.elephantwalk.com
Though it's "not fusion", this trio's "separate Cambodian and French menus" prove to be "a match made in heaven", with their "terrific choice of new, traditional", vegetarian, gluten-free and "healthy" dishes, all "flat-out delicious" and "punching way above their price point"; with diners ranging from "business" folk, "groups" of "friends", "first dates" and "families", there's "never a dull moment" in the "attractive", "exotic" environs, which come complete with "pleasant", "attentive service."

El Oriental de Cuba *Cuban*   24 | 13 | 20 | $17

Jamaica Plain | 416 Centre St. (S. Huntington Ave.) | 617-524-6464 | www.elorientaldecuba.com
"For a simple, hearty meal" of "authentic", "inexpensive" Cuban food "made with love", "you can't go wrong" with this "neighborhood spot" in Jamaica Plain; "enthusiastic servers" provide "fast", "easygoing" service in the casual digs, which are decked out with "pictures of old and new Havana."

El Pelón Taqueria *Mexican*   25 | 13 | 19 | $12

Brighton | 2197 Commonwealth Ave. (Lake St.) | 617-779-9090 | www.elpelon.com
"It's nice to have it back" say ta-cohorts who were "in mourning" when this formerly Fenway-set Mexican joint closed due to a fire; Boston College students are particularly happy with its new Brighton location, "tiny" and "sterile" as it may be, for the menu remains filled with "authentic delights", the counter service continues to be "quick" and the prices still "can't be beat."

El Sarape *Mexican*   26 | 17 | 22 | $28

Braintree | 5 Commercial St. (Washington St.) | 781-843-8005 | www.elsarape.com
"Don't dismiss" this Braintree spot because of its "cheesy", "cramped" quarters – if you do, you'll miss out on "outstandingly fla-

vorful" Mexican meals offered at "affordable" rates; during the week, it's a place to "chillax" with the aid of "strong margaritas", while on weekends, the atmosphere is more "fun", thanks in part to the "loud" live music.

Emma's *Pizza*
25 | 14 | 18 | $20

Kendall Square | 40 Hampshire St. (Portland St.) | Cambridge | 617-864-8534 | www.emmaspizza.com

You can "go every night and not have the same pizza twice" at this Kendall Square parlor that offers "imaginative toppings" of "your choice" or in "artful combinations" plus "crispy-cracker crusts" at "reasonable prices"; just "be prepared to wait", because the "space is very small" and "always packed" – and "don't expect a speedy turnaround" from the "mediocre" staff.

Emperor's Garden *Chinese*
21 | 17 | 16 | $22

Chinatown | 690 Washington St. (Kneeland St.) | 617-482-8898

It's "hard to top the variety and value" of the "delicious, authentic Chinese specialties" served at this "ex-theater" in Chinatown where "dim sum rules" ("it's empty at other times"); the setting looks "right out of a movie" and its "cavernous" size allows for "quick seating", though truth be told, it "really needs a face-lift."

Equator *Eclectic/Thai*
▽ 22 | 21 | 21 | $22

South End | 1721 Washington St. (Mass. Ave.) | 617-536-6386 | www.equatorrestaurantma.com

"Kick-ass Thai" is "oddly" paired with steaks and Italian pastas at this Eclectic "on the edge of the South End" that's a nonetheless "reliable" choice for a "good-value" meal; the "enjoyable atmosphere" features "understated lighting" and service that's "quick."

Erawan of Siam *Thai*
20 | 20 | 17 | $26

Waltham | 469 Moody St. (High St.) | 781-899-3399

"Completely reliable" say supporters of this "neighborhood Thai" in Waltham, whose "delicious" standards are served in a "spacious, comfortable", "lovely interior" filled with traditional decorations; "great service" and "reasonable prices" further make it "terrific."

Erbaluce Ⓜ *Italian*
26 | 20 | 25 | $53

Park Square | 69 Church St. (bet. Piedmont & Shawmut Sts.) | 617-426-6969 | www.erbaluce-boston.com

"Unlike any other Italian restaurant in Boston", this "jewel" in "an obscure" Park Square location is a "tour de force" for "gracious" chef Charles Draghi and his "outstanding" "out-of-the-box" fare in which "fresh herbs permeate"; just as "unique" is the "wonderful" wine list, and everything's presented by a "superb" staff, in a "low-key, elegant room" and for prices that are "worth the splurge."

Estragon Ⓢ *Spanish*
23 | 21 | 22 | $40

South End | 700 Harrison Ave. (bet. Canton & E. Brookline Sts.) | 617-266-0443 | www.estragontapas.com

"Not in the trendier part of the South End", this spot is nevertheless "a must for anyone who loves Spanish" tapas, both "mouthwatering" "standards" and "off-the-wall choices"; furthermore, the "art deco" interior is "charming", and the "friendly staff" is "well-versed" in the "wonderful wine list", "great cocktails" and "delicious sangrias."

Euno *Italian*   22 | 21 | 22 | $45

North End | 119 Salem St. (Cooper St.) | 617-573-9406 | www.eunoboston.com

"Refined" is the word on this North End nook's Italian fare, and "reliable" is another; the "cozy" street-level dining room boasts a "nice atmosphere", not to mention an "attentive staff", but for an "extra dose of romantic ambiance", sit in the candlelit "grotto downstairs."

Ⓩ EVOO *Eclectic*   26 | 22 | 24 | $49

Kendall Square | 350 Third St. (Broadway) | Cambridge | 617-661-3866 | www.evoorestaurant.com

In its "exciting new" Kendall Square location with "lovely" decor and a patio, this Eclectic remains a "bastion of creative, local", "flavor-rich food" (the "farm-fresh" ingredients "make a big difference"), which is complemented by a "diverse" wine selection and "professional, courteous" service; it's "on the expensive side", but most consider it an "outstanding value for the quality", especially those who've selected the "excellent" prix fixe.

Exchange Street Bistro *Eclectic*   21 | 21 | 18 | $34

Malden | 67 Exchange St. (bet. Commercial & Main Sts.) | 781-322-0071 | www.exchangestreetbistro.com

"One of the classier spots in the area", this "godsend" prepares Eclectic cuisine that's a "welcome" "upgrade from the usual Malden fare", and it's "reasonably priced" too; "a level of sophistication" is also evident at the bar, which is "trendy" "after work" for "huge", "skillfully prepared" cocktails.

Fajitas & 'Ritas *Tex-Mex*   16 | 15 | 15 | $19

Downtown Crossing | 25 West St. (bet. Tremont & Washington Sts.) | 617-426-1222 | www.fajitasandritas.com

"If you're in the mood for ultracasual" Tex-Mex eats and "crazy-addictive margaritas" for "cheap", this Downtown Crossing "dive" does the job; sure, the south-of-the-border fare is strictly "for gringos" (read: "a bit bland") and service can be "blatantly rude", but it's "fun" for "an after-work gathering" if you're in the area.

Farm Bar & Grille ☻ *American/BBQ*   – | – | – | M

Essex | 233 Western Ave. (Scotts Way) | 978-768-0000 | www.farmbargrille.com

With an "interesting", "excellent selection" of "moderately priced" American bar standards and BBQ ("they smoke their own ribs, chicken, etc."), plus a big patio and "play space in the yard" (with volleyball and horseshoe courts alongside a vegetable garden), this Essex eatery is "great for casual family dining"; meanwhile, adults enjoy the "huge bar" area whose "atmosphere hops" with "lots of TVs" and live music on weekends.

Federal, The   *Pizza/Sandwiches*   23 | 21 | 20 | $32

Beacon Hill | 204 Cambridge St. (bet. Joy & S. Russell Sts.) |
617-391-0025 | www.thefederalboston.com

"Excellent pizza" made "thin and crusty with lots of cheese" plus
"fantastic sandwiches" filled with "quality meats and veggies" are
the wares of this "cheap eats" spot in Beacon Hill; it's "a nice change
of pace for those working in the area", but it's "too bad there isn't
more sitting room" in the brick-and-wood dining room.

51 Lincoln   ▨   *American*   24 | 20 | 23 | $48

Newton | 51 Lincoln St. (Columbus St.) | 617-965-3100 |
www.51lincolnnewton.com

Delivering "a Downtown experience" in Newton Highlands (and "for
less money"), this "casual-upscale" spot shines with the "inspired",
"terrific", seasonal New American fare of a chef whose artwork also
adorns the walls, plus "superb cocktails" and "efficient, warm" service;
the "charming", "cozy" main room gets "noisy" sometimes, so if that
grates, ask for the "rustic, clandestine" downstairs wine room;
P.S. the signature watermelon steak appetizer is "unbelievable."

Figs   *Italian/Pizza*   24 | 18 | 19 | $34

Beacon Hill | 42 Charles St. (bet. Chestnut & Mt. Vernon Sts.) |
617-742-3447
Charlestown | 67 Main St. (bet. Monument Ave. & Winthrop St.) |
617-242-2229
www.toddenglish.com

"Sooo freakin' good" anoint "pizza snobs" of the "creative", "thin-
crust" pies sold for "reasonable prices" at these "warm", "casual"
parlors from celebrity chef Todd English whose "small but tasty
menu of casual Italian dishes" is also "amazing" (all ferried by a
"friendly" staff); the Beacon Hill offshoot is "a lot more cozy" than
the Charlestown original, but both are "cramped" and so "popular",
there's "often a wait."

Filippo Ristorante   *Italian*   ▽ 19 | 19 | 19 | $36

North End | 283 Causeway St. (Endicott St.) | 617-742-4143 |
www.filipporistorante.com

"When going to the Garden", take a detour to the "'60s" via this
"throwback" Italian at "the very end of the North End", offering
"great food" at "great prices"; though the experience is "not refined", the service is "friendly" and the setting boasts a "fascinating
history", which is "mounted on the walls."

Finale   ◑   *Dessert*   21 | 19 | 18 | $23

Park Square | Park Plaza Hotel | 1 Columbus Ave. (Park Plaza) |
617-423-3184
Harvard Square | 30 Dunster St. (bet. Mass. Ave. & Mt. Auburn St.) |
Cambridge | 617-441-9797
Brookline | Coolidge Corner | 1306 Beacon St. (Harvard St.) |
617-232-3233
www.finaledesserts.com

"Better than sex" sigh surveyors about this trio's "totally decadent",
"heaven-on-earth" sweets served in casual cafe settings, for which

there's "often a wait" ("in a pinch, you can order from the take-out counter"); "some nice, light" lunch and dinner fare is also on offer, plus "divine" hot beverages, cocktails and "flights of dessert wines", and while everything's "a little on the expensive side", it's "so worth the cost" – and "the calories."

Finz *Seafood*   21 | 20 | 19 | $36
Salem | Pickering Wharf | 76 Wharf St. (Derby St.) | 978-744-8485 | www.hipfinz.com

"Watch the boats go by" while enjoying a "well-prepared seafood feast" at this Salem "hot spot" with a "nice waterfront" deck, a "comfortable" interior and "good" prices; "during the summer", all the "noisy" "crowds" mean you can "expect to wait for a seat" – so to pass the time, "elbow" your way up to the "happening" bar, order a "yummy drink" and check out all of the "singles."

Fire & Ice *Eclectic*   15 | 14 | 14 | $26
Back Bay | 205 Berkeley St. (St. James Ave.) | 617-482-3473
Harvard Square | 50 Church St. (bet. Brattle St. & Mass. Ave.) | Cambridge | 617-547-9007
www.fire-ice.com

At these "noisy" "all-you-can-eat places" in the Back Bay and Harvard Square, you put your choice of "raw" "meats, veggies, noodles and sauces" "in a bowl", bring them to an "enormous flat-top grill" and "wait for the finished dish" to come back from the servers; just "choose wisely", as the quality of the ingredients swings from "high" to "low", which causes foodies to call it "overpriced"; P.S. decorwise, it "needs a makeover."

Firefly's *BBQ*   19 | 15 | 18 | $25
Quincy | 516 Adams St. (bet. Alrick Rd. & Furnace Brook Pkwy.) | 617-471-0011 Ⓜ
Framingham | Super Stop N' Shop Plaza | 235 Old Connecticut Path (Rte. 126) | 508-820-3333 Ⓜ
Marlborough | 350 E. Main St. (Concord Rd.) | 508-357-8883
www.fireflysbbq.com

"Finger-lickin' delicious" deem devotees of this threesome's "basic" BBQ, served with "tons of sauces" in "casual", "family-friendly", kind of "chain-y" environs; connoisseurs opine you'd only think it's "awesome if you've never been south of Providence", but still, it's hard to argue with such "oversized portions" and "decent prices."

Fireplace, The *New England*   21 | 21 | 21 | $40
Brookline | 1634 Beacon St. (Washington St.) | 617-975-1900 | www.fireplacerest.com

"Sparks fly" at this "cozy" Brookline bistro where "tasty, interesting" seasonal New England "comfort food" is served at "tables in front of the namesake fireplace" ("hot", literally) and an "awesome bar" area that presents "sophisticated drinks" and live entertainment; the prices are possibly "above what you might expect", but they're "worth it" for the "quality", which includes staffers who "know the menu well" (they're "charming" too).

FOOD | DECOR | SERVICE | COST

Fish Bones *Seafood*
22 | 17 | 21 | $35

Chelmsford | 34 Central Sq. (Rte. 110) | 978-250-0101 | www.fishbonesofchelmsford.com

"You might think about splitting some dishes" if you're a light eater at this "terrific" Chelmsford seafood venue where not only are the portions "generous", they're "reasonably priced"; a few say that the New England–styled environs "suffer" because they're "cramped" and perhaps too "hopping", although what some decry as "noisy", others applaud as "lively."

NEW 5 Corners Kitchen Ⓜ *French*
26 | 20 | 23 | $43

Marblehead | 2 School St. (Essex St.) | 781-631-5550 | www.5cornerskitchen.com

Marblehead "needed" a new "fine-dining choice", and this French addition is "taking the town by storm" with its "flawlessly executed" seasonal bistro fare and relatively reasonable prices; "cozy", "spare" environs with "lots of hard surfaces" mean it can get "quite loud in there", but the "delightful" staffers go a long way toward making everyone feel "comfortable."

Five Guys *Burgers*
20 | 10 | 15 | $11

Dedham | Dedham Mall | 170 Providence Hwy. (Bryant St.) | 781-326-1158
Swampscott | 980 Paradise Rd. (Vinnin St.) | 781-595-1300
Walpole | 104 Providence Hwy. (High Plain St.) | 508-660-9850
NEW Hanover | 1207 Washington St. (Mill St.) | 781-829-6770
Foxboro | Gillette Stadium | 269 Patriot Pl. (Boston-Providence Tpke.)
Randolph | 7 Warren St. (N. Main St.) | 781-963-0600
NEW Canton | 95 Washington St. (Sharon St.) | 781-828-4204
NEW Framingham | 301 Cochituate Rd. (Ring Rd.) | 508-879-7500
NEW Natick | 821 Worcester Rd. (Park Ave.) | 508-650-5100
www.fiveguys.com

"Juicy, greasy, tasty" burgers "with all the trimmings" "blow away" the competition according to fans of this "presidential favorite" that's also prized for its "farm-to-fryer" fries and "free peanuts while you wait"; so even if doubters "don't get the hype", these "bare-bones" but "cheery" franchises are "taking the world by storm."

Flash's ❶ *American*
∇ 19 | 15 | 17 | $24

Park Square | 310 Stuart St. (bet. Arlington & Berkeley Sts.) | 617-574-8888 | www.flashscocktails.com

"Super-creative cocktails" and a "great location" near Park Square make this "pleasant" American bar "not a bad place to hang out with friends" "after work or before the theater"; "great sandwiches" are the highlights of the "something-for-everyone" menu, and while other items are "hit-or-miss", at least everything's "reasonably priced."

Flat Iron Tapas Bar & Lounge *American*
– | – | – | M

West End | Bulfinch Hotel | 107 Merrimac St. (Causeway St.) | 617-778-2900 | www.flatironboston.com

"What a pleasant surprise" say discovers of this West End hotel lounge located "between the Garden and Government Center" (it's "one of the more upscale offerings in this bar-y part of town"), serving "inventive, well-executed" New American tapas; "great service", "cozy, comfortable" digs and "affordable" tabs complete the picture; P.S. "good breakfast too."

Fleming's Prime Steakhouse & Wine Bar *Steak*

| 25 | 22 | 25 | $62 |

Park Square | 217 Stuart St. (bet. Arlington & Charles Sts.) | 617-292-0808 | www.flemingssteakhouse.com

Beef eaters savor the "delicious" steaks, "unique" wines by the glass and "subdued" ambiance at this "chain-chic" Park Square chophouse that offers a "high level of service", showing impressive "attention to detail" all around; while the tabs are "prime" too, there's an "affordable happy hour" that makes for a "perfect after-office wind-down spot."

Flora Ⓜ *American*

| 24 | 23 | 24 | $45 |

Arlington | 190 Massachusetts Ave. (Chandler St.) | 781-641-1664 | www.florarestaurant.com

"Upscale" "without a hint of snobbery", this "charming restaurant" set in a former Arlington bank cooks "inventive", "reliably superb" New American fare whose seasonality is "a plus", as is the "reasonable" price point; "marvelous" service and an "attractive", "uncluttered" setting add to a "thoroughly enjoyable dining experience" that's suitable for everything from a "date night" to a "special occasion."

Florentine Cafe *Italian*

| ▽ 22 | 18 | 20 | $48 |

North End | 333 Hanover St. (Prince St.) | 617-227-1777 | www.florentinecafeboston.com

For "a great way to experience the North End", specifically the "streaming pedestrian traffic on Hanover Street", request a "window table" ("best in summer when the windows are open") at this Italian "treasure"; "delicious" dishes and "nice decor" are two more features that solidify its status as a "reliable" "respite."

🟥 Flour Bakery & Café *Bakery*

| 27 | 17 | 19 | $15 |

Seaport District | 12 Farnsworth St. (Congress St.) | 617-338-4333
South End | 1595 Washington St. (Rutland St.) | 617-267-4300
NEW **Central Square** | 190 Massachusetts Ave. (Albany St.) | Cambridge | 617-225-2525
www.flourbakery.com

"If you can stand" the "mile-long line", this "deluxe" bakery trio from Joanne Chang provides "the sweetest reward": "heaven-sent" pastries such as the "gooiest sticky buns" plus "amazing sandwiches", "quiches, soups and more" at "reasonable prices"; though "sometimes flippant", the "staff excels at handling the complicated orders" – just "don't count on getting a table at lunch", "get it to go."

Forty Carrots *American*

| 20 | 15 | 18 | $18 |

Chestnut Hill | Bloomingdale's at Chestnut Hill Mall | 225 Boylston St./ Rte. 9 W. (Hammond Pond Pkwy.) | 617-630-6640

Fro-yo that makes "hearts go pitter-patter" caps off "quick, healthy", "flavorful" New American sandwiches, salads and soups with "a lot of organic choices" at this "bright, sunny" cafe in the Bloomingdale's at the Chestnut Hill Mall; indeed, it's "great" for a lunch or snack "while shopping", though probably not worth a special trip.

NEW Foundry on Elm *American*

| - | - | - | M |

Somerville | 255 Elm St. (Chester St.) | 617-628-9999 |
www.foundryonelm.com

Among the solid watering holes and restaurants in college-friendly
Davis Square comes this American focused on craft beers (more
than two dozen) and seasonal fare made with many local ingredients; the warm setting's tiled floors, wood paneling and raw bar create an upscale feel, while the prices bear in mind that Tufts is just
around the corner.

NEW Four Green Fields *American/Irish*

| - | - | - | M |

Financial District | 1 Boston Pl. (bet. Court & Washington Sts.) |
617-367-4747 | www.fourgreenfields.com

Specializing in Irish pub fare (with a few American and international
twists), this Financial District arrival offers moderate prices, a long
dark-wood bar and live music on Sundays; the high ceilings don't exactly make the sprawling, bi-level setting (formerly a bank) feel
cozy, but photos and prints add warmth, and a patio adds extra appeal.

Franklin Café *American*

| 24 | 19 | 22 | $37 |

South Boston | 152 Dorchester Ave. (bet. 4th & 5th Sts.) |
617-269-1003 ●
South End | 278 Shawmut Ave. (Hanson St.) | 617-350-0010 ●
Gloucester | 118 Main St. (bet. Center & Hancock Sts.) | 978-283-7888
www.franklincafe.com

"Beyond reasonable prices" for "divine" New American "upscale"
"comfort food" make this a "staple of the South End", and its South
Boston offshoot is an equally "reliable" "standby", especially for a
"late-night supper" (the kitchen is open until 1:30 AM at both); the
earlier-to-bed Gloucester branch provides "a sophisticated place
for grown-ups" on Cape Ann, while all feature "attentive", "friendly
service", "dark" "bistro-pub" environs and a "boisterous vibe" that
often turns "loud, loud, loud."

Frank's Steak House *Steak*

| 18 | 14 | 20 | $31 |

Porter Square | 2310 Massachusetts Ave. (Rice St.) | Cambridge |
617-661-0666 | www.frankssteakhouse.com

"Nothing has changed" at this Porter Square steakhouse "since Don
Draper and the Mad Men were plying their trade", thus the "huge"
portions of "unfancy", "delicious" beef seem down-right "cheap" and
the "'50s" decor a bit "dreary"; indeed, it may be "nothing special"
overall, but "nostalgia" keeps its "older clientele" "coming back" –
whippersnappers, on the other hand, say "you get what you pay for."

Friendly Toast *American*

| 21 | 22 | 17 | $19 |

Kendall Square | One Kendall Square Complex | 1 Kendall Sq., Bldg. 300
(Hampshire St.) | Cambridge | 617-621-1200 | www.thefriendlytoast.com

"Kitsch to the max" is everywhere at this "supercharged" Kendall
Square "hipster heaven", from the "diner" setting festooned with
"more junk than an episode of *Hoarders*" to the "free-spirited",
"avant-garde" American fare served in "Flintstonian portions"; service from the "slacker staff" is pretty much "a mess", and there's of-

ten an "unbearable" wait for weekend brunch, both of which mean it's possibly "to be avoided when nursing a hangover" – however, "awesome" cocktails make it "a good place to get one."

⛨ Fugakyu ● *Japanese*   24 | 21 | 21 | $39
Brookline | 1280 Beacon St. (Harvard St.) | 617-738-1268
⛨ Fugakyu Café *Japanese*
Sudbury | 621 Boston Post Rd./Rte. 20 (Horse Pond Rd.) | 978-443-1998
www.fugakyucafe.com

"Sushi mavens daydream" about the "expansive menu" of "expertly prepared, attractively presented" Japanese fare at this "beautiful" Brookline restaurant that's "a little pricey but not really that bad"; "efficient" servers navigate "a warren" of "comfortable" seating areas on "multiple floors", including several "traditional private dining rooms" for which you should "prepare to take your shoes off"; P.S. the small, "warm and welcoming" Sudbury cafe provides similar "high quality."

Full Moon *American*   19 | 15 | 21 | $27
Huron Village | 344 Huron Ave. (bet. Chilton & Fayerweather Sts.) | Cambridge | 617-354-6699 | www.fullmoonrestaurant.com

You "gotta love kids to enjoy" this Huron Village New American, because it's an "unabashedly child-friendly" "madhouse" – and "a godsend" for parents who get a "grown-up meal" while the little ones stay sequestered in a "great play area" in "viewing distance of all the tables"; some feel the "decor looks a little tired", but not the "accommodating" staffers – so "give them an extra tip."

Galleria Umberto ◪⌨ *Pizza*   26 | 9 | 15 | $11
North End | 289 Hanover St. (bet. Prince & Richmond Sts.) | 617-227-5709

"Locals rightfully rave" about this "definitive North End experience", a "no-nonsense, cafeteria arrangement" providing "dirt-cheap", "amazing Sicilian pizza", arancini and calzones for lunch; "get here early" not only to "avoid painful lines", but because "they literally put down the gate when they sell out", and it's often "well before closing time at 2:30 PM."

NEW Gallows, The *American*   20 | 23 | 23 | $40
South End | 1395 Washington St. (Union Park St.) | 617-425-0200 | www.thegallowsboston.com

"Rich", "interesting" "gastro-pubbish" New American dishes like "creative poutines" are the draw at this "hip newcomer to the trendy South End", with a "modern rustic" decor scheme and generally "value"-minded prices; "friendly, competent" servers get good marks, but the cocktails lose points because a few folks feel they are, while "yummy", "too measured."

Game On! Sport Café *Pub Food*   15 | 18 | 17 | $24
Fenway | 82 Lansdowne St. (Brookline Ave.) | 617-351-7001 | www.gameonboston.com

Chow down on "reasonably priced", "typical sports-bar fare" while watching "lots and lots" of "TVs showing a variety" of games at this "fun spot" attached to Fenway Park, and "get there early", because it gets "crazy busy", especially "when the Red Sox are playing"; rounding out the experience are "nice" bartenders and "great people-watching."

Z Garden at The Cellar *American*   26 | 17 | 21 | $34
Harvard Square | The Cellar | 991 Massachusetts Ave. (Dana St.) | Cambridge | 617-230-5880 | www.gardenatthecellar.com
"Imaginatively, intelligently prepared" New American fare with real local and seasonal cred – some "produce comes from the chef's father's farm" – makes this a "huge asset" for Harvard Square, and the "prices are gentle enough to make it a weekly outing"; by choosing the "great" downstairs bar (with its own "sensational" menu), you can usually "avoid the wait" for the "quaint", "unassuming" upstairs dining room, for which no reservations are accepted (both areas boast "friendly" servers).

Gargoyles on the Square Ⓜ *American*   24 | 20 | 22 | $44
Somerville | 219 Elm St. (Grove St.) | 617-776-5300 | www.gargoylesrestaurant.com
"You read some of the menu descriptions", featuring ingredients you've "never heard of", and "think 'what?'" – but everything at this "ambitious" Somerville New American is "usually splendid", and though "a bit on the expensive side", delivers a "high bang for the buck"; whether you sit in the "homey, comfortable" dining room or the "fun", "crowded bar", the service is "competent and friendly", plus the "inventive" "drinks are big and strong."

NEW Garlic 'n Lemons ◗ *Lebanese*   ∇ 24 | 9 | 20 | $14
Brighton | 133 Harvard Ave. (bet. Brighton & Commonwealth Aves.) | 617-783-8100 | www.garliclemons.com
"Spectacular shawarma, falafel" and kebabs are sold for "very affordable" tabs at this "warm", "delicious" Lebanese addition to Brighton; there's a "helpful staff" to deliver the "authentic" wares, but many find the "stark", "utilitarian" digs "more conducive to eating and running" – or takeout.

Gaslight Brasserie du Coin ◗ *French*   22 | 24 | 21 | $39
South End | 560 Harrison Ave. (Waltham St.) | 617-422-0224 | www.gaslight560.com
"*Très délicieux*" "classic brasserie fare" and a "fun, youthful vibe" with "joie de vivre" are both "deeply satisfying" at this "South End hot spot" displaying "surprisingly reasonable prices"; "outstanding" cocktails are the best of the beverages, while "high ceilings" and "classic" "white tiles" highlight the "expansive", "delightful" and often "noisy" mise-en-scène.

G Bar & Kitchen Ⓢ *American*   ∇ 19 | 20 | 19 | $47
Swampscott | 256 Humphrey St. (Blaney St.) | 781-596-2228 | www.gbarandkitchen.com
Groupies say the "'G' is for 'gusto'" at this "gem" that supplies "the underserved seaside community of Swampscott" with "very good" New American cuisine that's only a little "expensive"; what's more,

service is "attentive" in the "attractive room with high ceilings, flocked wallpaper, splashes of red and lime" and chandeliers, and while it's often "crowded", it feels "pleasant" "rather than frantic."

Gennaro's Five North Square *Italian*   ∇ 24 | 20 | 23 | $35

North End | 5 North Sq. (Prince St.) | 617-720-1050 | www.5northsquare.com

From its "nice location" "overlooking North Square" in the North End, this eatery offers a "terrific variety" of classic Italian fare such as "delicious pizza and excellent antipasti" at reasonable rates; the mellow upstairs dining room and livelier street level, with a small granite bar, both provide welcoming settings for "splendid" meals.

Geoffrey's Cafe ◑ *American*   22 | 20 | 22 | $27

Back Bay | 142 Berkeley St. (Columbus Ave.) | 617-424-6711 | www.geoffreyscafebar.com

After a stint in Roslindale Square, post-Survey this New American cafe moved back to the Back Bay, outdating the Decor score but serving the same "well-priced menu" of "delicious" "fancied-up comfort food" and "amazing, original" cocktails; also making the trip are many of the "friendly", "attentive" staffers, who add to the "fun atmosphere", especially during the weekend disco brunch.

Ghazal *Indian*   ∇ 23 | 17 | 21 | $23

Jamaica Plain | 711 Centre St. (bet. Burroughs St. & Harris Ave.) | 617-522-9500 | www.ghazalboston.com

"Wonderful aromas greet you at the door" of this moderately priced spot in Jamaica Plain delivering some "tasty", "innovative takes on classic Indian", especially at the lunch buffet, filled with "many varied dishes, beautifully prepared"; the warm dining room features candlelight at night, and "attentive service" is provided by a "nice staff."

⊠ Giacomo's ⊯ *Italian/Seafood*   25 | 16 | 20 | $33

North End | 355 Hanover St. (bet. Fleet & Prince Sts.) | 617-523-9026
South End | 431 Columbus Ave. (bet. Holyoke & W. Newton Sts.) | 617-536-5723

Be ready to "stand out in the elements" for a "long" time, because this "North End institution" known for "wonderful Italian seafood dishes" that are "generous with the portions and with the garlic" doesn't take reservations – and once you finally get seated in the "crowded, cramped", "no-decor" dining room, prepare to be "rushed"; there's a bit less "hassle" at the slightly larger South End offshoot, but you should still "expect to wait" – the near-"bargain" bills make it "well worth" "the fuss"; P.S. both are cash only.

⊠ Gibbet Hill Grill *New England/Steak*   25 | 26 | 24 | $41

Groton | 61 Lowell Rd. (Lovers Ln.) | 978-448-2900 | www.gibbethill.com

"Jump in the car" and venture "way out to sleepy, cow-heavy Groton" where this "gem" in an "old barn" serves "outstanding" New England fare with an "emphasis on locally grown" ingredients, plus "grilled-to-perfection" steaks, all for "true-value" tabs; a "friendly, professional staff" keeps watch over the "truly magical setting" whose "warm ambiance dazzles", particularly for a "special night out."

Ginger Exchange, The *Asian*

 20 | 17 | 18 | $26

Inman Square | 1287 Cambridge St. (bet. Hampshire & Prospect Sts.) |
Cambridge | 617-250-8618 | www.thegingerexchange.com

Supporters say the "eclectic Asian cuisine" starring "innovative"
sushi is "solid" and "not unreasonably priced" at this Inman Square
sophomore that also supplies a "great beer list"; on the other hand,
skeptics say it's "rather average" while opining "less variety on the
menu would probably improve the quality."

Ginza *Japanese*

 23 | 15 | 20 | $34

Chinatown | 16 Hudson St. (bet. Beach & Kneeland Sts.) | 617-338-2261 |
www.ginza-boston.com
Brookline | 1002 Beacon St. (Crystal St.) | 617-566-9688

"Beautifully crafted sushi" plus a "variety of excellent cooked" fare
at "average" prices comprise the "broad menu" at these "reliable",
separately owned Brookline and Chinatown Japaneses; "friendly
servers" navigate the "relaxed" environs, which on Hudson Street
include a "tatami room" and 3:30 AM weekend closing times.

Glenn's Ⓜ *Eclectic*

- | - | - | E

Newburyport | 44 Merrimac St. (Green St.) | 978-465-3811 |
www.glennsrestaurant.com

A "standby" in Newburyport, this quaint, dark Eclectic eatery
adorned with local art employs a "friendly staff" to ferry its "impressive" fare while providing "terrific" live music on Sunday evenings; if
some find it a little pricey, habitués say there's better "value" to be
found if you sit at the bar and "order a few items to share."

Globe Bar & Cafe ◑ *American*

▽ 16 | 13 | 16 | $19

Back Bay | 565 Boylston St. (bet. Clarendon & Dartmouth Sts.) |
617-778-6993 | www.globebarandcafe.com

"If it's nice outside" and you're "in the Copley area", this Back Bay
American offers a patio where the people-watching is "great"; ok,
inside can be "noisy", the food is "mediocre" and the service can
swing from "fast" to "surly", but on the upside, prices are affordable,
and if anything, it's a "nice place to have a drink or two at the bar."

Glory Ⓩ *American*

▽ 21 | 20 | 20 | $46

Andover | 19 Essex St. (bet. Brooks & Central Sts.) | 978-475-4811 |
www.gloryrestaurant.com

"Yummy" New American fare that's "a little more creative than elsewhere" in Andover draws diners to this warmly decorated venue,
while the prospect of "striking up an interesting conversation with
locals" makes the "great bar" a magnet to nightlifers; however, the
few folks who find the whole endeavor "tired" (and "too dark")
"wonder whether it's worth the overprice."

Golden Temple ◑ *Chinese*

 20 | 19 | 20 | $33

Brookline | 1651 Beacon St. (bet. University & Winthrop Rds.) |
617-277-9722 | www.healthyfreshfood.com

Chinese food like how you "remember" from your "childhood" (if you
were a child in "the 1950s") is still "going strong" at this Brookline

"stalwart" that also "offers many healthy choices" on its "huge menu"; it's "a bit pricey" for its ilk, but the cost includes a "trendy", "tasteful" room design, "attentive" service and a "hopping bar" area where DJs spin Thursday–Saturday and "the drinks will keep you drunk for days."

Good Life ⑧ American
16 | 17 | 18 | $23

Downtown Crossing | 28 Kingston St. (bet. Bedford & Summer Sts.) | 617-451-2622 | www.goodlifebar.com

Known mostly as a "cool place" for "great" "after-work drinks", "dance parties", "live music" and other "fun nighttime" activities, this beams-and-brick Downtown Crossing venue also offers American fare for lunch and dinner; and while some praise the eats as "surprisingly well prepared", others plead "good god, no" and stick to booze.

Gourmet Dumpling House ● Chinese
25 | 10 | 14 | $21

Chinatown | 52 Beach St. (bet. Harrison Ave. & Oxford St.) | 617-338-6223 | www.gourmetdumpling.com

"You may sell your soul for the homemade dumplings" at this Chinatown Chinese whose whole "huge" menu is "amazing", and "cheap too; some "suggest takeout" since "there's always a line" for the "no-reservations", "tightly packed", "nothing-special" dining room where, to top it off, "service is a little slow."

Grafton Street Pub & Grill American
19 | 18 | 18 | $28

Harvard Square | 1230 Massachusetts Ave. (Bow St.) | Cambridge | 617-497-0400 | www.graftonstreetcambridge.com

"Satisfying" "elevated pub food" is delivered for "fair prices" by a "friendly", "knowledgeable staff" at this New American "student hangout" in Harvard Square; when the "upbeat" environs turn "noisy and crowded", especially in the "trendy bar" area, peace-seekers head to the "quieter setting in the back" or the sidewalk patio.

Grain & Salt Indian/Pakistani
▽ 23 | 17 | 22 | $26

Allston | 431 Cambridge St. (Denby Rd.) | 617-254-3373 | www.grainnsalt.com

Spice-aholics dig that the Indian and Pakistani cuisine is "not Americanized" at this Allston "gem" whose "excellent", "upscale" "regional cuisine" is served amid "nice" red-and-gold decor; "gracious, helpful" staffers and moderate prices are further embellishments.

Grand Chinatown ● Chinese
- | - | - | M

North Quincy | 21A-25 Billings Rd. (Hancock St.) | 617-472-6868

For Chinese eats that are "just as good as in town", North Quincy folk are pleased to have this "fairly new", moderately priced "alternative"; though it's quite "spacious", the casual environs still get "noisy", perhaps with the help of the beer and wine that's also on offer.

Gran Gusto Italian
- | - | - | M

Porter Square | 90 Sherman St. (Garden St.) | Cambridge | 617-441-0400 | www.grangustocambridge.com

"Outstanding, real Neapolitan-style pizza" has Porter Square denizens recommending this casual "neighborhood gem" where all of the "wonderful" seasonal Italian fare, including homemade pastas, is affordably priced; the "attractive", rustic setting includes a "friendly staff" and "pleasant outdoor seating during warm weather."

❷ Grapevine *American/Italian* 27 | 20 | 25 | $45

Salem | 26 Congress St. (Derby St.) | 978-745-9335 | www.grapevinesalem.com

"Probably the North Shore's best restaurant", this "reliable" Salem "occasion destination" presents a "frequently changing menu" of "fantastic", "innovative" New American fare alongside a "good wine list"; the "cozy" dining room is "delightful and romantic" and the garden is "nice" come summer, but some prefer to "sit in the bar area" with its "less-expensive menu" and "attentive bartenders."

Grasshopper *Asian/Vegan* 22 | 12 | 18 | $20

Allston | 1 N. Beacon St. (Cambridge St.) | 617-254-8883 | www.grasshoppervegan.com

When they're "cravin'" Asian, Allston vegans vamoose to this place where the "ersatz meats" are "great" and "value" priced; "there isn't really any atmosphere", unless you count the "friendly" folks who work here and the "alt-emo students" who eat here.

Green Briar *Irish/Pub Food* - | - | - | I

Brighton | 304 Washington St. (Cambridge St.) | 617-789-4100 | www.greenbriarpub.com

Collegiate types, expats and accented servers rub shoulders at this "terrific" Brightonian whose Irish pub fare delivers a whole lot of "value"; there's a patio when the weather's warm and DJs, "traditional Irish music" and a "great Sunday brunch" on weekends.

Green Papaya *Thai* 22 | 14 | 20 | $23

Waltham | 475 Winter St. (bet. 1st & 2nd Aves.) | 781-487-9988

"Don't show up at noon and expect to find a parking space" near this Waltham Thai, for despite its "bleak strip-mall" setting and "spare environs", it's a "popular" "power-lunch" spot for "lots of folks from the venture-capital community"; "super-quick" service and tabs that are easy on the expense account are the major draws, but it's also appreciated that the fare, though "cookie-cutter", is "satisfying."

Green Street *New England* 22 | 17 | 21 | $37

Central Square | 280 Green St. (bet. Magazine & Pearl Sts.) | Cambridge | 617-876-1655 | www.greenstreetgrill.com

Outside it "looks like a dump", but inside this Central Square edifice is a "trendy restaurant" with an "ever-changing menu" of affordable, "high-quality" New England "comfort food" plus "amazing cocktails" ("ask for the secret drink menu"); with "friendly service" and an "unpretentious" vibe, it's "good for a romantic, cozy date", though when "jovial groups" arrive, expect noise levels to go "a bit high."

Greg's Restaurant 🅩 *American/Italian* ▽ 18 | 8 | 14 | $25

Watertown | 821 Mt. Auburn St. (Belmont St.) | 617-491-0122

In business since 1933, this Watertown Italian-American "institution" has been using the "same recipes for years", which some find "great" "for the price" and others deem "bland" (maybe the "orange plastic cheese spread they offer as an appetizer" "dulled" their palate); as for the decor, regulars suggest "let's chip in and buy Greg a new rug."

Grendel's Den ◐ American
17 | 15 | 17 | $20

Harvard Square | 89 Winthrop St. (JFK St.) | Cambridge |
617-491-1160 | www.grendelsden.com

This "underground institution" in Harvard Square offers "one of the best deals in town": a twice-daily (once on Friday and Saturday) "happy-hour special" in which everything on the "decent" American "comfort" menu is half off; no matter when you show up, prices are "affordable", plus there's a "good beer selection" and "always something amusing to watch", from "funky decor" to "hipster" patrons; P.S. "on a nice day, eat outside."

☒ Grill 23 & Bar Steak
27 | 24 | 26 | $67

Back Bay | 161 Berkeley St. (Stuart St.) | 617-542-2255 |
www.grill23.com

Backers of this Back Bay steak "classic" say "the other big names" will "never dethrone" it and its "phenomenal" beef, "terrific sides" and "massive wine list", all of which are administered by "outstanding" "pro" servers in "impressive", "clubby" environs; the tables upstairs, where there's also a "great little bar", are "quieter" than the "loud, crowded" main level, while tabs are "pricey" everywhere you go – and thankfully, "worth every penny."

Grotto Italian
26 | 19 | 23 | $40

Beacon Hill | 37 Bowdoin St. (bet. Beacon & Cambridge Sts.) |
617-227-3434 | www.grottorestaurant.com

"Basement dining room, penthouse food" sums up this Beacon Hill "hideaway" serving "rich", "terrific Northern Italian" cuisine in "adorable, tiny", "romantic" digs patrolled by a "courteous staff"; everything's "well priced for the quality", but for a "fantastic bargain", choose the nightly three-course prix fixe – it's quite possibly the "best deal in the city."

Haley House
Bakery Café ☒ American/Bakery
▽ 22 | 15 | 20 | $16

Roxbury | 12 Dade St. (Washington St.) | 617-445-0900 |
www.haleyhouse.org

"Make a difference" by patronizing this "cozy", "urban" Roxbury American bakery and cafe, which helps people in need "get back on their feet" by "training" them for culinary careers; as a bonus, the "great variety" of pastries, sandwiches, salads and Thursday-only dinners are "delicious", "portioned for leftovers" and inexpensive.

Halfway Cafe Pub Food
17 | 12 | 20 | $19

Dedham | 174 Washington St. (VFW Pkwy.) | 781-326-3336 ◐
Watertown | 394 Main St. (Westminster Ave.) | 617-926-3595
Marshfield | 1840 Ocean St. (Webster St.) | 781-834-3040
Holbrook | 200 S. Franklin St. (bet. Adams St. & Technical Park Dr.) |
781-767-2900

(continued)

(continued)

Halfway Cafe

Canton | Cobbs Corner Plaza | 95 Washington St. (Sharon St.) | 781-821-0944

Marlborough | 820 Boston Post Rd./Rte. 20 (Dicenzo Blvd.) | 508-480-0688

www.thehalfwaycafe.com

The "big portions" of "cheap" pub food "never disappoint" at these sports bars – or so say the "casual" crowds who come to "hang out" and watch the "many TVs showing every conceivable sports event within a thousand miles"; the settings are indeed "dives", but the atmosphere is "family-friendly", thanks in part to "welcoming" staffers who ensure the free "bottomless bowls of popcorn" stay filled.

Z Hamersley's Bistro *French*　　28 | 25 | 26 | $61

South End | 553 Tremont St. (Clarendon St.) | 617-423-2700 | www.hamersleysbistro.com

"Bravo, Gordon!" cheer champions of this South End classic's "terrific" celebrity chef-owner, who's "almost always visible in the open kitchen" prepping "extraordinary" seasonal French bistro fare that includes the "to-die-for" signature roast chicken ("famous for a reason"); the "country atmosphere" is "the epitome of grace and elegance", just like the "charming, low-key" but "efficient" servers, and while the meal is "expensive", the "outstanding wine list" showcases many "reasonable prices."

Harry's Restaurant ●☞ *Diner*　　∇ 22 | 11 | 19 | $22

Westborough | 149 Turnpike Rd./Rte. 9 (Lyman St.) | 508-366-8302 | www.harrysrestaurant.com

"Good eats at a fair price" should be the motto of this "old-fashioned diner" in Westborough whose highlights include "delicious breakfasts", "excellent fried seafood" and "tempting homemade desserts"; after 60-plus years in business, the decor "could use a freshen-up", but otherwise, it "never disappoints."

Haru ● *Japanese*　　20 | 21 | 20 | $39

Back Bay | 55 Huntington Ave. (Ring Rd.) | 617-536-0770 | www.harusushi.com

"Located below the shops at Prudential Center", this "classy sushi joint" is the lone Boston outpost of a "hip" NYC chain churning out "interesting twists" in an "inviting" environment featuring a "lively bar" and "pleasing" service; though many deem the prices "reasonable", some feel the quality "doesn't warrant the cost."

Harvard Gardens ● *American*　　17 | 17 | 17 | $30

Beacon Hill | 316 Cambridge St. (Grove St.) | 617-523-2727 | www.harvardgardens.com

"With MGH across the street", this Beacon Hill "staple" reminds some of a "medical frat house" where "doctors and nurses wearing scrubs" "mingle at the bar" while downing "good", "standard" American fare and "tasty drinks"; a few "young professionals" feel it's "classy" enough for a "first date", no matter how "casual" the atmosphere is.

⊠ Harvest *American*
25 | 23 | 23 | $53

Harvard Square | 44 Brattle St. (Church St.) | Cambridge | 617-868-2255 | www.harvestcambridge.com

"Timeless and fabulous", this "civilized" "haven in Harvard Square" "utilizes local suppliers" for its "tremendous" New American cuisine, which is enhanced by an "extensive wine list" and "personable" staff; a "plush", "elegant" interior and "lovely courtyard" foster the feeling that the "high prices" are "worth the splurge"; P.S. head to the "fantastic bar" for "lighter fare" and lighter tabs.

Haveli *Indian*
- | - | - | I

Inman Square | 1248-1250 Cambridge St. (Prospect St.) | Cambridge | 617-497-6548 | www.royalbharatinc.com

A "longtime pillar of Inman Square dining", this "reliable" Indian presents a "nice" setting filled with tapestries and authentic decorations, plus "gracious service"; "reasonable prices" make it a "good value", especially the daily buffet lunch.

NEW Haven, The ⦿ *Scottish*
∇ 23 | 20 | 24 | $28

Jamaica Plain | 2 Perkins St. (Centre St.) | 617-524-2836 | www.thehavenjp.com

"A wee bit of the Highlands" comes to Jamaica Plain via this "brilliant" newcomer, an "authentic Scottish" spot serving "scrumptious" meat pies, "delicious Scotch eggs and haggis" alongside "obscure beers"; expats can often be found among the "hipster clientele" in the "comfortable", publike environs, which benefit from "friendly service."

Hei La Moon *Chinese*
- | - | - | I

Chinatown | 88 Beach St. (Lincoln St.) | 617-338-8813 | www.heilamoon.com

A "constant parade of carts with tasty morsels" zooms around the immense, busting dining room of this Chinatown dim sum specialist; the red-and-gold banquet-style interior "does not look like much", but it's still "worth a try", especially because the tabs are pretty "inexpensive" – just be sure to "come early" for the "biggest selection."

Helmand *Afghan*
25 | 21 | 21 | $37

East Cambridge | 143 First St. (Bent St.) | Cambridge | 617-492-4646 | www.helmandrestaurantcambridge.com

"Exotic yet approachable" "explosions of tastes" make for an "amazing cultural experience" at this "welcoming" Afghan venue in East Cambridge, whose "reliable menu" is such an "incredible value" – and suited to "meat lovers and vegetarians alike" – it's "perpetually packed"; "reserved, formal" servers traverse the "cozy, romantic" setting, which features a central wood-burning brick oven where "wonderful" bread is baked.

Hen House, The *American*
- | - | - | I

Dorchester | 1033 Massachusetts Ave. (Proctor St.) | 617-442-9464 | www.thehenhouseboston.com

"Good chicken 'n' waffles" and wings with a "great selection of dipping sauces" are indicative of the inexpensive "greasy-spoon" fare churned out at this low-key Dorchester haunt whose 4 AM weekend closing time makes it's "great for late-night snacks"; but "mediocre" service and a "tough" location mean it may be best to opt for takeout.

Henrietta's Table *New England*   23 | 21 | 22 | $41

Harvard Square | Charles Hotel | 1 Bennett St. (Eliot St.) | Cambridge | 617-661-5005 | www.charleshotel.com

"For an academic power breakfast", lunch or dinner – and an especially "lavish" buffet brunch – this "tried-and-true", "casual" Harvard Square hotel haunt fits the bill with "dependable, farm-to-table" "nouveau New England" eats whose cost, the majority maintains, is "moderate" (even most of those who feel it's "a little pricey" deem it "well worth the money"); "efficient service" is the order of the day, both in the "light and airy", "crowded and loud" "country"-esque interior or on the "relaxing" "piazza"-like patio.

Highland Kitchen *American*   25 | 20 | 23 | $30

Somerville | 150 Highland Ave. (Central St.) | 617-625-1131 | www.highlandkitchen.com

Somervilleans value the "variety of price points" available at this "bustling neighborhood joint" as much as they appreciate the "rich", "scrumptious" seasonal New American preparations and the "amazingly creative cocktails" mixed up at the "buzzing" bar; "kind, efficient servers" work a "funky", "cool" setting that's often "positively mobbed", especially during "fantastic" regularly scheduled "events like karaoke, live music and even a spelling bee."

Hillstone *American*   ▽ 25 | 22 | 24 | $34

Faneuil Hall | Faneuil Hall Mktpl. | 60 State St. (Congress St.) | 617-573-9777 | www.hillstone.com

Folks in the Faneuil Hall area are "continually surprised by how good the food is" at this upscale-looking yet affordable Traditional American chain where, "believe it or not", the sushi is "excellent" too; service also "exceeds expectations", and both the indoor and outdoor bars are "yuppie heavens" for "reasonably priced wines" "after work."

Hilltop Steak House *Steak*   16 | 13 | 17 | $34

Saugus | 855 Broadway/Rte. 1 (Lynn Fells Pkwy.) | 781-233-7700 | www.hilltopsteakhouse.com

"Plastic cows on the front lawn" and a "giant neon cactus" mark this Saugus "tradition" that "still has a huge following" for its "big portions" of "average" "old-school" steakhouse fare and "generous" cocktails that "won't break your wallet"; ok, servers "rush" the "hordes" like they're "herding cattle" and the "kitschy" setting has "seen better days" (actually, "better decades"), but it's "worth one visit", if anything, "for the sheer novelty."

Himalayan Bistro *Indian/Nepalese*   22 | 16 | 21 | $26

West Roxbury | 1735 Centre St. (Manthorne Rd.) | 617-325-3500 | www.himalayanbistro.net

"Fantastic flavors you will not taste anyplace else" come via the "aromatic Nepalese" cuisine that's offered alongside "delectable"

Indian cooking at this West Roxbury "change of pace" with a "calm" if somewhat "sterile" atmosphere; "the owner and staff are eager to please and will happily explain" the more "exotic" dishes, and while "value" is found throughout, the "wonderful" "lunch buffet is a bargain."

Hi-Rise Bread Co. *Bakery/Sandwiches*   24 | 14 | 13 | $15

Harvard Square | 56 Brattle St. (bet. Hilliard & Story Sts.) | Cambridge | 617-492-3003 ⊞
Huron Village | 208 Concord Ave. (Huron Ave.) | Cambridge | 617-876-8766
www.hi-risebread.com

In the "Cambridge Hall of Fame", these Huron Village and Harvard Square bakery/cafes deserve a place for their "irresistible baked goods", "fabulous sandwiches" and other "delicious treats"; indeed, it's "hard to stay away", even though it's "often difficult to get a seat" and you have to deal with "grumpy" service from the "hipper-than-thou" counter help and "expensive" tabs (it's "known locally as the 'high-price'").

Hong Kong ● *Chinese*   13 | 12 | 14 | $21

Harvard Square | 1238 Massachusetts Ave. (Bow St.) | Cambridge | 617-864-5311 | www.hongkongharvard.com

"A fuzzy night of scorpion bowls is a rite of passage" at this Chinese "Harvard Square standby" since 1954, whose "busy-on-weekends" upstairs disco is often an "odd spectacle" to behold; the "Americanized" dishes range from "average" to "substandard", but for a "midnight grease fix", it does the trick for cheap.

House of Blues ●⊠Ⓜ *Southern*   15 | 20 | 18 | $32

Fenway | 15 Lansdowne St. (bet. Brookline Ave. & Ipswich St.) | 888-693-2583 | www.houseofblues.com

The seasonal Sunday "gospel brunch is the way to go" at this "rustic" "Southern-style" Fenway chain link with a "bluesy, jazzy" feel and frequent "fabulous" music by big touring acts; the moderately priced American regional fare plays "second fiddle", so "keep it basic" when you order, or just "stick with the booze and bands."

House of Siam *Thai*   22 | 15 | 19 | $26

South End | 542 Columbus Ave. (Worcester St.) | 617-267-1755
South End | 592 Tremont St. (Dartmouth St.) | 617-267-7426
www.houseofsiamboston.com

"Cheap as chips and tasty to boot", this pair of "friendly", "low-key" South End Thais are "standbys" for takeout, dining in or "fast delivery"; the Columbus Avenue original is kind of "shabby" to look at, while the Tremont Street branch is more modern (although "smaller"), but you can "go with confidence to either", especially for "can't-beat" lunch specials.

House of Tibet Kitchen Ⓜ *Tibetan*   ▽ 18 | 16 | 21 | $24

Somerville | Teele Sq. | 235 Holland St. (Broadway) | 617-629-7567

"Try yak for the first time" at this affordable Somerville spot where all of the "filling, flavorful" Tibetan fare is "prepared with care" and "well presented"; the tiny space is "run by a wonderfully welcoming family" that's there to assist those who "know nothing" about the exotic fare.

Hungry I, The *French*   22 | 22 | 22 | $51

Beacon Hill | 71½ Charles St. (bet. Mt. Vernon & Pinckney Sts.) | 617-227-3524 | www.hungryiboston.com

"If you can find" this French Beacon Hill basement "charmer", you're in for a real "treat", starting with a "petite, discreet" setting that "oozes romance" with "lovely" decor, multiple fireplaces and an "intimate garden"; "refined" country fare and "unobtrusive but attentive service" contribute to the "special-occasion" vibe – so "if she doesn't say yes" after an evening here, "give up."

❑ Hungry Mother Ⓜ *Southern*   26 | 21 | 25 | $45

Kendall Square | 233 Cardinal Medeiros Ave. (Binney St.) | Cambridge | 617-499-0090 | www.hungrymothercambridge.com

"A splendid homage to fine Virginia kitchens", this "cozy, chic" Kendall Square spot spins "modern takes on traditional Southern cuisine", and while "the menu is limited", everything on it is "amazing" and "meticulously presented" by "people with demonstrable passion for their work" (they'll even "run across the street" to the theater and "purchase movie tickets for you at a discount"); fans forgive the slightly "high" prices because they're "reasonable for the quality", which is another reason they say it's "worth waiting three weeks for a reservation."

❑ Il Capriccio Ⓩ *Italian*   27 | 22 | 25 | $61

Waltham | 888 Main St. (Prospect St.) | 781-894-2234 | www.ilcapricciowaltham.com

Walthamites are "proud to have this gustatory gem" in the area and feel like they've hit the "big time" when dining on the "fancy", "creative" Northern Italian cuisine that's "pricey but incredible" and matched by a "phenomenal wine list"; the staff is "friendly and knowledgeable", while the "ambiance is fairly formal" in the "intimate", "windowless" environs, which feature some "semi-private nooks" that are "romantic places for special occasions."

Il Casale Ⓜ *Italian*   24 | 22 | 21 | $47

Belmont | 50 Leonard St. (Moore St.) | 617-209-4942 | www.ilcasalebelmont.com

The "best thing to happen to Belmont Center" in a long time, this "casual" "hot spot in an old firehouse" is "always mobbed" with "appreciative crowds" downing chef Dante de Magistris' "yummy" "rustic Italian" creations featuring a "delicious variety" of "bargain" small plates (though "prices run up" easily); "call for a reservation far in advance", and when you go, be ready to "shout to be heard" by the "well-trained" staff – or request a seat on the "lovely" patio.

Il Panino Express ⊘ *Italian*   22 | 12 | 14 | $18

North End | 264-266 Hanover St. (Parmenter St.) | 617-720-5720 | www.depasqualeventures.com

"Centrally located" on "the main drag" in the North End, this cash-only, "cafeteria-style" site serves "quick, cheap", "satisfying" Italian meals of the "pizza, pasta and sandwiches" variety; with such non-descript digs, most folks do takeout, though you can plop down at one of the "window seats" and "people-watch."

Incontro *Italian*   21 | 21 | 18 | $44

Franklin | 860 W. Central St. (Forge Pkwy.) | 508-520-2770 | www.incontrorestaurant.com

Housed in a "beautiful converted old stone mill", this Franklin destination does "enjoyable" if "a bit pricey" Italian dishes highlighted by "wonderful pizza" and delivered by a mostly "friendly" staff; for sit-down meals, there's a downstairs room that's "romantic but not stuffy", while for drinks and socializing, head to the "casual", "huge lounge area" upstairs with pool tables and a "beautiful bar"; P.S. "great" patio too.

Independent, The *American*   20 | 19 | 20 | $27

Somerville | 75 Union Sq. (Washington St.) | 617-440-6022 | www.theindo.com

"Solid food, outstanding drinks" sums up this "reasonably priced" Somerville "hipster haunt" whose "short menu" lies "somewhere between high-end bar food and mid-level American"; supplementing the restaurant is a bar side, featuring seasonally "rotating beers on tap", DJs spinning most nights and similarly "friendly" staffers and "old-timey decor."

India Pavilion *Indian*   ▽ 21 | 17 | 21 | $21

Central Square | 17-24 Central Sq. (Western Ave.) | Cambridge | 617-547-7463 | www.royalbharatinc.com

"One of the pioneers of Indian food in the area", this Central Square subcontinental is "still wonderful after all these years", particularly the "good-value lunch buffet"; it's a popular option for takeout, but since the "decor has vastly improved with recent renovations" – yielding "pleasant, relaxing", roomier environs – more folks are inclined to dine in.

India Quality *Indian*   24 | 14 | 22 | $24

Kenmore Square | 484 Commonwealth Ave. (Kenmore St.) | 617-267-4499 | www.indiaquality.com

"A Kenmore Square institution", particularly "before a Sox game", this Indian "model of consistency" "stands out" with "succulent" fare that's so "heavy-hitting", you "need to be rolled out of the place" when you're done eating; the "long, narrow" setting is "dated", but no one seems to mind in light of the "friendly, prompt" service and "reasonable prices."

Ironside Grill *American*   ▽ 15 | 14 | 16 | $30

Charlestown | 25 Park St. (Warren St.) | 617-242-1384 | www.ironside-grill.com

"A convenient place" "if you live in the area" or just got done checking out the nearby USS Constitution, this "fairly conventional" bar grills up "middle-of-the-road" American grub; but naysayers suggest it's "more expensive than it needs to be", so just "have a beer and watch a game."

	FOOD	DECOR	SERVICE	COST

Isabella *American* | 21 | 17 | 20 | $37 |

Dedham | 566 High St. (bet. Eastern Ave. & Washington St.) |
781-461-8485 | www.isabellarestaurant.com

"Before going to a movie next door", Dedhamites head to this
"splendid little place" to "sit cheek by jowl with their neighbors"
while dining on "delicious, artfully prepared" New American cuisine
at "reasonable prices"; the "casual", mural-adorned environment
may be getting a smidge "tired", but the "enjoyable" "buzz" and
"generally friendly" service compensate.

NEW Island Creek Oyster Bar ● *Seafood* | – | – | – | E |

Kenmore Square | Hotel Commonwealth | 500 Commonwealth Ave.
(Kenmore St.) | 617-532-5300 | www.islandcreekoysterbar.com

This chic seafood newcomer in the Hotel Commonwealth in
Kenmore Square couldn't get closer to the source – owner Skip
Bennett founded and operates Duxbury-based Island Creek
Oysters, whose beds provide many area restaurants with plump,
briny bivalves; the seaside-inspired setting is done up with oyster
shells behind gabion cages and a photo of Duxbury Bay, plus there's
a 25-seat bar offering raw fare and artisanal cocktails.

Island Hopper *Asian* | 18 | 15 | 19 | $24 |

Back Bay | 91 Massachusetts Ave. (bet. Commonwealth Ave. &
Newbury St.) | 617-266-1618 | www.islandhopperboston.com

"A little bit of everything" from Southeast Asia means there's
"something for everyone" at this "pleasant" Back Bay stop that commands "reasonable prices for the well-prepared offerings"; even
supporters suggest that the "exotic"-looking setting "needs redeco-
rating", but they also hope that the "sweet staff" stays just as it is;
P.S. "great takeout too."

NEW Istanbul'lu Ⓜ *Turkish* | ▽ 23 | 19 | 23 | $23 |

Somerville | 237 Holland St. (Broadway) | 617-440-7387 |
www.istanbul-lu.com

Acolytes "can't stop singing the praises" of this inexpensive
Somerville newcomer because they're "consistently wowed" by the
"lengthy menu" of "Turkish food made with fresh, flavorful ingredients"; though the space is "cramped", the atmosphere's "inviting"
thanks to a "friendly" staff that's adept at "guiding guests through
the many exotic offerings."

☒ Ithaki Mediterranean Cuisine *Greek/Mediterranean* | 27 | 24 | 26 | $48 |

Ipswich | 25 Hammatt St. (Depot Sq.) | 978-356-0099 |
www.ithakicuisine.com

From the "classic Greek dishes" to the more "interesting", "fusion"-
like Mediterranean meals, everything made at this "real find
in Ipswich" is "extraordinary", and it comes via "wonderful service"
to boot; the atmosphere has always been "relaxed but classy", but
it benefits from a recent expansion that brought "lovely updated
decor", so "run, don't walk to make a reservation – you will
not be disappointed."

NEW Jacky's Table *French* | 23 | 19 | 21 | $31

Brighton | 1414 Commonwealth Ave. (bet. Allston & Warren Sts.) | 617-274-8687 | www.chezjackyboston.com

A more "casual" offshoot of Petit Robert Bistro, this "solid" Brighton addition turns out "wonderful, old-school French bistro" cuisine paired with "fabulous" wines, with "lots of by-the-glass" options; "charming" Gallic staffers add appeal, and best of all, the prices are "so reasonable, you can go every week."

Jacob Wirth *American/German* | 18 | 19 | 18 | $29

Theater District | 31-37 Stuart St. (bet. Tremont & Washington Sts.) | 617-338-8586 | www.jacobwirth.com

Enter a "time warp" when you come to this "bustling, high-ceilinged" 1868 beer hall/"Boston landmark" in the Theater District doling out "hearty" "German staples" and some other New American food-stuffs, all at "reasonable prices"; "quick and friendly staffers", a "broad" brew selection and "unique" Friday night "piano sing-alongs" ensure the atmosphere's always "fun" and "festive."

Jae's *Asian* | 22 | 16 | 20 | $34

South End | 520 Columbus Ave. (Concord Sq.) | 617-421-9405 | www.jaescafe.com

"You can't go wrong" with anything on the "extensive menu" proffered at this South End Asian "treasure" offering everything from "solid" sushi to "Korean specialties" to "amazing Sichuan wings" and beyond; the "pleasant", casual space can often get "a little crowded" at night, while during the day, customers enjoy "bargain" lunch boxes (it's "not expensive" for dinner either); P.S. "great for takeout" too.

James's Gate *American/Irish* | 18 | 15 | 16 | $25

Jamaica Plain | 5-11 McBride St. (South St.) | 617-983-2000 | www.jamessgate.com

At this place in Jamaica Plain, the "pub side" offers "tasty" Irish accented eats like shepherd's pie plus a "decent beer selection" in a "somewhat cramped" "simple wood" atmosphere whose fireplace makes it feel "cozy in the winter"; on the "restaurant side", there's a slightly "more expensive" American menu that "needs to raise its game"; P.S. outdoor seating in summer.

Jamjuli *Thai* | 21 | 15 | 20 | $25

Newton | 1203 Walnut St. (Centre St.) | 617-965-5655 | www.jamjuli.com

The "spice is nice" at this "inexpensive" Thai "standby" "behind a quickie mart in Newton"; true, the decor is "tired", but the staff is "pleasant" and the quality's "reliable", so many locals "love it."

Jasmine Bistro Ⓜ *French/Hungarian* | 25 | 18 | 25 | $33

Brighton | 412 Market St. (Washington St.) | 617-789-4676

The "marvelous family" that runs this affordable Brighton attraction "takes pride" in serving its "interesting" "mixture" of "fine cuisines", featuring French, Hungarian and Middle Eastern; the "personalized service" includes a "great chef" who "often comes out to advise on the menu", making the "intimate" environs seem all the more "warm."

	FOOD	DECOR	SERVICE	COST

Jasper White's
Summer Shack *New England/Seafood* — 21 | 15 | 19 | $38

Back Bay | 50 Dalton St. (Boylston St.) | 617-867-9955
Huron Village | 149 Alewife Brook Pkwy. (Cambridge Park Dr.) |
Cambridge | 617-520-9500
Hingham | Derby Street Shoppes | 96 Derby St. (Cushing St.) |
781-740-9555
www.summershackrestaurant.com

"Real New England homestyle flavor" abounds in the "top-quality
seafood" – starring "an awesome selection of oysters" and "finger-
sucking-good" pan-roasted lobster – at these "casual oases" from
Boston's "original celebrity chef"; "informal, friendly" service
matches the "funky" settings with "children running about", and
while some "families" like that it "feels like a party", others are
bugged that they're paying "upscale prices" for "downscale decor."

Jer-Ne *American* — 19 | 22 | 22 | $56

Theater District | Ritz-Carlton Boston Common | 10 Avery St.
(Tremont St.) | 617-574-7176 | www.ritzcarlton.com

"As expected" from the Ritz-Carlton, the service is "pleasant" and the
art-adorned setting is "sophisticated" at this "relaxed" all-day Theater
District New American lounge/restaurant; but the "bistro-type food"
is merely "good", therefore perhaps "not worth" the "exorbitant price."

NEW Jerry Remy's *Pub Food* — 18 | 22 | 18 | $28

Fenway | 1265 Boylston St. (bet. Ipswich St. & Yawkey Way) |
617-236-7369
Seaport District | Liberty Wharf | 250 Northern Ave. (D St.) | 617-856-7369
www.jerryremys.com

From the eponymous "former Sox star"–turned–TV announcer, this
"big", "welcome addition to Fenway" is a "sports-enthusiast's type
of hangout", offering "memorabilia" and "more TV screens than
mission control" while serving "ample portions" of "decent", "well-
priced" "upscale pub grub"; an "efficient staff" "handles the crowds on
game days" when it's as "loud as the stadium" ("that's to be expected"); P.S. the similar Seaport District branch opened post-Survey.

Jerusalem Pita *Israeli* — 20 | 11 | 17 | $17

Brookline | 10 Pleasant St. (bet. John & Waldo Sts.) | 617-739-2400 |
www.jerusalempita.com

"A wide variety" of kosher Israeli food ("tasty" falafel, "fabulous
pita") is "served with a smile" at this small, "casual", "pleasant
place" "outside of busy Coolidge Corner"; though many feel tabs are
at "a competitive price point", quite a few surveyors calculate it's
"expensive for what it is" – nevertheless, it's probably "the only
place in the area where you can get" this kind of fare.

Jillian's ❶ *Pub Food* — 16 | 17 | 16 | $27

Fenway | 145 Ipswich St. (Lansdowne St.) | 617-437-0300 |
www.jilliansboston.com

"Come to play pool", bowl, "catch a game" on TV or "just to imbibe"
(via the "full bar with a good beer selection") at this "big, noisy"

sports haven across from Fenway Park that's "always a lot of fun"; the pub grub is "an afterthought", but it's "decent" enough, and affordable too.

Jimmy's Steer House *Steak*   20 | 16 | 21 | $29

Arlington | 1111 Massachusetts Ave. (Quincy St.) | 781-646-4450 | www.jimmysarlington.com
Saugus | 114 Broadway (bet. Rte. 129 & Walnut St.) | 781-233-8600 | www.jimmyssaugus.com

"Older folks" fawn "you can always count on Jimmy" for "decent steaks" at "great prices", plus "competent, friendly" service, at these "steady", "old-school" "meat-and-potatoes kind of places" in Arlington and Saugus; sure, there's "virtually no ambiance", but "if you accept it for what it is, you won't be disappointed."

Joe & Maria's *Italian*   – | – | – | M

Norwood | 434 Providence Hwy. (bet. Everett & Neponset Sts.) | 781-769-5730 | www.joeandmarias.com

"Fabulous" contemporary Italian cuisine is available with "worthwhile" wine pairings at this "hidden jewel" in Norwood, a place where it's "easy to relax" thanks in part to "prompt and pleasant" service, not to mention "reasonable prices"; if you're looking for a livelier time, "don't miss" the "fun" bar.

Joe's American Bar & Grill *American*   17 | 18 | 19 | $30

NEW **Back Bay** | 181 Newbury St. (Exeter St.) | 617-536-4200 ◗
North End | 100 Atlantic Ave. (Commercial Wharf) | 617-367-8700 ◗
Braintree | South Shore Plaza | 250 Granite St. (I-95, exit 6) | 781-848-0200
Dedham | 985 Providence Hwy. (bet. Rtes. 1 & 128) | 781-329-0800
Peabody | Northshore Mall | 210 Andover St./Rte. 114 (Rte. 128) | 978-532-9500
Woburn | 311 Mishawum Rd. (Commerce Way) | 781-935-7200
Hanover | Merchants Row | 2087 Washington St./Rte. 53 (Rte. 123) | 781-878-1234
Franklin | 466 King St. (Union St.) | 508-553-9313
Framingham | Shoppers World | 1 Worcester Rd./Rte. 9 (bet. I-90 & Rte. 30) | 508-820-8389
www.joesamerican.com

You "always know what to expect" at this local American chain: "reliable", "classic" "upscale pub food" (like "good burgers") doled out in "generous portions" and listed on a menu featuring "choices for the whole family" and "decent prices"; the "comfortable", "informal", usually "crowded" environs all offer "social" bars and service that "tries hard to be attentive and generally succeeds", and some even have "nice patios" too.

Joe Tecce's *Italian*   19 | 16 | 18 | $34

North End | 61 N. Washington St. (Cooper St.) | 617-742-6210 | www.joetecces.com

"Bring the family" and "relax" at this "very old" Italian in the North End, where "great", "classic" "red sauce" is "served unpretentiously" by a "friendly" staff; the "kitschy" atmosphere (grapes, statues) may be "dated", but "that's what makes it fun" to many – and a "tired" "tourist trap" to others.

John Harvard's Brew House *Pub Food*   16 | 17 | 17 | $25

Harvard Square | 33 Dunster St. (bet. Mass. Ave. & Mt. Auburn St.) | Cambridge | 617-868-3585
Framingham | Shoppers World | 1 Worcester Rd./Rte. 9 (Ring Rd.) | 508-875-2337
www.johnharvards.com

"Terrific beer" is all you need to know about this "casual" brewpub chain dispensing a "wide selection" of "craft-brewed" suds to wash down "ok" "comfort food"; though it can "feel like a frat house" ("expect a drinking crowd"), it's perfectly "adequate" as an "after-work hangout" thanks mainly to the "reasonable prices."

Johnny D's Uptown Ⓜ *American*   20 | 15 | 19 | $24

Somerville | 17 Holland St. (College Ave.) | 617-776-2004 | www.johnnyds.com

"Great musicians" and drinks are the "main attractions" at night at this Somerville venue with "album covers on the walls", but the American pub grub "ain't so bad either", and it's "reasonably priced" too; however, come the weekend, the "famous" oatmeal and "creative" pancakes are on par with the live jazz during the "out-of-this-world" brunch, at which the "staff makes you feel right at home" no matter how "busy" it gets.

Johnny's Luncheonette *Diner*   19 | 15 | 18 | $19

Newton | 30 Langley Rd. (bet. Beacon & Centre Sts.) | 617-527-3223 | www.johnnysluncheonette.com

"The decor may be cheesy", but the eats are "hearty and tasty" at this Newton "throwback" doling out "old-time diner" "comfort food", "Jewish deli specialties" and "yummy breakfasts all day" for "cheap"; "be prepared for long waits", particularly on weekend mornings when the "tight" digs are "crowded and noisy" and the "young, friendly servers" do their best to be "prompt."

José's *Mexican*   19 | 15 | 19 | $24

Huron Village | 131 Sherman St. (bet. Rindge Ave. & Walden St.) | Cambridge | 617-354-0335 | www.josesmex.com

With "low-key" vibes and "low-cost" tabs, this "serviceable" Huron Village Mexican makes for an "easy night out for a family", with "solid" *comida* and a "great selection of tequilas"; the "brightly colored" decor is "appropriate" for this type of place, and the "service is pretty speedy."

Joshua Tree *Pub Food*   15 | 14 | 16 | $20

Allston | 1316 Commonwealth Ave. (bet. Griggs & Redford Sts.) | 617-566-6699 | www.joshuatreeallston.com
Somerville | 256 Elm St. (Davis Sq.) | 617-623-9910 | www.joshuatreesomerville.com

If you're in "college" and "into sports", these "generic" "hangouts" in Allston and Somerville provide "lots of TVs" to "catch a game", plus "standard pub food" and "crazy" "deep-fried" desserts to soak up the "reasonably priced beers"; if you've graduated, it can also be a "fun place to meet friends after work", that is if you can shrug off the "indifferent" service.

NEW Journeyman *American* | - | - | - | E |

Somerville | 9 Sanborn Ct. (Somerville Ave.) | 617-718-2333 | www.journeymanrestaurant.com

"Something fresh and different" has arrived in Somerville: this New American whipping up locally sourced, pricey, weekly changing tasting menus (three, five or seven courses) for dinner only Wednesday–Sunday – and early word is they're "amazing, innovative and beautifully presented"; "interesting wines and enthusiastic people" abound in the cool, minimalist dining room where the best seats for gourmet gawking are at a concrete counter overlooking the open kitchen.

JP Seafood Cafe *Japanese/Korean* | 22 | 12 | 20 | $24 |

Jamaica Plain | 730 Centre St. (Harris Ave.) | 617-983-5177 | www.jpseafoodcafe.com

This Jamaica Plain "standby" "satisfies both palate and pocket" with "consistently well-prepared sushi" and other Japanese and Korean items, some of which "you don't find elsewhere", at "reasonable prices"; a "loyal neighborhood clientele" enjoys the "friendly, casual" service more than the "faded" decor ("freshen up!"), but ultimately, many "like it better for takeout."

J's at Nashoba Valley Winery M *American* | ▽ 24 | 24 | 24 | $50 |

Bolton | 100 Wattaquadock Hill Rd. (Berlin Rd.) | 978-779-9816 | www.nashobawinery.com

"Beautiful orchard views" from both the "lovely terrace" and "cozy-farmhouse" interior are alone "worth the drive to Bolton" and this "quiet", "romantic" winery restaurant, but the "terrific, imaginative" New American fare – with "adventurous" pairings of "Nashoba's wonderful fruit wines" – is its own attraction; prices are "not inexpensive", but the three-course dinner prix fixe and "superlative brunch" are "real bargains" comparatively.

Jumbo Seafood *Chinese/Seafood* | 22 | 15 | 18 | $29 |

Newton | 10 Langley Rd. (Centre St.) | 617-332-3600 | www.jumboseafoodrestaurant.com

New Jumbo Seafood ◐ *Chinese/Seafood*

Chinatown | 5 Hudson St. (bet. Beach & Kneeland Sts.) | 617-542-2823 | www.newjumboseafoodrestaurant.com

"Pick your own fish" from the tanks at these by and large "pleasant" Cantonese fish houses where everything's "well prepared", some things are "comparatively inexpensive" and others are "priced too high"; the Chinatown original is a "pro" in a neighborhood of many competitors, while the separately owned Newton iteration sets a suburban "standard" with white tablecloths, an attractive bar and the bonus of "excellent" weekend dim sum.

Kama Lounge ● *Eclectic*

- | - | - | M

Quincy | 39 Cottage Ave. (bet. Dennis Ryan Pkwy. & Hancock St.) |
617-773-3002 | www.kama-lounge.com

"Inventive" Eclectic tapas make for "great" light sustenance at this
"casual" but "slick lounge in Quincy Center", which also delivers
specialty cocktails in its black-and-gold environment; it's "happening" on weekends when it "turns into a club" with DJs and dancing.

Karoun ⊠Ⓜ *Armenian/Mideastern*

20 | 17 | 19 | $37

Newton | 839 Washington St. (Walnut St.) | 617-964-3400 |
www.karoun.net

"Entertainment and dining in one locale" is the selling point of this
"lovely" Newton venue offering "wonderful belly dancers" on weekends alongside its daily slate of "decent", "reasonably priced" Middle
Eastern fare and more "unusual Armenian" selections; though some
find the decor "hokey", it's nevertheless a "fun spot", especially with
a "large group" and particularly with the aid of the "nice" staff.

Kashmir *Indian*

24 | 20 | 20 | $32

Back Bay | 279 Newbury St. (Gloucester St.) | 617-536-1695 |
www.kashmirrestaurant.com

"Prepare to have your taste buds delighted" at this "elegant" Back
Bay "find" where "satisfying" Indian with "wonderful fiery sauces" is
served in a "calming", "beautiful" setting by an "experienced staff";
there's "great people-watching" from the "delightful" patio, and
though it's "a little pricey" for the type, it's "definitely more affordable than most places" on "chic Newbury Street."

Kathmandu Spice *Nepalese*

23 | 18 | 20 | $24

Arlington | 166 Massachusetts Ave. (Lake St.) | 781-316-1755 |
www.kathmanduspice.com

"Fresh", "hearty" and "yummy" is how surveyors describe the "exotic
Nepalese" cuisine whipped up at this "laid-back" Arlington attraction whose decor is as "pleasant and warm" as the staff is "nice"; most
impressive is how "reasonably priced" the menu is, chiefly the "wonderful lunch buffet" whose "great value" makes it "not to be missed."

Kaya House ● *Japanese/Korean*

- | - | - | M

Porter Square | 1924 Massachusetts Ave. (Porter Rd.) | Cambridge |
617-497-5656

"Come with friends" to this "great" Korean BBQ "mainstay" in Porter
Square, where you get "loads of yummy food" – including sushi and
lunchtime bento boxes – for not a lot of money; the "cozy, Asian"-in-
flected environs feature a "patio for sunny days" and a "friendly staff."

Kayuga ● *Japanese/Korean*

∇ 18 | 12 | 19 | $25

Brookline | 1030 Commonwealth Ave. (Babcock St.) | 617-566-8888 |
www.kayuga.com

Kayuga II *Japanese/Korean*

Arlington | 444 Massachusetts Ave. (Medford St.) | 781-648-7878

With a 1:30 AM nightly closing time, this "convenient", casual
Brookline option is a "haven for late-night sushi fixes", mainly

among "college students" who also value the "many other" Japanese and Korean items on sale for "reasonable prices"; with "bland decor", some brush the Arlington offshoot off as "nothing spectacular", though office types concede it's still a "good place for lunch with co-workers."

Kaze ◑ *Japanese* ▽ 24 | 20 | 21 | $27

Chinatown | 1 Harrison Ave. (Essex St.) | 617-338-8283 | www.kazeshabushabu.com

"Lots of fun for a date" or with "the kids", this informal Chinatown venue offers shabu-shabu, in which you cook your own "diverse array of fresh veggies and tender meats" in a "variety of soup bases" "right at the table", resulting in meals that are as "healthy" as they are "hearty"; newbies need not worry: the "great" staff makes sure "you don't hurt yourself on the table burners."

Kebab Factory *Indian* 24 | 16 | 19 | $25

Somerville | 414 Washington St. (Beacon St.) | 617-354-4996 | www.thekebabfactory.net

"Not a factory and not limited to kebabs", this Somerville site stocks "a wide variety" of "terrific Indian food", especially in its "stellar", "ever so tasty and cheap" daily lunch buffet; despite the "attentive service", a few find the industrial-looking digs too "tiny", so they get it to go.

Khao Sarn Cuisine *Thai* 24 | 19 | 20 | $27

Brookline | 250 Harvard St. (Beacon St.) | 617-566-7200 | www.khaosarnboston.com

A "wide selection" of "ecstasy-inducing" Thai is "skillfully prepared with fresh ingredients and colorful spices" at this "Coolidge Corner treasure" where the tabs are "inexpensive" and the portions are "generous"; it's "dependable" for takeout, but with "gracious" service and "tasteful", "serene", "somewhat upscale" decor, it's also "great for a date."

King & I *Thai* 22 | 13 | 21 | $24

Beacon Hill | 145 Charles St. (Cambridge St.) | 617-227-3320 | www.kingandi-boston.com

"Loves it!" roars the "MGH crowd" ("you see a lot of people wearing scrubs") about this Beacon Hill haunt and its "generous portions" of "consistent" Thai cuisine doled out "quick" and for "more than reasonable prices"; some even report getting the "royal treatment" from "friendly" staffers, which makes up for the fact that there's "not much atmosphere."

KingFish Hall *Seafood* 22 | 21 | 19 | $46

Faneuil Hall | Faneuil Hall Mktpl. | 188 Faneuil Hall Mktpl. (S. Market St.) | 617-523-8862 | www.toddenglish.com

"Inventive, delicious" preparations of seafood "right out of the ocean" make this a "Todd English success", despite service that can swing from "accommodating" to "overtaxed" when it's "crowded"; sure, its setting in Faneuil Hall is "touristy", but that's why there's such "fun people-watching" inside the "funky, lively", fishy environs and out on the patio where there's "lots" of tables (incidentally, the location's also why the prices are "high").

Kings ● *Pub Food* ▽ 19 | 19 | 16 | $30
Back Bay | Kings Bowling Alley | 50 Dalton St. (Scotia St.) | 617-266-2695 | www.kingsbackbay.com
NEW Dedham | 950 Providence Hwy. (Elm St.) | 781-329-6000 | www.kingsdedham.com

For a bowling alley, the "enhanced" pub fare is "surprisingly awesome" at this Back Bay and Dedham "place to spend a night", where the "young" "staff aims to please"; a "few bars", sports on TV and occasional live music complete the "fun concept."

Kingston Station *American* 20 | 18 | 19 | $29
Downtown Crossing | 25 Kingston St. (bet. Bedford & Summer Sts.) | 617-482-6282 | www.kingstonstation.com

You'll "never leave hungry" from this "large", "sophisticated" Downtown Crossing "gathering spot" where "knowledgeable servers" convey "something-for-everyone" Americana that's priced affordably; with "all the tile", it looks "like an old subway station" (or "a bathroom"), and it's just as "bustling", "crowded and loud", especially at the bar "after work."

KO Prime *Steak* 25 | 22 | 23 | $63
Downtown Crossing | Nine Zero Hotel | 90 Tremont St. (Beacon St.) | 617-772-0202 | www.koprimeboston.com

"Taste buds tingle at the mere thought" of Ken Oringer's "chic" steakhouse in a boutique hotel near Downtown Crossing where you too will be "ko'd by the quality" of the "copious amounts of cow" ("marrow, brain" and everything else); the "fantastic customer service" extends from the "funky", "hopping" bar to the "elegant, sophisticated" dining area – just be ready to "blow some dough" wherever you end up.

Koreana *Japanese/Korean* 21 | 16 | 19 | $30
Central Square | 154-158 Prospect St. (Broadway) | Cambridge | 617-576-8661 | www.koreanaboston.com

"Fun, interactive evenings out" occur at this place between Central and Inman Squares that's usually "crowded" with folks who find cooking their own Korean BBQ on tabletop grills "entertaining" (sushi is also served); expect an "awesome" sake and drinks list, a "charming, attentive staff", "not much decor" and tabs that a few find "on the pricey side."

Kouzina ☒Ⓜ *Greek/Mediterranean* 23 | 16 | 22 | $38
Newton | 1649 Beacon St. (Windsor Rd.) | 617-558-7677 | www.kouzinarestaurant.com

In an "unlikely" corner of Newton (specifically, Waban), this "welcoming", "family-owned" and "family-friendly" "gem" serves a "wonderful combination of Mediterranean and Greek food", some "innovative", some classic, all "well priced" and "consistent"; though "warm in the summer", the "quaint" space can be "drafty in the winter", and "noisy and slightly crowded" year-round.

Kowloon ● *Asian* | 15 | 16 | 16 | $26

Saugus | 948 Broadway/Rte. 1 (Main St.) | 781-233-0077 | www.kowloonrestaurant.com

"Like an 800-lb. sumo wrestler named Buddy", this "kitschy" 60-year-old Saugus "mega-restaurant" is "so over-the-top ridiculous, you have to love it" and its "tacky" "Polynesian" setting featuring "fountains, bamboo", "tiki huts", a ship's deck–cum–bandstand and seating for "a zillion people"; "you don't go" for the "greasy", "fake" yet somehow "great" Asian eats, but they are necessary to mitigate the effects of the scorpion bowls; P.S. on top of all that, you can "catch a comedy show" upstairs.

⊠ La Campania ⊠ *Italian* | 28 | 24 | 25 | $59

Waltham | 504 Main St. (bet. Cross & Heard Sts.) | 781-894-4280 | www.lacampania.com

"People come from far and wide" for this "transporting culinary experience" in Waltham, a "charming" "gem" creating both "inventive and traditional" "Italian country" dishes, "all splendid" and priced for those who "can afford luxury" (though the "staggering wine list" displays many "affordable" options); the "professional" staff is as "warm" as the "beautiful", "rustic" "farmhouse"-like setting, but just "make sure you have a reservation", "even for the bar."

La Cantina Italiana *Italian* | ▽ 20 | 14 | 19 | $30

Framingham | 911 Waverly St. (Winter St.) | 508-879-7874

"Dependable" "old-school" Italian cooking priced for "great value" makes this "solid" spot with "cheesy" decor "easy to do" "if you have kids" in Framingham; it can be "crowded" and "noisy", but the "attentive" staff provides "fast service" that gets you "in and out quick."

La Casa de Pedro *Venezuelan* | 21 | 21 | 21 | $33

Watertown | 343 Arsenal St. (School St.) | 617-923-8025 | www.lacasadepedro.com

"Pedro is a charming host" at his "lively" "bit of Latin America" in Watertown's Arsenal complex, and "you won't regret it" if you let him decide "what you should have" among the "super" "fish and beef"-centric Venezuelan cuisine, which flaunts "inventive" "riffs", comes in "large portions" and is affordably priced; there's a "nice" patio weather permitting, while the "bright colors", palm trees and weekend live music make inside feel like "South Beach" whatever the season.

La Famiglia Giorgio *Italian* | 22 | 15 | 21 | $33

North End | 112 Salem St. (bet. Cooper & Prince Sts.) | 617-367-6711 | www.lafamigliagiorgio.com

"Leftovers are guaranteed" (like, "three meals'" worth) at this "small", "informal" North End Italian whose "tremendous" portions mean the "tasty" red-sauce dishes are "excellent values"; the "friendly", "homey" setting – marked by brick walls, murals and a "staff that makes you feel like you're part of the family" – makes it "an ideal gathering place", especially with "a group."

La Galleria 33 *Italian*

▽ 21 | 17 | 24 | $38

North End | 125 Salem St. (Prince St.) | 617-723-7233 |
www.lagalleria33.com

Though sometimes "not as crowded as the places on
Hanover Street", this North End Italian is often "packed" and
"loud" with "tourists" trying its "generous portions" of "well-
executed", "great-value" Italian fare; the "rustic" setting is
"cute" with its "nice brick walls", and the staff is "excellent" with
its "welcoming" demeanor.

Lala Rokh *Persian*

23 | 21 | 23 | $43

Beacon Hill | 97 Mt. Vernon St. (Cedar St.) | 617-720-5511 |
www.lalarokh.com

"Exceptional" staffers prove "helpful in guiding new diners" through
the "amazingly fragrant", "intensely spiced", "seriously delicious"
Persian cuisine prepared at this "unique gem" in a "renovated
brownstone" on Beacon Hill; the "elegant", "refreshingly quiet"
"cluster of small rooms" are as suitable for "romance" as a "cozy"
"gathering of friends" – to be sure, it's "an experience to
share and remember."

La Morra *Italian*

25 | 19 | 24 | $46

Brookline | 48 Boylston St. (bet. Cypress St. & Harvard Ave.) |
617-739-0007 | www.lamorra.com

At this "gem" with an "unlikely" location "outside Brookline Village",
à la carte meals get off to an "intriguing" start with "tasty" Northern
Italian tapas, then continue with "superb", "homey yet sophisticated" entrees plus "interesting" wines – however, the four-course
"*prezzo fisso* is such a bargain, it's hard not to order it"; "small,
cramped" and often "quite noisy", the setting nevertheless feels
"warm and welcoming" thanks to "appealing" brick-and-beams
decor and "attentive", "pleasant" service.

Lam's *Asian*

19 | 13 | 18 | $23

Newtonville | 825 Washington St. (Walnut St.) | 617-630-5222 |
www.lamsrestaurant.com

"Something magical is brewing in the pots" of this "welcoming"
"neighborhood Asian" in Newtonville doling out "generous portions" of "affordable" Thai and Vietnamese–centric alimentation;
however, there's "not a lot of energy in the room", despite the fact
that it's teeming with "warm pink" tones and "pleasant" staffers.

⧫ L'Andana *Italian*

27 | 25 | 24 | $54

Burlington | 86 Cambridge St. (Arlington Rd.) | 781-270-0100 |
www.landanagrill.com

For an "exquisite dining experience without the city hassles",
Burlington gourmets hit this "amazing" Jamie Mammano venue
offering "flawlessly executed" Tuscan fare that's both "sophisticated" and "comforting"; a "wonderful" staff that "doesn't hurry you
along" plus "lovely", "upscale" environs make it conducive to "a celebration with your significant other or a small group" – "of course,
you'll still pay city prices."

	FOOD	DECOR	SERVICE	COST

Landing, The *American*　　18 | 19 | 21 | $36

Manchester-by-the-Sea | 7 Central St. (School St.) |
978-526-7494 | www.thelandingat7central.com
Marblehead | 81 Front St. (State St.) | 781-631-1878 |
www.thelandingrestaurant.com

"Great service" comes from a "friendly" staff at this "classic"
American tavern duo where if you "stick to the basics, you'll not be
disappointed" (seafood is particularly "well prepared"); the "unpretentious" Manchester-by-the-Sea iteration is a "super locals' spot"
that "tourists love" too, while the Marblehead "institution" boasts
"spectacular" views, especially from a "wonderful deck" that "literally hangs over the harbor."

Lansdowne Pub, The ● *American/Irish*　▽ 16 | 18 | 16 | $24

Fenway | 9 Lansdowne St. (Ipswich St.) | 617-247-1222 |
www.lansdownepubboston.com

"Fun" if "typical" is how baseball fans describe this dimly lit Fenway
"pre- and post-game watering hole" offering beer and affordable
American-Irish pub fare amid handcrafted wood furniture imported
from the Emerald Isle; the plates are "mediocre" and service can be
"painfully slow", but that doesn't keep it from getting "loud" and
"rowdy", especially Thursdays–Saturdays when there's live music.

La Paloma Ⓜ *Mexican*　　19 | 14 | 20 | $25

Quincy | 195 Newport Ave. (Hobart St.) | 617-773-0512
NEW **Kingston** | 114 Main St. (bet. Mayflower & Prospect Sts.) |
781-936-8172
www.lapalomarestaurant.com

The "price is right" at this "friendly" Quincy "standby" and its new
Kingston offshoot, both providing "cheesy, filling" Mexican meals
that are for the most part "traditional", although you may spy "a few
unusual dishes"; besides "sombreros hanging on the walls", there
isn't much going on in the adornments department, although after a
few "killer margaritas", some folks describe the decor as "largely
inspired by Jose Cuervo."

La Summa *Italian*　　23 | 18 | 24 | $35

North End | 30 Fleet St. (bet. Atlantic Ave. & Hanover St.) | 617-523-9503 |
www.lasumma.com

For something "not as trendy", "less touristy" and more "reasonably
priced" than other North End eateries, take a "trip off Hanover
Street" to this "old-time Italian" where the Sicilian-centric fare is
"unpretentious" though nevertheless "amazing"; a "warm", "homey
feel" is evoked in the "unassuming" digs thanks to "nicely spaced tables" and, moreover, an "attentive staff."

Lavender Asian Cuisine *Asian*　▽ 23 | 21 | 25 | $26

Sudbury | Sudbury Plaza | 519A Boston Post Rd. (Highland Ave.) |
978-579-9988 | www.lavenderasiancuisine.com

Though some say its "strip-mall location detracts from the allure",
once inside this Sudbury Pan-Asian "all guests are greeted like
they're regulars" and met with "sleek" decor featuring a blue-pearl-

topped bar and a Great Wall of China illustration; the inexpensive, sushi-free fare is "excellent" whether you eat in and partake in the "lively karaoke scene" (Thursdays–Saturdays) or get it to go.

La Verdad ● *Mexican*   21 | 15 | 16 | $25

Fenway | 1 Lansdowne St. (Ipswich St.) | 617-421-9595 | www.laverdadtaqueria.com

"Gourmet tacos" and "awesome" tequilas make for "delicious" "pre-Sox grazing and drinking" at this Fenway Mexican from Ken Oringer, so yes, it's often "crazy" (the take-out counter in front is an "alternative to waiting for a table" – so is going "when there isn't a game"); however, a cynical contingent says, with service that's "sliding downhill" and tabs that are "overpriced" for a "hole-in-the-wall", "'the truth' is that the jig is up."

La Voile *French/Mediterranean*   24 | 22 | 23 | $50

Back Bay | 259 Newbury St. (bet. Fairfield & Gloucester Sts.) | 617-587-4200 | www.lavoileboston.net

"You can almost smell the salt air of a Southern French town" at this "delightful find" in the Back Bay where "expatriate" guests converse with their "fabulous" compatriots on the staff while perusing the "memorable" Gallic-Mediterranean menu and "wonderful" wine list; with an interior that displays "charming" "nautical decor" and a "sunken patio" that presents "people-watching", the setting is a plus, but tabs that are "pricey" are a bit of a detriment.

Ledge Kitchen & Drinks *American*   15 | 21 | 16 | $33

Dorchester | 2261 Dorchester Ave. (bet. Richmond & Washington Sts.) | 617-698-2261 | www.ledgeboston.com

It's "all about" the "amazing patio" at this moderately priced, contemporary New American in Dorchester's Lower Mills neighborhood; the "trendy comfort food" "isn't stellar" and service can be "indifferent", but nevertheless, the place is often "crowded" and "noisy", the latter due to "too many" TVs "playing different things", not to mention the effects of the "hip drinks."

NEW Legal C Bar *Seafood*   22 | 18 | 21 | $34

Dedham | Legacy Pl. | 950 Providence Hwy. (Elm St.) | 781-234-6500 | www.legalcbar.com

There's "nothing to crab about" at this "Legal lite" in Dedham's Legacy Place, which "aims to be hipper" than its progenitor with "cool decor" ("love the bathrooms!"), an "upscale, active bar scene" and a "modern", "limited menu" listing "reasonable prices" and "smaller portion options"; what's the same is the "unerring quality" of the seafood, "interesting wines by the glass", "upbeat staff", "madding crowds" and "noise."

☑ Legal Sea Foods *Seafood*   22 | 18 | 21 | $41

Back Bay | Copley Pl. | 100 Huntington Ave. (bet. Dartmouth & Exeter Sts.) | 617-266-7775
Back Bay | Prudential Ctr. | 800 Boylston St. (Fairfield St.) | 617-266-6800
Park Square | 26 Park Plaza (Columbus Ave.) | 617-426-4444

(continued)

Legal Sea Foods

Waterfront | Long Wharf | 255 State St. (Atlantic Ave.) | 617-227-3115
Harvard Square | 20 University Rd. (Eliot St.) | Cambridge | 617-491-9400
Kendall Square | 5 Cambridge Ctr. (bet. Ames & Main Sts.) | Cambridge | 617-864-3400
Chestnut Hill | Chestnut Hill Shopping Ctr. | 43 Boylston St. (Hammond Pond Pkwy.) | 617-277-7300
Peabody | Northshore Mall | 210 Andover St./Rte. 114 (Rte. 128) | 978-532-4500
Framingham | 50-60 Worcester Rd./Rte. 9 (bet. Concord & Speen Sts.) | 508-766-0600
Burlington | Burlington Mall | 75 Middlesex Tpke. (Rte. 128) | 781-270-9700
www.legalseafoods.com
Additional locations throughout the Boston area

Again voted Boston's Most Popular restaurant, this "trustworthy" seafood chain "reigns supreme" thanks to a "huge variety" of "consistently fresh" fish, not to mention the smarts to "adapt to changing times and changing tastes" with "innovative touches" (e.g. what may be the "best" gluten-free menu "in the world") while ensuring "solid value"; the decor of each branch is "different" (ditto the service, though staffers generally "know their stuff"), but when all is said and done, the "location doesn't matter" – "they're everywhere" because "they know what they're doing."

Le Lyonnais   🅜 *French*   ▽ 23 | 20 | 21 | $47

Acton | 416 Great Rd./Rte. 2A (Rte. 27) | 978-263-9068 | www.lelyonnaisacton.com

A "most delightful experience" is found at this "charming" restaurant set in a rustic Acton house built in 1850, where "reliable" French plates are offered for relatively "affordable" prices; some antsy folks feel the fare can be "slow finding its way out of the kitchen", while others are more forgiving because they suspect "everything's from scratch."

Le's   *Vietnamese*   21 | 12 | 17 | $18

Allston | 137 Brighton Ave. (Harvard Ave.) | 617-783-2340
Harvard Square | 36 Dunster St. (Mt. Auburn St.) | Cambridge | 617-864-4100
Chestnut Hill | Atrium Mall | 300 Boylston St. (Florence St.) | 617-928-0900
www.lesrestaurant.com

"A lot of flavor for a little money" is the hallmark of this trio of "popular", "no-nonsense" Vietnamese eateries where "heaping bowls" of "fantastic pho" are the stars among the "yummy" "standards"; it's so "quick" and "reliable", no one really minds that the staff can be "not very friendly" and the "atmosphere leaves much to be desired."

🆉 L'Espalier   *French*   27 | 27 | 27 | $97

Back Bay | 774 Boylston St. (bet. Exeter & Fairfield Sts.) | 617-262-3023 | www.lespalier.com

"If heaven were a restaurant", it would be this "regal experience" in the Back Bay, where chef Frank McClelland's "exquisite", "inventive" New French cuisine is "perfectly paired" with "outstanding wines";

though longtimers "miss" the "old-world charm" of the former brownstone, modernists dig the newish location's "sleek, modern" setting; meanwhile, everyone appreciates staffers who "treat you like a king" – but then again, "they should since you're paying a king's ransom" (it's "worth every penny"); P.S. the prix fixe lunch may be "the best midday deal in Boston."

Les Zygomates 🖂 *French/Mediterranean*   22 | 22 | 21 | $41

Leather District | 129 South St. (Essex St.) | 617-542-5108 | www.winebar.com

"If you can't get to Paris", this "lively" Leather District bistro is a "*très bon*" backup, with "terrific" French-Med dishes, "great value", "fine service" and an "extensive wine selection"; "fabulous live jazz" and "spacious" digs (marked by exposed brick, beams, ductwork and a zinc bar) make it a "solid after-work choice", while semi-private alcoves mean it's a "cool, sexy" place for a "date."

Lexx *American*   19 | 19 | 20 | $32

Lexington | 1666 Massachusetts Ave. (bet. Grant St. & Wallis Ct.) | 781-674-2990 | www.lexx-restaurant.com

"Pleasant" staffers, a "varied menu" of "tasty" New American fare and "fine wines" are what you'll find at this Lexington "neighborhood gem" offering a "cozy", "upscale atmosphere" (slate floors, contemporary art) for "reasonable prices"; ok, so it's possibly "not worth much effort to get there" if you're not nearby, but locals keep it "always packed" since it "fills an area need", especially as a "place for a business lunch."

Lil Vinny's Ristorante *Italian*   ∇ 23 | 15 | 21 | $35

Somerville | 525 Medford St. (Broadway) | 617-628-8466 | www.lilvinnys.com

"Giant portions" of "pasta like mom used to cook" are delivered by "friendly" staffers who make "great recommendations" at this family-run Somerville Southern Italian "treasure" (a sibling of Vinny's at Night); consider getting there early, because with such "reasonable prices" (and despite there being "no ambiance"), the "small space" "gets crowded and noisy quickly."

Limoncello *Italian*   22 | 18 | 21 | $42

North End | 190 North St. (Richmond St.) | 617-523-4480 | www.ristorantelimoncello.com

"Large by neighborhood standards", this "bright", "family-friendly" North End Italian with "traditional decor" gets "clogged with tourists" due to its location on the Freedom Trail as well as its "midrange", "reliable" cuisine; the "friendly staff" can make "great suggestions" about the "broad menu" and wine list, and you should remember to "top off the meal with the owner's homemade limoncello."

Lineage *American*   25 | 21 | 24 | $44

Brookline | Coolidge Corner | 242 Harvard St. (Beacon St.) | 617-232-0065 | www.lineagerestaurant.com

"Imaginative", "market-driven" New American cuisine is the output of this "gem" in Brookline's Coolidge Corner, where the consensus is that "prices can be high for what's basically a neighborhood restaurant", but they're "fair" considering that "everything's prepared with care and skill"; "unobtrusive" service comes from "knowledgeable, friendly" staffers in both the "lovely", "serene" dining room and the "sublime" bar where a fire keeps folks "toasty warm" in winter.

Littlest Bar, The *Pub Food*   ∇ 18 | 18 | 20 | $27

Financial District | 102 Broad St. (Wharf St.) | 617-542-8469

"Hey, you moved, you are no longer the littlest bar" chide regulars of this spot now in roomier, "cute" Financial District digs and still serving "solid, simple", well-priced pub grub that "goes down well with a pint"; "good service" makes it "a great place to go after work", while live Irish music makes it a fun spot to hit on a Saturday night.

Living Room, The ● *American*   16 | 20 | 17 | $37

Waterfront | 101 Atlantic Ave. (Richmond St.) | 617-723-5101 | www.thelivingroomboston.com

"Like hanging out in your own living room", "only you don't have to clean up afterward" is the word on this Waterfront venue bedecked with "cushy chairs" and couches, a "go-to" for happy hour (when apps are half price), "watching sports" or just "meeting up with friends"; indeed, the "focus" is on the "impressive", "expensive" cocktails, but there's also New American fare that some deem "quite good" – and others bemoan is not "as nice as the decor."

Local, The *American*   19 | 17 | 18 | $31

West Newton | 1391 Washington St. (bet. Elm St. & Mass. Tpke.) | 617-340-2160 | www.thelocalnewton.com

"It's called The Local for a reason" say West Newton diners of this "high-energy" New American gastropub where it's likely you'll "see neighbors", and the staff "always makes you feel welcome"; menu options are "somewhat limited", but the fare "satisfies", and at a "digestible price point" no less.

☑ Locke-Ober ⌧ *American/Continental*   25 | 25 | 26 | $66

Downtown Crossing | 3 Winter Pl. (bet. Tremont & Washington Sts.) | 617-542-1340 | www.lockeober.com

"Step back in time" via this "formal" 1875 Downtown Crossing "legend" where "business moguls, political bigwigs" and "commoners" who want to "feel like Brahmins" feast on chef Lydia Shire's "indulgent", "retro" Continental dishes, some "involving tableside finishing touches", others with "pleasing" New American "updates"; the "gorgeous" "original decor" and "polished, professional service" befit the tabs, which are unsurprisingly "expensive" considering "this is one seriously elegant night out."

NEW Lolita Cocina & Tequila Bar ● *Mexican*   - | - | - | M

Back Bay | 271 Dartmouth St. (bet. Boylston & Newbury Sts.) | 617-369-5609 | www.lolitaboston.com

This sexy, red velvet–accented Mexican in a subterranean Back Bay space doubles as a dinner destination and late-night tequila

lounge – a rustic cabinet displaying top brands from its 200-plus selection separates the open dining room from the sunken lounge; the
not-too-pricey south-of-the-border fare is served in both areas, as
are sassy margaritas made with freshly squeezed juices.

☒ Longfellow's Wayside Inn *New England*
19 | **25** | **22** | **$43**

Sudbury | Longfellow's Wayside Inn | 72 Wayside Inn Rd. (Rte. 20) |
978-443-1776 | www.wayside.org

"You feel as though you've arrived in the early 1700s" at this "ever-
charming" Sudbury "landmark" in one of America's oldest inns;
whether the "hearty", "old-fashioned" New England fare is "delicious"
or "unremarkable" may not matter much, because most folks strictly
"come for the ambiance", which includes "kind" servers occasionally in "period dress", "Colonial decor" and "beautiful grounds."

Lord Hobo ● *American*
16 | **15** | **16** | **$29**

Inman Square | 92 Hampshire St. (Windsor St.) | Cambridge |
617-250-8454 | www.lordhobo.com

Samplers of this Inman Square New American gastropub say it's
"great for the beer geek" due to its "amazing" list; but it's "not great
for the beer geek's wallet" because the brews and the "inconsistent"
grub are "overpriced", plus the dim, red environs might be "in need
of sound absorption."

L'Osteria *Italian*
24 | **17** | **21** | **$39**

North End | 104 Salem St. (Cooper St.) | 617-723-7847 |
www.losteria.com

"Flavorful, traditional but never tiresome" Italian fare is the
métier of this North End "real deal" that's been "consistent" for a
quarter of a century; though the service gets mixed reviews
("friendly" vs. "indifferent"), surveyors are unanimous in their
praise of the "good value."

Lotus Blossom *Chinese/Japanese*
22 | **20** | **21** | **$29**

Sudbury | 394 Boston Post Rd./Rte. 20 (Station Rd.) | 978-443-0200 |
www.lotuscuisine.com

"Even the pickiest eater will love" this Sudbury spot, a "clapboard
house hiding contemporary Asian rooms" and a "big, diverse menu"
of "well-prepared", "high-quality" Chinese fare and sushi; "reasonable prices" make it "perfect for family outings", especially because
everything's delivered "quickly" – conversely, the service "never
seems rushed" even though the venue's "always busy."

Lower Depths ●⌿ *Pub Food*
▽ **17** | **14** | **18** | **$17**

Kenmore Square | 476 Commonwealth Ave. (W. Charlesgate) |
617-266-6662

"Beer, beer, beer" – "if you want it, they've got it" at this "down-and-
dirty" Kenmore Square go-to for brews and pub grub "before or after
a game"; debit-devotees dis the "totally impractical cash-only"
policy, but with such "cheap eats" (including "$1 Fenway franks"),
you won't need much of it; P.S. outdoor-types enjoy "sitting on the
patio on a sunny day."

LTK *Eclectic*
21 | 18 | 19 | $38

Seaport District | 225 Northern Ave. (D St.) | 617-330-7430 |
www.legalseafoods.com

Being that it's Legal Sea Food's test kitchen, expect a "more cutting-edge", sometimes "experimental" culinary approach at this "funky" Seaport District Eclectic with a "fun", "busy bar" and a "personable", "well-informed" staff; it's a bit "out of the way" for some – nevertheless it's "always crowded", especially "after work" when the energy's "terrific."

Lucca *Italian*
23 | 22 | 22 | $51

Back Bay | 116 Huntington Ave. (Garrison St.) | 617-247-2400
North End | 226 Hanover St. (Richmond St.) | 617-742-9200
www.luccaboston.com

"Definitely not your mom-and-pop red-sauce joint", this North End eatery creates "upscale", "highly tasty" Northern Italian meals, which the "excellent" staffers pair with "exceptional" wines; there's an "enjoyable" bar scene and "primo tables by the front window" on the main level, below which resides a "less noisy" wine cellar, but regardless of where you sit, it's "not cheap"; P.S. the Back Bay offshoot serves a seasonal menu that jumps all over The Boot in "stunning" (some say "spartan") surroundings.

Lucia *Italian*
23 | 20 | 22 | $38

North End | 415 Hanover St. (Charter St.) | 617-367-2353 |
www.luciaboston.com
Winchester | 5-13 Mt. Vernon St. (bet. Main & Washington Sts.) |
781-729-0515 | www.luciaristorante.com

"Reliable", "authentic" Italian fare is dished out in "superb portions" at this "intimate" North End eatery and its Winchester sibling, the latter offering a similar experience "without the city parking and crowds"; though quite a few numbers-crunchers find them to be "a little pricey", they remain "crowd-pleasers" thanks to the "attentive, friendly" staffs and "wonderful", recently spiffed up settings.

Lucky's Lounge *American*
19 | 16 | 18 | $27

Seaport District | 355 Congress St. (A St.) | 617-357-5825 |
www.luckyslounge.com

"If Frank Sinatra were around, he'd loosen his tie" at this "friendly" Seaport District "hidden gem" (literally: it's "subterranean" and has "no sign") that's chock-a-bloc with "1950s kitsch" and "cool" "regulars" downing "great", "reasonably priced" American grub and "generous cocktails"; come for the live music, especially on Saturdays and Sundays when tributes to Ol' Blue Eyes play at brunch and dinner, but "don't go for conversation" 'cause it's usually "loud."

 Lumière *French*
28 | 23 | 27 | $57

Newton | 1293 Washington St. (Waltham St.) | 617-244-9199 |
www.lumiererestaurant.com

Exhibiting "panache" plus a "real devotion to all things local, sustainable and green", "genius" chef-owner Michael Leviton presents New French fare as "art" (and with "wonderful wine pairings") at his "classy", recently expanded "West Newton gem"; "impeccable service" makes it a "good choice for that special occasion", and while it's a "little pricey", it costs "less" than if it were located Downtown.

Lyceum, The *Eclectic* 23 | 22 | 23 | $43

Salem | 43 Church St. (Washington St.) | 978-745-7665 | www.thelyceum.com

"Changes for the better" proliferate at this "casual yet classy" Salem "standard" boasting "lovely", "wonderful new decor" and a fresh Eclectic menu that's "well cooked" and "beautifully presented"; thankfully, the "old Colonial architecture" has been preserved (it's in the circa-1843 building from which Alexander Graham Bell made the first telephone call), and when you add in "top-notch" service and "not-inexpensive but good-value" pricing, it's no wonder locals deem it "hard to beat" for a "lunch, dinner, holiday party, small wedding reception or séance."

Machu Picchu *Peruvian* 21 | 13 | 18 | $24

Somerville | 25 Union Sq. (Stone Ave.) | 617-623-7972 | www.machuchicken.com

Somerville | 307 Somerville Ave. (bet. Hawkins St. & Warren Ave.) | 617-628-7070 | www.machupicchuboston.com

"Genuine Peruvian food" is found at these Somerville sibs where the decor "won't transport you", but the "wide selection" of "large, satisfying", "inexpensive" dishes ("distinctive" rotisserie chicken and ceviche among them) sure will; everything's proffered by a "helpful" staff – though there are grumblings that "meals can take a long time for reasons as mysterious as the ruins that give the place its name."

Maddie's Sail Loft *New England/Seafood* ∇ 14 | 14 | 17 | $26

Marblehead | 15 State St. (bet. Front & Washington Sts.) | 781-631-9824

"Still the same old Maddie's, thankfully" say Marblehead diners of this 1942 "classic" doling out New England seafood in a downstairs pub and upstairs dining room filled with "plastic and plywood"; though the fare is generally "good", "you don't really come here to eat" – you come for "cocktails the size of small planets" and to "watch the locals interact", including "some salty dogs at the bar."

Maggiano's Little Italy *Italian* 19 | 18 | 19 | $35

Park Square | 4 Columbus Ave. (bet. Boylston & Stuart Sts.) | 617-542-3456 | www.maggianos.com

"Bring a crowd and eat family-style for the best experience" at this "steady Eddie" Italian chain in Park Square delivering "gargantuan portions" of "comforting" fare for "reasonable" tabs; its "Little Italy" style (e.g. checkered tablecloths) and "raucous" environs are hits with fans who argue that even if the "assembly-line" food is "nothing special, the total experience is great"; P.S. "be ready for a wait."

Mamma Maria *Italian* 25 | 24 | 24 | $57

North End | 3 North Sq. (Clinton St.) | 617-523-0077 | www.mammamaria.com

"Tucked away in a charming townhouse" with several "elegant", "intimate", "peaceful" dining rooms, this "upscale Italian" is "certainly

	FOOD	DECOR	SERVICE	COST

one of the classier", more "romantic" North End options, and its "gourmet" fare is "worth every penny"; what's more, there's "excellent service" and an "interesting wine selection" to shore up its reputation as "a truly elegant place for that special evening."

Mantra *French/Indian* | 21 | 22 | 19 | $44 |

Downtown Crossing | 52 Temple Pl. (bet. Tremont & Washington Sts.) | 617-542-8111 | www.mantrarestaurant.com

With vaulted ceilings, marble floors and columns, this former bank in Downtown Crossing presents a "snazzy", "upscale" environment for its "imaginative" Indian-French fusion fare, which a few find "disappointing", but more deem "nicely done"; it may be "a little expensive", but the lunch buffet can be a "great bargain", just like the pre-theater prix fixe – however, "if you go late" on weekends, know that it "becomes a nightclub."

Marco Cucina Romana Ⓜ *Italian* | 23 | 19 | 23 | $46 |

North End | 253 Hanover St., 2nd fl. (bet. Cross & Richmond Sts.) | 617-742-1276 | www.marcoboston.com

Chef Marc Orfaly's "superb" Roman-inspired cuisine gets paired with "interesting wine specials" at this second-floor eatery whose "charming" atmosphere is "old-world North End" all the way; people-watchers like to nab a "table by the windows" "overlooking Hanover Street", but there are so "few" seats in general, most folks are happy to just snag a reservation.

Mare *Italian/Seafood* | 26 | 21 | 23 | $53 |

North End | 135 Richmond St. (North St.) | 617-723-6273 | www.marenatural.com

A coastal Italian "oasis in a sea of tomato sauce", this off-the-main-drag North Ender specializes in "creative, high-quality" seafood and other "fantastic" dishes based on "organic" ingredients and complemented by "excellent wines"; the "knowledgeable staff" and "intimate", "modern" digs with "great views of sidewalk passersby" get nods, so the only things to gripe about are the "lack of a full bar" and the "expensive" prices (but they're "so worth it").

Market *American* | 26 | 24 | 23 | $57 |

Theater District | W Boston | 100 Stuart St. (Tremont St.) | 617-310-6790 | www.marketbyjgboston.com

Celebrity chef Jean-Georges Vongerichten's "greatest hits" are the stars of this "glitzy" New American in the Theater District's W Boston, where "beautiful people" start with "fantastic cocktails" in the "lively bar", then proceed to the "modern" dining room for "scrumptious plates served with style" by "exemplary" staffers; but the best part may be the prices: "surprisingly reasonable" "for what it is."

Marliave *Continental/Italian* | 18 | 18 | 18 | $36 |

Downtown Crossing | 10 Bosworth St. (Tremont St.) | 617-422-0004 | www.marliave.com

"It feels like old Boston, but tastes like new" at this circa-1875 Downtown Crossing duplex that's been "revitalized" with an "extensive menu" of "upscale", "delicious" Continental-Italian "comfort food" and "renovated" digs that maintain an "amazing" "air of historical ambiance"; the "ample bar" downstairs can get "noisy" (an effect of the "amazing old-fashioned cocktails", no doubt), the "lovely" "upstairs dining room is dark and romantic", and when "weather permits", the patio is a "beautiful oasis."

Martsa's on Elm Ⓜ *Tibetan*

∇ 21 | 13 | 18 | $22

Somerville | 233A Elm St. (Grove St.) | 617-666-0660
It's "such a treat" to "stumble upon" this "funky", "serene" Davis Square Tibetan where newbies can opt for "family-style dining to sample multiple dishes" from the "fantastic" menu; the "casual" digs "could use an upgrade in ambiance", but the "lots of students" who frequent it don't mind, what with such bargain tabs.

Mary Chung ⊄ *Chinese*

22 | 7 | 16 | $19

Central Square | 464 Massachusetts Ave. (Brookline St.) | Cambridge | 617-864-1991
"On most days, Mary herself presides over the festivities" at this Central Square "hole-in-the-wall", which has been doling out "outstanding", "authentic, spicy" Sichuan fare to an "always crowded" house of "students, families and professors" for nearly three decades; it's cash only, but you won't need a lot of it – here's where you get "perhaps the most bang for your buck in the culinary universe."

Masa *Southwestern*

21 | 21 | 20 | $35

South End | 439 Tremont St. (Appleton St.) | 617-338-8884
Woburn | 348A Cambridge Rd. (Rte. 3A) | 781-938-8886
www.masarestaurant.com
Woburn heat-seekers are "so glad" this "brightly decorated" "piece of Southwest heaven" "came to the suburbs" because, like the "lively", "reliable" South End flagship, it's "not afraid to make it spicy"; the "happiest of happy hours" draws droves for "bargain tapas" alongside a "fancy-shmancy tequila selection", and "salsa dancing on Thursday nights" is a real "fun night out", but the "super-crowded" "brunch is where it's at", especially for "penny-pinching gourmands."

Masala Art *Indian*

24 | 21 | 21 | $34

Needham | Needham Ctr. | 990 Great Plain Ave. (Chestnut St.) | 781-449-4050 | www.masala-art.com
"Wow, what flavors!" marvel Needhamites of this "upscale Indian" whose "distinctive, imaginative" preparations are offered in a "comfortable", "gorgeous" "fine-dining atmosphere"; a few respondents calculate it's "priced a bit high" because the "portions could be more generous", however, most feel tabs are "not too bad", especially for the "steal" of a lunch buffet; P.S. "try the Spice Bar" for "private, customized" cooking demos.

Ma Soba *Asian*

20 | 18 | 20 | $32

Beacon Hill | 156 Cambridge St. (Hancock St.) | 617-973-6680 | www.masobaboston.com
Though "not groundbreaking", this Beacon Hill Pan-Asian is a "solid", "consistent" option for a "great selection" of "decent sushi",

etc., served in "large portions" by a generally "efficient" staff; a "convenient" location makes it a "regular stop before Celtics games", while prices that "aren't horrible" mean it's suitable for a "work lunch."

Masona Grill Ⓜ *American/Peruvian* | 24 | 17 | 23 | $40 |

West Roxbury | 4-6 Corey St. (bet. Hastings & Park Sts.) | 617-323-3331 | www.masonagrill.net

"Can there be a more hidden gem than this backstreet West Roxbury bistro?" ask devotees who return "again and again" for its "unique, carefully prepared" New American fare and "Peruvian specialties" like "wonderful ceviche"; what's more, service is "knowledgeable" and prices are "reasonable", which is why most easily overlook the fact that it's a "hole-in-the-wall."

Massimino's Cucina Italia *Italian* | 23 | 18 | 23 | $38 |

North End | 207 Endicott St. (Commercial St.) | 617-523-5959 | www.massiminosboston.com

"Keeping it real" in the North End, this "off-the-beaten-track" Italian presents a "satisfying extravaganza" of "old-school" red sauce, which is "reasonably priced" and brought in "fabulous portions" by "witty" staffers; just know that the occasional "jostling" is inevitable, as the "small" (some call it "claustrophobic") setting gets crowded with "tourists" and sports fans before a "Bruins or Celtics game."

Matt Murphy's Pub ⊅ *Pub Food* | 22 | 16 | 18 | $25 |

Brookline | 14 Harvard St. (bet. Kent St. & Webster Pl.) | 617-232-0188 | www.mattmurphyspub.com

"You'll go as much for the food as for the really good selection of beers" at this "charming, dark, cozy" Brookline Village pub known for its "simple", "reliable" "classic Irish" cooking, "hearty portions" and "homemade ketchup"; what's more, the "staff is so much fun" and the tabs are affordable – it's just "too bad about the cash-only policy."

Maurizio's *Italian* | 24 | 17 | 24 | $46 |

North End | 364 Hanover St. (Clark St.) | 617-367-1123 | www.mauriziosboston.com

At this "Sardinian sensation" in the North End, the "gracious, helpful" staff makes guests feel like they're "dining in the home of favorite friends" who are serving "plentiful" portions of fare "perfectly prepared" by a "master"; the "intimate" environment is strictly "no-frills", but that doesn't deter fans from making it "crowded" and, therefore, "loud."

Max & Dylans | 19 | 17 | 19 | $28 |
Kitchen & Bar *American*

Charlestown | 1 Chelsea St. (City Sq.) | 617-242-7400
Downtown Crossing | 15 West St. (bet. Tremont & Washington Sts.) | 617-423-3600
www.maxanddylans.com

"A laid-back atmosphere" befits the "modestly priced" American "comfort food" proffered at this pair where most "people like" the "great mac 'n' cheese choices" above all else – well, excepting the "interesting, eclectic" cocktail selection possibly; the Downtown Crossing locale, with "several floors" and "risqué photos" of women, is "good" for pre-theater, while the more "family-friendly" Charlestown outpost is a boon for "tourists" "after they visit the Navy Yard."

Maxwells 148 ⊠Ⓜ *Asian/Italian* 24 | 24 | 26 | $45

Natick | 148 E. Central St. (Speen St.) | 508-907-6262 | www.maxwells148.com

An "amazing", "artful blend" of Asian and Italian cuisines, plus "diverse wines" and "fantastic cocktails" (the fig-infused vodka is "legendary") make this "serious restaurant" a "diamond in the rough" – the 'rough' being "a downscale strip mall" in Natick; the chef's "attention to detail" extends beyond the kitchen, as he "regularly checks in with tables" (just like the "impeccable" servers) in the "upscale", "hip" dining room, whose "big-city-in-the-'burbs" vibe suits the "heavy prices."

McCormick & Schmick's *Seafood* 21 | 20 | 20 | $46

Faneuil Hall | Faneuil Hall Mktpl. | N. Market Bldg. (North St.) | 617-720-5522
Park Square | Park Plaza Hotel | 34 Columbus Ave. (Arlington St.) | 617-482-3999
www.mccormickandschmicks.com

An "enjoyable" choice for "business and pleasure", these "upscale" seafood chain links in Faneuil Hall and Park Square offer a "daily changing" menu of "freshly caught" fare in an "upbeat" atmosphere marked by "warm, dark paneling"; though it feels too "stamped-out-of-a-mold" for some, "professional" service is a plus and the "happy-hour bar menu" wins over the after-work crowd.

Mela *Indian* 24 | 20 | 21 | $29

South End | 578 Tremont St. (bet. Public Alley 701 & Union Park) | 617-859-4805 | www.melarestaurant.com

You get "lots of food for your money" (especially via the cheap lunch buffet) at this South End Indian where "all the staples" are "consistently well made"; furthermore, there's "cheerful service from the long-term staff" and "upscale" decor that's "modern with a touch of old-world charm" – it's just "too bad" they don't "dim the lights in the evening."

Melting Pot *Fondue* 19 | 17 | 18 | $45

Park Square | Park Plaza Hotel | 76 Arlington St. (Columbus Ave.) | 617-357-7007
Bedford | 213 Burlington Rd. (Network Dr.) | 781-791-0529
Framingham | 92 Worcester Rd. (Price Way) | 508-875-3115
www.meltingpot.com

"It's all about sharing" and "cooking your own food" at this chain serving "every kind of fondue" (including "delicious" chocolate pots) for meals that usually turn into "two-hour events"; while it's a "romantic" "treat" for "younger couples" and "fun to do with a group", critics contend it's "overpriced" and "gimmicky."

	FOOD	DECOR	SERVICE	COST

🛛 NEW Menton *French/Italian* 28 | 27 | 29 | $145

Seaport District | 354 Congress St. (A St.) | 617-737-0099 |
www.mentonboston.com

Barbara Lynch's latest "temple" of French-Italian gastronomy,
located in the Seaport District, makes an auspicious Survey debut
by earning the No. 1 scores for both Service and Decor thanks to its
"unparalleled" staff and "elegant", "sophisticated" setting of earthy
greens, grays and wood tones; the "phenomenal" prix fixe-only
cuisine, each course a "visual delight and a taste sensation" paired
with "divine" wines, also "sets a new standard", as do tabs you may
have to "mortgage your house" to pay – indeed, this ranks as the
Survey's "priciest restaurant."

🛛 Meritage 🗷🅼 *American* 26 | 26 | 26 | $68

Waterfront | Boston Harbor Hotel | 70 Rowes Wharf (Atlantic Ave.) |
617-439-3995 | www.meritagetherestaurant.com

It's "oenophile heaven" at this New American "destination" in a
Waterfront hotel, where chef Daniel Bruce preps a "marvelous
menu" that couples his "full and half plates" (each a "beautiful taste
symphony") with "excellent wine pairing choices"; sure, you'll pay
"top dollar", but it's "worth it", especially when factoring in the "exquisite harbor views", "chic", "romantic" setting and "professional,
courteous" staffers who "perform their job like a dance."

Met Back Bay *American/Steak* 19 | 20 | 17 | $32

NEW **Back Bay** | 279 Dartmouth St. (Newbury St.) | 617-267-0451 |
www.metbackbay.com

Met Bar & Grill *American/Steak*

Dedham | Legacy Pl. | 400 Legacy Pl. (Providence Hwy.) | 781-467-1234
Natick | Natick Collection | 1245 Worcester St. (Speen St.) | 508-651-0003
www.metbarandgrill.com

Though there's a "steak focus" at these "cool", "modern" Metropolitan
Club spin-offs in the Natick Collection and Dedham's Legacy Place,
the "fun burger bar" that encourages "yummy" "creative combos" is
the "core attraction"; surveyors split on whether tabs are "reasonable" or "overpriced for what you get"; P.S. the Back Bay iteration
opened post-Survey.

Metropolis Cafe *Eclectic* 24 | 21 | 22 | $40

South End | 584 Tremont St. (bet. Clarendon & Dartmouth Sts.) |
617-247-2931 | www.metropolisboston.com

"Charming" and "romantic", "tightly packed" yet "relaxed", this South
Ender with a "European feel" employs a "pleasant", "attentive" staff
to serve its "innovative", "reliable" Eclectic cuisine "with a focus on
seasonal ingredients"; "nice wines" and "gentle prices" are more
reasons it's a "regular habit" for "locals" and "pre-theater" diners alike.

Metropolitan Club *American/Steak* 20 | 20 | 19 | $52

Chestnut Hill | 1210 Boylston St. (Hammond St.) | 617-731-0600 |
www.metclubandbar.com

While "not exactly metropolitan", this Chestnut Hill haunt with an
"upscale pub atmosphere" draws a "trendy crowd" to its dining room

and "fun bar area" for "pretty good" steaks and other New American bites; however, those with issues, including service that "hasn't been very attentive", exclaim "how dare they charge what they do!"

Middle East, The ● *Mideastern* | 19 | 15 | 17 | $20 |

Central Square | 472-480 Massachusetts Ave. (Brookline St.) | Cambridge | 617-492-9181 | www.mideastclub.com

"Still great after all these years", this Central Square "staple" is a "small" Middle Eastern restaurant with "not much atmosphere" attached to a "famous" "large music venue" boasting a "welcoming community feel"; the mainly Lebanese specialties are "fairly good" tastewise and "great deals" pricewise, but really, you "come here" for the "completely awesome" "independent live acts"; P.S. occasional "belly dancing is an added bonus."

Middlesex Lounge ⊠ *Eclectic* | ▽ 20 | 20 | 19 | $20 |

Central Square | 315 Massachusetts Ave. (Blanche St.) | Cambridge | 617-868-6739 | www.middlesexlounge.us

"More like a club with food", this "hip", "crowded" spot in Central Square owned by the neighboring Miracle of Science nevertheless garners compliments for its "delicious" Eclectic small plates; the "cool couches" that dot the "minimalist", "easy-on-the-eyes" environs can be "hard to eat on", but again, it's more about "mingling and hanging out" here – not to mention the "hopping" dance floor.

Midwest Grill *Brazilian/Steak* | 21 | 14 | 18 | $31 |

Inman Square | 1124 Cambridge St. (bet. Elm & Norfolk Sts.) | Cambridge | 617-354-7536
Saugus | 910 Broadway (Rte. 1) | 781-231-2221
www.midwestgrillrestaurant.com

"Gentlemen bearing spears" with an "endless supply" of beef, sausage, etc. patrol these Brazilian rodizios in Cambridge and Saugus, where "serious carnivores" attempt to "eat their weight in meat" (though the quality is up for debate, i.e. "tasty" vs. "overcooked"); the "all-you-can-eat" set-price meals include a "buffet of diverse sides" and salads, which makes it a "good value" – as long as you "bring your game" and "feast."

Miel *French* | 22 | 23 | 23 | $48 |

Waterfront | InterContinental Boston | 510 Atlantic Ave. (Congress St.) | 617-217-5151 | www.intercontinentalboston.com

Both the "lovely" Waterfront-facing patio and "old-world French" dining room at this InterContinental Hotel brasserie are "enjoyable, relaxing" places to "unwind, have a drink" and dine on "tasty", "beautifully presented" Provençal cuisine; the tabs can be a bit "pricey", but they buy "gracious" service too.

Mike's City Diner ⊅ *Diner* | 20 | 13 | 19 | $15 |

South End | 1714 Washington St. (Springfield St.) | 617-267-9393

"Massive amounts" of "good old-fashioned" diner fare are dished out by a "friendly" staff at this South End "greasy spoon" that nourishes a real "local cast of characters"; it's not surprising to find "a line out the door on weekends", but it's "worth the wait" to get so "astoundingly stuffed" for such a "great price"; P.S. breakfast, lunch and cash only.

Miracle of Science Bar & Grill ◐ *Pub Food* 19 | 18 | 16 | $20

Central Square | 321 Massachusetts Ave. (State St.) | Cambridge | 617-868-2866 | www.miracleofscience.us

"Brainiacs" from MIT are the primary customer base of this "just-kitschy-enough" Central Square pub where the "awesome burgers" and other "simple", "reliable" grub are listed on a "clever" "periodic-table" menu; the "decent beer selection" helps ensure a "fun" time is had by all, but since it's such "a small place", one has to wonder: why is it so "hard to find your server"?

Mission Bar & Grill ◐ *Pub Food* ▽ 18 | 16 | 17 | $23

MFA | 724 Huntington Ave. (Tremont St.) | 617-566-1244 | www.themissionbar.com

"Impressive", "straightforward" pub food, a "decent beer selection" and a "nice cocktail menu" lure "scrubs" "from the nearby hospitals" in droves to this "small", "upbeat" "neighborhood standby" near the MFA; indeed, it's sometimes "hard to find a table" inside, where the game's usually on the two large TVs and, during the warmer months, windows running "the full length" of the place are opened, making for "nice, breezy" meals.

Z Mistral *French/Mediterranean* 28 | 25 | 26 | $70

South End | 223 Columbus Ave. (bet. Berkeley & Clarendon Sts.) | 617-867-9300 | www.mistralbistro.com

"Flashes of brilliance" illuminate this South End "legend" where dinner is an "event" thanks to chef Jamie Mammano's "imaginative", "sublime" French-Mediterranean cuisine paired with "glorious wines", "creative" cocktails and "terrific service"; an "elegant but not overly formal" aura permeates the "dramatic" high-ceilinged dining room and a "cool vibe" dominates the "chic bar" though it all comes at tabs that practically necessitate "a paycheck."

M.J. O'Connor's *Pub Food* 17 | 18 | 17 | $29

Park Square | Park Plaza Hotel | 27 Columbus Ave. (Arlington St.) | 617-482-2255

Seaport District | Westin Boston Waterfront Hotel | 425 Summer St. (bet. A & D Sts.) | 617-443-0800

www.mjoconnors.com

Dark-wood decor including a bar imported from the Emerald Isle sets the tone at this "typical Irish" pub in Park Square and its offshoot with "kind of an odd location" in a Seaport District hotel; the grub may be "unremarkable", but it's "decent" and "fairly priced", plus it's offered alongside a "great beer selection" and via brogue-sporting staffers, many of whom are "sweet."

Montien *Japanese/Thai* 21 | 16 | 19 | $29

Theater District | 63 Stuart St. (Tremont St.) | 617-338-5600 | www.montien-boston.com

For pre-show supping, this Theater District spot "graciously accommodates curtain times" while dispensing "dependable" Thai cuisine and "pleasant" sushi at prices that are a "great value" (especially the "lunch combos"); the cozy, neon-lit space is "always crowded and noisy", so folks with abodes in the area "usually get takeout."

Moonstones *Eclectic*   ▽ 20 | 22 | 22 | $39

Chelmsford | 185 Chelmsford St./Rte. 110 (Stedman St.) | 978-256-7777 | www.moonstones110.com

When they "want to get dressed up" and stay in Chelmsford, suburbanites head to this "trendy", "high-end" venue whose "fusion-oriented" Eclectic menu features an "extensive" selection of small dishes; if they're looking to just "hang out" with their neighbors, the "great bar with friendly servers" and "fabulous" cocktails is "a cool place" in and of itself.

Mooo . . . *Steak*   26 | 25 | 26 | $67

Beacon Hill | XV Beacon Hotel | 15 Beacon St. (bet. Bowdoin & Somerset Sts.) | 617-670-2515 | www.mooorestaurant.com

"Had enough of old-school steakhouses?" – then hit this "happening" beefery in a Beacon Hill hotel, where the vibe is "swanky" "without being too stuffy" thanks to "cow decor" and a "silly name"; additionally, the vittles are "magnificent", the wine list "superb", the cocktails "artful" and the service "attentive" and "knowledgeable", all of which adds up to a "memorable experience" that's "worth the splurge" (tip: "eating at the bar saves you money").

Morse Fish *Seafood*   ▽ 19 | 9 | 21 | $17

South End | 1401 Washington St. (Union Park) | 617-262-9375 | www.morsefish.com

Don't let the "bare-bones" decor "fool you" – a "treasure" trove of "quality and reasonable prices" lies within this South End fish market and counter-serve eatery offering a "large menu" of broiled and fried preparations; "cheerful service" also reels 'em in, although most get "takeout" or provisions to "cook at home."

☑ Morton's The Steakhouse *Steak*   25 | 22 | 24 | $67

Back Bay | Exeter Plaza | 699 Boylston St. (Exeter St.) | 617-266-5858
Seaport District | World Trade Center E. | 2 Seaport Ln. (bet. Congress St. & Northern Ave.) | 617-526-0410
www.mortons.com

A steakhouse "standard-bearer", this "big-ticket" chain offers "excellently prepared" cuts of beef and "grand sides" "served professionally" amid an atmosphere of "wealth and class" (the "Seaport location offers the best ambiance", as the Back Bay iteration is in a basement); some find it a bit "staid" and wish they'd "lose the raw-meat presentation" and "high" wine pricing, but the many who love its "traditional" ways consider it "one of the best."

Mother Anna's *Italian*   23 | 16 | 21 | $34

North End | 211 Hanover St. (Cross St.) | 617-523-8496 | www.motherannas.com

"Sunday dinners at grandma's house" are hosted seven days a week at this "family-run" North End Italian "icon", which has been dispensing its "generous portions" of "amazing" "home-cooked" "red sauce" since 1937; it's "not the fanciest place around", but the setting is secondary compared to the "reasonable prices", "friendly, knowledgeable" service and patio seating ("great for people-watching").

Mr. Bartley's Burger Cottage 🗷🍽 *Burgers* | 24 | 12 | 15 | $17 |

Harvard Square | 1246 Massachusetts Ave. (Plympton St.) | Cambridge | 617-354-6559 | www.mrbartley.com

If "burgers are the foundation of civilization", then "Mr. Bartley is a founding father" proclaim patty-partisans of this Harvard Square "tradition" where the "reasonably priced" namesakes are as "ginormous" as the "jam-packed" "communal tables" are "tiny" ("check your 'personal bubble' at the door"); it's "frenzied", "cash-only" and bathroom-less, but "everyone should go" "at least once" to experience the "endless choices" (each "amusingly named" after a political or pop-culture icon), "legendary shakes" and "surly" service.

Mr. Crepe *French* | 21 | 15 | 16 | $12 |

Somerville | 51 Davis Sq. (bet. Elm St. & Highland Ave.) | 617-623-0661 | www.mrcrepe.com

"Paris" meets "funky" Somerville at this counter-serve spot vending "inexpensive", "delicious" "crêpes in a wide variety of sweet and savory combinations"; service is "quick", but it's small and often "crowded", so consider yourself lucky if you can "sit by the windows" to "people-watch" the "hipsters of David Square."

Mr. Sushi *Japanese* | 21 | 13 | 19 | $27 |

Arlington | 693 Massachusetts Ave. (bet. Central & Water Sts.) | 781-643-4175
Brookline | 329 Harvard St. (Babcock St.) | 617-731-1122 | www.mrsushibrookline.com

"Perfectly acceptable and convenient" sums up this "no-frills" Japanese duo in Arlington and Brookline, where "no lines" create a "relaxing atmosphere" and "fair prices" mean you can let the "little ones" experiment with sushi (furthermore, the staff is "nice to kids"); sure, it's "nothing to write home about", but "if you live in the area", its "gets the job done."

MuLan Taiwanese Cuisine Ⓜ *Taiwanese* | 24 | 9 | 17 | $19 |

Kendall Square | 228 Broadway (Clark St.) | Cambridge | 617-441-8813 | www.mulan.4t.com

Those are "authentic" (not to mention "addictive") Taiwanese specials on the "large, unusual menu" at this "reasonably priced" Chinese "dive" in Kendall Square, so if you're not familiar, "bring along a regular", "do your research beforehand" or "ask for recommendations" from staffers – they'll be happy to oblige, although they may also "intimidate you to finish your meal", since the place is "very busy."

NEW Mumbai Chopstix ❶ *Chinese/Indian* | 19 | 20 | 18 | $31 |

Back Bay | 254 Newbury St. (bet. Fairfield & Gloucester Sts.) | 617-927-4444

"If you like it hot", you'll probably cotton to this "wonderful addition" to the Back Bay, offering "interesting", "inventive" Indian-Chinese cuisine at moderate prices; the two-story townhouse setting is filled with a "friendly staff" and "arty" decor with elements that are both traditional (Mumbai murals, Buddhas) and modern (Lucite chairs).

Muqueca ⓜ *Brazilian* `25` `19` `22` `$23`

Inman Square | 1008 Cambridge St. (Elm St.) | Cambridge | 617-354-3296 | www.muquecarestaurant.com

Recently "moved to bigger digs" in Inman Square, this "lively", "colorful" Brazilian still excels in "yummy" seafood "stews that come out of the kitchen bubbling" in clay pots, piled into "generous portions" and sold at "extraordinary bargain" prices; the "friendly" staff is the same, and so is its license for beer-and-wine only.

Myers + Chang *Asian* `24` `20` `22` `$35`

South End | 1145 Washington St. (E. Berkeley St.) | 617-542-5200 | www.myersandchang.com

"Inspiring", "innovative" Asian tapas are served in a "hip" Far East-leaning setting at this "edgy and excellent" South Ender by restaurateur Christopher Myers and chef Joanne Chang; servers stay "friendly" even when the vibe gets "frantic", and while the "small portions" can "make it more expensive than it appears", if you "sit at the bar overlooking the woks", you're also getting a "show" along with your meal.

Naked Fish *Cuban/Seafood* `20` `18` `19` `$34`

Waltham | 455 Totten Pond Rd. (3rd Ave.) | 781-684-0500 | www.nakedfish.com

For "something a little different", Walthamites have this seafooder whose "Cuban concoctions" (including "fun drinks") make a "delightful" "change from the usual"; it's "not a bad value for the money" either, which, along with the "high energy level" (and despite the "feels-like-a-chain" setting), means "families should feel comfortable" here.

Namaskar *Indian* ▽ `19` `18` `19` `$25`

Somerville | 234 Elm St. (Grove St.) | 617-623-9955 | www.namaskarcuisine.com

Davis Square surveyors who previously skipped this Indian in favor of "higher profile" neighbors says they "won't overlook it again" now that they've sampled its "terrific", "reasonably priced" fare; bonus points are bestowed because there's "never a wait", service is "pleasant", "portions are generous" and there's a "great lunch buffet" to boot.

Navy Yard Bistro & Wine Bar *American* `24` `21` `23` `$36`

Charlestown | Sixth St. (1st Ave.) | 617-242-0036 | www.navyyardbistro.com

The "secluded" Charlestown Navy Yard is the "unlikely setting" of this "intimate", "atmospheric" "treasure" where "incredibly good prices" are charged for both the "excellent" New American fare and the "good wines"; the staff adds to the "friendly neighborhood atmosphere" inside and out where there are a "few tables" for "when the weather is nice."

	FOOD	DECOR	SERVICE	COST

Nebo ⊠ *Italian*
| 20 | 20 | 21 | $33 |

North End | 90 N. Washington St. (Thacher St.) | 617-723-6326 |
www.neborestaurant.com

"Simply tasty pastas and pizzas" (including "lots of gluten-free options") are the forte of this "contemporary" North End Italian that's "great" "pre-game" since it's "close to the Garden"; those who've hit the extensive antipasti selection too hard warn the "little dishes add up to big dollars", but all things considered, it's a "great value."

☑ Neighborhood Restaurant & Bakery ⊘ *Portuguese*
| 26 | 18 | 21 | $15 |

Somerville | 25 Bow St. (bet. Somerville Ave. & Summer St.) |
617-623-9710

"If heaven were an unpretentious 'from-scratch' family restaurant", it would be this Portuguese daytime-only bakery in Somerville, where "heaping plates of delicious food" are served for "a steal" in a "quirky" interior with "limited seating" and on a "grapevine-covered patio" in warmer months; lunch is offered, but it's "famous" for breakfast, when the "long waits" to get in are allayed by "coffee and treats" from the "thoughtful owners."

☑ Neptune Oyster *Seafood*
| 28 | 20 | 22 | $47 |

North End | 63 Salem St. (Cross St.) | 617-742-3474 |
www.neptuneoyster.com

A "pearl" "floating among red sauce" joints, this "classy", "divine" North End fishery specializes in "unreal lobster rolls", either "drenched with melted butter" or "New England–style with mayo", plus "superb raw-bar" selections and "creative seafood concoctions", which the "knowledgeable staff" can help pair with "interesting wines"; however, be prepared for "expensive" checks, "sardine-can digs" and a "no-reservations" policy that leads to "frustrating waits" – all "well worth it."

NewBridge Cafe ⊘ *American*
| 26 | 8 | 18 | $24 |

Chelsea | 650 Washington Ave. (Woodlawn Ave.) | 617-884-0134 |
www.newbridgecafe.com

"Amazing" steak, turkey and lamb tips are the claims to fame of this "satisfying" Chelsea American grill where the "salads are just as tasty" and the portions are "cheap and plentiful"; the "cozy" setting is "not fancy at all" (in fact, it's "sort of depressing"), but it makes no difference since the "fast service" keeps it an "eat-and-run" kind of place.

New Ginza *Japanese*
| 23 | 17 | 21 | $39 |

Watertown | 63-65 Galen St. (Aldrich Rd.) | 617-923-2100 |
www.newginzaboston.com

"Ultrafresh ingredients" are "expertly prepared" at this "reliable, high-quality sushi" joint in Watertown, where the atmosphere is as "laid-back" as the decor is "nothing to write home about"; "gracious, respectful" staffers help cultivate "loyal customers" who keep it "crowded", especially "on weekends" and even though they "wish it were cheaper."

New Jang Su BBQ Ⓜ *Korean*

— | — | — | M

Burlington | 260 Cambridge St. (Arthur Woods Ave.) | 781-272-3787
"Knock-your-socks-off" Korean barbecue that you "grill at the table" and bibimbop that's "just right" are the fortes of this Burlington venue; the prices are appropriately affordable, which is consolation for the "bland pseudo-Asian decor" and sometimes "missing-in-action staff."

New Mother India Ⓜ *Indian*

22 | 15 | 18 | $27

Waltham | 336 Moody St. (Gordon St.) | 781-893-3311 |
www.newmotherindia.com
"Calm" atmospherics contrast "vibrant" flavors at this "reliable" Waltham Indian whose "bountiful portions" are doled out in an "informal", "spacious" setting; if the "service is a little cold", the "management is cordial", and the "value" negates all quibbles, especially for the "great lunch buffet", which gets bonus points from vegetarians.

New Shanghai *Chinese*

▽ 21 | 13 | 19 | $26

Chinatown | 21 Hudson St. (Kneeland St.) | 617-338-6688 |
www.newshanghairestaurant.com
"The Peking duck is the special" (and "quite a treat") at this "white-tablecloth restaurant" in Chinatown, but "quality and freshness" shine through in all of the Sino dishes served, and better still, they're affordable; though "casual", the staff is "accommodating", even when the setting is "extremely crowded."

Nico *Italian*

▽ 24 | 18 | 23 | $41

North End | 417 Hanover St. (Battery St.) | 617-742-0404 |
www.nicoboston.com
"Old-school Italian" fare is "thoughtfully prepared" with "contemporary flair" at this "busy" North Ender that employs a "responsive staff"; chandeliers and red curtains make the "quaint" dining room feel "romantic", but a few opine that the TVs at the bar give the place "a slightly cheap feel" (at least the tabs are appropriately moderate).

9 Tastes *Thai*

21 | 14 | 17 | $20

Harvard Square | 50 JFK St. (Winthrop St.) | Cambridge | 617-547-6666 |
www.9taste.com
"Swarming with undergrads and grad students", this basement "hole-in-the-wall" is a "Harvard Square staple" for "sumptuous" curries and "harder-to-find Thai treats"; what's more, the prices are so "affordable" (especially for the "satisfying lunch specials"), most are "willing to forgo good service."

ZNEW Noche ◗ *American*

22 | 26 | 22 | $44

South End | 3 Appleton St. (Tremont St.) | 617-482-0117 |
www.noche-boston.com
"Dark wood, white seats" and "gorgeous" contemporary accoutrements comprise the "clever decor" at this New American newcomer in the South End, which cultivates "hot-spot" status with "unique cocktails" and a "hipster"-heavy crowd; but while some deem the fare "fabulous", others say that, compared to the "stunning" setting, it "lacks an identity", "especially at the price."

Noir *American* ∇ 20 | 21 | 19 | $34

Harvard Square | Charles Hotel | 1 Bennett St. (Eliot St.) |
Cambridge | 617-661-8010 | www.noir-bar.com

As its name suggests, this upscale lounge in Harvard Square's
Charles Hotel is a dark, dim nest for night owls indulging in "great
drinks" and "good" New American "munchies"; some say it's
roundly "overhyped", but nevertheless, it's usually "hard to find a table for two", especially just "after work."

No Name *Seafood* 19 | 10 | 17 | $26

Seaport District | 15 W. Fish Pier St. (Northern Ave.) | 617-338-7539 |
www.nonamerestaurant.com

"If you're looking for this week's fashionable fish dish, look elsewhere", because this "ancient", "bare-bones" Seaport District "old
faithful" is all about "down-to-earth" seafood preparations shoveled
onto "paper plates" and served by "snappy", "sassy" staffers; sure,
modernists call it a "tired" stop for "tourists", but the majority of
surveyors appreciates it as an "awesome", "low-priced" "tradition."

☒ No. 9 Park ☒ *French/Italian* 27 | 25 | 27 | $77

Beacon Hill | 9 Park St. (bet. Beacon & Tremont Sts.) | 617-742-9991 |
www.no9park.com

"Meticulously prepared" French-Italian plates deliver "tastes and
textures beyond compare" at "genius" chef Barbara Lynch's "elegant" flagship on Beacon Hill, where the "revelatory" meals are enhanced by "brilliant wine pairings", "exceptional cocktails" and
service that goes "the whole nine yards"; you probably "won't get
stuffed on the portions" and you'll likely get a jolt of "sticker shock",
but it's "well worth it" for such a "joyful experience."

Noodle Street *Asian* 20 | 15 | 19 | $17

Boston University | 627 Commonwealth Ave. (bet. Granby &
Sherborn Sts.) | 617-536-3100 | www.noodlestreet.com

"Can't beat it" aver BU students about this Asian noodle shop that
proffers a comprehensive menu with "create-it-yourself" options,
with everything coming out "hot and delicious", "healthy" and "economical"; what's more, "service is great" whether you dine in amid
the "strange mix of license plates and street signs" or get it to-go.

North Street Grille Ⓜ *American* ∇ 24 | 16 | 18 | $34

North End | 229 North St. (Lewis St.) | 617-720-2010 |
www.northstreetgrille.com

Dinners are "spectacular", but weekend brunch is flat-out "outstanding" at this "great" North End New American; though there's
"almost no decor" to speak of, nobody's complaining, especially
when the affordable bill comes.

North 26 *New England* ∇ 25 | 24 | 24 | $40

Faneuil Hall | Millennium Bostonian | 26 North St. (Clinton St.) |
617-557-3640 | www.millenniumhotels.com

"Divine" New England fare featuring "bangin' bites" at the bar is the
specialty of this "crisp", "cool", minimalist eatery in the Millennium

Bostonian Hotel, which boasts vistas of Faneuil Hall and its vicinity; a "fantastic" staff demonstrates "attention to detail" as it delivers the dishes, wines and moderate tabs.

☑ Not Your Average Joe's *American* | 19 | 17 | 20 | $26 |

Arlington | 645 Massachusetts Ave. (Pleasant St.) | 781-643-1666
Needham | 109 Chapel St. (bet. Great Plain Ave. & May St.) | 781-453-9300
Watertown | 55 Main St. (Church St.) | 617-926-9229
Newburyport | Firehouse Ctr. | 1 Market Sq. (State St.) | 978-462-3808
Beverly | Commodore Plaza | 45 Enon St. (bet. Hoover Ave. & Lincoln St.) | 978-927-8950
Methuen | The Loop | 90 Pleasant Valley St. (Milk St.) | 978-974-0015
Randolph | 16 Mazzeo Dr. (West St.) | 781-961-7200
Dartmouth | 61 State Rd. (bet. Slocom Rd. & Suffolk Ave.) | 508-992-5637
Westborough | 291 Turnpike Rd. (Otis St.) | 508-986-2350
Burlington | 4C Wayside Rd. (Cambridge St.) | 781-505-1303
www.notyouraveragejoes.com
Additional locations throughout the Boston area

"If you have any room" after you "gorge" on the "incredible" focaccia with "seasoned olive oil" – which the "friendly", "willing" staff brings "as soon as you sit down" – this "pleasantly informal" local chain further "satisfies" with "something-for-everyone", ever-"evolving" American eats; a contrary contingent belittles it as indeed "just average", but the majority calls it a "wonderful value" that "never lets you down" – no wonder it's "always jam-packed."

☑ Oak Room *Steak* | 24 | 27 | 25 | $65 |

Back Bay | Fairmont Copley Plaza | 138 St. James Ave. (bet. Dartmouth St. & Trinity Pl.) | 617-267-5300 | www.theoakroom.com

"Luxurious meals" fetch "luxurious prices" at this "quintessential Brahmin" Back Bay chophouse, which most calculate as "worth every penny", what with the "falling-off-your-plate" portions and "wonderful" "professional" service; fittingly, the "ornately decorated", "clubby" setting ("dark"-wood paneling, "oversized chairs") is "hoity-toity to the max" and as appropriate for an "old-fashioned business dinner" as for a "special occasion."

Oceana *American/Seafood* | 22 | 20 | 21 | $52 |

Waterfront | Boston Marriott Long Wharf | 296 State St. (Atlantic Ave.) | 617-227-3838 | www.oceanaatlongwharf.com

"Exotic choices", particularly of seafood, mingle with "nicely prepared" American standards ("everything from burgers to steak") at this Marriott Long Wharf eatery, a cruise-ship look-alike with "a great view" of the Waterfront plus "friendly service"; it's "costly", but "good for the traveling family", especially the "nice breakfast buffet" offering a "made-to-order omelet station."

Oceanaire Seafood Room *Seafood* | 24 | 24 | 23 | $55 |

Financial District | 40 Court St. (Tremont St.) | 617-742-2277 | www.theoceanaire.com

"First-rate seafood" "impresses" fin fans at this "high-end" Financial District chain link delivering "creative" preparations of "fresh fish" matched by "excellent" wines; the group-friendly surroundings in a converted bank with "marble and vaulted ceiling" are "stunning" and the "knowledgeable" staff ensures you feel "catered to", so most guests are "happy" to make the "splurge."

Oga's *Japanese*
| 25 | 18 | 20 | $41 |

Natick | 915 Worcester St./Rte. 9 (Rte. 27) | 508-653-4338 |
www.ogasnatick.com

"Innovation goes far beyond expectations" at this Natick "oasis" where the "extremely fresh", "beautifully presented" sushi boasts "complexity, subtlety" and "lower price tags" than some other high-profile Japanese spots; "genteel dining is available" in the "modern" space ("darn nice for a suburban strip mall on a busy highway"), while aficionados "love watching the chefs prepare at the bar."

☑ Oishii Ⓜ *Japanese*
| 27 | 17 | 22 | $54 |

Chestnut Hill | 612 Hammond St. (Boylston St.) | 617-277-7888 |
www.oishiiboston.com
Sudbury | Mill Vill. | 365 Boston Post Rd./Rte. 20 (Concord Rd.) |
978-440-8300 | www.oishiitoo.com

☑ Oishii Boston ◑Ⓜ *Japanese*
South End | 1166 Washington St. (E. Berkeley St.) | 617-482-8868 |
www.oishiiboston.com

"True artistry" is on display in the "extravagant", "sublime" sushi crafted at this trio of "vibrant Japanese gems" where the service is mostly "kind" and "attentive"; while the scene is "chic yet serene" in the South End, you're "confined as tightly as the maki" at the Chestnut Hill original (where there's "usually a wait") and the setting is a "sparse", "tiny, dark cave" in Sudbury, but whichever you choose, you might "need to sell some stocks" first – and it's "worth every penny."

☑ Oleana *Mediterranean*
| 28 | 24 | 25 | $54 |

Inman Square | 134 Hampshire St. (bet. Elm & Norfolk Sts.) |
Cambridge | 617-661-0505 | www.oleanarestaurant.com

"Exotic-spice" "guru" Ana Sortun makes "taste buds sing" at this Inman Square "diamond" where she weaves "layers of flavors" into "adventurous" Arabic-Mediterranean dishes that "emphasize locally grown" ingredients; the "enthusiastic servers" are "helpful with choosing a wine" from the "excellent" list, but just know that reservations are nearly "impossible to obtain" for the "cramped" but "warm" interior, while in summer, you have to "get there early" to score a table on the "lovely" patio, which doesn't accept bookings at all.

Olé Mexican Grill *Mexican*
| 24 | 19 | 20 | $30 |

Inman Square | 11 Springfield St. (Cambridge St.) | Cambridge |
617-492-4495 | www.olegrill.com

Olecito *Mexican*
Boston University | 700 Commonwealth Ave. (bet. Cummington & Hinsdale Sts.) | 617-353-7257 Ⓢ Ⓜ
Inman Square | 12 Springfield St. (Cambridge St.) | Cambridge |
617-876-1374 ⅌

(continued)

(continued)

Olecito

Brookline | 6 Cypress St. (Washington St.) | 617-739-1408
www.olecito.net

"Guacamole made tableside" gets things off to a "scrumptious" start at this "bright", "upscale" Mexican grill in Inman Square, where the rest of the menu features "fantastic", "gourmet" regional fare; "fabulous" margaritas help keep the atmosphere "jolly" even when service goes from "pleasant" to "brusque", and though some feel the tabs are a bit "overpriced", there's Olecito for "inexpensive takeout."

Olivadi ⓜ *Italian*

▽ 20 | 19 | 22 | $36

Norwood | 32 Guild St. (Central St.) | 781-762-9090 |
www.olivadirestaurant.com

"Off the beaten path" in Norwood Center resides this "find" where the "extensive" midpriced menu of Italian classics with modern twists "exceeds expectations", just like the "good service"; suncolored walls, wood-and-tile floors and exposed brick evoke Tuscany, but the highlight of the space is a partially open kitchen with a woodburning pizza oven and a granite chef's table.

Om *American*

16 | 23 | 18 | $43

Harvard Square | 92 Winthrop St. (JFK St.) | Cambridge | 617-576-2800 |
www.omrestaurant.com

"Whimsical, trendy" Asian-influenced decor matches the menu at this Harvard Square New American with a "sexy", "clublike atmosphere" downstairs and a more traditional dining room upstairs where "large windows" frame "a view of the street below"; the "creative drinks" are "quite good", but as for the dishes, while some find them "well prepared", just as many deem them "disappointing" in taste, "small" in size and therefore "over" in price.

Orinoco: A Latin Kitchen ⓜ *Venezuelan*

23 | 18 | 20 | $31

South End | 477 Shawmut Ave. (W. Concord St.) | 617-369-7075
Brookline | 22 Harvard St. (Webster St.) | 617-232-9505
www.orinocokitchen.com

The flavors are as "bold" as the buzz is "loud" at this "festive", "reasonably priced" Venezuelan in the South End, where "hungry people wait" (no reservations) for one of the "handful of tables" to indulge in "not-to-be-missed arepas", "to-die-for bacon-wrapped dates" and "exotic concoctions" from the bar, all delivered by an "engaging staff"; the second location, bigger than its parent, offers "something different and special in Brookline."

Orleans *American*

17 | 18 | 19 | $28

Somerville | 65 Holland St. (Wallace St.) | 617-591-2100 |
www.orleansrestaurant.com

"Great music" (live on Thursdays and Fridays, DJs on Saturdays), a number of TVs, "good drinks", "friendly" service and a summertime patio make this Davis Square joint a "place to hang out"; there's a full American menu too, and if it's "nothing to rave about", at least it's "reliable" and "value" priced.

Orta 🅼 *Italian* ▽ 19 | 18 | 20 | $33

Hanover | 75 Washington St./Rte. 53 (Columbia Rd.) | 781-826-8883 | www.ortarestaurant.com

A Neapolitan "gem" in a "busy strip mall", this trattoria near Hanover in Pembroke prepares "solid", "reasonably priced" "little bites", pizzas and full entrees; the "knowledgeable servers" and Italian wine list also please, as does the rustic dining room with tile floors and a brick oven, which manages to feel "relaxed and comfortable" despite the fact that it's often "unbelievably crowded."

Osushi *Japanese* 21 | 17 | 19 | $39

Back Bay | Westin Copley Pl. | 10 Huntington Ave. (Dartmouth St.) | 617-266-2788 | www.osushirestaurant.com

"Creative rolls" served in "intimate" "modern-minimalist" digs is the congruous assessment of this sushi spot in a Back Bay hotel mall; but even if the "limited menu" is "well prepared", it's "overpriced" say surveyors whose comments about the staff vacillate between "dedicated" and "o service wherefore art thou?"

Other Side Cafe ⬤ *Sandwiches* 20 | 17 | 16 | $18

Back Bay | 407 Newbury St. (Mass. Ave.) | 617-536-8437 | www.theothersidecafe.com

"Grunge" lives on at this "cheap" bi-level Back Bay "hipster heaven" where "carnivores, vegetarians and vegans" alike find plenty of "healthy, fresh goodies" on the "extensive" sandwich menu; the "odd" setting, "loud" din, "graffiti-covered bathrooms" and "pierced" staffers are "not for the faint of heart", but at least the latter "will never rush you" – then again, maybe they're just being "dismissive."

Out of the Blue 🅼 *Italian/Seafood* 24 | 16 | 22 | $30

Somerville | 215 Elm St. (Grove St.) | 617-776-5020 | www.outofthebluerestaurant.com

"Amazing seafood" with loads of "North End-style Italian" influence (particularly in the "outstanding" pasta dishes) saves Davis Square denizens a "trip to the city" at this "reasonably priced" "neighborhood joint"; though "nothing fancy" decorwise, the "attentive staff" and "many familiar faces" of the clientele ensure the atmosphere is always "inviting."

🅉 O Ya 🅂🅼 *Japanese* 29 | 23 | 27 | $118

Leather District | 9 East St. (South St.) | 617-654-9900 | www.oyarestaurantboston.com

"Have you recently won a small fortune?" – then you have "the means" to enjoy this "cozy", unmarked izakaya in the Leather District, where "atomic" "bursts of texture and tastes" come from "every beautiful bite" of the "off-the-charts innovative" sushi, winner of Boston's No. 1 Food rating; suggestions from the "extensive sake list" by the "upbeat", "spot-on" staffers are just as "amazing" as the fare, but a caveat: even if you opt for the "luxurious" omakase and its "zillion tiny courses", it's possible you will still "leave hungry", as everything "comes in amuse-bouche portions" – nonetheless, it's an "unforgettable" meal.

Pagliuca's *Italian*
22 | 13 | 19 | $34

North End | 14 Parmenter St. (Hanover St.) | 617-367-1504 |
www.pagliucasrestaurant.com

Nothing "fancy-shmancy", just "terrific red sauce" – ladled out in "large portions" and sold for "bang-for-the-buck" prices – is what's on the menu at this "quintessential North End" Southern Italian; the "wait is sometimes long" for the "nothing-special", "tight" dining room, but once seated, the "warmth of the staff" makes you "feel like you're in someone's house" partaking in a "joyous meal."

Pairings *American*
▽ 21 | 23 | 19 | $35

Park Square | Park Plaza Hotel | 50 Park Plaza (bet. Arlington & Charles Sts.) | 617-262-3473 | www.pairingsboston.com

"Expectations were high" for this brightly colored sophomore in the Park Plaza Hotel, whose "concept" comprises pairing each of its New American small plates with wines in either 3- or 6-oz. pours; and while some call it a "wonderful experience" for "little money", others say they were "underwhelmed" and the fee was "pricey."

Palm, The *Steak*
24 | 21 | 24 | $63

Back Bay | Westin Copley Pl. | 200 Dartmouth St. (bet. St. James Ave. & Stuart St.) | 617-867-9292 | www.thepalm.com

"Perfect" lobster, "superb" steaks and "hefty" cocktails are the signatures of this "bustling" Back Bay chophouse chain link, where a "dark men's-club" look and "wonderful atmosphere" are enhanced by "caricatures of celebs" on the walls; "impeccable", "old-school" service seals the deal, so while it's "not cheap", it's "worth it."

Palmers ☒ *American*
▽ 22 | 17 | 20 | $32

Andover | 18 Elm St. (bet. High St. & Post Office Ave.) | 978-470-1606 | www.palmers-restaurant.com

"Consistent" "quality" and "large portions" make this Andover American a "good value"; downstairs there's a pub, with a "fun bar scene", live music (Thursdays–Saturdays) and its own selection of "well-prepared" vittles, while upstairs, there are three dining rooms with beamed ceilings and fireplaces ("eh" mutter design-mavens).

Panificio *Italian*
▽ 21 | 14 | 16 | $21

Beacon Hill | 144 Charles St. (bet. Cambridge & Revere Sts.) | 617-227-4340 | www.panificioboston.com

"Great for breakfast and lunch", this "small", "relaxed" Beacon Hill Italian bakery/cafe serves "reasonably priced" sandwiches, soups, salads and pizzas in an earth-toned room with mahogany trim; but it's "busy" and "tough to get a seat sometimes", which is why many "locals" keep it on their "good-for-takeout" list, especially at dinnertime.

NEW Papagayo Mexican Kitchen & Tequila Bar *Mexican*
- | - | - | I

Seaport District | 283 Summer St. (bet. D St. & Dorchester Ave.) | 617-423-1000 | www.papagayoboston.com

A bar offering more than 100 different types of tequilas and a slew of margaritas is the centerpiece of this funky Mexican arrival in the

Seaport District; open for lunch, dinner and Sunday brunch, it serves a menu of classics such as tacos and fajitas, all for under $20 – and often much less.

Papa Razzi *Italian* | 19 | 18 | 20 | $33 |

Back Bay | 159 Newbury St. (Dartmouth St.) | 617-536-9200 ◗
Chestnut Hill | The Mall at Chestnut Hill | 199 Boylston St. (Hammond Pond Pkwy.) | 617-527-6600
Hanover | Merchants Row | 2087 Washington St./Rte. 53 (Rte. 123) | 781-982-2800
Framingham | 155 Worcester Rd. (bet. Caldor Rd. & Walsh St.) | 508-848-2300
Wellesley | 16 Washington St. (Rte. 128, exit 21) | 781-235-4747
Burlington | 2 Wall St. (Rte. 3A) | 781-229-0100 ◗
Concord | 768 Elm St. (Concord Tpke.) | 978-371-0030
www.paparazzitrattoria.com

It's a "formula restaurant but the formula works" assure the "families", "groups" of "friends", "co-workers", "singles and couples" who keep this "dependable" (read: "predictable") Italian chain "always crowded"; the fare is "reasonably priced", and with "smart service" and "comfortable settings" thrown into the mix, no wonder it's a "regular stop" for "low-stress", "casual dining."

Paramount *American* | 22 | 14 | 17 | $21 |

Beacon Hill | 44 Charles St. (Mt. Vernon St.) | 617-720-1152 | www.paramountboston.com

"Seemingly everyone in Beacon Hill" "grabs a tray" and "waits" on the "long" though "fast" "weekend lines" for "yummy" "cafeteria-style" American breakfasts at this "local favorite" where, almost like magic, "you get a table" at exactly the moment you need it; "at night, it turns into a regular restaurant" offering "cozy dinners" at an equally "good value."

Paris Creperie *French* | 21 | 11 | 17 | $12 |

Brookline | 278 Harvard St. (Beacon St.) | 617-232-1770 | www.thepariscreperie.com

"Myriad sweet or savory fillings" are available in "delicious crêpes" that are "generously" sized and "reasonably priced" at this Brookline cafe; since everything's "made to order" and the "tiny" digs get "crowded", "you may have to wait" when it's busy – which is often.

Parish Cafe ◗ *Sandwiches* | 23 | 16 | 18 | $24 |

Back Bay | 361 Boylston St. (bet. Arlington & Berkeley Sts.) | 617-247-4777
South End | 493 Massachusetts Ave. (Tremont St.) | 617-391-0501
www.parishcafe.com

"Boston's top chefs" designed the "imaginative" "gourmet" sandwiches assembled at this pair of "awesome, unique" venues where the "fantastic drinks" and "copious beer offerings" are just as much of a draw; the Back Bay flagship is "crowded and noisy", especially during warmer months when the patio offers "prime people-watching", and the offshoot is a "great addition to the South End" – even though fans still can't come to a consensus whether tabs are "reasonable" or "overpriced for what you're getting."

	FOOD	DECOR	SERVICE	COST

Parker's *New England*

24 | 25 | 24 | $47

Downtown Crossing | Omni Parker House | 60 School St. (Tremont St.) | 617-227-8600 | www.omnihotels.com

"The only place to go for Parker House rolls and Boston cream pie" is this "glorious" Downtown Crossing restaurant where "the elegance of another era" thrives via "old-time", "pricey" New England eats, "beautiful", "formal" digs and "wonderful service"; "if you're looking for something innovative, go elsewhere", but to experience a piece of "incredible history", this is the spot.

☑ NEW Parsons Table ☒ *American*

27 | 21 | 26 | $48

Winchester | 34 Church St. (bet. School St. & Waterfield Rd.) | 781-729-1040 | www.parsons-table.com

"Catch was great but this is superb" cheer surveyors of chef Chris Parsons' "more casual", "rustic" reimagining of his fish-focused forerunner, where he now prepares New American "comfort foods with modern, creative spins" and "nods to local sourcing", all "while keeping prices in line"; thankfully, the "same great everything" else is still around, specifically the "attentive but unobtrusive service."

Pasha *Turkish*

▽ 22 | 17 | 20 | $28

Arlington | 669A Massachusetts Ave. (Water St.) | 781-648-5888 | www.pashaturkish.com

Arlington diners are "always amazed that the check is so low for such an abundance of food" at this Turkish undertaking where the "delicious" fare is paired with "good wines", coffee and tea from the Middle East; "friendly service" and a "pleasant, international-feeling setting" are two more reasons it's "worth revisiting."

Passage to India *Indian*

22 | 15 | 19 | $26

Porter Square | 1900 Massachusetts Ave. (Somerville Ave.) | Cambridge | 617-497-6113
Salem | 157 Washington St. (Rte. 114) | 978-832-2200
www.passageindia.com

At these separately owned, "pleasantly atmospheric" Indians, the midpriced "traditional" fare is "well seasoned" and the service is mostly "friendly"; the Porter Square location presents a "good lunch buffet", while the Salem outpost has a bar area that "takes pressure off the over-worked dining room."

Patou *Thai*

▽ 20 | 17 | 21 | $30

Belmont | 69 Leonard St. (Alexander Ave.) | 617-489-6999 | www.patouthai.com

"All the usual suspects" are augmented with "off-the-beaten-path" choices at this "solid" Belmont Thai offering "great value" to suburbanites; the "spare" interior with blue walls is "fine", the "patio out back is fun in warm weather" and the fare is "good for takeout as well."

Pazzo *Italian*

21 | 19 | 17 | $42

Back Bay | 269 Newbury St. (bet. Fairfield & Gloucester Sts.) | 617-267-2996 | www.pazzoboston.com

Two "adorable, cozy" floors and a "nice" patio offering prime Back Bay people-watching set the stage for "delicious Italian fare" at this "pleasant" place, which is surprisingly "reasonably priced" considering the Newbury Street location; while servers are generally "knowledgeable", sometimes one can "pull a disappearing act worthy of Houdini", "a shame" because everything else is "really enjoyable."

Peach Farm ● *Chinese/Seafood*   25 | 8 | 16 | $24
Chinatown | 4 Tyler St. (Beach St.) | 617-482-3332

You might be "intimidated" by the "cramped" "hole-in-the-wall" setting of this Chinatown basement, but just "close your eyes" and dig into the "incredible", "inexpensive" Cantonese cuisine, especially the "wonderful" seafood fished "fresh" out of the tank; indeed, "don't come if you need peace and quiet and romance" – but do come if you want "fast and hot" eats at 3 AM.

Peking Cuisine *Chinese*   - | - | - | I
Newton | 870 Walnut St. (Beacon St.) | 617-969-0888

Newtonites head to this "friendly" neighborhood eatery in a strip mall for "consistently excellent Chinese food" that's "especially good if you like it hot"; as for the service, customers marvel at the staff's "phenomenal memory" when they're recognized.

Pellana *Steak*   ∇ 25 | 25 | 24 | $63
Peabody | 9 Rear Sylvan St. (bet. Andover & Endicott Sts.) | 978-531-4800 | www.pellanasteakhouse.com

Peabody people say there's "no need to travel into Boston for a fine steakhouse" thanks to this "clubby" mahogany-paneled "gem" set in a strip mall (somewhat incongruously); "pleasant, efficient" staffers are on hand to deliver the "big", "tender" beef and "great wines", but all that big-city polish comes at a price: your wallet will "hurt for days."

Pellino's *Italian*   ∇ 24 | 17 | 25 | $46
Marblehead | 261 Washington St. (bet. Atlantic Ave. & Pleasant St.) | 781-631-3344 | www.pellinos.com

"Anxious to please" staffers set the "warm" tone at this family-run Marblehead Italian whose "excellent" Tuscan menu shines with "great homemade pastas"; as for the decor, regulars "love" the recently renovated dining room (bedecked with paneling and booths backed by lattice work) as much as the new mahogany bar.

Penang *Malaysian*   21 | 18 | 17 | $27
Chinatown | 685 Washington St. (Kneeland St.) | 617-451-6373 | www.penangusa.com

"When hunger pangs call for Malaysian", hit this "crowded", "cheerful" Chinatown eatery where the "big portions" are "always fresh and delicious"; the bamboo-bedecked decor is a bit "hokey looking" and the service can go from "efficient" to "rushed", but nevertheless, "you'll feel good knowing that your wallet wasn't hijacked."

☑ Petit Robert Bistro *French*   23 | 20 | 21 | $40
Kenmore Square | 468 Commonwealth Ave. (W. Charlesgate) | 617-375-0699
South End | 480 Columbus Ave. (Rutland Sq.) | 617-867-0600
(continued)

(continued)
Petit Robert Bistro
Needham | 45 Chapel St. (Highland Ave.) | 781-559-0532 |
www.petitrobertbistro.com

Z NEW Petit Robert Central Ⓢ *French*
Downtown Crossing | 101 Arch St. (Summer St.) | 617-737-1777 |
www.petitrobertcentral.com

"Long for Paris" no more via a visit to one of these "well-known French" stops delivering "wonderful, gutsy bistro-style fare" for "reasonable prices" in "authentic", "noisy", "crowded" settings where diners are "packed in like sardines"; the staffers in particular "make you think you're in France" – they're "not overly attentive or friendly", but they're "there when you need them" (plus, many have "adorable" "accents").

P.F. Chang's China Bistro *Chinese* | 19 | 19 | 18 | $33 |
Back Bay | Prudential Ctr. | 800 Boylston St. (Fairfield St.) | 617-378-9961
Theater District | Transportation Bldg. | 8 Park Plaza (bet. Boylston & Stuart Sts.) | 617-573-0821
East Cambridge | Cambridgeside Galleria | 100 Cambridgeside Pl. (bet. 1st & 2nd Sts.) | Cambridge | 617-250-9965
Dedham | Legacy Pl. | 410 Legacy Pl. (Mt. Vernon St.) | 781-461-6060
Peabody | Northshore Mall | 210 Andover St. (Sylvan St.) | 978-326-2410
Natick | Natick Collection | 1245 Worcester St. (Speen St.) | 508-651-7724
www.pfchangs.com

"Light, delicious", "Americanized" Chinese food keeps fans "coming back" – especially for the "standout" lettuce wraps – to this "trendy", "stylish" chain; though not everyone is convinced ("overpriced", "ordinary", "loud"), the "consistent" service is a plus, as is the "smart" menu "catering to people with allergies" and other needs.

Pho Hoa *Vietnamese* | 24 | 13 | 18 | $15 |
Chinatown | 17 Beach St. (Washington St.) | 617-423-3934 |
www.phohoa.com
Dorchester | 1370 Dorchester Ave. (Kimball St.) | 617-287-9746 |
www.phohoarestaurant.com
North Quincy | 409 Hancock St. (Billings Rd.) | 617-328-9600 |
www.phohoa.com

"No frills, just good food" is what's ladled out at these separately owned sites where, unsurprisingly, "spectacular pho" is the specialty among the "traditional" "Vietnamese treats"; they're "not fancy" places and the service seems "perfunctory" (though to be fair, "fast"), but it's hard to find fault with someplace so "cheap" and "generous."

Pho Lemongrass *Vietnamese* | 20 | 15 | 19 | $23 |
Brookline | 239 Harvard St. (Webster St.) | 617-731-8600 |
www.pholemongrass.com

"Decent pho at decent prices" sums up this "welcoming", "reliable" Coolidge Corner Vietnamese whose "personal" service "attracts a steady crowd" of "regulars"; while blasé diners dismiss it as "nothing transporting" with somewhat "cheesy" decor, even they agree it's "good enough for a quick fix."

Pho n' Rice *Thai/Vietnamese*
▽ 21 | 10 | 19 | $17

Somerville | 289 Beacon St. (Sacramento St.) | 617-864-8888 |
www.phonrice.com

"What a find!" declare Somerville diners of this "little family joint"
and its "well-prepared and -presented, fresh and appealing" Thai-
Vietnamese vittles that appear on a "large menu"; the "lunch combos" are a particular "bargain", whether eating in the unassuming
space, doing "cheap takeout" or getting it delivered.

Pho Pasteur *Vietnamese*
24 | 10 | 16 | $17

Chinatown | 682 Washington St. (Beach St.) | 617-482-7467 |
www.phopasteurboston.net

Still "the standard" for "awesome pho" in Chinatown, this "grungy"
Vietnamese venue doles out dishes that are "cheap" and "huge"; the
staffers are "spotty", but give them a break – they're "run ragged at
lunchtime" and still "get you in and out" "quick", "happy and satiated."

Piattini *Italian*
24 | 18 | 22 | $33

Back Bay | 226 Newbury St. (bet. Exeter & Fairfield Sts.) | 617-536-2020 |
www.piattini.com

Small dishes that "deliver a lot of flavor" plus "great wines" are the
hallmarks of this Back Bay Italian where the "European"-feeling dining room furnished with "copper tables" is a "charming" "escape
from the rush" of the Back Bay (if a "squeeze on busy nights") and
the "sunken patio" is "lovely for watching hipsters go by"; added attractions include a "knowledgeable, caring staff" and prices that
seem "discounted" for Newbury Street.

Picante Mexican Grill *Californian/Mexican*
▽ 22 | 13 | 18 | $14

Central Square | 735 Massachusetts Ave. (bet. Inman & Prospect Sts.) |
Cambridge | 617-576-6394 | www.picantemex.com

"Come for the burritos, but stay for the salsa bar" (laden with a
"great selection" at all spice levels) at this "hole-in-the wall type
Mexican eatery" with a pronounced Californian accent in Central
Square; whether you choose to "eat in or take out" of the basic,
"self-serve" digs, it's "fast" and "inexpensive."

Picco *Dessert/Pizza*
24 | 18 | 20 | $25

South End | 513 Tremont St. (Berkeley St.) | 617-927-0066 |
www.piccorestaurant.com

"The kid in you rejoices" at this "charming" South End parlor that
makes pizzas with "terrific toppings" and "exquisite crusts", plus
"premium ice cream" that "sends you to your knees", all served
alongside "rotating microbrews" and "decent wines"; that "ideal formula" coupled with "reasonable prices" means its "always busy"
with "families" – good thing the staff works "pretty quick."

Piccola Venezia *Italian*
22 | 18 | 21 | $33

North End | 263 Hanover St. (bet. Cross & Richmond Sts.) |
617-523-3888 | www.piccolaveneziaboston.com

"Traditional" "Italian comfort food" at "reasonable" prices is the stock
in trade of this North End eatery where "large portions" are doled out

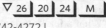

by a "friendly staff"; the "casual" dining room with exposed brick and antique bar is spacious, and therefore "great" for a "group."

Piccolo Nido 🗷 *Italian* ▽ 26 | 20 | 24 | M

North End | 257 North St. (Lewis St.) | 617-742-4272 | www.piccolonido.com

"Nothing glitzy" is found at this "charming", rustic, "off-the-beaten-path" North Ender, just "good old-fashioned Italian" dishes "made fresh" and affordable; the "feisty owner" can be a "gracious host" as he "works the room" and makes sure everything's "wonderful" – "get to know" him and "he'll make your return visits more special."

Pierrot Bistrot Français 🗷 *French* 24 | 19 | 24 | $46

Beacon Hill | 272 Cambridge St. (Anderson St.) | 617-725-8855 | www.pierrotbistrot.com

"Words fail to describe the delight" Francophiles feel at this "uncompromisingly Gallic bistro" on Beacon Hill, where "even the simplest dishes on the menu turn out well", and "without wallet-draining prices"; "the owner ensures that diners are greeted and treated very special" by the "helpful" staff, and if some folks find the setting "a bit cramped" and "creepy" (due to the "multitude" of clown images), that's "authenticity" for you.

Pigalle 🅼 *French* 26 | 23 | 25 | $55

Theater District | 75 S. Charles St. (bet. Stuart St. & Warrenton Pl.) | 617-423-4944 | www.pigalleboston.com

"Innovative touches" raise the "bistro fare" to "sublime" heights at this "high-end French experience" in the Theater District, where the wines are just as "amazing" and the "chef's menu is a real experience" (if you're not "rushing to make a curtain"); a "polished" staff works the "intimate", "lovely room", which is "not too loud", thus "perfect for a special occasion" that's "well worth" the "expensive" tabs.

Pinocchio's Pizza & Subs ⬤ *Pizza* 23 | 8 | 15 | $9

Harvard Square | 74 Winthrop St. (JFK St.) | Cambridge | 617-876-4897 | www.pinocchiospizza.net

"Fight through the crowd of students" for the "fantastic Sicilian" slices that makes this "cheap" Harvard Square pizzeria an "institution", especially late at night (until 2 AM); there are "a few tables", but with "tacky" "murals of its namesake fairy tale" and "curt service", most folks consider it "strictly a take-out place."

Pit Stop Bar-B-Q ⬤🗷🅼 *BBQ* - | - | - | I

Mattapan | 888A Morton St. (Evans St.) | 617-436-0485

"When the urge strikes", barbecue fanatics hit this "small" Mattapan shack for "really saucy" ribs and such, which are "smoked behind the counter"; just remember: there's "no decor, no service, no drinks" and four seats, so just plan to take it back to your car.

Pizzeria Regina *Pizza* 24 | 12 | 16 | $18

North End | 11½ Thacher St. (Margin St.) | 617-227-0765 ⬤
🆕🆕🆕 **Allston** | 353 Cambridge St. (Braintree St.) | 617-783-2300 ⬤
Back Bay | Prudential Ctr. | 800 Boylston St. (Ring Rd.) | 617-424-1115

(continued)

Pizzeria Regina

Leather District | South Station | Grand Concourse (Essex St.) | 617-261-6600
Faneuil Hall | Faneuil Hall Mktpl. | 226 Faneuil Hall Mktpl. (Congress St.) | 617-742-1713
Braintree | South Shore Plaza | 250 Granite St. (I-95, exit 6) | 781-848-8700
Medford | Station Landing | 44 Station Landing (Revere Beach Pkwy.) | 781-306-1222
Watertown | Arsenal Mall | 485 Arsenal St. (Elm St.) | 617-926-5300
Peabody | Northshore Mall | 210 Andover St. (Cross St.) | 978-538-9700
Burlington | Burlington Mall | 1131 Middlesex Tpke. (Rte. 128) | 781-270-4212
www.pizzeriaregina.com
Additional locations throughout the Boston area

"Hungry hordes" happily "wait" in "long lines" for this "unchanged-in-decades" Boston "original" "deep in the heart" of the North End, where the "Stradivarius of pizza ovens" infuses the "taste of heaven" into thin-crust pies that are delivered by "no-nonsense, no-warmth" waitresses; the setting may be "not too aesthetically pleasing", but "no other Regina location" (mostly in "mall food courts") "compares" – or is "worth bothering with."

Pleasant Cafe ● *American/Italian*   ∇ 21 | 11 | 20 | $19

Roslindale | 4515 Washington St. (Beech St.) | 617-323-2111 | www.pleasantcafe.com

"So old school, it's trendy", this "understated" 1937 Roslindale "classic" presents "decor that hasn't changed in years", "budget" tabs and "delightful" American and Italian eats, especially the "famous" pizza; vinyl booths and TVs surround the casual bar, which doles out "cheap beer" and pleasant vibes.

Plough & Stars *Eclectic/Pub Food*   23 | 20 | 18 | $23

Central Square | 912 Massachusetts Ave. (Hancock St.) | Cambridge | 617-576-0032 | www.ploughandstars.com

"A local favorite", this "funky, friendly" Central Square watering hole delivers a "surprisingly delicious" lineup of "dressed-up" Eclectic "bar food" along with a "great beer selection" and "terrific live music", usually blues, rock or country; despite some quibbles about cost ("reasonable" vs. "terrible value"), the "tiny" quarters are perpetually packed, especially during Sunday's "amazing" chicken and fish fry.

Poe's Kitchen at the Rattlesnake ● *Mexican*   ∇ 21 | 16 | 17 | $30

Back Bay | 384 Boylston St. (bet. Arlington & Berkeley Sts.) | 617-859-8555 | www.rattlesnakebar.com

Since chef Brian Poe took the helm of this Back Bay mainstay two years ago, most folks find "the food is actually good now", with "creative" South American–inflected Mexican eats complemented by margaritas and sangria; "lackluster" service and a "dark" interior are still sore spots, although the ample roof deck is a "huge plus" and a natural magnet for nine-to-fivers.

Polcari's *Italian* | 19 | 17 | 17 | $27 |

Woburn | 309 Montvale Ave. (bet. Central & Washington Sts.) | 781-938-1900
Saugus | 92 Broadway/Rte. 1 (Walnut St.) | 781-233-3765
www.polcaris.com

Customers "count on" these Saugus and Woburn Italians for "enormous portions" of "basic" fare at "decent prices"; though critics call the food "blah" and service "average", the memorabilia-laden digs are "family-friendly", and it's also a fallback for "takeout."

Pomodoro ₱ *Italian* | 25 | 18 | 21 | $40 |

North End | 319 Hanover St. (bet. Prince & Richmond Sts.) | 617-367-4348 | www.pomodoroboston.com
Brookline | 24 Harvard St. (Washington St.) | 617-566-4455

Though it's "only as big as a closet", fans are more than happy to "squeeze their way into" this "charming" North End eatery offering the kind of "simple, wonderful" Italian fare that makes you "feel like you're visiting a neighbor's house for dinner"; the "larger" Brookline Village sibling may be more "inviting", although both boast similarly "variable" service and a "cash-only" policy that rubs some the wrong way, especially since it's "not cheap."

Ponzu *Asian*   ∇ | 23 | 16 | 20 | $31 |

Waltham | 286 Moody St. (Gordon St.) | 781-736-9188 | www.theponzu.com

Surveyors sing the praises of this Waltham "sleeper" turning out "excellent", "varied" Asian tapas, mains and "fresh" sushi, all in "novel" presentations and for affordable prices; even if the yellow-and-lacquer setting's "nothing spectacular", service is "quick" and "friendly", so most "never tire" of it.

Pops *American* | 20 | 19 | 20 | $39 |

South End | 560 Tremont St. (Clarendon St.) | 617-695-1250 | www.popsrestaurant.net

"A neighborhood hangout", this South End eatery earns a "thumbs-up" for its "tasty", "interesting" New American comfort fare served in a "cozy" bistro-style space with white tile floors, a marble bar and a "lovely" patio; moderate prices are an added perk, although a few find service "inconsistent" and wonder if it's "lost its pop" in recent years.

Porcini's *Mediterranean* | 20 | 15 | 22 | $39 |

Watertown | 68 School St. (Arsenal St.) | 617-924-2221 | www.porcinis.com

"Regulars" rely on this Watertown mainstay for "well-priced" Med dishes set down by an "attentive", "family-friendly" staff; though the "dark", "old-school" decor is "pleasant" enough, critics call it "boring but dependable" and are left "wishing the food was just a bit edgier."

NEW Port 305 *American* | - | - | - | M |

North Quincy | Marina Bay | 305 Victory Rd. (Miwra Haul Rd.) | 617-302-4447 | www.port305marinabay.com

Though this casual waterfront American in North Quincy is still new on the scene, fans call it "exactly what Marina Bay was missing" with breezy outdoor seating plus a "fabulous" bar scene replete with TVs and DJs on Friday nights; the traditional-leaning menu is dubbed "hit-or-miss", but at least the price is right.

NEW Posto *Italian/Pizza*

25 | 24 | 24 | $30

Somerville | 187 Elm St. (Tenney St.) | 617-625-0600 | www.pizzeriaposto.com

This "delightful, little" Davis Square Italian newcomer scores well for its "fabulous" Neapolitan pies and "phenomenal" pastas and apps prepared with "sustainable ingredients" and backed by "amazing" cocktails and wines; service is "attentive", prices moderate and the "rustic", "farm-chic" environs bristle with "energy", so the only drawback is the no-reservations policy.

Post 390 *American*

20 | 25 | 20 | $42

Back Bay | 406 Stuart St. (Clarendon St.) | 617-399-0015 | www.post390restaurant.com

Eric Brennan's "high-end comfort" cuisine served by a mostly "attentive" staff draws "well-heeled" patrons to this "large, two-level" Back Bay American that's also a "perfect spot for a classy cocktail" thanks to a "lively bar"; but while the "unique" space boasts some "truly impressive" features ("multiple fireplaces", two open kitchens, black glazed columns, wood-slatted walls), critics contend "the decor promises more than the food delivers", hence the prices seem "inflated."

Prana Café, The Ⓜ *Vegan*

- | - | - | I

Newton | 292 Centre St. (Jefferson St.) | 617-527-7726 | www.eatatprana.com

"Come with an open mind" instruct acolytes of this Newton vegan purveying a midpriced menu of mostly raw fare deemed "darn tasty" to many; the spare, modern space is done up in aqua and couches, plus there's a separate kids' room with toys and bean bag chairs.

☒ Prezza *Italian*

27 | 22 | 24 | $55

North End | 24 Fleet St. (Hanover St.) | 617-227-1577 | www.prezza.com

"The place to be seen" in the North End is this "lively", "high-end" Italian that delivers "shockingly delicious" cuisine enhanced by "great wines" ("wow") and a "talented", "professional" staff; the setting's "sleek and sophisticated", but given the "expense account"–caliber tabs, many "save it for special occasions."

Publick House, The *Belgian/Pub Food*

20 | 19 | 17 | $29

Brookline | 1648 Beacon St. (Washington St.) | 617-277-2880 | www.eatgoodfooddrinkbetterbeer.com

"Don't ask for a Bud" at this Brookline tavern known for its near-"endless" array of "obscure" beers poured by a "knowledgeable" crew in "charming", "old-school" digs appointed with Colonial touches; there's also an "inspired" menu of Belgian pub grub featuring a "crave"-worthy mac 'n' cheese, though many find the mood marred by constant "crowds"; P.S. The Monk's Cell, an adjacent tap room, is quieter.

	FOOD	DECOR	SERVICE	COST

Punjab *Indian* 24 | 21 | 19 | $30

Arlington | 485 Massachusetts Ave. (Mystic St.) | 781-643-0943 | www.punjabarlington.com

"Some of the best Indian food around" turns up at this Arlington entry featuring "sophisticated", "wonderfully spiced" fare including a "chicken curry to make you lick your plate"; the "swank", "modern" setting with a full bar feels "upscale" for the genre (ditto the prices), although "uneven" service is a sore spot for some.

Punjabi Dhaba ●⇦ *Indian* 24 | 8 | 14 | $14

Inman Square | 225 Hampshire St. (Cambridge St.) | Cambridge | 617-547-8272 | www.royalbharatinc.com

If you want "absolutely fabulous" Indian food and "don't care about ambiance", try this Inman Square "hole-in-the-wall", a mainstay for "grad students and hipsters" offering "authentic", "no-frills" "street fare"; granted, it's "crowded, small" and you'll need to order from the counter, but all is forgiven for the "cheap" tabs.

Punjab Palace *Indian* 24 | 17 | 22 | $21

Allston | 109 Brighton Ave. (bet. Harvard Ave. & Linden St.) | 617-254-1500 | www.punjabpalace.com

This "inexpensive" Allston Indian specializes in "top-notch" takes on "all the classics", and they're "willing to bring the heat if you can handle it"; service is "attentive", tabs are "inexpensive" and the "simply decorated" space features "entertaining" Bollywood flicks playing on the TVs.

Purple Cactus Burrito & ▽ 19 | 13 | 17 | $12
Wrap Bar *Eclectic/Mexican*

Jamaica Plain | 674 Centre St. (Seaverns Ave.) | 617-522-7422 | www.thepurplecactus.com

For "fast" Mex in Jamaica Plain, this order-at-the-counter "wrap joint" offers a "nice selection" of burritos with an "all-natural, hippie-dippy" bent as well as "healthy, homemade" soups, salads and other Eclectic items; a bright, casual space and cheap tabs make it a "neighborhood" standby that's "frequented by many."

NEW Q Restaurant *Mongolian/Japanese* – | – | – | M

Chinatown | 660 Washington St. (bet. Beach & Essex Sts.) | 617-773-5888 | www.thequsa.com

Formerly located in Quincy, this revamped spot specializing in Mongolian hot pots and Japanese fare now resides in Chinatown, making it a convenient locale for a business lunch, pre- or post-theater dinner or late-night cocktails (the bar's open till 2 AM); the sleek setting's neutral tones and dim lighting add a Zen-like elegance, whether you're eating at the sushi bar or at a table.

☒ Radius ☒ *French* 26 | 25 | 25 | $72

Financial District | 8 High St. (bet. Federal & Summer Sts.) | 617-426-1234 | www.radiusrestaurant.com

Still a "revelation" swear fans of this Financial District "adventure" where "rock-star" chef Michael Schlow's "exceptional", "awe-inspiring" New French cuisine is set down by a "polished" staff in an "elegant" white room equally suited to "business lunches" or "long, romantic dinners"; those irked by "big bills" for "small portions" ("bring a microscope") should take heed of the "more casual" mood and menu – starring a "great burger" – at the bar.

Rami's *Mideastern*
24 | 8 | 16 | $15

Brookline | 324 Harvard St. (Babcock St.) | 617-738-3577 | www.ramisboston.com

"If Israeli-style falafel is what you crave", this kosher Brookliner does it in "snappy", "inexpensive" fashion while also offering "addictive shawarma" and other "great Middle Eastern food"; with "small" digs that are "always crowded and noisy" and just "a few tables", it's "not designed for lingering", so most get it to go.

Rani *Indian*
21 | 19 | 19 | $26

Brookline | 1353 Beacon St. (Harvard St.) | 617-734-0400 | www.ranibistro.com

"A delightful oasis of calm in the middle of Coolidge Corner", this "upscale", "sophisticated" Indian prepares a "reasonably priced" menu that fans consider "a cut above", partially due to its "wonderful" Hyderabadi specialties; the "courteous" owner can "regularly" be seen "behind the bar" as he oversees the "blazingly fast service."

Redbones BBQ *BBQ*
24 | 15 | 19 | $25

Somerville | 55 Chester St. (Elm St.) | 617-628-2200 | www.redbones.com

"Roll your sleeves up, because it is going to get messy" at this "always-packed" "hub of ribs culture" in Davis Square, where the "gut-bustingly great", "melt-off-the-bone" BBQ is "well priced" and "worth every calorie"; service is generally "pleasant" on both levels, though many folks feel the "atmosphere is better downstairs" where the decor is more "funky" and "if you can't decide" among the "ton" of beers, you can "spin a giant wheel and let the fates decide."

Red Fez ❶ *Mideastern*
18 | 19 | 19 | $33

South End | 1222 Washington St. (Perry St.) | 617-338-6060 | www.theredfez.com

Boosters of this "giant" South End "hangout" with a "Moroccan vibe" and a "terrific patio" say the "crowd is fun", the "staff is friendly" and the "traditional and creative Middle Eastern" fare is "delicious", especially the many small plates; "an extensive martini list" and live music and belly dancing on weekends all add to the "blast", which is especially "great with a group."

Red House Ⓜ *Eclectic*
21 | 21 | 21 | $40

Harvard Square | 98 Winthrop St. (bet. Eliot & JFK Sts.) | Cambridge | 617-576-0605 | www.theredhouse.com

With a "lovely patio in summer" and a variety of "cozy" interior rooms, complete with "fires blazing in the winter", this Eclectic set in a "lovingly restored house" is as "comfortable" for "dinner with friends" as it is for "romantic liaisons"; the "rustic" cuisine is "tasty and reliable", and with "fair prices" and generally "classy service" to sweeten the deal, no wonder it's so "popular" – yet surprisingly, it's "one of the quieter places in Harvard Square."

Redline ⊠ *American*   ▽ 16 | 19 | 19 | $23

Harvard Square | 59 JFK St. (bet. Eliot & Winthrop Sts.) | Cambridge | 617-491-9851 | www.redlinecambridge.com

Particularly popular among "grad students", this Harvard Square "college bar"–cum–"dance club" also "happens to serve food" of the "casual" New American variety, and it's affordable and often "better than expected" to boot; but really, it's mostly just a "place to hang out" over "great drinks", DJ-spun tunes and the occasional live act.

Red Robin *American*   16 | 15 | 17 | $18

Foxboro | Gillette Stadium | 290 Patriot Pl. (Rte. 1) | 508-698-0030 | www.redrobin.com

"A burger lover's paradise", this Foxboro outpost of the national American chain specializes in "great" patties paired with "bottom-less baskets of tempting fries" or "yummy onion rings"; "geared toward families with young children", it's a "casual, easy place" for "a quick bite" at an "alright price."

Red Rock Bistro *American*   20 | 19 | 16 | $43

Swampscott | 141 Humphrey St./Rte. 129 (Redington St.) | 781-595-1414 | www.redrockbistro.com

The "awesome view" of the ocean and the Boston skyline is "the best part" of this Swampscott New American whose seafood-centric menu is "generally quite good", while the cocktail and wine selection is "extensive"; though service swings from "great" to "could be better" to downright "snotty", and both food and drink "may be a little too pricey", the "chic atmosphere" makes it "worth a visit", especially for brunch or a "sunset dinner."

NEW Regal Beagle, The *American*   21 | 19 | 21 | $32

Brookline | 308 Harvard St. (Babcock St.) | 617-739-5151 | www.thebeaglebrookline.com

"Even the most mundane things" seem "exciting and new" at this "welcome addition to the Brookline scene", where "creative cocktails add to the fun" of a New American comfort menu that "changes seasonally"; though a few aesthetes find the space "a little awkward" (i.e. "dark and narrow"), others call it "comfortable, cozy" and delightfully "quirky", with a fittingly "friendly staff."

⊡ Rendezvous *Mediterranean*   26 | 20 | 25 | $47

Central Square | 502 Massachusetts Ave. (Brookline St.) | Cambridge | 617-576-1900 | www.rendezvouscentralsquare.com

"Hands-on chef-owner" Steve Johnson "even grows things on the roof" of this "innovative", "ingredient-driven", seasonal Mediterranean endeavor in Central Square, making it a veritable "locavore heaven"; "housed in a former Burger King", the now "quietly modern" setting is enlivened by an "active bar", the source of "great cocktails", and "friendly" staffers who deliver what most calculate as relatively "modest bills."

⚡ Rialto *Italian* 26 | 25 | 26 | $68

Harvard Square | Charles Hotel | 1 Bennett St. (Eliot St.) | Cambridge |
617-661-5050 | www.rialto-restaurant.com

"Whimsical interpretations" of Italian cuisine spotlighting seasonal
"New England ingredients" are turned out with "elegance and flair"
at "wonderful chef" Jody Adams' "solid performer" in Harvard
Square; though a few diners admit to being "overwhelmed" by
the cost, especially when considering the sometimes "skimpy
portions", the prices do befit the "swanky", "romantic" digs
and "professional" servers.

Rincon Limeno *Peruvian* - | - | - | I

East Boston | 409 Chelsea St. (Shelby St.) | 617-569-4942 |
www.rinconlimenorestaurant.com

"Authentic-to-the-core Peruvian food" featuring "the most generous ceviche portions north of Lima" are sold for inexpensive fees at
this small, informal East Bostonian run by an "accessible" owner
who's "willing to explain the menu" to newbies; offal-lovers relish
that "you can actually order beef heart here", but rest assured,
vegetarians have "plenty of options" too.

Rino's Place ⑤ *Italian* ▽ 29 | 13 | 23 | $31

East Boston | 258 Saratoga St. (Putnam St.) | 617-567-7412 |
www.rinosplace.com

"Unbelievable ravioli" is the signature among the "fantastic", "imaginative" Italian dishes doled out at this East Boston "foodie secret"
where the servers "welcome" you "like old friends, even if you've
never been there"; since it's "small" (some say "uncomfortable"
too), it can be "difficult to obtain a table", so "go early or late" or be
prepared to "wait" – It's "worth" It, not least of all because it "won't
break the bank."

Ristorante Damiano ● *Italian* ▽ 26 | 20 | 24 | $36

North End | 307 Hanover St. (bet. Prince & Richmond Sts.) |
617-742-0020 | www.ristorantedamiano.com

"Superlative" Italian small plates pair with "spot-on wines" at this
North Ender with "high ceilings", exposed brick, an open kitchen,
windows that open onto Hanover Street and service that's "attentive
without being intrusive"; prices are generally "fair", but given
the "*piattini* concept", if you're "hungry", expect to really "run
up the bill."

Ristorante Fiore *Italian* 21 | 19 | 21 | $40

North End | 250 Hanover St. (bet. Cross & Parmenter Sts.) |
617-371-1176 | www.ristorantefiore.com

"If it's summer, ask for the roof deck" or the "little patio" at this
"pleasant" North End "red-sauce" Italian "mainstay", as some find
the interior a little too "cozy" (and subsequently, the noise level too
"high"); wherever they sit, everyone leaves "stuffed, satisfied", in-
toxicated by the "fairly extensive" wines and appreciative of the
"knowledgeable, friendly staff that makes you feel like you're part
of the *famiglia*."

Ristorante Pavarotti *Italian*   `- | - | - | M`

Reading | 601 Main St./Rte. 28 (Haven St.) | 781-670-9050 |
www.ristorantepavarotti.com

Reading locals cite this "small" Italian's "adorable", "inviting" dining
room, featuring tiled floors, soft lighting, white linens and windows
overlooking the town center; they also say the native Calabrian
chef's midpriced cuisine is "very good", which, along with service
that makes everyone feel "comfortable", makes it "worth a try" if
you're in the area.

Ristorante Villa Francesca *Italian*   `▽ 23 | 23 | 22 | $40`

North End | 150 Richmond St. (Hanover St.) | 617-367-2948 |
www.ristorantevillafrancesca.com

"Everything's made to order" at this "classic" Italian, a longtime
"solid performer" in the North End; the "quaint" dining room features tin ceilings, windows that open onto the street and tables that
some say are "a little too close", the last of which matters not since
the prices are "reasonable for what you get."

Riva *Italian*   `▽ 26 | 20 | 23 | $38`

Scituate | 116 Front St. (Otis Pl.) | 781-545-5881 | www.rivarestaurant.net

"Foodies and kids" alike like the "excellent" Italian menu with an
"emphasis on seafood" and "local vegetables" at this "intimate" harborside trattoria in Scituate; "hearty portions", not to mention
"friendly service", further make it "worth the price" – and it's not even
expensive; P.S. in the warmer months, try for the "comfortable" patio.

River Gods *Eclectic*   `22 | 23 | 18 | $23`

Central Square | 125 River St. (Central Sq.) | Cambridge |
617-576-1881 | www.rivergodsonline.com

"More bar than restaurant", this "funky, little" spot in Central Square
works the "Gothic" angle with church-pew seating, gargoyle fixtures
and granite angels throughout; the Eclectic, booze-friendly menu is
"well done", well priced and features "lots of options for vegetarians
and meat eaters alike", while frequent DJs are an added perk.

Robinwood *American*   `- | - | - | I`

Jamaica Plain | 536 Centre St. (Robinwood Ave.) | 617-524-7575 |
www.robinwoodcafegrille.com

Neighborhood types tout this "budget"-friendly arrival in Jamaica
Plain where a "likable" staff churns out "filling", "diner-style"
American eats (all-day breakfasts); though "big portions" and an
"old-fashioned" vibe are certainly appealing, the eating's a tad too
"ordinary" for some.

Rod Dee ⊄ *Thai*   `24 | 9 | 15 | $14`

NEW **Porter Square** | 1906 Massachusetts Ave. (Somerville Ave.) |
Cambridge | 617-374-9252
Brookline | 1671 Beacon St. (Winthrop Rd.) | 617-738-1455
www.roddee.net

For "tasty" Thai at "rock-bottom" prices, try this cash-only canteen
in Brookline dispensing "authentic, flavorful" fare in "unbelievable"

portions; the food comes out "fast", but with only a few tables and "minimal ambiance and comfort" (and no alcohol), "takeout" is recommended; P.S. the Porter Square branch is new.

Ronnarong Thai Tapas Bar 🗷 *Thai* ▽ 22 | 19 | 20 | $25

Somerville | 255 Washington St. (bet. Bonner Ave. & Sanborn Ct.) | 617-625-9296 | www.ronnarongthai.com

Thai cooking "with flair" distinguishes this "cute, little" Union Square eatery turning out "creative" tapas-style plates and mains plus "cool cocktails"; adding to the allure are modest prices, "helpful" service from a "hipster" staff and a "cozy" setting decked out with lotus-shaped light fixtures.

Roobar Ⓜ *American* 19 | 17 | 16 | $37

Plymouth | Cordage Park | 10 Cordage Park Circle (Court St.) | 508-746-4300 | www.theroobar.com

See review in Cape Cod Directory.

Rosebud Diner *Diner* 15 | 17 | 16 | $16

Somerville | 381 Summer St. (bet. Cutter Ave. & Grove St.) | 617-666-6015 | www.rosebuddiner.com

"A classic old-time diner", this Davis Square mainstay housed in a vintage dining car slings "typical" "greasy-spoon" fare, notably the all-day breakfasts and Bloody Marys with a "heavy pour"; "cheap" tabs and "fast" (and occasionally "hilarious") service from a longtime staff increase its appeal.

Rowes Wharf Sea Grille *Seafood* 23 | 25 | 24 | $62

Waterfront | Boston Harbor Hotel | 70 Rowes Wharf (Atlantic Ave.) | 617-856-7744 | www.roweswharfseagrille.com

"Gorgeous harbor views" form the backdrop for this "pricey" respite in the Waterfront's Boston Harbor Hotel that's "especially nice in the summer if you can nab an outside table"; factor in "expertly prepared" seafood, service that's "beyond reproach" and a "beautiful" nautically inspired room, and for most it's "a pleasure to dine here"; P.S. afternoon tea is also popular.

Royal East *Chinese* 23 | 15 | 20 | $23

Central Square | 782-792 Main St. (Windsor St.) | Cambridge | 617-661-1660 | www.royaleast.com

"Ask the owner for recommendations" and you can't go wrong at this "popular" Chinese in Central Square, a "dependable" bet for cooking that's "a cut above" the competition; "inexpensive" prices, share-worthy portions and a "roomy" (if plain) space make it ideal for groups.

Rubin's *Deli* 19 | 9 | 15 | $23

Brookline | 500 Harvard St. (Kenwood St.) | 617-731-8787 | www.rubinskosher.com

One of "the only places to get a tongue sandwich" in Brookline is this circa-1928 all-day kosher deli known for its "real-deal" "stuff-your-belly" Jewish noshes; despite complaints that it's "tired", "run-down" and "pricey" to boot ("oy vey"), most leave "happy" nonetheless.

	FOOD	DECOR	SERVICE	COST

RumBa ● *Eclectic* ▽ 19 | 24 | 21 | $43

Waterfront | InterContinental Boston | 510 Atlantic Ave.
(bet. Congress St. & Seaport Blvd.) | 617-747-1000 |
www.intercontinentalboston.com

An "unparalleled rum selection" is the lure at this "super-swank"
lobby bar in the InterContinental Hotel on the Waterfront attracting
a "lively" crowd for "finely made" drinks and snacky Eclectic eats;
the cushy decor evoking an island estate incorporates leather club
chairs and Louis Vuitton trunks, so it's probably no surprise that
it's "pricey" too.

NEW Russell House Tavern ● *American* 21 | 22 | 19 | $36

Harvard Square | 14 JFK St. (bet. Brattle & Mt. Auburn Sts.) |
Cambridge | 617-500-3055 | www.russellhousecambridge.com

"A welcome addition to Harvard Square", this "warm", "well-
appointed" New American gastropub features "inventive",
"well-executed" fare – from oysters and housemade charcuterie to
short ribs Wellington – abetted by an "impressive beer and cocktail
list"; the clientele, mostly "free of students", appreciates the
moderate prices and "cozy" vibe, although service "missteps"
can occasionally detract.

Rustic Kitchen *Italian* 20 | 21 | 20 | $38

Theater District | Radisson Hotel Boston | 210 Stuart St. (bet. Arlington &
Charles Sts.) | 617-423-5700
Hingham | Derby Street Shoppes | 94 Derby St. (Cushing St.) |
781-749-2700
www.rustickitchen.biz

"Homey" sums up this Hingham and Theater District Italian duo, a
"reliable" bet for "huge portions" of "homemade pastas" and pizzas in
a "relaxed", "unpretentious" atmosphere; despite some quibbles
about "inconsistent" execution, service is "prompt" "before a show",
and those with more time tout the Hingham branch's "nice patio."

☒ Ruth's Chris Steak House *Steak* 26 | 24 | 24 | $64

Downtown Crossing | Old City Hall | 45 School St. (Province St.) |
617-742-8401 | www.ruthschris.com

Loyalists "love the sizzling platters" of "oh-so-good buttery
steaks" and "winning" sides at this "top-quality" chophouse
chain link in Downtown Crossing's Old City Hall; delivering "old-
style service" in a "traditional" setting, it's "expensive" (and "not
for the dieter"), but "utterly reliable", especially when you're "entertaining friends and clients."

Sabur *Mediterranean* 23 | 22 | 21 | $34

Somerville | 212 Holland St. (bet. Claremon & Moore Sts.) |
617-776-7890 | www.saburrestaurant.com

"A neighborhood gem", this "unique" spot in Somerville's Teele
Square purveys "exotic", "delicious" fare "from a variety of
Mediterranean lands", the Balkans, Greece and North Africa among
them; prices are "affordable", and the "atmospheric" setting draped
with handmade textiles is particularly "cozy" "when the fire's going."

NEW Sake Japanese Restaurant *Japanese* — — — M

Braintree | 910 Washington St. (Holbrook Ave.) | 781-849-1900 |
www.sakesushibraintree.com

At this intimate Japanese arrival in Braintree, servers dressed in
kimonos deliver a midpriced menu of sushi, sashimi, tempura and
teriyaki (though you'll have to bring your own sake, as there's no
liquor license); the minimal setting features tile floors and sparsely
decorated yellow walls, and seating options include tables in the
dining room and an eight-seat sushi bar where you can watch the
chefs at work.

Sakurabana 🖪 *Japanese* 22 | 13 | 19 | $32

Financial District | 57 Broad St. (Milk St.) | 617-542-4311 |
www.sakurabanaonline.com

Financial District diners tout this "traditional", "reliable" Japanese
as a "great place to go for a lunch meeting" with an "extensive selection" of "quick", "fairly priced" sushi and sashimi; despite the "total
lack" of decor, it's "always crowded", "so go early" or risk getting
seated in "the dungeon" (aka the basement); P.S. things are less
frenetic at dinnertime.

Z Salts 🖪🖪 *American/French* 27 | 23 | 26 | $61

Central Square | 798 Main St. (bet. Cherry & Windsor Sts.) |
Cambridge | 617-876-8444 | www.saltsrestaurant.com

"To-die-for duck for two" is the signature dish at this "sophisticated", "intimate" Central Square spot, but everything on the
French–New American menu is "innovative" and "exquisitely prepared" (the chef "sources local ingredients", some of which come
from the restaurant's "own farm"); it's "expensive" to be sure, but
"worth every penny", not least of all for the "impeccable" service
and "classy decor."

Salvatore's *Italian* 21 | 18 | 18 | $34

Seaport District | 225 Northern Ave. (D St.) | 617-737-5454 ◐
NEW Medford | 55 High St. (Governors Ave.) | 781-393-9333
NEW Lawrence | 354 Merrimack St. (Blue Star Memorial Hwy.) |
978-291-0220
www.salvatoresrestaurants.com

"Humongous portions" ensure "you won't leave hungry" from
this "casual" Italian with a "varied" menu of "great pizzas" and
"fresh pastas", plus "modern" decor, "polite, prompt service"
and a "friendly, comfortable bar"; sure, it's "not a destination",
but it's "handy if you're in the Seaport District", especially since
the tabs are "quite reasonable"; P.S. the Lawrence and Medford
branches weren't surveyed.

NEW Sam's *American/French* 20 | 24 | 21 | $43

Seaport District | 60 Northern Ave., 2nd fl. (Courthouse Way) |
617-295-0191 | www.samsatlouis.com

"Sublime" second-floor views of Boston Harbor from the "attractive" dining room's "floor-to-ceiling windows" and the "great patio"
are the lures at this American-French addition to the Seaport

District; while disenchanted diners say the setting's "potential" "hasn't been realized yet" in the food, the majority commends the "delicious" bistro dishes, "none of which are terribly expensive"; BTW, shout-outs go to the "terrific", "generous" cocktails.

Sandrine's *French*   24 | 22 | 23 | $49

Harvard Square | 8 Holyoke St. (bet. Mass. Ave. & Mt. Auburn St.) | Cambridge | 617-497-5300 | www.sandrines.com

An "Alsatian emphasis" sets this "formal" yet "comfortable" Harvard Square French bistro apart, as does its mix of "filling and excellent" dishes, "some traditional, some more nouvelle" and all delivered by "professional" staffers who prove to be especially "helpful" with matches from the "nice wine list"; while tabs can be "a bit pricey" at dinner, the lunch fees are "low enough for a splurging college student."

S&S *Deli*   19 | 13 | 17 | $21

Inman Square | 1334 Cambridge St. (bet. Hampshire & Prospect Sts.) | Cambridge | 617-354-0777 | www.sandsrestaurant.com

"Nothing's changed in years" at this circa-1919 Inman Square "fixture" famed for its "vast", midpriced menu of all-day deli "standards" and "classic" Sunday brunch; most overlook the "shabby", "hectic" digs and occasionally "grouchy" service because that's "all part of the charm."

Santarpio's Pizza *Pizza*   25 | 8 | 14 | $18

East Boston | 111 Chelsea St. (bet. Paris Pl. & Porter St.) | 617-567-9871 ●≢

NEW Peabody | 71 Newbury St. (Dearborn Rd.) | 978-535-1811 www.santarpiospizza.com

"After landing at Logan", pie partisans "have to stop" at this "been-around-forever" "grimy" East Boston "dive" that "never fails to amaze" with its "revelatory" thin-crust pizza, not to mention the "heavenly" lamb and sausage; "arrogant" servers have to be tolerated, but if you "become a 'regla'", you might more generously call them "charmingly terrible" – either way "can you go wrong with the price?"; P.S. the much roomier Peabody branch was not surveyed.

Saporito's Ⓜ *Italian*   ▽ 28 | 19 | 27 | $41

Hull | 11 Rockland Circle (George Washington Blvd.) | 781-925-3023 | www.saporitoscafe.com

In "what looks like a ramshackle, abandoned house by the bay" in Hull, "magic is created" in the form of "high-quality" Northern Italian dishes, which are "beautifully presented" by a "friendly and knowledgeable staff"; like the exterior, the "intimate" interior is "not fancy" with "somewhat uncomfortable seating" (take care not to "slide off" the wooden booth benches), but still, for a "memorable night", it "never disappoints."

Sapporo *Japanese/Korean*   – | – | – | M

Newton | 81 Union St., downstairs (Beacon St.) | 617-964-8044

"Vast", "varied" choices aplenty draw "lots of regulars" to this "affordable" Newton Center den delivering "delicious" Korean and sushi standards via "friendly" staffers who also serve sake and Asian beers; no one's really bothered by the basement setting since they feel "always welcome", while in summer, there's some outdoor seating for fresh-air seekers.

Saraceno *Italian*   24 | 19 | 23 | $46

North End | 286 Hanover St. (bet. Parmenter & Prince Sts.) | 617-227-5353 | www.saracenos.com

"Each little dining room has its own charm" at this "real Italian treat" in the North End, from the "romantic basement" to the ground floor where there's "a view of the action on the street" to the glassed-in rooftop, and the "locals make it so colorful" too; wherever you take your "flavorful" "red-gravy" meal, you can count on "fair prices" and "warm" staffers to "make you feel special."

Sauciety *American*   - | - | - | E

Seaport District | Westin Boston Waterfront Hotel | 425 Summer St. (D St.) | 617-532-4670 | www.sauciety.com

Dark woods and earth tones dominate the dining room at this New American in the Seaport District's Westin Boston Waterfront, whose "cute" "concept" involves pairing each course with an assortment of sauces; but it "falls a little flat" for some (the sauces could "be better"), and on top of that, it's "overpriced" for serving "too small portions."

Scampo *Italian*   25 | 24 | 24 | $57

Beacon Hill | Liberty Hotel | 215 Charles St. (Cambridge St.) | 617-536-2100 | www.scampoboston.com

It's "quite the scene" at this "cutting-edge" Italian in Beacon Hill's Liberty Hotel, where "amazing talent" Lydia Shire showcases a "delicious", "wildly eclectic" menu in a "bustling", "historic", "former-jail" setting; on the downside, the acoustics are "unbelievably noisy" and the prices are "expensive", P.S. "don't miss the mozzarella bar."

Scarlet Oak Tavern *Steak*   21 | 24 | 22 | $42

Hingham | 1217 Main St. (Whiting St.) | 781-749-8200 | www.scarletoaktavern.com

Regulars rely on this "lovely tavern" in Hingham, an "updated" "farmhouse" known for its bustling bar with a fireplace that's "cozy on a cold winter's day"; perhaps the steakhouse fare "won't wow you", but it's "solid" enough, and a "gracious" staff keeps the overall mood "convivial."

Scollay Square *American*   19 | 17 | 21 | $37

Beacon Hill | 21 Beacon St. (Bowdoin St.) | 617-742-4900 | www.scollaysquare.com

The "strong drinks" and plenty of beers make it "all the better for legislating" at this politico favorite in the heart of Beacon Hill, where "upscale" American pub grub is served in a lofty space loaded with Boston memorabilia; it's "convenient and quick" if you're looking to get in and out, although lingering on the "great patio" is also appealing in warm weather.

| | FOOD | DECOR | SERVICE | COST |

Scoozi *Italian*

17 | 15 | 18 | $25

Back Bay | 235 Newbury St. (Fairfield St.) | 617-247-8847
NEW Fenway | 580 Commonwealth Ave. (Beacon St.) | 617-536-7777
www.scooziboston.com

"Tasty panini, salads" and pizzas sold at "reasonable" prices define these casual Italians, a Back Bay branch that boasts a "great" "people-watching" patio and an offshoot on the BU campus, a "great place to dine" before a game at nearby Fenway or to "relax after exams."

Scutra ⓩ *Eclectic*

25 | 23 | 24 | $42

Arlington | 92 Summer St. (Mill St.) | 781-316-1816 |
www.scutra.com

Locals feel "lucky to have" this "unlikely" Arlington "gem" in their neck of the woods, thanks to its "wonderful", moderately priced Eclectic dishes and "good wines"; a husband-and-wife team oversees the "accommodating" service and "warm" ambiance, so despite its somewhat "out-of-the-way" locale, most will "definitely go back."

Second
Street Café ⓩ🍽 *American/Sandwiches*

▽ 23 | 11 | 17 | $14

East Cambridge | 89 Second St. (bet. Hurley & Spring Sts.) | Cambridge | 617-661-1311 | www.2ndstcafe.com

"An easygoing vibe" pervades this "cute" East Cambridge American breakfast-and-lunch cafe where "really good sandwiches" and such are served by "friendly" staffers amid vintage soda-shop barstools, ice-cream parlor chairs and an old wooden counter; a Monday–Friday schedule makes it a "big fave with the courthouse crowd", while locals "wish it were open on weekends."

Seiyo *Japanese*

▽ 22 | 21 | 23 | $38

South End | 1721C Washington St. (Mass. Ave.) | 617-447-2183 |
www.seiyoboston.com

"Perfectly positioned between cheap takeout and the ridiculously expensive sushi places", this South End Japanese rolls "high-quality" maki in "simple" industrial-chic digs overseen by "friendly, helpful" staffers; indeed, it's "amazing" considering the "not-unreasonable prices", and the availability of "some unique and affordable wines" in the "cute" "attached shop makes it even better."

ⓩ Sel de la Terre *French*

23 | 21 | 22 | $45

Back Bay | 774 Boylston St. (Fairfield St.) | 617-266-8800
Waterfront | 255 State St. (Atlantic Ave.) | 617-720-1300
Natick | Natick Collection | 1245 Worcester St. (Speen St.) |
508-650-1800
www.seldelaterre.com

"Owned by the L'Espalier folks", these "lovely" spots serve up "profoundly flavored, classic" Provençal bistro cuisine in settings displaying varying degrees of "modern" and "French cottage", all with on-site bakeries – hence, "the bread basket alone is worth the visit"; the "warm staff" offers "excellent advice on wine pairings" from the "fantastic", "affordable" list, but as for the food tabs, surveyors split on whether they're a "good value" or "overpriced."

Serafina Ristorante *Italian*   ▽ 16 | 17 | 18 | $43

Concord | 195 Sudbury Rd. (Thoreau St.) | 978-371-9050 |
www.serafinaristorante.com

"Large groups of regulars at the bar" and tables fill this "pleasant"-
looking Concord Northern Italian, and while some of them find the fare
"very good", others deem it "expensive" for being merely "mediocre";
no matter, it remains an "'in' place" judging by the "noisy" scene.

75 Chestnut *American*   21 | 21 | 22 | $37

Beacon Hill | 75 Chestnut St. (bet. Brimmer & River Sts.) | 617-227-2175 |
www.75chestnut.com

"Everyone gets treated like a local" at this "quintessential Beacon
Hill restaurant" whipping up "reliable", "yummy" American comfort
food in "warm", "cozy" digs that make for a "romantic first date"
(that is, when the "charming bar" isn't too "noisy"); best of all,
"when the bill arrives, you feel like you've gotten an incredible
value", especially during the "scrumptious" Sunday brunch, which
features "relaxing" live jazz September–June.

Shabu-Zen *Japanese*   23 | 16 | 19 | $24

Allston | 80 Brighton Ave. (Reedsdale St.) | 617-782-8888
Chinatown | 16 Tyler St. (bet. Beach & Kneeland Sts.) | 617-292-8828
www.shabuzen.com

"Entertaining" to cook and "lots of fun to eat" assure acolytes of this
Chinatown spot and its sibling offering "do-it-yourself", "healthy"
shabu-shabu hot-pot meals comprising "tasty broths", "delicious
vegetables and thinly sliced meats"; the Allston branch is "enormous", but both are "comfortable" "for groups" (and abet ice-
breaking for "first dates"), with "adequate service" and prices that
are "pretty unbelievable for what you get."

Shanghai Gate *Chinese*   21 | 13 | 15 | $21

Allston | 204 Harvard Ave. (Commonwealth Ave.) | 617-566-7344
A "plethora of Shanghainese delights" awaits at this "different-
from-the-usual" Allston storefront doling out "big portions" that
seem even more "generous for the price"; sure, sometimes "it's hard
to enjoy a meal when the staff is mean to you", but thick-skinned
types just ignore the "rude"-ness (and the "nothing-much decor")
and concentrate on the "authentic" eats.

Shangri-La Ⓜ *Taiwanese*   23 | 8 | 15 | $21

Belmont | 149 Belmont St. (Grove St.) | 617-489-1488
Taiwanese dim sum is served in a "brusque" manner by "people who
couldn't care less" at this "tiny" Belmont storefront; nevertheless, it's
"lively and often crowded" (you may have to "wait on weekends")
because the bites are "expertly prepared" and "reasonably priced."

Shanti: Taste of India *Indian*   ▽ 28 | 22 | 26 | $27

Dorchester | 1111 Dorchester Ave. (Savin Hill Ave.) | 617-929-3900 |
www.shantiboston.com

"Likely overlooked" because of its "unassuming location" on Dot
Ave., this "hidden gem" is praised for Indian fare of "stunning quality

and value" on a menu where all the "typical specialties are represented" along with a "rotating out-of-the-ordinary dish or two"; "lovely, personal service" and "reasonable prices" seal the deal.

Shawarma King ⊄ Lebanese | 21 | 6 | 17 | $14 |

Brookline | 1383 Beacon St. (bet. Park & Winchester Sts.) | 617-731-6035 | www.thebestshawarmaking.com

"Fantastic" shawarma, kebabs, hummus and other "great" Lebanese fare – and "lots of it"– are doled out for "cheap" at this small "Brookline old-timer"; both service and the "cramped" setting are "less than to be desired", but take-out service is "efficient", so get it to go.

Shea's Riverside New England (fka Tom Shea's) | 19 | 19 | 21 | $39 |

Essex | 122 Main St./Rte. 133 (Rte. 22) | 978-768-6931 | www.sheasriversideessex.com

Formerly Tom Shea's, this New England eatery has new owners and a "great" interior renovation that added a bar where "fun" 'tenders "make a mean cocktail"; what remains is the "romantic", "beautiful" views of the Essex River, especially from the patio, and while the menu is roundly "well prepared, delicious" and "worth the price", regulars advise "it'd be a shame to order anything other than fish."

Sherborn Inn, The New England | 19 | 19 | 19 | $40 |

Sherborn | The Sherborn Inn | 33 N. Main St./Rte. 16 (Rte. 27) | 508-655-9521 | www.sherborninn.com

Boasting a "lovely" "country atmosphere" in both the "classy" dining room and a "comfortable tavern" with a fireplace and "local buzz", this eatery in the restored 19th-century Sherborn Inn offers "tasty" "traditional" New England eats that are "priced right" in light of the "good portions"; though the vibe is "informal", it can seem quite "romantic" too, especially on Thursday evenings when there's live jazz.

Shogun ▥ Japanese | ▽ 20 | 13 | 16 | $30 |

Newton | 1385 Washington St. (Elm St.) | 617-965-6699 | www.shogunwestnewton.com

Though the sushi served at this "little storefront" in Newton is "fairly standard", it's "fresh" and "consistent"; on the downside, the "cramped" setting "could benefit from a remodel" and the staff is "sparse" and "slow" – still, many locals "never hesitate" to go, probably because it's so "reasonably priced."

Sibling Rivalry American | 23 | 22 | 22 | $54 |

South End | 525 Tremont St. (Berkeley St.) | 617-338-5338 | www.siblingrivalryboston.com

It's a "family affair" at this "elegant, sophisticated" South End New American where brothers David and Bob Kinkead put forward "dueling menus" "offering two versions of the same main ingredients" – and though there are complaints of "inconsistencies", most palates deem the "pricey" dishes "amazing"; overall the "cool concept" is "lots of fun", even if only for "great drinks" and "nibbles" at the "beautiful bar", and especially on the "pleasant" patio come summer.

	FOOD	DECOR	SERVICE	COST

Sichuan Garden *Chinese* | 23 | 16 | 17 | $26 |

Brookline | 295 Washington St. (Harvard St.) | 617-734-1870
Woburn | 2 Alfred St. (Rte. 95) | 781-935-8488
www.sichuangarden2.com

You "don't have to travel across the globe" for "authentic Sichuan food" because this twosome offers "vibrant" variations on a "mile-long menu" filled with "spicy" dishes "you've probably never heard of"; the Woburn locale boasts a "charming" setting in an "old mansion", the Brookline location "needs a face-lift", while both are "not expensive."

Sichuan Gourmet *Chinese* | 25 | 13 | 19 | $24 |

NEW Brookline | 1004 Beacon St. (bet. Carlton & St. Mary's Sts.) | 617-277-4227
Billerica | 502 Boston Rd. (bet. Concord & Tower Farm Rds.) | 978-670-7339
Framingham | 271 Worcester Rd./Rte. 9 (bet. Ordway & Pierce Sts.) | 508-626-0248
www.laosichuan.com

If you're game for "authentic" Chinese dishes that "take no prisoners when it comes to spicy", "stick to the Sichuan specialties" says the "cult following" of this "inexpensive" Sino trio; few mind that "the decor is nothing to write home about", as is evidenced by the "always packed" digs where "frantic" staffers deliver "lightning-fast service."

Sidney's Grille *American* | ▽ 21 | 19 | 22 | $36 |

Central Square | Le Meridien Hotel | 20 Sidney St. (Green St.) | Cambridge | 617-577-0200 | www.sidneysgrille.com

"Good, reliable food" is served in all-you-can-eat breakfast buffets and à la carte lunches and dinners at this midpriced Central Square New American in the Le Meridian Hotel; equally pleasing is the decor, with beech wood and abstract lighting fixtures that extend through the sprawling, high-ceilinged space onto a balcony.

Silvertone Bar & Grill 🅂 *American* | 21 | 17 | 19 | $26 |

Downtown Crossing | 69 Bromfield St. (Tremont St.) | 617-338-7887 | www.silvertonedowntown.com

"Comfort food" in a "comforting atmosphere" sums up this "dim", basement-set Downtown Crossing American tavern and grill where "fun" and "friendly bartenders" offer "great cocktails" and beers to wash down the "filling" grub; it's "almost always crowded", which is hardly surprising considering that "it won't cost you a mint."

NEW Simple Truth *American* | - | - | - | M |

Harvard Square | Hotel Veritas | 1 Remington St. (bet. Harvard St. & Mass. Ave.) | Cambridge | 617-520-5000 | www.thehotelveritas.com

This intimate lobby lounge in Harvard Square's boutique Hotel Veritas offers two sleek, curvaceous sofas in addition to a small complement of chairs inside, plus a quartet of patio tables outside; as for the sips and snacks, 'local' is the name of the game, with moderately priced New England brews and craft spirits from Berkshire Mountain Distillers, plus American charcuterie and cheese plates spotlighting provender from regional farms and dairies.

	FOOD	DECOR	SERVICE	COST

Singh's Café *Indian*
▽ 22 | 17 | 21 | $29

Wellesley Hills | 312 Washington St. (Maugus Ave.) | 781-235-1666 | www.singhscafe.com

"Homesick" Indians say they're satisfied with the "solid" subcontinental fare that's dished out by a "friendly, efficient" staff at this "quiet" Wellesley Hills eatery where "not the same dishes you see at every other buffet" draw adventure-seekers at lunchtime; "the decor and layout are weird" to some, but a full bar, "fast" service and "reasonable prices" compensate for any shortcomings.

Siros *Italian*
20 | 19 | 20 | $44

North Quincy | Marina Bay | 307 Victory Rd. (Marina Dr.) | 617-472-4500 | www.sirosrestaurants.com

"Summertime and the living is breezy" sing surveyors about this Italian with "nice outdoor seating" overlooking Quincy's Marina Bay; it's somewhat "pricey", but "consistent execution" means the "quality" fare "never disappoints", plus "the service is friendly" too.

606 Congress *American*
20 | 21 | 21 | $45

Seaport District | Renaissance Boston Waterfront Hotel | 606 Congress St. (D St.) | 617-476-5606 | www.606congress.com

Many a guest of the Renaissance Boston Waterfront Hotel tout its main eatery's "refined", "minimalist decor", "helpful" service, "fine" New American fare and "creative" drinks; detractors dis it as "overpriced for the quality", but if nothing else, it's a "perfectly serviceable" "place to bring clients" when in the Seaport District.

62 Restaurant & Wine Bar Ⓜ *Italian*
25 | 22 | 23 | $43

Salem | 62 Wharf St. (Derby St.) | 978-744-0062 | www.62restaurant.com

"All of your senses will be pleased" at this "modern Italian" in Salem, where the "inventively prepared" fare is as "beautiful" as it is "delicious", the "housemade pastas are a standout" and the "intimate" location on Pickering Wharf is "unique"; what's more, there's a friendly and knowledgeable" staff, plus "wonderful wines" and drinks, all of which helps justify the "high cost."

Skellig, The *Pub Food*
▽ 17 | 16 | 17 | $19

Waltham | 240 Moody St. (Pine St.) | 781-647-0679 | www.theskellig.com

An "all-around good pub", this Waltham Emerald Isle establishment "feels authentic" with "dark" bar decor, "great" grub, proper pints and a selection of bottled beers; when "sports on TV" isn't being ogled, there's live music spanning traditional Irish to rock – for which the aurally sensitive advise "bring your earplugs."

Skipjack's *Seafood*
20 | 17 | 20 | $39

Back Bay | 199 Clarendon St. (bet. Boylston St. & St. James Ave.) | 617-536-3500

Newton | 55 Needham St. (Rte. 128) | 617-964-4244

Foxboro | Patriot Pl. | 226 Patriot Pl. (Washington St.) | 508-543-2200 www.skipjacks.com

"Known as the 'other'" "corporate-seafood" purveyor, this trio "competes well" with "satisfying", "dependable" "fresh" fish, including "many interesting preparations" (like "excellent" bento boxes), at prices that quite a few numbers-crunchers feel are a "better value"; "informal settings" speak to its "family-friendly" reputation, which is shored up with "knowledgeable" service that "hustles", plus "comfortable" vibes.

Sky American
16 | 19 | 17 | $39

Norwood | 1369 Providence Hwy. (Sumner St.) | 781-255-8888 | www.sky-restaurant.com

Boosters of this Norwood New American tout "creative" fare that's "consistently good" and ferried by "wonderful" staffers amid "beautiful" upscale contemporary decor; however, critics wave it off as "trying to be something it isn't" due to "ok", "overpriced" dishes – at least there's a "great wine list" to mitigate their "disappointment."

Smith & Wollensky Steak
22 | 22 | 22 | $64

Back Bay | The Castle at Park Sq. | 101 Arlington St. (Columbus Ave.) | 617-423-1112 | www.smithandwollensky.com

Beef eaters hit this "big-time" chophouse chain link for "succulent" steaks matched by a "breathtaking" wine list in a "grand", "gorgeous" setting in the Back Bay's "cool" "old Armory"; the "old-boy service" strikes some as "arrogant", but others admire its "NYC edge" and say it's worth going "even without an expense account."

Sofia Italian/Steak
∇ 21 | 23 | 19 | $35

West Roxbury | 1430 VFW Pkwy. (Spring St.) | 617-469-2600 | www.sofiaboston.com

"You don't have to spend a lot" to get "upscale" beef when you visit this "moderately priced" West Roxbury Italian chophouse, an "oasis" with an "attentive staff"; the fireplace-equipped "lounge provides a nice ambiance for drinks and appetizers" with lively companions, while the "attractive", clubby, dark-brown dining room features booths for "quiet dinner conversation" among couples and small groups.

☒ Sofra Bakery & Café Mideastern
27 | 16 | 18 | $18

Huron Village | 1 Belmont St. (Mt. Auburn St.) | Cambridge | 617-661-3161 | www.sofrabakery.com

"Anyplace that Ana Sortun touches is golden", and this "casual" Huron Village Middle Eastern cafe is no exception, with its "huge variety" of "inspired", "delectable" light meals and pastries flaunting "exotic flavors" (at "half the price" of Oleana); it's "always busy", and the "cramped quarters" and "haphazard counter service" yield "long lines of rabid foodies fighting for a table", so it's best to "get it to go" or, in summer, "find a table outdoors."

Sol Azteca Mexican
21 | 19 | 19 | $29

Fenway | 914A Beacon St. (bet. Park Dr. & St. Mary's St.) | 617-262-0909
Newton | 75 Union St. (Beacon St.) | 617-964-0920
www.solaztecarestaurants.com

"Still reliable after all these years", these "traditional", "upbeat", separately owned Fenway and Newton cantinas prepare "authentic Mexican cuisine" with "fresh ingredients", complemented with "to-die-for" sangria and margaritas; gourmets shrug that the fare is "nothing special", but they still get their south-of-the-border fix here because of the "friendly service", fees that "won't break the bank" and "fun patio" in summer.

Solea Restaurant & Tapas Bar *Spanish* 22 | 20 | 20 | $37

Waltham | 388 Moody St. (Cushing St.) | 781-894-1805 | www.solearestaurant.com

"It's hard not to get carried away" at this "lively" Waltham sibling of Dalí, where the "extensive" menu of "tasty", "modestly priced" Spanish tapas is complemented by "fabulous sangria"; "great for groups", the "festive", "always crowded" dining room features windows that open onto the street in warm weather, a "great" bar and servers who are "all smiles."

Solstice *American* ▽ 25 | 23 | 22 | $47

Kingston | 63 Summer St. (bet. Evergreen & Pottle Sts.) | 781-585-2221 | www.restaurantsolstice.com

Situated in an "old railroad station", this "upscale" New American "oasis" in Kingston is right "on track", what with the "high-quality", "gourmet" fare, "superb wines" and "great crowd" that relishes it; "although it's a little pricey, the meal usually satisfies", as does the "friendly and attentive" staff.

Soma 🗷 *Mediterranean* ▽ 22 | 21 | 22 | $39

Beverly | 256 Cabot St. (bet. Dane & Hale Sts.) | 978-524-0033 | www.somabeverly.com

"So many great tastes" abound in the midpriced modern Mediterranean meals that are prepped with "an emphasis on local ingredients" at this "stylish" site near Beverly's North Shore Music Theatre; "amazing cocktails" mixed by "fabulous bartenders" help to keep the warmly colored setting "upbeat", and the "attentive, friendly staff adds to the experience."

Sonsie *Eclectic* 20 | 21 | 20 | $43

Back Bay | 327 Newbury St. (bet. Hereford St. & Mass. Ave.) | 617-351-2500 | www.sonsieboston.com

"You might see your favorite Boston athlete" at this "trendy" "place to hang" in the Back Bay, where a "personable" staff serves "casual, tasty" Eclectic fare to the "beautiful people" in the "cute" dining room "overlooking Newbury Street", the "gorgeous wine cellar" or at the "upscale", "busy" mahogany bar, from where "strong drinks" come; for such a "hyped scene", the prices are quite "affordable."

Sophia's Grotto *Mediterranean* 23 | 21 | 22 | $32

Roslindale | 22R Birch St. (bet. Belgrade Ave. & Corinth St.) | 617-323-4595 | www.sophiasgrotto.com

In the summer, the patio is "always festive", and "when it gets colder", the "cozy dining room" beckons at this "cute", "family-friendly" Roslindale Mediterranean that employs a "warm", "knowledgeable" staff; however, "good prices" for the "palate-pleasing" fare and "nice wines by the glass" make it a "perfectly acceptable" choice whatever the weather.

Sorella's ⌷ *American*   24 | 13 | 17 | $15

Jamaica Plain | 386-388 Centre St. (Sheridan St.) | 617-524-2016
"It's impossible to not find something" on the "immense, legendary" menu at this Jamaica Plain American where "huge portions" of "superbly prepared", "creative breakfast offerings" are served until 2 PM daily; the "occasionally gruff" staffers "make no apologies" for the no-frills interior or the "slow service", which leads to "lines out the door" – yet devotees "keep coming back", partially because "you can't beat the price."

Sorelle *Coffeehouse/Sandwiches*   23 | 18 | 22 | $14

Charlestown | 1 Monument Ave. (Main St.) | 617-242-2125 ⌷
Charlestown | 100 City Sq. (Chelsea St.) | 617-242-5980
www.sorellecafe.com
"Exceptional homemade muffins and scones", "fabulous sandwiches" and "great soups" augment what may be the "best coffee in Charlestown" at this java-joint duo; the cash-only Monument Avenue original is "tiny", while the City Square spin-off boasts a wine bar, "alfresco dining in good weather" and a credit-card machine, but wherever you end up, the "servers are pleasant" and the prices are "sure to please."

☒ Sorellina *Italian*   27 | 27 | 26 | $67

Back Bay | 1 Huntington Ave. (Dartmouth St.) | 617-412-4600 | www.sorellinaboston.com
"Nothing but superlatives" rain down on Jamie Mammano's "chic", "lively" Back Bay "temple" where "sumptuous", "elegant" Italian dishes are conveyed by "detail-oriented" staffers in a "beautifully sophisticated", "spacious" black-and-white dining room filled with "lovely light-paneled murals"; it's the sort of "decadently sublime experience" you save for "when you need to impress someone" – and you should "save up" plenty of dough for it too.

Sorento's ☒ *Italian/Persian*   ▽ 25 | 20 | 21 | $32

Marlborough | 128 Main St. (bet. Court & Florence Sts.) | 508-486-0090 | www.sorentos.com
"Sometimes excellent" say surveyors of the pizzas and pastas that come from this Marlborough Italian, but they're "not sure about" the Persian items – perhaps simply because they didn't expect to see them here; nevertheless, costs are "reasonable", and the warm-wood-dominated setting can feel "romantic" if the stars are in alignment.

Sorriso ☒ *Italian*   21 | 20 | 20 | $37

Leather District | 107 South St. (bet. Beach & Essex Sts.) | 617-259-1560 | www.sorrisoboston.com
The brick-oven "pizza is always on the mark" at this "well-priced" Leather District trattoria where the rest of the rustic Italian "selection changes seasonally" and everything's enhanced with "tasty" picks from a "good-value" wine list; the "personable, attentive" staff can either be "quick" or conducive to a leisurely, "romantic" meal (for best results, ask for one of the "cozy booths").

	FOOD	DECOR	SERVICE	COST

Soul Fire *BBQ*   22 | 14 | 19 | $20

Allston | 182 Harvard Ave. (Commonwealth Ave.) | 617-787-3003 |
www.soulfirebbq.com

"Herds of carnivores hankering for smoky deliciousness" gather at
this "spacious", "well-priced" Allston joint for classics slathered
with "sauces galore" and sided with "to-die-for mac 'n' cheese"; the
"funky", soul-music-inspired setting is enhanced by "friendly",
"chatty" staffers who cheerfully deliver all-you-can-eat wings on
Monday nights, an "awesome" deal.

Sound Bites *American/Mideastern*   23 | 14 | 18 | $17

Somerville | 704 Broadway (Boston Ave.) | 617-623-8338
Somerville | 711 Broadway (bet. Josephine & Willow Aves.) |
617-623-9464
www.soundbitesrestaurant.com

A "breakfast classic", this Somerville American eatery at 704
always has "long lines on weekends", which are "worth" it for the
"sublime pancakes", "huge selection of omelets" and "coffee
bar" with a "vast array of choices", everything "available all day"
and for "cheap"; the "dinerlike" space has a real "community"
feel, thanks mainly to those "divine" members of the staff;
P.S. Middle Eastern plates and pizza take the spotlight at the grill
across the street.

South End Buttery ● *American/Bakery*   22 | 20 | 19 | $30

South End | 314 Shawmut Ave. (Union Park) | 617-482-1015 |
www.southendbuttery.com

You'll have to "navigate the dogs and strollers tied up out front" for
the "delicious pastries", "flavorful" breakfast, lunch and dinner sa-
vories plus "fine" coffee served at this "environmentally and socially
responsible" South End New American that "hops at all times of
day"; though "a bit cramped", the setup (bakery in front, bistro in
back) is "charming", with "stone walls, a fireplace and comfy chairs",
while the prices are "reasonable."

South Street Diner ● *Diner*   ▽ 17 | 13 | 18 | $16

Leather District | 178 Kneeland St. (South St.) | 617-350-0028 |
www.southstreetdiner.com

"If you want food at 4 AM after a night of drinking" around the
Leather District, there's this "popular", "low-lit and divey" 24/7
diner; as for the quality of the "typical fare", it "does the job", just
like the "quick" staff ("thanks for keeping it real").

Spice Thai Cuisine *Thai*   ▽ 19 | 18 | 19 | $24

Harvard Square | 24 Holyoke St. (Mt. Auburn St.) | Cambridge |
617-868-9560 | www.spicethaicuisine.com

"As advertised", the "solid Thai food" comes spicy at this Harvard
Square eatery, while milder palates appreciate that "you can have
your selections cooled down" if you ask the "nice" staffers; "great"
"lunch specials make it a popular destination for students", who
also like that it looks "upscale" enough "for a date, without
the upscale prices."

	FOOD	DECOR	SERVICE	COST

Spiga Trattoria Italiana ⊠ *Italian* | 22 | 20 | 22 | $39

Needham | 18 Highland Circle (bet. Highland Ave. & Needham St.) |
781-449-5600 | www.spigaitaliana.com

"North End–style Italian" comes to Needham via this "reliable" spot
whose "lousy location" "in the middle of a parking lot" is rescued by its
"charming" interior and courtyard; the fees may be a bit "expensive"
all things considered, yet groupies gush they're "worth every cent."

Splash Ultra Lounge & Burger Bar ●⊠Ⓜ *Burgers* | ▽ 17 | 22 | 16 | $32

Leather District | 150 Kneeland St. (bet. Lincoln & South Sts.) |
617-426-6397 | www.splash150kneeland.com

On "summer nights", this "classy", "unique little club" in the Leather
District offers an "unforgettable", cabana-lined, "wading pool"-
blessed roof deck that's "cool" for "pricey" drinks; the multilevel interior includes billiard tables and "just ok" patties from a burger bar.

Sportello *Italian* | 25 | 19 | 22 | $42

Seaport District | 348 Congress St. (Farnsworth St.) | 617-737-1234 |
www.sportelloboston.com

"Barbara Lynch shows her incredible range" with this "fancy luncheon-
ette" in the Seaport District, where most guests grab a seat at the
"gleaming white" wraparound counter (those who find it "awkward"
try for one of the few tables) for "innovative", "exquisitely prepared"
Italian cuisine; the "well-informed" staffers help set a "casual"
tone – which some complain contradicts the "less-than-casual
prices"; P.S. "don't miss the decadent desserts" in the bakery section.

⊠ Square Café *American* | 25 | 26 | 24 | $48

Hingham | 150 North St. (bet. Central & Main Sts.) | 781-740-4060 |
www.thesquarecafe.com

Like "the quiet kid at the back of the Hingham dining-scene class-
room", this "popular" New American "scores the best grades in the
class" thanks to its "delicious", "creative" menu, "generous, well-
made" drinks and "fine service"; commuters are especially enamored of it, as the "quaint" setting, comprised of a "tiny bar area" and
a "cozy", banquette-filled dining room, is a "refreshing change" from
the "frantic" pace of the city.

Stanhope Grille *American* | ▽ 20 | 22 | 22 | $45

Back Bay | Back Bay Hotel | 350 Stuart St. (Berkeley St.) | 617-532-3827 |
www.thedoylecollection.com

"Tantalizing" New American fare at "reasonable prices" comes from
the kitchen of this "pleasant" earth-toned eatery with "tasteful lighting" in the Back Bay Hotel; for some, it "doesn't quite live up to its
promise", but "outdoor dining is a plus", as is the "attentive service."

Stars on Hingham Harbor *Diner* | 18 | 11 | 16 | $27

Hingham | 3 Otis St./Rte. 3A (North St.) | 781-749-3200 |
www.starshingham.com

"Amazing breakfasts" are the highlight of the "enormous selection"
of "solid" fare sold at this "fun, retro" Hingham diner, "a great place

to bring the whole family" since it's affordable (and even though the "bar side gets noisy"); the "pretty" view of the harbor is a bonus, but you should "be prepared to wait" to see it.

NEW Stats Bar & Grille *Pub Food*   ▽ 21 | 15 | 19 | $25

South Boston | 77 Dorchester St. (W. Broadway) | 617-268-9300 | www.statsboston.com

"Better-than-average bar food", "a good beer and drinks list" and "nice" pub decor ensure this "great new addition" to Southie stays "always busy"; true, it may be "slightly more expensive" than the norm, but sports fiends are too busy gawking at the "TVs aplenty" to care.

Stella *Italian*   24 | 22 | 22 | $46

South End | 1525 Washington St. (W. Brookline St.) | 617-247-7747 | www.bostonstella.com

"Good times" happen at this "hopping" South End Italian where "outstanding" cuisine is conveyed alongside "great cocktails" in a "Miami"-"minimalist" setting bedecked with "molded white-plastic" furnishings; prices are "reasonable" for the area, and if you're one of the folks who suggests "something should be done about dampening the noise level", you should "eat outside" "when the weather's right."

Stellina *Italian*   23 | 18 | 21 | $39

Watertown | 47 Main St./Rte. 20 (Pleasant St.) | 617-924-9475 | www.stellinarestaurant.com

Watertown surveyors "always want to go back for more" of this Italian's "dependable", "inspired cooking", especially since "new items" appear "regularly" on the seasonal menu; the "lovely, simple" interior tends to be "noisy", but "nothing beats the patio" (sporting a "garden and fountain") "on a warm summer evening" – meanwhile, "pleasant", "helpful" service and "reasonable prices" are deal sweeteners throughout.

Stephanie's on Newbury *American*   20 | 20 | 20 | $38

Back Bay | 190 Newbury St. (Exeter St.) | 617-236-0990 | www.stephaniesonnewbury.com

Stephi's on Tremont *American*

South End | 571 Tremont St. (bet. Clarendon & Dartmouth Sts.) | 617-236-2063 | www.stephisontremont.com

"Trendy and warm" describes the bi-level interior, but the "best seat in the house" is actually out on the patio at this "mainstay" of "quality people-watching" in the Back Bay, where the New American "comfort food" is "decent", "decently priced" and served in "generous" portions; it's "always packed" (and "noisy"), so "expect a wait" – or hit up its more "relaxed" sibling in the South End.

Steve's Greek Restaurant *Greek*   19 | 11 | 16 | $21

Back Bay | 316 Newbury St. (Hereford St.) | 617-267-1817 | www.stevesgreek.com

Faneuil Hall | Faneuil Hall Mktpl. | 1 Faneuil Hall Sq. (bet N. & S. Market Sts.) | 617-263-1166

"Quick, cheap and, most importantly, delicious" sums up this "little Greek cafe" in the Back Bay where you'll find "suits side-by-side with "sandals" chowing on "basic" Hellenic "comfort food"; the "cramped diner-style seating area" is "nothing to speak of" and the staff is "not always friendly", so consider takeout, "a great option"; P.S. similar stuff is available at the Faneuil Hall to-go stall.

Stockyard *Steak*

18 | 16 | 19 | $31

Brighton | 135 Market St. (N. Beacon St.) | 617-782-4700 | www.stockyardrestaurant.com

"Less pretentious" than some others, this "popular" Brighton steakhouse grills up "huge portions" of "hearty" "food for the meat-and-potatoes gang" at "relatively inexpensive" fees; the "dark, cavernous" setting is "a meat-market in more than one way", specifically the "noisy" mahogany bar where "everyone checks everyone out" over "delicious, potent" cocktails.

NEW Stoddard's Fine Food & Ale Ⓜ *American*

19 | 21 | 17 | $35

Downtown Crossing | 48 Temple Pl. (bet. Tremont & Washington Sts.) | 617-426-0048 | www.stoddardsfoodandale.com

"You get a sense of history" at this "cool", "dark" Downtown Crossing American newcomer set in an "old corset shop" with pressed-tin ceilings, exposed brick and "antiques"; as for its wares, there's an "impressive beer selection" and "yummy creative cocktails" administered by "professional" bartenders, plus fare that's "good, hearty", but maybe a little "pricier than it should be" – and sometimes "slow" coming out of the kitchen.

Stone Hearth Pizza *Pizza*

‒ | ‒ | ‒ | M

Porter Square | 1782 Massachusetts Ave. (Somerville Ave.) | Cambridge | 617-492-1111
Belmont | 57 Leonard St. (Concord Ave.) | 617-484-1700
Needham | 974 Great Plain Ave . (Highland Ave.) | 781-433-0600
www.stonehearthpizza.com

"Great pizzas" are "made to order" in the authentic Neapolitan manner (flash-baked in the super-hot namesake oven) with "excellent", mostly organic and local ingredients at this trio of relaxed (yet often noisy) parlors where gourmet salads round out the offerings; staffers who are "nice to kids", "generous glasses of wine" and "affordable" tabs make it a "weekly" stop for many "families."

Strega Restaurant & Lounge Ⓜ *Italian*

▽ 19 | 23 | 21 | $28

Salem | 94 Lafayette St. (Peabody St.) | 978-741-0004 | www.stregasalem.com

"Good for pre-theater" since it's "right next door" to the Salem Theatre Company, this midpriced venue presents an "awesome" setting with jewel tones and a large mahogany bar in which to serve "decent" Italian fare; there's "hopping nightlife as well", so some audience members continue their evening here after the show.

Strega Ristorante *Italian*

23 | 17 | 20 | $54

North End | 379 Hanover St. (bet. Clark & Fleet Sts.) | 617-523-8481 | www.stregaristorante.com

(continued)

(continued)

NEW **Strega Waterfront** *Italian*

Seaport District | Fan Pier | One Marina Park Dr. (Northern Ave.) | 617-345-3992 | www.stregawaterfront.com

"Where else can you slurp up your red sauce" while watching "mob movies" on TV than at this North Ender where "caricatures of wise guys" (aka the "helpful" waiters) ferry "huge portions" of "amazing" fare; sure, "there's something hokey" about it (some "expect classier decor for the price"), but on the upside, there's a chance you'll "catch a Hollywood or sports star" there; P.S. the new, unsurveyed Seaport District branch boasts a grander white-tablecloth setting sprinkled with 1930s Vegas–style glamour.

Strip-T's Ⓩ *American*   ∇ 21 | 12 | 20 | $20

Watertown | 95 School St. (Arsenal St.) | 617-923-4330 | www.stripts.com
Though it "looks like a dive", this "cozy", "casual" Watertown American maintains a "welcoming, friendly" atmosphere thanks to its "customer-pleasing" staffers, who serve up "fresh salads and great sandwiches at lunchtime", plus "nice home-cooked meals" for dinner; add "modest prices" to the mix, and it's no surprise that it gets "too crowded sometimes."

Suffolk Grille *American*   - | - | - | M

Canton | 2790 Washington St./Rte. 138 (Blue Hill River Rd.) | 339-237-4700 | www.suffolkgrille.com
Its location near Route 93 in Canton makes this "cozy", moderately priced American a convenient spot for classy business lunches, and it also hosts a lively after-work-drinks crowd at a horseshoe-shaped granite bar; a mural depicting a Colonial scene and an "inviting fireplace in winter" lend extra character to the interior.

Sugar & Spice *Thai*   20 | 16 | 19 | $19

Porter Square | 1933 Massachusetts Ave. (Davenport St.) | Cambridge | 617-868-4200 | www.sugarspices.com
Perhaps the "diner-style" decor makes this "laid-back" Porter Square eatery seem "generic", but "don't be put off" or else you'll miss out on "vibrant", "spicy" Thai fare that's "reasonably priced" too; though "most seem to go for takeout", those who do dine in get the bonus of "attentive", "friendly" service.

Suishaya ☾ *Japanese/Korean*   ∇ 19 | 12 | 18 | $24

Chinatown | 2 Tyler St. (Beach St.) | 617-423-3848
"Yum!" yell supporters of the "large" menu of "Korean comfort food" and "quality sushi" at this affordable Chinatown "bar-restaurant hybrid", which draws night owls with a 2 AM closing time; but "meh" grunt detractors who dis "subpar" fare and "zero atmosphere."

Sultan's Kitchen Ⓩ *Turkish*   23 | 9 | 13 | $17

Financial District | 116 State St. (Broad St.) | 617-570-9009 | www.sultans-kitchen.com
"What this sultan doesn't know about his native cuisine isn't worth knowing" rave regulars of this "divine", affordable Turkish "pioneer"

in the Financial District; unfortunately, you often have to "wait in line", endure "gruff counter service" then stake out one of the "few tables" to experience it – still, many a devotee would "would walk over coals" to get their "kebab fix" here.

Summer Winter *American*   25 | 23 | 22 | $53

Burlington | Boston Marriott Burlington | 1 Mall Rd. (I-95, exit 33B) | 781-221-6643 | www.markandclarkrestaurants.com

The "culinary garden" in a "greenhouse outside of the dining room makes its point loud and clear": "you're eating fresh" at this Burlington Marriott "diamond", a sibling of "foodie paradise" Arrows in Ogunquit, Maine, serving Clark Frasier and Mark Gaier's "innovative", "scrumptious" New American dishes; there's "plenty of room to stretch out" in the "tasteful" setting, which helps to keep the vibe "relaxing" if the menu's "city prices" grate.

Sunset Cafe *American/Portuguese*   ▽ 24 | 16 | 17 | $20

Inman Square | 851 Cambridge St. (bet. Harding & Hunting Sts.) | Cambridge | 617-547-2938 | www.thesunsetcafe.net

"Outstanding" Portuguese and American cuisine is turned out at this Inman Square spot with live fado music on weekends; service can be "spotty" (i.e. "friendly" but "slow") and the setting "feels old" ("they need more comfortable chairs!"), but fans find it easy to forgive its shortcomings, with much credit going to the "bargain-basement prices."

Sunset Grill & Tap ● *Mexican/Pub Food*   19 | 16 | 18 | $21

Allston | 130 Brighton Ave. (Harvard Ave.) | 617-254-1331

Sunset Cantina ● *Mexican/Pub Food*

Boston University | 916 Commonwealth Ave. (bet. Pleasant & St. Paul Sts.) | 617-731-8646
www.allstonsfinest.com

"Ah, decisions" sigh hops-hounds at this "hectic" Allston brew "mecca" whose "unbelievable" variety of "over 500 beers" is paired with an "astonishing" selection of "decent" pub grub; at the BU cantina, the emphasis is on a "fantastic tequila selection" and "casual Mexican food" doled out in "ample portions", but like its larger sibling, the atmosphere's "fun", the staff is "knowledgeable" and the prices are "inexpensive."

Super Fusion   26 | 9 | 19 | $29
Cuisine *Japanese*

Brookline | 690A Washington St. (Beacon St.) | 617-277-8221
Watertown | 54 Mt. Auburn St. (bet. Main & Summer Sts.) | 617-393-0008
www.superfusionsushi.com

"Incredibly fresh", "creative" sushi in "oversized pieces" plus "fantastic appetizers" are "priced well for the quality" at this Brookline BYOB whose "cramped" setting with "only a few tables" "screams 'takeout!'" – hence, most folks "get it to go"; the Watertown location is larger and "more attractive", but the fare and "friendly, accommodating" staff are "the same."

	FOOD	DECOR	SERVICE	COST

Sushi-Teq 🅱🅼 *Asian* ▽ 24 | 21 | 19 | $51

Waterfront | InterContinental Boston | 510 Atlantic Ave.
(bet. Congress St. & Seaport Blvd.) | 617-747-1000 |
www.intercontinentalboston.com

"East meets Southwest" at this "interesting concept" in the Waterfront's InterContinental Hotel, where "work-of-art", "high-priced" sushi is complemented by a "great" selection of tequila shots and cocktails; patio seating overlooking the harbor is "nice" in summer, while the contemporary dining room is a bit "cramped", though it does afford the same view.

Sweet Basil ⊅ *Italian* 26 | 17 | 22 | $32

Needham | 942 Great Plain Ave. (Highland Ave.) | 781-444-9600 |
www.sweetbasilneedham.com

"Massive portions of lavishly garlicked Italian" come via an "engaging", "always-present" chef-owner at this "fabulous", "affordable" Needham BYOB whose "attentive" staff also "could not be nicer"; unfortunately, they "don't take reservations" (or credit cards) and the setting is "tight" and "tiny", so don't be surprised by "long lines" "outside on weekends" – not to worry, it's "worth the wait."

Sweet Tomatoes *Pizza* 24 | 9 | 16 | $15

West Newton | 1279 Washington St. (Watertown St.) | 617-630-8666
Needham | 320 Chestnut St. (bet. Clyde & Lincoln Sts.) |
781-444-9644
Newton | 47 Langley Rd. (Beacon St.) | 617-558-0222 🅱🅼
www.sweettomatoespizza.com

"If you like designer pizza", head to one of these parlors for "addictive" "thin-crust" iterations with "tons" of "tasty toppings"; however, given that there's "no atmosphere", "not enough seating" and "inattentive service", the pies are "best taken home to eat."

Symphony Sushi *Japanese* 23 | 14 | 20 | $31

Fenway | 45 Gainsborough St. (Huntington Ave.) | 617-262-3888 |
www.symphonysushi.com

With a "location convenient to Symphony Hall and the Huntington Theatre Company", this Fenway "neighborhood spot" presents "well-above-average sushi" to an "always-busy" house heavy with ticket-holders who appreciate that the "pleasant" staff "keeps things moving"; "Northeastern students" also dig it, particularly because the tabs are "relatively cheap."

Taberna de Haro 🅱 *Spanish* 25 | 20 | 20 | $39

Brookline | 999 Beacon St. (St. Mary's St.) | 617-277-8272 |
www.tabernaboston.com

"This is the real thing" declare tapas aficionados of this "fun" Brookline Spaniard where the "fabulous" fare is paired with "out-of-this-world" sangria and a seemingly "infinite" variety of "well-priced" Iberian wines; as usual with this type of place, "all those little plates add up to a big bill", but nevertheless, the "warm" space is "always crowded", thanks in part to the "gracious", "knowledgeable" staff and the "bonus" of a warm-weather patio.

Tacos El Charro *Mexican*
▽ 25 | 12 | 21 | $20

Jamaica Plain | 349 Centre St. (Hyde Sq.) | 617-522-2578

The Mexican fare dished out at this casual, inexpensive Jamaica Plain taqueria has groupies moaning "yum", and the sangria is just as "delicious" (beer and wine only); walls festooned with guitars and sombreros lend the setting an "authentic feeling", which is clinched by "mariachi players on the weekends" – and "once that starts, you can't really talk."

Tacos Lupita *Mexican/Salvadoran*
25 | 6 | 14 | $11

Revere | 107 Shirley Ave. (bet. Nahant & Walnut Aves.) | 781-284-2430
Somerville | 13 Elm St. (Porter St.) | 617-666-0677 ⊟
Lynn | 129 Munroe St. (Washington St.) | 781-593-6437
Lawrence | 505 Broadway (Manchester St.) | 978-681-4517 Ⓜ

"It certainly tastes like someone's grandmother is in the kitchen" at this foursome of mostly take-out cantinas specializing in "unbelievably tasty" Mexican and Salvadorian staples; sure, each branch is a "spartan" "hole-in-the-wall" and service can be "crabby", but "wow, what a deal."

Taiwan Cafe ●⊟ *Taiwanese*
24 | 7 | 17 | $17

Chinatown | 34 Oxford St. (Beach St.) | 617-426-8181

"Super-authentic", often "truly spicy" Taiwanese cuisine is delivered at this "no-frills", lunch-to-late-night Chinatown cafe that "doesn't hold back on the strange but delicious delicacies" (e.g. "frogs' legs", "fermented tofu"); service "varies", but that's no issue considering the "portions are enormous" and "prices simply cannot be beat" – just come bearing cash.

Tamarind Bay Bistro & Bar *Indian*
23 | 17 | 19 | $33

Harvard Square | 75 Winthrop St. (JFK St.) | Cambridge | 617-491-4552

Tamarind Bay Coastal Indian Kitchen *Indian*

Brookline | 1665 Beacon St. (Winthrop Rd.) | 617-277-1752
www.tamarind-bay.com

"Upscale Indian food with a modern edge" and "incandescently brilliant flavors" is what you'll find at this Harvard Square and Brookline duo, the former a "subterranean", "cramped and dark" setting, the "seafood-heavy" latter a "charming" venue with a "wall of windows" that "opens up" in warm weather; "service is variable" at both, while prices are "a little high for the genre" though generally "worth it for the high quality."

Tangierino ● *Moroccan*
22 | 25 | 20 | $44

Charlestown | 83 Main St. (Pleasant St.) | 617-242-6009 |
www.tangierino.com

"Moroccan immersion" occurs at this "cool", "lush", "inviting" Charlestown destination where the "exotic", "expensive" eats are loaded with "lots of interesting spices" and the "belly dancing adds some fun"; after your meal, "head down to the nightclub" for cigar and hookah smoking plus cocktails from a "small bar" helmed by keeps who, like their upstairs counterparts, are "accommodating and attentive."

Tango *Argentinean/Steak*

22 | 20 | 22 | $38

Arlington | 464 Massachusetts Ave. (Swan Pl.) | 781-443-9000 | www.tangoarlington.com

"A true gaucho experience" comes for a "reasonable price" at this "meat-lovers' paradise" in Arlington, grilling up "delectable" Argentinean steaks piled in "plentiful" portions and complemented by a "great wine list" ("Malbecs!"); to top it all off, the "attentive" staff seems to "care so much about your experience"; P.S. supporters are "happy" that it recently "expanded" and added a bar.

Tanjore *Indian*

22 | 15 | 18 | $22

Harvard Square | 18 Eliot St. (Bennett St.) | Cambridge | 617-868-1900 | www.tanjoreharvardsq.com

Whether during the "excellent lunch buffet" or dinner featuring "interesting regional specialties", this "casual", "friendly" Harvard Square Indian lets folks "take their time", which diners appreciate despite having to look at "utilitarian" decor; factor in "great value", and no wonder it's the "preferred" subcontinental stop for many.

Tantric *Indian*

24 | 21 | 22 | $29

Theater District | 123 Stuart St. (Tremont St.) | 617-367-8742 | www.tantricbistro.com

"Hip music and wonderful smells swirling around you" set the stage for "scrumptious", "indulgent" Indian fare at this "large" Theater District destination whose bar turns out "creative martinis"; it's "a great place to go before" a show because the "helpful" staff keeps things moving, but it's also conducive to a "leisurely" meal, so "check it out on other nights too."

Tapéo *Spanish*

23 | 22 | 22 | $37

Back Bay | 266 Newbury St. (bet. Fairfield & Gloucester Sts.) | 617-267-4799 | www.tapeo.com

Go with a "group", order "wave after wave" of "tapas from heaven" and "keep the sangria coming" at this "lively" Back Bay Spaniard where there are "no losers" among the "wide variety" of small plates; "pleasant, knowledgeable" folks staff the "lovely" surroundings that include "patio seating in the summer", and while "prices are reasonable", take care because "the bill can mount up if one is ravenous."

Taqueria Mexico *Mexican*

24 | 11 | 20 | $18

Waltham | 24 Charles St. (bet. Moody & Prospect Sts.) | 781-647-0166 | www.taqueriamexico.com

"Almost no money" gets you "large helpings" of "incredible" Mexican *comida* at this "somewhat drab", "little hole-in-the-wall" in Waltham; there's a "wide variety of choices" on the menu, which the "friendly" staff can help you navigate before bringing your selections out "quick."

⛋ Taranta *Italian/Peruvian*

26 | 21 | 24 | $49

North End | 210 Hanover St. (Cross St.) | 617-720-0052 | www.tarantarist.com

Chef-owner José Duarte's "charming" spot "stands out among the other restaurants in the North End" for its "intriguing, innovative" fusion of Peruvian and Southern Italian cuisines with an "emphasis on organic ingredients" (plus a "primarily organic wine list") offered on three "modern, cozy" floors festooned with "dark wood, upholstered banquettes" and some "nice window-side seats"; yes, it's "pricey", but service that's "most attentive and never rushed" adds value.

Tartufo *Italian* ▽ 22 | 18 | 22 | $42

Newton | 22 Union St. (bet. Beacon St. & Langley Rd.) | 617-244-8833 | www.tartuforestaurant.com

An "accommodating", "friendly" staff serves an "enthusiastic clientele" "great" Abruzzese cuisine at this "piece of the North End" in Newton, whose prices are, all things considered, rather "inexpensive"; a granite-topped bar and tables are complemented by warm, rustic walls and lighting, all conspiring to create a "nice atmosphere."

Tasca *Spanish* 23 | 22 | 21 | $27

Brighton | 1612 Commonwealth Ave. (Washington St.) | 617-730-8002 | www.tascarestaurant.com

Such a "bargain" is the "extensive" selection of "awesome tapas" (not to mention "reasonably priced, diverse wine list") at this Brighton Spaniard with an "old-world atmosphere", "you feel like you're stealing from them"; "pleasant service" and "generous discounts" if you "sign up for the e-mail list" are two more reasons it's "easy to become a regular" here.

Tashi Delek ⓈⰀ *Tibetan* - | - | - | M

Brookline | 236 Washington St. (bet. Davis Ave. & Davis Ct.) | 617-232-4200 | www.tashidelekboston.com

"Impress your friends" with "a genuine find" by bringing them to this "remarkable Tibetan treat" in Brookline, and definitely "try the dumplings" (momos) – they're "outstanding"; "the service here is excellent" and the traditional atmosphere is "warm", but the best feature may be that it's "cheap."

Tastings Wine Bar & Bistro Ⓜ *Eclectic* ▽ 21 | 22 | 22 | $44

Foxboro | Patriot Pl. | 201 Patriot Pl. (overlooking Gillette Stadium) | 508-203-9463 | www.tastingswinebarandbistro.com

"In the middle of football madness", you'll find this airy, warm Foxboro wine bar and eatery that pairs "delicious" small and large Eclectic plates with "incredible wines", hundreds of bottles of which are displayed on a wall; floor-to-ceiling windows that frame a "nice view of all the activity at Patriot Place" and a "friendly" staff earn points, but still, some surveyors feel the experience is "a little overpriced."

ℕ𝔼𝕎 Tasty Burger ● *Burgers* - | - | - | I

Fenway | 1301 Boylston St. (Yawkey Way) | 617-425-4444 | www.tastyburger.com

This winsome burger joint located near Fenway Park and open until 2 AM nightly offers a menu of house-ground tenderloin patties, fries, shakes, beer and wine, plus rotating blackboard specials like a $10 burger-fries-and-beer combo; set in a former gas station, the setting features a pool table, jukebox and mahogany bar, plus there's a take-out window for on-the-go grub grabs.

	FOOD	DECOR	SERVICE	COST

Tavern in the Square *American*   15 | 15 | 16 | $25

NEW **Allston** | 161 Brighton Ave. (Harvard Ave.) | 617-782-8100
Central Square | 730 Massachusetts Ave. (bet. Inman & Prospect Sts.) |
Cambridge | 617-868-8800
Porter Square | Porter Exchange Mall | 1815 Massachusetts Ave.
(Roseland St.) | Cambridge | 617-354-7766
Salem | 189 Washington St. (New Derby St.) | 978-740-2337
www.taverninthesquare.com

"Plenty of TVs" make these "spacious", "noisy" American sports pubs
the place for "throngs of college" kids to "cheer on their local sports
team", despite the fact that the otherwise "generic" decor "needs
upgrading"; though occasionally "attentive", there can be "some
stunning lapses in the service", and the quality of the "basic" grub also
varies, from "great" to "mediocre" to "just drink and forget the food."

Tavern on the Water *American*   12 | 18 | 14 | $26

Charlestown | Charlestown Navy Yard | 1 Pier 6 Eighth St. (1st Ave.) |
617-242-8040 | www.tavernonthewater.com

"You're not necessarily going for the food" (it's "subpar", hence
"overpriced") at this "casual" American in the Charlestown Navy
Yard, you're going for the "spectacular view of Boston Harbor" plus
"potent drinks" that fuel the "singles-bar" scene; as for the atmosphere, "if the weather is good and you get a seat outside, it's sublime", but inside is "somewhat shabby."

Tavolino *Italian*   20 | 20 | 19 | $35

Foxboro | Patriot Pl. | 274 Patriot Pl. (Washington St.) | 508-543-6543
Westborough | 33 E. Main St. (bet. Prospect & Willow Sts.) | 508-366-8600
www.tavolinorestaurant.us

"Thin-crust" pizza with "unique combinations" of toppings is the
"fabulous" specialty of this casual duo in Foxboro's Patriot Place and
Westborough, which also lists pastas and other Italian eats on its
menu; football-goers say it's "a bit pricey for a pre-game meal", but
thanks in part to a "lovely environment" with a "great bar", it gets
"busy", especially on weekends.

Tavolo *Italian*   24 | 21 | 23 | $33

Dorchester | The Carruth | 1918 Dorchester Ave. (Ashmont St.) |
617-822-1918 | www.tavoloristorante.com

The "softball-size meatballs" are "not to be missed" at this "modestly
priced" Dorchester Italian where chef Chris Douglass is "always
coming up with something delicious and fresh"; "calmer" than
Ashmont Grill, its "sister restaurant across the street", it's nevertheless "lively", with "super service", a "big, open, comfortable" feel
and a "warm, friendly" bar that's a "great place to dine solo" and
"meet fun people from the neighborhood."

Teatro *Italian*   23 | 21 | 22 | $44

Theater District | 177 Tremont St. (bet. Avery & West Sts.) |
617-542-6418 | www.teatroboston.com

The "mix 'n' match small plates", augmented by "interesting", "flavorful" entrees, make this "well-priced" Theater District Italian

"wonderful" "before seeing a show" if you don't want to be "too stuffed", and there are "delicious drinks" and a "nice wine selection" to go with; "dim lighting and candles" help craft a "sexy atmosphere" in the former synagogue, but "oy, the noise!" – prepare to "scream" to the "person across the table."

Technique ☒ *American* — | — | — | M

East Cambridge | Athenaeum Bldg. | 215 First St. (bet. Athenaeum St. & Linskey Way) | Cambridge | 617-218-8088 | www.bostonculinaryarts.com

"On-the-job training" for enrollees of the famous Le Cordon Bleu occurs in "two open kitchens staffed by student cooks and overseen by faculty chefs" at this "interesting experience" in East Cambridge, where the New England–centric New American fare is "inventive", "affordable" and conveyed by "helpful" staffers (coeds themselves); sure, there are "occasional blunders", but most folks gladly "cut them some slack."

NEW Telegraph Hill — | — | — | M
Kitchen & Bar ☒Ⓜ *American*

South Boston | 289 Dorchester St. (bet. Old Colony Ave. & Rev. Burke St.) | 212-680-0012 | www.telegraphhillboston.com

This cozy American tavern tucked into a former bookie hang in Southie dispenses more than a dozen microbrews on tap from a sleek bar, plus burgers, sandwiches, panini and po' boys; with entrees clocking in under $20, you might even escape with more to spare for next time.

Temple Bar ❶ *American* 21 | 21 | 20 | $34

Porter Square | 1688 Massachusetts Ave. (Sacramento St.) | Cambridge | 617-547-5055 | www.templebarcambridge.com

"Well-flavored", "reliable" New American fare complements "designer cocktails" and a "solid" selection of wines at this "trendy" Porter Square "respite" with lots of "comfortable booths", "warm" colors plus an "informed" staff; the "fantastic" brunch is a weekend draw, and insiders say it's "best to go in nice weather, when the windows are opened."

Tempo ☒ *American* 22 | 17 | 19 | $41

Waltham | 474 Moody St. (Maple St.) | 781-891-9000 | www.tempobistro.com

"Culinary creativity" on a menu with "so many" "delicious", "well-prepared" choices makes this Waltham New American an "amazing" "find" for most; however, others cite "erratic" results, both in food and service, as the reason it's "overpriced", though there are happy-hour specials at the "great", "loud" bar.

☒ Ten Tables *American/European* 27 | 20 | 25 | $50

Jamaica Plain | 597 Centre St. (Pond St.) | 617-524-8810
Harvard Square | 5 Craigie Circle (Concord Ave.) | Cambridge | 617-576-5444
www.tentables.net

"True to its name", this Jamaica Plain "extravaganza" has just 10 tables, and while the "tight" digs strike some as "romantic", others as "claustrophobic" (a new attached bar "adds some space"), most agree that the "creative" European–New American dishes employing "locally grown produce" are "absurdly delicious"; the "noisy" "basement location" of the beer-and-wine-only Harvard Square offshoot has "more than 10 tables", but similarly "beautifully prepared" fare, "upbeat servers" and "excellent value"; P.S. "make reservations" "a zillion years in advance."

Teranga *Senegalese* ▽ 22 | 20 | 23 | $32

South End | 1746 Washington St. (Mass. Ave.) | 617-266-0003 | www.terangaboston.com

"Eye-opening" is how enthusiasts describe this "wonderful surprise" in the South End, the "only Senegalese restaurant in Boston", whose "unusual", "swoon"-inducing cuisine is served amid true "African ambiance" (including a sapele-and-zebrawood bar dispensing beer and wine); "large", "well-priced" portions and "gracious" service complete the picture.

Terramia Ristorante *Italian* 26 | 19 | 23 | $46

North End | 98 Salem St. (Parmenter St.) | 617-523-3112 | www.terramiaristorante.com

"Foodies" from "across the world" agree that this North End Italian provides a "simply divine" "culinary experience", with "seasonally changing fare" and "pastas without compare" – and it "won't bust the bank either"; a "professional staff" lends a "pleasant and warm" feeling to "crowded" quarters in which you're "packed tight as sardines" ("who cares?"); P.S. no dessert, but there are all sorts of "bakeries and gelaterias nearby."

Thai Basil *Thai* 21 | 15 | 18 | $26

Back Bay | 132 Newbury St. (bet. Clarendon & Dartmouth Sts.) | 617-578-0089

"You get plenty of delicious food" for "cheap" at this Back Bay "below-ground-level" Thai that's a "standby after shopping on Newbury Street" (and when you're not "worried about being seen"); the "decor is nothing special", but the service is "super fast", meaning you'll get in and out "quick."

Thaitation *Thai* ▽ 26 | 15 | 23 | $23

Fenway | 129 Jersey St. (bet. Park Dr. & Queensberry St.) | 617-585-9909 | www.thaitation.com

"Sumptuous" and "spicy" Thai sustenance "satisfies" diners for a "great price" at this Fenway eatery that's especially "fabulous" "before going to see the Red Sox"; some chafe at the "silly name", but everything else is fine here, from the "informative" staff to the casual setting that's "quiet enough to encourage leisurely conversation"; P.S. outdoor seating in warm weather.

NEW Think Tank ◑🅱 *American/Asian* - | - | - | M

Kendall Square | 1 Kendall Sq. (B'way) | Cambridge | 617-500-3031 | www.thinktankcambridge.com

Dubbing itself a 'bistrotheque', this Kendall Square newcomer serves a trendy, reasonably priced New American menu (featuring numerous Southeast Asian influences) in a stylishly retro space; scenesters sip inventive cocktails while grooving along to regularly scheduled live and DJ music, plus there are vintage video games, TVs and a photo booth to keep the young and restless occupied.

☑ 1369 Coffeehouse ⌷ *Coffeehouse* | 21 | 18 | 20 | $9 |

Central Square | 757 Massachusetts Ave. (Pleasant St.) | Cambridge | 617-576-4600
Inman Square | 1369 Cambridge St. (Springfield St.) | Cambridge | 617-576-1369
www.1369coffeehouse.com

"Emblematic of the Cambridge coffee-shop" "social scene", these "buzzing" spots in Central and Inman Squares draw "hipster" "intellectuals" who "linger endlessly" over "awesome" hot and iced beverages and "yummy" sandwiches, soups, quiches and baked goods that garner Boston's No. 1 Bang for the Buck rating; "tattooed baristas" add to the "authentic urban-college atmosphere", but it's "so popular" (and "cramped"), "good luck getting a seat."

NEW Tico ⓈⓂ *American/Latin* | - | - | - | M |

Back Bay | 222 Berkeley St. (bet. Boylston St. & St. James Ave.) | 617-351-0400 | www.ticoboston.com

The latest from the prolific Michael Schlow (Alta Strada, Radius, Via Matta), this Back Bay American offers a midpriced, mostly small-plates menu that reflects the chef-owner's travels through Spain, Mexico and other parts of Latin America; the hip setting includes rustic touches such as haciendalike chandeliers and a faux tin ceiling, plus there's an exhibition kitchen visible from most seats.

Tivoli's ⓈⓂ *French/Italian* | - | - | - | E |

Malden | 121 Exchange St. (Washington St.) | 781-321-5559 | www.tivolisrestaurant.com

"Tucked away on a backstreet" in Malden, this "intimate", "quiet" bistro serves a "limited selection" of "good" French-Italian dishes; it's an especially "nice choice for a rainy or snowy evening" when a "warm and friendly atmosphere" coupled with a "hearty dish" can be quite "comforting."

Tomasso Trattoria & Enoteca *Italian* | 23 | 20 | 21 | $44 |

Southborough | 154 Turnpike Rd./Rte. 9 (Breakneck Hill Rd.) | 508-481-8484 | www.tomassotrattoria.com

"An ever-changing selection" of "scrumptious" Italian fare, "designed for sharing", plus a "wonderful wine list" and "pleasant" setting make this a "refreshing choice" for Southborough; service opinions range from "excellent" to "mediocre", but it's the price comments that swing most wildly: "great value", "moderate", "a little expensive", "overpriced" and everything in between.

☑ Top of the Hub ● *American* | 20 | 26 | 22 | $55 |

Back Bay | Prudential Ctr. | 800 Boylston St., 52nd fl. (Ring Rd.) | 617-536-1775 | www.topofthehub.net

"Spectacular" Boston vistas still "wow" at this "famous" New American on the 52nd floor of the Back Bay's Prudential Center, "a go-to" for locals "to celebrate" as well as a "must for out-of-town visitors"; the decor is as "beautiful" as the scenery, the staff is "professional" and as for the food, the prevailing opinion is it's "much, much better than most people" think it is – but you're "definitely paying for the view"; P.S. you can "save yourself some money" by just having "snappy drinks" in the lounge, featuring "live music each night."

NEW Top Steakhouse *Brazilian/Steak*   – | – | – | M

Peabody | 72 Walnut St. (Harris St.) | 978-532-1530 | www.topsteakbar.com

The Brazilians know their steak and they know how to party – both of which come into play at this Peabody newcomer serving a Brazilian buffet, churrascaria meats carved tableside, plus a few Continental items like lasagna; the casual dining room, decorated with black-and-white prints, makes a nice first stop before heading to the bar upstairs for live music Thursday–Sunday, or to the one adjacent to the dining room for a nightcap.

Z Toro *Spanish*   27 | 21 | 21 | $43

South End | 1704 Washington St. (Mass. Ave.) | 617-536-4300 | www.toro-restaurant.com

"A treat for your senses" awaits at Ken Oringer's rustic, "trendy" South End Spaniard specializing in both "authentic and inventive", "lick-the-plate-delicious tapas" ("don't miss the house specialty, grilled corn"); though "annoyances" abound – "no reservations", "insanely long waits", "absurd" "crowds", "noise" and, ironically, dishes "so good, you keep ordering and the price creeps up fast" – they're "well worth it" for such a "sizzling" time; P.S. things move "more quickly" if you can snag a seat at the "cool bar", which dispenses "avant-garde cocktails."

Tory Row *American/European*   17 | 18 | 17 | $24

Harvard Square | 3 Brattle St. (Mass. Ave.) | Cambridge | 617-876-8769 | www.toryrow.us

A "fantastic location" in the "heart" of Harvard Square means "you can't beat" the "people-watching" at this "sleek" gastropub peddling European–New American "bites" that land somewhere between "well prepared" and "substandard", but are "affordable"; the "small", "thoughtful" beer selection gets hops-hounds in the door, but some feel that the "communal seating" at "tall tables" is "not comfortable" for a long stay.

Z Tosca **M** *Italian*   26 | 26 | 25 | $49

Hingham | 14 North St. (Mill St.) | 781-740-0080 | www.toscahingham.com

"Imaginative", "fantastic", "outstanding" – "a thesaurus-full of superlatives" is earned by this Hingham Italian, which epicures estimate is "on par with all of the great restaurants in Boston" (ditto the "top prices"); "spot-on service", a "warm, friendly environment" and a "thriving bar scene" with "live jazz every weekend" shore up its rep as "as good as it gets in the suburbs."

	FOOD	DECOR	SERVICE	COST

Toscano *Italian* — 25 | 23 | 24 | $49

Beacon Hill | 41-47 Charles St. (bet. Chestnut & Mt. Vernon Sts.) | 617-723-4090 | www.toscanoboston.com

Beacon Hill Italophiles "can't get enough of this place" and its "superb" "Tuscan delights", not to mention the "fine" selection of wines; the "cozy, dignified atmosphere" scattered with "carved wood panels" and leather seems even "more pleasurable with marvelous service", which on top of everything else, makes it "worth every penny" (prices are a bit "high").

🆕 Towne *Eclectic* — 21 | 24 | 20 | $57

Back Bay | 900 Boylston St. (Gloucester St.) | 617-247-0400 | www.towneboston.com

Culinary pioneers Lydia Shire and Jasper White charted the "imaginative" Eclectic offerings at this "trendy" Back Bay "hot spot" for "fancy people", and even though "you have to be Magellan to figure your way around the menu", the spoils are frequently "fantastic" (and "expensive") – just hope you get one of the "attentive" servers to "help you navigate" it and not a "distracted" one; the "chic", "big" bi-level setting is "crazy-loud" everywhere, but "the roar" coming from the bar is sheer "madness."

Townsend's ❶ *American* — ▽ 21 | 22 | 23 | $35

Hyde Park | 81 Fairmount Ave. (Truman Pkwy.) | 617-333-0306 | www.townsendsrestaurant.com

On "a chilly fall or frigid winter night", "a roaring fire" makes this Hyde Park New American with high ceilings, black granite counters and "fancy dark-wood decor" feel "as warm and welcoming as the owner/hosts" and their "friendly" staff; everyone feels the mid-priced "comfort food served with contemporary flair" is "tasty", but suds-aholics say it's a "second cousin" to the "great beer selection."

Trata 🅐 *American* — _ | - | - | I

Harvard Square | 49 Mt. Auburn St. (Plympton St.) | Cambridge | 617-349-1650

"Generously sized" brick-oven pizzas with "excellent" thin crusts and toppings are the standouts among the "reliable" American grub offered at this "small", "comfortable" Harvard Square American whose bar holds an "interesting" beer selection; a "European" setting, with exposed-brick walls and tall windows that open onto the street, plus "generally friendly" service are other bonuses, but the biggest pull is the cheap price point.

Trattoria di Monica *Italian* — 25 | 19 | 20 | $46

North End | 67 Prince St. (Salem St.) | 617-720-5472

Vinoteca di Monica *Italian*

North End | 143 Richmond St. (bet. Hanover & North Sts.) | 617-227-0311
www.monicasboston.com

"Yummy" homemade pastas with "amazing sauces" are the highlights of this North End duo where the "reasonable portions" of "consistently excellent Italian" mean you get generally good "value for your money"; compared to the "larger" vinoteca, with an "intelligent wine list", the trattoria is "tiny" ("OMG, could they cram in any more tables?"), while both employ servers who range from "helpful" to "pompous."

Trattoria Il Panino *Italian*   24 | 16 | 20 | $36
North End | 11 Parmenter St. (Hanover St.) | 617-720-1336 |
www.trattoriailpanino.com

"Fresh ingredients", "plenty of buzz", "friendly" service and an "awe"-inspiring amount of "home cooking" delivered from a kitchen the size of a "postage" stamp add up to a "great experience" at this "consistently *delizioso*" North End Italian; some are piqued by the "dark", "small" quarters, but the "patio can't be beat in summer."

Trattoria Pulcinella *Italian*   ∇ 24 | 23 | 24 | $44
Huron Village | 147 Huron Ave. (Concord Ave.) | Cambridge |
617-491-6336 | www.trattoriapulcinella.net

"Incredible in every way", this Huron Village venue with a "wonderful selection" of Italian cuisine "prepared simply and with loving care" is "'that place' all the locals hope stays hidden", especially since it only contains "a few small tables"; an "excellent", "reasonably priced" wine list featuring bottles exclusively from The Boot is another reason it's "unique" for the area.

⊠ Trattoria Toscana ⊠ *Italian*   26 | 19 | 26 | $41
Fenway | 130 Jersey St. (Park Dr.) | 617-247-9508

"Simple", "small" surroundings put the "emphasis on the food" at this "charming" "treasure", "the place to go for authentic, unpretentious, neighborhoody Tuscan food" and matching wines brought by a "warm", "friendly" staff in the Fenway; "no reservations" and "long waits" are "downsides", but factor in the comparatively "bargain" bills, and it's "well worth the trouble."

Tremont 647/Sister Sorel *American*   20 | 17 | 21 | $38
South End | 647 Tremont St. (W. Brookline St.) | 617-266-4600 |
www.tremont647.com

An "offbeat, informal party atmosphere" prevails at this "reliable, not-expensive" South End eatery and its adjoining bar, doling out "well-prepared" New American fare alongside "creative cocktails and a decent wine list"; for an "unbelievable value", swing by for $2 tacos on Tuesdays, or come for the "fantastic" brunch and do like the "spirited" staff: "wear your PJs"; P.S. a post-Survey renovation outdates the Decor score.

Tresca *Italian*   24 | 22 | 23 | $51
North End | 233 Hanover St. (Cross St.) | 617-742-8240 |
www.trescanorthend.com

"Solid and trendy", this North End eatery proffers "Italian classics" that are "fit for foodies" and ferried by "fabulous" staffers in "cozy" digs that exude "old-world charm"; wines and drinks are just as delicious as the fare, but still, a few dollar-watchers deem the tabs "overpriced" no matter how "exquisite" the eats are.

	FOOD	DECOR	SERVICE	COST

Trident Booksellers & Cafe ● *Eclectic* | 20 | 18 | 19 | $19 |

Back Bay | 338 Newbury St. (Mass. Ave.) | 617-267-8688 |
www.tridentbookscafe.com

"Bookworms and people-watchers" aver that this "understated" all-day Back Bay bookstore/coffee shop/Eclectic cafe is a "fun" place for "light meal" from an "extensive menu" of "homey, satisfying" grub from which "you get your money's worth"; the staff remains "friendly" even when the "crunchy" digs get "crowded", especially during the "great" brunch.

Trina's Starlite Lounge ● *American* | 20 | 20 | 20 | $24 |

Inman Square | 3 Beacon St. (Cambridge St.) | Cambridge | 617-576-0006 | www.trinastarlitelounge.com

"Dive on the outside, pretty sweet on the inside", this "funky" Inman Square American lounge metes out "kick-ass comfort food" listed on a "limited" menu that's designed to complement the real stars of the show: "formidable cocktails" mixed by a "friendly staff"; "hipsters hanging from the rafters" and "affordable" tabs make it a "great place" to "party" "any night of the week", especially "if you love hot dogs."

☒ Troquet ☒Ⓜ *American/French* | 26 | 21 | 25 | $67 |

Theater District | 140 Boylston St. (bet. Charles & Tremont Sts.) | 617-695-9463 | www.troquetboston.com

A "wide variety" of "magnificent", "reasonably priced" wines by the glass and half-glass makes this bi-level Theater District bistro an oenophile's "Oz", while "exciting" pairings with the "progressive" New American–French bistro cuisine boasting "tantalizing flavors galore" help justify the fare's "high cost"; "formal but not stuffy service" complements the "understated but elegant" setting, the highlight of which is a "beautiful view" of the Common.

Tryst *American* | 24 | 21 | 23 | $42 |

Arlington | 689 Massachusetts Ave. (Rte. 60) | 781-641-2227 | www.trystrestaurant.com

"Just the right amount of city sensibility" suffuses this "classy option for dinner or weekend brunch" in Arlington, whose "lovely, carefully prepared New American" fare is "worth the cost", particularly when factoring in the "attentive, caring" service; there are "sedate, family-oriented tables in the rear" that also work "for a romantic dinner", while it's all about "bustle and buzz" at the "amazing bar", which manages to be at once "comfortable and trendy."

Tupelo Ⓜ *Southern* | 24 | 17 | 23 | $32 |

Inman Square | 1193 Cambridge St. (Tremont St.) | Cambridge | 617-868-0004 | www.tupelo02139.com

A "serious" approach to "delicious", "down-home Southern cooking" belies the "casual atmosphere" at this "awesome" Inman Square outpost that "doesn't break the bank"; wine and beer "served in glass jars" and true "hospitality" from the "fantastic" staff make the setting, though "small", "crowded" and "too noisy for intimate conversation", "more fun than you can shake a stick at."

	FOOD	DECOR	SERVICE	COST

NEW Turbine
Wine Bar 🖉🅜 *American/Asian*

| - | - | - | M |

Lynn | 56 Central Sq. (Blake St.) | 781-780-7301 | www.turbinewinebar.com

Set in a beautifully renovated 1890s building in Downtown Lynn, this wine bar offers a moderately priced menu of American and Asian-fusion cuisine to accompany more than 40 wines by the glass, all enjoyed in a minimalist, industrial-chic setting with bamboo floors, stainless-steel tables and soft pendant lighting; it's a shining example of urban transformation in a neighborhood that was once a shoe-manufacturing mecca.

Turner Fisheries 🖉 *Seafood*

| 20 | 21 | 21 | $49 |

Back Bay | Westin Copley Pl. | 10 Huntington Ave. (Dartmouth St.) | 617-424-7425 | www.turnersboston.com

With a "great location" in the Back Bay's Westin Copley Place, this "modern, sleek fishery" boasts a contingent that enthuses about the "consistent", "fresh", "delicious" seafood (e.g. "excellent chowder") and a staff that does "a wonderful job making sure you're taken care of"; however, there are also a fair amount of dissenters who are "frustrated" by "mediocre" meals, too "expensive" tabs and "bored" servers.

Turner's Seafood
Grill & Market 🅜 *Seafood*

| 23 | 18 | 22 | $34 |

Melrose | 506 Main St. (bet. Essex & Foster Sts.) | 781-662-0700 | www.turners-seafood.com

"Melrose's happenin' spot" is this "quintessential New England" fish restaurant with nautical-themed wood decor, a "never-disappointing" menu featuring everything "from classic seafood-shack to upscale" preparations, a "wide range of prices" and "great cocktail and raw bars"; unsurprisingly, it's "noisy" and "can be tough to find a table", but the "friendly staff" and "owners go out of their way to make your experience a good one."

Tuscan Grill *Italian*

| 21 | 18 | 20 | $48 |

Waltham | 361 Moody St. (bet. Spruce & Walnut Sts.) | 781-891-5486 | www.tuscangrillwaltham.com

It's "so good" say allies of this "rustic" Waltham "safe spot" whose "great grilled meats" are the stars of the mostly "moderately priced", "consistently well-prepared" Northern Italian menu, which is enhanced by a "wonderful selection of wines" and ferried by a "caring, knowledgeable" staff; but it's also "so small", so expect a "crowded, chaotic" vibe and an "often sizable wait."

Tu y Yo *Mexican*

| 24 | 16 | 22 | $30 |

Somerville | 858 Broadway (Powderhouse Circle) | 617-623-5411
Needham | 66 Chestnut St. (School St.) | 781-453-1000
www.tuyyo2.com

"Remarkable" recipes "handed down for generations" and "prepared *con amor*" is the selling point of this "affordable" Somerville cantina and its Needham offshoot, both "great places to go for dishes you can't find at any ol' Mexican restaurant" ("try the grasshopper"); adorned with a "spartan" amount of decor meant to evoke 18th-century Mexico, the venue boasts "the feel of a family-owned restaurant where the family cares about the food and their guests."

28 Degrees ⓜ *American* | 19 | 24 | 20 | $37 |

South End | 1 Appleton St. (Tremont St.) | 617-728-0728 |
www.28degrees-boston.com

"Luxe attention to detail" ("techno" design elements, "flowing curtains", "cool bathrooms") sets the "trendy" stage at this South End lounge whose "claim to fame" is an "impressive list" of "delicious specialty cocktails" that fuel many a "girls' night out" and "dates"; though some say the New American small plates are "terrific" and "fun to share", a few foodies dismisses them as "afterthoughts."

21st Amendment *Pub Food* | 17 | 18 | 18 | $21 |

Beacon Hill | 150 Bowdoin St. (bet. Beacon & Mt. Vernon Sts.) |
617-227-7100 | www.21stboston.com

With the State House "right across the street", this "neighborhood pub" is "often rife with politicos, aspiring politicos" and more of the "Beacon Hill elite" who, "after-work", like a "strong, well-made drink" along with "typical", "inexpensive" pub food; the "dark, cozy tavern" environs please, as does the "fast and friendly service."

29 Newbury *American* | 20 | 19 | 20 | $40 |

Back Bay | 29 Newbury St. (bet. Arlington & Berkeley Sts.) |
617-536-0290 | www.29newbury.com

"After a day of shopping", "get a seat near the windows" or on the "lovely patio" and "enjoy the human scenery" that parades in front of this "casual", "see-and-be-seen" "Newbury Street fixture" offering a "reasonably priced", "something-for-everyone" New American menu; ok, so maybe the "stuck-in-the-'80s decor" "needs an update", but the "attentive staff" can stay just as it is.

ⓩ T.W. Food *American/French* | 28 | 22 | 27 | $58 |

Huron Village | 377 Walden St. (Concord Ave.) | Cambridge |
617-864-4745 | www.twfoodrestaurant.com

At this "extraordinary" Huron Village "hideaway", toque Tim Wiechmann's "sublime", seasonal New American–New French fare is "thoughtfully prepared" with local ingredients and "layers of complexity", then paired with wines from a "creative" list; the "casual", "minimalist" setting is "tight but charming" and conducive to "personal attention" from the "knowledgeable", "impeccable" staff, another element that makes it "worth the extra cost."

224 Boston Street *American* | 21 | 19 | 22 | $37 |

Dorchester | 224 Boston St. (Mass. Ave.) | 617-265-1217 |
www.224bostonstreet.com

This "charming neighborhood restaurant" with a "cool bar" in Dorchester employs "knowledgeable, friendly" staffers to deliver its "delicious" seasonal New American "comfort food with a creative streak"; so "intimate" are the digs (and so "moderate" are the prices) that there's occasionally "a wait", though more room is available "when it's warmer" and the "great patio" is open.

Typhoon *Asian*

▽ 18 | 15 | 17 | $32

Back Bay | 725 Boylston St. (bet. Exeter & Fairfield Sts.) | 617-859-8181
NEW Hingham | 25 Shipyard Dr. (Lincoln St.) | 781-749-8484
www.typhoonboston.com

Everyone appreciates this "casual" eatery's "great" Back Bay location with a "patio right in Copley Square", but the fare – Asian with a Japanese-focused, sushi-centric slant – gets mixed marks ("very good" to "just ok" to "boring"); the same goes for the cost ("cheap" vs. "expensive"), the service ("quick" vs. "nontimely") and the setting ("beautiful" vs. "silly"); P.S. there's a relatively new Hingham offshoot.

UBurger *Burgers*

22 | 13 | 17 | $12

Boston University | 1022 Commonwealth Ave. (bet. Babcock St. & Winslow Rd.) | 617-487-4855 ●
Kenmore Square | 636 Beacon St. (Kenmore St.) | 617-536-0448
www.uburgerboston.com

"Fantastic burgers" augmented by an "incredible amount of topping options" plus "noteworthy" fries, onion rings that are "the bomb" and "yummy frappes" are the hallmarks of this duo with "quick counter service"; "cheap" prices attract "pre-Fenway" folk to the Kenmore Square location and "college students" to the BU version, though probably not the "basic settings."

UFood Grill *Health Food*

17 | 11 | 15 | $12

Downtown Crossing | 530 Washington St. (DeLafayette Ave.) | 617-451-0043
Fenway | LandMark Ctr. | 201 Brookline Ave. (Park Dr.) | 857-254-0082
Watertown | 222 Arsenal St. (bet. Beechwood Ave. & Louise St.) | 617-923-7676
www.ufoodgrill.com

"Havens for healthy eaters", this "speedy, efficient", "counter-service" trio doles out "fast food" that's "not as bad for you" as others of its ilk (e.g. "unfries", turkey burgers, fro-yo), or so says the posted "nutritional content"; skeptics, however, assert the "bland" fodder is "not nearly as healthy as it claims" and "a little pricey" for what it is.

Umbria Prime 🗷 *Italian/Steak*

23 | 22 | 22 | $60

Financial District | 295 Franklin St. (Broad St.) | 617-338-1000 | www.umbriaprime.com

With a "prime location" in the Financial District, this "not-cheap" venue grills up "excellent" steaks with "Italian flair" plus "wonderful" pizzas and "scrumptious" pastas; the "sleek", "testosterone-driven" space includes a bar, lounge and nightclub on multiple floors, plus "pleasant, friendly" staffers.

⛉ Uni *Japanese*

28 | 23 | 25 | $70

Back Bay | Eliot Hotel | 370 Commonwealth Ave. (Mass. Ave.) | 617-536-7200 | www.cliorestaurant.com

"Exotic", "excellent", "expensive" are just some descriptors for the "impeccably fresh" sashimi prepared at this "cutting-edge" Ken Oringer sibling to Clio in the Back Bay's Eliot Hotel, where "stylish decor fills the cozy corners of the intimate dining area"; the "great attention to detail" in the "constantly changing" fare extends to the "huge cocktail list" as well as "fabulous" staffers who are adept at "suggesting something to make your eyes twinkle."

Union Bar & Grille *American*　24 | 23 | 24 | $46

South End | 1357 Washington St. (bet. Union Park & Waltham Sts.) | 617-423-0555 | www.unionrestaurant.com

"Linger in joyful conversation" in "tufted-leather circular booths" over "consistent", "beautifully prepared" New American fare at this "gorgeous", "clubby" South End "mainstay" with "smart service"; for being so "chic", it's quite affordable, with a "fabulous" prix fixe brunch that's "one of the best" "deals" in the city.

☑ Union Oyster　21 | 21 | 20 | $42

House *New England/Seafood*

Faneuil Hall | 41 Union St. (bet. Hanover & North Sts.) | 617-227-2750 | www.unionoysterhouse.com

The "oldest restaurant in continuous service in the U.S.", this Faneuil Hall–area "antique" is a "must-do for tourists", with its "arguably perfect" chowder, "reliable oysters" readied by "fabulous" shuckers and other "cooked-as-requested" New England seafood, not to mention its "maze" of "creaky stairs", "nooks and crannies"; but it's also "worth your time" "if you're a local", at least for "historical value" – just know that "prices have risen substantially" since 1826.

Upper Crust *Pizza*　21 | 12 | 16 | $16

Back Bay | 222 Newbury St. (Fairfield St.) | 617-262-0090
Beacon Hill | 20 Charles St. (Beacon St.) | 617-723-9600
West Roxbury | 1727 Centre St. (bet. Esther & Manthorne Rds.) | 617-323-6400
Fenway | 1330 Boylston St. (bet. Jersey & Kilmarnock Sts.) | 617-266-9210
South End | 683 Tremont St. (W. Newton St.) | 617-927-0090
Harvard Square | 49 Brattle St. (Church St.) | Cambridge | 617-497-4111
Brookline | 286 Harvard St. (Beacon St.) | 617-734-4900
Lexington | 41 Waltham St. (Mass. Ave.) | 781-274-0089
Waltham | 435 Moody St. (Chestnut St.) | 781-736-0044
Watertown | 94 Main St. (Cross St.) | 617-923-6060
www.theuppercrustpizzeria.com
Additional locations throughout the Boston area

Partisans of this pizza chain say that toppings "more diverse than the U.N.", crusts that are at once "thin, crisp and chewy" and "enormous slices" mean it "lives up to the hype" – but they also advise "don't eat in", because while "watching them throw the dough up in the air" is "fun", "most locations are small, cramped and uncomfortable"; a party of perfectionists declare it "overrated" and "overpriced", but loyalists are "happy" it's "constantly expanding."

Upstairs on the Square *American*　24 | 24 | 23 | $49

Harvard Square | 91 Winthrop St. (JFK St.) | Cambridge | 617-864-1933 | www.upstairsonthesquare.com

"Like falling down the rabbit hole", the "whimsical", "adorable" Monday Club Bar (festooned in "pink, gold", "turquoise, zebra", an "abundance of mirrors") at this Harvard Square New American provides a "fairy-tale experience", while the "jewel"-like Soirée Room on the top floor is a "more formal", "pricier" "feast for the eyes"; indeed, the "experience between upstairs and downstairs is like night and day", but the service is universally "impeccable", just as the cuisine is altogether "luxe and delicious."

NEW Vapiano _Italian_   18 | 20 | 14 | $22

Theater District | 191 Stuart St. (Charles St.) | 857-445-0236 | www.vapiano-boston.com

The "unique, cafeteria-style" concept – in which "different stations" provide "many options" of "made-to-order" pastas, pizzas, panini and salads – "takes some getting used to" at this "moderately priced", "cool"-looking Theater District premiere of an Italian chain from Germany, and converts call it a "nice and easy alternative", especially for a "quick" lunch; others, however, aren't keen on the "work" involved, especially when it yields "bland" chow.

Veggie Planet _Pizza/Vegetarian_   22 | 12 | 16 | $16

Harvard Square | Club Passim | 47 Palmer St. (Church St.) | Cambridge | 617-661-1513 | www.veggieplanet.net

"You'll never miss" the meat at this "groovy" Harvard Square basement spinning "creative" vegetarian pizzas that are "flavorful", "healthy" and "inexpensive"; some, though, "take it or leave it" because the setting is "small and uncomfortable", plus "service is intermittent", especially when there's live music being performed at the attached "legendary folk-music mecca", Club Passim.

Via Lago 🅢 _American_   22 | 15 | 20 | $24

Lexington | 1845 Massachusetts Ave. (Bedford St.) | 781-861-6174 | www.vialagocatering.com

"Gourmet take-out" breakfasts and lunches (e.g. "fancy sandwiches and pastries") are whipped up at this "unassuming", "reasonably priced" counter-serve storefront in Downtown Lexington; at night, it "transforms into a shockingly good" "full-service" American restaurant, which is so "small", it can be "tough to get a table" or a seat at the "new little bar."

Via Matta 🅢 _Italian_   25 | 22 | 24 | $54

Park Square | 79 Park Plaza (Arlington St.) | 617-422-0008 | www.viamattarestaurant.com

"Oh, what food! what service!" exalt enthusiasts of Michael Schlow's "stylish" Park Square Italian where "sophisticated", "carefully crafted" meals are paired with a "superlative wine list" by "professional" staffers; "the air is electric" in the "sleek", white dining room and separate bar, while the patio is "secluded from street traffic", and though you "need a deep wallet" wherever you sit, it's "worth it."

Vicki Lee's Ⓜ _Bakery/Sandwiches_   23 | 19 | 19 | $18

Belmont | 105 Trapelo Rd. (Common St.) | 617-489-5007 | www.vickilees.com

"Bringing some zip" to Belmont's Cushing Square, this "adorable" bakery's "genius" chef fashions "scrumptious", "over-the-top gorgeous" cakes and pastries, plus casual breakfast and lunch sandwiches, etc., that are equally "wonderful", though "exorbitantly priced", all things considered; nevertheless, fans "wish" it had "longer hours."

Victoria's Diner *Diner*
19 | 15 | 19 | $16

Roxbury | 1024 Massachusetts Ave. (New Market Sq.) | 617-442-5965 | www.victoriasdiner.com

"All social strata collide" at this "greasy spoon" in Roxbury delivering "cheap", "delicious" diner grub that can be anything to anybody, including a "special treat" for early birds, the "ultimate hangover cure" for late-risers and an "amazing" "late-night option" for partyers (it's open 24/7 Thursdays–Saturdays).

Village Fish *Italian/Seafood*
22 | 14 | 18 | $31

Needham | 970 Great Plain Ave. (bet. Chapel St. & Dedham Ave.) | 781-449-0544

"Simply prepared", "wonderful seafood" mostly served in a skillet is the specialty of this "unpretentious" Needham Italian promising "fair prices" and "prompt service"; the "small", "almost dinerlike" setting, marked by nautical paintings, "can get noisy", so if you're looking for quiet, regulars recommend "asking for a booth near the back."

Village Smokehouse *BBQ*
21 | 15 | 19 | $28

Brookline | 1 Harvard St. (Washington St.) | 617-566-3782 | www.villagesmokehouse.com

"If y'all favor Texas BBQ", then this Brookline Villager is the place to "satisfy that craving" via "finger-licking good" vittles that've been "slow cooked" in an "open pit", then delivered with "lightning speed" for "good prices"; although a few feel the "low-key" setting with "checked tablecloths" "needs to be updated", as it stands, you don't mind "getting messy" in these digs (witness the roll of paper towels at each table).

Village Sushi & Grill *Japanese/Korean*
∇ 22 | 15 | 19 | $30

Roslindale | 14 Corinth St. (Birch St.) | 617-363-7874 | www.villagesushiandgrill.com

The sushi and Korean cuisine turned out at this Roslindale "neighborhood place" is "shockingly good" for its "no-atmosphere" location; indeed, "don't try to impress a date" here, but do bring the family, because it's "kid-friendly" and reasonably priced.

Vin & Eddie's Ⓜ *Italian*
∇ 21 | 14 | 18 | $51

Abington | 1400 Bedford St. (bet. Rtes. 58 & 139) | 781-871-1469

"In the wilds of Abington", this "standby" has been offering "quality", upscale Northern Italian fare and a solid selection of international wines since 1955; and while some longtime patrons find the mural-marked setting "romantic", others scoff it "needs an overhaul."

Vinny's at Night *Italian*
24 | 14 | 21 | $29

Somerville | 76 Broadway (Hathorn St.) | 617-628-1921 | www.vinnysonbroadway.com

Never mind its "kitschy", "unusual setting" in "the back of a convenience store", this "off-the-beaten-path" Somerville Sicilian whips up "absolutely delicious" dishes like "killer homemade pastas" whose "big portions" equal a "great value" ("one of the best bets is the antipasto table" – "delicious!"); since it doesn't take reservations, you should expect "long waits on occasion" and have faith that the "great" staff is working to turn those tables.

Vlora ● *Mediterranean*   20 | 19 | 21 | $34

Back Bay | 545 Boylston St. (bet. Clarendon & Dartmouth Sts.) | 617-638-9699 | www.vloraboston.com

"A bit hard to find" in its basement setting, this "easy-on-the-eyes" "contemporary" destination infuses "creative" Albanian touches into "tasty" Med dishes, which are "beautifully presented" by "eager-to-please" staffers, complemented by a "great wine selection" and priced to provide a "break from the Back Bay expense-account culture"; a vocal minority feels "it misses the mark somehow", but still, props are given for "trying hard."

Volle Nolle ☒⌐ *Sandwiches*   ▽ 26 | 16 | 25 | $12

North End | 351 Hanover St. (Fleet St.) | 617-523-0003

"Unforgettable" sandwiches and "addictive" chocolate chip cookies and brownies prove to be "great for kids and families", and priced right too, at this "funky", cash-only North End shop with tin ceilings and chocolate-colored walls; "the woman who runs it" has her fair share of fans too – apparently, she's the "nicest."

Wagamama *Noodle Shop*   18 | 15 | 17 | $20

Back Bay | Prudential Ctr. | 800 Boylston St. (Fairfield St.) | 617-778-2344
Faneuil Hall | Faneuil Hall Mktpl. | Quincy Mkt. (Congress St.) | 617-742-9242
Harvard Square | 57 JFK St. (Winthrop St.) | Cambridge | 617-499-0930
www.wagamama.us

A "British phenom", these "funky" "cafeteria"-style noodle shops "quickly" ladle out "made-to-order" ramen, soups and stir-fries that fans "slurping" away at the "communal tables" pronounce "yummy"; some palates are "underwhelmed by the taste", and truth be told, "you could get the real deal in Chinatown minus the inflated price tag", but "on a cold day", it "works" "in a pinch."

Walden Grille *American*   ▽ 16 | 18 | 17 | $36

Concord | 24 Walden St. (Main St.) | 978-371-2233 | www.waldengrille.com

"Nicely prepared" if "unremarkable" New American dishes feed "regulars", especially "for lunch", at this "reasonable" Concord grill in a former firehouse, whose "decor could use updating"; other locals who come here "by default" because "there are so few places to eat" in the area lament that it "could be so much more" if only its "promise" was fulfilled.

Warren Tavern *American*   19 | 21 | 18 | $27

Charlestown | 2 Pleasant St. (Main St.) | 617-241-8142 | www.warrentavern.com

"Paul Revere's pub fare" turns out to be rather "enjoyable", and "value"-priced, at this Charlestown American tavern from 1780, a "fun", "spooky little space" with low, slanted ceilings and floorboards that really "feels like it may very well be one of the birthplaces of our nation"; however, with a "drinking crowd of locals and tourists" and TVs at the bar, some preservationists bemoan "efforts to make it into yet another sports bar."

Washington Square Tavern *American* | 22 | 20 | 21 | $34 |

Brookline | 714 Washington St. (Beacon St.) | 617-232-8989 | www.washingtonsquaretavern.com

"Dependable" "comfort food" prepared with "some imagination", "excellent" brews and "great wine deals" is what's happening at this "lively" Brookline American, a "cozy" setting "lined with dark wood and books"; "the owner knows everyone in the neighborhood" so it's unsurprisingly "popular with locals" who appreciate the "fair prices" – and don't mind the occasional "long wait."

West End Johnnie's M *Eclectic* | ∇ 18 | 23 | 17 | $31 |

West End | 138 Portland St. (Causeway St.) | 617-227-1588 | www.westendjohnnies.com

The movie, "sports and historical memorabilia" (from the collection of the eponymous owner) displayed on both levels of this Eclectic "pre- or post-Garden" hangout in the West End is "awesome", and Sunday's live reggae brunch is just as "fun" – and "loud"; the eats, on the other hand, are "nothing to write home about", though certainly "decent", and thankfully moderately priced.

West on Centre *American* | 19 | 19 | 21 | $33 |

West Roxbury | 1732 Centre St. (Belgrade Ave.) | 617-323-4199 | www.westoncentreboston.com

"Go West, young man . . . and lady" advise advocates of this American "nice surprise in West Roxbury", where a "friendly" staff roams, a "cozy" fireplace roars and the "charming" bar harbors locals "watching games"; as for the "varied menu" (with "varying prices"), there are "some great choices" and some that "sound better than they taste."

West Side Lounge *American* | 21 | 19 | 22 | $36 |

Porter Square | 1680 Massachusetts Ave. (bet. Shepard & Wendell Sts.) | Cambridge | 617-441-5566 | www.westsidelounge.com

"Fabulous, seasonal cocktail creations" made by bartenders who are "consummate professionals" plus "excellent small plates" make this "hip, little" Porter Square American "neighborhood hangout" with "art on the walls" "the kind of place for which eating at the bar was invented"; the regular menu is "great" at the "laid-back" tables too, and just as "moderately priced."

NEW Whiskey Priest *Irish/Pub Food* | 12 | 17 | 16 | $31 |

Seaport District | 150 Northern Ave. (D St.) | 617-426-8111 | www.thewhiskeypriestpub.com

"Being new to the area, one would think this place would try a bit harder", but as it stands now, the Irish pub grub is "subpar" and many staffers are "scatter-brained" (though "nice"); what it does have going for it is an "amazing view" from its Seaport District perch, so if you come, sit near the windows inside (among the "abundance of televisions") or on the "great roof deck" and "stick to the scotch" – the "giant bar" has more than a hundred types.

Wine Cellar ☒ *Continental/Fondue* ▽ 22 | 19 | 19 | $48

Back Bay | 30 Massachusetts Ave. (bet. Beacon & Marlborough Sts.) | 617-236-0080 | www.bostoncellar.com

"Fairly romantic" atmospherics are enhanced by murals of an old New England street and an "extensive" list of "excellent wines" at this "cozy" Back Bay spot where a "helpful staff" makes "great suggestions" about the Continental cuisine; the menu's métier is fondue, and while some diners deem the meats "lackluster", others would return for an "all-cheese" meal, despite the fact that it may be "overpriced."

NEW W Lounge ● *American* 19 | 25 | 20 | $42

Theater District | W Boston | 100 Stuart St. (Tremont St.) | 617-261-8700

It's "quite a scene" at this "swanky", "energetic" hotel lounge in the Theater District, where the "young and hip" "wait in line" to sample "fab" cocktails and "delicious" if "limited" New American snacks; leather couches, "amazing decor" and "personable" service make it a "great place for a girls' night out – if the girls have good-paying day jobs."

Wonder Spice Cafe *Cambodian/Thai* 20 | 14 | 18 | $20

Jamaica Plain | 697 Centre St. (Burroughs St.) | 617-522-0200

"Basic" but "reliable" Cambodian and Thai fare are doled out by a "friendly", "efficient" staff at this "reasonably priced" Jamaica Plain stop; the "decor could be updated" inside and the "little alley" patio delivers "no great atmo" either, so no wonder it's "popular for takeout."

Woodman's *Seafood* 23 | 11 | 14 | $28

Essex | 121 Main St. (Rte. 128) | 978-768-6057 | www.woodmans.com

The devoted make "annual pilgrimages" to this "no-frills", "shabby" Essex "institution" that "claims to have invented the fried clam" to brave "lines that wind around the block" (in summer) for a "fantastic" seafood "fry fest" and "unbelievable" lobsters, both in rolls and in the rough; it may be "expensive" for a "self-service" spot where you "clean up after yourself", but it's all "worth it for a memorable New England experience."

Woodward ● *American* 21 | 22 | 20 | $44

Financial District | Ames Hotel | 1 Court St. (State St.) | 617-979-8200 | www.woodwardatames.com

"Exciting" New American "comfort food" "sized for sharing" is what's on the menu at this "fab" black-and-white bi-level tavern in the lobby of the Financial District's Ames Hotel, a "gorgeous reuse of a historic building"; however, with such "unique, delicious" cocktails, "lounge lizards" suspect "it's a better bar than restaurant", an estimation that's supported by the occasional "attitude" from the staff and the "boisterous" scene (you might "go deaf during dinner").

	FOOD	DECOR	SERVICE	COST

Woody's Grill & Tap *American* | 23 | 16 | 21 | $22 |

Fenway | 58 Hemenway St. (Westland Ave.) | 617-375-9663

Between the "friendly service" and the "comfortable" "home-away-from-home" atmosphere, this American grill in the Fenway invites "students and faculty" to "relax" and watch a game on the many televisions; to keep them content are "excellent" "wood-fired pizzas" and "tons of delicious beers on tap", not to mention cheap fees.

Xinh Xinh *Vietnamese* | 25 | 8 | 20 | $16 |

Chinatown | 7 Beach St. (Washington St.) | 617-422-0501

This Chinatown "hole-in-the-wall" "doesn't mess around" with such things as decor – "delicious, huge bowls of pho" and other "fantastic" Vietnamese victuals, "that's what matters!"; what's more, "the price is nice", just like the "wonderful folks who run it" and the "friendly" staff.

NEW Yak & Yeti *Indian/Nepalese* | - | - | - | M |

Somerville | 719 Broadway (Boston Ave.) | 617-284-6227 | www.yakandyeticafe.com

Adventurous palates and vegetarians alike dub this Somerville newcomer "a real find" for its Indian and Nepalese cuisine from various regions, packed with exotic curries and flavors; the weekday lunch buffet and set menus please affordability-seekers, while the comfortable, modern setting satisfies suppers looking for a unique date spot.

Yama *Japanese* | 23 | 17 | 22 | $34 |

Andover | 63 Park St. (bet. Florence & Whittier Sts.) | 978-749-9777 | www.yamaandover.com Ⓜ

Wellesley | 245 Washington St. (Rte. 9) | 781-431-8886 | www.yamawellesley.com

"Yama is yummy!" yowl supporters of these "reliable", individually owned Andover and Wellesley sushi haunts where "both the standards and the inventive rolls", not to mention the cooked items, are "as good as places that are twice the cost"; the decor "could probably use a little makeover", but the "friendly, efficient" staffers are fine as is; P.S. Washington Street is BYO, "so plan accordingly."

NEW Yard House ☻ *American* | 19 | 18 | 18 | $30 |

Dedham | Legacy Pl. | 950 Providence Hwy. (Elm St.) | 781-326-4644 | www.yardhouse.com

"Loud crowds" of "sports fans" and brew "aficionados" declare this "industrial"-looking national chain outpost in Dedham's Legacy Place "the place to be", what with its "more TVs than a Best Buy" and so many tap beers they "don't even know where to start"; as for the American menu (with "tons of variety"), though it may very well be a "second thought", it's "surprisingly good", "filling" and "affordable."

Za *Pizza* | 24 | 20 | 23 | $23 |

NEW Kendall Square | 350 Third St. (Dorchester St.) | Cambridge | 617-452-9292

Arlington | 138 Massachusetts Ave. (Milton St.) | 781-316-2334 | www.zarestaurant.com

"Ingenious" "designer" pizzas and "gourmet salads" are crafted to look like "pieces of art" and constructed with "local, organic products" at this "contemporary", "family-friendly" Arlington spot with a new Kendall Square spin-off, the latter sharing a bar and patio with EVOO (owned by the same folks); "frequent menu changes" and generally "great value" keep the "adventurous" "coming back", and the "engaging" staff helps set a "pleasant" tone, which is good since everything "takes a little time" to be "made fresh."

Zabaglione *Italian*   ∇ 28 | 17 | 24 | $43
Ipswich | 10 Central St. (Market St.) | 978-356-5466

Café Zabaglione *Italian*
Ipswich | 1 Market St. (Central St.) | 978-356-6484
www.zabaglioneristorante.com

A "fine choice of dishes and wines" topped by "heavenly" desserts makes Ipswich folks feel like they're "eating in Italy" at this "tiny" but "wonderful" Central Street dinner spot; the portions are "heaping", but still it's a "little pricey", so if you're looking to spend less, head to the "casual" cafe around the corner, serving "excellent" lunches too.

Zaftigs Delicatessen *Deli*   21 | 16 | 19 | $22
Brookline | 335 Harvard St. (bet. Babcock & Stedman Sts.) |
617-975-0075 | www.zaftigs.com

"Wonderful overstuffed sandwiches" and breakfast "served all day" in "mega portions" (e.g. "to-die-for" banana-stuffed French toast) are among the "old-fashioned cholesterol" doled out at this "friendly" Jewish-style (though non-kosher) deli in Brookline; many a penny-pincher pegs it as "overpriced" and a few foodies feel the grub's "bland", but you wouldn't know it from the "long lines, especially during weekend brunch."

Zebra's Bistro and Wine Bar *American*   24 | 22 | 24 | $44
Medfield | 21 North St. (Rte. 109) | 508-359-4100 | www.zebrasbistro.com

"Fine diners with diverse tastes" are catered to by a "personable" staff at this "hip, warm" "urban restaurant" in Medfield, which augments its "fantastic" New American cuisine with "some amazing sushi"; the "upscale" experience extends to the "nice" bar, which "offers a full menu", "froufrou" cocktails and an "extensive wine list."

Zen *Japanese*   ∇ 23 | 18 | 20 | $35
Beacon Hill | 21A Beacon St. (bet. Bowdoin & Somerset Sts.) |
617-371-1230 | www.zensushibar.com

When the "yen for sushi" strikes, Beacon Hill fish fans quell it with a visit to this "awesome" Japanese where "special attention is paid to each delicate, delectable morsel"; aesthetes judge the bi-level digs as "dated", but you "don't go there for the atmosphere" – it's the "quick service" and "pretty reasonable" tabs that attract.

Zócalo Cocina Mexicana *Mexican*   24 | 19 | 22 | $26
NEW **Back Bay** | 35 Stanhope St. (bet. Chambers Pl. & Clarendon St.) |
617-456-7849 | www.zocalobrighton.com
Arlington | 203A Broadway (bet. Adams & Foster Sts.) | 781-643-2299 |
www.zocaloarlington.com 🚫

"Creative and original *platos de Mexico*", particularly the "fantastic guacamole made tableside", "sing with flavor" at these Arlington and Back Bay *casas* of "high-end" (yet moderately priced) regional cuisine; the margaritas are just as "different and delicious" as the dishes, and they help to keep the atmosphere "chill", as do the "helpful" servers.

Zoe's *Chinese*   22 | 16 | 20 | $23

Somerville | 296 Beacon St. (Eustis St.) | 617-864-6265
"More authentic than many", this Chinese "standby" in Somerville prepares a "wide variety of regional dishes" that's notable for its "tasty", "peppery" Sichuan specialties; the "downscale setting" is no issue to surveyors who are more enamored with "pleasant service" and "extremely reasonable prices."

Zuzu! *Eclectic/Mideastern*   ∇ 19 | 18 | 17 | $26

Central Square | The Middle East | 474 Massachusetts Ave. (Brookline St.) | Cambridge | 617-864-3278 | www.zuzubar.com
"A bit of everything" is served at this Eclectic-Mideastern lounge with "funky" decor in Central Square, all of it "reasonably priced", most of it "delicious"; since it's part of the adjacent The Middle East (they also share a kitchen), partyers declare that "the real reason to go" is later at night, when it "brims with hipsters" and DJs or the occasional live band play "something for everybody."

Cape Cod

TOP FOOD		TOP DECOR	
28	Bramble Inn | *American*	29	Belfry Inne | *American*
	PB Boulangerie Bistro | *French*	28	28 Atlantic | *American*
	Abba | *Mediterranean/Thai*		Red Inn | *New Eng.*
27	Glass Onion, The | *American*	27	Ocean House | *American*
	Cape Sea Grille | *American*		Marshside | *American/Seafood*

⏣ Abba *Mediterranean/Thai* `28` `23` `25` `$53`

Orleans | 89 Old Colony Way (West Rd.) | 508-255-8144 |
www.abbarestaurant.com

At this Orleans "standout", voted Cape Cod's Most Popular restaurant, "flavorful surprises" abound in Erez Pinhas' "luscious", "innovative" Med-Thai cuisine; "cheerful" staffers can suggest pairings from the "well-edited wine list" featuring "hard-to-find" varieties and more "moderate prices" than the "expensive-but-worth-it" fare; though "charming", the old-house setting is "cramped", which is why summerers try for the terrace and "locals love it best off-season."

Academy Ocean Grille *Eclectic/Seafood* `21` `18` `20` `$40`

Orleans | 2 Academy Pl. (bet. Main St. & Orleans-Chatham Rd.) |
508-240-1585 | www.academyoceangrille.com

"Competently prepared, fairly priced" Eclectic seafood is the draw at this "casual", "homey" Orleans grill whose features include an "intimate" if "basic" dining room with a fireplace, a "quaint bar" and a "pleasant patio"; though there are reports of "lackluster service", for the most part, staffers are "friendly and helpful."

Adrian's *American/Italian* ▽ `18` `16` `20` `$38`

North Truro | Outer Reach Resort | 535 Rte. 6 (Pilgrim Heights Rd.) |
508-487-4360 | www.adriansrestaurant.com

"Spectacular views" of the bay, affordable prices and a "child-friendly" atmosphere keep families returning to this North Truro longtimer offering "quality" American breakfasts and Italian dinners with "no pretentions"; housed in the Outer Reach Resort, the setting screams "motel" to some – nevertheless, for an alfresco meal "on the deck" "after the beach", it's a "treasure."

Alberto's Ristorante *Italian* `21` `20` `21` `$39`

Hyannis | 360 Main St. (Barnstable Rd.) | 508-778-1770 | www.albertos.net

"You can always find something to please your mood" and palate at this "welcoming", "dependable" Northern Italian in Hyannis, where the prices are always "reasonable", but the "sunset dinners" are a particularly "outstanding value"; "snag a seat outside" or, for "romantic", "old-world charm", a table by one of seven fireplaces.

Amari Bar & Ristorante *Italian* `22` `22` `22` `$37`

East Sandwich | 674 Rte. 6A/Old King's Hwy. (Jones Ln.) |
508-375-0011 | www.amarirestaurant.com

"Never a bad meal, whatever you order" assure acolytes of this East Sandwich year-round Italian "hidden gem" with rustic Tuscan decor, a fireplace, live entertainment Fridays and Saturdays and, best of all, "reasonable prices."

Anthony's Cummaquid Inn Ⓜ *Continental* | 17 | 18 | 19 | $45 |

Yarmouth Port | 2 Main St./Rte. 6A (Willow St.) | 508-362-4501 | www.pier4.com

"Beautiful" views of the bay are "the best part" of this Yarmouth Port Continental, with the "wonderful popovers" coming in second; and while some surveyors say it serves "tasty" fare in a "romantic" interior, "longtime patrons" lament it "used to be a must-go place for special occasions, but has slipped" due to "expensive" yet "plainly average food" and "run-down" digs.

Aqua Grille *American/Seafood* | 19 | 19 | 19 | $40 |

Sandwich | 14 Gallo Rd. (Town Neck Rd.) | 508-888-8889 | www.aquagrille.com

"Go for the view" and "good variety" at this "casual", "traditional" venue overlooking the canal in Sandwich, a popular lunch stop for those heading to the Upper Cape; the "dependable" menu of New American seafood boasts some "creative recipes" with "German twists", and everything's brought by "accommodating" servers.

Ardeo *Mediterranean* | 19 | 16 | 19 | $31 |

South Yarmouth | Union Plaza | 23 Whites Path (Station Ave.) | 508-760-1500
Brewster | 280 Underpass Rd. (Snow Rd.) | 508-896-4200
Hyannis | 644 Main St. (Sea St.) | 508-790-1115
Yarmouth Port | 81 Kings Circuit (Rte. 6A) | 508-362-7730 Ⓜ
www.ardeocapecod.com

This "casual", "reliable" Cape Cod Mediterranean mini-chain boasts a "loyal following among locals" for its "large variety", "huge portions" and "fine service"; the Brewster branch is a "great option for famished cyclists", as it's "located right off the Cape Cod Rail Trail", the Yarmouth iteration offers a "relaxed" setting on a golf course, while all are spots to "bring the family" because the "prices are right."

ⓩ Arnold's Lobster & Clam Bar ⊅ *Seafood* | 24 | 12 | 15 | $24 |

Eastham | 3580 Rte. 6 (Old Orchard Rd.) | 508-255-2575 | www.arnoldsrestaurant.com

"Every summer", "you must at least once" "brave the frightening lines" that seemingly "go all the way to the next town" for the "awesome lobster rolls", "to-die-for fried clams", "killer onion rings" and "nice raw-bar options" doled out at this Eastham "seafood shack"; indeed, it's "worth the wait" and relatively "pricey" tabs, especially considering there's alcohol (a rarity), ice cream and mini golf too.

Asia *Asian* | ▽ 21 | 18 | 22 | $29 |

Mashpee | Mashpee Commons | 3 Greene St. (Steeple St.) | 508-477-8883 | www.mashpeeasia.com

"Groups of friends" are grateful for this Pan-Asian in Mashpee Commons because there's "a little something for everyone" (especially sushi, Chinese and Korean) and the "dishes usually come out fresh, hot" and "quick"; sure, the modern "decor could be livelier", but most folks won't quibble, as the prices are so reasonable.

Barley Neck Inn *American*   20 | 21 | 21 | $37

East Orleans | 5 Beach Rd. (Main St.) | 508-255-0212 | www.barleyneck.com

"Ever reliable" American fare, reasonable prices, "great" service and three "cozy", "romantic" dining rooms make this "informal but not too casual" East Orleans year-rounder in a "historic" sea captain's house a "hangout for locals"; there's also a "popular" attached pub, dubbed Joe's Beach Road Bar & Grill, which boasts a "good wine list", "creative, generous drinks" and live music on weekends.

Barnstable Restaurant & Tavern *New England*   19 | 18 | 19 | $32

Barnstable | 3176 Main St. (Railroad Ave.) | 508-362-2355 | www.barnstablerestaurant.com

"Take the family" for "reasonably priced", "stick-to-your-ribs", Cape Cod–centric cuisine and a healthy serving of "history" at this "cozy", "olde New England"–style tavern in Barnstable; a "friendly staff" and "pleasant outdoor dining in the summer" add to the "nice" vibes.

Baxter's Boathouse *Seafood*   20 | 20 | 17 | $30

Hyannis | 177 Pleasant St. (South St.) | 508-775-4490 | www.baxterscapecod.com

"Get a table with a view" and prepare for "nonstop action" at this "busy", "informal" waterside fish joint where your attention will be split between "watching the boats go in and out of Hyannis Harbor" and shielding your "standard" fried seafood (offered alongside "a few healthier grilled alternatives") from "seagulls"; "take the kids", "they'll have fun" – though you might be peeved by prices that are somewhat "high" for what it is.

Bayside Betsy's *American*   18 | 18 | 20 | $30

Provincetown | 177 Commercial St. (Winthrop St.) | 508-487-6566 | www.baysidebetsys.com

If you don't mind being "crammed in like sardines", this P-towner with "divine" bay views is "a fun place" – and the all-day New American fare is "better than ever", as evidenced by a three-point leap in the Food score; "there is a Betsy", and she's "always welcoming", just like her "great staff", which includes bartenders who mix "stiff drinks" in the front bar.

Bee-Hive Tavern *American*   19 | 17 | 19 | $29

East Sandwich | 406 Rte. 6A (Atkins Rd.) | 508-833-1184 | www.thebeehivetavern.com

"Cape-to-mainland" summer travelers tout the "convenient location" of this "comfortable, cozy" Colonial tavern in East Sandwich, which serves "solid", "dependable", "not-fancy" Traditional American dishes that locals call "warm-me-up food" in winter; affordable prices mean it's especially "good for families with children", and the "friendly" service doesn't hurt either.

	FOOD	DECOR	SERVICE	COST

☑ Belfry Inne & Bistro 🅼 *American* | 27 | 29 | 27 | $56 |

Sandwich | Belfry Inne | 8 Jarves St. (bet. Main St. & Rte. 6A) |
508-888-8550 | www.belfryinn.com

As "close to heaven" as you can get in Sandwich, this New American
in a "beautiful former church" laden with "delightfully interesting"
stained-glass windows earns the Cape's No. 1 Decor score; and hal-
lelujah, the "food is fabulous", the staff commits "no sins" and
there's live music on weekends, all of which helps to make the "expensive" experience "worth it."

Betsy's Diner *Diner* | 16 | 14 | 18 | $18 |

Falmouth | 457 Main St. (bet. King St. & Nye Rd.) | 508-540-0060
"It's all about quantity" at this "'50s"-style diner in Falmouth, where
a "neon sign says 'eat heavy', and they mean it" (e.g. the "bargain
breakfasts" "will carry you until dinner"); red vinyl booths with mini
jukeboxes make it a "fun place to go with the family", and as for the
quality, "stick to the basics, and you'll be happy."

Bistro at Crowne Pointe 🅼 *American* ▽ | 23 | 23 | 23 | $46 |

Provincetown | Crowne Pointe Historic Inn & Spa | 82 Bradford St.
(Prince St.) | 508-487-6767 | www.crownepointe.com

"Amazing views" of Provincetown's Pilgrim Monument from the
"glassed-in porch" are highlights of the "serene setting" at this "intimate" New American "in a historic" High Victorian inn and spa;
while expensive, the prices seem "not outrageous" considering that
the "food is superb" and the "service is impeccable"; P.S. breakfasts
are available to registered guests only.

🆕 Black Cat Tavern, The *Seafood* | 20 | 20 | 20 | $35 |

Hyannis | 165 Ocean St. (bet. Bay St. & Bond Ct.) | 508-778-1233 |
www.blackcattavern.com

"The newest of Dave Colombo's trio of eateries" (he owns Roadhouse
Cafe and Colombo's, also in Hyannis), this seafooder is a "great place"
to grab a "solid, tasty meal" "pre- or post-ferry" since it's "conveniently
located" across the street from the harbor; prices are reasonable,
and with "interesting beers on tap" and "fun music most nights", the
"relaxing" piano bar is a "good" spot "to bring out-of-towners."

Blackfish *American* | 25 | 21 | 23 | $47 |

Truro | 17 Truro Center Rd. (Castle Rd.) | 508-349-3399
With an "interesting" setting in a "cozy" former Truro blacksmith
shop (marked by exposed brick and lanterns), this "classy", "expensive" New American is a "real treat" for "terrific", "innovative" seafood, particularly the "rich" signature tuna Bolognese, all
accompanied by "attentive service"; there's a "good bar scene" to
boot, which exacerbates the "noisy" acoustics.

Bleu *French* | 27 | 22 | 23 | $45 |

Mashpee | Mashpee Commons | 10 Market St. (Nathan Ellis Hwy.) |
508-539-7907 | www.bleurestaurant.com

"Wonderful", "innovative" creations as well as "many bistro-fare
options" "never disappoint" at this French venue in the Mashpee

Commons, where lunch is a "bargain" and the $25 prix fixe dinner (Sundays–Wednesdays) "can't be beat"; a "solid wine list", "graceful service" and "chic decor" featuring "beautiful vintage posters", antiques and many shades of *bleu* are some more reasons why mainlanders say "it's worth a trip to the Cape just to eat" here.

Blue Moon Bistro ⊠ *Mediterranean*   24 | 18 | 22 | $40

Dennis | 605 Main St./Rte. 6A (Old Bass River Rd.) | 508-385-7100 | www.bluemoonbistro.net

"Tiny but special" is what devotees have to say about this Dennis "destination" where a chef who "knows his stuff" preps "delightful" Mediterranean dishes with an "emphasis on local ingredients" (the fare "may be a tad pricey", but it's "worth it"); factor in "prompt service" and a "nice wine list", and you've got a winning combination, especially for those attending a show at the nearby Cape Cod Center for the Arts.

Bookstore & Restaurant *Seafood*   20 | 16 | 20 | $34

Wellfleet | 50 Kendrick Ave. (Commercial St.) | 508-349-3154 | www.wellfleetoyster.com

"Go for sunsets" or "breakfasts on the front porch facing the bay" at this affordable seafooder in Wellfleet with a used bookstore attached, because the interior is a little "old and dusty"; nevertheless, even on a rainy day or in winter, it's a "fun, quirky" choice for "local", "reliable", "not-fancy" fish and "inventive cocktails" delivered by an "attentive staff."

☒ Bramble Inn *American*   28 | 25 | 28 | $69

Brewster | Bramble Inn | 2019 Main St./Rte. 6A (bet. Breakwater Rd. & Crocker Ln.) | 508-896-7644 | www.brambleinn.com

"Absolutely superb" New American cuisine and "impeccable" staffers earn Cape Cod's No. 1 Food and Service scores at this "beautiful", "quaint" 1861 inn in Brewster; comprised of several "small dining rooms" filled with "elegant antiques", it's "slightly formal" for the "casual Cape" (you'll "want to dress up") – and "steeply priced" to boot – but it's "worth it" for a "special meal."

Brazilian Grill *Brazilian*   24 | 17 | 23 | $33

Hyannis | 680 Main St. (bet. Sea & Stevens Sts.) | 508-771-0109 | www.braziliangrill-capecod.com

"Come hungry" for dinner at this all-you-can-eat Brazilian churrascaria in Hyannis, where the "endless supply" of rodizio meats (carved "directly onto your plate" by "fun waiters") is "fabulous" as well as a "great value", just like the "amazing" salad bar; it's a "must-do lunch spot" too, as the "incredible variety" is "exactly the same", but the tabs are "less expensive."

☒ Brewster Fish House *Seafood*   26 | 20 | 23 | $44

Brewster | 2208 Main St./Rte. 6A (Stonehenge Dr.) | 508-896-7867 | www.brewsterfish.com

"Always fabulous, sometimes even sublime" seafood is ferried by "attentive" servers at this "popular" Brewster fish monger where the fees are only "a bit pricey"; the "only bummer" is the "no-reservations policy", which equals "painfully long waits" for the "slightly twee" setting's "few seats" (there's "a teeny bar", but that "also gets packed").

Bubala's by the Bay *Eclectic/Seafood*   16 | 15 | 17 | $32

Provincetown | 183-85 Commercial St. (bet. Court & Winthrop Sts.) | 508-487-0773 | www.bubalas.com

So what if this "casual" P-town spot's "predictable" Eclectic seafood is merely "decent" and service can be "disinterested"? – it's "always packed" thanks to the "great views" of the bay from the otherwise "unprepossessing" interior and the "passing parade of humanity" on Commercial Street from the "much nicer outdoor cafe", not to mention the "fair prices."

Buca's Tuscan Roadhouse *Italian*   23 | 20 | 23 | $46

Harwich | 4 Depot Rd. (Main St.) | 508-432-6900 | www.bucasroadhouse.com

"A wow culinary experience" awaits at this "classy", "cozy" Harwich "gem" where the Northern Italian menu features "imaginative takes", the "staff is knowledgeable" and the "Tuscan-inspired decor" with checked cloths is "charming"; it may be somewhat "expensive", but the "fantastic", "extensive wine list" features "reasonable values"; P.S. "on a cold winter night", "try to get a seat by the fire."

☑ Cape Sea Grille *American*   27 | 25 | 25 | $54

Harwich Port | 31 Sea St. (Main St.) | 508-432-4745 | www.capeseagrille.com

"Innovative", seasonal New American fare starring "amazing fish" coupled with "exceptional service" makes this Harwich Port venue a "perennial favorite" for a "splurge"; the "cheerful", "lovely setting in an old house" features a porch ("great if you can get" a seat there), plus it's "close to the beach", so "walk down to the water after dinner to take full advantage of the location."

Captain Frosty's *New England/Seafood*   21 | 9 | 16 | $17

Dennis | 219 Main St./Rte. 6A (S. Yarmouth Rd.) | 508-385-8548 | www.captainfrosty.com

"You're not going for the decor" (it's "cheesy") at this clam shack, you're there for "huge portions" of "fairly priced", "nothing-fancy" "fresh fish freshly fried", plus "great burgers" and soft-serve ice cream; Dennis locals deem it "a must" after a "hard day at the beach", while passers-through appreciate it as an easy pit stop when "trying to cope with the traffic."

Captain Kidd, The *Pub Food*   ∇ 16 | 17 | 17 | $36

Woods Hole | 77 Water St. (Luscombe Ave.) | 508-548-8563 | www.thecaptainkidd.com

"It's about location" at this "Woods Hole institution" where parents "return with their kids and grandkids" to sup on "dependable", moderately priced pub grub while waiting for the Martha's Vineyard ferry; the rustic, nautical setting is a bit "dark", but the "great views" of Eel Pond and "boisterous" vibe around the "old-fashioned bar" sure do brighten things up.

Captain Linnell House *American*   24 | 25 | 25 | $53

Orleans | 137 Skaket Beach Rd. (West Rd.) | 508-255-3400 |
www.linnell.com

This 1950 Orleans "stalwart has kept its luster and charm" with an
"amazing setting in an old sea captain's house", "upscale", "beautifully
presented" American fare and a "mature, knowledgeable staff"; the
multiple dining "rooms are cozy, especially in the cooler weather"
when the fireplaces are employed, and when the "lovely gardens"
are in bloom, the "breathtaking views" set a "romantic" mood.

Captain Parker's Pub *New England*   21 | 15 | 21 | $28

West Yarmouth | 668 Rte. 28 (W. Yarmouth Rd.) | 508-771-4266 |
www.captainparkers.com

"Vacationers and locals" flock to this "affordable" year-round pub in
West Yarmouth for the "thick, rich clam chowder", though it's also a
"solid place for steaks, prime rib" and other New England dishes; between the "busy bar" and the "family-friendly" dining area, it gets quite
"noisy", so check your hope for a "quiet conversation" at the door.

Catch of the Day *Seafood*   25 | 12 | 19 | $30

Wellfleet | 975 Rte. 6 (Marconi Beach Rd.) | 508-349-9090 |
www.wellfleetcatch.com

This "super" summer spot in Wellfleet "lives up to its name" with
seafood you "would swear was just brought in from the shores minutes
before" ("it probably was"); wine and beer make "eating in a roadside
fish store" more palatable, but "better yet, stop by when you leave the
beach", grab a "bargain" early-bird special (representative of the altogether "great prices") and bring it back to the sand for sunset.

Chapin's Fish 'n Chips &   ▽ 19 | 17 | 19 | $29
Beach Bar *Seafood*

Dennisport | 228 Lower County Rd. (Shad Hole Rd.) | 508-394-6900 |
www.chapinsbeachbar.com

"Despite its name", this "no-frills" Dennisport seafooder is not on
the beach, but it does offer "consistent" fish 'n' chips 'n' such and an
"active bar scene"; moderate prices mean it's "family-friendly" – the
"kids can play outside while their parents sip their drinks."

Chapoquoit Grill *Mediterranean*   21 | 16 | 21 | $32

West Falmouth | 410 W. Falmouth Hwy./Rte. 28A (Brick Kiln Rd.) |
508-540-7794 | www.chapoquoitgrill.com

"Locals know" this West Falmouth Mediterranean as "a reliable spot
for dinner or just pizza", the latter garnering praise for "great" "wood-
grilled", "thin crusts" and "creative" toppings; it may "not have
much atmosphere", but the "fireplace makes you feel like you're in a
country inn", plus the service is "friendly" and the "value" "terrific."

Chart Room *New England/Seafood*   18 | 19 | 20 | $42

Cataumet | 1 Shipyard Ln. (Shore Rd.) | 508-563-5350 |
www.chartroomcataumet.com

If you "love eating on the water" and don't mind "long waits", make
this "loud, crowded" Cataumet "institution" part of your "summer

FOOD | DECOR | SERVICE | COST

adventure"; though "not anything special", the New England seafood is "ok" ("the best item", a "large" variation of the "incredible lobster salad", "isn't on the menu"), but sipping a "delightful mudslide" while "sitting outside" and "watching the sunset" is a "ritual."

☒ Chatham Bars Inn *American* | 23 | 26 | 25 | $58 |

Chatham | Chatham Bars Inn | 297 Shore Rd. (Seaview St.) | 508-945-0096 | www.chathambarsinn.com

There are "so many options to pick from" at this "quintessential" luxury inn in Chatham, among them an "elegant", "formal main room" where "decadent" New American fare is matched by "wonderful" ocean vistas, a "warm, inviting tavern", the "fun", "casual" Beach House Grill (a "must on a night with a traditional clambake") and the new, seafood-focused Harbor View Room; wherever you wind up, you're sure to find "gracious service" and "splurge"-worthy tabs.

Chatham Squire *Eclectic* | 19 | 16 | 20 | $31 |

Chatham | 487 Main St. (Chatham Bars Ave.) | 508-945-0945 | www.thesquire.com

"Convivial" and "casual", this Chatham "neighborhood place" is "dependable" for "pub staples" and "surprising" Eclectic dinner specials, which "can be truly excellent"; whether you sup in the rustic dining room or eat while "watching a game" on TV in the "sometimes raucous" tavern, where the walls are adorned with "license plates from all of the states", "it won't break the bank."

Chillingsworth ☒ *French* | 26 | 25 | 24 | $71 |

Brewster | 2449 Main St./Rte. 6A (Foster Rd.) | 508-896-3640 | www.chillingsworth.com

An "extraordinary dining experience" awaits at this "Brewster gem", which crafts "beautifully thought-out" prix fixe meals of "classic French cuisine with a contemporary twist" complemented by "fine wines" and "wonderful, professional service"; the "special-occasion" pricing is commensurate with the elegant setting in an over-three-centuries-old estate ("no sea views" or "nautical" tchotchkes here), but "something a bit more casual and less expensive" can be found in the adjacent bistro.

Ciro & Sal's *Italian* | 17 | 16 | 17 | $44 |

Provincetown | 4 Kiley Ct. (Commercial St.) | 508-487-6444 | www.ciroandsals.com

This P-town venue has a "long history" of serving "local families" and vacationers "traditional Italian fare" that some deem "outstanding" and others dis as "mediocre" (but "oh that garlic!"); in a similar vein, while many dig the "cozy", "rustic" "underground-grotto setting" with exposed brick, hanging Chianti jugs and "fireplaces to keep you warm" in winter, a few label it a "dark" "cave."

Clancy's *American* | 21 | 19 | 20 | $34 |

Dennisport | 8 Upper County Rd. (bet. Rtes. 28 & 134) | 508-394-6661 | www.clancysrestaurant.com

Though "nothing fancy", the "all-American menu" with "great" seafood, "ample portions", "reasonable prices" and "libations to boot" incite sometimes "torturous" lines to get into this "friendly, upbeat" (read: "noisy") Dennisport dining room; it's "especially nice for lunch" "if you can get an outdoor seat", "relax" and enjoy a libation while "waving to the kayakers" on Swan River.

Cobie's Clam Shack 🚫 *Seafood* 22 | 7 | 15 | $20

Brewster | 3260 Main St. (Linnell Landing Rd.) | 508-896-7021 | www.cobies.com

Strollers would "walk a mile for the fried clams", bikers make it a detour "when riding on the Cape Cod Rail Trail" and sun-worshipers stock up on "nice beach food" at this "reasonably priced" 1948 Brewster seafood shanty; you might have to endure a "long wait in season", but the staffers at the window hustle to be "quick", so be a sport and "contribute to their college funds."

Colombo's *Italian* - | - | - | M

Hyannis | 544 Main St. (Bassett Ln.) | 508-790-5700 | www.columboscafe.com

"Plentiful, flavorful" pizzas, pastas and other casual Italian fare are offered at a "good price" at this "family-friendly" cafe and bakery in Downtown Hyannis; some prefer to sit outside in summer, as "it tends to get loud" in the informal interior, and everyone says "save room for desserts: just looking at them in the case will make you drool."

Cooke's Seafood *Seafood* 19 | 11 | 17 | $22

Orleans | 1 S. Orleans Rd./Rte. 28 (Rte. 6A) | 508-255-5518
Hyannis | 1120 Iyannough Rd./Rte. 132 (Bearses Way) | 508-775-0450 | www.cookesseafood.com
Mashpee | 7 Ryans Way (Great Neck Rd.) | 508-477-9595 | www.cookesseafood.com

With "no servers" and "no decor to speak of", this Cape Cod seafood trio is "not exactly fine dining", but for "simple, good, cheap" fish served "quick", it's "a must" – and in some households, "legendary"; "you have to be in the mood" for a "cafeteria-style", "seat-yourself" experience, but you "can get beer" or wine, and that's a "big plus."

Coonamessett Inn *New England* 21 | 21 | 21 | $40

Falmouth | Coonamessett Inn | 311 Gifford St. (Jones Rd.) | 508-548-2300 | www.capecodrestaurants.org

Like a "trustworthy friend", this eatery in a Falmouth country inn is "reliable" for "old-fashioned" New England cuisine "pleasantly served"; lunches, dinners and the "extensive Sunday" brunch buffets are all equally "relaxing" thanks to the "lovely" interior and views of the "picturesque" grounds.

NEW Dalla Cucina *Italian* ▽ 20 | 20 | 20 | $43

Provincetown | 404 Commercial St. (Law St.) | 508-487-5404 | www.dallacucinaptown.com

It's still "working out" some "kinks", but overall, this "high-end Italian" newcomer to Provincetown's East End is "off to a great start", as there are "no losers on the menu"; the red, black and white interior displays local artwork on the walls, plus there's "outdoor dining in good weather" and a working fireplace.

	FOOD	DECOR	SERVICE	COST

Dan'l Webster Inn *American*   21 | 25 | 23 | $42

Sandwich | Dan'l Webster Inn | 149 Main St. (bet. Jarvis St. &
Rte. 130) | 508-888-3622 | www.danlwebsterinn.com

"Impress a tourist" with the "pure New England" experience offered
at this "beautiful", "historic" Sandwich inn where a "genuine, warm"
staff serves "well-prepared" New American cuisine at "can't-beat
prices" in an "elegant dining room", a "cozy tavern" and a glass-
enclosed conservatory; "leave time for a walk in the garden", especially after the "excellent Sunday brunch" buffet, and show your love
to the "octogenarian crowd" that frequents it.

Devon's *American*   25 | 18 | 22 | $53

Provincetown | 401½ Commercial St. (Washington Ave.) |
508-487-4773 | www.devons.org

Fans flock to this all-day "oasis in Provincetown" for "imaginative"
New American cuisine served in a "tiny cottage" with a front patio
that's "perfect for people-watching", "sea breezes" and "elbow
room" (the interior can feel "cramped"); the "eponymous owner
presides over the front-of-house" and staffers who are so "cheerful", they'll "put a smile on your face" even after you've seen the "expensive" bill (it's "worth it").

Dockside, The *New England*   17 | 14 | 16 | $32

Hyannis | 110 School St. (South St.) | 774-470-1383 |
www.thedocksidehyannis.com

The "decor is good if you're seated outside" on the "great deck" at
this haunt "overlooking Hyannis Harbor"; though the New England
breakfasts, lunches and dinners are merely "ok", they're well priced,
and in the very least, the spot is a convenient "stop for a drink and a
bite" if you're heading to the nearby Nantucket ferry.

Dolphin *American/Seafood*   22 | 17 | 20 | $35

Barnstable | 3250 Main St./Rte. 6A (Hyannis Rd.) | 508-362-6610

It's "not cutting-edge", just a "great place to take the family" for
"consistently good" "classic" American and seafood dishes tout admirers of this "unpretentious", over-50-year-old "watering hole" in
Barnstable; even if the decor appears "old and tired", that's canceled
out by the "friendly" staffers and tabs that won't "empty your wallet."

D'Parma Italian Table ● *Italian*   22 | 19 | 20 | $27

West Yarmouth | 175 Main St./Rte. 28 (Higgins Crowell Rd.) |
508-771-7776 | www.dparmarestaurant.com

"Tasty" "traditional red-sauce Italian" dishes are listed on an "extensive menu" at this "great" eatery in West Yarmouth; the "casual setting" offers a full bar and "reasonable prices", the latter element one
of the main reasons parents with kids in tow cheer "love it!"

Dunbar Tea Room *British/Tearoom*   21 | 25 | 20 | $23

Sandwich | Dunbar Tea Shop | 1 Water St. (Main St.) | 508-833-2485 |
www.dunbarteashop.com

At this "authentic English" tearoom in an early 1800s Sandwich car-
riage house, the edibles include "wonderful" "fresh soups, sand-

wiches" and salads, plus "yummy" pastries such as "warm scones"; "cheerful and prompt" service makes it the kind of place you'll feel comfortable bringing your "grandnieces."

Edwige *American*
26 | 19 | 23 | $47

Provincetown | 333 Commercial St. (Freeman St.) | 508-487-2008 | www.edwigeatnight.com

For "fabulous fun" and "inventive", "high-style" New American eats in a "quintessential P-town" atmosphere, head upstairs to this breakfast and dinner destination, which also features "professional, friendly servers" and "amazing" "signature cocktails"; there's a "small outdoor area", but on a "hot day", head inside where the recent "addition of air-conditioning" is a boon (the "only problem here" is what some deem "uncomfortable seating").

Enzo *French*
∇ 21 | 22 | 19 | $38

Provincetown | Enzo Guest House | 186 Commercial St. (Court St.) | 508-487-7555 | www.enzolives.com

This "upscale" Provincetown Provençal in a "pretty" Victorian guest house serves its "pleasant, tasty", moderately priced fare in a dining room that some rate as "romantic" and others deem "dated"; either way, one thing is indisputable: the front patio is where all the "fun" is.

Fairway Restaurant & Pizzeria *American/Italian*
17 | 12 | 20 | $25

North Eastham | 4295 State Hwy./Rte. 6 (Brackett Rd.) | 508-255-3893 | www.fairwaycapecod.com

"Line up" for the "superb breakfasts" whipped up at this "busy", "no-frills", tavernlike North Eastham American-Italian eatery that's still "going after 30-plus years"; come dinner, "stick with the pizza", as the rest of the midpriced menu is just "average"; P.S. no lunch.

Fanizzi's by the Sea *American/Italian*
19 | 19 | 21 | $38

Provincetown | 539 Commercial St. (Hancock St.) | 508-487-1964 | www.fanizzisrestaurant.com

"Views to die for", "reliable", "nothing-fancy" American and Italian seafood and "great service" sums up this "casual" P-townie, a "handy place when you're down in the East End"; "it's a favorite with locals", as it's "open year-round" and the prices are "reasonable."

Far Land Provisions *Deli*
∇ 19 | 8 | 17 | $16

Provincetown | 150 Bradford St. (Conwell St.) | 508-487-0045 | www.farlandprovisions.com

"Generous, high-quality" "sandwiches for breakfast and lunch", "homemade breads and pastries" plus an "assortment" of prepared foods come from "nice people" at this Provincetown deli; there are "a few seats inside and some chairs outside", but it's really a "to-go" kind of place – the eats are "perfect to bring to the beach."

Fazio's Trattoria *Italian*
∇ 21 | 16 | 21 | $29

Hyannis | 294 Main St. (Center St.) | 508-775-9400 | www.fazio.net

Hyannis diners "say '*grazie*'" to this "cozy" year-round trattoria for its "delicious" "homemade pastas", "crusty bread" and other "old-fashioned Italian mainstays"; sidewalk dining in summer is coveted, and if the interior's a bit "drab" (even when the gas fireplace is on), the "staff makes up for that."

Finely JP's *American*   21 | 19 | 21 | $39
Wellfleet | 554 Rte. 6 (Castanga Dr.) | 508-349-7500
"Predictable and durable", this "Wellfleet fixture" cranks out "solid", "fairly priced" seafood-focused New American cuisine in "classy", modern-leaning digs and on a deck; the "friendly staff" and "great drinks" are two more aspects that its longtime patrons "count on."

Fishmonger's Cafe *American/Seafood*   20 | 20 | 19 | $33
Woods Hole | 56 Water St. (Luscombe Ave.) | 508-540-5376
"Get a window seat" and "watch the drawbridge while you eat" breakfast, lunch or dinner at this New American "on the channel" in Woods Hole; the "interesting", "creative" menu sports plenty of "good fresh fish", the "friendly, patient" staffers set a "lively" tone and, perhaps most importantly, the moderate tabs keep the atmosphere worry-free.

Five Bays Bistro *American*   23 | 20 | 20 | $46
Osterville | 825 Main St. (Wianno Ave.) | 508-420-5559 | www.fivebaysbistro.com
"You'll feel like you're part of tony Osterville's 'in' crowd if you can get a table" at this "sophisticated", "upscale" New American with high ceilings, white tablecloths and "wonderful" fare; the "noisy" "bar scene" and "overall bustling atmosphere" make it feel more "South End" than "chowder Cape" – that is until you notice the "parade" of "preppies" with "Beemers."

Friendly Fisherman's *Seafood*   22 | 9 | 18 | $24
North Eastham | 4580 Rte. 6 (Oak Rd.) | 508-255-6770
Look for the "picnic tables and a children's swing set" when you "drive up" to this "no-frills" North Eastham "seafood shack" serving "fresh and tasty" "fried standards" and an "excellent lobster roll"; for home cooking, "very good raw materials" are available from the "fish market next door", but no booze, so BYO if you plan to eat here.

Front Street *Continental/Italian*   25 | 19 | 24 | $50
Provincetown | 230 Commercial St. (Masonic Pl.) | 508-487-9715 | www.frontstreetrestaurant.com
"Make sure you book early" to get into this P-town "hot spot" housed in a "charming", "cozy" Victorian vending "superb" Italian and Continental dishes (e.g. "heavenly tea-smoked duck"), which are offered along with an "awesome wine list" and "warm, efficient service"; true, it's somewhat "costly", but it's worth it because "it never fails to please."

Gina's by the Sea Ⓜ *Italian*   21 | 15 | 21 | $38
Dennis | 134 Taunton Ave. (Chapin Beach Rd.) | 508-385-3213 | www.ginasbythesea.com
"Only the Chianti bottles are missing" at this "old-school Italian" "institution" set in the "dunes of Dennis", a "crowded", "decades-

old" throwback that, like the "enjoyable" menu, "never changes" ("why mess with success?"); if it's "too hot" inside, "eat on the porch" and cool off in the "sea breeze."

☑ Glass Onion, The ☒ *American*   27 | 27 | 27 | $50

Falmouth | 37 N. Main St. (Locust St.) | 508-540-3730 | www.theglassoniondining.com

This Falmouth New American is "memorable" for its "inventive, delicious" dishes, "great service" and "romantic", "casually elegant" 1920s setting with wainscoting and sea-foam-green walls; the "no-reservations policy is a problem", but having to "wait" on the "lovely porch" with a drink isn't all that bad.

☑ Impudent Oyster *Seafood*   23 | 19 | 22 | $44

Chatham | 15 Chatham Bars Ave. (Main St.) | 508-945-3545

"You may want to fast before" dining at this "crowded-in-summer, cozy-in-winter" Chatham "gem" "in an old church", because the "inventive", "outstanding" seafood comes in "huge" portions (start with the 'devils on horseback' – they're "pure heaven"); the "upscale" environs boast a "great bar scene" and a staff that "aims to please", and while some feel "lunch is a better value than dinner", either way, "you can't go wrong."

Inaho ☒ *Japanese*   26 | 22 | 21 | $43

Yarmouth Port | 157 Main St./Rte. 6A (S. Yarmouth Rd.) | 508-362-5522 | www.inahocapecod.com

"Exceptional" "works-of-art" sushi keep this Yarmouth Port "favorite" "always packed", so "better make a reservation", because even with one, there are sometimes "long waits"; seating's "tight" and it "can be noisy" in the "old house", but the atmosphere is usually "fun" – despite occasionally "disorganized" service.

Island Merchant *American/Caribbean*   - | - | - | M

Hyannis | 302 Main St. (bet. Barnstable Rd. & Center St.) | 508-771-1337 | www.theislandmerchant.com

Set at the otherwise "quiet end of Main Street in Hyannis", this colorful, faux palm tree–festooned venue "rocks in the summer" with live music ("which can be deafening") "many evenings" plus a "creative", "reasonably priced" New American menu bursting with "great" Caribbean flavors and paired with "woo hoo!" rum punch; in winter, "locals" are reeled in with movie nights and $2 cheeseburger specials after 10 PM.

JT's Seafood *Seafood*   20 | 13 | 19 | $30

Brewster | 2689 Main St./Rte. 6A (Winslow Landing Rd.) | 508-896-3355 | www.jt-seafood.com

The "fried clams are as tasty as ever", as is the rest of the seafood at this Brewster cottage, an "easy summer pleasure" for "families" thanks to ice cream for the kids, beer and wine for mom and dad ("just don't expect much of a selection") and affordability for all; you order at the counter and find a "dining-room, back-deck or front-patio table", but to "avoid the lines and waits", "takeout is your best option."

Karoo Kafe S African
22 | 14 | 20 | $18

Provincetown | 338 Commercial St. (Center St.) | 508-487-6630 |
www.karookafe.com

"Creative, delicious, reliable" and "cheap" sums up this South
African "hole-in-the-wall" in P-town, whose fare (including game)
makes for an "adventurous" "alternative to clam chowder and lobster rolls"; "warm" staffers serve inside the "kitschy", "brightly colored room" and on the deck, and you can also buy some "authentic"
"ingredients to take home."

La Cucina Sul Mare Italian
24 | 19 | 24 | $42

Falmouth | 237 Main St. (Walker St.) | 508-548-5600 |
www.lacucinasulmare.com

For "a bit of Boston's North End" in Falmouth, check out this "reliable" year-rounder where "friendly" staffers ladle "huge portions"
of "*sooo* good" Italian fare in "warm" but "tight quarters"; the "no-
reservations policy makes for long waits", so "get there early" – or
try it for lunch, a better "bargain."

L'Alouette French
26 | 21 | 24 | $57

Harwich Port | 787 Main St./Rte. 28 (Julien Rd.) | 508-430-0405 |
www.lalouettebistro.com

"Conversation"-seekers appreciate that this "superb", somewhat
"old fashioned"–looking Harwich Port venue is "not too loud" as
much as gourmets are thankful that the "classic French" bistro cuisine
"never disappoints"; furthermore, the "staff is knowledgeable", plus
the wine list is "impressive", but like the fare, it "tends to be pricey."

Landfall Seafood
18 | 21 | 19 | $40

Woods Hole | 2 Luscombe Ave. (Water St.) | 508-548-1758

"Fantastic" "views of Woods Hole Harbor exceed the culinary experience" at this "traditional" seafood spot, but it nevertheless "chugs
along year after year" (since 1946) because it's "reliable" and generally a "good value"; inside, you "feel like you're in an old ship" with
an "excellent bar" and "peppy" staffers, whose customers skew toward folks "waiting for the ferry to the Vineyard" or munching "after
a long day on the beach."

Liam's at Nauset Beach Seafood
20 | 11 | 12 | $19

East Orleans | 239 Beach Rd. (Surf Path) | 508-255-3474

"Impossibly thin, crispy and golden" "onion rings from heaven"
("how do they do it?") are the musts at this "snack shack" "steps
from the surf at Nauset Beach" in East Orleans, which also sells
"awesome" fried seafood; "long lines make it a bit of a drag, but that's
the only downside" – if you don't count the "aggressive seagulls."

Lobster Pot Eclectic/Seafood
22 | 16 | 20 | $42

Provincetown | 321 Commercial St. (Standish St.) | 508-487-0842 |
www.ptownlobsterpot.com

A "must-eat in P-town", this "reliable" seafood landmark cooks up
"classic, no-nonsense" seafood dishes with Eclectic influences on
two floors displaying "gorgeous" bay views and decor that looks like

it "pre-dates the Pilgrims"; "relatively reasonable prices" are another aspect that draws "big crowds" ("prepare for a queue at peak periods"), around which the "staff flies", "always helpful and pleasant."

Lorraine's *Mexican* ▽ 17 | 12 | 14 | $40

Provincetown | 133 Commercial St. (Pleasant St.) | 508-487-6074 | www.lorrainesrestaurant.com

P-towners who've been dining at this "dark" Mexican "for years" say it can be "wonderful", "mediocre" or "ersatz" (therefore "priced ridiculously"); but if you're craving "international foods", you don't have many "choices on the Cape", so just "cram" yourself into an "uncomfortable wooden booth", order up shots from the "huge tequila list" and "take yer chances."

Lyric *American* 25 | 23 | 23 | $48

Yarmouth Port | 43 Main St./Rte. 6A (Willow St.) | 774-330-0000 | www.lyriccapecod.com

You're in for a "memorable treat" at this "romantic" New American inside a "Cape Cod cottage" in Yarmouth Port, where the cuisine may be "a little pricey", but it's "imaginative" and ultimately "superb"; along with the "professional, pleasant service", the "live music" – from Thursday–Saturday evenings' piano bar and Sunday's jazz brunch – abets a "transcendent experience."

Mac's Seafood Market & Grill *Seafood* 25 | 17 | 19 | $36

Wellfleet | 265 Commercial St. (Kendrick Ave.) | 508-349-0404

Mac's Shack *Seafood*

Wellfleet | 91 Commercial St. (Railroad Ave.) | 508-349-6333 www.macsseafood.com

"Unique flair" shows up in the "high-quality seafood", including "superb sushi", prepared at these Wellfleet "successes" where you "sit at a picnic table in the sand (if you're lucky enough to get a seat)" at the BYOB market or "cram in" at the equally "casual" shack (where some feel the wine is the most "reasonably priced" thing offered, comparatively); wherever you wind up, be prepared to "wait a long time to get in" (no reservations).

Marshland Restaurant *American* 20 | 12 | 20 | $20

Sandwich | 109 Rte. 6A (Tupper Rd.) | 508-888-9824

Sandwich | 315 Cotuit Rd. (Rte. 130) | 508-888-9747 www.marshlandrestaurant.com

Sandwich "locals love" these diners' "big portions" of "well-prepared, reliable" Traditional American fare as much as their "easygoing ambiance" ("come as you are, flip-flops are fine"); better still, "the prices fit most budgets", particularly those for the "fabulous breakfasts."

Marshside, The *American/Seafood* 19 | 27 | 23 | $34

Dennis | 28 Bridge St. (bet. Rtes. 28 & 134) | 508-385-4010 | www.themarshside.com

"Spectacular" environs boasting "beautiful views through floor-to-ceiling windows" and a "great bar area" make for an all-around "lovely setting" at this American-seafood spot in East Dennis; if the "casual" "menu doesn't match the location", at least it's "solid, dependable" and priced to be "family-friendly"; P.S. "they need to take reservations", but they don't, so "expect a wait for a table."

Mattakeese Wharf Waterfront Restaurant *Seafood*

| 18 | 21 | 21 | $39 |

Barnstable | 273 Millway Rd. (Commerce Rd.) | 508-362-4511 | www.mattakeese.com

"Bring your camera" to capture the "great views of Barnstable Harbor" at this "rustic" seafood eatery from 1970; "decent" prices make it easy to take the "family" "before a whale-watching cruise", but better still, leave the kids with a sitter, come later and "watch the sun go down with a nice cocktail."

Mews *American*

| 26 | 25 | 27 | $52 |

Provincetown | 429 Commercial St. (Lovetts Ct.) | 508-487-1500 | www.mews.com

"Make reservations at least two weeks in advance" or run the risk of "missing out" on this "true gem" in P-town's East End, where the "outstanding", "innovative" New American fare is offered along with "impeccable service", "an amazing array of vodkas" and "lovely views" of the harbor; choose between the "lively bar, the demure lower dining room and the upstairs cafe", the latter offering "a friendly buzz and less expensive" prices.

Mezza Luna *Italian*

| 22 | 20 | 23 | $32 |

Buzzards Bay | 253 Main St. (Perry Ave.) | 508-759-4667 | www.mezzalunarestaurant.com

"Everyone in your family, from your children to your grandparents", will find something "satisfying" at this midrange, "reliable, traditional red-sauce" Italian that's open year-round in Buzzards Bay; "beautifully redone and redecorated" after the original was destroyed in a fire a few years ago, the venue boasts two cozy fireplaces, a patio and a "great bar."

Misaki   *Japanese*

| ▽ 25 | 18 | 22 | $30 |

Hyannis | 379 W. Main St. (Pitchers Way) | 508-771-3771 | www.misakisushi.com

"Ignore the outside appearance" and the "not-fancy" interior of this year-round Japanese in Hyannis and treat yourself to fish "so fresh, you'd swear there was a boat parked in the back" – and "what a value" it is!; "efficient" staffers are on hand, and they're so "friendly", some locals liken the place to a "*Cheers* for sushi."

Moby Dick's *Seafood*

| 24 | 13 | 20 | $30 |

Wellfleet | 3225 Rte. 6 (Gull Pond Rd.) | 508-349-9795 | www.mobydicksrestaurant.com

It's "always packed and for good reason" at this "family-pleasing" Wellfleet "clam shack" that doles out "sparklingly fresh" "fried and broiled" seafood in a "casual" "fake-ship" setting; owners who are "always there to ensure that you're satisfied", "charming", "helpful" staffers and "reasonable prices" are three more reasons there's "always a line", so "go early or late" – and "don't forget to bring your own alcohol."

Naked Oyster Bistro & Raw Bar *Seafood*   25 | 18 | 21 | $48

Hyannis | 410 Main St. (Pearl St.) | 508-778-6500 |
www.nakedoyster.com

A recent "move to Main Street" is the big news about this "upper-class, hip" Hyannis haunt creating "delicious, innovative seafood dishes with an emphasis on the freshest local ingredients" and "lots of oyster choices"; it's a "bit pricey" and the "noise level can be pretty fierce" due to a "vibrant bar crowd several celebrants deep", but even those in the "plain back dining area" say a meal here is "always a big hit."

Napi's *Eclectic*   20 | 20 | 20 | $40

Provincetown | 7 Freeman St. (Bradford St.) | 508-487-1145 |
www.napis-restaurant.com

"Fun, fun, fun" is what's on offer at this "Provincetown institution" where "paintings" and "masks" comprise the "funky" yet "inviting" backdrop for a "vast" menu of "competent", "reasonably priced" Eclectic fare; "helpful", "friendly servers" are another aspect that "never changes."

Nauset Beach Club *Italian*   23 | 20 | 20 | $54

East Orleans | 222 Main St. (Beach Rd.) | 508-255-8547 |
www.nausetbeachclub.com

"Carefully prepared pastas and seafood are the strengths" of this year-round "fine-dining" Northern Italian in East Orleans, where a new chef is getting "creative with fresh ingredients"; with "enthusiastic, friendly service" and "warm", "highly civilized" environs, "it's not a cheap night out", but more reasonable is the three-course early-bird prix fixe (before 6 PM on Fridays and Saturdays, all night the rest of the week).

☒ Not Your Average Joe's *American*   19 | 17 | 20 | $26

Hyannis | Cape Cod Mall | 793 Iyannough Rd. (Airport Rd.) |
508-778-1424 | www.notyouraveragejoes.com
See review in Boston Directory.

Ocean House Ⓜ *American*   27 | 27 | 27 | $54

Dennisport | 425 Old Wharf Rd. (Depot St.) | 508-394-0700 |
www.oceanhouserestaurant.com

"Wow", "the food is just as spectacular as the view" at this "literally on-the-beach" Dennisport destination where the service is "polished" and a "Pan-Asian influence is evident" ("but not overdone") in the "worth-every-penny" New American cuisine; for the most "romantic dinner", "get a seat near a window" around sunset, or just join the "active scene" at the bar – it's "easier" than getting a prime-time reservation.

Ocean Terrace *American*   ▽ 19 | 21 | 19 | $45

Brewster | Ocean Edge Resort | 2907 Main St./Rte. 6A (off Rte. 124) |
508-896-9000 | www.oceanedge.com

A "great view" of Cape Cod Bay from the expansive terrace is "the real attraction" of this American eatery in Brewster's

Ocean Edge Resort; but there are also three intimate, elegant interior rooms plus "good" food, not to mention pricey tabs that befit the resort setting.

Optimist Café, The *American/British* `- | - | - | I`

Yarmouth Port | 134 Rte. 6A (Willow St.) | 508-362-1024 |
www.optimistcafe.com

For something "a little different", take your favorite young ladies to this "funky", "quirky gingerbread house" in Yarmouth Port, where the fare has a "nice" American-British bent; breakfast and lunch are served, but "afternoon tea" is its real claim to fame, and everything's inexpensively priced.

Orleans Inn *American* `16 | 19 | 20 | $38`

Orleans | Orleans Inn | 21 Rte. 6A (Orleans Rotary) | 508-255-2222 |
www.orleansinn.com

"Glorious views" from the deck "make the entire meal worthwhile" at this "cozy" Orleans American in a "converted mansion by the water"–turned–"family-friendly inn"; on second thought, the "attentive service" deserves a nod too – it's just the food that's "nothing special" (at least it's "not too expensive").

Osteria La Civetta *Italian* `27 | 23 | 23 | $41`

Falmouth | 133 Main St. (Post Office Rd.) | 508-540-1616 |
www.osterialacivetta.com

"You'll say 'bravo!' to the chef" after experiencing the "fabulous homemade pastas" and other "addictive" Northern Italian eats at this "real deal" in Falmouth, where the "recent expansion" of the "charming setting" includes a "beautiful new wine bar with a great vibe"; some diners are "surprised" just how "genuine" it all is, but how could it not be? – "the owners are from Bologna!"

Oyster Company
Raw Bar & Grill *Seafood* `24 | 19 | 21 | $37`

Dennisport | 202 Depot St. (Rte. 28) | 508-398-4600 |
www.theoystercompany.com

"Oysters are the star" – after all, "they farm their own" – but the rest of the seafood is just as "terrific" at this "hidden pearl" in Dennisport; historically "free from tourists", it gets "packed with locals" who belly up to the zinc bar for "great martinis" or take a table for "reasonably priced" meals, including early-bird winter "specials that will leave you and your wallet as happy as a clam."

Paddock *American/New England* `22 | 20 | 21 | $41`

Hyannis | West End Rotary | 20 Scudder Ave. (Main St.) |
508-775-7677 | www.paddockcapecod.com

If you're "attending an event at the Melody Tent" in Hyannis, this is the "old standby" for "reliable, classic old New England" and New American dishes, as well as "reasonable prices" and "attentive service that begins with a friendly greeting"; even people who find the fare "mediocre" and the setting a "'60s throwback" patronize it because it's so "convenient" – you can "walk right across the street" to see your show.

FOOD | DECOR | SERVICE | COST

Pain D'Avignon *Bakery/French* 26 | 16 | 18 | $33

Hyannis | 15 Hinckley Rd. (Iyannough Rd.) | 508-778-8588 |
www.paindavignon.com

"Divine bread" and croissants get folks into this "out-of-the-way" bakery near the Hyannis airport, but the attached Café Boulangerie's "terrific" French bistro fare, plus a full bar, gets them to stay for lunch and dinner; inside is at once "cramped" and resembling a "warehouse", but the patio's "cute", plus the staff is "nice" and the prices are "reasonable."

ⓩ NEW PB Boulangerie Bistro Ⓜ *French* 28 | 21 | 21 | $40

Wellfleet | 15 Lecount Hollow Rd. (Rte. 6) | 508-349-1600 |
www.pbboulangeriebistro.com

"Two chefs from France" offer "phenomenal" bakery items and "*magnifique*" (and pricey) bistro dinners – with "a well-edited, fairly priced wine list and unreal desserts" – at this "informal" yet "sophisticated" Wellfleet two-for-one, which in its first year has garnered the Cape's No. 2 Food score; the "only negative": they're "overwhelmed by their success", "so get there early before they run out" – "no matter how long the line is", just join it and "prepare to be dazzled."

Pearl *Seafood* 17 | 17 | 19 | $37

Wellfleet | 250 Commercial St. (Kendrick Ave.) | 508-349-2999 |
www.wellfleetpearl.com

"Fair prices", a "water view" and a convenient Wellfleet Harbor location make this "family-friendly" seafood-selling sophomore a draw for tourists; but locals offer a second opinion, saying it's "expensive for what you get" considering the "food is nothing to write home about" and the interior is a little "dark."

Pisces *Mediterranean/Seafood* 27 | 19 | 23 | $56

Chatham | 2653 Main St. (Forest Beach Rd.) | 508-432-4600 |
www.piscesofchatham.com

"Incredible seafood" with Med flair makes this pricey place in an "antique" Chatham house a "treasure"; for such a "small place", the "wine list is nice", and with a "softly decorated" "beach atmosphere" and "friendly staff", "memorable" evenings are virtually guaranteed.

Port, The *New England/Seafood* 23 | 23 | 21 | $44

Harwich Port | 541 Main St./Rte. 28 (Sea St.) | 508-430-5410 |
www.theportrestaurant.com

The "younger crowd" calls this "cosmopolitan" New England seafood spot in Harwich Port "*the* place to be" for a "hip" scene, "great drinks" and "adventurous food"; unsurprisingly, the tabs are "pricey", the sound is "noisy" and some of the staffers "have an attitude" – but to be fair, others are "pleasant" and most are "attractive."

Red Inn *New England* 26 | 28 | 24 | $54

Provincetown | Red Inn | 15 Commercial St. (W. Vine St.) |
508-487-7334 | www.theredinn.com

"Breathtaking" water views and a "glorious setting away from the crowds" make this "elegant" "grown-up venue" in an "old"

Provincetown inn an "icon", as does its "fabulous", "high-end" New England cuisine and "efficient, attentive staff"; for the most "memorable", "romantic" experience, "arrive early to get a seat on the deck" for a drink and a "dreamy sunset."

Red Pheasant *American/French*   27 | 24 | 25 | $52

Dennis | 905 Main St./Rte. 6A (Elm St.) | 508-385-2133 | www.redpheasantinn.com

Located "a short distance from the Cape Playhouse, making it a perfect spot for a pre-show dinner", this "adorable" "antique barn" in Dennis prepares "yummy", "upscale" French–New American fare and employs an "amiable" staff to serve it; since it's been around since 1977, it's "a sentimental favorite" for locals who request a "table with a garden view" in the summer or near one of the "great fireplaces" in winter and toast with something from the "outstanding wine selection."

Regatta of Cotuit at the Crocker House *American*   26 | 25 | 24 | $59

Cotuit | Crocker House | 4631 Falmouth Rd./Rte. 28 (Rte. 130) | 508-428-5715 | www.regattarestaurant.com

"For excellent fine dining on the Cape", come to this "historic home-turned-restaurant" in Cotuit offering "outstanding New American cuisine" and "fabulous service" in seven "lovely", "fancy" dining rooms; for a "more casual ambiance", chose the "cozy" tavern where, like the patio, diners can pick from the "regular menu" or a separate selection of "inspired" "lighter fare."

Roadhouse Cafe *Seafood/Steak*   22 | 20 | 23 | $38

Hyannis | 488 South St. (Main St.) | 508-775-2386 | www.roadhousecafe.com

"Huge portions, tasty eats and fair prices" are the draws at this long-time year-round steak-and-seafood house in Hyannis, where the upscale dining rooms and more casual bistro are all bedecked with nautical paraphernalia and fireplaces; it's "always good" for an evening "with your loved one", but "for a great time" with revelers, "dine at the bar", which often hosts live music.

Roobar *American*   19 | 17 | 16 | $37

Falmouth | 285 Main St. (Cahoon Ct.) | 508-548-8600 | www.theroobar.com

"Hopping" with a "young crowd", this "bar with food" in Falmouth is a "great choice" for "creative" New American dining; sure, it's "noisy" and service sometimes "lacks", but there's "value in the menu" and, more importantly, "the cocktails are good"; P.S. the Plymouth branch is under separate ownership.

Ross' Grill *American*   24 | 23 | 23 | $41

Provincetown | 237 Commercial St. (bet. Gosnold St. & Masonic Pl.) | 508-487-8878 | www.rossgrillptown.com

Don't let its location on the second floor of a Provincetown mini mall "put you off", for this New American is adept at "artfully prepared", "reliable" fare that's "higher end" but still "reasonably priced";

"many wines by the glass", "attentive service", "sleek" decor and "spectacular" harbor views complete the experience, for which "making reservations well in advance is highly recommended."

Sal's Place *Italian/Mediterranean* ▽ 18 | 13 | 15 | $38

Provincetown | 99 Commercial St. (bet. Cottage & Mechanic Sts.) | 508-487-1279 | www.salsplaceofprovincetown.com

"If you're hungry", go to this "affordable" "old-school Italian place" (with a Med bent) "on the water" in P-town's West End, because the dishes are "huge", plus they're "delicious", particularly the "over-sized pizzas"; even if service can be "inefficient", it's still a "fun stop" for alfresco dining with "picturesque views of the harbor."

Scargo Café *American* 21 | 20 | 21 | $36

Dennis | 799 Main St./Rte. 6A (bet. Corporation Rd. & Hope Ln.) | 508-385-8200 | www.scargocafe.com

With a "great location close to the Cape Playhouse", this "venerable" Dennis "delight" is a "good buy" for "reliable" New American vittles in a "lovely", "inviting" setting; it's "usually crowded" with "vacationers" in the summer, while winter finds plenty of "locals" "sitting by the fire" and "chatting" with the "efficient" staff.

Siena *Italian* 22 | 20 | 22 | $35

Mashpee | Mashpee Commons | 17 Steeple St. (Rte. 28) | 508-477-5929 | www.siena.us

"After going to a movie next door", get virtually "two meals for the price of one" at this "solid", "spacious" year-round Italian in Mashpee Commons, because "the portions are monstrous" (the "menu's extensive" too); its "kid-friendly" rep means it sure "can get noisy", but that's no big deal to folks who "rely on" it and its "good service."

Sir Cricket's Fish & Chips ⊅ *Seafood* 24 | 8 | 17 | $20

Orleans | 38 Rt. 6A (Orleans Rotary) | 508-255-4453

"Fried seafood to drool over", plus "unbelievable" lobster rolls and scallops made with "fish from the market next door" by a "friendly staff" is the claim to fame of this "hole-in-the-wall" Orleans "clam shack" that's just as renowned for its "great prices"; there's only "three or four tables" in the "not-fancy" digs, so plan to get it to go.

Squealing Pig, The *Pub Food* 20 | 18 | 20 | $24

Provincetown | 335 Commercial St. (Freeman St.) | 508-487-5804 | www.squealingpigtown.com

"Even if it's more of a drinking than eating establishment", this "friendly" P-town pub still earns some squeals for the "thoughtful food" it prepares to go along with the "great beer selection"; it's often "raucous" with partyers who "sing along with the band" in summer, while off-season, it's an "essential" part of life for locals.

Stir Crazy Ⓜ *Cambodian* ▽ 20 | 15 | 19 | $29

Pocasset | 570 MacArthur Blvd./Rte. 28 (Portside Dr.) | 508-564-6464 | www.stircrazyrestaurant.com

"A welcome Asian respite from fried seafood" is available in an "out-of-the-way" Pocasset location, namely this "find" featuring "reliable", "lovingly prepared" Cambodian cuisine; and with "huge portions" for affordable rates, it turns out to be one of the "best values on the Cape", especially for a "family meal."

Terra Luna *American*   23 | 20 | 23 | $52

North Truro | 104 Shore Rd. (Windigo Ln.) | 508-487-1019 |
www.theterraluna.com

"Meeting the standards of fussy foodies", this "casual, friendly", seasonal "standout" in North Truro specializes in "reliable, delicious" New American fare and "first-rate mixology"; "reservations are a must" since the "small" dining room in a former stagecoach stop quickly "fills up with locals and vacationers", all of whom lend the place a "nice buzz."

Trevi Café & Wine Bar *Mediterranean*   25 | 21 | 22 | $38

Mashpee | Mashpee Commons | 25 Market St. (Fountain St.) |
508-477-0055 | www.trevicafe.com

"From tapas to a full meal", everything's a "treat" at this Mediterranean in Mashpee Commons offering "lots of variety for a reasonable price" plus an "excellent wine selection", which the "knowledgeable staff" can guide you through; there's "nice seating outside" overlooking the fountain in warm weather, while the interior is equally sought after for "great romantic dinners" and nights out with the family.

Twenty-Eight Atlantic *American*   27 | 28 | 26 | $70

Chatham | Wequassett Resort & Golf Club | 2173 Orleans Rd./Rte. 28
(Pleasant Bay Rd.) | 508-430-3000 | www.wequassett.com

You have "an excuse to dress up" when you sup at this "elegant" New American in Chatham's Wequassett Resort, which features "superb food", "gracious" staffers who are at your "beck and call" and "stunning views of Pleasant Bay"; whether you have breakfast, lunch or dinner in the "huge", "beautifully appointed dining room with a yachtlike ambiance" or just have drinks on the "spectacular" patio adjacent to the pool, it's "always first class" (and never cheap).

Van Rensselaer's *American/Seafood*   17 | 13 | 19 | $34

Wellfleet | 1019 Rte. 6 (bet. Marconi Beach & Old Wharf Rds.) |
508-349-2127 | www.vanrensselaers.com

Wellfleet locals "depend" on this all-day "family restaurant" "year after year" for "moderately priced", seafood-focused American fare that, while "nothing exciting", is "well prepared" (breakfasts are "terrific", and dinner entrees include access to the "great salad bar"); regulars suggest the decor "could use some updating" – just as long as you "never take away the friendly and concerned owners."

Vining's Bistro *Eclectic*   ▽ 23 | 16 | 20 | $40

Chatham | Gallery Bldg. | 595 Main St. (Seaview St.) | 508-945-5033 |
www.viningsbistro.net

Follow the "aroma from the wood-burning grill" at this bistro that's "somewhat hidden" "over a group of stores" in Chatham – it's "worth finding", as the "innovative" Eclectic meats and seafood "never disappoint for quality and reliability"; the "pleasant service" includes bartenders who know "how to make a drink" and what's good on the "excellent wine list."

Waterford Café & Tavern, The *American*   – | – | – | M

Provincetown | Waterford Inn | 386 Commercial St. (bet. Law & Pearl Sts.) | 508-487-6400 | www.thewaterfordinn.com

"Cozy in bad weather, lovely outdoors in nice" ("ask for the rooftop deck" for "fabulous views"), this airy P-town American in a quaint inn is as "great" for lunch after gallery hopping as it is for a dinner "date"; adding to the charming ambiance is piano music every night except Monday and a gospel brunch on Sunday.

Wicked Fire Kissed Pizza *American/Pizza*   25 | 20 | 23 | $29

Mashpee | South Cape Vill. | 35 South St. (bet. Joys St. & Shellback Way) | 508-477-7422 | www.wickedrestaurant.com

"Inventive" "pizzas that are a cut above most parlors (especially on the Cape)" are prepped alongside other "solid" American dishes based on "quality ingredients" at this dispenser of "high-end comfort" in Mashpee; despite its "simple" appearance, the vibe is "hot and hip", so "get there early or you'll have to wait."

Wicked Oyster *American/Seafood*   23 | 20 | 21 | $43

Wellfleet | 50 Main St. (Rte. 6) | 508-349-3455 | www.thewickedo.com

"Wicked good" fish that seemingly "hops from the ocean onto your plate" makes for "scrumptious dinners" at this "reliable" Wellfleet New American in a "lovely", "casual" "old house"; it's also a "must for breakfast", but whatever meal you take here, the prices are "more reasonable than you would think" given all the "wealthy vacationers" who frequent it.

Wild Goose Tavern *American*   ▽ 21 | 23 | 21 | $37

Chatham | Chatham Wayside Inn | 512 Main St. (bet. Chatham Bars Ave. & Library Ln.) | 508-945-5590 | www.wildgoosetavern.com

"Beautiful painted scenes of Chatham" fill this "big, reliable" Traditional American with a patio in "the center of town", where the "diverse menu" offers "both pub grub and exciting fish entrees"; fans "love it for lunch while shopping", plus it's "family-friendly" for dinner and "pleasant" for drinks at the bar too.

Winslow's Tavern *American*   21 | 25 | 23 | $41

Wellfleet | 316 Main St. (bet. Bank St. & Holbrook Ave.) | 508-349-6450 | www.winslowstavern.com

In a "beautifully renovated mansion" in the "center of Wellfleet", this "crisp-white", "elegant" New American houses "relatively large" environs that include a "phenomenal patio" and a bar that hosts "great music"; service is for the most part "outstanding" and the seafood-heavy fare "commendable", but the biggest selling point may be that tabs are "reasonably priced for the area."

Martha's Vineyard

	FOOD	DECOR	SERVICE	COST

TOP FOOD

28 Larsen's Fish Mkt. | *Seafood*
L'Étoile | *French*
Détente | *American*
26 Bite | *Seafood*
Art Cliff Diner | *Diner*

TOP DECOR

26 Outermost Inn | *American*
L'Étoile | *French*
Lambert's Cove Inn | *American*
25 State Road Rest. | *American*
Sweet Life | *American/French*

Alchemy *American*

23	21	22	$46

Edgartown | 71 Main St. (bet. School & Summer Sts.) |
508-627-9999

The "magic continues" at this Edgartown year-rounder where the "rich and famous" and the "want-to-be-seen" join locals for "awesome, interesting" New American dinners served by "skilled" staffers; some feel the "best tables" are outside because the "light and airy" interior is often "noisy", while others are attracted to the "fun" upstairs bar, a "great place to meet for drinks" and "lower-cost" snacks.

☑ Art Cliff Diner *Diner*

26	16	21	$20

Vineyard Haven | 39 Beach Rd. (Five Corners) | 508-693-1224

"Go early or off-season to avoid the hordes" who create the "long, long lines" outside this "tiny" "throwback to the '40s" in Vineyard Haven, where "local fishermen" "rub elbows with celebrities" while digging into "huge portions" of "outstanding" diner breakfasts; lunch is equally "delicious and reasonable", while the recent addition of a food truck (5 PM-2 AM) makes it a nighttime and "wee hours" "destination" too.

Atlantic Fish & Chop House ❷ *Seafood/Steak*

21	24	21	$49

Edgartown | 2 Main St. (Water St.) | 508-627-7001 | www.atlanticmv.com

"Right on Edgartown Harbor", this steak-and-seafood house boasts an interior with a "splashy" "yacht-club feel" and "amazing views if you can snag a waterside table" outside; "everything from inexpensive bar food to high-end gourmet fare" is offered, and though there are "no surprises", it's all "serviceable" and served in "large portions"; in fact, the only complaint comes from locals who think the "hot" nightlife scene, complete with "loud music", "doesn't fit in with the relaxed island vibe."

Atria *American*

26	23	24	$68

Edgartown | 137 Main St. (bet. Green Ave. & Pine St.) |
508-627-5850 | www.atriamv.com

In this "attractive old house" in Edgartown, the "local, seasonal" New American fare is "tremendous", just like the "bright, simple" interior, "romantic" "wraparound porch" and "lovely" garden; in the "more casual" brick-lined basement bar, the "hamburgers are stupendous", not to mention the "best deal" (compared to the "pricey" main menu) – meanwhile, "knowledgeable, friendly service" pervades throughout.

Beach Plum Inn *American*

22 | 24 | 21 | $61

Menemsha | Beach Plum Inn | 50 Beach Plum Ln. (Night Heron Ln.) | 508-645-9454 | www.beachpluminn.com

"Book a table before sunset" and revel in the "romantic ambiance and gorgeous views" of Menemsha Harbor at this New American in an "elegant" "inn with lovely gardens"; as for the "high-priced" cuisine, though some surveyors deem it "delicious", a few critics feel it's "gone downhill", which a drop in the Food score supports – just like a five-point dip in the Service score backs reports of "amateurish" staffers.

Bite, The ♥ *Seafood*

26 | 9 | 16 | $20

Menemsha | 29 Basin Rd. (North Rd.) | 508-645-9239 | www.thebitemenemsha.com

"Who needs decor" when you can eat "swimmingly fresh", "fab" fried seafood "down the street at the beach"? – or so ask fans of this "ultimate clam shack" in Menemsha, where "there's always a line" and practically "never" a seat at its two lone picnic tables; just "be sure to stop by the ATM" and the liquor store before you go, because it's a cash-only, BYO affair.

Black Dog Tavern *American*

19 | 18 | 18 | $34

Vineyard Haven | 20 Beach St. Ext. (Water St.) | 508-693-9223 | www.theblackdog.com

This "tavern that launched a T-shirt empire" (thanks to the "cool black Lab" logo) continues to sell "serviceable", "sensibly priced" American eats amid "rustic decor" and "hypnotic" "harbor views"; breakfasts are still its "raison d'être", but lunches and dinners are just as "reliable", and especially "cozy" in winter "by the roaring fireplace"; P.S. beer and wine are offered now that Vineyard Haven is no longer a dry town.

Blue Canoe *Seafood*

∇ 16 | 19 | 19 | $35

Vineyard Haven | 52 Beach Rd. (Lagoon Pond Rd.) | 508-693-3332 | www.bluecanoegrill.com

"Hidden away from the hustle and bustle" of Vineyard Haven's "walk-by shops", this "casual, small" harborside seafooder offers "earnest service" and a recently implemented beer and wine list; but with fare that swings between "scrumptious" and "only ok", some surveyors speculate the owners are "still figuring out how to make the rest of it as great as the views" (especially those from the second-floor deck).

Chesca's *American/Italian*

24 | 21 | 23 | $53

Edgartown | 38 N. Water St. (Winter St.) | 508-627-1234 | www.chescasmv.com

"High-quality Italian and American food", "great" service and a "pretty setting" draw "loud" "crowds" to this "excellent" choice in Edgartown, where the tabs are somewhat "expensive", but the "generous portions" add "value"; "the wait can be a drag" (no reservations), so if you don't "go early", just "relax on the rockers on the front porch sipping wine" – the delay will "fly by."

	FOOD	DECOR	SERVICE	COST

Chilmark Tavern *American*   24 | 23 | 23 | $51

Chilmark | 9 State Rd. (bet. Lagemann Ln. & South Rd.) | 508-645-9400 | www.chilmarktavern.com

Grab "your best wine" and "run", don't walk, to this "wonderful" choice in Chilmark, whose "excellent" New American cuisine is based on "top-quality", "locally sourced" ingredients; the "mixer bar (you bring the booze, they supply the mixings) is a nice touch", as is the "friendly" staff, and if the country-chic interior can get "noisy" and the prices are a bit "high", all other aspects render it "well worth the drive up-island."

Deon's Restaurant *American/Caribbean*   − | − | − | M

Oak Bluffs | 53 Circuit Ave. (Narragansett Ave.) | 508-696-0001 | www.deonsrestaurant.com

With a "convenient" location in the heart of Oak Bluffs, this casual venue imbues New American cuisine with Caribbean flair, the latter evident in the surroundings also; "great deals offset" the "tad pricey" menu, and "good drinks" can counteract the effects of sometimes "too noisy" acoustics, like when DJs spin on Friday and Saturday evenings.

Détente *American*   28 | 22 | 25 | $69

Edgartown | Nevin Sq. | Winter St. (bet. Summer & Water Sts.) | 508-627-8810 | www.detentemv.com

"Exquisitely prepared" New American cuisine is the raison d'être of this "refined" Edgartonian where the menu is "built around seasonal, local foods", "served in a stylish manner" by "helpful, engaging" staffers and "worth" the "high prices"; the "romantic", "nicely decorated" interior has recently "expanded" to the second floor, but the "best seats" are in the garden ("you need to request it when you make the reservation").

Giordano's ⴆ *Italian*   23 | 17 | 21 | $31

Oak Bluffs | 18 Lake Ave. (Circuit Ave.) | 508-693-0184 | www.giosmv.com

"Doing something right" for "80 years and counting", this "great, family-style" Oak Bluffs Italian offers the "rare-on-island" combo of "huge portions" of "reliable pizza", "excellent fried clams" and such at "reasonable prices"; parents appreciate that there are "lots of kids" so "nobody notices how noisy yours are", but still "wish it would start taking credit cards" so they don't have to remember the cash *and* the diaper bag.

Home Port *Seafood*   21 | 18 | 19 | $46

Menemsha | 512 North Rd. (Basin Rd.) | 508-645-2679 | www.homeportmv.com

"Excellent-quality" "lobsters and the view" are the main draws at this BYOB seafood mainstay in Menemsha, whose newish owners have implemented "some food upgrades", including a "raw bar on the deck", while carrying on the "good value"; skirt the "noisy" dining room by "getting takeout from the back porch" and heading to the nearby beach for a "wonderful" sunset.

Il Tesoro at the Terrace *Italian*   ▽ 19 | 27 | 22 | $69

Edgartown | The Charlotte Inn | 27 S. Summer St. (Main St.) |
508-939-3840 | www.iltesoro.net

"Set in a beautifully lit glass conservatory dripping with ferns", this
Italian in an Edgartown luxury inn crafts a "romantic atmosphere"
with a "dress code"; and while some find the fare "great", those with
complaints (ranging from "not that special" to "unduly complex")
call it "overpriced", particularly the specials ("be careful!").

Jimmy Seas Pan Pasta *Italian*   23 | 11 | 18 | $39

Oak Bluffs | 38 Kennebec Ave. (Post Office Sq.) | 508-696-8550

"Unpretentious and reliable", this 20-year-old Oak Bluffs Italian
sautés "huge, mouthwatering portions" of seafood-laden pasta at
comparatively "inexpensive" prices (so "rare" on the Vineyard!);
"tight seating is an understatement" and you should expect a "long
wait", so "get there early" and don't forget the mints, because the
three main ingredients are "garlic, garlic, garlic."

Lambert's Cove Inn Ⓜ *American*   23 | 26 | 24 | $58

West Tisbury | Lambert's Cove Inn | 90 Manaquayak Rd.
(Lambert's Cove Rd.) | 508-693-2298 | www.lambertscoveinn.com

"Swooning" surveyors trumpet the "tranquil" "country setting" of this
American dining room in a "gracious" West Tisbury inn; "attentive"
servers ferry the "wholesome" fare, which most laud as "outstanding"
but a vocal minority opines could be "more reliable" considering
tabs that are "expensive" despite having to bring your own wine.

🅉 Larsen's Fish Market *Seafood*   28 | 13 | 23 | $24

Menemsha | 56 Basin Rd. (North Rd.) | 508-645-2680 |
www.larsensfishmarket.com

"You'd have to swim in the ocean" to find "fresher" seafood than
what's offered for "great prices" at this "hectic take-out window" in a
seasonal Menemsha fish market, ranked No. 1 for Food on Martha's
Vineyard; "pleasant people behind the counter" work hard to speed up
the "lines" that form, especially pre-sunset when everyone wants "the
best oysters, clams and lobsters on the island" to bring to the beach.

Lattanzi's *Italian*   21 | 17 | 19 | $33

Edgartown | Old Post Office Sq. (bet. Main & Winter Sts.) |
508-627-8854 | www.lattanzis.com

Tuscan accents abound both in the decor and in the fare at this
Edgartown Italian with a "fancy dining room", "terrific" eats, "helpful" service and the option to make reservations; if you come for the
"casual side", which can't be booked, expect "long waits", as its
"amazing", "gourmet", brick-oven pizzas are a "real draw"; meanwhile, service is "helpful" throughout (including the patio).

Le Grenier *French*   24 | 17 | 22 | $59

Vineyard Haven | 92 Main St. (bet. Church St. & Colonial Ln.) |
508-693-4906 | www.legrenierrestaurant.com

"Take two Lipitors" before dining at this Vineyard Haven "dowager"
delivering "expertly rendered" "old-fashioned" (read: "heavy")

	FOOD	DECOR	SERVICE	COST

"French classics" in a second-floor room with a "sea breeze, classical music" and decor that "hasn't changed in years"; the "cognoscenti" that frequents it appreciates that "you always feel a valued guest", but "it's no longer BYOB", so "expect to pay more than before."

L'Étoile *French*   28 | 26 | 26 | $68

Edgartown | 22 N. Water St. (Winter St.) | 508-627-5187 | www.letoile.net

"Solicitous without being obsequious" service, "marvelous" New French cuisine and a "warm" ambiance make for a "winning combination" at this Edgartown endeavor; whether you choose the "lovely" dining room, the "great" bar (with its own menu) or the "nice garden", a "most pleasant experience" is virtually guaranteed – and made even better if "someone else is paying."

Lure Grill *American*   22 | 23 | 22 | $56

Edgartown | Winnetu Oceanside Resort | 31 Dunes Rd. (Katama Rd.) | 508-627-3663 | www.luremv.com

"What a treat to eat" at this New American where the ocean "view from the deck is awesome" (and preferable to the "bland dining room") and the prices for the "great food and wonderful drinks" are a "deal" given the "expensive resort location"; "unpretentious service" informs the "relaxing atmosphere", and the "delightful sunset water taxi from Edgartown adds a lot to the experience."

Net Result *Seafood*   24 | 11 | 18 | $22

Vineyard Haven | Tisbury Mktpl. | 79 Beach Rd. (Lagoon Pond Rd.) | 508-693-6071 | www.mvseafood.com

"Impeccable" seafood, "delicious sushi" and "no decor" are what's found at this "great fish market" in "the see-and-be-seen epicenter of Vineyard Heaven" with "quick" counter service and "picnic tables in the parking lot"; sure, it's no place to dine, but it fills a "need", plus it's "reasonably priced for the island."

Newes from America *Pub Food*   20 | 21 | 20 | $27

Edgartown | Kelley House | 23 Kelley St. (N. Water St.) | 508-627-4397 | www.kelley-house.com

"Close your eyes and it's 1776" at this subterranean spot in Edgartown's Kelley House, with brick walls, beamed ceilings, fireplaces and "nothing fancy" foodwise, "just typical pub food done right", plus a "great beer selection"; it's a "quaint" and "comfortable" place to "watch TV and meet your neighbors", and best of all, "you won't be robbed."

Offshore Ale Co. *Pub Food*   20 | 19 | 19 | $28

Oak Bluffs | 30 Kennebec Ave. (Healey Way) | 508-693-2626 | www.offshoreale.com

With "great" burgers, pizzas and other grub plus "music and winter coziness" (when the "large fireplace" is employed), this brewpub in Oak Bluffs is a year-round "island favorite"; "kids love throwing the peanut shells on the floor", while adults appreciate the "pretty good housemade brews", "reasonable prices" and the "friendly" vibe – too bad it's "too crowded and noisy during the summer."

⚡ Outermost Inn Ⓜ *American* | 23 | 26 | 23 | $73 |

Aquinnah | Outermost Inn | 81 Lighthouse Rd. (State Rd.) |
508-645-3511 | www.outermostinn.com

"Come for dinner, stay for the view" at this New American whose
"magical" setting perched on the Gay Head Cliffs in Aquinnah earns
Martha's Vineyard's No. 1 Decor score; sip a "drink on the patio"
during a "spectacular sunset" before indulging in a "fabulous" prix
fixe meal, which is served by a "seasoned" staff that "aims to
please", helping to make the "pricey" fees seem worth it.

Oyster Bar Grill *Seafood/Steak* | 24 | 21 | 23 | $46 |

Oak Bluffs | 57 Circuit Ave. (Kennebec St.) | 508-693-6600 |
www.oysterbargrill.net

"Delicious" steaks and seafood plus a "great raw bar" entice at this
upscale, "historical" Oak Bluffs year-rounder with a late-night bar;
the "service is not bad and the decor is nice" with its clubby look featuring artwork, pillars, tin ceilings and plenty of room to spread out.

Saltwater *Eclectic* | ▽ 21 | 25 | 21 | $56 |

Vineyard Haven | Tisbury Mktpl. | 79 Beach Rd. (Lagoon Pond Rd.) |
508-338-4666 | www.saltwaterrestaurant.com

"Stunning" "views of a small lagoon" and a "contemporary space"
are "the major sell" at this Vineyard Haven Eclectic whose "creative
menu" boasts an "excellent variety of seafood"; "fine service" is another feature for which fans are "glad to pay" the pricey bill.

Sharky's Cantina ◗ *Mexican* | 16 | 15 | 18 | $28 |

Edgartown | 266 Upper Main St. (Chase Rd.) | 508-627-6565
Oak Bluffs | 31 Circuit Ave. (Narragansett Ave.) | 508-693-7501
www.sharkyscantina.com

"Good margs" and "fun" vibes are why folks keep these Edgartown
("warehouse") and Oak Bluffs ("scaled-down") joints "hopping", for
the Mex fare, while "decent" and "reasonably priced", is "not authentic
by any means"; staffers are "friendly but seem overworked, or at least
badly outnumbered", and as for the decor, well, "nice attempt."

Sidecar Café & Bar *New England* | - | - | - | M |

Oak Bluffs | 16 Kennebec Ave. (Lake Ave.) | 508-693-6261 |
www.sidecarcafeandbar.com

"Cool guys and hot girls" always have a "fun time" at this "secret
fave" in Oak Bluffs, where the "amazing" New England menu sates
"all types of eaters"; an "inviting bar" and "great art" on the
pumpkin-colored walls help craft a "welcoming atmosphere."

Slice of Life *American* | ▽ 26 | 15 | 23 | $28 |

Oak Bluffs | 50 Circuit Ave. (bet. Lake & Samoset Aves.) | 508-693-3838 |
www.sliceoflifemv.com

As "yummy" as it is "casual", this "friendly", "busy little" New
American cafe in Oak Bluffs doles out three meals a day, in "generous portions" and for gentle rates; visitors say "it makes a perfect
ending to a beach day", while locals "depend" on it as a "nice place
to meet friends" since it's open year-round.

Square Rigger Restaurant *Seafood*   - | - | - | M

Edgartown | 225 Edgartown Vineyard Haven Rd. (bet. Beach &
Dark Woods Rds.) | 508-627-9968 | www.squareriggerrestaurant.com
"Don't ignore" this seafood spot in Edgartown, as the "traditional"
menu lists "many choices" that provide "an enjoyable meal for any
appetite" (try it "when the parents are visiting"); its setting in an old
house may not be fancy, but it sure is quaint, and when factoring in
service and price, advocates aver it's "great all around."

State Road Restaurant *American*   25 | 25 | 24 | $65

West Tisbury | 688 State Rd. (Caldwell Ln.) | 508-693-8582 |
www.stateroadmv.com
There's a reason folks are "obsessed" with this all-day West Tisbury
New American: the "excellent cuisine" includes "produce from right
outside the back door", the rustic farmhouse setting is "lovely" (if
"noisy") and the "staff is timely and nice"; just be sure to "book
early" because it's "one of the toughest reservations on the island";
P.S. tabs are "expensive", though "BYOB saves you some money."

Sweet Life Café *American/French*   25 | 25 | 24 | $69

Oak Bluffs | 63 Circuit Ave. (bet. Narragansett & Pequot Aves.) |
508-696-0200 | www.sweetlifemv.com
"One of Oak Bluffs' special restaurants", this "perennial favorite" in
a rehabbed Victorian presents "wonderful" American-French fare in
a "beautiful" interior and garden that's "pure magic"; "sticker
shock" has been reported, but it's mitigated by the "gracious", "professional service" and all-around quality.

Water St. *New England*   ▽ 26 | 23 | 26 | $54

Edgartown | Harbor View Hotel & Resort | 131 N. Water St. (Cottage St.) |
508-627-7000 | www.harbor-view.com
"Have a drink" on "the fabulous porch" with a "beautiful view of the
harbor", then move into the "coastal interior" (dark woods, white
columns) at this New Englander in a "wonderful" Edgartown hotel,
where "you can't go wrong" with anything on the "fantastic menu";
like the "nicely appointed dining room", the adjacent, more casual
and less expensive Henry's Bar offers "professional service."

Zapotec *Southwestern*   21 | 14 | 19 | $25

Oak Bluffs | 14 Kennebec Ave. (Lake Ave.) | 508-693-6800
"In the heart of Oak Bluffs", this "cozy" cantina whips up "great fish
tacos" and other "tasty" Southwest sustenance accompanied by
"frosty" margaritas; service is generally "accommodating" and "prices
won't break the bank", making it an "overall fun" "joint to hang out."

Zephrus *American*   19 | 18 | 20 | $45

Vineyard Haven | Mansion House | 9 Main St. (State Rd.) |
508-693-3416 | www.zephrus.com
"Well-located" "near the Vineyard Haven ferry, this New American
harbors "decently priced", "well-prepared, creative" fare "made
with island-fresh ingredients", plus beer and wine ("finally!"); inside
is "pleasant" enough, but the place to be is the "terrific" patio.

Nantucket

TOP FOOD

28 Pearl | *Asian*
   Òran Mór | *Eclectic*
27 Company/Cauldron | *American*
   Topper's | *American*
   Straight Wharf | *Seafood*

TOP DECOR

29 Galley Beach | *Eclectic*
28 Topper's | *American*
27 Pearl | *Asian*
26 Brant Point Grill | *Seafood/Steak*
   Summer House | *American*

American Seasons *American*　　26 | 22 | 23 | $67

Nantucket | 80 Centre St. (Easton St.) | 508-228-7111 |
www.americanseasons.com

Chef-owner Michael LaScola pairs his "sumptuous", seasonal New American fare with a "unique catalog of some of America's finest wines" at this "superb" Nantucket eatery where a "smiling staff" delivers the "expensive" dishes; "the patio is lovely", and while most deem the "shabby-chic" interior "romantic", be prepared to "use your phone for light" to "read the menu", as it's "dim" in here.

Arno's *American*　　20 | 18 | 19 | $38

Nantucket | 41 Main St. (bet. Centre & Federal Sts.) | 508-228-7001 |
www.arnos.net

As a four-point rise in the Food score attests, this "family-friendly" Downtown New American's "casual" lunches and dinners have "grown in quality", even as they remain priced for "good value for Nantucket" – but as always, "breakfast is the best meal", and the "most popular"; meanwhile a "wine bar has added class" to the "eclectic" setting.

Black-Eyed Susan's ⊄ *American*　　25 | 15 | 21 | $38

Nantucket | 10 India St. (Centre St.) | 508-325-0308 |
www.black-eyedsusans.com

"Scrumptious" breakfasts and "ethereal" dinners are the "rewards" for waiting on the "long lines" at this "quirky", "friendly" Nantucket New American where "BYO makes it reasonable" pricewise; inside may be "nothing to look at", but the "small" back patio is "a nice option"; P.S. "reservations only for the 6 PM seating" and no credit cards.

Boarding House *American*　　25 | 23 | 23 | $59

Nantucket | 12 Federal St. (India St.) | 508-228-9622 |
www.boardinghousenantucket.com

You'll "feel at home" at this "lovely" Nantucket New American where "friendly" staffers convey "excellent" Med-tinged fare, for which you should make sure you have a "big credit limit"; its "busy corner" location means there's "great people-watching" on the patio, and the "hot bar scene" is a single's dream, but the basement dining room, well, it "feels like a basement"; P.S. "weekend brunch is a must."

Brant Point Grill *Seafood/Steak*　　24 | 26 | 24 | $63

Nantucket | White Elephant Hotel | 50 Easton St. (Harbor View Way) |
508-228-2500 | www.whiteelephanthotel.com

"Gorgeous views" of a "lovely garden", Children's Beach and the "ferries coming and going" in Nantucket Harbor are "romantic" in the evening and even "better" in the sunlight at this "fabulous" all-day steak-and-seafooder in a "luxury" inn; but the fare is equally "visually appealing" and tastes "wonderful" too (brunch is particularly "awesome"), with "a wine list to match" plus fittingly "attentive service" and "expensive" prices.

Brotherhood of Thieves *American* | 21 | 19 | 20 | $33 |

Nantucket | 23 Broad St. (bet. Centre & Federal Sts.) | 508-228-2551 | www.brotherhoodofthieves.com
"Relatively inexpensive" tabs for "great burgers" and other "hearty" American pub dishes draw the wallet-conscious to this Nantucket "staple" with "friendly service" and a "historic tavern" vibe, especially downstairs; during the summer, the "patio is a respite from the bustle of Downtown", while in the winter, fireplaces keep locals "cozy."

Centre Street Bistro *American* | ▽ 26 | 15 | 22 | $42 |

Nantucket | Meeting House | 29 Centre St. (bet. Chestnut & India Sts.) | 508-228-8470 | www.nantucketbistro.com
For such an "expensive area", the "prices are phenomenal" at this "homey" Nantucket New American BYO whose kitchen "turns out some very tasty surprises"; the interior is a "cozy" spot for just 20 people at time, and there's more room outside where "you can sit in the sun watching the people pass by."

Chanticleer *French* | 25 | 25 | 23 | $71 |

Siasconset | 9 New St. (Park Ln.) | 508-257-6231 | www.thechanticleer.net
"Pure magic" is conjured at this "'Sconset stunner" where New French dishes are ferried by "attentive" servers; "leisurely lunches" and dinners are as "delightful" inside where the vibe is "European elegance" as they are outside in the "beautiful" rose garden, but no matter how "fine" and "fancy" the fare is, many feel it's "overpriced."

Club Car *Continental* | 24 | 22 | 23 | $68 |

Nantucket | 1 Main St. (Easy St.) | 508-228-1101 | www.theclubcar.com
The piano player "attracts a lively singing crowd" to the bar – a 19th-century railway club car – and the "excellent" Continental cuisine and "wonderful wine selection" draw diners to the "old world"–"classy" "white-tablecloth" dining room at this "loads-of-fun" "Nantucket classic"; with a "friendly staff" along for the ride, it's a "can't miss", even if it is a "little pricey" (maybe even "overpriced").

Company of the Cauldron *American* | 27 | 24 | 25 | $79 |

Nantucket | 5 India St. (bet. Centre & Federal Sts.) | 508-228-4016 | www.companyofthecauldron.com
"Heavenly food accompanied by live harp music" (on many nights) sums up this "romantic" Nantucket "gem" that offers two seatings per evening and an "innovative, wonderful" set New American menu that "varies each night" (the roster of dishes is "posted weekly" on-line, so you can "book the day that interests you most"); true, it's "expensive, but worth it" when factoring in the "wonderful staff" – in fact, the only complaint is that you're "packed in like sardines."

FOOD | DECOR | SERVICE | COST

Corazon del Mar   Latin

25 | 20 | 22 | $50

Nantucket | 21 S. Water St. (bet. Broad & Oak Sts.) | 508-228-0815 | www.corazonnantucket.com

"Hard-core addictions to everything on the menu" have developed at this colorful, "innovative" Pan-Latin place on Nantucket, where "great ceviche" is the bait at the downstairs raw bar and virtually "every kind of tequila" is the draw upstairs (beware the sometimes "excruciating noise level" here); service is generally "gracious and knowledge-able", and if it's "slightly overpriced", "what isn't on the island?"

DeMarco   Italian

23 | 19 | 22 | $62

Nantucket | 9 India St. (bet. Centre & Federal Sts.) | 508-228-1836 | www.demarcorestaurant.com

That this Northern Italian has "survived in a fish town" for over 30 years just about "tells it all", but still, surveyors want you to know about its "wonderful", "reliable" fare and "charming" setting in an 1800s home; sure, there's typically "outrageous Nantucket pricing", but most cop to having "always a lovely night here."

Dune   American

22 | 19 | 21 | $59

Nantucket | 20 Broad St. (bet. Centre & Federal Sts.) | 508-228-5550 | www.dunenantucket.com

"Geared to the sophisticated palate", this "upscale" Nantucket "pleasure" prepares "solid" New American dishes in a "modern" setting of "simple chairs, unadorned tables, soothing colors and soft lighting"; service "tries hard to accommodate", and while tabs are "a little pricey", they're thankfully "not as expensive as others" of this ilk.

Easy Street   Seafood

- | - | - | M

Nantucket | Steamboat Wharf | 31 Easy St. (Broad St.) | 508-228-5031 | www.easystreetnantucket.com

Set on Nantucket's Steamboat Wharf, this 1973 seafood purveyor reopened in 2009 after operating as a different restaurant for more than a decade, affording a "pleasant, easy" option for "good" eats on the water; what's more, it's a "great value" – just don't expect too much from the staff, as word is the "food outweighs the service."

Even Keel Cafe   American

19 | 14 | 18 | $26

Nantucket | 40 Main St. (Federal St.) | 508-228-1979 | www.evenkeelcafe.com

An affordable price point is one reason this Nantucket New American is "crowded and noisy" from breakfast till dinner – it's "reliable, un-pretentious, easy" and "kid-friendly too"; a meal or coffee at the counter is "always entertaining", but it can't compare to the "pass-ing show" if you snag a "window table" (to "get away from the hustle and bustle of Main Street", ask for the "quaint courtyard" in back).

Fifty-Six Union   Eclectic

23 | 23 | 23 | $57

Nantucket | 56 Union St. (E. Dover St.) | 508-228-6135 | www.fiftysixunion.com

A "hideaway on the edge of town", this Nantucket Eclectic beckons with "outstanding" culinary creations, "warm welcomes" from the "wonderful" staff and owners who are "really involved"; what's more, the "classy", "romantic" seating options "never disappoint", be it one of the two art-filled interior dining rooms or the garden.

Figs at 29 Fair by Todd English *Mediterranean*

| 26 | 25 | 25 | $54 |

Nantucket | 29 Fair St. (Martins Ln.) | 508-228-7800 | www.thesummerhouse.com

"Thoroughly hyped", this recently Todd English-ized Mediterranean "exceeds expectations" with "absolutely fabulous" designer pizzas et al. brought by "friendly but professional" servers; everyone thinks the "quintessential Nantucket dining room with antiques, exposed beams and fireplaces" is "romantic" regardless of whether they find the tabs "overpriced" or a "bargain."

Fog Island Cafe *American*

| 23 | 15 | 21 | $27 |

Nantucket | 7 S. Water St. (India St.) | 508-228-1818 | www.fogisland.com

"You'll love the huevos and coffee" at this "reliable, simple" Nantucket New American breakfast beacon, which also dishes out "consistently good" lunches in a "cozy" setting with a "pleasant, low-key" vibe; "reasonable prices" and a "friendly staff" buttress its rep as a "great family place" where "even when there's a wait, it's worth it!"

☑ Galley Beach *Eclectic*

| 24 | 29 | 26 | $77 |

Nantucket | 54 Jefferson Ave. (N. Beach St.) | 508-228-9641 | www.galleybeach.net

Nantucket's top-rated Decor is found at this "chic" sandside Eclectic eatery boasting "unrivaled" views of the sound (and "gorgeous sunsets", natch) from walls of windows plus a bar on the beach; "out-of-this-world food" and "fantastic service" are part of the package, but just remember that an experience this "sophisticated" "comes with a price", so be sure to "bring the Gold Card."

Jetties, The *Italian/New England*

| ▽ 17 | 19 | 20 | $28 |

Nantucket | 4 Bathing Beach Rd. (Hulbert Ave.) | 508-228-2279 | www.thejetties.com

"No need to bring a picnic to the beach" thanks to this "fun" Italian-New Englander set right on the sand on Nantucket; it's about "as casual as you can get", as "the kids can play while waiting for their pizza" and adults can indulge in "frozen drinks" on the deck while swaying along to the occasional "great" live musician.

Le Languedoc Bistro Ⓜ *French*

| 23 | 23 | 23 | $58 |

Nantucket | Le Languedoc Inn | 24 Broad St. (bet. Centre & Federal Sts.) | 508-228-2552 | www.lelanguedoc.com

"Each morsel is worth savoring" at this "magnificent" French splurge on Nantucket, whether you dine in the "casual downstairs bistro" (where there's a "small", "friendly" bar too), the "quiet", "elegant" dining room upstairs (some say it's "a bit stiff") or outdoors (the "only way to go" on a "warm evening"); "wonderful people" "graciously serve" the fare and "lovely wines", but just remember to "reserve early" if you want to experience them or "don't expect to get a table."

Lo La 41° ● *Eclectic*
25 | 24 | 23 | $56

Nantucket | 15 S. Beach St. (bet. Broad & Easton Sts.) | 508-325-4001 | www.lola41.net

"Celebutantes" and ordinary "young" people alike have "no reservations" bestowing "raves" upon this "contemporary" Nantucket "hot spot", as "everything" on the Eclectic menu is "unique and tasty", from the "excellent burger" to the "phenomenal sushi"; just know that "you need reservations" to get a seat, plus lots of dough and "elbow pads", because it's "pricey" and "crowded", especially at the "hopping", "noisy" bar.

NEW Millie's *Californian/Mexican*
▽ 19 | 17 | 15 | $31

Nantucket | 326 Madaket Rd. (Baltimore St.) | 508-228-8435 | www.milliesnantucket.com

"Go west, young man" – that is Nantucket's West End – for "inventive tacos, quesadillas" and "amazing sunsets", which are offered at this Cali-Mex cafe where folks put up with service that's "a bit slow" because the "decent prices" are an outright "bargain" for the island; there's "live music several times a week" also – "too bad no one can hear it" over the "deafening", "zoo"-like decibel levels.

Nantucket Lobster Trap *Seafood*
22 | 16 | 18 | $48

Nantucket | 23 Washington St. (Coffin St.) | 508-228-4200 | www.nantucketlobstertrap.com

"Dress casual, kick back and eat so much lobster" you might "explode" ("you'll die happy") at this "no-frills" Nantucket seafooder whipping up "good old-fashioned clambake-type food"; "helpful" staffers make "those with children" feel comfortable, but know that the "outside bar gets rowdy with college-age kids" – so maybe leave the kids at home, because "that's where the fun is!"

☑ Òran Mór *Eclectic*
28 | 24 | 24 | $67

Nantucket | 2 S. Beach St., 2nd fl. (bet. Broad & Water Sts.) | 508-228-8655 | www.oranmorbistro.com

"Fabulous", "unique" Eclectic fare distinguishes this "ultimate romantic hideaway tucked in a charming second-story location" where the "classic decor is in line with its historic-home" setting and the staffers are "dedicated and professional"; though it commands "typically outrageous Nantucket prices", it's all so "memorable", "you'll want to go again" as soon as possible – in fact, it "should be called Oran More!"

☑ Pearl *Asian*
28 | 27 | 25 | $77

Nantucket | 12 Federal St. (India St.) | 508-228-9701 | www.thepearlnantucket.com

"Taste sensations" "you are unlikely to find elsewhere" (like the "work-of-art wok-fried lobster") earn Nantucket's No. 1 Food rating at this "slick" Asian where the drinks at the "stylish bar" are just as "great" and the "owners are friendly and generous"; "prices are pretty substantial", but that goes with the territory, i.e. the "gorgeous" "NYC chic–meets–Nantucket charm" decor.

Pi Pizzeria *Pizza*

| 23 | 16 | 18 | $31 |

Nantucket | 11 W. Creek Rd. (bet. Orange & Pleasant Sts.) | 508-228-1130 | www.pipizzeria.com

"Shhh . . . don't tell anyone" about the "great wood-fired pizza" spun at this "solid", "casual" Nantucket Neapolitan boasting "ingredients so fresh, you'd think they were picked hours earlier", plus prices that "won't break the bank" and a "courteous staff"; the "wait for a table" is already "a challenge", what with the no-reservations policy and "intimate" digs – which is why many "mostly do takeout."

Queequeg's *Eclectic*

| 25 | 20 | 23 | $51 |

Nantucket | 6 Oak St. (bet. Federal & Water Sts.) | 508-325-0992 | www.queequegsnantucket.com

"Nestled on a wee side street" in Nantucket town, this "dependable" "hideaway" offers "innovative, well-prepared" all-day Eclectic fare in "cocoonlike" quarters; the "friendly", "helpful service" adds to the "pleasant surprise", which includes "nice outdoor dining" on a deck and comparatively "reasonable" prices.

Ropewalk, The *Seafood*

| 18 | 20 | 18 | $40 |

Nantucket | 1 Straight Wharf (Main St.) | 508-228-8886 | www.theropewalk.com

"Glorious views of the harbor" plus "nice sea breezes" make this Nantucket seafood purveyor perched "at the end of a wharf" a "perfect" "informal" spot for a "fully satisfying" breakfast, lunch or dinner; inside, there's a "ramshackle set of 'fish shack' dining rooms", but the best "people-watching" is at the "fun bar" and on the patio.

Sconset Café ⊄ *American/Eclectic*

| 25 | 20 | 24 | $37 |

Siasconset | 8 Main St. (Post Office Sq.) | 508-257-4008 | www.sconsetcafe.com

"Get away from the busy-ness of Nantucket town" at this "delight-ful" American-Eclectic "oasis" in "Sconset, specializing in "classy breakfasts", "wonderful lunches" and "innovative" dinners; though "a little cheaper than the usual ACK outing" (thanks to BYO with a wine store next door), the "quaint", "low-key" setting definitely is not – rather, it's something "right out of a romantic novel."

Sea Grille *Seafood*

| 23 | 19 | 24 | $44 |

Nantucket | 45 Sparks Ave. (bet. Pleasant St. & Sanford Rd.) | 508-325-5700 | www.theseagrille.com

"Variety" is this spice of this year-round Nantucketeer whose "large menu" stars an "amazing range" of "well-prepared" seafood plus "meat and vegetarian options", all "at a great price"; "friendly service" and a "comfortable", "attractive" "old-school" setting are two more reasons why many locals "call it home."

Ships Inn *American*

| ▽ 27 | 25 | 29 | $52 |

Nantucket | Ships Inn | 13 Fair St. (Lucretia Mott Ln.) | 508-228-0040 | www.shipsinnnantucket.com

Everything about this "gem" "in the lower level of an old inn" "on the edge of town" is "so elegant", from the "beautifully presented", "luscious, gourmet" New American cuisine to the service to the "intimate" setting; "as with most Nantucket restaurants", it's "pricey", but that makes no difference to its "steady following" who particularly adore "snuggling here on a blustery night."

Slip 14 *American* ▽ 19 | 16 | 18 | $48

Nantucket | 14 Old South Wharf (New Whale St.) | 508-228-2033 | www.slip14.com

The decor needn't be anything more than "simple" when you've got "breathtaking" views such as those on display from inside and outside this "pleasant, casual" Nantucket New American; the "enjoyable, unpretentious" menu highlights "well-prepared" seafood that's comparatively "not expensive" and "served with a smile" alongside "fun, fruity drinks", all of which virtually guarantees "a relaxed meal."

Straight Wharf *Seafood* 27 | 25 | 26 | $68

Nantucket | 6 Harbor Sq. (Orange St.) | 508-228-4499 | www.straightwharfrestaurant.com

"Beautiful" environs and "killer views" from the dining porch set the stage for "artistic", "absolutely delightful" seafood complemented by "excellent" wines and "attentive service" at this "wonderful experience on the water on Nantucket"; of course, fare this "outstanding" comes at "a high price", but "go once and you'll be addicted – even in this economy"; P.S. after your meal, join the "younger crowd" at the "vibrant bar."

Summer House *American* 25 | 26 | 25 | $70

Siasconset | Summer House | 17 Ocean Ave. (Magnolia Ave.) | 508-257-9976 | www.thesummerhouse.com

Todd English's "inventive" cuisine "blows minds" at this Nantucket New American with a "romantic" Siasconset setting comprised of an "attractive", "formal" dining room, a porch and a "picture-perfect" poolside bistro "overlooking the Atlantic Ocean"; there's also a "fantastic piano bar", a "fabulous wine list" and "friendly service" that makes everyone feel "well cared for", all of which helps to create "magical evenings" – and command fees that are "so expensive."

Sushi by Yoshi *Japanese* 23 | 14 | 19 | $40

Nantucket | 2 E. Chestnut St. (Water St.) | 508-228-1801 | www.sushibyyoshi.com

"If you need a sushi fix on Nantucket, this is the place", as the fish is "always fresh", plus it's served by a "friendly, helpful staff" and offered at "decent prices" to boot ("BYOB is a plus"); those who feel "the decor leaves much to be desired" "sit at the bar and watch" the chefs at work or get their meal to go – after all, the place is quite "quaint" and utterly "popular."

Topper's *American* 27 | 28 | 27 | $81

Nantucket | Wauwinet Inn | 120 Wauwinet Rd. (north of Polpis Rd.) | 508-228-8768 | www.wauwinet.com

"Extravagant" in every way, this all-day New American in Nantucket's "historic", "secluded" Wauwinet Inn ferries its guests on a "romantic, relaxing" water taxi from town, then plies them with

FOOD | DECOR | SERVICE | COST

"incredible" cuisine and a "superb wine selection" in a "charming", "serene" dining room or on a "casually elegant patio"; the expense makes it "a once-in-a-lifetime experience" for some, but it's "worth it", and besides, with the "premium price" comes "premium service."

Town *Eclectic*   ▽ 24 | 25 | 24 | $59

Nantucket | 4 E. Chestnut St. (bet. Federal & Water Sts.) | 508-325-8696 | www.townnantucket.com

Possibly "the most exotic spot on the island", this "aims-to-please" Eclectic presents a "unique menu" with Asian, Indian and North African influences that represent a "nice break" from "typical Nantucket fare", and an "amazing" one at that; with "romantic", Eastern-influenced decor and an "inviting patio", it's "lovely both inside and out", plus it's "intimate enough" for "date night" and "fun" to "go with the girls."

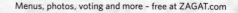

BOSTON/
CAPE COD & THE ISLANDS
INDEXES

LOCATION MAPS

All places are in Boston area unless otherwise noted (CC=Cape Cod; MV=Martha's Vineyard; Nan=Nantucket).

Cuisines

Includes names, locations and Food ratings.

AFGHAN

Helmand | **E Cambridge** 25

AFRICAN

Teranga | **S End** 22

AMERICAN

🆕 Abbey, The | **Brookline** –
Abby Park | **Milton** 19
Adrian's | **CC** 18
Alchemy | **MV** 23
🔢 Alibi | **Beacon Hill** 19
American Seasons | **Nan** 26
Amrheins | **S Boston** 19
🆕 Anthem | **Faneuil Hall** 19
Aqua Grille | **CC** 19
Arno's | **Nan** 20
🔢 Art Cliff | **MV** 26
Ashmont Grill | **Dorchester** 23
Atria | **MV** 26
Audubon Circle | **Kenmore Sq** 21
Aura | **Seaport Dist** 22
Avenue One | **D'town Cross** 19
🆕 Back Bay Social | **Back Bay** 18
Bakers' Best | **Newton** 22
Bambara | **E Cambridge** 21
🔢 Barker Tavern | **Scituate** 27
Barley Neck Inn | **CC** 20
🆕 Barlow's | **Seaport Dist** 16
Bayside Betsy's | **CC** 18
Beach Plum | **MV** 22
Beacon St. Tavern | **Brookline** 19
Beehive | **S End** 20
Bee-Hive Tavern | **CC** 19
🔢 Belfry Inne | **CC** 27
🔢🆕 Bergamot | **Somerville** 27
Betsy's Diner | **CC** 16
Big Papi's | **Framingham** 13
Biltmore B&G | **Newton** 21
Birch St. Bistro | **Roslindale** 20
Bistro/Crowne Pointe | **CC** 23
Black Cow | **multi.** 20
Black Dog | **MV** 19
Black-Eyed Susan's | **Nan** 25
Blackfish | **CC** 25
Black Sheep | **Kendall Sq** 21
Blarney Stone | **Dorchester** 20

Blu | **Theater Dist** 21
Blue on Highland | **Needham** 20
Blue22 | **Quincy** 14
Boarding House | **Nan** 25
🆕 Bondir | **Central Sq** –
🔢 Bramble Inn | **CC** 28
Brenden Crocker's | **Beverly** 26
🔢 Bristol Lounge | **Back Bay** 26
Brotherhood/Thieves | **Nan** 21
Burtons | **multi.** 21
Cafe 47 | **Back Bay** 19
Cafeteria | **Back Bay** 18
🆕 Canary Sq. | **Jamaica Plain** –
🔢 Cape Sea | **CC** 27
Capt. Linnell | **CC** 24
CBS Scene Rest. & Bar | **Foxboro** –
🆕 Center Café | **Needham** 20
Central Kitchen | **Central Sq** 23
Centre St. Bistro | **Nan** 26
Charley's | **multi.** 18
🔢 Chatham Bars | **CC** 23
🔢 Cheesecake Factory | **multi.** 18
Chesca's | **MV** 24
Chilmark Tavern | **MV** 24
Church | **Fenway** 20
🆕 Citizen Public | **Fenway** –
City Bar | **multi.** 19
City Table | **Back Bay** 22
Clancy's | **CC** 21
Clink | **Beacon Hill** 19
Club Cafe | **S End** 19
Coda | **S End** 21
Company/Cauldron | **Nan** 27
Corner Tavern | **Back Bay** –
Courtyard/Boston Library | 18
  Back Bay
🆕 Cutty's | **Brookline** 25
Cygnet | **Beverly** 23
Daedalus | **Harv Sq** 18
Dalya's | **Bedford** 21
Dan'l Webster | **CC** 21
Dbar | **Dorchester** 23
Deon's | **MV** –
Détente | **MV** 28
🆕 Deuxave | **Back Bay** –
Devlin's | **Brighton** 20

Devon's | **CC**	25
Dillon's | **Back Bay**	16
District | **Leather Dist**	–
Dog Bar | **Gloucester**	–
Dogwood Café | **Jamaica Plain**	20
Dolphin | **CC**	22
Drink | **Seaport Dist**	21
☒ Duckworth's | **Gloucester**	27
Dune | **Nan**	22
☒ Eastern Stand. | **Kenmore Sq**	23
☒ Ecco | **E Boston**	27
Edwige | **CC**	26
88 Wharf | **Milton**	19
Even Keel | **Nan**	19
Fairway | **CC**	17
Fanizzi's | **CC**	19
Farm Bar | **Essex**	–
51 Lincoln | **Newton**	24
Finely JP's | **CC**	21
Fishmonger's | **CC**	20
Five Bays | **CC**	23
Flash's | **Park Sq**	19
Flat Iron | **W End**	–
Flora | **Arlington**	24
Fog Island | **Nan**	23
Forty Carrots | **Chestnut Hill**	20
NEW Foundry/Elm | **Somerville**	–
NEW Four Green Fields | **Financial Dist**	–
Franklin | **multi.**	24
Friendly Toast | **Kendall Sq**	21
Full Moon | **Huron Vill**	19
NEW Gallows | **S End**	20
☒ Garden at Cellar | **Harv Sq**	26
Gargoyles | **Somerville**	24
G Bar | **Swampscott**	19
Geoffrey's | **Back Bay**	22
☒ Glass Onion | **CC**	27
Globe Bar | **Back Bay**	16
Glory | **Andover**	21
Good Life | **D'town Cross**	16
Grafton St. Pub | **Harv Sq**	19
☒ Grapevine | **Salem**	27
Greg's | **Watertown**	18
Grendel's Den | **Harv Sq**	17
Haley House | **Roxbury**	22
Harvard Gdns. | **Beacon Hill**	17
☒ Harvest | **Harv Sq**	25
Hen House | **Dorchester**	–
Highland Kitchen | **Somerville**	25
Hillstone | **Faneuil Hall**	25
Independent | **Somerville**	20
Ironside Grill | **Charlestown**	15
Isabella | **Dedham**	21
Island Merchant | **CC**	–
Jacob Wirth | **Theater Dist**	18
James's Gate | **Jamaica Plain**	18
Jer-Ne | **Theater Dist**	19
Joe's American | **multi.**	17
Johnny D's | **Somerville**	20
NEW Journeyman | **Somerville**	–
J's/Nashoba | **Bolton**	24
Kingston | **D'town Cross**	20
Lambert's Cove | **MV**	23
Landing | **multi.**	18
Lansdowne | **Fenway**	16
Ledge | **Dorchester**	15
Lexx | **Lexington**	19
Lineage | **Brookline**	25
Living Room | **Waterfront**	16
Local | **W Newton**	19
☒ Locke-Ober | **D'town Cross**	25
Lord Hobo | **Inman Sq**	16
Lucky's | **Seaport Dist**	19
Lure Grill | **MV**	22
Lyric | **CC**	25
Market | **Theater Dist**	26
Marshland | **CC**	20
Marshside | **CC**	19
Masona Grill | **W Roxbury**	24
Max/Dylan | **multi.**	19
☒ Meritage | **Waterfront**	26
Met Back/B&G | **multi.**	19
Metropolitan | **Chestnut Hill**	20
Mews | **CC**	26
Mike's | **S End**	20
Mr. Bartley's | **Harv Sq**	24
Navy Yard | **Charlestown**	24
☒**NEW** Noche | **S End**	22
Noir | **Harv Sq**	20
North St. Grille | **N End**	24
☒ Not Average Joe's | **multi.**	19
Oceana | **Waterfront**	22
Ocean House | **CC**	27
Ocean Terrace | **CC**	19
Om | **Harv Sq**	16
Optimist Café | **CC**	–
Orleans | **Somerville**	17
Orleans Inn | **CC**	16
☒ Outermost Inn | **MV**	23

Paddock	**CC**	22
Pairings	**Park Sq**	21
Palmers	**Andover**	22
Paramount	**Beacon Hill**	22
NEW Parsons Table	**Winchester**	27
Pleasant Cafe	**Roslindale**	21
Pops	**S End**	20
NEW Port 305	**N Quincy**	–
Post 390	**Back Bay**	20
Redline	**Harv Sq**	16
Red Pheasant	**CC**	27
Red Robin	**Foxboro**	16
Red Rock	**Swampscott**	20
NEW Regal Beagle	**Brookline**	21
Regatta/Cotuit	**CC**	26
Robinwood	**Jamaica Plain**	–
Roobar	**multi.**	19
Ross' Grill	**CC**	24
NEW Russell Hse.	**Harv Sq**	21
Z Salts	**Central Sq**	27
NEW Sam's	**Seaport Dist**	20
Sauciety	**Seaport Dist**	–
Scargo Café	**CC**	21
Scollay Sq.	**Beacon Hill**	19
Sconset Café	**Nan**	25
Second St. Café	**E Cambridge**	23
75 Chestnut	**Beacon Hill**	21
Ships Inn	**Nan**	27
Sibling Rivalry	**S End**	23
Sidney's	**Central Sq**	21
Silvertone B&G	**D'town Cross**	21
NEW Simple Truth	**Harv Sq**	–
606 Congress	**Seaport Dist**	20
Sky	**Norwood**	16
Slice of Life	**MV**	26
Slip 14	**Nan**	19
Solstice	**Kingston**	25
Sorella's	**Jamaica Plain**	24
Sound Bites	**Somerville**	23
South/Buttery	**S End**	22
South St. Diner	**Leather Dist**	17
Z Square Café	**Hingham**	25
Stanhope Grille	**Back Bay**	20
State Road	**MV**	25
Stephanie's	**multi.**	20
NEW Stoddard's	**D'town Cross**	19
Strip-T's	**Watertown**	21
Suffolk Grille	**Canton**	–
Summer House	**Nan**	25
Summer Winter	**Burlington**	25
Sunset Cafe	**Inman Sq**	24
Sweet Life	**MV**	25
Tavern in Sq.	**multi.**	15
Tavern/Water	**Charlestown**	12
Technique	**E Cambridge**	–
NEW Telegraph Hill	**S Boston**	–
Temple Bar	**Porter Sq**	21
Tempo	**Waltham**	22
Z Ten Tables	**multi.**	27
Terra Luna	**CC**	23
NEW Think Tank	**Kendall Sq**	–
NEW Tico	**Back Bay**	–
Z Top of Hub	**Back Bay**	20
Topper's	**Nan**	27
Tory Row	**Harv Sq**	17
Townsend's	**Hyde Park**	21
Trata	**Harv Sq**	–
Tremont 647/Sorel	**S End**	20
Trina's	**Inman Sq**	20
Z Troquet	**Theater Dist**	26
Tryst	**Arlington**	24
NEW Turbine	**Lynn**	–
28 Atlantic	**CC**	27
28 Degrees	**S End**	19
21st Amendment	**Beacon Hill**	17
29 Newbury	**Back Bay**	20
Z T.W. Food	**Huron Vill**	28
224 Boston St.	**Dorchester**	21
Union B&G	**S End**	24
Upstairs/Square	**Harv Sq**	24
Van Rensselaer's	**CC**	17
Via Lago	**Lexington**	22
Walden Grille	**Concord**	16
Warren	**Charlestown**	19
Washington Sq.	**Brookline**	22
Waterford Café/Tav.	**CC**	–
West/Centre	**W Roxbury**	19
West Side	**Porter Sq**	21
Wicked Fire Kissed	**CC**	25
Wicked Oyster	**CC**	23
Wild Goose	**CC**	21
Winslow's Tavern	**CC**	21
NEW W Lounge	**Theater Dist**	19
Woodward	**Financial Dist**	21
Woody's Grill	**Fenway**	23
NEW Yard House	**Dedham**	19
Zebra's Bistro	**Medfield**	24
Zephrus	**MV**	19

AMERICAN (REGIONAL)

NEW Darryl's | S End	-

ARGENTINEAN

Tango | Arlington	22

ARMENIAN

Karoun | Newton	20

ASIAN

Z All Seasons | Malden	27
Asia | CC	21
Betty's Wok | MFA	17
Billy Tse | multi.	21
Z Blue Ginger | Wellesley	27
Blue22 | Quincy	14
NEW Brother's Crawfish | Dorchester	-
NEW Budda C | Brookline	20
Grasshopper | Allston	22
Island Hopper | Back Bay	18
Jae's | S End	22
Kowloon | Saugus	15
Lam's | Newtonville	19
Lavender Asian | Sudbury	23
Ma Soba | Beacon Hill	20
Maxwells 148 | Natick	24
Myers + Chang | S End	24
Noodle St. | Boston U	20
Z Pearl | Nan	28
Ponzu | Waltham	23
NEW Think Tank | Kendall Sq	-
NEW Turbine | Lynn	-
Typhoon | multi.	18

BAKERIES

Athan's Café | multi.	22
Bakers' Best | Newton	22
Z Flour Bakery | multi.	27
Haley House | Roxbury	22
Hi-Rise | multi.	24
Z Neighborhood | Somerville	26
Pain D'Avignon | CC	26
Panificio | Beacon Hill	21
South/Buttery | S End	22
Vicki Lee's | Belmont	23

BARBECUE

Bison County | Waltham	18
Z Blue Ribbon BBQ | multi.	26
Z East Coast | Inman Sq	26
Farm Bar | Essex	-
Firefly's | multi.	19
Pit Stop BBQ | Mattapan	-
Redbones | Somerville	24
Soul Fire | Allston	22
Village Smokehse. | Brookline	21

BELGIAN

Publick House | Brookline	20

BRAZILIAN

Brazilian Grill | CC	24
Café Belô | multi.	24
Café Brazil | Allston	22
Don Ricardo's | S End	20
Midwest | multi.	21
Muqueca | Inman Sq	25
NEW Top Steak | Peabody	-

BRITISH

Cornwall's | Kenmore Sq	16
Dunbar Tea | CC	21
Optimist Café | CC	-

BURGERS

B. Good | multi.	18
Boston Burger | Somerville	23
Brotherhood/Thieves | Nan	21
Charlie's Kitchen | Harv Sq	17
Christopher's | Porter Sq	21
Five Guys | multi.	20
Miracle of Science | Central Sq	19
Mr Bartley's | Harv Sq	24
Red Robin | Foxboro	16
Splash Ultra | Leather Dist	17
NEW Tasty Burger | Fenway	-
UBurger | multi.	22

CAJUN

Border Cafe | multi.	20

CALIFORNIAN

Caliterra | Financial Dist	15
Cottage | Wellesley Hills	19
NEW Millie's | Nan	19
Picante | Central Sq	22

CAMBODIAN

Z Elephant Walk | multi.	23
Stir Crazy | CC	20
Wonder Spice | Jamaica Plain	20

CARIBBEAN

Deon's	**MV**	-
Island Merchant	**CC**	-

CHILEAN

Chacarero	**D'town Cross**	25

CHINESE

(* dim sum specialist)

Bernard's	**Chestnut Hill**	25
Bistro Chi	**Quincy**	-
Changsho	**Porter Sq**	21
Chau Chow*	**multi.**	22
Chef Chow's	**Brookline**	20
China Blossom	**North Andover**	-
China Pearl*	**multi.**	21
China Sky	**Wellesley**	22
CK Shanghai	**Wellesley**	24
NEW East by NE	**Inman Sq**	22
East Ocean	**Chinatown**	25
Emperor's Gdn.*	**Chinatown**	21
Golden Temple	**Brookline**	20
Gourmet Dumpling	**Chinatown**	25
Grand Chinatown	**N Quincy**	-
Hei La Moon*	**Chinatown**	-
Hong Kong	**Harv Sq**	13
Jumbo	**multi.**	22
Lotus Blossom	**Sudbury**	22
Mary Chung	**Central Sq**	22
NEW Mumbai Chop	**Back Bay**	19
New Shanghai	**Chinatown**	21
Peach Farm	**Chinatown**	25
Peking Cuisine	**Newton**	-
P.F. Chang's	**multi.**	19
Royal East	**Central Sq**	23
Shanghai Gate	**Allston**	21
Shangri-La*	**Belmont**	23
Sichuan Gdn.	**multi.**	23
Sichuan Gourmet	**multi.**	25
Zoe's	**Somerville**	22

COFFEEHOUSES

Caffe Paradiso	**N End**	19
Darwin's	**Harv Sq**	21
Sorelle	**Charlestown**	23
Z 1369 Coffee	**multi.**	21
Trident	**Back Bay**	20

COFFEE SHOPS/ DINERS

Z Art Cliff	**MV**	26
Betsy's Diner	**CC**	16
Charlie's Kitchen	**Harv Sq**	17
Charlie's Sandwich	**S End**	22
Deluxe Town	**Watertown**	22
Harry's	**Westborough**	22
Johnny's Lunch.	**Newton**	19
Mike's	**S End**	20
Robinwood	**Jamaica Plain**	-
Rosebud	**Somerville**	15
South St. Diner	**Leather Dist**	17
Stars on Hingham	**Hingham**	18
Victoria's	**Roxbury**	19

CONTINENTAL

Anthony Cummaquid	**CC**	17
Cafe Escadrille	**Burlington**	21
Club Car	**Nan**	24
Front St.	**CC**	25
Z Locke-Ober	**D'town Cross**	25
Marliave	**D'town Cross**	18
Wine Cellar	**Back Bay**	22

CRÊPES

Mr. Crepe	**Somerville**	21
Paris Creperie	**Brookline**	21

CUBAN

Chez Henri	**Harv Sq**	24
El Oriental/Cuba	**Jamaica Plain**	24
Naked Fish	**Waltham**	20

DELIS

Bottega	**multi.**	23
Darwin's	**Harv Sq**	21
Far Land Provisions	**CC**	19
Rubin's	**Brookline**	19
S&S	**Inman Sq**	19
Zaftigs	**Brookline**	21

DESSERT

Z Bristol Lounge	**Back Bay**	26
Caffe Paradiso	**N End**	19
Z Cheesecake Factory	**multi.**	18
Finale	**multi.**	21
Z Flour Bakery	**multi.**	27
Hi-Rise	**multi.**	24
Picco	**S End**	24

ECLECTIC

Academy Ocean	**CC**	21
Blue Room	**Kendall Sq**	24
Boloco	**multi.**	19

☑ Bond	**Financial Dist**	22
Bravo	**MFA**	20
Bubala's	**CC**	16
Bullfinchs	**Sudbury**	21
Café at Taj	**Back Bay**	21
Centre St. Café	**Jamaica Plain**	25
Chatham Squire	**CC**	19
Christopher's	**Porter Sq**	21
Columbus Café	**S End**	20
☑ Cuchi Cuchi	**Central Sq**	23
Deep Ellum	**Allston**	23
Delux Cafe	**S End**	20
Equator	**S End**	22
☑ EVOO	**Kendall Sq**	26
Exchange St. Bistro	**Malden**	21
Fifty-Six Union	**Nan**	23
Fire & Ice	**multi.**	15
☑ Galley Beach	**Nan**	24
Glenn's	**Newburyport**	-
Kama	**Quincy**	-
Lobster Pot	**CC**	22
Lo La 41°	**Nan**	25
LTK	**Seaport Dist**	21
Lyceum	**Salem**	23
Metropolis	**S End**	24
Middlesex	**Central Sq**	20
Moonstones	**Chelmsford**	20
Napi's	**CC**	20
☑ Òran Mór	**Nan**	28
Plough & Stars	**Central Sq**	23
Purple Cactus	**Jamaica Plain**	19
Queequeg's	**Nan**	25
Red House	**Harv Sq**	21
River Gods	**Central Sq**	22
RumBa	**Waterfront**	19
Saltwater	**MV**	21
Sconset Café	**Nan**	25
Scutra	**Arlington**	25
Sonsie	**Back Bay**	20
Tastings Wine/Bistro	**Foxboro**	21
Town	**Nan**	24
NEW Towne	**Back Bay**	21
Trident	**Back Bay**	20
Vining's	**CC**	23
West End Johnnie's	**W End**	18
Zuzu!	**Central Sq**	19

ERITREAN

Asmara	**Central Sq**	22

ETHIOPIAN

Addis Red Sea	**multi.**	22
Asmara	**Central Sq**	22

EUROPEAN

NEW Ceia Kitchen/Bar	**Newburyport**	-
☑ Eastern Stand.	**Kenmore Sq**	23
☑ Ten Tables	**multi.**	27
Tory Row	**Harv Sq**	17

FONDUE

Melting Pot	**multi.**	19
Wine Cellar	**Back Bay**	22

FRENCH

Bleu	**CC**	27
Bon Savor	**Jamaica Plain**	22
Butcher Shop	**S End**	25
Chanticleer	**Nan**	25
Chillingsworth	**CC**	26
☑ Clio	**Back Bay**	27
☑ Elephant Walk	**multi.**	23
Enzo	**CC**	21
Hungry I	**Beacon Hill**	22
Jasmine	**Brighton**	25
Le Grenier	**MV**	24
Le Languedoc	**Nan**	23
Le Lyonnais	**Acton**	23
☑ L'Espalier	**Back Bay**	27
L'Étoile	**MV**	28
☑ Lumière	**Newton**	28
Mantra	**D'town Cross**	21
☑ NEW Menton	**Seaport Dist**	28
Miel	**Waterfront**	22
☑ Mistral	**S End**	28
Mr. Crepe	**Somerville**	21
☑ No. 9 Park	**Beacon Hill**	27
Paris Creperie	**Brookline**	21
Pigalle	**Theater Dist**	26
☑ Radius	**Financial Dist**	26
Red Pheasant	**CC**	27
☑ Salts	**Central Sq**	27
Sandrine's	**Harv Sq**	24
☑ Sel de la Terre	**Back Bay**	23
Sweet Life	**MV**	25
Tivoli's	**Malden**	-
☑ T.W. Food	**Huron Vill**	28

FRENCH (BISTRO)

NEW Aka Bistro	**Lincoln**	25
☑ Aquitaine	**multi.**	23

Beacon Hill | **Beacon Hill**	23
Bistro du Midi | **Back Bay**	23
Chez Henri | **Harv Sq**	24
NEW Cognac Bistro | **Brookline**	–
Z Craigie on Main | **Central Sq**	27
NEW 5 Corners | **Marblehead**	26
Z Hamersley's | **S End**	28
NEW Jacky's | **Brighton**	23
L'Alouette | **CC**	26
Les Zygomates | **Leather Dist**	22
Pain D'Avignon | **CC**	26
Z NEW PB Boulangerie | **CC**	28
Z Petit Robert | **multi.**	23
Pierrot Bistrot | **Beacon Hill**	24
NEW Sam's | **Seaport Dist**	20
Z Sel de la Terre | **multi.**	23
Z Troquet | **Theater Dist**	26

FRENCH (BRASSERIE)

Brasserie Jo | **Back Bay**	21
Gaslight Brasserie | **S End**	22
La Voile | **Back Bay**	24

GERMAN

Jacob Wirth | **Theater Dist**	18

GREEK

Aegean | **multi.**	20
Demos | **multi.**	17
Z Ithaki Med. | **Ipswich**	27
Kouzina | **Newton**	23
Steve's Greek | **multi.**	19

HEALTH FOOD

(See also Vegetarian)	
UFood | **multi.**	17

HUNGARIAN

Jasmine | **Brighton**	25

INDIAN

Bhindi Bazaar | **Back Bay**	20
Bukhara | **Jamaica Plain**	22
Cafe of India | **Harv Sq**	20
Coriander | **Sharon**	25
Diva Indian | **Somerville**	22
Dosa Factory | **Central Sq**	22
Ghazal | **Jamaica Plain**	23
Grain & Salt | **Allston**	23
Haveli | **Inman Sq**	–
Himalayan | **W Roxbury**	22

India Pavilion | **Central Sq**	21
India Quality | **Kenmore Sq**	24
Kashmir | **Back Bay**	24
Kebab Factory | **Somerville**	24
Mantra | **D'town Cross**	21
Masala Art | **Needham**	24
Mela | **S End**	24
NEW Mumbai Chop | **Back Bay**	19
Namaskar | **Somerville**	19
New Mother India | **Waltham**	22
Passage to India | **multi.**	22
Punjab | **Arlington**	24
Punjabi Dhaba | **Inman Sq**	24
Punjab Palace | **Allston**	24
Rani | **Brookline**	21
Shanti India | **Dorchester**	28
Singh's | **Wellesley Hills**	22
Tamarind Bay | **multi.**	23
Tanjore | **Harv Sq**	22
Tantric | **Theater Dist**	24
NEW Yak & Yeti | **Somerville**	–

IRISH

Burren | **Somerville**	17
Doyle's | **Jamaica Plain**	17
Druid | **Inman Sq**	24
NEW Four Green Fields | **Financial Dist**	–
Green Briar | **Brighton**	–
James's Gate | **Jamaica Plain**	18
Lansdowne | **Fenway**	16
Matt Murphy's | **Brookline**	22
Skellig | **Waltham**	17
NEW Whiskey Priest | **Seaport Dist**	12

ISRAELI

Jerusalem Pita | **Brookline**	20
Rami's | **Brookline**	24

ITALIAN

(N=Northern; S=Southern)	
Abbondanza | **Everett**	23
Adrian's | **CC**	18
Alberto's | **N** | **CC**	21
Al Dente | **N End**	22
Z NEW Alma Nove | **Hingham**	22
Alta Strada | **Wellesley**	22
Amari | **CC**	22
Amelia's Kitchen | **Somerville**	18
Amelia's Trattoria | **Kendall Sq**	21

Anchovies | **S End**	19
Angelo's | **Stoneham**	27
Antico Forno | S | **N End**	23
Antonio's Cucina | **Beacon Hill**	23
Appetito | **Newton**	17
Artú | **multi.**	22
Assaggio | **N End**	23
Bacco | **N End**	21
Basta Pasta | **multi.**	22
Bella Luna/Milky Way | **Jamaica Plain**	19
Bella's | **Rockland**	–
Bertucci's | **multi.**	18
Bina Osteria | **D'town Cross**	18
Bin 26 | **Beacon Hill**	21
☑ Bistro 5 | N | **W Medford**	27
Bon Caldo | **Norwood**	20
Bottega | N | **multi.**	23
Bricco | **N End**	25
Bridgeman's | N | **Hull**	24
Buca's Tuscan | N | **CC**	23
Butcher Shop | **S End**	25
Caffe Tosca | **Hingham**	24
Caliterra | **Financial Dist**	15
Canestaro | **Fenway**	16
Cantina Italiana | **N End**	22
☑ Carlo's Cucina | **Allston**	26
☑ Carmen | **N End**	27
Chesca's | **MV**	24
Ciro & Sal's | **CC**	17
Colombo's | **CC**	–
Comella's | **multi.**	–
☑ Coppa | **S End**	26
Daily Catch | S | **multi.**	24
NEW Dalla Cucina | **CC**	20
Dante | **E Cambridge**	24
Davide Rist. | **N End**	25
Da Vinci | **Park Sq**	24
☑ Davio's | N | **multi.**	25
☑ Delfino | **Roslindale**	26
DeMarco | N | **Nan**	23
Donatello | **Saugus**	22
D'Parma Italian Table | **CC**	22
Erbaluce | **Park Sq**	26
Euno | **N End**	22
Fairway | **CC**	17
Fanizzi's | **CC**	19
Fazio's | **CC**	21
Figs | **multi.**	24
Filippo | **N End**	19
Florentine Cafe | **N End**	22
Front St. | **CC**	25
Gennaro's Five N. | **N End**	24
☑ Giacomo's | **multi.**	25
Gina's | **CC**	21
Giordano's | **MV**	23
Gran Gusto | **Porter Sq**	–
☑ Grapevine | **Salem**	27
Greg's | **Watertown**	18
Grotto | N | **Beacon Hill**	26
☑ Il Capriccio | N | **Waltham**	27
Il Casale | **Belmont**	24
Il Panino | **N End**	22
Il Tesoro/Terrace | **MV**	19
Jetties | **Nan**	17
Jimmy Seas | **MV**	23
Joe & Maria's | **Norwood**	–
Joe Tecce's | S | **N End**	19
☑ La Campania | **Waltham**	28
La Cantina | **Framingham**	20
La Cucina/Mare | **CC**	24
La Fam. Giorgio | **N End**	22
La Galleria 33 | **N End**	21
La Morra | N | **Brookline**	25
☑ L'Andana | N | **Burlington**	27
La Summa | S | **N End**	23
Lattanzi's | N | **MV**	21
Lil Vinny's | S | **Somerville**	23
Limoncello | **N End**	22
L'Osteria | **N End**	24
Lucca | N | **multi.**	23
Lucia | **multi.**	23
Maggiano's | **Park Sq**	19
Mamma Maria | **N End**	25
Marco Romana | **N End**	23
Mare | **N End**	26
Marliave | **D'town Cross**	18
Massimino's Cucina | **N End**	23
Maurizio's | **N End**	24
Maxwells 148 | **Natick**	24
☑**NEW** Menton | **Seaport Dist**	28
Mezza Luna | **CC**	22
Mother Anna's | **N End**	23
Nauset Beach | N | **CC**	23
Nebo | **N End**	20
Nico | **N End**	24
☑ No. 9 Park | **Beacon Hill**	27
Olivadi | **Norwood**	20
Orta | **Hanover**	19
Osteria/Civetta | N | **CC**	27

Out of the Blue | **Somerville**	24
Pagliuca's | S | **N End**	22
Panificio | **Beacon Hill**	21
Papa Razzi | **multi.**	19
Pazzo | **Back Bay**	21
Pellino's | N | **Marblehead**	24
Piattini | **Back Bay**	24
Piccola Venezia | **N End**	22
Piccolo Nido | **N End**	26
Pi Pizzeria | S | **Nan**	23
Pleasant Cafe | **Roslindale**	21
Polcari's | **multi.**	19
Pomodoro | **multi.**	25
NEW Posto | **Somerville**	25
Z Prezza | **N End**	27
Z Rialto | **Harv Sq**	26
Rino's Place | **E Boston**	29
Rist. Damiano | **N End**	26
Rist. Fiore | **N End**	21
Rist. Pavarotti | **Reading**	-
Rist. Villa Francesca | **N End**	23
Riva | **Scituate**	26
Rustic Kitchen | **multi.**	20
Sal's Place | **CC**	18
Salvatore's | **multi.**	21
Saporito's | N | **Hull**	28
Saraceno | **N End**	24
Scampo | **Beacon Hill**	25
Scoozi | **multi.**	17
Serafina | N | **Concord**	16
Siena | **CC**	22
Siros | **N Quincy**	20
62 Rest. & Wine Bar | **Salem**	25
Sofia | **W Roxbury**	21
Z Sorellina | **Back Bay**	27
Sorento's | **Marlborough**	25
Spiga Trattoria | **Needham**	22
Sportello | **Seaport Dist**	25
Stella | **S End**	24
Stellina | **Watertown**	23
Strega Lounge | **Salem**	19
Strega Rist./Water | **multi.**	23
Sweet Basil | **Needham**	26
Z Taranta | S | **N End**	26
Tartufo | S | **Newton**	22
Tavolino | **multi.**	20
Tavolo | **Dorchester**	24
Teatro | **Theater Dist**	23
Terramia | **N End**	26
Tivoli's | **Malden**	-

Tomasso | **Southborough**	23
Z Tosca | **Hingham**	26
Toscano | N | **Beacon Hill**	25
Tratt. Il Panino | **N End**	24
Tratt. Monica/Vinoteca | **N End**	25
Z Tratt. Toscana | N | **Fenway**	26
Tratt. Pulcinella | **Huron Vill**	24
Tresca | **N End**	24
Tuscan Grill | N | **Waltham**	21
Umbria Prime | **Financial Dist**	23
NEW Vapiano | **Theater Dist**	18
Via Matta | **Park Sq**	25
Village Fish | **Needham**	22
Vin & Eddie's | N | **Abington**	21
Vinny's/Night | S | **Somerville**	24
Zabaglione | **Ipswich**	28

JAPANESE

(* sushi specialist)

Aji* | **Newtonville**	23
NEW Aka Bistro* | **Lincoln**	25
Apollo Grill* | **Chinatown**	19
NEW Basho* | **Fenway**	23
Blue Fin* | **multi.**	22
Cafe Sushi* | **Harv Sq**	22
China Sky* | **Wellesley**	22
Chung Ki Wa* | **Medford**	23
Douzo* | **Back Bay**	25
Z Fugakyu* | **multi.**	24
Ginger Ex.* | **Inman Sq**	20
Ginza* | **multi.**	23
Haru* | **Back Bay**	20
Inaho* | **CC**	26
JP Seafood* | **Jamaica Plain**	22
Kaya House* | **Porter Sq**	-
Kayuga | **multi.**	18
Kaze | **Chinatown**	24
Koreana* | **Central Sq**	21
Lotus Blossom* | **Sudbury**	22
Misaki* | **CC**	25
Montien* | **Theater Dist**	21
Mr. Sushi* | **multi.**	21
Net Result* | **MV**	24
New Ginza* | **Watertown**	23
Oga's* | **Natick**	25
Z Oishii* | **multi.**	27
Osushi* | **Back Bay**	21
Z O Ya* | **Leather Dist**	29
NEW Q Restaurant* | **Chinatown**	-
NEW Sake Japanese* | **Braintree**	-

Sakurabana*	**Financial Dist**	22	Athan's Café	**multi.**	22
Sapporo*	**Newton**	–	Avila	**Theater Dist**	23
Seiyo*	**S End**	22	Bar 10	**Back Bay**	21
Shabu-Zen	**multi.**	23	Bia Bistro	**Cohasset**	25
Shogun*	**Newton**	20	Blue Moon	**CC**	24
Suishaya*	**Chinatown**	19	ꭓ Bosphorus	**Inman Sq**	–
Super Fusion*	**multi.**	26	Café Mangal	**Wellesley**	26
Sushi by Yoshi*	**Nan**	23	Caffe Bella	**Randolph**	26
Sushi-Teq*	**Waterfront**	24	Casablanca	**Harv Sq**	21
Symphony Sushi*	**Fenway**	23	Chapoquoit Grill	**CC**	21
ꭓ Uni	**Back Bay**	28	Chiara	**Westwood**	24
Village Sushi*	**Roslindale**	22	C. Tsar's	**Newton**	–
Wagamama	**multi.**	18	Figs at 29 Fair	**Nan**	26
Yama*	**multi.**	23	ꭓ Ithaki Med.	**Ipswich**	27
Zen*	**Beacon Hill**	23	Kouzina	**Newton**	23

JEWISH

Zaftigs	**Brookline**	21

La Voile | **Back Bay** 24
Les Zygomates | **Leather Dist** 22
ꭓ Mistral | **S End** 28
ꭓ Oleana | **Inman Sq** 28
Pisces | **CC** 27

KOREAN

(* barbecue specialist)

Apollo Grill*	**Chinatown**	19
Chung Ki Wa*	**Medford**	23
JP Seafood	**Jamaica Plain**	22
Kaya House*	**Porter Sq**	–
Kayuga	**multi.**	18
Koreana*	**Central Sq**	21
New Jang Su*	**Burlington**	–
Sapporo	**Newton**	–
Suishaya	**Chinatown**	19
Village Sushi	**Roslindale**	22

Porcini's | **Watertown** 20
ꭓ Rendezvous | **Central Sq** 26
Sabur | **Somerville** 23
Sal's Place | **CC** 18
Soma | **Beverly** 22
Sophia's | **Roslindale** 23
Trevi Café | **CC** 25
Vlora | **Back Bay** 20

MEXICAN

**KOSHER/
KOSHER-STYLE**

Jerusalem Pita	**Brookline**	20
Rami's	**Brookline**	24
Rubin's	**Brookline**	19

LEBANESE

Byblos	**Norwood**	24
Cafe Barada	**Porter Sq**	24
ꭐꭐꮤ Garlic 'n Lemons	**Brighton**	24
Shawarma King	**Brookline**	21

MALAYSIAN

Penang	**Chinatown**	21

MEDITERRANEAN

ꭓ Abba	**CC**	28
ꭓ Alibi	**Beacon Hill**	19
ꭓ ꭐꭐꮤ Alma Nove	**Hingham**	22
Ardeo	**CC**	19

Angela's Café | **E Boston** 25
Baja Betty's | **Brookline** 23
Cantina la Mex. | **Somerville** 24
Casa Romero | **Back Bay** 22
Cilantro | **Salem** 21
Dorado | **Brookline** 24
El Pelón Taqueria | **Brighton** 25
El Sarape | **Braintree** 26
José's | **Huron Vill** 19
La Paloma | **multi.** 19
La Verdad | **Fenway** 21
ꭐꭐꮤ Lolita Cocina | **Back Bay** –
Lorraine's | **CC** 17
ꭐꭐꮤ Millie's | **Nan** 19
Olé/Olecito | **multi.** 24
ꭐꭐꮤ Papagayo | **Seaport Dist** –
Picante | **Central Sq** 22
Poe's/Rattlesnake | **Back Bay** 21
Purple Cactus | **Jamaica Plain** 19
Sharky's | **MV** 16

Sol Azteca | **multi.** 21
Sunset Grill/Cantina | **multi.** 19
Tacos El Charro | **Jamaica Plain** 25
Tacos Lupita | **multi.** 25
Taqueria Mexico | **Waltham** 24
Tu y Yo | **multi.** 24
Zócalo Cocina | **multi.** 24

MIDDLE EASTERN

Café Algiers | **Harv Sq** 16
Cafe Jaffa | **Back Bay** 21
Middle East | **Central Sq** 19
Red Fez | **S End** 18
☑ Sofra Bakery | **Huron Vill** 27
Sound Bites | **Somerville** 23
Zuzu! | **Central Sq** 19

MONGOLIAN

🆕 Q Restaurant | **Chinatown** -

MOROCCAN

Tangierino | **Charlestown** 22

NEPALESE

Coriander | **Sharon** 25
Himalayan | **W Roxbury** 22
Kathmandu Spice | **Arlington** 23
🆕 Yak & Yeti | **Somerville** -

NEW ENGLAND

☑ Asana | **Back Bay** 22
Barnstable | **CC** 19
Café Fleuri | **Financial Dist** 24
Capt. Frosty's | **CC** 21
Capt. Parker's | **CC** 21
Chart Room | **CC** 18
Coonamessett | **CC** 21
Dockside, The | **CC** 17
☑ Durgin-Park | **Faneuil Hall** 20
Fireplace | **Brookline** 21
☑ Gibbet Hill | **Groton** 25
Green St. | **Central Sq** 22
Henrietta's | **Harv Sq** 23
Jasper White's | **multi.** 21
Jetties | **Nan** 17
☑ Longfellow's | **Sudbury** 19
Maddie's Sail | **Marblehead** 14
North 26 | **Faneuil Hall** 25
Paddock | **CC** 22
Parker's | **D'town Cross** 24
Port | **CC** 23

Red Inn | **CC** 26
Shea's Riverside | **Essex** 19
Sherborn Inn | **Sherborn** 19
Sidecar Café | **MV** -
☑ Union Oyster | **Faneuil Hall** 21
Water St. | **MV** 26

NOODLE SHOPS

Wagamama | **multi.** 18

NORTH AFRICAN

Baraka Cafe | **Central Sq** 25

NUEVO LATINO

Betty's Wok | **MFA** 17

PAKISTANI

Grain & Salt | **Allston** 23

PAN-LATIN

Corazon del Mar | **Nan** 25
🆕 Tico | **Back Bay** -

PERSIAN

Lala Rokh | **Beacon Hill** 23
Sorento's | **Marlborough** 25

PERUVIAN

Don Ricardo's | **S End** 20
Machu Picchu | **Somerville** 21
Masona Grill | **W Roxbury** 24
Rincon Limeno | **E Boston** -
☑ Taranta | **N End** 26

PIZZA

Antico Forno | **N End** 23
🆕 Benevento's | **N End** 21
Bertucci's | **multi.** 18
Bluestone Bistro | **Brighton** 18
Cambridge 1 | **multi.** 22
Ducali | **N End** 19
Emma's | **Kendall Sq** 25
Fairway | **CC** 17
Federal | **Beacon Hill** 23
Figs | **multi.** 24
Galleria Umberto | **N End** 26
Gran Gusto | **Porter Sq** -
Lattanzi's | **MV** 21
Nebo | **N End** 20
Picco | **S End** 24
Pinocchio's | **Harv Sq** 23
Pi Pizzeria | **Nan** 23

Pizzeria Regina | **multi.**	24
Pleasant Cafe | **Roslindale**	21
Polcari's | **multi.**	19
NEW Posto | **Somerville**	25
Santarpio's | **multi.**	25
Scoozi | **multi.**	17
Stone Hearth Pizza | **multi.**	-
Sweet Tomatoes | **multi.**	24
Upper Crust | **multi.**	21
Veggie Planet | **Harv Sq**	22
Wicked Fire Kissed | **CC**	25
Woody's Grill | **Fenway**	23
Za | **multi.**	24

POLISH

Café Polonia | **multi.**	24

PORTUGUESE

Atasca | **Kendall Sq**	20
Casa Portugal | **Inman Sq**	23
Z Neighborhood | **Somerville**	26
Sunset Cafe | **Inman Sq**	24

PUB FOOD

NEW Amer. Craft | **Brookline**	17
Black Cow | **multi.**	20
Blarney Stone | **Dorchester**	20
Boston Beer | **multi.**	18
Brighton Beer | **Brighton**	16
Brownstone | **Back Bay**	15
Bukowski | **multi.**	18
Burren | **Somerville**	17
Cambridge Brewing | **Kendall Sq**	16
Cambridge Common | **Harv Sq**	18
Capt. Kidd | **CC**	16
Cheers | **multi.**	14
Coolidge Corner | **Brookline**	17
Cornwall's | **Kenmore Sq**	16
Doyle's | **Jamaica Plain**	17
Druid | **Inman Sq**	24
Game On! | **Fenway**	15
Green Briar | **Brighton**	-
Halfway Cafe | **multi.**	17
NEW Jerry Remy's | **multi.**	18
Jillian's | **Fenway**	16
John Harvard's | **multi.**	16
Johnny D's | **Somerville**	20
Joshua Tree | **multi.**	15
Kings | **multi.**	19
Lansdowne | **Fenway**	16
Littlest | **Financial Dist**	18

Lower Depths | **Kenmore Sq**	17
Matt Murphy's | **Brookline**	22
Miracle of Science | **Central Sq**	19
Mission B&G | **MFA**	18
M.J. O'Connor's | **multi.**	17
Newes/America | **MV**	20
Offshore Ale | **MV**	20
Plough & Stars | **Central Sq**	23
Publick House | **Brookline**	20
Skellig | **Waltham**	17
Squealing Pig | **CC**	20
NEW Stats B&G | **S Boston**	21
Sunset Grill/Cantina | **multi.**	19
21st Amendment | **Beacon Hill**	17
Warren | **Charlestown**	19
NEW Whiskey Priest | **Seaport Dist**	12

RUSSIAN

Café St. Petersburg | **Newton**	21

SALVADORAN

Tacos Lupita | **multi.**	25

SANDWICHES

All Star | **Inman Sq**	23
Chacarero | **D'town Cross**	25
NEW Cutty's | **Brookline**	25
Federal | **Beacon Hill**	23
Z Flour Bakery | **multi.**	27
Haley House | **Roxbury**	22
Hi-Rise | **multi.**	24
Other Side | **Back Bay**	20
Parish Cafe | **multi.**	23
Second St. Café | **E Cambridge**	23
Sorelle | **Charlestown**	23
Vicki Lee's | **Belmont**	23
Volle Nolle | **N End**	26

SCOTTISH

NEW Haven | **Jamaica Plain**	23

SEAFOOD

Academy Ocean | **CC**	21
Z Anthony's | **Seaport Dist**	18
Aqua Grille | **CC**	19
Z Arnold's Lobster | **CC**	24
Atlantica | **Cohasset**	20
Atlantic Fish/Chop | **MV**	21
Z Atlantic Fish | **Back Bay**	24

Back Eddy | **Westport**	23	Mare | **N End**	26
☑ B&G Oysters | **S End**	26	Marshside | **CC**	19
Barking Crab | **Seaport Dist**	17	Mattakeese Wharf | **CC**	18
NEW Barracuda | **D'town Cross**	–	McCormick/Schmick | **multi.**	21
Baxter's | **CC**	20	Moby Dick's | **CC**	24
Bite | **MV**	26	Morse Fish | **S End**	19
NEW Black Cat Tavern | **CC**	20	Naked Fish | **Waltham**	20
Blue Canoe | **MV**	16	Naked Oyster | **CC**	25
Bookstore & Rest. | **CC**	20	Nantucket Lobster | **Nan**	22
Boston Sail | **Waterfront**	18	☑ Neptune Oyster | **N End**	28
Brant Point | **Nan**	24	Net Result | **MV**	24
☑ Brewster Fish | **CC**	26	No Name | **Seaport Dist**	19
Bubala's | **CC**	16	Oceana | **Waterfront**	22
Capt. Frosty's | **CC**	21	Oceanaire | **Financial Dist**	24
Captain's Table | **Wellesley**	24	Out of the Blue | **Somerville**	24
Catch of the Day | **CC**	25	Oyster BG | **MV**	24
Chapin's | **CC**	19	Oyster Co. | **CC**	24
Chart House | **Waterfront**	20	Peach Farm | **Chinatown**	25
Chart Room | **CC**	18	Pearl | **CC**	17
Clam Box | **Ipswich**	24	Pisces | **CC**	27
Cobie's Clam | **CC**	22	Port | **CC**	23
Cooke's | **CC**	19	Roadhouse | **CC**	22
Courthouse | **E Cambridge**	24	Ropewalk | **Nan**	18
Daily Catch | **multi.**	24	Rowes Wharf | **Waterfront**	23
Dolphin | **CC**	22	Sea Grille | **Nan**	23
Dolphin Seafood | **multi.**	19	Sir Cricket's | **CC**	24
☑ East Coast | **Inman Sq**	26	Skipjack's | **multi.**	20
East Ocean | **Chinatown**	25	Square Rigger | **MV**	–
Easy Street | **Nan**	–	Straight Wharf | **Nan**	27
Fanizzi's | **CC**	19	Tamarind Bay | **multi.**	23
Finz | **Salem**	21	Turner Fish | **Back Bay**	20
Fish Bones | **Chelmsford**	22	Turner's Seafood | **Melrose**	23
Fishmonger's | **CC**	20	☑ Union Oyster | **Faneuil Hall**	21
Friendly Fisherman | **CC**	22	Van Rensselaer's | **CC**	17
☑ Giacomo's | **multi.**	25	Village Fish | **Needham**	22
Home Port | **MV**	21	Wicked Oyster | **CC**	23
☑ Impudent Oyster | **CC**	23	Woodman's | **Essex**	23
NEW Island Creek | **Kenmore Sq**	–		
Jasper White's | **multi.**	21	**SMALL PLATES**	
JT's Seafood | **CC**	20	(See also Spanish tapas specialist)	
Jumbo | **multi.**	22	Bar 10 | Med. | **Back Bay**	21
KingFish Hall | **Faneuil Hall**	22	☑ Bond | Eclectic | **Financial Dist**	22
Landfall | **CC**	18	☑ Coppa | Italian | **S End**	26
☑ Larsen's Fish | **MV**	28	☑ Cuchi Cuchi | Eclectic |	23
NEW Legal C Bar | **Dedham**	22	**Central Sq**	
☑ Legal Sea | **multi.**	22	District | Amer. | **Leather Dist**	–
Liam's | **CC**	20	Drink | Amer. | **Seaport Dist**	21
Lobster Pot | **CC**	22	Flat Iron | Amer. | **W End**	–
Mac's | **CC**	25	Kama | Eclectic | **Quincy**	–
Maddie's Sail | **Marblehead**	14	La Morra | Italian | **Brookline**	25
		Masa | SW | **S End**	21

Meritage | Amer. | **Waterfront**	26
Middlesex | Eclectic | **Central Sq**	20
Noir | Amer. | **Harv Sq**	20
Pairings | Amer. | **Park Sq**	21
Piattini | Italian | **Back Bay**	24
Rist. Damiano | Italian | **N End**	26
Trevi Café | Med. | **CC**	25

SOUTH AFRICAN

Karoo Kafe | **CC**	22

SOUTH AMERICAN

Bon Savor | **Jamaica Plain**	22

SOUTHERN

NEW Brother's Crawfish | **Dorchester**	-
House of Blues | **Fenway**	15
Hungry Mother | **Kendall Sq**	26
Tupelo | **Inman Sq**	24

SOUTHWESTERN

Masa | **multi.**	21
Zapotec | **MV**	21

SPANISH

(* tapas specialist)

BarLola* | **Back Bay**	17
Dalí* | **Somerville**	25
Estragon* | **S End**	23
Solea* | **Waltham**	22
Taberna/Haro* | **Brookline**	35
Tapéo* | **Back Bay**	23
Tasca* | **Brighton**	23
Toro* | **S End**	27

STEAKHOUSES

Abe & Louie's | **Back Bay**	26
Atlantic Fish/Chop | **MV**	21
Bokx | **Newton Lower Falls**	21
Brant Point | **Nan**	24
Capital Grille | **multi.**	26
Coach Grill | **Wayland**	24
Davio's | **multi.**	25
Fleming's Prime | **Park Sq**	25
Frank's Steak | **Porter Sq**	18
Gibbet Hill | **Groton**	25
Grill 23 | **Back Bay**	27
Hilltop Steak | **Saugus**	16
Jimmy's Steer | **multi.**	20
KO Prime | **D'town Cross**	25
Met Back/B&G | **multi.**	19

Metropolitan | **Chestnut Hill**	20
Midwest | **multi.**	21
Mooo… | **Beacon Hill**	26
Morton's | **multi.**	25
Oak Room | **Back Bay**	24
Oyster BG | **MV**	24
Palm | **Back Bay**	24
Pellana | **Peabody**	25
Roadhouse | **CC**	22
Ruth's Chris | **D'town Cross**	26
Scarlet Oak | **Hingham**	21
Smith/Wollensky | **Back Bay**	22
Sofia | **W Roxbury**	21
Stockyard | **Brighton**	18
Tango | **Arlington**	22
NEW Top Steak | **Peabody**	-
Umbria Prime | **Financial Dist**	23

TAIWANESE

MuLan Taiwanese | **Kendall Sq**	24
Shangri-La | **Belmont**	23
Taiwan Cafe | **Chinatown**	24

TEAROOMS

Dunbar Tea | **CC**	21
Optimist Café | **CC**	-

TEX-MEX

Anna's | **multi.**	23
Boca Grande | **multi.**	21
Boloco | **multi.**	19
Border Cafe | **multi.**	20
Cactus Club | **Back Bay**	17
Fajitas/'Ritas | **D'town Cross**	16

THAI

Abba | **CC**	28
Amarin Thailand | **multi.**	21
Bamboo | **Brighton**	23
Bangkok Bistro | **Brighton**	18
Bangkok Blue | **Back Bay**	20
Bangkok City | **Back Bay**	23
Brown Sugar/Similans | **multi.**	24
Chilli Duck | **Back Bay**	21
Dok Bua | **Brookline**	23
Equator | **S End**	22
Erawan/Siam | **Waltham**	20
Green Papaya | **Waltham**	22
House of Siam | **S End**	22
Jamjuli | **Newton**	21
Khao Sarn | **Brookline**	24

King & I | **Beacon Hill** 22
Montien | **Theater Dist** 21
9 Tastes | **Harv Sq** 21
Patou | **Belmont** 20
Pho n' Rice | **Somerville** 21
Rod Dee | **multi.** 24
Ronnarong | **Somerville** 22
Spice Thai | **Harv Sq** 19
Sugar & Spice | **Porter Sq** 20
Thai Basil | **Back Bay** 21
Thaitation | **Fenway** 26
Wonder Spice | **Jamaica Plain** 20

TIBETAN

House of Tibet | **Somerville** 18
Martsa's/Elm | **Somerville** 21
Tashi Delek | **Brookline** –

TURKISH

Brookline Family | **Brookline** 22
Café Mangal | **Wellesley** 26

NEW Istanbul'lu | **Somerville** 23
Pasha | **Arlington** 22
Sultan's Kitchen | **Financial Dist** 23

VEGETARIAN

(* vegan)
NEW Clover Food Lab | **Harv Sq** –
Grasshopper* | **Allston** 22
Prana Café* | **Newton** –
Veggie Planet | **Harv Sq** 22

VENEZUELAN

La Casa/Pedro | **Watertown** 21
Orinoco | **multi.** 23

VIETNAMESE

Le's | **multi.** 21
Pho Hoa | **multi.** 24
Pho Lemongrass | **Brookline** 20
Pho n' Rice | **Somerville** 21
Pho Pasteur | **Chinatown** 24
Xinh Xinh | **Chinatown** 25

Locations

Includes names, cuisines, Food ratings and, for locations that are mapped, top list with map coordinates.

Boston

ALLSTON/ BOSTON U./ BRIGHTON

Athan's Café	Bakery/Med.	22
Bamboo	Thai	23
Bangkok Bistro	Thai	18
Bluestone Bistro	Pizza	18
Brighton Beer	Pub	16
Brown Sugar/Similans	Thai	24
Café Belô	Brazilian	24
Café Brazil	Brazilian	22
☑ Carlo's Cucina	Italian	26
Deep Ellum	Eclectic	23
Devlin's	Amer.	20
El Pelón Taqueria	Mex.	25
NEW Garlic 'n Lemons	Lebanese	24
Grain & Salt	Indian/Pakistani	23
Grasshopper	Asian/Vegan	22
Green Briar	Irish/Pub	-
NEW Jacky's	French	23
Jasmine	French/Hungarian	25
Joshua Tree	Pub	15
Le's	Viet.	21
Noodle St.	Asian	20
Ole/Olecito	Mex.	24
Pizzeria Regina	Pizza	24
Punjab Palace	Indian	24
Shabu-Zen	Japanese	23
Shanghai Gate	Chinese	21
Soul Fire	BBQ	22
Stockyard	Steak	18
Sunset Grill/Cantina	Mex./Pub	19
Tasca	Spanish	23
Tavern in Sq.	Amer.	15
UBurger	Burgers	22

BACK BAY

(See map on page 260)

TOP FOOD

Uni	Japanese	D1	28
L'Espalier	French	D4	27
Clio	French	D1	27
Sorellina	Italian	D5	27
Grill 23	Steak	D7	27

LISTING

☑ Abe & Louie's	Steak	26
☑ Asana	New Eng.	22
☑ Atlantic Fish	Seafood	24
NEW Back Bay Social	Amer.	18
Bangkok Blue	Thai	20
Bangkok City	Thai	23
BarLola	Spanish	17
Bar 10	Med.	21
B. Good	Burgers	18
Bhindi Bazaar	Indian	20
Bistro du Midi	French	23
Boloco	Eclectic/Tex-Mex	19
Bottega	Italian/Deli	23
Brasserie Jo	French	21
☑ Bristol Lounge	Amer.	26
Brownstone	Pub	15
Bukowski	Pub	18
Cactus Club	Tex-Mex	17
Cafe 47	Amer.	19
Café at Taj	Eclectic	21
Cafe Jaffa	Mideast.	21
Cafeteria	Amer.	18
☑ Capital Grille	Steak	26
Casa Romero	Mex.	22
Charley's	Amer.	18
☑ Cheesecake Factory	Amer.	18
Chilli Duck	Thai	21
City Bar	Amer.	19
City Table	Amer.	22
☑ Clio	French	27
Corner Tavern	Amer.	-
Courtyard/Boston Library	Amer.	18
NEW Deuxave	Amer.	-
Dillon's	Amer.	16
Douzo	Japanese	25
Fire & Ice	Eclectic	15
Geoffrey's	Amer.	22
Globe Bar	Amer.	16
☑ Grill 23	Steak	27
Haru	Japanese	20
Island Hopper	Asian	18
Jasper White's	New Eng./Seafood	21
Joe's American	Amer.	17
Kashmir	Indian	24
Kings	Pub	19

La Voile	*French/Med.*	24
🅱 Legal Sea	*Seafood*	22
🅱 L'Espalier	*French*	27
NEW Lolita Cocina	*Mex.*	-
Lucca	*Italian*	23
Met Back/B&G	*Amer./Steak*	19
🅱 Morton's	*Steak*	25
NEW Mumbai Chop	*Chinese/Indian*	19
🅱 Oak Room	*Steak*	24
Osushi	*Japanese*	21
Other Side	*Sandwiches*	20
Palm	*Steak*	24
Papa Razzi	*Italian*	19
Parish Cafe	*Sandwiches*	23
Pazzo	*Italian*	21
P.F. Chang's	*Chinese*	19
Piattini	*Italian*	24
Pizzeria Regina	*Pizza*	24
Poe's/Rattlesnake	*Mex.*	21
Post 390	*Amer.*	20
Scoozi	*Italian*	17
🅱 Sel de la Terre	*French*	23
Skipjack's	*Seafood*	20
Smith/Wollensky	*Steak*	22
Sonsie	*Eclectic*	20
🅱 Sorellina	*Italian*	27
Stanhope Grille	*Amer.*	20
Stephanie's	*Amer.*	20
Steve's Greek	*Greek*	19
Tapéo	*Spanish*	23
Thai Basil	*Thai*	21
NEW Tico	*Amer./Latin*	-
🅱 Top of Hub	*Amer.*	20
NEW Towne	*Eclectic*	21
Trident	*Eclectic*	20
Turner Fish	*Seafood*	20
29 Newbury	*Amer.*	20
Typhoon	*Asian*	18
🅱 Uni	*Japanese*	28
Upper Crust	*Pizza*	21
Vlora	*Med.*	20
Wagamama	*Noodles*	18
Wine Cellar	*Continental/Fondue*	22
Zócalo Cocina	*Mex.*	24

BEACON HILL

(See map on page 258)

TOP FOOD

No. 9 Park	*French/Italian*	**D6**	27
Grotto	*Italian*	**A6**	26

Mooo...	*Steak*	**C6**	26
Scampo	*Italian*	**A2**	25
Toscano	*Italian*	**D2**	25

LISTING

🅱 Alibi	*Amer./Med.*	19
🅱 Anna's	*Tex-Mex*	23
Antonio's Cucina	*Italian*	23
Artú	*Italian*	22
Beacon Hill	*French*	23
Bin 26	*Italian*	21
Cheers	*Pub*	14
Clink	*Amer.*	19
Federal	*Pizza/Sandwiches*	23
Figs	*Italian/Pizza*	24
Grotto	*Italian*	26
Harvard Gdns.	*Amer.*	17
Hungry I	*French*	22
King & I	*Thai*	22
Lala Rokh	*Persian*	23
Ma Soba	*Asian*	20
Mooo...	*Steak*	26
🅱 No. 9 Park	*French/Italian*	27
Panificio	*Italian*	21
Paramount	*Amer.*	22
Pierrot Bistrot	*French*	24
Scampo	*Italian*	25
Scollay Sq.	*Amer.*	19
75 Chestnut	*Amer.*	21
Toscano	*Italian*	25
21st Amendment	*Pub*	17
Upper Crust	*Pizza*	21
Zen	*Japanese*	23

CHARLESTOWN

Figs	*Italian/Pizza*	24
Ironside Grill	*Amer.*	15
Max/Dylan	*Amer.*	19
Navy Yard	*Amer.*	24
Sorelle	*Coffee/Sandwiches*	23
Tangierino	*Moroccan*	22
Tavern/Water	*Amer.*	12
Warren	*Amer.*	19

CHELSEA/ EAST BOSTON/ REVERE

Angela's Café	*Mex.*	25
Billy Tse	*Asian*	21
🅱 Ecco	*Amer.*	27
NewBridge	*Amer.*	26

Rincon Limeno | *Peruvian* — ⌋
Rino's Place | *Italian* 29⌋
Santarpio's | *Pizza* 25⌋
Tacos Lupita | 25⌋
　Mex./Salvadoran

CHINATOWN/
LEATHER DIST.
(See map on page 258)

TOP FOOD

O Ya | *Japanese* | **H9** 29⌋
Peach Farm | *Chinese/Seafood* | **H7** 25⌋
Xinh Xinh | *Viet.* | **H6** 25⌋
Gourmet Dumpling | *Chinese* | **H7** 25⌋
East Ocean | *Chinese/Seafood* | **H6** 25⌋

LISTING

Apollo Grill | *Japanese/Korean* 19⌋
Chau Chow | *Chinese* 22⌋
China Pearl | *Chinese* 21⌋
District | *Amer.* — ⌋
East Ocean | *Chinese/Seafood* 25⌋
Emperor's Gdn. | *Chinese* 21⌋
Ginza | *Japanese* 23⌋
Gourmet Dumpling | *Chinese* 25⌋
Hei La Moon | *Chinese* — ⌋
Jumbo | *Chinese/Seafood* 22⌋
Kaze | *Japanese* 24⌋
Les Zygomates | *French/Med.* 22⌋
New Shanghai | *Chinese* 21⌋
🛛 O Ya | *Japanese* 29⌋
Peach Farm | *Chinese/Seafood* 25⌋
Penang | *Malaysian* 21⌋
Pho Hoa | *Viet.* 24⌋
Pho Pasteur | *Viet.* 24⌋
Pizzeria Regina | *Pizza* 24⌋
NEW Q Restaurant | — ⌋
　Japanese/Mongolian
Shabu-Zen | *Japanese* 23⌋
Sorriso | *Italian* 21⌋
South St. Diner | *Diner* 17⌋
Splash Ultra | *Burgers* 17⌋
Suishaya | *Japanese/Korean* 19⌋
Taiwan Cafe | *Taiwanese* 24⌋
Xinh Xinh | *Viet.* 25⌋

DORCHESTER/
MATTAPAN/ROXBURY/
WEST ROXBURY

Ashmont Grill | *Amer.* 23⌋
Blarney Stone | *Pub* 20⌋

NEW Brother's Crawfish | — ⌋
　Asian/Southern
Chau Chow | *Chinese* 22⌋
Comella's | *Italian* — ⌋
Dbar | *Amer.* 23⌋
Haley House | *Amer./Bakery* 22⌋
Hen House | *Amer.* — ⌋
Himalayan | *Indian/Nepalese* 22⌋
Ledge | *Amer.* 15⌋
Masona Grill | *Amer./Peruvian* 24⌋
Pho Hoa | *Viet.* 24⌋
Pit Stop BBQ | *BBQ* — ⌋
Shanti India | *Indian* 28⌋
Sofia | *Italian/Steak* 21⌋
Tavolo | *Italian* 24⌋
224 Boston St. | *Amer.* 21⌋
Upper Crust | *Pizza* 21⌋
Victoria's | *Diner* 19⌋
West/Centre | *Amer.* 19⌋

DOWNTOWN
CROSSING
(See map on page 258)

TOP FOOD

Ruth's Chris | *Steak* | **C8** 26⌋
Chacarero | 25⌋
　Chilean/Sandwiches | **E8**
Locke-Ober | 25⌋
　Amer./Continental | **E7**
KO Prime | *Steak* | **D7** 25⌋
Parker's | *New Eng.* | **C7** 24⌋

LISTING

Avenue One | *Amer.* 19⌋
NEW Barracuda | *Seafood* — ⌋
B. Good | *Burgers* 18⌋
Bina Osteria | *Italian* 18⌋
Boloco | *Eclectic/Tex-Mex* 19⌋
Chacarero | *Chilean/Sandwiches* 25⌋
Fajitas/'Ritas | *Tex-Mex* 16⌋
Good Life | *Amer.* 16⌋
Kingston | *Amer.* 20⌋
KO Prime | *Steak* 25⌋
🛛 Locke-Ober | *Amer./Continental* 25⌋
Mantra | *French/Indian* 21⌋
Marliave | *Continental/Italian* 18⌋
Max/Dylan | *Amer.* 19⌋
Parker's | *New Eng.* 24⌋
🛛 Petit Robert | *French* 23⌋
🛛 Ruth's Chris | *Steak* 26⌋
Silvertone B&G | *Amer.* 21⌋

NEW Stoddard's	*Amer.*	19
UFood	*Health*	17

FANEUIL HALL
(See map on page 256)

TOP FOOD
Pizzeria Regina	*Pizza*	**F6**	24
KingFish Hall	*Seafood*	**G6**	22
Union Oyster	*New Eng./Seafood*	**E5**	21
McCormick/Schmick	*Seafood*	**F6**	21
Durgin-Park	*New Eng.*	**F6**	20

LISTING
NEW Anthem	*Amer.*	19
Bertucci's	*Italian*	18
Cheers	*Pub*	14
Z Durgin-Park	*New Eng.*	20
Hillstone	*Amer.*	25
KingFish Hall	*Seafood*	22
McCormick/Schmick	*Seafood*	21
North 26	*New Eng.*	25
Pizzeria Regina	*Pizza*	24
Steve's Greek	*Greek*	19
Z Union Oyster	*New Eng./Seafood*	21
Wagamama	*Noodles*	18

FENWAY/ KENMORE SQUARE/ MFA
(See map on page 264)

TOP FOOD
Tratt. Toscana	*Italian*	**E6**	26
India Quality	*Indian*	**A7**	24
Petit Robert	*French*	**B7**	23
Woody's Grill	*Amer.*	**D9**	23
Elephant Walk	*Cambodian/French*	**C2**	23
Eastern Stand.	*Amer./Euro.*	**B6**	23
Basho	*Japanese*	**D5**	23
Symphony Sushi	*Japanese*	**F10**	23
UBurger	*Burgers*	**A7**	22
Audubon Circle	*Amer.*	**C3**	21
Bravo	*Eclectic*	**G7**	20

LISTING
Audubon Circle	*Amer.*	21
NEW Basho	*Japanese*	23
Bertucci's	*Italian*	18
Betty's Wok	*Asian/Nuevo Latino*	17
Boca Grande	*Tex-Mex*	21

Boloco	*Eclectic/Tex-Mex*	19
Boston Beer	*Pub*	18
Bravo	*Eclectic*	20
Burtons	*Amer.*	21
Cambridge 1	*Pizza*	22
Canestaro	*Italian*	16
Church	*Amer.*	20
NEW Citizen Public	*Amer.*	-
Cornwall's	*British/Pub*	16
Z Eastern Stand.	*Amer./Euro.*	23
Z Elephant Walk	*Cambodian/French*	23
Game On!	*Pub*	15
House of Blues	*Southern*	15
India Quality	*Indian*	24
NEW Island Creek	*Seafood*	-
NEW Jerry Remy's	*Pub*	18
Jillian's	*Pub*	16
Lansdowne	*Amer./Irish*	16
La Verdad	*Mex.*	21
Lower Depths	*Pub*	17
Mission B&G	*Pub*	18
Z Petit Robert	*French*	23
Scoozi	*Italian*	17
Sol Azteca	*Mex.*	21
Symphony Sushi	*Japanese*	23
NEW Tasty Burger	*Burgers*	-
Thaitation	*Thai*	26
Z Tratt. Toscana	*Italian*	26
UBurger	*Burgers*	22
UFood	*Health*	17
Upper Crust	*Pizza*	21
Woody's Grill	*Amer.*	23

FINANCIAL DISTRICT
(See map on page 256)

TOP FOOD
Radius	*French*	**K5**	26
Café Fleuri	*New Eng.*	**I6**	24
Oceanaire	*Seafood*	**G3**	24
Umbria Prime	*Italian/Steak*	**I7**	23
Sultan's Kitchen	*Turkish*	**G6**	23

LISTING
Boloco	*Eclectic/Tex-Mex*	19
Z Bond	*Eclectic*	22
Café Fleuri	*New Eng.*	24
Caliterra	*Cal./Italian*	15
NEW Four Green Fields	*Amer./Irish*	-
Littlest	*Pub*	18

Oceanaire	*Seafood*	24
☑ Radius	*French*	26
Sakurabana	*Japanese*	22
Sultan's Kitchen	*Turkish*	23
Umbria Prime	*Italian/Steak*	23
Woodward	*Amer.*	21

JAMAICA PLAIN

Bella Luna/Milky Way	*Italian*	19
Bon Savor	*French/S Amer.*	22
Bukhara	*Indian*	22
NEW Canary Sq.	*Amer.*	-
Centre St. Café	*Eclectic*	25
Dogwood Café	*Amer.*	20
Doyle's	*Irish/Pub*	17
El Oriental/Cuba	*Cuban*	24
Ghazal	*Indian*	23
NEW Haven	*Scottish*	23
James's Gate	*Amer./Irish*	18
JP Seafood	*Japanese/Korean*	22
Purple Cactus	*Eclectic/Mex.*	19
Robinwood	*Amer.*	-
Sorella's	*Amer.*	24
Tacos El Charro	*Mex.*	25
☑ Ten Tables	*Amer./Euro.*	27
Wonder Spice	*Cambodian/Thai*	20

NORTH END

(See map on page 256)

TOP FOOD

Neptune Oyster	*Seafood*	**D5**	28
Carmen	*Italian*	**D6**	27
Prezza	*Italian*	**C7**	27
Taranta	*Italian/Peruvian*	**D5**	26
Mare	*Italian/Seafood*	**D6**	26

LISTING

Al Dente	*Italian*	22
Antico Forno	*Italian/Pizza*	23
Artú	*Italian*	22
Assaggio	*Italian*	23
Bacco	*Italian*	21
NEW Benevento's	*Pizza*	21
Billy Tse	*Asian*	21
Bricco	*Italian*	25
Caffe Paradiso	*Coffee*	19
Cantina Italiana	*Italian*	22
☑ Carmen	*Italian*	27
Daily Catch	*Italian/Seafood*	24
Davide Rist.	*Italian*	25

Ducali	*Pizza*	19
Euno	*Italian*	22
Filippo	*Italian*	19
Florentine Cafe	*Italian*	22
Galleria Umberto	*Pizza*	26
Gennaro's Five N.	*Italian*	24
☑ Giacomo's	*Italian/Seaood*	25
Il Panino	*Italian*	22
Joe's American	*Amer.*	17
Joe Tecce's	*Italian*	19
La Fam. Giorgio	*Italian*	22
La Galleria 33	*Italian*	21
La Summa	*Italian*	23
Limoncello	*Italian*	22
L'Osteria	*Italian*	24
Lucca	*Italian*	23
Lucia	*Italian*	23
Mamma Maria	*Italian*	25
Marco Romana	*Italian*	23
Mare	*Italian/Seafood*	26
Massimino's Cucina	*Italian*	23
Maurizio's	*Italian*	24
Mother Anna's	*Italian*	23
Nebo	*Italian*	20
☑ Neptune Oyster	*Seafood*	28
Nico	*Italian*	24
North St. Grille	*Amer.*	24
Pagliuca's	*Italian*	22
Piccola Venezia	*Italian*	22
Piccolo Nido	*Italian*	26
Pizzeria Regina	*Pizza*	24
Pomodoro	*Italian*	25
☑ Prezza	*Italian*	27
Rist. Damiano	*Italian*	26
Rist. Fiore	*Italian*	21
Rist. Villa Francesca	*Italian*	23
Saraceno	*Italian*	24
Strega Rist./Water	*Italian*	23
☑ Taranta	*Italian/Peruvian*	26
Terramia	*Italian*	26
Tratt. Il Panino	*Italian*	24
Tratt. Monica/Vinoteca	*Italian*	25
Tresca	*Italian*	24
Volle Nolle	*Sandwiches*	26

PARK SQUARE

(See map on page 260)

TOP FOOD

Erbaluce	*Italian*	**D8**	26
Davio's	*Italian/Steak*	**D8**	25

Via Matta	*Italian*	**C8**	25
Fleming's Prime	*Steak*	**D8**	25
Da Vinci	*Italian*	**D7**	24

LISTING

Da Vinci	*Italian*	24
☑ Davio's	*Italian/Steak*	25
Erbaluce	*Italian*	26
Finale	*Dessert*	21
Flash's	*Amer.*	19
Fleming's Prime	*Steak*	25
☑ Legal Sea	*Seafood*	22
Maggiano's	*Italian*	19
McCormick/Schmick	*Seafood*	21
Melting Pot	*Fondue*	19
M.J. O'Connor's	*Pub*	17
Pairings	*Amer.*	21
Via Matta	*Italian*	25

SEAPORT DISTRICT

☑ Anthony's	*Seafood*	18
Aura	*Amer.*	22
Barking Crab	*Seafood*	17
NEW Barlow's	*Amer.*	16
City Bar	*Amer.*	19
Daily Catch	*Italian/Seafood*	24
Drink	*Amer.*	21
☑ Flour Bakery	*Bakery*	27
NEW Jerry Remy's	*Pub*	18
LTK	*Eclectic*	21
Lucky's	*Amer.*	19
☑NEW Menton	*French/Italian*	28
M.J. O'Connor's	*Pub*	17
☑ Morton's	*Steak*	25
No Name	*Seafood*	19
NEW Papagayo	*Mex.*	-
Salvatore's	*Italian*	21
NEW Sam's	*Amer./French*	20
Sauciety	*Amer.*	-
606 Congress	*Amer.*	20
Sportello	*Italian*	25
Strega Rist./Water	*Italian*	23
NEW Whiskey Priest	*Irish/Pub*	12

SOUTH BOSTON

Amrheins	*Amer.*	19
Café Polonia	*Polish*	24
Franklin	*Amer.*	24
NEW Stats B&G	*Pub*	21
NEW Telegraph Hill	*Amer.*	-

SOUTH END

(See map on page 260)

TOP FOOD

Hamersley's	*French*	**G7**	28
Mistral	*French/Med.*	**E7**	28
Oishii	*Japanese*	**G9**	27
Toro	*Spanish*	**J5**	27
Flour Bakery	*Bakery*	**I6**	27

LISTING

Addis Red Sea	*Ethiopian*	22
Anchovies	*Italian*	19
☑ Aquitaine	*French*	23
☑ B&G Oysters	*Seafood*	26
Beehive	*Amer.*	20
Butcher Shop	*French/Italian*	25
Charlie's Sandwich	*Diner*	22
Club Cafe	*Amer.*	19
Coda	*Amer.*	21
Columbus Café	*Eclectic*	20
☑ Coppa	*Italian*	26
NEW Darryl's	*Amer.*	-
Delux Cafe	*Eclectic*	20
Don Ricardo's	*Brazilian/Peruvian*	20
Equator	*Eclectic/Thai*	22
Estragon	*Spanish*	23
☑ Flour Bakery	*Bakery*	27
Franklin	*Amer.*	24
NEW Gallows	*Amer.*	20
Gaslight Brasserie	*French*	22
☑ Giacomo's	*Italian/Seaood*	25
☑ Hamersley's	*French*	28
House of Siam	*Thai*	22
Jae's	*Asian*	22
Masa	*SW*	21
Mela	*Indian*	24
Metropolis	*Eclectic*	24
Mike's	*Diner*	20
☑ Mistral	*French/Med.*	28
Morse Fish	*Seafood*	19
Myers + Chang	*Asian*	24
☑NEW Noche	*Amer.*	22
☑ Oishii	*Japanese*	27
Orinoco	*Venez.*	23
Parish Cafe	*Sandwiches*	23
☑ Petit Robert	*French*	23
Picco	*Dessert/Pizza*	24
Pops	*Amer.*	20
Red Fez	*Mideast.*	18
Seiyo	*Japanese*	22

Menus, photos, voting and more – free at ZAGAT.com

Sibling Rivalry | *Amer.*	23
South/Buttery | *Amer./Bakery*	22
Stella | *Italian*	24
Stephanie's | *Amer.*	20
Teranga | *Senegalese*	22
☑ Toro | *Spanish*	27
Tremont 647/Sorel | *Amer.*	20
28 Degrees | *Amer.*	19
Union B&G | *Amer.*	24
Upper Crust | *Pizza*	21

THEATER DISTRICT

(See map on page 258)

TOP FOOD

Troquet | *Amer./French* | **G4**	26
Pigalle | *French* | **I4**	26
Market | *Amer.* | **H5**	26
Tantric | *Indian* | **H4**	24
Avila | *Med.* | **H4**	23

LISTING

Avila | *Med.*	23
Blu | *Amer.*	21
Boloco | *Eclectic/Tex-Mex*	19
Jacob Wirth | *Amer./German*	18
Jer-Ne | *Amer.*	19
Market | *Amer.*	26
Montien | *Japanese/Thai*	21
P.F. Chang's | *Chinese*	19
Pigalle | *French*	26
Rustic Kitchen | *Italian*	20
Tantric | *Indian*	24
Teatro | *Italian*	22
☑ Troquet | *Amer./French*	26
NEW Vapiano | *Italian*	18
NEW W Lounge | *Amer.*	19

WATERFRONT

(See map on page 256)

TOP FOOD

Meritage | *Amer.* | **I8**	26
Sel de la Terre | *French* | **G8**	23
Rowes Wharf | *Seafood* | **H8**	23
Legal Sea | *Seafood* | **G8**	22
Oceana | *Amer./Seafood* | **G8**	22

LISTING

Boston Sail | *Seafood*	18
Chart House | *Seafood*	20
☑ Legal Sea | *Seafood*	22
Living Room | *Amer.*	16

☑ Meritage | *Amer.*	26
Miel | *French*	22
Oceana | *Amer./Seafood*	22
Rowes Wharf | *Seafood*	23
RumBa | *Eclectic*	19
☑ Sel de la Terre | *French*	23
Sushi-Teq | *Asian*	24

WEST END

Boston Beer | *Pub*	18
Flat Iron | *Amer.*	-
West End Johnnie's | *Eclectic*	18

Cambridge

CAMBRIDGEPORT/ EAST CAMBRIDGE

☑ Anna's | *Tex-Mex*	23
Bambara | *Amer.*	21
Boca Grande | *Tex-Mex*	21
☑ Cheesecake Factory | *Amer.*	18
Courthouse | *Seafood*	24
Dante | *Italian*	24
Helmand | *Afghan*	25
P.F. Chang's | *Chinese*	19
Second St. Café | *Amer./Sandwiches*	23
Brown Sugar/Similans | *Thai*	24
Technique | *Amer.*	-

CENTRAL SQUARE

(See map on page 262)

TOP FOOD

Craigie on Main | *French* | **H9**	27
Salts | *Amer./French* | **H10**	27
Flour Bakery | *Bakery* | **I10**	27
Rendezvous | *Med.* | **H8**	26
Baraka Cafe | *African* | **H8**	25

LISTING

Asmara | *Eritrean/Ethiopian*	22
Baraka Cafe | *African*	25
Basta Pasta | *Italian*	22
Bertucci's | *Italian*	18
NEW Bondir | *Amer.*	-
Central Kitchen | *Amer.*	23
☑ Craigie on Main | *French*	27
☑ Cuchi Cuchi | *Eclectic*	23
Dosa Factory | *Indian*	22
☑ Flour Bakery | *Bakery*	27
Green St. | *New Eng.*	22

India Pavilion	*Indian*	21
Koreana	*Japanese/Korean*	21
Mary Chung	*Chinese*	22
Middle East	*Mideast.*	19
Middlesex	*Eclectic*	20
Miracle of Science	*Pub*	19
Picante	*Cal./Mex.*	22
Plough & Stars	*Eclectic/Pub*	23
☑ Rendezvous	*Med.*	26
River Gods	*Eclectic*	22
Royal East	*Chinese*	23
☑ Salts	*Amer./French*	27
Sidney's	*Amer.*	21
Tavern in Sq.	*Amer.*	15
☑ 1369 Coffee	*Coffee*	21
Zuzu!	*Eclectic/Mideast.*	19

HARVARD SQUARE

(See map on page 262)

TOP FOOD

Ten Tables	*Amer./Euro.*	**B1**	27
Garden at Cellar	*Amer.*	**F6**	26
Rialto	*Italian*	**E3**	26
Harvest	*Amer.*	**D3**	25
Sandrine's	*French*	**E4**	24

LISTING

Bertucci's	*Italian*	18
B. Good	*Burgers*	18
Boloco	*Eclectic/Tex-Mex*	19
Border Cafe	*Cajun/Tex-Mex*	20
Café Algiers	*Mideast.*	16
Cafe of India	*Indian*	20
Cafe Sushi	*Japanese*	22
Cambridge Common	*Pub*	18
Cambridge 1	*Pizza*	22
Casablanca	*Med.*	21
Charlie's Kitchen	*Diner*	17
Chez Henri	*Cuban/French*	24
NEW Clover Food Lab	*Veg.*	-
Daedalus	*Amer.*	18
Darwin's	*Coffee/Deli*	21
Dolphin Seafood	*Seafood*	19
Finale	*Dessert*	21
Fire & Ice	*Eclectic*	15
☑ Garden at Cellar	*Amer.*	26
Grafton St. Pub	*Amer.*	19
Grendel's Den	*Amer.*	17
☑ Harvest	*Amer.*	25
Henrietta's	*New Eng.*	23
Hi-Rise	*Bakery/Sandwiches*	24

Hong Kong	*Chinese*	13
John Harvard's	*Pub*	16
☑ Legal Sea	*Seafood*	22
Le's	*Viet.*	21
Mr. Bartley's	*Burgers*	24
9 Tastes	*Thai*	21
Noir	*Amer.*	20
Om	*Amer.*	16
Pinocchio's	*Pizza*	23
Red House	*Eclectic*	21
Redline	*Amer.*	16
☑ Rialto	*Italian*	26
NEW Russell Hse.	*Amer.*	21
Sandrine's	*French*	24
NEW Simple Truth	*Amer.*	-
Spice Thai	*Thai*	19
Tamarind Bay	*Indian*	23
Tanjore	*Indian*	22
☑ Ten Tables	*Amer./Euro.*	27
Tory Row	*Amer./Euro.*	17
Trata	*Amer.*	-
Upper Crust	*Pizza*	21
Upstairs/Square	*Amer.*	24
Veggie Planet	*Pizza/Veg.*	22
Wagamama	*Noodles*	18

HURON VILLAGE

Bertucci's	*Italian*	18
Full Moon	*Amer.*	19
Hi-Rise	*Bakery/Sandwiches*	24
Jasper White's	*New Eng./Seafood*	21
José's	*Mex.*	19
☑ Sofra Bakery	*Mideast.*	27
Tratt. Pulcinella	*Italian*	24
☑ T.W. Food	*Amer./French*	28

INMAN SQUARE

(See map on page 262)

TOP FOOD

Oleana	*Med.*	**E10**	28
East Coast	*BBQ/Seafood*	**D9**	26
Muqueca	*Brazilian*	**D10**	25
Punjabi Dhaba	*Indian*	**D9**	24

LISTING

All Star	*Sandwiches*	23
NEW Bosphorus	*Med.*	-
Bukowski	*Pub*	18
Casa Portugal	*Portug.*	23
Druid	*Irish/Pub*	24
NEW East by NE	*Chinese*	22

☑ East Coast	*BBQ/Seafood*	26
Ginger Ex.	*Asian/Japanese*	20
Haveli	*Indian*	–
Lord Hobo	*Amer.*	16
Midwest	*Brazilian/Steak*	21
Muqueca	*Brazilian*	25
☑ Oleana	*Med.*	28
Olé/Olecito	*Mex.*	24
Punjabi Dhaba	*Indian*	24
S&S	*Deli*	19
Sunset Cafe	*Amer./Portug.*	24
☑ 1369 Coffee	*Coffee*	21
Trina's	*Amer.*	20
Tupelo	*Southern*	24

KENDALL SQUARE

Amelia's Trattoria	*Italian*	21
Atasca	*Portug.*	20
Black Sheep	*Amer.*	21
Blue Room	*Eclectic*	24
Cambridge Brewing	*Pub*	16
Emma's	*Pizza*	25
☑ EVOO	*Eclectic*	26
Friendly Toast	*Amer.*	21
☑ Hungry Mother	*Southern*	26
☑ Legal Sea	*Seafood*	22
MuLan Taiwanese	*Taiwanese*	24
NEW Think Tank	*Amer./Asian*	–
Za	*Pizza*	24

PORTER SQUARE

Addis Red Sea	*Ethiopian*	22
☑ Anna's	*Tex-Mex*	23
Blue Fin	*Japanese*	22
Boca Grande	*Tex-Mex*	21
Cafe Barada	*Lebanese*	24
Changsho	*Chinese*	21
Christopher's	*Eclectic*	21
☑ Elephant Walk	*Cambodian/French*	23
Frank's Steak	*Steak*	18
Gran Gusto	*Italian*	–
Kaya House	*Japanese/Korean*	–
Passage to India	*Indian*	22
Rod Dee	*Thai*	24
Stone Hearth Pizza	*Pizza*	–
Sugar & Spice	*Thai*	20
Tavern in Sq.	*Amer.*	15
Temple Bar	*Amer.*	21
West Side	*Amer.*	21

Nearby Suburbs

ARLINGTON/ BELMONT/ WINCHESTER

☑ Blue Ribbon BBQ	*BBQ*	26
Comella's	*Italian*	–
Flora	*Amer.*	24
Il Casale	*Italian*	24
Jimmy's Steer	*Steak*	20
Kathmandu Spice	*Nepalese*	23
Kayuga	*Japanese/Korean*	18
Lucia	*Italian*	23
Mr. Sushi	*Japanese*	21
☑ Not Average Joe's	*Amer.*	19
☑ NEW Parsons Table	*Amer.*	27
Pasha	*Turkish*	22
Patou	*Thai*	20
Punjab	*Indian*	24
Scutra	*Eclectic*	25
Shangri-La	*Taiwanese*	23
Stone Hearth Pizza	*Pizza*	–
Tango	*Argent./Steak*	22
Tryst	*Amer.*	24
Vicki Lee's	*Bakery/Sandwiches*	23
Za	*Pizza*	24
Zócalo Cocina	*Mex.*	24

BRAINTREE/ MILTON/QUINCY

Abby Park	*Amer.*	19
Basta Pasta	*Italian*	22
Bertucci's	*Italian*	18
Bistro Chi	*Chinese*	–
Blue22	*Amer./Asian*	14
☑ Cheesecake Factory	*Amer.*	18
China Pearl	*Chinese*	21
88 Wharf	*Amer.*	19
El Sarape	*Mex.*	26
Firefly's	*BBQ*	19
Grand Chinatown	*Chinese*	–
Joe's American	*Amer.*	17
Kama	*Eclectic*	–
La Paloma	*Mex.*	19
Pho Hoa	*Viet.*	24
Pizzeria Regina	*Pizza*	24
NEW Port 305	*Amer.*	–
NEW Sake Japanese	*Japanese*	–
Siros	*Italian*	20

BROOKLINE

NEW Abbey, The | *Amer.*	–
NEW Amer. Craft | *Pub*	17
Z Anna's | *Tex-Mex*	23
Athan's Café | *Bakery/Med.*	22
Baja Betty's | *Mex.*	23
Beacon St. Tavern | *Amer.*	19
Boca Grande | *Tex-Mex*	21
Bottega | *Italian/Deli*	23
Brookline Family | *Turkish*	22
NEW Budda C | *Asian*	20
Chef Chow's | *Chinese*	20
NEW Cognac Bistro | *French*	–
Comella's | *Italian*	–
Coolidge Corner | *Pub*	17
NEW Cutty's | *Amer./Sandwiches*	25
Daily Catch | *Italian/Seafood*	24
Dok Bua | *Thai*	23
Dorado | *Mex.*	24
Finale | *Dessert*	21
Fireplace | *New Eng.*	21
Z Fugakyu | *Japanese*	24
Ginza | *Japanese*	23
Golden Temple | *Chinese*	20
Jerusalem Pita | *Israeli*	20
Kayuga | *Japanese/Korean*	18
Khao Sarn | *Thai*	24
La Morra | *Italian*	25
Lineage | *Amer.*	25
Matt Murphy's | *Pub*	22
Mr. Sushi | *Japanese*	21
Olé/Olecito | *Mex.*	24
Orinoco | *Venez.*	23
Paris Creperie | *French*	21
Pho Lemongrass | *Viet.*	20
Pomodoro | *Italian*	25
Publick House | *Belgian/Pub*	20
Rami's | *Mideast.*	24
Rani | *Indian*	21
NEW Regal Beagle | *Amer.*	21
Rod Dee | *Thai*	24
Rubin's | *Deli*	19
Shawarma King | *Lebanese*	21
Sichuan Gdn. | *Chinese*	23
Sichuan Gourmet | *Chinese*	25
Super Fusion | *Japanese*	26
Taberna/Haro | *Spanish*	25
Tamarind Bay | *Indian*	23
Tashi Delek | *Tibetan*	–
Upper Crust | *Pizza*	21

Village Smokehse. | *BBQ*	21
Washington Sq. | *Amer.*	22
Zaftigs | *Deli*	21

CHESTNUT HILL

Z Aquitaine | *French*	23
Bernard's | *Chinese*	25
Bertucci's | *Italian*	18
Z Capital Grille | *Steak*	26
Charley's | *Amer.*	18
Z Cheesecake Factory | *Amer.*	18
Comella's | *Italian*	–
Forty Carrots | *Amer.*	20
Z Legal Sea | *Seafood*	22
Le's | *Viet.*	21
Metropolitan | *Amer./Steak*	20
Z Oishii | *Japanese*	27
Papa Razzi | *Italian*	19

DEDHAM/
HYDE PARK/
ROSLINDALE

Z Aquitaine | *French*	23
B. Good | *Burgers*	18
Birch St. Bistro | *Amer.*	20
Z Delfino | *Italian*	26
Five Guys | *Burgers*	20
Halfway Cafe | *Pub*	17
Isabella | *Amer.*	21
Joe's American | *Amer.*	17
Kings | *Pub*	19
NEW Legal C Bar | *Seafood*	22
Met Back/B&G | *Amer./Steak*	19
P.F. Chang's | *Chinese*	19
Pleasant Cafe | *Amer./Italian*	21
Sophia's | *Med.*	23
Townsend's | *Amer.*	21
Village Sushi | *Japanese/Korean*	22
NEW Yard House | *Amer.*	19

LEXINGTON

Lexx | *Amer.*	19
Upper Crust | *Pizza*	21
Via Lago | *Amer.*	22

MEDFORD/
SOMERVILLE

Amelia's Kitchen | *Italian*	18
Z Anna's | *Tex-Mex*	23
Z NEW Bergamot | *Amer.*	27
Bertucci's | *Italian*	18
Z Bistro 5 | *Italian*	27

Boloco	*Eclectic/Tex-Mex*	19
Boston Burger	*Burgers*	23
Burren	*Irish/Pub*	17
Café Belô	*Brazilian*	24
Cantina la Mex.	*Mex.*	24
Chung Ki Wa	*Japanese/Korean*	23
Dalí	*Spanish*	25
Diva Indian	*Indian*	22
NEW Foundry/Elm	*Amer.*	-
Gargoyles	*Amer.*	24
Highland Kitchen	*Amer.*	25
House of Tibet	*Tibetan*	18
Independent	*Amer.*	20
NEW Istanbul'lu	*Turkish*	23
Johnny D's	*Amer.*	20
Joshua Tree	*Pub*	15
NEW Journeyman	*Amer.*	-
Kebab Factory	*Indian*	24
Lil Vinny's	*Italian*	23
Machu Picchu	*Peruvian*	21
Martsa's/Elm	*Tibetan*	21
Mr. Crepe	*French*	21
Namaskar	*Indian*	19
☑ Neighborhood	*Portug.*	26
Orleans	*Amer.*	17
Out of the Blue	*Italian/Seafood*	24
Pho n' Rice	*Thai/Vietnamese*	21
Pizzeria Regina	*Pizza*	24
NEW Posto	*Italian/Pizza*	25
Redbones	*BBQ*	24
Ronnarong	*Thai*	22
Rosebud	*Diner*	15
Sabur	*Med.*	23
Salvatore's	*Italian*	21
Sound Bites	*Amer./Mideast.*	23
Tacos Lupita	*Mex./Salvadoran*	25
Tu y Yo	*Mex.*	24
Vinny's/Night	*Italian*	24
NEW Yak & Yeti	*Indian/Nepalese*	-
Zoe's	*Chinese*	22

NEEDHAM/NEWTON/ WABAN

Aji	*Japanese*	23
Amarin Thailand	*Thai*	21
Appetito	*Italian*	17
Bakers' Best	*Amer.*	22
Bertucci's	*Italian*	18
Biltmore B&G	*Amer.*	21
Blue on Highland	*Amer.*	20
☑ Blue Ribbon BBQ	*BBQ*	26

Bokx	*Steak*	21
Café St. Petersburg	*Russian*	21
NEW Center Café	*Amer.*	20
Comella's	*Italian*	-
C. Tsar's	*Med.*	-
51 Lincoln	*Amer.*	24
Jamjuli	*Thai*	21
Johnny's Lunch.	*Diner*	19
Jumbo	*Chinese/Seafood*	22
Karoun	*Armenian/Mideast.*	20
Kouzina	*Greek/Med.*	23
Lam's	*Asian*	19
Local	*Amer.*	19
☑ Lumière	*French*	28
Masala Art	*Indian*	24
☑ Not Average Joe's	*Amer.*	19
Peking Cuisine	*Chinese*	-
☑ Petit Robert	*French*	23
Prana Café	*Vegan*	-
Sapporo	*Japanese/Korean*	-
Shogun	*Japanese*	20
Skipjack's	*Seafood*	20
Sol Azteca	*Mex.*	21
Spiga Trattoria	*Italian*	22
Stone Hearth Pizza	*Pizza*	-
Sweet Basil	*Italian*	26
Sweet Tomatoes	*Pizza*	24
Tartufo	*Italian*	22
Tu y Yo	*Mex.*	24
Village Fish	*Italian/Seafood*	22

WALTHAM/ WATERTOWN

Aegean	*Greek*	20
Bison County	*BBQ*	18
Deluxe Town	*Diner*	22
Demos	*Greek*	17
☑ Elephant Walk	*Cambodian/French*	23
Erawan/Siam	*Thai*	20
Green Papaya	*Thai*	22
Greg's	*Amer./Italian*	18
Halfway Cafe	*Pub*	17
☑ Il Capriccio	*Italian*	27
☑ La Campania	*Italian*	28
La Casa/Pedro	*Venez.*	21
Naked Fish	*Cuban/Seafood*	20
New Ginza	*Japanese*	23
New Mother India	*Indian*	22
☑ Not Average Joe's	*Amer.*	19
Pizzeria Regina	*Pizza*	24

Ponzu | *Asian*	23
Porcini's | *Med.*	20
Skellig | *Pub*	17
Solea | *Spanish*	22
Stellina | *Italian*	23
Strip-T's | *Amer.*	21
Super Fusion | *Japanese*	26
Taqueria Mexico | *Mex.*	24
Tempo | *Amer.*	22
Tuscan Grill | *Italian*	21
UFood | *Health*	17
Upper Crust | *Pizza*	21

Outlying Suburbs

NORTH OF BOSTON

Abbondanza | *Italian*	23
☑ All Seasons | *Asian*	27
Angelo's | *Italian*	27
Black Cow | *Amer./Pub*	20
Blue Fin | *Japanese*	22
Border Cafe | *Cajun/Tex-Mex*	20
Brenden Crocker's | *Amer.*	26
Burtons | *Amer.*	21
Café Belô | *Brazilian*	24
Café Polonia | *Polish*	24
NEW Ceia Kitchen/Bar | *European*	-
☑ Cheesecake Factory | *Amer.*	18
China Blossom | *Chinese*	-
Cilantro | *Mex.*	21
Clam Box | *Seafood*	24
Cygnet | *Amer.*	23
Dog Bar | *Amer.*	-
Donatello | *Italian*	22
☑ Duckworth's | *Amer.*	27
Exchange St. Bistro | *Eclectic*	21
Farm Bar | *Amer./BBQ*	-
Finz | *Seafood*	21
Fish Bones | *Seafood*	22
NEW 5 Corners | *French*	26
Five Guys | *Burgers*	20
Franklin | *Amer.*	24
G Bar | *Amer.*	19
Glenn's | *Eclectic*	-
Glory | *Amer.*	21
☑ Grapevine | *Amer./Italian*	27
Hilltop Steak | *Steak*	16
☑ Ithaki Med. | *Greek/Med.*	27
Jimmy's Steer | *Steak*	20
Joe's American | *Amer.*	17
Kowloon | *Asian*	15

Landing | *Amer.*	18
☑ Legal Sea | *Seafood*	22
Lyceum | *Eclectic*	23
Maddie's Sail | *New Eng./Seafood*	14
Masa | *SW*	21
Midwest | *Brazilian/Steak*	21
Moonstones | *Eclectic*	20
☑ Not Average Joe's | *Amer.*	19
Palmers | *Amer.*	22
Passage to India | *Indian*	22
Pellana | *Steak*	25
Pellino's | *Italian*	24
P.F. Chang's | *Chinese*	19
Pizzeria Regina | *Pizza*	24
Polcari's | *Italian*	19
Red Rock | *Amer.*	20
Rist. Pavarotti | *Italian*	-
Boston Beer | *Pub*	18
Salvatore's | *Italian*	21
Santarpio's | *Pizza*	25
Shea's Riverside | *New Eng.*	19
Sichuan Gdn. | *Chinese*	23
Sichuan Gourmet | *Chinese*	25
62 Rest. & Wine Bar | *Italian*	25
Soma | *Med.*	22
Strega Lounge | *Italian*	19
Tacos Lupita | *Mex./Salvadoran*	25
Tavern in Sq. | *Amer.*	15
Tivoli's | *French/Italian*	-
NEW Top Steak | *Brazilian/Steak*	-
NEW Turbine | *Amer./Asian*	-
Turner's Seafood | *Seafood*	23
Woodman's | *Seafood*	23
Yama | *Japanese*	23
Zabaglione | *Italian*	28

SOUTH OF BOSTON

☑ NEW Alma Nove | *Italian/Med.*	22
Atlantica | *Seafood*	20
Back Eddy | *Seafood*	23
☑ Barker Tavern | *Amer.*	27
Bella's | *Italian*	-
B. Good | *Burgers*	18
Bia Bistro | *Med.*	25
Bon Caldo | *Italian*	20
Bridgeman's | *Italian*	24
Burtons | *Amer.*	21
Byblos | *Lebanese*	24
Caffe Bella | *Med.*	26
Caffe Tosca | *Italian*	24
CBS Scene Rest. & Bar | *Amer.*	-

Chiara | *Med.*	24
Coriander | *Indian/Nepalese*	25
☑ Davio's | *Italian/Steak*	25
Five Guys | *Burgers*	20
Halfway Cafe | *Pub*	17
Boston Beer | *Pub*	18
Incontro | *Italian*	21
Jasper White's | *New Eng./Seafood*	21
Joe & Maria's | *Italian*	-
Joe's American | *Amer.*	17
La Paloma | *Mex.*	19
☑ Not Average Joe's | *Amer.*	19
Olivadi | *Italian*	20
Orta | *Italian*	19
Papa Razzi | *Italian*	19
Red Robin | *Amer.*	16
Riva | *Italian*	26
Roobar | *Amer.*	19
Rustic Kitchen | *Italian*	20
Saporito's | *Italian*	28
Scarlet Oak | *Steak*	21
Skipjack's | *Seafood*	20
Sky | *Amer.*	16
Solstice | *Amer.*	25
☑ Square Café | *Amer.*	25
Stars on Hingham | *Diner*	18
Suffolk Grille | *Amer.*	-
Tastings Wine/Bistro | *Eclectic*	21
Tavolino | *Italian*	20
☑ Tosca | *Italian*	26
Typhoon | *Asian*	18
Vin & Eddie's | *Italian*	21

WEST OF BOSTON

Aegean | *Greek*	20
NEW Aka Bistro | *French/Japanese*	25
Alta Strada | *Italian*	22
Amarin Thailand | *Thai*	21
Bertucci's | *Italian*	18
Big Papi's | *Amer.*	13
☑ Blue Ginger | *Asian*	27
Border Cafe | *Cajun/Tex-Mex*	20
Bullfinchs | *Eclectic*	21
Café Belô | *Brazilian*	24
Cafe Escadrille | *Continental*	21
Café Mangal | *Med./Turkish*	26
☑ Capital Grille | *Steak*	26
Captain's Table | *Seafood*	24
☑ Cheesecake Factory | *Amer.*	18
China Sky | *Chinese/Japanese*	22
CK Shanghai | *Chinese*	24

Coach Grill | *Steak*	24
Comella's | *Italian*	-
Cottage | *Cal.*	19
Dalya's | *Amer.*	21
Dolphin Seafood | *Seafood*	19
Firefly's | *BBQ*	19
Five Guys | *Burgers*	20
☑ Fugakyu | *Japanese*	24
☑ Gibbet Hill | *New Eng./Steak*	25
Halfway Cafe | *Pub*	17
Harry's | *Diner*	22
Joe's American | *Amer.*	17
John Harvard's | *Pub*	16
J's/Nashoba | *Amer.*	24
La Cantina | *Italian*	20
☑ L'Andana | *Italian*	27
Lavender Asian | *Asian*	23
☑ Legal Sea | *Seafood*	22
Le Lyonnais | *French*	23
☑ Longfellow's | *New Eng.*	19
Lotus Blossom | *Chinese/Japanese*	22
Maxwells 148 | *Asian/Italian*	24
Melting Pot | *Fondue*	19
Met Back/B&G | *Amer./Steak*	19
New Jang Su | *Korean*	-
☑ Not Average Joe's | *Amer.*	19
Oga's | *Japanese*	25
☑ Oishii | *Japanese*	27
Papa Razzi | *Italian*	19
P.F. Chang's | *Chinese*	19
Pizzeria Regina | *Pizza*	24
☑ Sel de la Terre | *French*	23
Serafina | *Italian*	16
Sherborn Inn | *New Eng.*	19
Sichuan Gourmet | *Chinese*	25
Singh's | *Indian*	22
Sorento's | *Italian/Persian*	25
Summer Winter | *Amer.*	25
Tavolino | *Italian*	20
Tomasso | *Italian*	23
Walden Grille | *Amer.*	16
Yama | *Japanese*	23
Zebra's Bistro | *Amer.*	24

Far Outlying Areas

CAPE COD

☑ Abba | *Med./Thai*	28
Academy Ocean | *Eclectic/Seafood*	21
Adrian's | *Amer./Italian*	18

Alberto's	*Italian*	21	Edwige	*Amer.*	26
Amari	*Italian*	22	Enzo	*French*	21
Anthony Cummaquid	*Continental*	17	Fairway	*Amer./Italian*	17
Aqua Grille	*Amer./Seafood*	19	Fanizzi's	*Amer./Italian*	19
Ardeo	*Med.*	19	Far Land Provisions	*Deli*	19
☑ Arnold's Lobster	*Seafood*	24	Fazio's	*Italian*	21
Asia	*Asian*	21	Finely JP's	*Amer.*	21
Barley Neck Inn	*Amer.*	20	Fishmonger's	*Amer./Seafood*	20
Barnstable	*New Eng.*	19	Five Bays	*Amer.*	23
Baxter's	*Seafood*	20	Friendly Fisherman	*Seafood*	22
Bayside Betsy's	*Amer.*	18	Front St.	*Continental/Italian*	25
Bee-Hive Tavern	*Amer.*	19	Gina's	*Italian*	21
☑ Belfry Inne	*Amer.*	27	☑ Glass Onion	*Amer.*	27
Betsy's Diner	*Diner*	16	☑ Impudent Oyster	*Seafood*	23
Bistro/Crowne Pointe	*Amer.*	23	Inaho	*Japanese*	26
NEW Black Cat Tavern	*Seafood*	20	Island Merchant	*Amer./Carib.*	-
Blackfish	*Amer.*	25	JT's Seafood	*Seafood*	20
Bleu	*French*	27	Karoo Kafe	*S African*	22
Blue Moon	*Med.*	24	La Cucina/Mare	*Italian*	24
Bookstore & Rest.	*Seafood*	20	L'Alouette	*French*	26
☑ Bramble Inn	*Amer.*	28	Landfall	*Seafood*	18
Brazilian Grill	*Brazilian*	24	Liam's	*Seafood*	20
☑ Brewster Fish	*Seafood*	26	Lobster Pot	*Eclectic/Seafood*	22
Bubala's	*Eclectic/Seafood*	16	Lorraine's	*Mex.*	17
Buca's Tuscan	*Italian*	23	Lyric	*Amer.*	25
☑ Cape Sea	*Amer.*	27	Mac's	*Seafood*	25
Capt. Frosty's	*New Eng./Seafood*	21	Marshland	*Amer.*	20
Capt. Kidd	*Pub*	16	Marshside	*Amer./Seafood*	19
Capt. Linnell	*Amer.*	24	Mattakeese Wharf	*Seafood*	18
Capt. Parker's	*New Eng.*	21	Mews	*Amer.*	26
Catch of the Day	*Seafood*	25	Mezza Luna	*Italian*	22
Chapin's	*Seafood*	19	Misaki	*Japanese*	25
Chapoquoit Grill	*Med.*	21	Moby Dick's	*Seafood*	24
Chart Room	*New Eng./Seafood*	18	Naked Oyster	*Seafood*	25
☑ Chatham Bars	*Amer.*	23	Napi's	*Eclectic*	20
Chatham Squire	*Eclectic*	19	Nauset Beach	*Italian*	23
Chillingsworth	*French*	26	☑ Not Average Joe's	*Amer.*	19
Ciro & Sal's	*Italian*	17	Ocean House	*Amer.*	27
Clancy's	*Amer.*	21	Ocean Terrace	*Amer.*	19
Cobie's Clam	*Seafood*	22	Optimist Café	*Amer./British*	-
Colombo's	*Italian*	-	Orleans Inn	*Amer.*	16
Cooke's	*Seafood*	19	Osteria/Civetta	*Italian*	27
Coonamessett	*New Eng.*	21	Oyster Co.	*Seafood*	24
NEW Dalla Cucina	*Italian*	20	Paddock	*Amer./New Eng.*	22
Dan'l Webster	*Amer.*	21	Pain D'Avignon	*Bakery/French*	26
Devon's	*Amer.*	25	☑ NEW PB Boulangerie	*French*	28
Dockside, The	*New Eng.*	17	Pearl	*Seafood*	17
Dolphin	*Amer./Seafood*	22	Pisces	*Med./Seafood*	27
D'Parma Italian Table	*Italian*	22	Port	*New Eng./Seafood*	23
Dunbar Tea	*British/Tea*	21	Red Inn	*New Eng.*	26

Red Pheasant | *Amer./French* — 27

Regatta/Cotuit | *Amer.* — 26

Roadhouse | *Seafood/Steak* — 22

Roobar | *Amer.* — 19

Ross' Grill | *Amer.* — 24

Sal's Place | *Italian/Med.* — 18

Scargo Café | *Amer.* — 21

Siena | *Italian* — 22

Sir Cricket's | *Seafood* — 24

Squealing Pig | *Pub* — 20

Stir Crazy | *Cambodian* — 20

Terra Luna | *Amer.* — 23

Trevi Café | *Med.* — 25

28 Atlantic | *Amer.* — 27

Van Rensselaer's | *Amer./Seafood* — 17

Vining's | *Eclectic* — 23

Waterford Café/Tav. | *Amer.* — -

Wicked Fire Kissed | *Amer./Pizza* — 25

Wicked Oyster | *Amer./Seafood* — 23

Wild Goose | *Amer.* — 21

Winslow's Tavern | *Amer.* — 21

MARTHA'S VINEYARD

Alchemy | *Amer.* — 23

🔁 Art Cliff | *Diner* — 26

Atlantic Fish/Chop | *Seafood/Steak* — 21

Atria | *Amer.* — 26

Beach Plum | *Amer.* — 22

Bite | *Seafood* — 26

Black Dog | *Amer.* — 19

Blue Canoe | *Seafood* — 16

Chesca's | *Amer./Italian* — 24

Chilmark Tavern | *Amer.* — 24

Deon's | *Amer./Carib.* — -

Détente | *Amer.* — 28

Giordano's | *Italian* — 23

Home Port | *Seafood* — 21

Il Tesoro/Terrace | *Italian* — 19

Jimmy Seas | *Italian* — 23

Lambert's Cove | *Amer.* — 23

🔁 Larsen's Fish | *Seafood* — 28

Lattanzi's | *Italian* — 21

Le Grenier | *French* — 24

L'Étoile | *French* — 28

Lure Grill | *Amer.* — 22

Net Result | *Seafood* — 24

Newes/America | *Pub* — 20

Offshore Ale | *Pub* — 20

🔁 Outermost Inn | *Amer.* — 23

Oyster BG | *Seafood/Steak* — 24

Saltwater | *Eclectic* — 21

Sharky's | *Mex.* — 16

Sidecar Café | *New Eng.* — -

Slice of Life | *Amer.* — 26

Square Rigger | *Seafood* — -

State Road | *Amer.* — 25

Sweet Life | *Amer./French* — 25

Water St. | *New Eng.* — 26

Zapotec | *SW* — 21

Zephrus | *Amer.* — 19

NANTUCKET

American Seasons | *Amer.* — 26

Arno's | *Amer.* — 20

Black-Eyed Susan's | *Amer.* — 25

Boarding House | *Amer.* — 25

Brant Point | *Seafood/Steak* — 24

Brotherhood/Thieves | *Amer.* — 21

Centre St. Bistro | *Amer.* — 26

Chanticleer | *French* — 25

Club Car | *Continental* — 24

Company/Cauldron | *Amer.* — 27

Corazon del Mar | *Latin* — 25

DeMarco | *Italian* — 23

Dune | *Amer.* — 22

Easy Street | *Seafood* — -

Even Keel | *Amer.* — 19

Fifty-Six Union | *Eclectic* — 23

Figs at 29 Fair | *Med.* — 26

Fog Island | *Amer.* — 23

🔁 Galley Beach | *Eclectic* — 24

Jetties | *Italian/New Eng.* — 17

Le Languedoc | *French* — 23

Lo La 41° | *Eclectic* — 25

NEW Millie's | *Cal./Mex.* — 19

Nantucket Lobster | *Seafood* — 22

🔁 Òran Mór | *Eclectic* — 28

🔁 Pearl | *Asian* — 28

Pi Pizzeria | *Pizza* — 23

Queequeg's | *Eclectic* — 25

Ropewalk | *Seafood* — 18

Sconset Café | *Amer./Eclectic* — 25

Sea Grille | *Seafood* — 23

Ships Inn | *Amer.* — 27

Slip 14 | *Amer.* — 19

Straight Wharf | *Seafood* — 27

Summer House | *Amer.* — 25

Sushi by Yoshi | *Japanese* — 23

Topper's | *Amer.* — 27

Town | *Eclectic* — 24

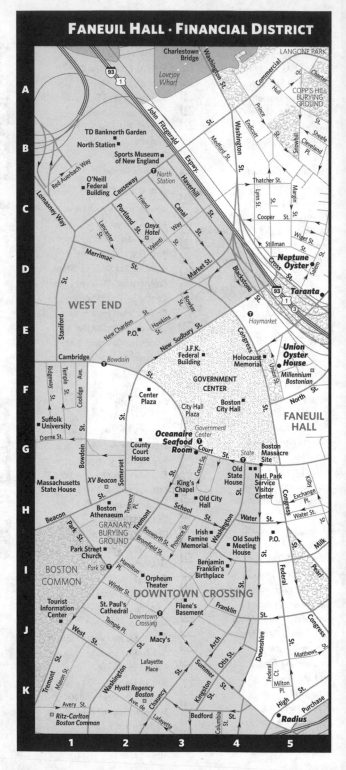

Menus, photos, voting and more – free at ZAGAT.com

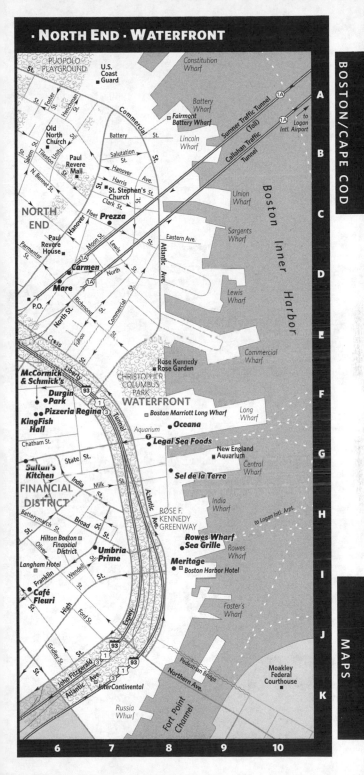

· NORTH END · WATERFRONT

PUOPOLO
PLAYGROUND

U.S. Coast
Guard

Constitution
Wharf

Battery
Wharf

Fairmont
Battery Wharf

Lincoln
Wharf

Commercial St.

Old
North
Church

Battery St.

Salutation St.

Hanover Ave.

Harris St.

St. Stephen's
Church

Clark St.

Union
Wharf

NORTH
END

Prezza

Fleet St.

Hanover St.

Moon St.

Lewis St.

Eastern Ave.

Sargents
Wharf

Paul
Revere
House

Carmen

North St.

Atlantic Ave.

Lewis
Wharf

Mare

Parmenter St.

Richmond St.

Commercial St.

P.O.

Cross St.

Fulton St.

Rose Kennedy
Rose Garden

Commercial
Wharf

CHRISTOPHER
COLUMBUS
PARK

McCormick
& Schmick's

Durgin
Park

Pizzeria Regina

WATERFRONT

Boston Marriott Long Wharf

Long
Wharf

KingFish
Hall

Chatham St.

Aquarium

Oceana

Legal Sea Foods

Sultan's
Kitchen

State St.

India St.

Milk St.

New England
Aquarium

Central
Wharf

FINANCIAL
DISTRICT

Sel de la Terre

Batterymarch St.

Broad St.

Atlantic Ave.

ROSE F.
KENNEDY
GREENWAY

India
Wharf

Hilton Boston
Financial
District

Oliver St.

Umbria
Prime

Rowes Wharf
Sea Grille

to Logan Intl. Arpt.

Langham Hotel

Wendell St.

Meritage

Rowes
Wharf

Franklin St.

Boston Harbor Hotel

Café
Fleuri

High St.

Ford St.

Foster's
Wharf

Gridley St.

Expwy.

John Fitzgerald

Atlantic Ave.

InterContinental

Pedestrian Bridge

Northern Ave.

Moakley
Federal
Courthouse

Russia
Wharf

Fort Point Channel

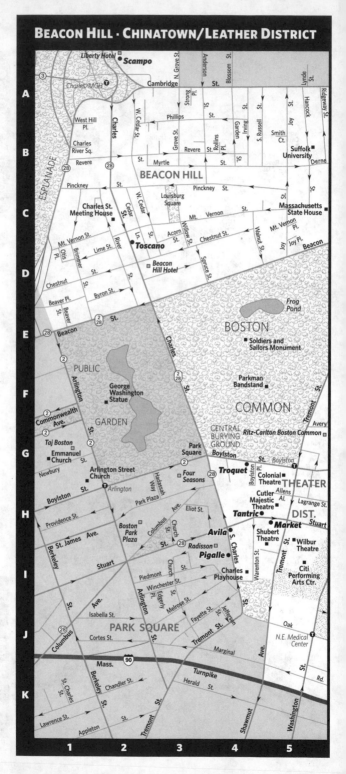

BEACON HILL · CHINATOWN/LEATHER DISTRICT

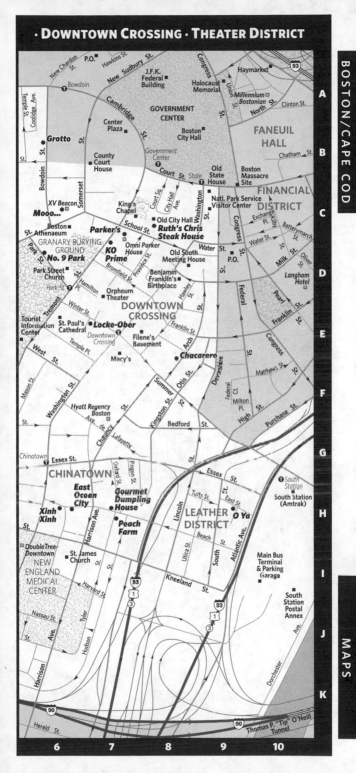

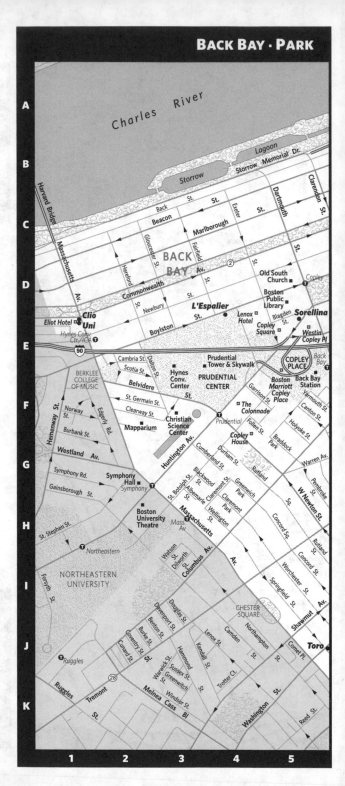

Menus, photos, voting and more – free at ZAGAT.com

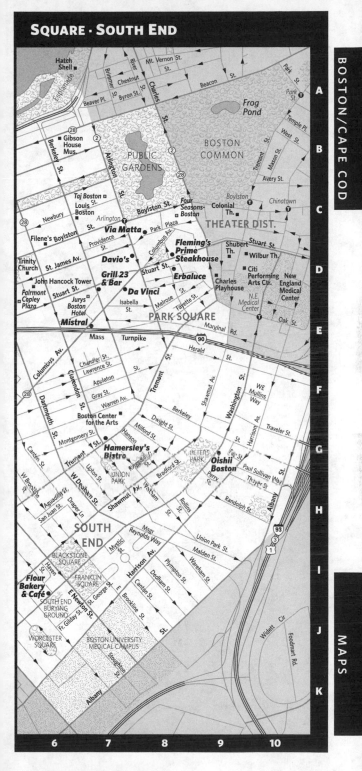

SQUARE · SOUTH END

Hatch Shell

Esplanade

Mt. Vernon St.

Brimmer

River St.

Chestnut St.

Byron St.

Beacon St.

Beaver Pl.

Charles St.

Park St.

Park St.

Frog Pond

Temple Pl.

West St.

Gibson House Mus.

Berkeley St.

PUBLIC GARDENS

Arlington St.

BOSTON COMMON

Tremont St.

Mason St.

Avery St.

Boylston

Chinatown

Taj Boston

Louis Boston

St. James St.

Arlington

Boylston St.

Four Seasons Boston

Colonial Th.

THEATER DIST.

Newbury

Filene's Boylston

Via Matta

Park Plaza

Columbus Av.

Fleming's Prime Steakhouse

Shubert Th.

Wilbur Th.

Stuart St.

Trinity Church

St. James Av.

Providence St.

Davio's

Stuart St.

Erbaluce

Charles Playhouse

Citi Performing Arts Ctr.

New England Medical Center

John Hancock Tower

Grill 23 & Bar

Da Vinci

N.E. Medical Center

Fairmont Copley Plaza

Stuart St.

Isabella St.

Melrose St.

Fayette St.

Jurys Boston Hotel

Mistral

PARK SQUARE

Marginal Rd.

Oak St.

Mass

Turnpike

90

Herald

St.

Columbus Av.

Clarendon St.

Chandler St.

Lawrence St.

Appleton St.

Gray St.

Warren Av.

St.

Tremont St.

Shawmut Av.

Washington St.

WE Mullins Way

Dartmouth St.

Berkeley St.

Dwight St.

Milford St.

Harrison Av.

Traveler St.

Boston Center for the Arts

Montgomery St.

Hanson St.

Rutland St.

Canton St.

Tremont

Hamersley's Bistro

W Dedham St.

Upton St.

UNION PARK

Bradford St.

Shawmut Av.

Gresham St.

PETERS PARK

Perry St.

Oishii Boston

Fox St.

Paul Sullivan Way

Thayer St.

Albany St.

Rollins St.

Randolph St.

W. Brookline St.

SOUTH END

Aguadilla St.

San Juan St.

Draper Ln

Mystic St.

Msgr. Reynolds Way

Harrison Av.

Union Park St.

Malden St.

Wareham St.

93

3

1

BLACKSTONE SQUARE

Haven St.

FRANKLIN SQUARE

Plympton St.

Flour Bakery & Café

E Newton St.

St. George St.

Canton St.

Dedham St.

Brookline St.

SOUTH END BURYING GROUND

Fr. Gilday St.

WORCESTER SQUARE

BOSTON UNIVERSITY MEDICAL CAMPUS

St.

Stoughton St.

Widett Cir

Foodmart Rd.

Albany St.

6   7   8   9   10

A B C D E F G H I J K

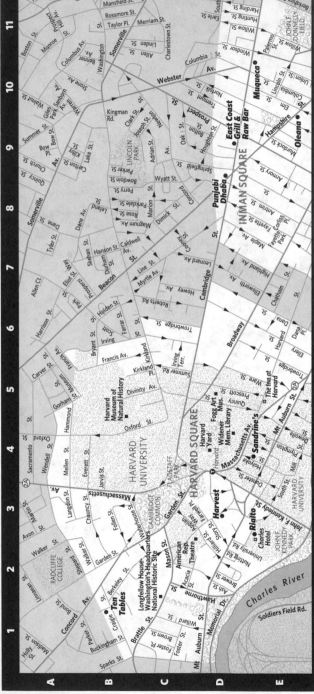

Menus, photos, voting and more – free at ZAGAT.com

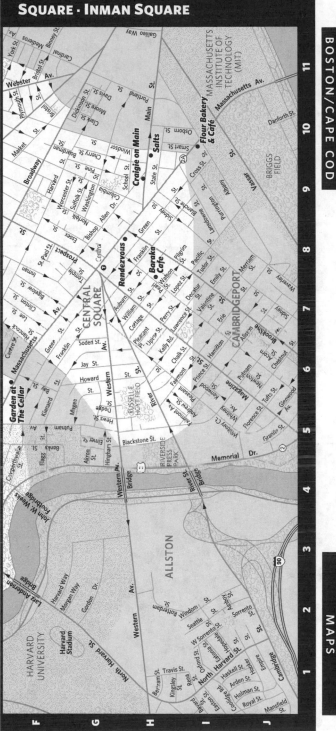

SQUARE · INMAN SQUARE

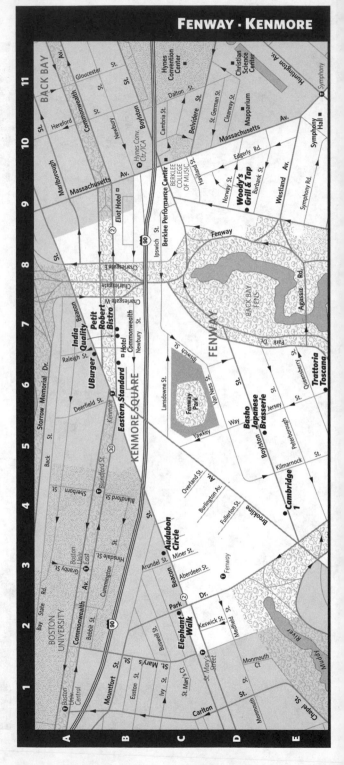

Menus, photos, voting and more - free at ZAGAT.com

SQUARE · MFA

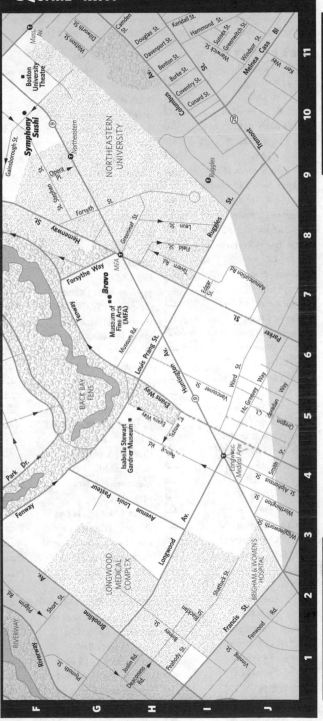

Special Features

Listings cover the best in each category and include names, locations and Food ratings. Multi-location restaurants' features may vary by branch.

BREAKFAST
(See also Hotel Dining)

Arno's | Nan	20
⦿ Art Cliff | MV	26
Bakers' Best | Newton	22
Bayside Betsy's | CC	18
Betsy's Diner | CC	16
Black Dog | MV	19
Black-Eyed Susan's | Nan	25
Brookline Family | Brookline	22
Centre St. Bistro | Nan	26
Chacarero | D'town Cross	25
Charlie's Sandwich | S End	22
Deluxe Town | Watertown	22
Edwige | CC	26
Even Keel | Nan	19
Fairway | CC	17
⦿ Flour Bakery | S End	27
Fog Island | Nan	23
Haley House | Roxbury	22
Harry's | Westborough	22
Hi-Rise | multi.	24
Johnny's Lunch. | Newton	19
Mike's | S End	20
⦿ Neighborhood | Somerville	26
Optimist Café | CC	-
Panificio | Beacon Hill	21
Paramount | Beacon Hill	22
Rosebud | Somerville	15
Rubin's | Brookline	19
S&S | Inman Sq	19
Sconset Café | Nan	25
Sorella's | Jamaica Plain	24
Sorelle | Charlestown	23
Sound Bites | Somerville	23
South/Buttery | S End	22
South St. Diner | Leather Dist	17
Stars on Hingham | Hingham	18
Trident | Back Bay	20
Via Lago | Lexington	22
Vicki Lee's | Belmont	23
Victoria's | Roxbury	19
Wicked Oyster | CC	23

BRUNCH

⦿ Abe & Louie's | Back Bay	26
⦿ Aquitaine | multi.	23

Ashmont Grill | Dorchester	23
Bakers' Best | Newton	22
Beacon Hill | Beacon Hill	23
Beehive | S End	20
Blue Room | Kendall Sq	24
Bon Savor | Jamaica Plain	22
Bullfinchs | Sudbury	21
Café Fleuri | Financial Dist	24
Centre St. Café | Jamaica Plain	25
Charley's | multi.	18
Church | Fenway	20
Club Cafe | S End	19
Columbus Café | S End	20
Coonamessett | CC	21
Delux Cafe | S End	20
⦿ East Coast | Inman Sq	26
Friendly Toast | Kendall Sq	21
Gargoyles | Somerville	24
Geoffrey's | Back Bay	22
Haley House | Roxbury	22
⦿ Harvest | Harv Sq	25
Henrietta's | Harv Sq	23
Johnny D's | Somerville	20
J's/Nashoba | Bolton	24
KingFish Hall | Faneuil Hall	22
⦿ Legal Sea | Harv Sq	22
Lucky's | Seaport Dist	19
Lyceum | Salem	23
Masa | multi.	21
Metropolis | S End	24
Mews | CC	26
North St. Grille | N End	24
Oceana | Waterfront	22
Olé/Olecito | Inman Sq	24
Panificio | Beacon Hill	21
Sabur | Somerville	23
S&S | Inman Sq	19
⦿ Sel de la Terre | Waterfront	23
75 Chestnut | Beacon Hill	21
Sidney's | Central Sq	21
Sonsie | Back Bay	20
South/Buttery | S End	22
Stephanie's | Back Bay	20
Temple Bar | Porter Sq	21
Topper's | Nan	27
Tremont 647/Sorel | S End	20

Tryst | **Arlington**	24
Union B&G | **S End**	24
Upstairs/Square | **Harv Sq**	24
West End Johnnie's | **W End**	18
West Side | **Porter Sq**	21
Zaftigs | **Brookline**	21

BUFFET

(Check availability)

Amrheins | **S Boston**	19
Bhindi Bazaar | **Back Bay**	20
Blue Room | **Kendall Sq**	24
Brazilian Grill | **CC**	24
Bukhara | **Jamaica Plain**	22
Café Belô | **Somerville**	24
Café Fleuri | **Financial Dist**	24
Cafe of India | **Harv Sq**	20
Caliterra | **Financial Dist**	15
Changsho | **Porter Sq**	21
China Blossom | **North Andover**	-
Coonamessett | **CC**	21
Coriander | **Sharon**	25
Dan'l Webster | **CC**	21
Diva Indian | **Somerville**	22
Fire & Ice | **multi.**	15
Firefly's | **multi.**	19
Flora | **Arlington**	24
Ghazal | **Jamaica Plain**	23
Haveli | **Inman Sq**	-
Henrietta's | **Harv Sq**	23
Himalayan | **W Roxbury**	22
India Pavilion | **Central Sq**	21
I's/Nashoba | **Bolton**	24
Kashmir | **Back Bay**	24
Kathmandu Spice | **Arlington**	23
Kebab Factory | **Somerville**	24
Lotus Blossom | **Sudbury**	22
Mantra | **D'town Cross**	21
Martsa's/Elm | **Somerville**	21
Masala Art | **Needham**	24
Mela | **S End**	24
Midwest | **multi.**	21
Namaskar | **Somerville**	19
New Mother India | **Waltham**	22
Oceana | **Waterfront**	22
Parker's | **D'town Cross**	24
Passage to India | **Porter Sq**	22
Rani | **Brookline**	21
Shanti India | **Dorchester**	28
Sidney's | **Central Sq**	21

Singh's | **Wellesley Hills**	22
606 Congress | **Seaport Dist**	20
Sky | **Norwood**	16
Sunset Grill/Cantina | **Allston**	19
Tamarind Bay | **Harv Sq**	23
Tanjore | **Harv Sq**	22
Tantric | **Theater Dist**	24
Tashi Delek | **Brookline**	-
Tavern in Sq. | **multi.**	15
NEW Top Steak | **Peabody**	-
Van Rensselaer's | **CC**	17
Water St. | **MV**	26
NEW Whiskey Priest | **Seaport Dist**	12
NEW Yak & Yeti | **Somerville**	-

BUSINESS DINING

NEW Aka Bistro | **Lincoln**	25
Z NEW Alma Nove | **Hingham**	22
Z Aquitaine | **multi.**	23
Z Asana | **Back Bay**	22
Avenue One | **D'town Cross**	19
Bambara | **E Cambridge**	21
Beacon Hill | **Beacon Hill**	23
Bina Osteria | **D'town Cross**	18
Bistro du Midi | **Back Bay**	23
Blu | **Theater Dist**	21
Z Blue Ginger | **Wellesley**	27
Bokx | **Newton Lower Falls**	21
Z Bond | **Financial Dist**	22
H Bristol Lounge | **Back Bay**	26
Café Fleuri | **Financial Dist**	24
Caliterra | **Financial Dist**	15
Z Capital Grille | **multi.**	26
NEW Ceia Kitchen/Bar | **Newburyport**	-
City Table | **Back Bay**	22
Z Clio | **Back Bay**	27
Courtyard/Boston Library | **Back Bay**	18
Cygnet | **Beverly**	23
Z Davio's | **Foxboro**	25
Z Eastern Stand. | **Kenmore Sq**	23
88 Wharf | **Milton**	19
Fleming's Prime | **Park Sq**	25
Good Life | **D'town Cross**	16
Green Papaya | **Waltham**	22
Z Grill 23 | **Back Bay**	27
Z Hamersley's | **S End**	28
Z Harvest | **Harv Sq**	25
Henrietta's | **Harv Sq**	23

☑ Il Capriccio | **Waltham**	27
NEW Island Creek | **Kenmore Sq**	–
NEW Jacky's | **Brighton**	23
Jer-Ne | **Theater Dist**	19
Joe's American | **Back Bay**	17
KO Prime | **D'town Cross**	25
☑ Legal Sea | **multi.**	22
☑ L'Espalier | **Back Bay**	27
☑ Locke-Ober | **D'town Cross**	25
Lucca | **Back Bay**	23
Mantra | **D'town Cross**	21
Market | **Theater Dist**	26
McCormick/Schmick | **multi.**	21
☑**NEW** Menton | **Seaport Dist**	28
☑ Meritage | **Waterfront**	26
Met Back/B&G | **Back Bay**	19
Metropolitan | **Chestnut Hill**	20
☑ Mistral | **S End**	28
Mooo... | **Beacon Hill**	26
☑ Morton's | **multi.**	25
☑ No. 9 Park | **Beacon Hill**	27
North 26 | **Faneuil Hall**	25
☑ Oak Room | **Back Bay**	24
Oceanaire | **Financial Dist**	24
Olivadi | **Norwood**	20
Pairings | **Park Sq**	21
Palm | **Back Bay**	24
Papa Razzi | **multi.**	19
☑ Petit Robert | **D'town Cross**	23
NEW Port 305 | **N Quincy**	–
Post 390 | **Back Bay**	20
☑ Radius | **Financial Dist**	26
☑ Rialto | **Harv Sq**	26
Rowes Wharf | **Waterfront**	23
☑ Ruth's Chris | **D'town Cross**	26
Sandrine's | **Harv Sq**	24
☑ Sel de la Terre | **multi.**	23
Sidney's | **Central Sq**	21
606 Congress | **Seaport Dist**	20
Smith/Wollensky | **Back Bay**	22
Stephanie's | **S End**	20
Strega Rist./Water | **Seaport Dist**	23
Suffolk Grille | **Canton**	–
Summer Winter | **Burlington**	25
Tavolino | **Foxboro**	20
NEW Towne | **Back Bay**	21
Turner Fish | **Back Bay**	20
Turner's Seafood | **Melrose**	23
Upstairs/Square | **Harv Sq**	24
Woodward | **Financial Dist**	21

BYO

☑ Art Cliff | **MV**	26
Beach Plum | **MV**	22
Bite | **MV**	26
Black-Eyed Susan's | **Nan**	25
Café Mangal | **Wellesley**	26
Captain's Table | **Wellesley**	24
Centre St. Bistro | **Nan**	26
Chilmark Tavern | **MV**	24
Clam Box | **Ipswich**	24
Friendly Fisherman | **CC**	22
Home Port | **MV**	21
Lambert's Cove | **MV**	23
☑ Larsen's Fish | **MV**	28
Liam's | **CC**	20
Mac's | **CC**	25
Moby Dick's | **CC**	24
Net Result | **MV**	24
NEW Sake Japanese | **Braintree**	–
Sconset Café | **Nan**	25
State Road | **MV**	25
Super Fusion | **Brookline**	26
Sushi by Yoshi | **Nan**	23
Sweet Basil | **Needham**	26
Yama | **Wellesley**	23

CELEBRITY CHEFS

Jody Adams	
☑ Rialto | **Harv Sq**	26
Jamie Bissonnette/Ken Oringer	
☑ Coppa | **S End**	26
Jason Bond	
NEW Bondir | **Central Sq**	–
Eric Brennan	
Post 390 | **Back Bay**	20
Joanne Chang	
☑ Flour Bakery | **Central Sq**	27
Myers + Chang | **S End**	24
Dante de Magistris	
Dante | **E Cambridge**	24
Il Casale | **Belmont**	24
Todd English	
Figs | **multi.**	24
Figs at 29 Fair | **Nan**	26
KingFish Hall | **Faneuil Hall**	22
Clark Frasier/Mark Gaier	
Summer Winter | **Burlington**	25
Bob/David Kinkead	
Sibling Rivalry | **S End**	23

Michael Leviton	
🄩 Lumière | **Newton**	28
Barbara Lynch	
🄩 B&G Oysters | **S End**	26
Butcher Shop | **S End**	25
Drink | **Seaport Dist**	21
🄩 **NEW** Menton | **Seaport Dist**	28
🄩 No. 9 Park | **Beacon Hill**	27
Sportello | **Seaport Dist**	25
Jamie Mammano	
🄩 L'Andana | **Burlington**	27
🄩 Mistral | **S End**	28
🄩 Sorellina | **Back Bay**	27
Tony Maws	
🄩 Craigie on Main | **Central Sq**	27
Frank McClelland	
🄩 L'Espalier | **Back Bay**	27
Ken Oringer	
🄩 Clio | **Back Bay**	27
KO Prime | **D'town Cross**	25
La Verdad | **Fenway**	21
🄩 Toro | **S End**	27
🄩 Uni | **Back Bay**	28
Chris Parsons	
🄩 **NEW** Parsons Table | **Winchester**	27
Michael Schlow	
Alta Strada | **Wellesley**	22
🄩 Radius | **Financial Dist**	26
NEW Tico | **Back Bay**	-
Via Matta | **Park Sq**	25
Lydia Shire	
🄩 Locke-Ober | **D'town Cross**	25
Scampo | **Beacon Hill**	25
Lydia Shire/Jasper White	
NEW Towne | **Back Bay**	21
Ana Sortun	
🄩 Oleana | **Inman Sq**	28
🄩 Sofra Bakery | **Huron Vill**	27
Ming Tsai	
🄩 Blue Ginger | **Wellesley**	27
Jean-Georges Vongerichten	
Market | **Theater Dist**	26
Jasper White	
Jasper White's | **multi.**	21

CHILD-FRIENDLY

(Alternatives to the usual fast-food
places; * children's menu available)

Adrian's* | **CC**	18
Amarin Thailand | **multi.**	21

🄩 Anna's | **multi.**	23
Ardeo* | **CC**	19
Arno's* | **Nan**	20
🄩 Art Cliff | **MV**	26
Artú | **multi.**	22
🄩 Atlantic Fish* | **Back Bay**	24
Baja Betty's* | **Brookline**	23
Bakers' Best | **Newton**	22
Bamboo | **Brighton**	23
Bangkok Bistro | **Brighton**	18
Barking Crab* | **Seaport Dist**	17
Bee-Hive Tavern* | **CC**	19
Bertucci's* | **multi.**	18
B. Good | **multi.**	18
Bison County | **Waltham**	18
Black Dog* | **MV**	19
Blue Fin* | **multi.**	22
🄩 Blue Ribbon BBQ | **multi.**	26
Boca Grande | **multi.**	21
Boloco | **multi.**	19
Border Cafe* | **Saugus**	20
Bottega | **Brookline**	23
Brazilian Grill | **CC**	24
Brown Sugar/Similans | **Boston U**	24
Cafe Barada | **Porter Sq**	24
Café Belô | **Somerville**	24
Café Fleuri* | **Financial Dist**	24
Canestaro | **Fenway**	16
Cantina la Mex. | **Somerville**	24
Capt. Frosty's* | **CC**	21
Capt. Kidd* | **CC**	16
Charley's* | **multi.**	18
Chau Chow | **Chinatown**	22
Cheers* | **multi.**	14
Chef Chow's | **Brookline**	20
China Pearl | **Chinatown**	21
Clam Box | **Ipswich**	24
Coolidge Corner* | **Brookline**	17
Cottage* | **Wellesley Hills**	19
Courthouse | **E Cambridge**	24
Demos* | **multi.**	17
Dolphin Seafood* | **multi.**	19
Donatello | **Saugus**	22
🄩 Durgin-Park* | **Faneuil Hall**	20
Fifty-Six Union | **Nan**	23
Fire & Ice | **multi.**	15
Firefly's* | **multi.**	19
🄩 Flour Bakery | **S End**	27
Fog Island* | **Nan**	23
Frank's Steak* | **Porter Sq**	18

Full Moon* | **Huron Vill**	19
Galleria Umberto | **N End**	26
Golden Temple | **Brookline**	20
Grasshopper | **Allston**	22
Greg's | **Watertown**	18
Halfway Cafe* | **multi.**	17
Hilltop Steak* | **Saugus**	16
Hi-Rise | **Harv Sq**	24
Home Port* | **MV**	21
Il Panino | **N End**	22
Island Hopper | **Back Bay**	18
Jae's* | **S End**	22
Jasper White's* | **multi.**	21
Jetties* | **Nan**	17
Joe's American* | **multi.**	17
Johnny's Lunch.* | **Newton**	19
JP Seafood | **Jamaica Plain**	22
Karoo Kafe | **CC**	22
Kowloon* | **Saugus**	15
La Cantina* | **Framingham**	20
La Fam. Giorgio* | **N End**	22
☑ Legal Sea* | **multi.**	22
Le's* | **multi.**	21
Lobster Pot* | **CC**	22
☑ Longfellow's* | **Sudbury**	19
Lure Grill* | **MV**	22
Midwest | **Inman Sq**	21
Mike's | **S End**	20
Moby Dick's* | **CC**	24
Mr. Bartley's* | **Harv Sq**	24
Naked Fish* | **Waltham**	20
Nantucket Lobster* | **Nan**	22
☑ Neighborhood* | **Somerville**	26
New Jang Su | **Burlington**	-
No Name* | **Seaport Dist**	19
☑ Not Average Joe's* | **multi.**	19
Offshore Ale* | **MV**	20
Optimist Café* | **CC**	-
Out of the Blue | **Somerville**	24
Paddock* | **CC**	22
Panificio | **Beacon Hill**	21
Papa Razzi* | **multi.**	19
Paris Creperie | **Brookline**	21
Peach Farm | **Chinatown**	25
Peking Cuisine | **Newton**	-
Penang | **Chinatown**	21
P.F. Chang's* | **Theater Dist**	19
Pho Hoa | **multi.**	24
Pho Pasteur | **Chinatown**	24
Picante | **Central Sq**	22

Picco | **S End**	24
Pit Stop BBQ | **Mattapan**	-
Pizzeria Regina | **multi.**	24
Polcari's* | **multi.**	19
Punjab | **Arlington**	24
Purple Cactus* | **Jamaica Plain**	19
Redbones* | **Somerville**	24
Rubin's* | **Brookline**	19
S&S | **Inman Sq**	19
Scargo Café* | **CC**	21
Sconset Café | **Nan**	25
Sea Grille* | **Nan**	23
Shea's Riverside* | **Essex**	19
Sichuan Gdn. | **multi.**	23
Siena* | **CC**	22
Skipjack's* | **multi.**	20
Sky* | **Norwood**	16
Sorella's* | **Jamaica Plain**	24
Sorelle | **Charlestown**	23
Stars on Hingham | **Hingham**	18
Stir Crazy* | **CC**	20
Sunset Cafe* | **Inman Sq**	24
Tacos El Charro | **Jamaica Plain**	25
Tacos Lupita | **multi.**	25
Taqueria Mexico* | **Waltham**	24
Trident | **Back Bay**	20
☑ Union Oyster* | **Faneuil Hall**	21
Veggie Planet | **Harv Sq**	22
Via Lago* | **Lexington**	22
Victoria's* | **Roxbury**	19
Village Smokehse.* | **Brookline**	21
Woodman's* | **Essex**	23
Za | **Arlington**	24
Zaftigs* | **Brookline**	21

DELIVERY

Bamboo | **Brighton**	23
Bangkok Bistro | **Brighton**	18
Bangkok City | **Back Bay**	23
Bertucci's | **multi.**	18
Bluestone Bistro | **Brighton**	18
Brown Sugar/Similans | **Boston U**	24
Canestaro | **Fenway**	16
Chef Chow's | **Brookline**	20
Chilli Duck | **Back Bay**	21
Golden Temple | **Brookline**	20
9 Tastes | **Harv Sq**	21
Redbones | **Somerville**	24
Sichuan Gdn. | **Woburn**	23
Spice Thai | **Harv Sq**	19

Super Fusion | **Brookline**	26
Trident | **Back Bay**	20
Upper Crust | **multi.**	21
Zen | **Beacon Hill**	23

ENTERTAINMENT

(Call for days and times of performances)

Amari | guitarist | **CC**	22
Barley Neck Inn | live music | **CC**	20
☑ Belfry Inne | live music | **CC**	27
Bravo | jazz/piano | **MFA**	20
Bullfinchs | jazz | **Sudbury**	21
Burren | live music | **Somerville**	17
Byblos | belly dancing | **Norwood**	24
Café Brazil | guitar/karaoke | **Allston**	22
Café Fleuri | DJ/jazz | **Financial Dist**	24
Café St. Petersburg | piano | **Newton**	21
Chart Room | piano | **CC**	18
Church | bands | **Fenway**	20
Club Car | piano | **Nan**	24
Company/Cauldron | classical harpist | **Nan**	27
Dog Bar | live music | **Gloucester**	–
El Sarape | guitarist | **Braintree**	26
Fireplace | jazz/Latin | **Brookline**	21
Glenn's | blues/jazz | **Newburyport**	–
Good Life | bands/DJ | **D'town Cross**	16
Green Briar | bands/DJ | **Brighton**	–
Jacob Wirth | singalongs | **Theater Dist**	18
Jetties | live music | **Nan**	17
Johnny D's | live music/trivia | **Somerville**	20
Karoun | belly dancing | **Newton**	20
Kowloon | varies | **Saugus**	15
La Casa/Pedro | live music | **Watertown**	21
Les Zygomates | varies | **Leather Dist**	22
Lucky's | live music | **Seaport Dist**	19
Middle East | bands | **Central Sq**	19
Offshore Ale | Irish/jazz | **MV**	20
Orleans | band | **Somerville**	17
Red Fez | dancing/Mideastern music | **S End**	18
Redline | jazz | **Harv Sq**	16
Roadhouse | jazz/piano | **CC**	22

Skellig | live music | **Waltham**	17
Sunset Cafe | Brazilian/ Portuguese folk | **Inman Sq**	24
Tangierino | belly dancing | **Charlestown**	22
Tavern in Sq. | DJ | **Central Sq**	15
☑ Top of Hub | jazz | **Back Bay**	20
Tryst | jazz | **Arlington**	24
28 Degrees | DJs | **S End**	19
Veggie Planet | folk | **Harv Sq**	22
Warren | varies | **Charlestown**	19
Zuzu! | bands/DJs | **Central Sq**	19

FIREPLACES

☑ Abe & Louie's | **Back Bay**	26
Academy Ocean | **CC**	21
Aegean | **Watertown**	20
Alberto's | **CC**	21
Amari | **CC**	22
Anthony Cummaquid | **CC**	17
Aqua Grille | **CC**	19
☑ Asana | **Back Bay**	22
Atlantica | **Cohasset**	20
Atria | **MV**	26
Back Eddy | **Westport**	23
☑ Barker Tavern | **Scituate**	27
Barking Crab | **Seaport Dist**	17
Barley Neck Inn | **CC**	20
Beacon Hill | **Beacon Hill**	23
Beacon St. Tavern | **Brookline**	19
☑ Beltry Inne | **CC**	27
Big Papi's | **Framingham**	13
Bison County | **Waltham**	10
Bistro/Crowne Pointe | **CC**	23
Black Cow | **Newburyport**	20
Black Dog | **MV**	19
Black Sheep | **Kendall Sq**	21
Bon Caldo | **Norwood**	20
NEW Bondir | **Central Sq**	–
☑ Bristol Lounge | **Back Bay**	26
Brotherhood/Thieves | **Nan**	21
Buca's Tuscan | **CC**	23
Cafe Escadrille | **Burlington**	21
☑ Cape Sea | **CC**	27
Capt. Kidd | **CC**	16
Capt. Linnell | **CC**	24
Chanticleer | **Nan**	25
Chapoquoit Grill | **CC**	21
Chiara | **Westwood**	24
Chillingsworth | **CC**	26
Christopher's | **Porter Sq**	21

Ciro & Sal's	**CC**	17
NEW Citizen Public	**Fenway**	-
Coach Grill	**Wayland**	24
Coonamessett	**CC**	21
Cottage	**Wellesley Hills**	19
NEW Dalla Cucina	**CC**	20
Dalya's	**Bedford**	21
Dan'l Webster	**CC**	21
DeMarco	**Nan**	23
NEW Deuxave	**Back Bay**	-
Dillon's	**Back Bay**	16
Dog Bar	**Gloucester**	-
Dolphin	**CC**	22
Dolphin Seafood	**Natick**	19
Donatello	**Saugus**	22
Dunbar Tea	**CC**	21
Enzo	**CC**	21
Euno	**N End**	22
Exchange St. Bistro	**Malden**	21
Farm Bar	**Essex**	-
Fazio's	**CC**	21
Figs at 29 Fair	**Nan**	26
Finz	**Salem**	21
Fireplace	**Brookline**	21
Z Gibbet Hill	**Groton**	25
Gina's	**CC**	21
Glory	**Andover**	21
Z Grill 23	**Back Bay**	27
Z Harvest	**Harv Sq**	25
Helmand	**E Cambridge**	25
Hilltop Steak	**Saugus**	16
Hungry I	**Beacon Hill**	22
Il Tesoro/Terrace	**MV**	19
Incontro	**Franklin**	21
James's Gate	**Jamaica Plain**	18
Joe's American	**multi.**	17
Joshua Tree	**Allston**	15
J's/Nashoba	**Bolton**	24
Z La Campania	**Waltham**	28
La Fam. Giorgio	**N End**	22
L'Alouette	**CC**	26
Lambert's Cove	**MV**	23
Z L'Andana	**Burlington**	27
Landing	**Manchester/Sea**	18
Lansdowne	**Fenway**	16
Lattanzi's	**MV**	21
Z Longfellow's	**Sudbury**	19
L'Osteria	**N End**	24
Lure Grill	**MV**	22
Lyceum	**Salem**	23
Maddie's Sail	**Marblehead**	14
Marshside	**CC**	19
Met Back/B&G	**multi.**	19
Metropolitan	**Chestnut Hill**	20
Mews	**CC**	26
Mezza Luna	**CC**	22
Miel	**Waterfront**	22
Z Mistral	**S End**	28
M.J. O'Connor's	**multi.**	17
Nauset Beach	**CC**	23
Newes/America	**MV**	20
Ocean House	**CC**	27
Offshore Ale	**MV**	20
Z Oleana	**Inman Sq**	28
Olé/Olecito	**Inman Sq**	24
Z Òran Mór	**Nan**	28
Orleans Inn	**CC**	16
Orta	**Hanover**	19
Osushi	**Back Bay**	21
Z Outermost Inn	**MV**	23
Palmers	**Andover**	22
Porcini's	**Watertown**	20
Post 390	**Back Bay**	20
Red House	**Harv Sq**	21
Red Inn	**CC**	26
Red Pheasant	**CC**	27
Rist. Fiore	**N End**	21
Riva	**Scituate**	26
Roadhouse	**CC**	22
Ross' Grill	**CC**	24
Scampo	**Beacon Hill**	25
Scargo Café	**CC**	21
Scarlet Oak	**Hingham**	21
Shea's Riverside	**Essex**	19
Sherborn Inn	**Sherborn**	19
Ships Inn	**Nan**	27
Sky	**Norwood**	16
Smith/Wollensky	**Back Bay**	22
Sofia	**W Roxbury**	21
South/Buttery	**S End**	22
State Road	**MV**	25
Stephanie's	**Back Bay**	20
Stockyard	**Brighton**	18
Suffolk Grille	**Canton**	-
Summer House	**Nan**	25
Taberna/Haro	**Brookline**	25
Topper's	**Nan**	27
Townsend's	**Hyde Park**	21
28 Atlantic	**CC**	27
Upstairs/Square	**Harv Sq**	24

Warren | **Charlestown**	19
West/Centre | **W Roxbury**	19
Wicked Oyster | **CC**	23
Wild Goose | **CC**	21
NEW W Lounge | **Theater Dist**	19
Woodward | **Financial Dist**	21

HISTORIC PLACES

(Year opened; * building)

1700 | 28 Atlantic* | **CC**	27
1700 | Wicked Oyster* | **CC**	23
1707 | Longfellow's* | **Sudbury**	19
1709 | Figs at 29 Fair* | **Nan**	26
1720 | Chart House* | **Waterfront**	20
1740 | Dunbar Tea* | **CC**	21
1742 | Union Oyster* | **Faneuil Hall**	21
1745 | Newes/America* | **MV**	20
1750 | Landing* | **Manchester/Sea**	18
1750 | Scarlet Oak* | **Hingham**	21
1778 | Chillingsworth* | **CC**	26
1780 | Warren* | **Charlestown**	19
1786 | Red Pheasant* | **CC**	27
1790 | Lambert's Cove* | **MV**	23
1790 | Regatta/Cotuit* | **CC**	26
1796 | Coonamessett* | **CC**	21
1800 | Bistro/Crowne Pointe* | **CC**	23
1800 | DeMarco* | **Nan**	23
1800 | Durgin-Park* | **Faneuil Hall**	20
1800 | Mantra* | **D'town Cross**	21
1800 | Russell Hse.* | **Harv Sq**	21
1800 | Square Rigger* | **MV**	-
1802 | Red House* | **Harv Sq**	21
1805 | Red Inn* | **CC**	26
1805 | Terra Luna* | **CC**	23
1807 | Sal's Place* | **CC**	18
1825 | Piccolo Nido* | **N End**	26
1827 | Sherborn Inn* | **Sherborn**	19
1830 | Abba* | **CC**	28
1830 | Anthony Cummaquid* | **CC**	17
1831 | Ships Inn* | **Nan**	27
1835 | Capt. Linnell* | **CC**	24
1840 | Brotherhood/Thieves* | **Nan**	21
1840 | Hungry I* | **Beacon Hill**	22
1843 | Lyceum* | **Salem**	23
1848 | Stoddard's* | **D'town Cross**	19
1849 | Optimist Café* | **CC**	-
1850 | Dalya's* | **Bedford**	21
1850 | Dolphin* | **CC**	22

1850 | Le Lyonnais* | **Acton**	23
1856 | Parker's* | **D'town Cross**	24
1857 | Living Room* | **Waterfront**	16
1860 | Franklin* | **S End**	24
1860 | Jimmy Seas* | **MV**	23
1860 | Òran Mór* | **Nan**	28
1860 | Pisces* | **CC**	27
1860 | Sweet Life* | **MV**	25
1861 | Bramble Inn* | **CC**	28
1865 | Scargo Café* | **CC**	21
1865 | Wild Goose* | **CC**	21
1868 | Barley Neck Inn* | **CC**	20
1868 | Jacob Wirth | **Theater Dist**	18
1870 | Enzo* | **CC**	21
1875 | Club Car* | **Nan**	24
1875 | Cygnet* | **Beverly**	23
1875 | Locke-Ober | **D'town Cross**	25
1875 | Orleans Inn* | **CC**	16
1876 | Lobster Pot* | **CC**	22
1882 | Doyle's* | **Jamaica Plain**	17
1882 | L'Étoile* | **MV**	28
1890 | Amrheins | **S Boston**	19
1890 | Atria* | **MV**	26
1890 | Cambridge Brewing* | **Kendall Sq**	16
1890 | Fireplace* | **Brookline**	21
1891 | North St. Grille* | **N End**	24
1891 | Smith/Wollensky* | **Back Bay**	22
1896 | Slip 14* | **Nan**	19
1897 | Cape Sea* | **CC**	27
1899 | Scollay Sq.* | **Beacon Hill**	19
1900 | Capt. Kidd* | **CC**	16
1900 | Chatham Squire* | **CC**	19
1900 | Chez Henri* | **Harv Sq**	24
1900 | Club Cafe* | **S End**	19
1900 | Elephant Walk* | **Waltham**	23
1900 | Front St.* | **CC**	25
1900 | Mr. Bartley's* | **Harv Sq**	24
1900 | Santarpio's* | **E Boston**	25
1900 | Topper's* | **Nan**	27
1903 | Morse Fish | **S End**	19
1903 | Walden Grille* | **Concord**	16
1905 | Davide Rist.* | **N End**	25
1905 | Ocean Terrace* | **CC**	19
1906 | Tivoli's* | **Malden**	-
1906 | Upstairs/Square* | **Harv Sq**	24
1907 | Mother Anna's* | **N End**	23
1909 | Chanticleer* | **Nan**	25
1910 | Tosca* | **Hingham**	26

1912 | Courthouse | **E Cambridge** 24
1912 | Oak Room* | **Back Bay** 24
1914 | Chatham Bars | **CC** 23
1914 | Mr. Crepe* | **Somerville** 21
1914 | Woodman's | **Essex** 23
1915 | Strega Lounge* | **Salem** 19
1917 | No Name | **Seaport Dist** 19
1919 | S&S | **Inman Sq** 19
1920 | Caliterra* | **Financial Dist** 15
1920 | Nauset Beach* | **CC** 23
1920 | Rubin's* | **Brookline** 19
1923 | J's/Nashoba* | **Bolton** 24
1926 | Glass Onion* | **CC** 27
1926 | Pizzeria Regina | **N End** 24
1927 | Charlie's Sandwich | **S End** 22
1927 | Poe's/Rattlesnake* | 21
Back Bay
1928 | Union B&G* | **S End** 24
1930 | Centre St. Bistro* | **Nan** 26
1930 | Giordano's | **MV** 23
1930 | Harvard Gdns. | **Beacon Hill** 17
1931 | Cantina Italiana | **N End** 22
1931 | Home Port | **MV** 21
1933 | Green St.* | **Central Sq** 22
1933 | Greg's | **Watertown** 18
1935 | Clam Box* | **Ipswich** 24
1937 | Mezza Luna | **CC** 22
1937 | Paramount | **Beacon Hill** 22
1937 | Pleasant Cafe | **Roslindale** 21
1938 | Frank's Steak | **Porter Sq** 18
1938 | Gina's | **CC** 21
1940 | Even Keel* | **Nan** 19
1941 | Rosebud* | **Somerville** 15
1943 | Art Cliff* | **MV** 26
1946 | Harry's | **Westborough** 22
1946 | Landfall | **CC** 18
1946 | Maddie's Sail | **Marblehead** 14
1947 | Café at Taj | **Back Bay** 21
1947 | Deluxe Town* | 22
Watertown
1947 | South St. Diner* | 17
Leather Dist
1948 | Cobie's Clam | **CC** 22
1948 | Joe Tecce's | **N End** 19
1950 | Ciro & Sal's | **CC** 17
1950 | Fazio's* | **CC** 21
1950 | Kowloon | **Saugus** 15
1952 | Beach Plum | **MV** 22
1952 | Liam's | **CC** 20
1953 | La Cantina | **Framingham** 20

1954 | Hong Kong | **Harv Sq** 13
1955 | Casablanca | **Harv Sq** 21
1955 | Charlie's Kitchen | **Harv Sq** 17
1955 | Vin & Eddie's | **Abington** 21
1957 | Baxter's | **CC** 20
1959 | Golden Temple | **Brookline** 20
1960 | Caffe Paradiso | **N End** 19
1960 | China Blossom | –
North Andover
1960 | Marshland | **CC** 20
1961 | Hilltop Steak | **Saugus** 16

HOTEL DINING

Ames Hotel
  Woodward | **Financial Dist** 21
Back Bay Hotel
  Stanhope Grille | **Back Bay** 20
Beach Plum Inn
  Beach Plum | **MV** 22
Beacon Hill Hotel
  Beacon Hill | **Beacon Hill** 23
Belfry Inne
  🆉 Belfry Inne | **CC** 27
Boston Harbor Hotel
  🆉 Meritage | **Waterfront** 26
  Rowes Wharf | **Waterfront** 23
Boston Marriott Burlington
  Summer Winter | **Burlington** 25
Boston Marriott Long Wharf
  Oceana | **Waterfront** 22
Bramble Inn
  🆉 Bramble Inn | **CC** 28
Bulfinch Hotel
  Flat Iron | **W End** –
Charles Hotel
  Henrietta's | **Harv Sq** 23
  Noir | **Harv Sq** 20
  🆉 Rialto | **Harv Sq** 26
Charlotte Inn, The
  Il Tesoro/Terrace | **MV** 19
Chatham Bars Inn
  🆉 Chatham Bars | **CC** 23
Chatham Wayside Inn
  Wild Goose | **CC** 21
Colonnade Hotel
  Brasserie Jo | **Back Bay** 21
Coonamessett Inn
  Coonamessett | **CC** 21
Crowne Pointe Historic Inn
  Bistro/Crowne Pointe | **CC** 23

Dan'l Webster Inn
  Dan'l Webster | **CC**   21

Eliot Hotel
  Ⓩ Clio | **Back Bay**   27
  Ⓩ Uni | **Back Bay**   28

Fairmont Copley Plaza
  Ⓩ Oak Room | **Back Bay**   24

Four Seasons Hotel
  Ⓩ Bristol Lounge | **Back Bay**   26

Harbor View Hotel & Resort
  Water St. | **MV**   26

Hilton Boston Financial District
  Caliterra | **Financial Dist**   15

Hotel Commonwealth
  Ⓩ Eastern Stand. | **Kenmore Sq**   23
  𝗡𝗘𝗪 Island Creek | —
    Kenmore Sq

Hotel Veritas
  𝗡𝗘𝗪 Simple Truth | **Harv Sq**   —

Hyatt Regency Boston
  Avenue One | **D'town Cross**   19

Indigo, Hotel
  Bokx | **Newton Lower Falls**   21

InterContinental Boston
  Miel | **Waterfront**   22
  RumBa | **Waterfront**   19
  Sushi-Teq | **Waterfront**   24

Kelley House
  Newes/America | **MV**   20

Kendall Hotel
  Black Sheep | **Kendall Sq**   21

Lambert's Cove Inn
  Lambert's Cove | **MV**   23

Langham Hotel Boston
  Ⓩ Bond | **Financial Dist**   22
  Café Fleuri | **Financial Dist**   24

Le Languedoc Inn
  Le Languedoc | **Nan**   23

Le Meridien Hotel
  Sidney's | **Central Sq**   21

Lenox, The
  City Bar | **Back Bay**   19
  City Table | **Back Bay**   22

Liberty Hotel
  Ⓩ Alibi | **Beacon Hill**   19
  Clink | **Beacon Hill**   19
  Scampo | **Beacon Hill**   25

Longfellow's Wayside Inn
  Ⓩ Longfellow's | **Sudbury**   19

Mandarin Oriental
  Ⓩ Asana | **Back Bay**   22

Mansion House
  Zephrus | **MV**   19

Marlowe, Hotel
  Bambara | **E Cambridge**   21

Millennium Bostonian
  North 26 | **Faneuil Hall**   25

Nine Zero Hotel
  KO Prime | **D'town Cross**   25

Ocean Edge Resort
  Ocean Terrace | **CC**   19

Omni Parker House
  Parker's | **D'town Cross**   24

Orleans Inn
  Orleans Inn | **CC**   16

Outermost Inn
  Ⓩ Outermost Inn | **MV**   23

Outer Reach Resort
  Adrian's | **CC**   18

Park Plaza Hotel
  Finale | **Park Sq**   21
  McCormick/Schmick | **Park Sq**   21
  Melting Pot | **Park Sq**   19
  M.J. O'Connor's | **Park Sq**   17
  Pairings | **Park Sq**   21

Red Inn
  Red Inn | **CC**   26

Renaissance Boston Waterfront
Hotel
  606 Congress | **Seaport Dist**   20

Ritz-Carlton Boston Common
  Jer-Ne | **Theater Dist**   19

Royal Sonesta Hotel Boston
  Dante | **E Cambridge**   24

Seaport Hotel
  Aura | **Seaport Dist**   22

Sherborn Inn, The
  Sherborn Inn | **Sherborn**   19

Ships Inn
  Ships Inn | **Nan**   27

Summer House
  Summer House | **Nan**   25

Taj Boston
  Café at Taj | **Back Bay**   21

Waterford Inn
  Waterford Café/Tav. | **CC**   —

Wauwinet Inn
  Topper's | **Nan**   27

W Boston
  Market | **Theater Dist** 26
  NEW W Lounge | **Theater Dist** 19
Wequassett Resort & Golf Club
  28 Atlantic | **CC** 27
Westin Boston Waterfront
  Sauciety | **Seaport Dist** —
  City Bar | **Seaport Dist** 19
  M.J. O'Connor's | **Seaport Dist** 17
Westin Copley Pl.
  Bar 10 | **Back Bay** 21
  Osushi | **Back Bay** 21
  Palm | **Back Bay** 24
  Turner Fish | **Back Bay** 20
White Elephant Hotel
  Brant Point | **Nan** 24
Winnetu Oceanside Resort
  Lure Grill | **MV** 22
XV Beacon Hotel
  Mooo... | **Beacon Hill** 26

LATE DINING

(Weekday closing hour)
NEW Abbey, The | 1:30 | **Brookline** —
Abby Park | 12 AM | **Milton** 19
Anchovies | 1 AM | **S End** 19
NEW Anthem | varies | **Faneuil Hall** 19
Apollo Grill | 4 AM | **Chinatown** 19
Assaggio | 12 AM | **N End** 23
Atlantic Fish/Chop | 12:30 AM | **MV** 21
NEW Back Bay Social | 1:30 AM | **Back Bay** 18
BarLola | 1 AM | **Back Bay** 17
NEW Barlow's | 12:30 AM | **Seaport Dist** 16
NEW Barracuda | 1:30 AM | **D'town Cross** —
Bar 10 | 12 AM | **Back Bay** 21
NEW Basho | 1 AM | **Fenway** 23
Billy Tse | 12 AM | **Revere** 21
Bistro Chi | 1 AM | **Quincy** —
Bluestone Bistro | 12:45 AM | **Brighton** 18
Border Cafe | varies | **Harv Sq** 20
Boston Beer | 12 AM | **multi.** 18
Brasserie Jo | 1 AM | **Back Bay** 21
Brownstone | 2 AM | **Back Bay** 15
Bukowski | varies | **multi.** 18
Café Algiers | 12 AM | **Harv Sq** 16

Café Belô | 1 AM | **Framingham** 24
Caffe Paradiso | varies | **N End** 19
Cambridge Common | varies | **Harv Sq** 18
Cambridge 1 | 12 AM | **multi.** 22
NEW Canary Sq. | 1 AM | **Jamaica Plain** —
CBS Scene Rest. & Bar | 12:30 AM | **Foxboro** —
Charley's | varies | **Back Bay** 18
Charlie's Kitchen | varies | **Harv Sq** 17
Chau Chow | 3 AM | **Chinatown** 22
Christopher's | 12 AM | **Porter Sq** 21
NEW Citizen Public | 1 AM | **Fenway** —
City Bar | 2 AM | **multi.** 19
Coolidge Corner | 1:15 AM | **Brookline** 17
Z Coppa | 12:45 AM | **S End** 26
Corner Tavern | 12 AM | **Back Bay** —
Cornwall's | 12 AM | **Kenmore Sq** 16
Deep Ellum | 12 AM | **Allston** 23
Dog Bar | 1 AM | **Gloucester** —
D'Parma Italian Table | 12 AM | **CC** 22
Ducali | 1 AM | **N End** 19
Farm Bar | 1 AM | **Essex** —
Franklin | 1:30 AM | **multi.** 24
Z Fugakyu | 1:30 AM | **Brookline** 24
NEW Garlic 'n Lemons | varies | **Brighton** 24
Gaslight Brasserie | 1:30 AM | **S End** 22
Geoffrey's | 1 AM | **Back Bay** 22
Globe Bar | 12 AM | **Back Bay** 16
Golden Temple | 1 AM | **Brookline** 20
Gourmet Dumpling | 1 AM | **Chinatown** 25
Grand Chinatown | 12 AM | **N Quincy** —
Halfway Cafe | 1 AM | **Dedham** 17
Harry's | 1 AM | **Westborough** 22
Haru | 12 AM | **Back Bay** 20
Harvard Gdns. | 1 AM | **Beacon Hill** 17
NEW Haven | 12 AM | **Jamaica Plain** 23
Hong Kong | varies | **Harv Sq** 13
House of Blues | 12 AM | **Fenway** 15
NEW Island Creek | varies | **Kenmore Sq** —
Jillian's | 1:30 AM | **Fenway** 16

Menus, photos, voting and more – free at ZAGAT.com

Joe's American | 12 AM | **multi.** [17]
Jumbo | 1 AM | **Chinatown** [22]
Kama | 1 AM | **Quincy** [-]
Kaya House | varies | **Porter Sq** [-]
Kayuga | 1:30 AM | **Brookline** [18]
Kaze | 12 AM | **Chinatown** [24]
Kings | 12 AM, 2 AM | **multi.** [19]
Kowloon | 1 AM | **Saugus** [15]
Lansdowne | 1 AM | **Fenway** [16]
La Verdad | varies | **Fenway** [21]
Living Room | 12 AM | **Waterfront** [16]
NEW Lolita Cocina | 1 AM | [-]
   Back Bay
Lord Hobo | 1 AM | **Inman Sq** [16]
Lower Depths | 12:30 AM | [17]
   Kenmore Sq
Middle East | 12 AM | **Central Sq** [19]
Miracle of Science | 12 AM | [19]
   Central Sq
Mission B&G | 12 AM | **MFA** [18]
Z NEW Noche | varies | **S End** [22]
Z Oishii | 12 AM | **S End** [27]
Other Side | 12 AM | **Back Bay** [20]
Parish Cafe | varies | **multi.** [23]
Peach Farm | 3 AM | **Chinatown** [25]
Pinocchio's | varies | **Harv Sq** [23]
Pizzeria Regina | 1 AM | **Allston** [24]
Poe's/Rattlesnake | 12 AM | [21]
   Back Bay
Punjabi Dhaba | 12 AM | **Inman Sq** [24]
Red Fez | 12 AM | **S End** [18]
Rist. Damiano | 12 AM | **N End** [26]
RumBa | 1 AM | **Waterfront** [19]
NEW Russell Hse. | varies | [21]
   Harv Sq
Salvatore's | 12 AM | **Seaport Dist** [21]
Santarpio's | 12 AM | **E Boston** [25]
Sharky's | 12:30 AM | **MV** [16]
South St. Diner | varies | [17]
   Leather Dist
Splash Ultra | 2 AM | **Leather Dist** [17]
Suishaya | 2 AM | **Chinatown** [19]
Sunset Grill/Cantina | 1 AM | [19]
   multi.
Taiwan Cafe | 1 AM | **Chinatown** [24]
Tangierino | 12 AM | **Charlestown** [22]
NEW Tasty Burger | 2 AM | [-]
   Fenway
Temple Bar | 12 AM | **Porter Sq** [21]
NEW Think Tank | 12:30 AM | [-]
   Kendall Sq
Z Top of Hub | 1 AM | **Back Bay** [20]

Townsend's | 12 AM | **Hyde Park** [21]
Trident | 12 AM | **Back Bay** [20]
Trina's | 12 AM | **Inman Sq** [20]
UBurger | 12 AM | **Boston U** [22]
Vlora | 1 AM | **Back Bay** [20]
NEW W Lounge | 12 AM | [19]
   Theater Dist
Woodward | 1 AM | **Financial Dist** [21]
NEW Yard House | 12 AM | [19]
   Dedham

MEET FOR A DRINK

NEW Abbey, The | **Brookline** [-]
Z Abe & Louie's | **Back Bay** [26]
Alchemy | **MV** [23]
Z Alibi | **Beacon Hill** [19]
Z NEW Alma Nove | **Hingham** [22]
NEW Amer. Craft | **Brookline** [17]
NEW Anthem | **Faneuil Hall** [19]
Aqua Grille | **CC** [19]
Z Aquitaine | **Dedham** [23]
Z Asana | **Back Bay** [22]
Atlantic Fish/Chop | **MV** [21]
Audubon Circle | **Kenmore Sq** [21]
NEW Back Bay Social | **Back Bay** [18]
Bambara | **E Cambridge** [21]
Bar 10 | **Back Bay** [21]
NEW Basho | **Fenway** [23]
Baxter's | **CC** [20]
Beacon St. Tavern | **Brookline** [19]
Beehive | **S End** [20]
Bella Luna/Milky Way | [19]
   Jamaica Plain
NEW Benevento's | **N End** [21]
Big Papi's | **Framingham** [13]
Bina Osteria | **D'town Cross** [18]
Bin 26 | **Beacon Hill** [21]
Bistro du Midi | **Back Bay** [23]
NEW Black Cat Tavern | **CC** [20]
Black Cow | **multi.** [20]
Blue22 | **Quincy** [14]
Boarding House | **Nan** [25]
Bokx | **Newton Lower Falls** [21]
Z Bond | **Financial Dist** [22]
Bricco | **N End** [25]
Z Bristol Lounge | **Back Bay** [26]
NEW Budda C | **Brookline** [20]
Burren | **Somerville** [17]
Butcher Shop | **S End** [25]
Cactus Club | **Back Bay** [17]
Cafe 47 | **Back Bay** [19]

Cambridge 1 | **multi.**	22
NEW Canary Sq. | **Jamaica Plain**	–
Casablanca | **Harv Sq**	21
NEW Ceia Kitchen/Bar | **Newburyport**	–
Chez Henri | **Harv Sq**	24
Church | **Fenway**	20
NEW Citizen Public | **Fenway**	–
City Bar | **multi.**	19
Clink | **Beacon Hill**	19
Club Cafe | **S End**	19
Club Car | **Nan**	24
Colombo's | **CC**	–
Corazon del Mar | **Nan**	25
Corner Tavern | **Back Bay**	–
Cottage | **Wellesley Hills**	19
C. Tsar's | **Newton**	–
Daedalus | **Harv Sq**	18
Dante | **E Cambridge**	24
NEW Darryl's | **S End**	–
Z Davio's | **multi.**	25
Dbar | **Dorchester**	23
Delux Cafe | **S End**	20
NEW Deuxave | **Back Bay**	–
Dillon's | **Back Bay**	16
District | **Leather Dist**	–
Dog Bar | **Gloucester**	–
Doyle's | **Jamaica Plain**	17
Drink | **Seaport Dist**	21
Druid | **Inman Sq**	24
Z Eastern Stand. | **Kenmore Sq**	23
Z Ecco | **E Boston**	27
88 Wharf | **Milton**	19
Erbaluce | **Park Sq**	26
Estragon | **S End**	23
Firefly's | **Quincy**	19
NEW 5 Corners | **Marblehead**	26
Flash's | **Park Sq**	19
NEW Foundry/Elm | **Somerville**	–
NEW Four Green Fields | **Financial Dist**	–
Franklin | **multi.**	24
NEW Gallows | **S End**	20
Gaslight Brasserie | **S End**	22
Z Glass Onion | **CC**	27
Glenn's | **Newburyport**	–
Good Life | **D'town Cross**	16
Grafton St. Pub | **Harv Sq**	19
Z Grill 23 | **Back Bay**	27
Harvard Gdns. | **Beacon Hill**	17

NEW Haven | **Jamaica Plain**	23
Highland Kitchen | **Somerville**	25
Hillstone | **Faneuil Hall**	25
House of Blues | **Fenway**	15
Z Hungry Mother | **Kendall Sq**	26
Il Casale | **Belmont**	24
Independent | **Somerville**	20
NEW Island Creek | **Kenmore Sq**	–
NEW Jacky's | **Brighton**	23
James's Gate | **Jamaica Plain**	18
Jasper White's | **Hingham**	21
NEW Jerry Remy's | **Fenway**	18
Joe's American | **Back Bay**	17
John Harvard's | **multi.**	16
Joshua Tree | **multi.**	15
Kama | **Quincy**	–
Kings | **Back Bay**	19
Kingston | **D'town Cross**	20
Lansdowne | **Fenway**	16
Lavender Asian | **Sudbury**	23
La Voile | **Back Bay**	24
Ledge | **Dorchester**	15
NEW Legal C Bar | **Dedham**	22
Les Zygomates | **Leather Dist**	22
Littlest | **Financial Dist**	18
Living Room | **Waterfront**	16
Local | **W Newton**	19
Lo La 41° | **Nan**	25
NEW Lolita Cocina | **Back Bay**	–
Lord Hobo | **Inman Sq**	16
LTK | **Seaport Dist**	21
Lucky's | **Seaport Dist**	19
Mantra | **D'town Cross**	21
Market | **Theater Dist**	26
Marliave | **D'town Cross**	18
Masa | **multi.**	21
Matt Murphy's | **Brookline**	22
Max/Dylan | **multi.**	19
McCormick/Schmick | **multi.**	21
Met Back/B&G | **multi.**	19
Metropolitan | **Chestnut Hill**	20
NEW Millie's | **Nan**	19
Miracle of Science | **Central Sq**	19
Mission B&G | **MFA**	18
Z Mistral | **S End**	28
M.J. O'Connor's | **multi.**	17
Z Morton's | **Seaport Dist**	25
Nebo | **N End**	20
Z NEW Noche | **S End**	22
Noir | **Harv Sq**	20

☑ No. 9 Park | **Beacon Hill**	27
Oceanaire | **Financial Dist**	24
Olivadi | **Norwood**	20
Om | **Harv Sq**	16
Orleans | **Somerville**	17
Orta | **Hanover**	19
Pairings | **Park Sq**	21
NEW Papagayo | **Seaport Dist**	-
Parish Cafe | **Back Bay**	23
Pazzo | **Back Bay**	21
☑ Petit Robert | **D'town Cross**	23
Poe's/Rattlesnake | **Back Bay**	21
NEW Port 305 | **N Quincy**	-
NEW Posto | **Somerville**	25
Post 390 | **Back Bay**	20
Publick House | **Brookline**	20
Red Fez | **S End**	18
Redline | **Harv Sq**	16
NEW Regal Beagle | **Brookline**	21
River Gods | **Central Sq**	22
Roobar | **CC**	19
Ross' Grill | **CC**	24
Rowes Wharf | **Waterfront**	23
RumBa | **Waterfront**	19
NEW Russell Hse. | **Harv Sq**	21
☑ Ruth's Chris | **D'town Cross**	26
NEW Sam's | **Seaport Dist**	20
Scampo | **Beacon Hill**	25
Scollay Sq. | **Beacon Hill**	19
☑ Sel de la Terre | **multi.**	23
Silvertone B&G | **D'town Cross**	21
606 Congress | **Seaport Dist**	20
Skellig | **Waltham**	17
Sofla | **W Roxbury**	21
Solea | **Waltham**	22
Sonsie | **Back Bay**	20
☑ Sorellina | **Back Bay**	27
Splash Ultra | **Leather Dist**	17
NEW Stats B&G | **S Boston**	21
Stella | **S End**	24
Stephanie's | **multi.**	20
NEW Stoddard's | **D'town Cross**	19
Straight Wharf | **Nan**	27
Strega Rist./Water | **Seaport Dist**	23
Suffolk Grille | **Canton**	-
Sunset Grill/Cantina | **Boston U**	19
Sushi-Teq | **Waterfront**	24
Tastings Wine/Bistro | **Foxboro**	21
NEW Tasty Burger | **Fenway**	-
Tavern in Sq. | **multi.**	15
Tavern/Water | **Charlestown**	12
Tavolino | **Foxboro**	20
Tavolo | **Dorchester**	24
NEW Telegraph Hill | **S Boston**	-
Temple Bar | **Porter Sq**	21
NEW Tico | **Back Bay**	-
☑ Top of Hub | **Back Bay**	20
NEW Top Steak | **Peabody**	-
Tory Row | **Harv Sq**	17
Town | **Nan**	24
NEW Towne | **Back Bay**	21
Townsend's | **Hyde Park**	21
Trina's | **Inman Sq**	20
☑ Troquet | **Theater Dist**	26
NEW Turbine | **Lynn**	-
Turner's Seafood | **Melrose**	23
28 Degrees | **S End**	19
21st Amendment | **Beacon Hill**	17
Typhoon | **Hingham**	18
Union B&G | **S End**	24
NEW Vapiano | **Theater Dist**	18
Via Matta | **Park Sq**	25
Vlora | **Back Bay**	20
Washington Sq. | **Brookline**	22
Water St. | **MV**	26
West End Johnnie's | **W End**	18
West/Centre | **W Roxbury**	19
West Side | **Porter Sq**	21
NEW Whiskey Priest | **Seaport Dist**	12
Wild Goose | **CC**	21
NEW W Lounge | **Theater Dist**	19
Woodward | **Financial Dist**	21
NEW Yard House | **Dedham**	19

NEWCOMERS

Abbey, The | **Brookline**	-
Aka Bistro | **Lincoln**	25
☑ Alma Nove | **Hingham**	22
Amer. Craft | **Brookline**	17
Anthem | **Faneuil Hall**	19
Back Bay Social | **Back Bay**	18
Barlow's | **Seaport Dist**	16
Barracuda | **D'town Cross**	-
Basho | **Fenway**	23
Benevento's | **N End**	21
☑ Bergamot | **Somerville**	27
Black Cat Tavern | **CC**	20
Bondir | **Central Sq**	-
Bosphorus | **Inman Sq**	-

Brother's Crawfish | **Dorchester**	‑⏌
Budda C | **Brookline**	20
Canary Sq. | **Jamaica Plain**	‑⏌
Ceia Kitchen/Bar | **Newburyport**	‑⏌
Center Café | **Needham**	20
Citizen Public | **Fenway**	‑⏌
Clover Food Lab | **Harv Sq**	‑⏌
Cognac Bistro | **Brookline**	‑⏌
Comella's | **multi.**	‑⏌
C. Tsar's | **Newton**	‑⏌
Cutty's | **Brookline**	25
Dalla Cucina | **CC**	20
Darryl's | **S End**	‑⏌
Deuxave | **Back Bay**	‑⏌
East by NE | **Inman Sq**	22
5 Corners | **Marblehead**	26
Five Guys | **multi.**	20
Foundry/Elm | **Somerville**	‑⏌
Four Green Fields | **Financial Dist**	‑⏌
Gallows | **S End**	20
Garlic 'n Lemons | **Brighton**	24
Haven | **Jamaica Plain**	23
Island Creek | **Kenmore Sq**	‑⏌
Istanbul'lu | **Somerville**	23
Jacky's | **Brighton**	23
Jerry Remy's | **multi.**	18
Journeyman | **Somerville**	‑⏌
Legal C Bar | **Dedham**	22
Lolita Cocina | **Back Bay**	‑⏌
☒ Menton | **Seaport Dist**	28
Millie's | **Nan**	19
Mumbai Chop | **Back Bay**	19
☒ Noche | **S End**	22
Papagayo | **Seaport Dist**	‑⏌
☒ Parsons Table | **Winchester**	27
☒ PB Boulangerie | **CC**	28
Port 305 | **N Quincy**	‑⏌
Posto | **Somerville**	25
Q Restaurant | **Chinatown**	‑⏌
Regal Beagle | **Brookline**	21
Russell Hse. | **Harv Sq**	21
Sake Japanese | **Braintree**	‑⏌
Sam's | **Seaport Dist**	20
Santarpio's | **Peabody**	25
Simple Truth | **Harv Sq**	‑⏌
Stats B&G | **S Boston**	21
Stoddard's | **D'town Cross**	19
Tasty Burger | **Fenway**	‑⏌
Tavern in Sq. | **Allston**	15
Telegraph Hill | **S Boston**	‑⏌

Think Tank | **Kendall Sq**	‑⏌
Tico | **Back Bay**	‑⏌
Top Steak | **Peabody**	‑⏌
Towne | **Back Bay**	21
Turbine | **Lynn**	‑⏌
Vapiano | **Theater Dist**	18
Whiskey Priest | **Seaport Dist**	12
W Lounge | **Theater Dist**	19
Yak & Yeti | **Somerville**	‑⏌
Yard House | **Dedham**	19

OFFBEAT

☒ Alibi | **Beacon Hill**	19
All Star | **Inman Sq**	23
Baraka Cafe | **Central Sq**	25
Barking Crab | **Seaport Dist**	17
Betty's Wok | **MFA**	17
B. Good | **Back Bay**	18
NEW Brother's Crawfish | **Dorchester**	‑⏌
Bukowski | **multi.**	18
Butcher Shop | **S End**	25
Café Polonia | **S Boston**	24
Centre St. Café | **Jamaica Plain**	25
☒ Cuchi Cuchi | **Central Sq**	23
NEW Cutty's | **Brookline**	25
Dalí | **Somerville**	25
Dbar | **Dorchester**	23
Friendly Toast | **Kendall Sq**	21
Galleria Umberto | **N End**	26
NEW Gallows | **S End**	20
Green St. | **Central Sq**	22
NEW Haven | **Jamaica Plain**	23
Helmand | **E Cambridge**	25
Karoo Kafe | **CC**	22
Kings | **Back Bay**	19
LTK | **Seaport Dist**	21
Masala Art | **Needham**	24
NEW Mumbai Chop | **Back Bay**	19
Paramount | **Beacon Hill**	22
Pit Stop BBQ | **Mattapan**	‑⏌
Publick House | **Brookline**	20
Punjabi Dhaba | **Inman Sq**	24
Redbones | **Somerville**	24
Santarpio's | **E Boston**	25
Shabu-Zen | **Chinatown**	23
Sidecar Café | **MV**	‑⏌
Strip-T's | **Watertown**	21
Trident | **Back Bay**	20

Vinny's/Night | **Somerville**	24
Wine Cellar | **Back Bay**	22

OUTDOOR DINING

(G=garden; P=patio; S=sidewalk; T=terrace)

☑ Abe & Louie's | S | **Back Bay**	26
Academy Ocean | P | **CC**	21
Adrian's | T | **CC**	18
NEW Aka Bistro | T | **Lincoln**	25
Alberto's | P | **CC**	21
☑ NEW Alma Nove | P | **Hingham**	22
NEW Amer. Craft | S | **Brookline**	17
Ashmont Grill | P | **Dorchester**	23
Atasca | P | **Kendall Sq**	20
Atlantica | P | **Cohasset**	20
☑ Atlantic Fish | S | **Back Bay**	24
Atria | P | **MV**	26
Audubon Circle | P | **Kenmore Sq**	21
NEW Back Bay Social | S | **Back Bay**	18
Back Eddy | P, T | **Westport**	23
☑ B&G Oysters | G | **S End**	26
Bangkok Blue | P | **Back Bay**	20
Barking Crab | T | **Seaport Dist**	17
BarLola | P | **Back Bay**	17
NEW Barlow's | P | **Seaport Dist**	16
NEW Basho | S | **Fenway**	23
Baxter's | T | **CC**	20
Beacon St. Tavern | P | **Brookline**	19
Birch St. Bistro | P | **Roslindale**	20
Bistro du Midi | P | **Back Bay**	23
Black Cow | T | **Newburyport**	20
Blarney Stone | P | **Dorchester**	20
Bluestone Bistro | P | **Brighton**	18
Boarding House | P | **Nan**	25
Bookstore & Rest. | P, T | **CC**	20
Boston Burger | P | **Somerville**	23
Bottega | P | **Back Bay**	23
Brant Point | T | **Nan**	24
Bravo | T | **MFA**	20
Brotherhood/Thieves | P | **Nan**	21
Bubala's | P | **CC**	16
Bullfinchs | P | **Sudbury**	21
Cactus Club | S | **Back Bay**	17
Cafeteria | P | **Back Bay**	18
Caffe Tosca | P | **Hingham**	24
Canestaro | P | **Fenway**	16
Capt. Frosty's | P | **CC**	21
Casa Romero | P | **Back Bay**	22
Chanticleer | G | **Nan**	25

Charley's | G, P | **multi.**	18
Charlie's Kitchen | P | **Harv Sq**	17
Clam Box | T | **Ipswich**	24
Clancy's | T | **CC**	21
Columbus Café | P | **S End**	20
Cooke's | P | **CC**	19
Daily Catch | P | **Seaport Dist**	24
Dante | P | **E Cambridge**	24
Deep Ellum | P | **Allston**	23
Détente | G | **MV**	28
NEW Deuxave | S | **Back Bay**	–
Devlin's | P | **Brighton**	20
Devon's | P | **CC**	25
Dillon's | P | **Back Bay**	16
Dog Bar | P | **Gloucester**	–
Dunbar Tea | P | **CC**	21
Dune | P | **Nan**	22
☑ Eastern Stand. | P | **Kenmore Sq**	23
88 Wharf | P | **Milton**	19
Enzo | P, T | **CC**	21
Even Keel | P | **Nan**	19
☑ EVOO | P | **Kendall Sq**	26
Farm Bar | P | **Essex**	–
Fifty-Six Union | G | **Nan**	23
Finz | T | **Salem**	21
NEW Four Green Fields | P | **Financial Dist**	–
☑ Galley Beach | P | **Nan**	24
Grafton St. Pub | P | **Harv Sq**	19
☑ Grapevine | G | **Salem**	27
Green Briar | P | **Brighton**	–
☑ Hamersley's | P | **S End**	28
☑ Harvest | P | **Harv Sq**	25
Henrietta's | T | **Harv Sq**	23
Hi-Rise | P | **Harv Sq**	24
Hungry I | G | **Beacon Hill**	22
Il Casale | S | **Belmont**	24
Il Tesoro/Terrace | T | **MV**	19
Ironside Grill | P | **Charlestown**	15
James's Gate | P | **Jamaica Plain**	18
J's/Nashoba | P | **Bolton**	24
Karoo Kafe | T | **CC**	22
Kashmir | P | **Back Bay**	24
KingFish Hall | P | **Faneuil Hall**	22
La Casa/Pedro | P | **Watertown**	21
La Cucina/Mare | P | **CC**	24
Landing | P, T | **multi.**	18
Lattanzi's | G, P | **MV**	21
La Voile | P | **Back Bay**	24
Ledge | P | **Dorchester**	15

Le Languedoc | P | **Nan** 23

L'Étoile | P | **MV** 28

Lo La 41° | P | **Nan** 25

Mac's | S | **CC** 25

Marliave | P | **D'town Cross** 18

McCormick/Schmick | P | **Faneuil Hall** 21

Met Back/B&G | S | **Back Bay** 19

Miel | G, P | **Waterfront** 22

Mother Anna's | P | **N End** 23

NEW Mumbai Chop | S | **Back Bay** 19

Z Neighborhood | G | **Somerville** 26

North 26 | P | **Faneuil Hall** 25

Ocean Terrace | T | **CC** 19

Z Oleana | P | **Inman Sq** 28

Orinoco | S | **S End** 23

Orleans Inn | T | **CC** 16

Other Side | P, S | **Back Bay** 20

Pairings | S | **Park Sq** 21

Parish Cafe | P | **Back Bay** 23

Pazzo | P | **Back Bay** 21

Piattini | P | **Back Bay** 24

Poe's/Rattlesnake | S, T | **Back Bay** 21

Porcini's | P | **Watertown** 20

Red Fez | P | **S End** 18

Red House | P | **Harv Sq** 21

Red Rock | G, P | **Swampscott** 20

Rist. Fiore | P, T | **N End** 21

Riva | P | **Scituate** 26

Ropewalk | P | **Nan** 18

Rowes Wharf | T | **Waterfront** 23

NEW Russell Hse. | P | **Harv Sq** 21

Rustic Kitchen | P | **Hingham** 20

Z Ruth's Chris | P | **D'town Cross** 26

Salvatore's | P | **Seaport Dist** 21

NEW Sam's | P | **Seaport Dist** 20

Scampo | P | **Beacon Hill** 25

Scollay Sq. | P | **Beacon Hill** 19

Scoozi | P | **Back Bay** 17

Shea's Riverside | T | **Essex** 19

Sibling Rivalry | P | **S End** 23

Sidecar Café | P, S | **MV** ‒

Siena | P | **CC** 22

Siros | T | **N Quincy** 20

Sol Azteca | P | **multi.** 21

Sophia's | P | **Roslindale** 23

South/Buttery | P | **S End** 22

Stanhope Grille | P | **Back Bay** 20

Stella | P | **S End** 24

Stellina | G | **Watertown** 23

Stephanie's | S | **Back Bay** 20

Straight Wharf | P | **Nan** 27

Summer House | P | **Nan** 25

Sushi-Teq | P | **Waterfront** 24

Sweet Life | G | **MV** 25

Tantric | S | **Theater Dist** 24

Tapéo | S | **Back Bay** 23

Tavern/Water | P | **Charlestown** 12

Temple Bar | P | **Porter Sq** 21

Topper's | T | **Nan** 27

Town | P | **Nan** 24

Tratt. Il Panino | P | **N End** 24

Tremont 647/Sorel | P | **S End** 20

Trevi Café | P | **CC** 25

28 Atlantic | P | **CC** 27

28 Degrees | P | **S End** 19

29 Newbury | P | **Back Bay** 20

224 Boston St. | G | **Dorchester** 21

Typhoon | P | **multi.** 18

Via Matta | P | **Park Sq** 25

Village Sushi | P | **Roslindale** 22

Winslow's Tavern | P | **CC** 21

Wonder Spice | P | **Jamaica Plain** 20

Woodman's | G | **Essex** 23

Woodward | P | **Financial Dist** 21

NEW Yard House | P | **Dedham** 19

Za | P | **Kendall Sq** 24

Zen | P | **Beacon Hill** 23

PARKING

(V=valet, *=validated)

Z Abe & Louie's | V* | **Back Bay** 26

Al Dente* | **N End** 22

Z NEW Alma Nove | V | **Hingham** 22

Amarin Thailand* | **Newton** 21

Antico Forno* | **N End** 23

Z Aquitaine | V | **multi.** 23

Z Asana | V | **Back Bay** 22

Atlantica | V | **Cohasset** 20

Z Atlantic Fish | V | **Back Bay** 24

Aura* | **Seaport Dist** 22

Avenue One | V | **D'town Cross** 19

Avila | V* | **Theater Dist** 23

Bacco* | **N End** 21

NEW Back Bay Social | V | **Back Bay** 18

Bambara | V | **E Cambridge** 21

Z B&G Oysters | V | **S End** 26

NEW Barlow's* | **Seaport Dist** 16

NEW Barracuda | V | D'town Cross	–
Bar 10 | V | **Back Bay**	21
NEW Basho | V | **Fenway**	23
Beehive | V | **S End**	20
Bertucci's | V* | **multi.**	18
Big Papi's | V | **Framingham**	13
Billy Tse | V | **Revere**	21
Bin 26 | V | **Beacon Hill**	21
Bistro du Midi | V | **Back Bay**	23
Blu* | **Theater Dist**	21
Blue Room* | **Kendall Sq**	24
Bokx | V | **Newton Lower Falls**	21
⚫ Bond | V | **Financial Dist**	22
Brasserie Jo | V | **Back Bay**	21
Bravo* | **MFA**	20
Bricco | V* | **N End**	25
⚫ Bristol Lounge | V* | **Back Bay**	26
Butcher Shop | V | **S End**	25
Café Fleuri | V | **Financial Dist**	24
Cafeteria | V | **Back Bay**	18
Caffe Paradiso* | **N End**	19
Caliterra | V | **Financial Dist**	15
Cambridge Brewing* | **Kendall Sq**	16
Cambridge 1* | **Fenway**	22
Cantina Italiana | V* | **N End**	22
⚫ Capital Grille | V | **multi.**	26
Casablanca* | **Harv Sq**	21
Chart House | V | **Waterfront**	20
Chart Room | V | **CC**	18
⚫ Chatham Bars | V | **CC**	23
Chau Chow* | **Chinatown**	22
Cheers* | **Faneuil Hall**	14
⚫ Cheesecake Factory | V* | **multi.**	18
China Pearl* | **Chinatown**	21
NEW Citizen Public* | **Fenway**	–
City Table | V | **Back Bay**	22
Clink | V | **Beacon Hill**	19
⚫ Clio | V | **Back Bay**	27
Coonamessett | V | **CC**	21
⚫ Craigie on Main | V | **Central Sq**	27
⚫ Cuchi Cuchi | V | **Central Sq**	23
Daily Catch* | **N End**	24
Dante | V* | **E Cambridge**	24
NEW Darryl's | V | **S End**	–
Da Vinci | V | **Park Sq**	24
⚫ Davio's | V* | **Park Sq**	25
NEW Deuxave | V | **Back Bay**	–
District | V | **Leather Dist**	–
Donatello | V | **Saugus**	22
Douzo* | **Back Bay**	25
⚫ Durgin-Park* | **Faneuil Hall**	20
⚫ Eastern Stand. | V | **Kenmore Sq**	23
East Ocean* | **Chinatown**	25
⚫ Elephant Walk | V | **Fenway**	23
⚫ EVOO* | **Kendall Sq**	26
Exchange St. Bistro* | **Malden**	21
Fajitas/'Ritas* | **D'town Cross**	16
Filippo* | **N End**	19
Fire & Ice* | **Harv Sq**	15
Fishmonger's* | **CC**	20
Fleming's Prime | V* | **Park Sq**	25
⚫ Fugakyu | V | **Brookline**	24
NEW Gallows | V | **S End**	20
⚫ Giacomo's | V | **S End**	25
Golden Temple | V | **Brookline**	20
Good Life* | **D'town Cross**	16
Gourmet Dumpling* | **Chinatown**	25
⚫ Grill 23 | V | **Back Bay**	27
⚫ Hamersley's | V | **S End**	28
Haru* | **Back Bay**	20
⚫ Harvest | V* | **Harv Sq**	25
Henrietta's | V* | **Harv Sq**	23
Hillstone* | **Faneuil Hall**	25
House of Siam | V | **S End**	22
Hungry I | V | **Beacon Hill**	22
⚫ Hungry Mother* | **Kendall Sq**	26
Incontro | V | **Franklin**	21
NEW Jacky's | V | **Brighton**	23
Jacob Wirth* | **Theater Dist**	18
Jae's | V | **S End**	22
Jasper White's* | **Back Bay**	21
Jer-Ne | V | **Theater Dist**	19
Jillian's | V | **Fenway**	16
Joe's American | V | **N End**	17
Joe Tecce's | V | **N End**	19
John Harvard's* | **Harv Sq**	16
Joshua Tree | V | **Allston**	15
Jumbo* | **Chinatown**	22
Kashmir | V | **Back Bay**	24
KingFish Hall* | **Faneuil Hall**	22
Kings* | **Back Bay**	19
KO Prime | V | **D'town Cross**	25
La Fam. Giorgio* | **N End**	22
Lala Rokh | V | **Beacon Hill**	23
La Morra | V | **Brookline**	25
⚫ L'Andana | V | **Burlington**	27
⚫ Legal Sea | V* | **multi.**	22

Le's | V | **Chestnut Hill**	21
🔲 L'Espalier | V | **Back Bay**	27
Les Zygomates | V | **Leather Dist**	22
Lineage* | **Brookline**	25
Living Room | V* | **Waterfront**	16
🔲 Locke-Ober | V | **D'town Cross**	25
🆕 Lolita Cocina | V | **Back Bay**	–
L'Osteria* | **N End**	24
Lucca | V | **multi.**	23
Lucia | V | **N End**	23
Lyric | V | **CC**	25
Maggiano's | V | **Park Sq**	19
Mamma Maria | V | **N End**	25
Mantra | V | **D'town Cross**	21
Marco Romana* | **N End**	23
Mare* | **N End**	26
Market | V | **Theater Dist**	26
Marshside | V | **CC**	19
Masa | V | **S End**	21
Ma Soba* | **Beacon Hill**	20
Mattakeese Wharf | V | **CC**	18
Maurizio's | V* | **N End**	24
Max/Dylan | **D'town Cross**	19
McCormick/Schmick | V | **Park Sq**	21
Melting Pot | V | **Park Sq**	19
🔲🆕 Menton | V | **Seaport Dist**	28
🔲 Meritage | V* | **Waterfront**	26
Met Back/B&G | V | **Back Bay**	19
Metropolis | V | **S End**	24
Metropolitan | V | **Chestnut Hill**	20
Midwest | V | **Inman Sq**	21
Miel | V | **Waterfront**	22
🔲 Mistral | V | **S End**	28
M.J. O'Connor's | V | **Seaport Dist**	17
Mooo... | V | **Beacon Hill**	26
🔲 Morton's | V | **multi.**	25
Mother Anna's* | **N End**	23
New Shanghai* | **Chinatown**	21
Nico | V | **N End**	24
9 Tastes* | **Harv Sq**	21
🔲🆕 Noche | V | **S End**	22
Noir* | **Harv Sq**	20
🔲 No. 9 Park | V | **Beacon Hill**	27
North 26 | V | **Faneuil Hall**	25
🔲 Oak Room | V | **Back Bay**	24
Oceana | V* | **Waterfront**	22
Oceanaire | V | **Financial Dist**	24
Ocean House | V | **CC**	27
🔲 Oishii | V | **S End**	27
Om | V* | **Harv Sq**	16
Osushi | V | **Back Bay**	21
🔲 O Ya | V | **Leather Dist**	29
Paddock | V | **CC**	22
Pagliuca's* | **N End**	22
Pairings | V | **Park Sq**	21
Palm | V | **Back Bay**	24
Papa Razzi | V | **Back Bay**	19
Parker's | V* | **D'town Cross**	24
Peach Farm* | **Chinatown**	25
Penang* | **Chinatown**	21
🔲 Petit Robert | V* | **multi.**	23
P.F. Chang's* | **multi.**	19
Piccola Venezia* | **N End**	22
Pigalle* | **Theater Dist**	26
Pisces | V | **CC**	27
Pops | V | **S End**	20
Post 390 | V | **Back Bay**	20
🔲 Prezza | V | **N End**	27
🔲 Radius | V | **Financial Dist**	26
Red House* | **Harv Sq**	21
Red Pheasant | V | **CC**	27
🔲 Rendezvous | V | **Central Sq**	26
🔲 Rialto | V* | **Harv Sq**	26
Rist. Fiore | V | **N End**	21
Rist. Villa Francesca | V | **N End**	23
Roadhouse | V | **CC**	22
Rowes Wharf | V | **Waterfront**	23
RumBa | V | **Waterfront**	19
Rustic Kitchen | V | **Theater Dist**	20
🔲 Ruth's Chris | V | **D'town Cross**	26
Salvatore's* | **Seaport Dist**	21
🆕 Sam's* | **Seaport Dist**	20
Sandrine's* | **Harv Sq**	24
Saraceno* | **N End**	24
Sauciety | V* | **Seaport Dist**	–
Scampo | V | **Beacon Hill**	25
🔲 Sel de la Terre | V | **multi.**	23
75 Chestnut | V | **Beacon Hill**	21
Shabu-Zen* | **Chinatown**	23
Sibling Rivalry | V | **S End**	23
Sidney's | V | **Central Sq**	21
606 Congress | V | **Seaport Dist**	20
Skipjack's* | **Back Bay**	20
Sky | V | **Norwood**	16
Smith/Wollensky | V | **Back Bay**	22
Sonsie | V | **Back Bay**	20

🖪 Sorellina	V	**Back Bay**	27
Sorriso	V	**Leather Dist**	21
Splash Ultra	V	**Leather Dist**	17
Stanhope Grille	V	**Back Bay**	20
Stella	V	**S End**	24
Stephanie's	V	**Back Bay**	20
Strega Rist./Water	V	**N End**	23
Sunset Grill/Cantina*	**Boston U**	19
Sushi-Teq	V	**Waterfront**	24
Tangierino	V	**Charlestown**	22
Tanjore*	**Harv Sq**	22
🖪 Taranta*	**N End**	26
Tasca	V	**Brighton**	23
Tavern in Sq.*	**Porter Sq**	15
Teatro	V	**Theater Dist**	23
Terramia*	**N End**	26
NEW Think Tank*	**Kendall Sq**	–
Tivoli's*	**Malden**	–
🖪 Top of Hub*	**Back Bay**	20
🖪 Toro	V	**S End**	27
Toscano	V	**Beacon Hill**	25
NEW Towne	V	**Back Bay**	21
Townsend's	V	**Hyde Park**	21
Tratt. Monica/Vinoteca	V*	**N End**	25
Tremont 647/Sorel	V	**S End**	20
Tresca	V*	**N End**	24
🖪 Troquet	V	**Theater Dist**	26
Turner Fish	V	**Back Bay**	20
28 Degrees	V	**S End**	19
Umbria Prime	V	**Financial Dist**	23
🖪 Uni	V	**Back Bay**	28
Union B&G	V	**S End**	24
🖪 Union Oyster	V*	**Faneuil Hall**	21
Upstairs/Square	V*	**Harv Sq**	24
Via Matta	V	**Park Sq**	25
Vlora	V	**Back Bay**	20
West End Johnnie's	V	**W End**	18
Wine Cellar	V	**Back Bay**	22
Woodward	V	**Financial Dist**	21

PEOPLE-WATCHING

🖪 Alibi	**Beacon Hill**	19
🖪 NEW Alma Nove	**Hingham**	22
NEW Anthem	**Faneuil Hall**	19
🖪 Aquitaine	**Dedham**	23
🖪 Asana	**Back Bay**	22
Atlantic Fish/Chop	**MV**	21
NEW Back Bay Social	**Back Bay**	18
Bangkok Blue	**Back Bay**	20

Beehive	**S End**	20
Bella Luna/Milky Way	**Jamaica Plain**	19
Big Papi's	**Framingham**	13
Bina Osteria	**D'town Cross**	18
Bistro du Midi	**Back Bay**	23
NEW Black Cat Tavern	**CC**	20
Blu	**Theater Dist**	21
Boarding House	**Nan**	25
Bottega	**Back Bay**	23
Bricco	**N End**	25
Bukhara	**Jamaica Plain**	22
Butcher Shop	**S End**	25
Café at Taj	**Back Bay**	21
Cafeteria	**Back Bay**	18
Caffe Paradiso	**N End**	19
CBS Scene Rest. & Bar	**Foxboro**	–
Charley's	**multi.**	18
City Bar	**multi.**	19
🖪 Clio	**Back Bay**	27
NEW Clover Food Lab	**Harv Sq**	–
Club Cafe	**S End**	19
Cobie's Clam	**CC**	22
Corazon del Mar	**Nan**	25
Courtyard/Boston Library	**Back Bay**	18
🖪 Cuchi Cuchi	**Central Sq**	23
Dante	**E Cambridge**	24
🖪 Davio's	**multi.**	25
Devon's	**CC**	25
Drink	**Seaport Dist**	21
🖪 Eastern Stand.	**Kenmore Sq**	23
Edwige	**CC**	26
88 Wharf	**Milton**	19
Florentine Cafe	**N End**	22
NEW Foundry/Elm	**Somerville**	–
Franklin	**S End**	24
Friendly Toast	**Kendall Sq**	21
NEW Gallows	**S End**	20
Game On!	**Fenway**	15
Gaslight Brasserie	**S End**	22
Globe Bar	**Back Bay**	16
🖪 Grill 23	**Back Bay**	27
Highland Kitchen	**Somerville**	25
Il Casale	**Belmont**	24
NEW Island Creek	**Kenmore Sq**	–
Jetties	**Nan**	17
Joe's American	**Back Bay**	17
Kashmir	**Back Bay**	24
KingFish Hall	**Faneuil Hall**	22

Lansdowne | **Fenway**	16
La Voile | **Back Bay**	24
Ledge | **Dorchester**	15
Living Room | **Waterfront**	16
Lo La 41° | **Nan**	25
Lord Hobo | **Inman Sq**	16
LTK | **Seaport Dist**	21
Mantra | **D'town Cross**	21
Market | **Theater Dist**	26
Masa | **Woburn**	21
Max/Dylan | **Charlestown**	19
NEW Millie's | **Nan**	19
Z Mistral | **S End**	28
Mother Anna's | **N End**	23
Z No. 9 Park | **Beacon Hill**	27
Pairings | **Park Sq**	21
Parish Cafe | **Back Bay**	23
Pazzo | **Back Bay**	21
Z Pearl | **Nan**	28
Z Petit Robert | **D'town Cross**	23
Piattini | **Back Bay**	24
Poe's/Rattlesnake | **Back Bay**	21
Post 390 | **Back Bay**	20
Z Radius | **Financial Dist**	26
NEW Regal Beagle | **Brookline**	21
Roobar | **CC**	19
Ropewalk | **Nan**	18
Rowes Wharf | **Waterfront**	23
NEW Russell Hse. | **Harv Sq**	21
NEW Sam's | **Seaport Dist**	20
Scampo | **Beacon Hill**	25
Scollay Sq. | **Beacon Hill**	19
Sibling Rivalry | **S End**	23
Sidecar Café | **MV**	-
Sonsie | **Back Bay**	20
Z Sorellina | **Back Bay**	27
Splash Ultra | **Leather Dist**	17
Sportello | **Seaport Dist**	25
Stephanie's | **multi.**	20
NEW Stoddard's | **D'town Cross**	19
Strega Rist./Water | **Seaport Dist**	23
Tastings Wine/Bistro | **Foxboro**	21
NEW Tasty Burger | **Fenway**	-
Tavern in Sq. | **Salem**	15
Tavolino | **Foxboro**	20
Teatro | **Theater Dist**	23
Technique | **E Cambridge**	-
Temple Bar | **Porter Sq**	21
NEW Think Tank | **Kendall Sq**	-
NEW Tico | **Back Bay**	-

Tory Row | **Harv Sq**	17
NEW Towne | **Back Bay**	21
Tremont 647/Sorel | **S End**	20
Trident | **Back Bay**	20
Turner's Seafood | **Melrose**	23
28 Degrees | **S End**	19
29 Newbury | **Back Bay**	20
NEW Vapiano | **Theater Dist**	18
Via Matta | **Park Sq**	25
Wagamama | **Back Bay**	18
Water St. | **MV**	26
West End Johnnie's | **W End**	18
NEW W Lounge | **Theater Dist**	19
NEW Yard House | **Dedham**	19

PRIVATE ROOMS

(Restaurants charge less at off
times; call for capacity)

Z Belfry Inne | **CC**	27
Brotherhood/Thieves | **Nan**	21
Z Capital Grille | **multi.**	26
Capt. Linnell | **CC**	24
Chanticleer | **Nan**	25
Z Chatham Bars | **CC**	23
Chau Chow | **Chinatown**	22
China Pearl | **Chinatown**	21
Coonamessett | **CC**	21
Dan'l Webster | **CC**	21
Z East Coast | **Inman Sq**	26
Z Eastern Stand. | **Kenmore Sq**	23
Z Elephant Walk | **multi.**	23
Filippo | **N End**	19
Fleming's Prime | **Park Sq**	25
Z Fugakyu | **Brookline**	24
Golden Temple | **Brookline**	20
Z Grill 23 | **Back Bay**	27
Z Harvest | **Harv Sq**	25
Hungry I | **Beacon Hill**	22
Z Il Capriccio | **Waltham**	27
Kashmir | **Back Bay**	24
Kowloon | **Saugus**	15
Lala Rokh | **Beacon Hill**	23
Z Legal Sea | **multi.**	22
Z L'Espalier | **Back Bay**	27
Z Locke-Ober | **D'town Cross**	25
Lure Grill | **MV**	22
Mamma Maria | **N End**	25
Mantra | **D'town Cross**	21
McCormick/Schmick | **multi.**	21
Metropolitan | **Chestnut Hill**	20
Z Mistral | **S End**	28

Ⓩ Morton's | **Back Bay** 25
Ⓩ Òran Mór | **Nan** 28
Ⓩ Pearl | **Nan** 28
Ⓩ Radius | **Financial Dist** 26
Regatta/Cotuit | **CC** 26
Saraceno | **N End** 24
Sibling Rivalry | **S End** 23
Smith/Wollensky | **Back Bay** 22
Stella | **S End** 24
Tangierino | **Charlestown** 22
Ⓩ Taranta | **N End** 26
Topper's | **Nan** 27
🆕 Towne | **Back Bay** 21
Tremont 647/Sorel | **S End** 20
Turner Fish | **Back Bay** 20
Upstairs/Square | **Harv Sq** 24

RAW BARS

Ⓩ Arnold's Lobster | **CC** 24
Atlantic Fish/Chop | **MV** 21
Back Eddy | **Westport** 23
Ⓩ B&G Oysters | **S End** 26
🆕 Basho | **Fenway** 23
Bookstore & Rest. | **CC** 20
🆕 Citizen Public | **Fenway** -
🆕 Cognac Bistro | **Brookline** -
Corazon del Mar | **Nan** 25
Ⓩ East Coast | **Inman Sq** 26
Ⓩ Eastern Stand. | **Kenmore Sq** 23
Finz | **Salem** 21
Game On! | **Fenway** 15
Ⓩ Impudent Oyster | **CC** 23
Jasper White's | **multi.** 21
Jetties | **Nan** 17
KingFish Hall | **Faneuil Hall** 22
Ⓩ Larsen's Fish | **MV** 28
Ⓩ Legal Sea | **multi.** 22
Les Zygomates | **Leather Dist** 22
Lobster Pot | **CC** 22
Ⓩ Locke-Ober | **D'town Cross** 25
Mac's | **CC** 25
McCormick/Schmick | 21
   Faneuil Hall
Moby Dick's | **CC** 24
Naked Oyster | **CC** 25
Ⓩ Neptune Oyster | **N End** 28
Oceanaire | **Financial Dist** 24
Ⓩ Outermost Inn | **MV** 23
Oyster BG | **MV** 24
Oyster Co. | **CC** 24

Port | **CC** 23
Red Inn | **CC** 26
Ropewalk | **Nan** 18
Saltwater | **MV** 21
Skipjack's | **multi.** 20
Summer Winter | **Burlington** 25
Turner's Seafood | **Melrose** 23
28 Degrees | **S End** 19
Ⓩ Union Oyster | **Faneuil Hall** 21
Village Fish | **Needham** 22
Woodman's | **Essex** 23

ROMANTIC PLACES

Alberto's | **CC** 21
Ⓩ Alibi | **Beacon Hill** 19
Ⓩ🆕 Alma Nove | **Hingham** 22
Amari | **CC** 22
Ⓩ Aquitaine | **S End** 23
Ⓩ Asana | **Back Bay** 22
Assaggio | **N End** 23
Atasca | **Kendall Sq** 20
Atria | **MV** 26
Ⓩ Barker Tavern | **Scituate** 27
Barley Neck Inn | **CC** 20
BarLola | **Back Bay** 17
Beach Plum | **MV** 22
Ⓩ Belfry Inne | **CC** 27
Ⓩ🆕 Bergamot | **Somerville** 27
Bin 26 | **Beacon Hill** 21
Bistro/Crowne Pointe | **CC** 23
Bistro du Midi | **Back Bay** 23
Ⓩ Bistro 5 | **W Medford** 27
Boarding House | **Nan** 25
Bon Savor | **Jamaica Plain** 22
Brant Point | **Nan** 24
Ⓩ Bristol Lounge | **Back Bay** 26
Buca's Tuscan | **CC** 23
Ⓩ Cape Sea | **CC** 27
Capt. Linnell | **CC** 24
Ⓩ Carmen | **N End** 27
Casa Romero | **Back Bay** 22
🆕 Ceia Kitchen/Bar | -
   Newburyport
Chanticleer | **Nan** 25
Chez Henri | **Harv Sq** 24
Chillingsworth | **CC** 26
Chilmark Tavern | **MV** 24
City Bar | **multi.** 19
Ⓩ Clio | **Back Bay** 27
🆕 Cognac Bistro | **Brookline** -

Company/Cauldron | **Nan**	27
Ⓩ Coppa | **S End**	26
Ⓩ Craigie on Main | **Central Sq**	27
Ⓩ Cuchi Cuchi | **Central Sq**	23
Daily Catch | **Brookline**	24
Dalí | **Somerville**	25
Dalya's | **Bedford**	21
🆕 Darryl's | **S End**	-
Da Vinci | **Park Sq**	24
Détente | **MV**	28
🆕 Deuxave | **Back Bay**	-
Dune | **Nan**	22
Erbaluce | **Park Sq**	26
Estragon | **S End**	23
Euno | **N End**	22
Fifty-Six Union | **Nan**	23
Figs at 29 Fair | **Nan**	26
Finale | **multi.**	21
Fleming's Prime | **Park Sq**	25
Front St. | **CC**	25
Ⓩ Galley Beach | **Nan**	24
G Bar | **Swampscott**	19
Gennaro's Five N. | **N End**	24
Ghazal | **Jamaica Plain**	23
Ⓩ Glass Onion | **CC**	27
Glory | **Andover**	21
Grain & Salt | **Allston**	23
Ⓩ Grapevine | **Salem**	27
Grotto | **Beacon Hill**	26
Haveli | **Inman Sq**	-
Helmand | **E Cambridge**	25
Hungry I | **Beacon Hill**	22
Ⓩ Il Capriccio | **Waltham**	27
Il Casale | **Belmont**	24
Il Tesoro/Terrace | **MV**	19
🆕 Island Creek | **Kenmore Sq**	-
🆕 Jacky's | **Brighton**	23
Joe's American | **Back Bay**	17
J's/Nashoba | **Bolton**	24
Ⓩ La Campania | **Waltham**	28
Lala Rokh | **Beacon Hill**	23
Lambert's Cove | **MV**	23
Ⓩ L'Andana | **Burlington**	27
La Voile | **Back Bay**	24
Le Languedoc | **Nan**	23
Ⓩ L'Espalier | **Back Bay**	27
L'Étoile | **MV**	28
Lucca | **N End**	23
Ⓩ Lumière | **Newton**	28
Lure Grill | **MV**	22

Lyric | **CC**	25
Mamma Maria | **N End**	25
Marliave | **D'town Cross**	18
Ⓩ🆕 Menton | **Seaport Dist**	28
Ⓩ Meritage | **Waterfront**	26
Met Back/B&G | **Back Bay**	19
Mews | **CC**	26
Ⓩ🆕 Noche | **S End**	22
Noir | **Harv Sq**	20
Ⓩ Oak Room | **Back Bay**	24
Ocean House | **CC**	27
Ⓩ Oishii | **S End**	27
Ⓩ Oleana | **Inman Sq**	28
Olivadi | **Norwood**	20
Ⓩ Òran Mór | **Nan**	28
Orta | **Hanover**	19
Osteria/Civetta | **CC**	27
Ⓩ Outermost Inn | **MV**	23
Ⓩ O Ya | **Leather Dist**	29
Pagliuca's | **N End**	22
Ⓩ🆕 PB Boulangerie | **CC**	28
Ⓩ Petit Robert | **D'town Cross**	23
Pierrot Bistrot | **Beacon Hill**	24
Pigalle | **Theater Dist**	26
Ⓩ Prezza | **N End**	27
Ⓩ Radius | **Financial Dist**	26
Red House | **Harv Sq**	21
Red Inn | **CC**	26
🆕 Regal Beagle | **Brookline**	21
Ⓩ Rialto | **Harv Sq**	26
Rist. Damiano | **N End**	26
Rist. Pavarotti | **Reading**	-
RumBa | **Waterfront**	19
Ⓩ Salts | **Central Sq**	27
Ⓩ Sel de la Terre | **multi.**	23
75 Chestnut | **Beacon Hill**	21
Shea's Riverside | **Essex**	19
Sol Azteca | **Fenway**	21
Solea | **Waltham**	22
Sorriso | **Leather Dist**	21
Spiga Trattoria | **Needham**	22
Splash Ultra | **Leather Dist**	17
State Road | **MV**	25
Stephanie's | **S End**	20
Straight Wharf | **Nan**	27
Strega Rist./Water | **Seaport Dist**	23
Summer House | **Nan**	25
Sunset Cafe | **Inman Sq**	24
Sushi-Teq | **Waterfront**	24
Sweet Life | **MV**	25

Menus, photos, voting and more – free at ZAGAT.com

Tangierino | **Charlestown**	22
☑ Taranta | **N End**	26
Tasca | **Brighton**	23
☑ Top of Hub | **Back Bay**	20
Topper's | **Nan**	27
☑ Tosca | **Hingham**	26
Town | **Nan**	24
NEW Towne | **Back Bay**	21
Townsend's | **Hyde Park**	21
Tresca | **N End**	24
Trevi Café | **CC**	25
Trina's | **Inman Sq**	20
☑ Troquet | **Theater Dist**	26
Tryst | **Arlington**	24
28 Atlantic | **CC**	27
Umbria Prime | **Financial Dist**	23
☑ Uni | **Back Bay**	28
Upstairs/Square | **Harv Sq**	24
Via Matta | **Park Sq**	25
Vlora | **Back Bay**	20
Water St. | **MV**	26
West/Centre | **W Roxbury**	19
Wine Cellar | **Back Bay**	22
NEW W Lounge | **Theater Dist**	19
Zebra's Bistro | **Medfield**	24

SINGLES SCENES

☑ Abe & Louie's | **Back Bay**	26
☑ Alibi | **Beacon Hill**	19
Atlantic Fish/Chop | **MV**	21
NEW Back Bay Social | **Back Bay**	18
BarLola | **Back Bay**	17
Bella Luna/Milky Way | **Jamaica Plain**	12
Blue22 | **Quincy**	14
Boston Sail | **Waterfront**	18
Cactus Club | **Back Bay**	17
Cafe Escadrille | **Burlington**	21
Chatham Squire | **CC**	19
NEW Citizen Public | **Fenway**	-
City Bar | **multi.**	19
Club Car | **Nan**	24
Cottage | **Wellesley Hills**	19
Dbar | **Dorchester**	23
Dillon's | **Back Bay**	16
Fleming's Prime | **Park Sq**	25
Glenn's | **Newburyport**	-
Glory | **Andover**	21
Grafton St. Pub | **Harv Sq**	19
Hillstone | **Faneuil Hall**	25

House of Blues | **Fenway**	15
Joe's American | **Back Bay**	17
John Harvard's | **Harv Sq**	16
Joshua Tree | **Somerville**	15
Kama | **Quincy**	-
Lansdowne | **Fenway**	16
Living Room | **Waterfront**	16
Max/Dylan | **D'town Cross**	19
Met Back/B&G | **Back Bay**	19
Middlesex | **Central Sq**	20
M.J. O'Connor's | **Park Sq**	17
Orleans | **Somerville**	17
Poe's/Rattlesnake | **Back Bay**	21
Redline | **Harv Sq**	16
NEW Russell Hse. | **Harv Sq**	21
Sunset Grill/Cantina | **multi.**	19
Tavern in Sq. | **Porter Sq**	15
Temple Bar | **Porter Sq**	21
28 Degrees | **S End**	19
Village Fish | **Needham**	22
West End Johnnie's | **W End**	18
NEW W Lounge | **Theater Dist**	19
NEW Yard House | **Dedham**	19

SLEEPERS

(Good food, but little known)

Amari | **CC**	22
Angelo's | **Stoneham**	27
Bia Bistro | **Cohasset**	25
Bistro/Crowne Pointe | **CC**	23
Brenden Crocker's | **Beverly**	26
Cafe Sushi | **Harv Sq**	22
Centre St. Bistro | **Nan**	28
Chilmark Tavern | **MV**	24
Chung Ki Wa | **Medford**	23
Coriander | **Sharon**	25
D'Parma Italian Table | **CC**	22
Equator | **S End**	22
Friendly Fisherman | **CC**	22
Gennaro's Five N. | **N End**	24
Ghazal | **Jamaica Plain**	23
Grain & Salt | **Allston**	23
Haley House | **Roxbury**	22
NEW Haven | **Jamaica Plain**	23
NEW Istanbul'lu | **Somerville**	23
J's/Nashoba | **Bolton**	24
Karoo Kafe | **CC**	22
Kaze | **Chinatown**	24
Lavender Asian | **Sudbury**	23
Le Lyonnais | **Acton**	23

Lyric | **CC**	25
Misaki | **CC**	25
North 26 | **Faneuil Hall**	25
North St. Grille | **N End**	24
Oyster BG | **MV**	24
Palmers | **Andover**	22
Pellana | **Peabody**	25
Pellino's | **Marblehead**	24
Piccolo Nido | **N End**	26
Pi Pizzeria | **Nan**	23
Rist. Damiano | **N End**	26
Riva | **Scituate**	26
Second St. Café | **E Cambridge**	23
Seiyo | **S End**	22
Shanti India | **Dorchester**	28
Ships Inn | **Nan**	27
Singh's | **Wellesley Hills**	22
Slice of Life | **MV**	26
Solstice | **Kingston**	25
Soma | **Beverly**	22
Sorento's | **Marlborough**	25
Sunset Cafe | **Inman Sq**	24
Sushi by Yoshi | **Nan**	23
Sushi-Teq | **Waterfront**	24
Tacos El Charro | **Jamaica Plain**	25
Tartufo | **Newton**	22
Town | **Nan**	24
Tratt. Pulcinella | **Huron Vill**	24
Trevi Café | **CC**	25
Village Sushi | **Roslindale**	22
Vining's | **CC**	23
Volle Nolle | **N End**	26
Water St. | **MV**	26

THEME RESTAURANTS

CBS Scene Rest. & Bar | **Foxboro**	-
Cheers | **multi.**	14
Z Durgin-Park | **Faneuil Hall**	20
Fire & Ice | **multi.**	15
Jacob Wirth | **Theater Dist**	18
Kowloon | **Saugus**	15

TRENDY

NEW Aka Bistro | **Lincoln**	25
Alchemy | **MV**	23
Z Alibi | **Beacon Hill**	19
Ashmont Grill | **Dorchester**	23
Avila | **Theater Dist**	23
NEW Back Bay Social | **Back Bay**	18
Z B&G Oysters | **S End**	26

NEW Basho | **Fenway**	23
Beehive | **S End**	20
Z NEW Bergamot | **Somerville**	27
Bin 26 | **Beacon Hill**	21
NEW Bosphorus | **Inman Sq**	-
Bricco | **N End**	25
Butcher Shop | **S End**	25
Cafeteria | **Back Bay**	18
Caffe Tosca | **Hingham**	24
Cambridge 1 | **Harv Sq**	22
Church | **Fenway**	20
NEW Citizen Public | **Fenway**	-
City Bar | **multi.**	19
Clink | **Beacon Hill**	19
Dante | **E Cambridge**	24
NEW Darryl's | **S End**	-
Dbar | **Dorchester**	23
NEW Deuxave | **Back Bay**	-
District | **Leather Dist**	-
Douzo | **Back Bay**	25
Z Eastern Stand. | **Kenmore Sq**	23
Exchange St. Bistro | **Malden**	21
Five Bays | **CC**	23
NEW Foundry/Elm | **Somerville**	-
NEW Gallows | **S End**	20
Gargoyles | **Somerville**	24
Gaslight Brasserie | **S End**	22
KO Prime | **D'town Cross**	25
La Verdad | **Fenway**	21
Lineage | **Brookline**	25
NEW Lolita Cocina | **Back Bay**	-
Lord Hobo | **Inman Sq**	16
Lucky's | **Seaport Dist**	19
Mare | **N End**	26
Metropolitan | **Chestnut Hill**	20
Mooo... | **Beacon Hill**	26
Myers + Chang | **S End**	24
Noir | **Harv Sq**	20
Om | **Harv Sq**	16
Osushi | **Back Bay**	21
NEW Papagayo | **Seaport Dist**	-
Z Pearl | **Nan**	28
Pops | **S End**	20
Port | **CC**	23
Z Rendezvous | **Central Sq**	26
RumBa | **Waterfront**	19
NEW Russell Hse. | **Harv Sq**	21
NEW Sam's | **Seaport Dist**	20
Sonsie | **Back Bay**	20
Sophia's | **Roslindale**	23

☑ Sorellina | **Back Bay**	27
Sorriso | **Leather Dist**	21
Stella | **S End**	24
Sushi-Teq | **Waterfront**	24
Tavolo | **Dorchester**	24
Temple Bar | **Porter Sq**	21
NEW Think Tank | **Kendall Sq**	-
☑ Toro | **S End**	27
Tory Row | **Harv Sq**	17
NEW Towne | **Back Bay**	21
Tremont 647/Sorel | **S End**	20
Trina's | **Inman Sq**	20
28 Degrees | **S End**	19
29 Newbury | **Back Bay**	20
224 Boston St. | **Dorchester**	21
Via Matta | **Park Sq**	25
NEW W Lounge | **Theater Dist**	19

VIEWS

Adrian's | **CC**	18
☑**NEW** Alma Nove | **Hingham**	22
Anthony Cummaquid | **CC**	17
☑ Anthony's | **Seaport Dist**	18
Aqua Grille | **CC**	19
Ardeo | **CC**	19
☑ Asana | **Back Bay**	22
Atlantica | **Cohasset**	20
Atlantic Fish/Chop | **MV**	21
Audubon Circle | **Kenmore Sq**	21
Back Eddy | **Westport**	23
Barking Crab | **Seaport Dist**	17
Baxter's | **CC**	20
Bayside Betsy's | **CC**	18
Beach Plum | **MV**	22
Beacon Hill | **Beacon Hill**	23
Bistro/Crowne Pointe | **CC**	23
Bistro du Midi | **Back Bay**	23
Black Cow | **Newburyport**	20
Black Dog | **MV**	19
Blu | **Theater Dist**	21
Blue Canoe | **MV**	16
Bookstore & Rest. | **CC**	20
Boston Sail | **Waterfront**	18
Brant Point | **Nan**	24
Bravo | **MFA**	20
Bricco | **N End**	25
Bridgeman's | **Hull**	24
☑ Bristol Lounge | **Back Bay**	26
Bubala's | **CC**	16
Bukowski | **Inman Sq**	18

Café at Taj | **Back Bay**	21
☑ Cape Sea | **CC**	27
Capt. Kidd | **CC**	16
Capt. Linnell | **CC**	24
Capt. Parker's | **CC**	21
Chart House | **Waterfront**	20
Chart Room | **CC**	18
☑ Chatham Bars | **CC**	23
Clancy's | **CC**	21
Courtyard/Boston Library | **Back Bay**	18
Daily Catch | **Seaport Dist**	24
NEW Dalla Cucina | **CC**	20
Dante | **E Cambridge**	24
Devon's | **CC**	25
Dockside, The | **CC**	17
Easy Street | **Nan**	-
88 Wharf | **Milton**	19
Enzo | **CC**	21
Fanizzi's | **CC**	19
Finz | **Salem**	21
Fishmonger's | **CC**	20
☑ Galley Beach | **Nan**	24
☑ Gibbet Hill | **Groton**	25
Grafton St. Pub | **Harv Sq**	19
Boston Beer | **Hingham**	18
Home Port | **MV**	21
Jetties | **Nan**	17
J's/Nashoba | **Bolton**	24
Landfall | **CC**	18
Landing | **Marblehead**	18
☑ Legal Sea | **Waterfront**	22
Le Lyonnais | **Acton**	23
Liam's | **CC**	20
Lobster Pot | **CC**	22
Mamma Maria | **N End**	25
Marshside | **CC**	19
Mattakeese Wharf | **CC**	18
☑ Meritage | **Waterfront**	26
Mews | **CC**	26
Miel | **Waterfront**	22
NEW Millie's | **Nan**	19
Net Result | **MV**	24
No Name | **Seaport Dist**	19
☑ Not Average Joe's | **Newburyport**	19
Oceana | **Waterfront**	22
Ocean House | **CC**	27
Ocean Terrace | **CC**	19
Om | **Harv Sq**	16

Orleans Inn | **CC** — 16

Z Outermost Inn | **MV** — 23

NEW Port 305 | **N Quincy** — ⎯

Post 390 | **Back Bay** — 20

Red Inn | **CC** — 26

Red Pheasant | **CC** — 27

Red Rock | **Swampscott** — 20

Z Rialto | **Harv Sq** — 26

Rist. Fiore | **N End** — 21

Ropewalk | **Nan** — 18

Ross' Grill | **CC** — 24

Rowes Wharf | **Waterfront** — 23

Sal's Place | **CC** — 18

Saltwater | **MV** — 21

Salvatore's | **Seaport Dist** — 21

NEW Sam's | **Seaport Dist** — 20

Shea's Riverside | **Essex** — 19

Sherborn Inn | **Sherborn** — 19

Sidney's | **Central Sq** — 21

Siros | **N Quincy** — 20

Slip 14 | **Nan** — 19

Sonsie | **Back Bay** — 20

Straight Wharf | **Nan** — 27

Summer House | **Nan** — 25

Sushi-Teq | **Waterfront** — 24

Tavern/Water | **Charlestown** — 12

Z Top of Hub | **Back Bay** — 20

Topper's | **Nan** — 27

Tory Row | **Harv Sq** — 17

Z Troquet | **Theater Dist** — 26

Turner Fish | **Back Bay** — 20

28 Atlantic | **CC** — 27

Waterford Café/Tav. | **CC** — ⎯

Water St. | **MV** — 26

NEW Whiskey Priest | **Seaport Dist** — 12

Woodman's | **Essex** — 23

WATERSIDE

Z NEW Alma Nove | **Hingham** — 22

Anthony Cummaquid | **CC** — 17

Z Anthony's | **Seaport Dist** — 18

Aqua Grille | **CC** — 19

Atlantica | **Cohasset** — 20

Atlantic Fish/Chop | **MV** — 21

Back Eddy | **Westport** — 23

Barking Crab | **Seaport Dist** — 17

Baxter's | **CC** — 20

Bayside Betsy's | **CC** — 18

Black Cow | **Newburyport** — 20

Black Dog | **MV** — 19

Blue Canoe | **MV** — 16

Bookstore & Rest. | **CC** — 20

Brant Point | **Nan** — 24

Bridgeman's | **Hull** — 24

Bubala's | **CC** — 16

Capt. Kidd | **CC** — 16

Chart House | **Waterfront** — 20

Chart Room | **CC** — 18

Z Chatham Bars | **CC** — 23

Clancy's | **CC** — 21

Daily Catch | **Seaport Dist** — 24

Dante | **E Cambridge** — 24

Dockside, The | **CC** — 17

88 Wharf | **Milton** — 19

Fanizzi's | **CC** — 19

Finz | **Salem** — 21

Fishmonger's | **CC** — 20

Z Galley Beach | **Nan** — 24

Jetties | **Nan** — 17

Landfall | **CC** — 18

Landing | **multi.** — 18

Z Legal Sea | **Waterfront** — 22

Liam's | **CC** — 20

Lobster Pot | **CC** — 22

Lure Grill | **MV** — 22

Mews | **CC** — 26

Miel | **Waterfront** — 22

No Name | **Seaport Dist** — 19

Oceana | **Waterfront** — 22

Ocean House | **CC** — 27

Orleans Inn | **CC** — 16

Z Outermost Inn | **MV** — 23

NEW Port 305 | **N Quincy** — ⎯

Red Inn | **CC** — 26

Red Rock | **Swampscott** — 20

Riva | **Scituate** — 26

Ropewalk | **Nan** — 18

Ross' Grill | **CC** — 24

Sal's Place | **CC** — 18

Shea's Riverside | **Essex** — 19

Siros | **N Quincy** — 20

Slip 14 | **Nan** — 19

Straight Wharf | **Nan** — 27

Summer House | **Nan** — 25

Tavern/Water | **Charlestown** — 12

Topper's | **Nan** — 27

28 Atlantic | **CC** — 27

WINNING WINE LISTS

Z Abba | **CC** — 28
Z Abe & Louie's | **Back Bay** — 26
NEW Aka Bistro | **Lincoln** — 25
American Seasons | **Nan** — 26
Angelo's | **Stoneham** — 27
Z Anthony's | **Seaport Dist** — 18
Atria | **MV** — 26
Z NEW Bergamot | **Somerville** — 27
Bin 26 | **Beacon Hill** — 21
Bistro du Midi | **Back Bay** — 23
Blue Room | **Kendall Sq** — 24
Z Bramble Inn | **CC** — 28
Bravo | **MFA** — 20
Buca's Tuscan | **CC** — 23
Butcher Shop | **S End** — 25
Caffe Bella | **Randolph** — 26
Z Capital Grille | **multi.** — 26
Chanticleer | **Nan** — 25
Z Clio | **Back Bay** — 27
Dante | **E Cambridge** — 24
NEW Deuxave | **Back Bay** — -
Dune | **Nan** — 22
Fleming's Prime | **Park Sq** — 25
Z Grill 23 | **Back Bay** — 27
Z Hamersley's | **S End** — 28
Z Harvest | **Harv Sq** — 25
Z Il Capriccio | **Waltham** — 27
Il Casale | **Belmont** — 24
Z La Campania | **Waltham** — 28
Z Legal Sea | **Park Sq** — 22
Z L'Espalier | **Back Bay** — 27
Les Zygomates | **Leather Dist** — 22
Lucca | **multi.** — 23
Z Lumière | **Newton** — 28
Lure Grill | **MV** — 22
Mamma Maria | **N End** — 25
Mantra | **D'town Cross** — 21
Market | **Theater Dist** — 26
Z NEW Menton | **Seaport Dist** — 28
Z Meritage | **Waterfront** — 26
Z Mistral | **S End** — 28
Mooo... | **Beacon Hill** — 26
Z Neptune Oyster | **N End** — 28
Z No. 9 Park | **Beacon Hill** — 27
North 26 | **Faneuil Hall** — 25
Z Oleana | **Inman Sq** — 28
Pairings | **Park Sq** — 21
NEW Posto | **Somerville** — 25

Z Prezza | **N End** — 27
Z Radius | **Financial Dist** — 26
Ross' Grill | **CC** — 24
Z Salts | **Central Sq** — 27
Silvertone B&G | **D'town Cross** — 21
Smith/Wollensky | **Back Bay** — 22
Taberna/Haro | **Brookline** — 25
Tomasso | **Southborough** — 23
Topper's | **Nan** — 27
NEW Towne | **Back Bay** — 21
Tresca | **N End** — 24
Z Troquet | **Theater Dist** — 26
Z Uni | **Back Bay** — 28
Upstairs/Square | **Harv Sq** — 24
Via Matta | **Park Sq** — 25
Wine Cellar | **Back Bay** — 22

WORTH A TRIP

Belmont
  Il Casale — 24
  Shangri-La — 23
Cape Cod
  Z Abba — 28
  Z Bramble Inn — 28
  Buca's Tuscan — 23
  Chillingsworth — 26
  Inaho — 26
  Mac's — 25
  Mews — 26
  Red Pheasant — 27
  Regatta/Cotuit — 26
  28 Atlantic — 27
Hingham
  Z NEW Alma Nove — 22
Hull
  Bridgeman's — 24
  Saporito's — 28
Ipswich
  Zabaglione — 28
Kingston
  Solstice — 25
Lincoln
  NEW Aka Bistro — 25
Marblehead
  NEW 5 Corners — 26
Martha's Vineyard
  Atria — 26
  Beach Plum — 22
  Détente — 28

THE BERKSHIRES
RESTAURANT
DIRECTORY

TOP FOOD

27 Old Inn/Green | *American*
Blantyre | *American/French*
25 Wheatleigh | *American/French*
Nudel | *American*
Tratt. Rustica* | *Italian*

TOP DECOR

29 Blantyre | *American/French*
Wheatleigh | *American/French*
26 Old Inn/Green | *American*
25 Cranwell Resort | *American*
24 Old Mill | *American*

Aegean Breeze *Greek*

19 | 16 | 19 | $39

Great Barrington | 327 Stockbridge Rd. (bet. Cooper & Crissey Rds.) |
413-528-4001 | www.aegean-breeze.com

It's "not quite Santorini", but this "comfortable" Great Barrington Greek is "a reliable choice" for "tasty taverna food" like "wonderful" charcoal-grilled whole fish; white stucco decor with blue accents creates a "relaxing" backdrop for "friendly, informal service", and while a few find the menu "pricey", "terrific" daily specials offer "reasonable" value.

Allium *American*

18 | 19 | 17 | $46

Great Barrington | 42-44 Railroad St. (off Main St.) | 413-528-2118 |
www.mezzeinc.com

Fans of this "upscale" Great Barrington sibling of Williamstown's Mezze praise the "smashing", "ambitious" New American "comfort food for locavores" and "hip" digs; the less enthused complain that lately the "limited menu" "misses the mark", tabs are "a bit expensive" and service "varies from ok to clueless"; even so, it remains a "happening place."

Alta *Mediterranean*

21 | 18 | 22 | $44

Lenox | 34 Church St. (bet. Housatonic & Walker Sts.) | 413-637-0003 |
www.altawinebar.com

"Locals and visitors alike" head to this "congenial" Lenox eatery and wine bar for "delicious" Mediterranean fare and "top-notch" *vini* at "upper-moderate" prices; service is "lovely", while the "porch on a breezy summer night" suits "those of a certain age" who find the "pretty" but "generally crowded" interior on the "noisy" side.

Aroma Bar & Grill *Indian*

22 | 13 | 19 | $27

Great Barrington | 485 Main St. (South St.) | 413-528-3116 |
www.aromabarandgrill.com

"What a surprise!" declare Great Barrington denizens of this "rare find" "run by a lovely family", which prepares its "authentic" Indian fare "as spicy as you like"; "well-chosen wines" and "affordable" rates are pluses, and there's always takeout for those who don't care for the "informal" setting.

Baba Louie's Sourdough Pizza *Pizza*

24 | 13 | 18 | $23

Great Barrington | 286 Main St. (bet. Elm & Railroad Sts.) | 413-528-8100
NEW Pittsfield | 34 Depot St. (McKay St.) | 413-499-2400
www.babalouiespizza.com

"Superb" pizza with "paper-thin" sourdough crusts and "creative, sophisticated" toppings lead to "lines out the door" at this Great

---

* Indicates a tie with restaurant above

Barrington spot where "scrumptious" salads, soups and sandwiches round out the "bargain" menu; staffers "aim to please", and although it's "cramped", there's much more "elbow room" at the "attractive" Pittsfield newcomer.

Barrington Brewery & Restaurant American
14 | 14 | 17 | $24

Great Barrington | 420 Stockbridge Rd./Rte. 7 N. (Crissey Rd.) | 413-528-8282 | www.barringtonbrewery.net

"It's all about the beer" at this "bustling" Great Barrington microbrewery, but there's "something for everyone" in the way of food too, namely "plentiful" portions of "homey" American eats with "no pretense"; "quick service", "modest" tabs and a "casual" if "chaotic" vibe in a "rustic, barnlike" setting make it "fun" for "families."

Bistro Zinc French
21 | 22 | 19 | $48

Lenox | 56 Church St. (bet. Housatonic & Tucker Sts.) | 413-637-8800 | www.bistrozinc.com

"Sophisticated" Gallic fare pairs with "polished" decor at this Lenox bistro where patrons can sit in the "sleek" dining room or "be part of the buzz" at the bar; although a few are annoyed by "Manhattan prices" and the "attitude problem" of many of "the people you're supposed to be tipping" (others are "friendly and accommodating"), it's nevertheless a "go-to" "for a special night out", so "reserve early."

Bizen Japanese
24 | 18 | 19 | $40

Great Barrington | 17 Railroad St. (Rte. 7) | 413-528-4343

"Sparklingly fresh, creative" sushi and a "huge menu" of "memorable" grilled fare "worth" the price keep this "popular" Great Barrington Japanese "always packed"; the "can-be-spotty" service is made up for by "engaging" chef Michael Marcus (BTW, that's his "wonderful pottery on view"), while those who consider the "noisy", "close quarters" "less than Zen" find "the tatami rooms a boon", especially when splurging on the prix fixe kaiseki.

☑ Blantyre American/French
27 | 29 | 28 | $107

Lenox | Blantyre | 16 Blantyre Rd. (Rte. 20) | 413-637-3556 | www.blantyre.com

With a "romantic, intimate" setting that conjures "Gilded Age" "luxury" and staffers who give patrons the "royal treatment", this "outstanding" prix fixe–only French–New American dining room in a Lenox inn earns The Berkshires' No. 1 scores for Decor and Service; the fare "makes you swoon" as much as the "megabucks" needed to pay for it, yet "it's worth every penny" for an experience that's "special in every sense"; P.S. it's "formal", so jacket and tie required at dinner, and no children under 12.

Bombay Ⓜ Indian
22 | 14 | 18 | $30

Lee | Quality Inn | 435 Laurel St./Rte. 20 (Lake Rd.) | 413-243-6731 | www.fineindiandining.com

Indian fare that's "sizzling with flavor" and "prepared to your liking" draws Lee curryphiles to this "comfortable" spot where a lunch buffet that "can't be beat for value" is upstaged only by the "extraordinary" Sunday brunch; "service is willing", and if you "sit where you can view" Lake Laurel, it takes your mind off the "drab" decor.

Brix Wine Bar M *French*   23 | 20 | 22 | $42

Pittsfield | 40 West St. (bet. McKay & North Sts.) | 413-236-9463 | www.brixwinebar.com

"What's not to like?" asks the "younger crowd" who hie to this "hip" Pittsfield bistro for its "excellent" French bistro fare, "well-chosen wines", "reasonable prices" and "chic", "brick-lined" setting; "personable" service and an "*intime*" vibe help to make it "perfect for a date", as long as you don't mind a little "noise" (and a no-rez policy).

NEW Brulées M *American/European*   ∇ 21 | 23 | 22 | $33

Pittsfield | 41 North St. (bet. East & School Sts.) | 413-443-0500 | www.brulees.com

"Everyone's excited" about this "promising" midpriced Pittsfield newcomer offering a "good variety" of "great" American-European eats, ranging from its signature pan-seared scallops to steaks, seafood and pastas, plus vittles for vegetarians and young 'uns; the roomy, "comfortably elegant" digs include a lounge, which hosts live music on weekends.

Cafe Adam M *European*   23 | 17 | 20 | $43

Great Barrington | 325 Stockbridge Rd. (bet. Cooper & Crissey Rds.) | 413-528-7786 | www.cafeadam.org

"Skillful" chef-owner Adam Zieminski turns out a "small" but "fabulous" menu of "inspired" "European bistro cuisine" at this "comfortable" Great Barrington outpost; a "soothing" environment with a "nice porch" for when it's warm, "welcoming" staffers, "fair prices" and a "wonderful" "wine list that has real value" all factor into the "satisfying" experience.

Café Lucia ⊠M *Italian*   23 | 20 | 22 | $51

Lenox | 80 Church St. (bet. Franklin & Housatonic Sts.) | 413-637-2640 | www.cafelucialenox.com

"Sophisticated", "wonderful" Italian cooking ("you'll swoon for the osso buco") plus a staff that "aims to please" make this Lenox venue in an "elegant" 1839 farmhouse an "'in' spot", despite somewhat "elevated tariffs"; surveyors seeking "lots of energy" choose to sit inside, while those who find it too "cramped" and "noisy" (especially when they "pack them in during Tanglewood") ask for the "lovely deck"; P.S. closed in winter.

Castle Street Cafe *American/French*   20 | 18 | 20 | $41

Great Barrington | 10 Castle St. (Main St.) | 413-528-5244 | www.castlestreetcafe.com

"An old standby and deservedly so", this "reliable" Great Barrington American-French "charmer" draws "repeat customers" for "bargain" "quick bites" in the bar or "solid" bistro "standards" at more expensive tabs in the dining room; service is "warm", the wine list is "moderately priced" and "great" live jazz on weekends gives the "homey" digs a "festive" feel, so no wonder it's "still going strong."

	FOOD	DECOR	SERVICE	COST

Chez Nous *French*   24 | 20 | 24 | $48

Lee | 150 Main St. (Academy St.) | 413-243-6397 |
www.cheznousbistro.com

"Wonderful all around" declare Lee locals of this "delightful" destination where chef Franck Tessier's "fantastic" French bistro fare is
matched by spouse Rachel Portnoy's "scrumptious desserts", not to
mention her "charming" greetings; an "impressive", "well-priced
wine list" adds to the "good value", while "marvelous service" "without hauteur" and a setting in a "historic house" with "quiet, romantic
corners" add to the "appeal."

Church Street Cafe *American*   20 | 18 | 20 | $41

Lenox | 65 Church St. (bet. Franklin & Housatonic Sts.) | 413-637-2745 |
www.churchstreetcafe.biz

This "casual" 30-year-old gets "mobbed in summer" not only for its
convenient Lenox location (e.g. for "before-concert dining"), but because the New American fare is "reliably good"; a "most pleasant"
staff plus three "nice", "simple" dining rooms add up to a "relaxing"
mood, and even critics who complain it's "nothing to rave about"
with tabs that are "a little pricey" admit that the "porch is special."

Coyote Flaco Ⓜ *Mexican*   23 | 18 | 22 | $34

Williamstown | 505 Cold Spring Rd. (Bee Hill Rd.) | 413-458-4240 |
www.mycoyoteflaco.com

It's "not your usual Mexican fare" at this "inexpensive" Williamstown
chainlet link dishing up "wonderful", "creative" specialties in "generous portions"; "huge margaritas" and a flamenco guitarist on
Friday nights fuel a "fun" atmosphere, so it's a good thing the
staffers are "good sports."

Cranwell Resort,
Spa & Golf Club *American*   21 | 25 | 22 | $51

Lenox | 55 Lee Rd./Rte. 20 (Rte. 7) | 413-637-1364 |
www.cranwell.com

"Swellegant" sums up this "beautiful" Tudor-esque mansion resort
in Lenox, where "people come from all over" for "well-prepared"
New American fare served in an "unrushed" fashion in the "grand"
Wyndhurst or Music Room restaurants; those who don't want to "go
broke" "eat smart" at the more "moderate" Sloane's Tavern,
dispensing "publike" provisions, while calorie counters hit
the Spa Cafe.

Dakota Steakhouse *Steak*   17 | 17 | 18 | $36

Pittsfield | 1035 South St. (Dan Fox Dr.) | 413-499-7900 |
www.steakseafood.com

"You get a lot for your money" at this Pittsfield steakhouse
famed for its "pig-out Sunday buffet" brunch, "well-stocked
salad bar" and "generous" if "pedestrian" "proteins, be they seafood or land-based"; the "Western motif" complete with "stuffed
animals" may be "tired" and service can be "lackluster", but it
nevertheless "hits the spot", especially for "families", as it's
quite "child-friendly."

	FOOD	DECOR	SERVICE	COST

Dream Away Lodge ⓜ⊘ *American*   17 | 21 | 19 | $34

Becket | 1342 County Rd. (bet. Lenox-Whitney Place Rd. & McNerney Rd.) | 413-623-8725 | www.thedreamawaylodge.com
"A true original", this "oddball" New American "in the middle of no-where" in Becket puts the "kitsch in kitchen" with an affordable, "un-usual menu" running from burgers to tagines served by a "pleasant" crew; even those who consider the eats "average" admit the "hoote-nanny atmosphere" (a 19th century farm–cum–"old cathouse"–cum-speakeasy) "makes up for it", as does the nightly live music.

Elizabeth's ⊠ⓜ⊘ *Eclectic*   24 | 13 | 23 | $35

Pittsfield | 1264 East St. (Newell St.) | 413-448-8244
"Utterly delicious" pastas, "legendary salads" and one "tantalizing" fish and meat dish per night comprise the roster at this "off-the-beaten-track" Pittsfield Eclectic "institution" with a "devoted fan base"; a "dinerlike" setting prompts the question "what decor?", but tabs are "a true bargain" and chef-owner Tom Ellis is a "trip" who'll accept "an IOU" if you haven't got "good old cash or a check."

Fin *Japanese*   23 | 19 | 19 | $44

Lenox | 27 Housatonic St. (Church St.) | 413-637-9171 | www.finsushi.com
Even though it's "far from the ocean", this "easygoing" Lenox Japanese stocks sushi "so fresh it wiggles", along with some "cre-ative specials" among the cooked fare; such "big quality" helps off-set the "small", "noisy" digs dominated by a red lacquered bar, while takeout's an option when it's "hard to get into."

Firefly *American*   17 | 17 | 17 | $38

Lenox | 71 Church St. (Housatonic St.) | 413-637-2700 | www.fireflylenox.com
"Berkshires casual" is the style of this Lenox New American where "locals meet" in the "cozy" dining rooms or on the "pleasant" porch when it's warm; some say the midpriced fare is "imaginative" and "well prepared" while others claim it's "mediocre" – but there's con-sensus on the "erratic service" and the appeal of the "late-night bar."

Flavours of Malaysia ⓜ *Asian*   21 | 12 | 20 | $29

Pittsfield | 75 North St. (McKay St.) | 413-443-3188 | www.flavoursintheberkshires.com
An "elaborate" assortment of dishes from China, Malaysia, India and Thailand come "cooked to order" and as "spicy" as you like at this "wonderful" Pittsfield Asian; though "remodeling" wouldn't hurt and the live bands on weekends "change the atmosphere", the "accommodating" staff and "outstanding value" help make it "de-serving of the crowds it attracts."

Frankie's Ristorante Italiano *Italian*   18 | 18 | 20 | $41

Lenox | 80 Main St. (Cliftwood St.) | 413-637-4455 | www.frankiesitaliano.com
"Enjoyable" "red-sauce preparations" "entice" "families" to this "welcoming" Lenox Italian where a "young", "on-the-ball" staff serves in dining rooms warmed up with "old photos on the walls";

true, it's "not high end", but it's "not stuffy" either, just a "good spot" for those "on a budget"; P.S. the "porch in summer is a plus."

Gramercy Bistro *American/Eclectic*

| 23 | 21 | 22 | $43 |

North Adams | MASS MoCA | 87 Marshall St. (bet. River St. & Rte. 2) | 413-663-5300 | www.gramercybistro.com

After a move across the street to Mass MoCA, this "standout" chef-owned North Adams bistro now feeds "famished" museumgoers its "diverse menu" of "stellar" seasonal American-Eclectic fare; "reasonable pricing", an "attentive" crew, "comfortable" modern surroundings and a summertime patio all add to the "pleasure."

NEW Gypsy Joynt Ⓜ *American*

| ▽ 16 | 13 | 16 | $17 |

Great Barrington | 389 Stockbridge Rd. (Crissey Rd.) | 413-644-8811 | www.yallsjoynt.com

Great Barrington "locals love" to "hang out and relax" at this "deli-style" American newcomer where the affordable salads, sandwiches, pizzas and pastas are made with organic produce; some say the eats are "just ok", but the "friendly service", "delightfully random decor" and "great music" on weekends add up to a "funky good time."

Haven *American/Bakery*

| 23 | 15 | 16 | $21 |

Lenox | 8 Franklin St. (Main St.) | 413-637-8948 | www.havencafebakery.com

The "elite meet to eat" "wonderful", "high-end" breakfasts" and "flavorful, hearty" lunches (plus "indulgent" "homestyle" dinners in season) at this "low-key" American cafe and bakery in "trendy" Downtown Lenox; "gourmet coffees, teas" and "cocktails based on Berkshire mountains spirits" are also available in the "spacious, unassuming" room – and "oh yeah, they have wireless" too.

Hub, The Ⓢ *American*

| ∇ 23 | 21 | 22 | $36 |

North Adams | 55 Main St. (State St.) | 413-662-2500 | www.thehubrestaurant.com

Often "packed", this North Adams American "upscale diner" "lives up to its name" as a "hangout" that's "tough to beat" for "comfort food"; "professional" servers patrol the storefront setting where the eats are "priced right" and the house wines are a similarly "good value."

Isabella's Ⓜ *Italian*

| - | - | - | M |

North Adams | 896 State Rd. (bet. Georgia & Hawthorne Aves.) | 413-662-2239 | www.isabellasrest.com

"Good food and good service at a fair price" sums up this casual North Adams Italian turning out "reliable" regional standards that make it a "favorite place to bring the family"; soft colors create a "pleasant" mood in the yellow 19th-century farmhouse where every table overlooks the garden, while the porch offers "nice" seating in summer.

Jae's Spice *American/Asian*

| 22 | 23 | 20 | $40 |

Pittsfield | 297 North St. (bet. Summer & Union Sts.) | 413-443-1234 | www.eatatjaes.com

Don't worry if the "adventurous menu" of midpriced "designer" Pan-Asian fare at Jae Chung's "beautiful" Pittsfield "gem" "seems daunting", because "you can't go wrong" – there are even "tasty" "American choices" "for the non-chopstick crowd"; although it's "warehouse-sized", the "richly renovated" space has a "warm atmosphere", with the "bonus" of being "close to the Barrington Stage" theater and a "nice staff" to ensure you "make the curtain."

John Andrews   *American* | 24 | 22 | 23 | $54 |

South Egremont | Rte. 23 (Blunt Rd.) | 413-528-3469 | www.jarestaurant.com

A "nicely dressed, soft-spoken clientele" gathers at this "fine-dining rendezvous" "in the woods" of South Egremont to "sit back and enjoy" "superior" New American cooking served by an "informed, friendly" staff in "delightful", "romantic" surroundings; naturally, such a "celebratory" experience commands an "expensive" tab, although the budget-conscious claim "even the bar menu is a class act", and "more reasonable" to boot.

John Harvard's Brew House   *Pub Food* | 16 | 17 | 17 | $25 |

Hancock | Country Inn at Jiminy Peak | 37 Corey Rd., 3rd fl. (Brodie Mountain Rd.) | 413-738-5500 | www.johnharvards.com

See review in Boston Directory.

Jonathan's Bistro   *American* | 20 | 17 | 19 | $37 |

Lenox | Lenox Commons | 55 Pittsfield Rd. (bet. Dugway Rd. & Main St.) | 413-637-8022

"A pleasant surprise hidden in a shopping center", this "casual" Lenox New American turns out "something for all appetites", ranging from "tasty sandwiches" to "original" entrees; although a few find the fare "uneven", most say it's "on the mark" and laud the "lovely wine list", "good prices", "comfortable" digs and patio for summer dining.

La Terrazza   *American/Italian* | ∇ 23 | 24 | 20 | $55 |

Lenox | Gateways Inn | 51 Walker St. (bet. Church & Kemble Sts.) | 413-637-2532 | www.gatewaysinn.com

You "walk into what looks like someone's house" at this Italian-American eatery in Lenox's "lovely" Gateways Inn (it was the Procter mansion, back in the day); terra-cotta walls and soft music in the dining room create an "elegant" backdrop for somewhat pricey but "outstanding homemade pastas" and such, while the "excellent wine and spirits" include an extravagant selection of single-malt scotch.

Marketplace | - | - | - | I |
Kitchen   *American/Sandwiches*

Sheffield | 18 Elm Ct. (Main St.) | 413-248-5040 | www.marketplacekitchen.com

"Breakfast wraps that will fortify you until dusk", plus "terrific soups", "amazing burgers" and flatbread pizzas are among the American eats on offer at this Sheffield spin-off of Marketplace, the specialty foods shop nearby; the "diner"-style digs are cheery and the rates "inexpensive", especially on Tuesday nights when "home-cooked meals" that feed a family of four cost only $20.

	FOOD	DECOR	SERVICE	COST

Mezze Bistro + Bar *American* — 22 | 22 | 22 | $51

Williamstown | 777 Cold Spring Rd./Rte. 7 (Taconic Trail) |
413-458-0123 | www.mezzebistro.com

Now ensconced in an "inviting", "airy" 19th-century farmhouse (reflecting its farm-to-table philosophy), this "exciting" Williamstown New American still dispenses "sophisticated" dishes via staffers who "know the right pace"; even those who say it "lost its amiability" after the move, and complain of "inflated" prices and quality that's "slipped a bit", agree it's "the place to impress your out-of-town friends."

Mill on the Floss 🅜 *French* — 23 | 23 | 24 | $51

New Ashford | 342 Rte. 7 (Rte. 43) | 413-458-9123 |
www.millonthefloss.com

It's "a little old-fashioned" and "that's a good thing" declare the "discerning clientele" of this "long-established" New Ashford French "classic" where "everything is superb", from the "quality" "country fare" and "personal" service to the "glorious" 18th-century farmhouse setting; sure, it's "special" (read: pricey), but there's a nightly three-course prix fixe that's "the bargain of the century."

Mission Bar & Tapas ◐ *Spanish* — 23 | 19 | 22 | $30

Pittsfield | 438 North St. (Maplewood Ave.) |
www.missionbarandtapas.com

A "slice of SoHo in Downtown Pittsfield", this "trendy" Spanish "hangout" has "mastered" a menu of "tasty" tapas to match its "wonderful" Iberian wines – and for pretty "low prices" too; a staff that "aims to please" works the "funky", low-lit room where musicians and a "kitchen open until midnight" mean it stays "lively" until "late."

Morgan House *New England* — 15 | 16 | 17 | $39

Lee | Morgan House | 33 Main St. (Mass. Tpke., exit 2) |
413-243-3661 | www.morganhouseinn.com

"Comforting in an old country inn kind of way", this "friendly" spot in Lee has "been around for years", dishing up moderately priced, "traditional" New England fare in an early-19th-century onetime stagecoach stop; some complain the eats are "ordinary" and the vibe "touristy", but the "good bar crowd" might disagree.

Napa *Eclectic* — 18 | 19 | 17 | $41

Great Barrington | 293 Main St. (Church St.) | 413-528-4311 |
www.napagb.com

Smack "in the middle of everything" in Great Barrington, this "cool" Eclectic cafe and vino bar delivers a "well-priced" menu of "good, basic" fare, plus "wines from every region" to go with; the "pretty" digs exude a "New York feeling", abetted by sometimes "surly service" but enhanced by "great jazz on Friday nights."

🅩 Nudel 🅜 *American* — 25 | 15 | 21 | $41

Lenox | 37 Church St. (bet. Housatonic & Walker Sts.) |
413-551-7183 | www.nudelrestaurant.com

"Wow", "this man can cook!" exclaim those taking a "culinary romp" at chef Bjorn Somlo's "vibrant" New American enlivening "sleepy" Lenox with an "excellent", "ever-changing", midpriced menu of "ingenious cuisine", which highlights pastas (aka nudels) and "whatever's fresh" that day; the "no-reservations scenario" makes it "tough to get into" the "cubbyhole" of a space, so "show up early" or expect "a big wait."

☑ Old Inn on the Green American
 27 | 26 | 26 | $63

New Marlborough | Old Inn on the Green | 134 Hartsville-New Marlborough Rd./Rte. 57 (Rte. 272) | 413-229-7924 | www.oldinn.com

"You need a compass to find" this "idyllic" New Marlborough "treasure" set in a "romantic" 1760s inn, but once there you'll be "blown away" by chef-owner Peter Platt's "prodigious menu" of "fabulous" New American cuisine, voted No. 1 for Food in The Berkshires; a "superb wine list", "professional staff" and "lovely" rooms "lit only by candles and fireplaces" are part of the package, and while it'll "empty your pocketbook", "it's worth it" for such a "magical experience"; P.S. the $30 prix fixe offered on some nights is a "fantastic" "steal."

Old Mill American
24 | 24 | 25 | $47

South Egremont | 53 Main St. (Rte. 41) | 413-528-1421 | www.oldmillberkshires.com

It's "pure country charm" at this "quaint" South Egremont veteran turning out "first-rate" American fare via the "best-trained staff" in a "pretty" 1797 old mill with "crooked floors" and "a gorgeous fireplace"; one "drawback" is no reservations for fewer than five, but there's a "cozy bar to warm your cockles while you wait", or you can eat there from a lighter menu – it's "easier on the budget" and you "get the best of both worlds."

Once Upon a Table American/Continental
21 | 15 | 19 | $38

Stockbridge | The Mews | 36 Main St. (bet. Elm St. & Rte. 7) | 413-298-3870 | www.onceuponatablebistro.com

"Blessed with a loyal following", this "delightful" Stockbridge American-Continental "hidden away" in a mews beside the Red Lion Inn dispenses "well-prepared" dishes deemed "worth the squeeze" in the "intimate" (make that *very* small") setting; "quick service" means it's "good for lunch", while you "can take your time" at dinner, "if you can get in."

Perigee Eclectic/New England
19 | 18 | 20 | $46

Lee | 1575 Pleasant St. (bet. Church & Willow Sts.) | 413-394-4047 | www.perigee-restaurant.com

This "casual", "off-the-beaten-path" Lee sophomore offers Eclectic-New England fare (trademarked as Berkshire cuisine) that some say is "consistently good" and others find sometimes "too elaborate", with tabs a tad "high for the area"; still, given the "appealing" two-story setting and a "wonderful owner" heading up an "accommodating" staff, they probably just need time to "work out the kinks."

Pho Saigon Vietnamese
22 | 12 | 18 | $22

Lee | 5 Railroad St. (Main St.) | 413-243-6288

"Who'd have thought you'd find authentic Vietnamese in Lee?" ask astonished newcomers to this "tiny place" run by a "friendly, talkative owner" turning out "homestyle" pho and other dishes, plus "excellent pad Thai" to boot; yes, it's "low on decor, but high on taste and value", and it "hits the spot" after a "night of partying."

Prime Italian Steakhouse & Bar ● *Italian/Steak*
▽ 21 | 22 | 22 | $48

Lenox | 15 Franklin St. (Rte. 7) | 413-637-2998 | www.primelenox.com

"A good bet" for "red meat and red wine" plus "old favorite dishes" like chef-owner Gennaro Gallo's homemade gnocchi, this Lenox Southern Italian steakhouse beloved of the "business" set makes everyone "feel welcome"; yes, it's "pricey", but unsurprisingly so given the upscale touches that abound in both the fare and the "hip decor" with a backlit bar.

Red Lion Inn *New England*
18 | 22 | 21 | $46

Stockbridge | Red Lion Inn | 30 Main St./Rte. 102 (bet. Main & Water Sts.) | 413-298-5545 | www.redlioninn.com

Stockbridge's "grande dame", this 1773 inn simply "screams Norman Rockwell" while dispensing "safe" New England "classics" in the "fine, old", "formal" dining room, "rustic" Widow Bingham's Tavern or "casual" Lion's Den pub, where tariffs are "lower"; "service is top-notch", and even though grumps grumble it's "only for tourists", it's practically "mandatory" to "go once."

Rouge ☒ *French*
22 | 18 | 17 | $49

West Stockbridge | 3 Center St. (Rte. 41) | 413-232-4111 | www.rougerestaurant.com

Chef William Merelle's "mouthwatering" French cuisine coupled with spouse Maggie's "warm hospitality" make this West Stockbridge bistro a "popular" "go-to" for the "elite and hoi polloi alike"; a recent expansion doubled the rouge-accented space, although it still gets "jammed" in the "lively" bar where the less "expensive", "interesting tapas menu" is "a treat", leaving only "loud" decibels and sometimes "lackadaisical service" as issues.

Route 7 Grill *BBQ*
18 | 13 | 19 | $36

Great Barrington | 999 S. Main St. (bet. Brookside & Lime Kiln Rds.) | 413-528-3235 | www.route7grill.com

"Awfully good babyback ribs" are among the "well-priced", "finger-licking" fare at this "unpretentious" Great Barrington BBQ specialist focusing on "locally raised meats and produce"; "Texans" and others less enthused declare it "just ok" and the "cost not merited", but most enjoy the "nice buzz" in the "plain", "family-friendly" space, made cheery by its "raging fire" and "horseshoe bar."

Shiro Sushi & Hibachi *Japanese*
20 | 16 | 18 | $34

Great Barrington | 105 Stockbridge Rd. (bet. Blue Hill Rd. & Brooke Ln.) | 413-528-1898

Shiro Lounge *Japanese*

Pittsfield | 48 North St. (School St.) | 413-236-8111 | www.berkshiro.com

Sushi is "difficult to find in the Berkshires", but "the art is alive" at this Japanese duo purveying "first-class", "artistic" fare; true, the

	FOOD	DECOR	SERVICE	COST

digs have all "the ambiance of a tire shop", but the staff is "pleasant" and the prices moderate, plus the "hilarious" hibachi chefs grilling "bountiful" meals at the Great Barrington original "make it fun for the whole family."

Siam Square Thai Cuisine *Thai*   19 | 16 | 20 | $25

Great Barrington | 290 Main St. (Railroad St.) | 413-644-9119 | www.siamsquares.com

"The only game in town" for Thai, this "casual", somewhat "quiet" Great Barrington spot draws many "regulars" with its "wide array" of "terrific" fare featuring the occasional "kick"; it's "a good value" and the dishes come "served quickly and with a smile", making it "one of the best pre-movie" options around.

Stagecoach Tavern Ⓜ *American*   ∇ 17 | 23 | 20 | $40

Sheffield | Race Brook Lodge | S. Undermountain Rd./Rte. 41 (Berkshire School Rd.) | 413-229-8585 | www.stagecoachtavern.net

It's so "atmospheric", "you can imagine tying your horse outside" this "inviting" 1829 tavern in Sheffield, where a seasonal menu of "dependable" American fare comes served in "cozy", "candlelit" rooms with fireplaces, making it "perfect on a snowy night"; the "sweet" staff adds to the "convivial" vibe, while moderate tabs are another reason it's "worth going."

Sullivan Station   15 | 18 | 20 | $30
Restaurant Ⓜ *New England*

Lee | 109 Railroad St. (Mass. Tpke., exit 2) | 413-243-2082 | www.sullivanstationrestaurant.com

"A Lee standby", this restored "historic" onetime train depot is all "old-fashioned charm", from its "large portions" of affordable, "plain" New England eats to its "homey" digs with "decor featuring locomotive pictures and railroad nostalgia"; "lunch is always good" and just the ticket if you're with kids, especially when the Berkshire Scenic Railway toots by.

Sushi Thai Garden *Japanese/Thai*   ∇ 20 | 15 | 21 | $30

Williamstown | 27 Spring St. (Rte. 2) | 413-458-0004 | www.sushithaigarden.com

The "Thai food is hearty and hot" and the sushi "surprisingly good" at this "dependable" Williamstown spot; although the "tables are close together", the decor in the "casual" brick storefront setting is "fine", while "bargain" rates, "attentive service" and overall menu "variety" make it a "good place to go with a group of friends."

Taylor's Ⓩ *American*   - | - | - | M

North Adams | 34 Holden St. (Center St.) | 413-664-4500 | www.taylorsfinedining.net

White tablecloth restaurants are rare in North Adams, so this American near Mass MoCa serves as a "good place" for locals in search of reasonably priced steaks, seafood and pastas, as well as affordable comfort fare – and even sushi Thursdays–Saturdays; "inviting" brick-walled rooms and a staff that "works hard" are added attractions.

	FOOD	DECOR	SERVICE	COST

Trattoria Il Vesuvio *Italian* | 19 | 17 | 20 | $41 |

Lenox | 242 Pittsfield Rd. (bet. Lime Kiln & New Lenox Rds.) |
413-637-4904 | www.trattoria-vesuvio.com

Fans of this "reliable" Lenox Italian claim the menu of "traditional"
red sauce may "not change much", but it's as "comforting as a warm
blanket on a cold day", plus the "homemade bread is great"; the converted hundred-year-old stable is "cavernous" but cozy, thanks to
the wood-fired brick oven and "family-owned" feeling.

Trattoria Rustica *Italian* | 25 | 21 | 21 | $48 |

Pittsfield | 27 McKay St. (West St.) | 413-499-1192 |
www.trattoria-rustica.com

This "charming" Southern Italian is "worth a detour" to Pittsfield declare devotees of chef-owner Davide Manzo's "delicious", "sophisticated" cooking; the lantern-lit, brick-and-stone setting creates a
"romantic" vibe in winter, while courtyard dining is "wonderful" when
it's warm, so even though it's a little "expensive", it's a "special place."

Truc Orient Express *Vietnamese* | 22 | 19 | 20 | $32 |

West Stockbridge | 3 Harris St. (Main St.) | 413-232-4204

"A Berkshires legend", this "amazing", over-30-year-old West
Stockbridge Vietnamese offers its "splendid", "artfully presented" fare
for "great prices"; the owners provide a "quiet", "welcoming" mood
in "easygoing" digs, which are adorned with art from their homeland
and augmented with an "extraordinary" attached gift shop.

Viva ⓜ *Spanish* | 23 | 19 | 21 | $38 |

Glendale | 14 Glendale Rd. (Rte. 102) | 413-298-4433 |
www.vivaberkshires.com

"Excellent paella" and "wonderful tapas" are representative of the
"confident Spanish cooking" that draws Glendale denizens to this
"out-of-the-way" spot near the Norman Rockwell museum; an "unobtrusive" staff serves in the "spacious", colorful room where a
Picasso-like mural adds to the "fun" environment.

ⓩ Wheatleigh *American/French* | 25 | 29 | 27 | $93 |

Lenox | Wheatleigh | 11 Hawthorne Rd. (Hawthorne St.) |
413-637-0610 | www.wheatleigh.com

"Gatsby would have been proud" of Lenox's "magnificent" Italianate
mansion, where it's "class all the way", from rooms exuding "elegance by the cartload" to the "fabulous" New American–French fare
and "pampering" staff; a few fret about "prohibitive" tabs, but most
suggest you "take out a second mortgage" and "splurge", because
"life doesn't get much better than this"; P.S. jackets suggested.

Xicohtencatl *Mexican* | 21 | 19 | 20 | $33 |

Great Barrington | 50 Stockbridge Rd. (Rte. 7) | 413-528-2002 |
www.xicohmexican.com

"No average Mexican", this Great Barrington spot dispenses "inspired", "flavorful" eats via a "crowd-pleasing staff" "who can discuss the subtleties"; "lively decor", a "huge margarita list" and
"moderate prices" add to the "fun", while the patio is "mellow."

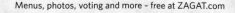
Menus, photos, voting and more - free at ZAGAT.com

THE BERKSHIRES
INDEXES

Cuisines

Includes names, locations and Food ratings.

AMERICAN

Allium | **Great Barr**	18
Barrington Brew | **Great Barr**	14
🅱 Blantyre | **Lenox**	27
NEW Brulées | **Pittsfield**	21
Castle St. | **Great Barr**	20
Church St. Cafe | **Lenox**	20
Cranwell Resort | **Lenox**	21
Dream Away | **Becket**	17
Firefly | **Lenox**	17
Gramercy | **N Adams**	23
NEW Gypsy Joynt | **Great Barr**	16
Haven | **Lenox**	23
Hub | **N Adams**	23
Jae's Spice | **Pittsfield**	22
John Andrews | **S Egremont**	24
Jonathan's | **Lenox**	20
La Terrazza | **Lenox**	23
Marketplace | **Sheffield**	-
Mezze Bistro | **Williamstown**	22
🅱 Nudel | **Lenox**	25
🅱 Old Inn/Green | **New Marl**	27
Old Mill | **S Egremont**	24
Once Upon | **Stockbridge**	21
Stagecoach Tav. | **Sheffield**	17
Taylor's | **N Adams**	-
🅱 Wheatleigh | **Lenox**	25

ASIAN

Flavours/Malaysia | **Pittsfield**	21
Jae's Spice | **Pittsfield**	22

BAKERY

Haven | **Lenox**	23

BARBECUE

Rte. 7 Grill | **Great Barr**	18

CONTINENTAL

Once Upon | **Stockbridge**	21

ECLECTIC

Elizabeth's | **Pittsfield**	24
Gramercy | **N Adams**	23
Napa | **Great Barr**	18
Perigee | **Lee**	19

EUROPEAN

NEW Brulées | **Pittsfield**	21
Cafe Adam | **Great Barr**	23

FRENCH

🅱 Blantyre | **Lenox**	27
Mill on Floss | **New Ashford**	23
🅱 Wheatleigh | **Lenox**	25

FRENCH (BISTRO)

Bistro Zinc | **Lenox**	21
Brix Wine | **Pittsfield**	23
Castle St. | **Great Barr**	20
Chez Nous | **Lee**	24
Rouge | **W Stockbridge**	22

GREEK

Aegèan Breeze | **Great Barr**	19

INDIAN

Aroma B&G | **Great Barr**	22
Bombay | **Lee**	22

ITALIAN

(S=Southern)

Café Lucia | **Lenox**	23
Frankie's Rist. | **Lenox**	18
Isabella's | **N Adams**	-
La Terrazza | **Lenox**	23
Prime Italian | S | **Lenox**	21
Tratt. Il Vesuvio | **Lenox**	19
Tratt. Rustica | S | **Pittsfield**	25

JAPANESE

(* sushi specialist)

Bizen* | **Great Barr**	24
Fin* | **Lenox**	23
Shiro* | **multi.**	20
Sushi Thai Gdn.* | **Williamstown**	20

MEDITERRANEAN

Alta | **Lenox**	21

MEXICAN

Coyote Flaco | **Williamstown**	23
Xicohtencatl | **Great Barr**	21

NEW ENGLAND

Morgan Hse. | **Lee**	15
Perigee | **Lee**	19
Red Lion Inn | **Stockbridge**	18
Sullivan Station | **Lee**	15

PIZZA

Baba Louie's | **multi.**	24

PUB FOOD

John Harvard's | **Hancock**	16

SANDWICHES

Marketplace | **Sheffield** —|

SPANISH

(* tapas specialist)

Mission Bar* | **Pittsfield** 23|
Viva* | **Glendale** 23|

STEAKHOUSES

Dakota Steak | **Pittsfield** 17|
Prime Italian | **Lenox** 21|

THAI

Siam Sq. Thai | **Great Barr** 19|
Sushi Thai Gdn. | **Williamstown** 20|

VIETNAMESE

Pho Saigon | **Lee** 22|
Truc Orient | **W Stockbridge** 22|

THE BERKSHIRES

CUISINES

Locations

Includes names, cuisines and Food ratings.

BECKET

Dream Away | *Amer.* <u>17</u>

GLENDALE

Viva | *Spanish* <u>23</u>

GREAT BARRINGTON

Aegean Breeze | *Greek* <u>19</u>
Allium | *Amer.* <u>18</u>
Aroma B&G | *Indian* <u>22</u>
Baba Louie's | *Pizza* <u>24</u>
Barrington Brew | *Amer.* <u>14</u>
Bizen | *Japanese* <u>24</u>
Cafe Adam | *Euro.* <u>23</u>
Castle St. | *Amer./French* <u>20</u>
🆕 Gypsy Joynt | *Amer.* <u>16</u>
Napa | *Eclectic* <u>18</u>
Rte. 7 Grill | *BBQ* <u>18</u>
Shiro | *Japanese* <u>20</u>
Siam Sq. Thai | *Thai* <u>19</u>
Xicohtencatl | *Mex.* <u>21</u>

HANCOCK

John Harvard's | *Pub* <u>16</u>

LEE

Bombay | *Indian* <u>22</u>
Chez Nous | *French* <u>24</u>
Morgan Hse. | *New Eng.* <u>15</u>
Perigee | *Eclectic/New Eng.* <u>19</u>
Pho Saigon | *Viet.* <u>22</u>
Sullivan Station | *New Eng.* <u>15</u>

LENOX

Alta | *Med.* <u>21</u>
Bistro Zinc | *French* <u>21</u>
🇿 Blantyre | *Amer./French* <u>27</u>
Café Lucia | *Italian* <u>23</u>
Church St. Cafe | *Amer.* <u>20</u>
Cranwell Resort | *Amer.* <u>21</u>
Fin | *Japanese* <u>23</u>
Firefly | *Amer.* <u>17</u>
Frankie's Rist. | *Italian* <u>18</u>
Haven | *Amer./Bakery* <u>23</u>
Jonathan's | *Amer.* <u>20</u>
La Terrazza | *Amer./Italian* <u>23</u>
🇿 Nudel | *Amer.* <u>25</u>

Prime Italian | *Italian/Steak* <u>21</u>
Tratt. Il Vesuvio | *Italian* <u>19</u>
🇿 Wheatleigh | *Amer./French* <u>25</u>

NEW ASHFORD

Mill on Floss | *French* <u>23</u>

NEW MARLBOROUGH

🇿 Old Inn/Green | *Amer.* <u>27</u>

NORTH ADAMS

Gramercy | *Amer./Eclectic* <u>23</u>
Hub | *Amer.* <u>23</u>
Isabella's | *Italian* <u>-</u>
Taylor's | *Amer.* <u>-</u>

PITTSFIELD

Baba Louie's | *Pizza* <u>24</u>
Brix Wine | *French* <u>23</u>
🆕 Brulées | *Amer./Euro.* <u>21</u>
Dakota Steak | *Steak* <u>17</u>
Elizabeth's | *Eclectic* <u>24</u>
Flavours/Malaysia | *Asian* <u>21</u>
Jae's Spice | *Amer./Asian* <u>22</u>
Mission Bar | *Spanish* <u>23</u>
Shiro | *Japanese* <u>20</u>
Tratt. Rustica | *Italian* <u>25</u>

SHEFFIELD

Marketplace | *Amer./Sandwiches* <u>-</u>
Stagecoach Tav. | *Amer.* <u>17</u>

SOUTH EGREMONT

John Andrews | *Amer.* <u>24</u>
Old Mill | *Amer.* <u>24</u>

STOCKBRIDGE

Once Upon | *Amer./Continental* <u>21</u>
Red Lion Inn | *New Eng.* <u>18</u>

WEST STOCKBRIDGE

Rouge | *French* <u>22</u>
Truc Orient | *Viet.* <u>22</u>

WILLIAMSTOWN

Coyote Flaco | *Mex.* <u>23</u>
Mezze Bistro | *Amer.* <u>22</u>
Sushi Thai Gdn. | *Japanese/Thai* <u>20</u>

Special Features

Listings cover the best in each category and include names, locations and Food ratings. Multi-location restaurants' features may vary by branch.

BRUNCH

Bombay	Lee	22
Cafe Adam	Great Barr	23
Dakota Steak	Pittsfield	17
☑ Wheatleigh	Lenox	25
Xicohtencatl	Great Barr	21

BUSINESS DINING

Allium	Great Barr	18
Cranwell Resort	Lenox	21
Jae's Spice	Pittsfield	22
La Terrazza	Lenox	23
Napa	Great Barr	18
Taylor's	N Adams	-

CATERING

Bizen	Great Barr	24
Bombay	Lee	22
Castle St.	Great Barr	20
John Andrews	S Egremont	24
Mezze Bistro	Williamstown	22

CHILD-FRIENDLY

(Alternatives to the usual fast-food places; * children's menu available)

Aegean Breeze	Great Barr	19
Baba Louie's	Great Barr	24
Barrington Brew*	Great Barr	14
Bistro Zinc*	Lenox	21
Café Lucia	Lenox	23
Castle St.	Great Barr	20
Church St. Cafe*	Lenox	20
Coyote Flaco*	Williamstown	23
Dakota Steak*	Pittsfield	17
Elizabeth's	Pittsfield	24
Marketplace	Sheffield	-
Morgan Hse.	Lee	15
Old Mill	S Egremont	24
Once Upon	Stockbridge	21
Red Lion Inn*	Stockbridge	18
Rouge	W Stockbridge	22
Rte. 7 Grill*	Great Barr	18
Shiro	Great Barr	20
Siam Sq. Thai	Great Barr	19
Sullivan Station*	Lee	15
Sushi Thai Gdn.	Williamstown	20
Tratt. Il Vesuvio*	Lenox	19
Xicohtencatl*	Great Barr	21

DINING ALONE

(Other than hotels and places with counter service)

Alta	Lenox	21
Baba Louie's	multi.	24
Cafe Adam	Great Barr	23
Castle St.	Great Barr	20
Coyote Flaco	Williamstown	23
Fin	Lenox	23
NEW Gypsy Joynt	Great Barr	16
Marketplace	Sheffield	-
Mission Bar	Pittsfield	23
Napa	Great Barr	18
Once Upon	Stockbridge	21
Pho Saigon	Lee	22
Rte. 7 Grill	Great Barr	18
Sullivan Station	Lee	15

ENTERTAINMENT

(Call for days and times of performances)

☑ Blantyre	piano	Lenox	27
Castle St.	jazz/piano	Great Barr	20
Dream Away	live music	Becket	17
Mission Bar	folk/indie rock	Pittsfield	23
Napa	jazz	Great Barr	18
Red Lion Inn	varies	Stockbridge	18

FIREPLACES

Aegean Breeze	Great Barr	19
Barrington Brew	Great Barr	14
☑ Blantyre	Lenox	27
Cranwell Resort	Lenox	21
Dakota Steak	Pittsfield	17
Dream Away	Becket	17
John Andrews	S Egremont	24
La Terrazza	Lenox	23
Mezze Bistro	Williamstown	22
Mill on Floss	New Ashford	23
Morgan Hse.	Lee	15
☑ Old Inn/Green	New Marl	27
Old Mill	S Egremont	24
Red Lion Inn	Stockbridge	18
Rte. 7 Grill	Great Barr	18
Stagecoach Tav.	Sheffield	17
Truc Orient	W Stockbridge	22
☑ Wheatleigh	Lenox	25

HISTORIC PLACES

(Year opened; * building)

1760	Old Inn/Green*	New Marl	27
1773	Red Lion Inn*	Stockbridge	18

1797 | Old Mill* | **S Egremont** 24
1810 | Dream Away* | **Becket** 17
1817 | Morgan Hse.* | **Lee** 15
1829 | Stagecoach Tav.* | **Sheffield** 17
1839 | Café Lucia* | **Lenox** 23
1840 | Jae's Spice* | **Pittsfield** 22
1841 | Chez Nous* | **Lee** 24
1852 | Church St. Cafe* | **Lenox** 20
1893 | Sullivan Station* | **Lee** 15
1893 | Wheatleigh* | **Lenox** 25
1894 | Cranwell Resort* | **Lenox** 21
1900 | Tratt. Il Vesuvio* | **Lenox** 19
1924 | Brix Wine* | **Pittsfield** 23

HOTEL DINING

Blantyre
  Z Blantyre | **Lenox** 27
Gateways Inn
  La Terrazza | **Lenox** 23
Morgan House
  Morgan Hse. | **Lee** 15
Old Inn on the Green
  Z Old Inn/Green | **New Marl** 27
Quality Inn
  Bombay | **Lee** 22
Race Brook Lodge
  Stagecoach Tav. | **Sheffield** 17
Red Lion Inn
  Red Lion Inn | **Stockbridge** 18
Wheatleigh
  Z Wheatleigh | **Lenox** 25

MEET FOR A DRINK

Alta | **Lenox** 21
Bistro Zinc | **Lenox** 21
Brix Wine | **Pittsfield** 23
NEW Brulées | **Pittsfield** 21
Castle St. | **Great Barr** 20
Chez Nous | **Lee** 24
Gramercy | **N Adams** 23
Jae's Spice | **Pittsfield** 22
Mission Bar | **Pittsfield** 23
Napa | **Great Barr** 18
Old Mill | **S Egremont** 24
Prime Italian | **Lenox** 21
Red Lion Inn | **Stockbridge** 18
Stagecoach Tav. | **Sheffield** 17

MICROBREWERIES

Barrington Brew | **Great Barr** 14

NEWCOMERS

Brulées | **Pittsfield** 21
Gypsy Joynt | **Great Barr** 16

OFFBEAT

Barrington Brew | **Great Barr** 14
Elizabeth's | **Pittsfield** 24
NEW Gypsy Joynt | **Great Barr** 16

OUTDOOR DINING

(G=garden; P=patio; T=terrace)
Aegean Breeze | P | **Great Barr** 19
Alta | T | **Lenox** 21
Barrington Brew | G | **Great Barr** 14
Cafe Adam | P | **Great Barr** 23
Café Lucia | G, T | **Lenox** 23
Church St. Cafe | T | **Lenox** 20
Firefly | P | **Lenox** 17
Frankie's Rist. | T | **Lenox** 18
Gramercy | P | **N Adams** 23
Isabella's | T | **N Adams** -
John Andrews | T | **S Egremont** 24
Jonathan's | P | **Lenox** 20
Z Old Inn/Green | T | **New Marl** 27
Red Lion Inn | P | **Stockbridge** 18
Rouge | T | **W Stockbridge** 22
Shiro | P | **Great Barr** 20
Sullivan Station | T | **Lee** 15
Tratt. Il Vesuvio | T | **Lenox** 19
Tratt. Rustica | P | **Pittsfield** 25
Xicohtencatl | T | **Great Barr** 21

PEOPLE-WATCHING

Allium | **Great Barr** 18
Alta | **Lenox** 21
Bistro Zinc | **Lenox** 21
Mezze Bistro | **Williamstown** 22

POWER SCENES

Bistro Zinc | **Lenox** 21
Mezze Bistro | **Williamstown** 22

PRIVATE ROOMS

(Restaurants charge less at off times; call for capacity)
Bizen | **Great Barr** 24
Z Blantyre | **Lenox** 27
Castle St. | **Great Barr** 20
Church St. Cafe | **Lenox** 20
Cranwell Resort | **Lenox** 21
Dakota Steak | **Pittsfield** 17
Mill on Floss | **New Ashford** 23
Red Lion Inn | **Stockbridge** 18
Rouge | **W Stockbridge** 22
Stagecoach Tav. | **Sheffield** 17
Z Wheatleigh | **Lenox** 25

PRIX FIXE MENUS

(Call for prices and times)
Bizen | **Great Barr** 24
Z Blantyre | **Lenox** 27
Z Old Inn/Green | **New Marl** 27
Z Wheatleigh | **Lenox** 25

QUIET CONVERSATION

☑ Blantyre	Lenox	27
Cranwell Resort	Lenox	21
Gramercy	N Adams	23
John Andrews	S Egremont	24
La Terrazza	Lenox	23
Mill on Floss	New Ashford	23
Stagecoach Tav.	Sheffield	17
Taylor's	N Adams	-
☑ Wheatleigh	Lenox	25

ROMANTIC PLACES

☑ Blantyre	Lenox	27
Chez Nous	Lee	24
Cranwell Resort	Lenox	21
John Andrews	S Egremont	24
Mill on Floss	New Ashford	23
☑ Old Inn/Green	New Marl	27
Taylor's	N Adams	-
Tratt. Rustica	Pittsfield	25
☑ Wheatleigh	Lenox	25

SENIOR APPEAL

Aegean Breeze	Great Barr	19
Cranwell Resort	Lenox	21
La Terrazza	Lenox	23
Morgan Hse.	Lee	15
Red Lion Inn	Stockbridge	18
Taylor's	N Adams	-

SINGLES SCENES

Alta	Lenox	21
Brix Wine	Pittsfield	23
Castle St.	Great Barr	20
Jae's Spice	Pittsfield	22
Napa	Great Barr	18
Prime Italian	Lenox	21
Sushi Thai Gdn.	Williamstown	20

SLEEPERS

(Good food, but little known)

Aroma B&G	Great Barr	22
Bombay	Lee	22
La Terrazza	Lenox	23
Mezze Bistro	Williamstown	22
Mill on Floss	New Ashford	23
Pho Saigon	Lee	22
Tratt. Rustica	Pittsfield	25
Truc Orient	W Stockbridge	22
Viva	Glendale	23

TAKEOUT

Aegean Breeze	Great Barr	19
Baba Louie's	Great Barr	24
Barrington Brew	Great Barr	14
Bistro Zinc	Lenox	21
Bizen	Great Barr	24

Café Lucia	Lenox	23
Castle St.	Great Barr	20
Church St. Cafe	Lenox	20
Dakota Steak	Pittsfield	17
John Andrews	S Egremont	24
Marketplace	Sheffield	-
Morgan Hse.	Lee	15
Once Upon	Stockbridge	21
Rouge	W Stockbridge	22
Shiro	Great Barr	20
Siam Sq. Thai	Great Barr	19
Stagecoach Tav.	Sheffield	17
Sushi Thai Gdn.	Williamstown	20
Truc Orient	W Stockbridge	22

TEEN APPEAL

Baba Louie's	multi.	24
Barrington Brew	Great Barr	14
Coyote Flaco	Williamstown	23
Dakota Steak	Pittsfield	17

TRENDY

Allium	Great Barr	18
Bistro Zinc	Lenox	21
Bizen	Great Barr	24
Brix Wine	Pittsfield	23
Cafe Adam	Great Barr	23
Castle St.	Great Barr	20
Fin	Lenox	23
Jae's Spice	Pittsfield	22
John Andrews	S Egremont	24
Mission Bar	Pittsfield	23
Napa	Great Barr	18
Prime Italian	Lenox	21
Rouge	W Stockbridge	22
Xicohtencatl	Great Barr	21

VIEWS

Bombay	Lee	22
Cranwell Resort	Lenox	21
☑ Wheatleigh	Lenox	25

WINNING WINE LISTS

Alta	Lenox	21
Brix Wine	Pittsfield	23
Cafe Adam	Great Barr	23
Castle St.	Great Barr	20
Chez Nous	Lee	24
Gramercy	N Adams	23
John Andrews	S Egremont	24
Jonathan's	Lenox	20
La Terrazza	Lenox	23
Mezze Bistro	Williamstown	22
Mission Bar	Pittsfield	23
☑ Old Inn/Green	New Marl	27

Wine Vintage Chart

This chart is based on our 0 to 30 scale. The ratings (by U. of South Carolina law professor **Howard Stravitz**) reflect vintage quality and the wine's readiness to drink. A dash means the wine is past its peak or too young to rate. Loire ratings are for dry whites.

Whites	95	96	97	98	99	00	01	02	03	04	05	06	07	08	09
France:															
Alsace	24	23	23	25	23	25	26	23	21	24	25	24	26	25	25
Burgundy	27	26	22	21	24	24	24	27	23	26	27	25	26	25	25
Loire Valley	-	-	-	-	-	-	-	26	21	23	27	23	24	24	26
Champagne	26	27	24	23	25	24	21	26	21	-	-	-	-	-	-
Sauternes	21	23	25	23	24	24	29	24	26	21	26	24	27	25	27
California:															
Chardonnay	-	-	-	-	22	21	25	26	22	26	29	24	27	25	-
Sauvignon Blanc	-	-	-	-	-	-	-	-	-	26	25	27	25	24	25
Austria:															
Grüner V./Riesl.	22	-	25	22	25	21	22	25	26	25	24	26	25	23	27
Germany:	21	26	21	22	24	20	29	25	26	27	28	25	27	25	25

Reds	95	96	97	98	99	00	01	02	03	04	05	06	07	08	09
France:															
Bordeaux	26	25	23	25	24	29	26	24	26	25	28	24	23	25	27
Burgundy	26	27	25	24	27	22	24	27	25	23	28	25	25	24	26
Rhône	26	22	23	27	26	27	26	-	26	25	27	25	26	23	26
Beaujolais	-	-	-	-	-	-	-	-	-	-	27	24	25	23	27
California:															
Cab./Merlot	27	25	28	23	25	-	27	26	25	24	26	23	26	23	25
Pinot Noir	-	-	-	-	-	-	25	26	25	26	24	23	27	25	24
Zinfandel	-	-	-	-	-	-	25	23	27	22	24	21	21	25	23
Oregon:															
Pinot Noir	-	-	-	-	-	-	-	26	24	26	25	24	23	27	25
Italy:															
Tuscany	25	24	29	24	27	24	27	-	25	27	26	26	25	24	-
Piedmont	21	27	26	25	26	28	27	-	24	27	26	25	26	26	-
Spain:															
Rioja	26	24	25	-	25	24	28	-	23	27	26	24	24	-	26
Ribera del Duero/ Priorat	26	27	25	24	25	24	27	-	24	27	26	24	26	-	-
Australia:															
Shiraz/Cab.	24	26	25	28	24	24	27	27	25	26	27	25	23	-	-
Chile:	-	-	-	-	25	23	26	24	25	24	27	25	24	26	-
Argentina:															
Malbec	-	-	-	-	-	-	-	-	-	25	26	27	25	24	-

ZAGATMAP

Boston Transit Map

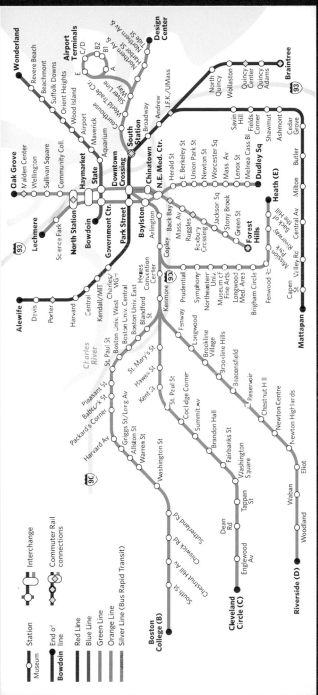

Key:

- ⊖ Station
- Museum
- ● End of line (Bowdoin)
- Red Line
- Blue Line
- Green Line
- Orange Line
- Silver Line (Bus Rapid Transit)
- ⊜ Interchange
- ◈ Commuter Rail connections

Most Popular Restaurants

Map coordinates follow each name. Those in the Greater Boston area lie in sections A-G (see adjacent map); Those in the suburbs, Cape Cod & the Islands lie in sections H-O (see reverse side of map).

BOSTON

1. Legal Sea Foods† (E-5)
2. Abe & Louie's (E-5)
3. Craigie on Main (C-3)
4. Blue Ginger (J-2)
5. Oleana (B-3)
6. L'Espalier (E-5)
7. No. 9 Park (D-7)
8. Capital Grille† (E-4)
9. Hamersley's Bistro (F-6)
10. B&G Oysters (F-6)
11. Mistral (E-6)
12. Aquitaine† (F-6)
13. Grill 23 & Bar (E-6)
14. Neptune Oyster (C-8)
15. Oishii† (F-6)
16. EVOO (C-5)
17. Lumière (J-2)
18. Ten Tables (A-1, J-3)
19. Union Oyster House (D-7)
20. Cheesecake Factory† (J-3)
21. Sel de la Terre† (D-8)
22. Anna's Taqueria† (G-1)
23. Giacomo's (C-8, F-5)
24. Elephant Walk† (F-3)
25. Sorellina (E-5)
26. Toro (G-6)
27. Hungry Mother (C-4)
28. Clio (E-4)
29. La Campania (J-2)
30. Eastern Standard (E-4)
31. Petit Robert Bistro† (E-4)
32. Blue Ribbon BBQ† (J-2, J-3)
33. Il Capriccio (J-2)
34. Atlantic Fish Co. (E-5)
35. O Ya (E-7)
36. Flour Bakery & Café† (G-6)
37. Locke-Ober (D-7)
38. Anthony's Pier 4 (D-8)
39. Bergamot (A-3)
40. East Coast Grill & Raw Bar* (B-3)
41. Radius (E-7)
42. Fugakyu (F-1, J-2)
43. Ruth's Chris (D-7)
44. Durgin-Park (D-7)
45. Davio's (E-6, K-2)
46. Rialto (B-1)
47. Harvest (B-1)
48. Not Your Average Joe's† (J-3)
49. Morton's (E-5, E-8)
50. Rendezvous (C-3)

CAPE COD & THE ISLANDS

1. Abba (L-7)
2. American Seasons (O-7)
3. Chatham Bars Inn (M-7)
4. Brewster Fish House (M-7)
5. Impudent Oyster* (M-7)
6. Straight Wharf (O-7)
7. Black-Eyed Susan's (O-7)
8. Arnold's Lobster (L-7)
9. Ocean House (M-6)
10. Cape Sea Grille (M-7)
11. Topper's (O-7)
12. Galley Beach (O-7)
13. Mews (K-6)
14. Brant Point Grill (O-7)
15. Twenty-Eight Atlantic* (M-7)
16. Art Cliff Diner (N-5)
17. Chillingsworth* (M-7)
18. Company of the Cauldron* (O-7)
19. Alchemy (N-5)
20. Lobster Pot* (K-6)
21. Red Inn (K-6)
22. Chart Room (M-4)

*Indicates tie with above   † Indicates multiple branches

This map is printed using SoyInks on paper containing a minimum 10% post-consumer waste fiber.